Better Homes and Gardens®

COMPLETE GUIDE TO GARDENING

© Copyright 1979 by Meredith Corporation, Des Moines, Iowa.
All Rights Reserved. Printed in the United States of America.
First Edition. Printing Number and Year: 25 24 23 22 21   96 95 94 93
Library of Congress Catalog Card Number: 79-51395
ISBN: 0-696-00041-5
ISBN: 0-696-02556-6 (trade paperback)

**BETTER HOMES AND
GARDENS® BOOKS**

Editor in Chief: James A. Autry
Editorial Director: Neil Kuehnl
Executive Art Director:
    William J. Yates

Editor: Gerald M. Knox
Art Director: Ernest Shelton
Associate Art Directors:
    Randall Yontz, Neoma Alt West
Copy and Production Editors:
    David Kirchner, Lamont Olson,
    David A. Walsh
Assistant Art Director:
    Harijs Priekulis
Senior Graphic Designer:
    Faith Berven
Graphic Designers: Linda Ford,
    Richard Lewis, Sheryl Veenschoten,
    Tom Wegner
Garden and Outdoor Living Editor:
    Beverly Garrett
Senior Garden Editors:
    Steven Coulter, Marjorie P. Groves,
    Russell O'Harra
Associate Garden Editors:
    Douglas A. Jimerson,
    CarolAnn Shindelar

Complete Guide to Gardening

Editor: Marjorie P. Groves
Graphic Designer: Harijs Priekulis
Copy and Production Editors:
    Paul S. Kitzke, David A. Walsh
Contributors: Lorraine Burgess,
    Michael Kressy, Donald R. Lewis,
    Ann Reilly, Kay Stroud

Thanks to O.M. Scott & Sons
and Netherlands Flower-bulb
Institute for some of the
illustrations in this book.

Gardening, in its various forms, is a tradition that spans hundreds of years and all continents. Yet, it is an ever-changing creative process, too. Gardeners must apply techniques that fit their particular situation. These techniques sometimes are promoted as new, but often turn out to be little more than innovative updates of good old common sense.

This book, like gardening, is both traditional and creative. In 1951, Better Homes and Gardens published a book called the *New Garden Book*. Developed by well-known garden editor Fleeta Brownell Woodroffe, it was an instant success. The *New Garden Book* went through two revisions and sold nearly three million copies.

Now Better Homes and Gardens replaces that book with the *Complete Guide to Gardening*. In this book, you'll find facts about modern plant and soil science; also in it is information collected from hundreds of current sources, yet presented in a way that returns us to an almost forgotten partnership with nature.

You'll find hundreds of photographs of the best home gardens in the country, along with descriptions of techniques developed by other gardeners that can be adapted to your own backyard. There are closeup pictures of plants, as well as ways they can be arranged to make a relaxing, pleasing setting. With the "how-to" drawings, beginners can learn to plan, plant, and enjoy gardening; experts will discover tips, techniques, and planting combinations. Gardeners of any skill will find many ways to do things better and easier.

Advice in this book is shaped to fit the peculiarities of your region and your weather, the uniqueness of your home and lot, and the special quality of your own tastes and personality.

Some people call gardening a form of magic, others call it a therapy. Still others say it's good exercise; some will call it only an excuse—an excuse to be outdoors or to slow down for a moment to nurture a houseplant. No matter what you call gardening, we hope this book helps you enjoy it.

Contents

Chapter 1
ABCs OF GOOD GARDENING ___ 6
Consider Your Climate ___ 8
Know Your Soil ___ 10
Compost: How To Make and Use It ___ 12
Plant Foods: How To Choose and Use ___ 14
Watering ___ 16
Mulches ___ 18

Chapter 2
LANDSCAPING ___ 20
Put Your House in Proper Setting ___ 22
Outdoor Living ___ 23
Gardens—None Too Small ___ 24
Making Your Own Plan ___ 26
Grading Slopes for Correct Drainage ___ 28
Analyzing Your Lot ___ 30
Choosing Plants ___ 32
The Master Plan ___ 34
Front Entrances ___ 36
Patio Surfaces ___ 38
Decks ___ 40
Where To Plant Trees ___ 42
Overhead Shelter ___ 44
Gaining Privacy with Hedges ___ 46
Privacy Fences ___ 48
Landscaping Ideas ___ 50

Chapter 3
LAWNS AND GROUND COVERS ___ 58
Preparing Soil for a New Lawn ___ 60
Cool Season Grasses (chart) ___ 62
Southern Warm Season Grasses (chart) ___ 63
Western Great Plains Dryland Grasses (chart) ___ 64
Starting a Lawn from Seed ___ 65
Perk Up Your Lawn ___ 66
Control of Weeds That May Invade Lawns ___ 68
Diseases of Lawn Grasses and Their Control ___ 72
Common Lawn Insects and Their Control ___ 73
Ground Covers ___ 75
Ground Covers (chart) ___ 78

Chapter 4
TREES ___ 86
Selecting a Tree To Fit Your Needs ___ 88
Tree Treasury (chart) ___ 94
How To Plant and Maintain Trees ___ 106
Pruning and Repairs ___ 108

Chapter 5
SHRUBS ___ 112
Shrub Shapes and Uses ___ 114
Flowering Shrubs ___ 116
Choosing and Planting a Hedge ___ 120
Deciduous Shrubs (chart) ___ 123
Coniferous Shrubs (chart) ___ 140
Broad-leaved Evergreen Shrubs ___ 142
How To Plant Shrubs ___ 151
How To Prune Shrubs ___ 152
Pruning Evergreens ___ 154

Chapter 6
VINES ___ 156
How To Select a Vine ___ 158
How To Train a Vine ___ 160
How To Start a Vine ___ 161
Annual Vines ___ 162
Annual Vines (chart) ___ 163
Perennial Vines ___ 165
Perennial Vines (chart) ___ 166

Chapter 7
PERENNIALS AND BIENNIALS ___ 170
Constant Color ___ 172
How To Propagate Perennials ___ 173
Perennials for Special Conditions ___ 175
Perennial Basics ___ 176
How To Plan Perennial Borders ___ 178
Perennial Descriptions and Preferred Locations ___ 181
How To Plan and Produce Constant Bloom ___ 182
Starting with Perennials ___ 184
Choose Perennials by Height ___ 184
Approximate Bloom Dates (chart) ___ 185
ABCs of Perennials (chart) ___ 186
ABCs of Biennials ___ 223

Chapter 8
ANNUALS ___ 226
Uses for Annual Flowers ___ 228
Problem-Solving Flowers ___ 232
Annuals—Portable Color ___ 236
Annuals in Your Border ___ 241
Getting Ready for Annuals ___ 242
Hanging Baskets ___ 246
Strawberry Jars ___ 248
Favorite Annuals ___ 250
Annual Flowers (chart) ___ 258

Chapter 9
BULBS _____ 268

Sunny, Hardy Bulbs _____ 270
Leading Types of Tulips _____ 272
Daffodils _____ 280
Hyacinths _____ 282
Hardy Favorites To Begin the Season _____ 284
Hardy Favorites To Extend the Season _____ 286
Hardy Bulb Know-how _____ 288
Hardy Lilies _____ 290
Tender Bulbs _____ 292
Other Favorite Tender Bulbs _____ 300
Bulbs in Pots Outdoors _____ 302

Chapter 10
ROSES _____ 304

Planting Roses _____ 306
Rose Types _____ 307
Care of Roses _____ 308
Pruning _____ 310
Protect Against Insects, Disease _____ 313
Uses of Roses _____ 314
Old Garden Roses _____ 321
Modern Roses _____ 326
Climbing Roses _____ 332
Miniature Roses _____ 334
Tree Roses _____ 335

Chapter 11
SPECIAL GARDENS _____ 336

Wildflowers _____ 339
Wildflowers (chart) _____ 340
Ferns _____ 344
Wildflowers in the Shade _____ 345
Wildflowers in Sunny Spots _____ 348
Fancy Grasses _____ 350
Attract Wildlife to Your Garden _____ 352
Planning a "Wild" Garden _____ 354
Herb Gardens _____ 356
ABCs of Herbs _____ 358
Rock Gardens _____ 362
Shady Gardens _____ 366
Desert Gardens _____ 368
Water Gardens _____ 370
Water Plants (chart) _____ 372
Container Gardening _____ 374
Flowers for Cutting _____ 379
Handling Cut Flowers _____ 381
Dried Flowers _____ 382

Chapter 12
VEGETABLES _____ 384

Planning Your Garden _____ 386
Growing Food in Containers _____ 396
Getting a Jump on the Season _____ 398
Planting How-to _____ 400
Vegetable Garden Care _____ 402
Space-Saving Ideas _____ 406
ABCs of Vegetables _____ 408
Storing Your Crops _____ 429

Chapter 13
FRUITS AND NUTS _____ 430

Fruit Tree Basics _____ 432
How To Prune Fruit Trees _____ 434
How To Prune Cane Fruits _____ 434
Espalier Basics _____ 436
Fruit Tips _____ 438
ABCs of Fruit _____ 440
ABCs of Nuts _____ 454

Chapter 14
HOUSEPLANTS _____ 456

Containing and Potting _____ 458
Care for Houseplants _____ 460
Propagation Techniques _____ 464
Houseplants Under Lights _____ 468
Foliage Houseplants (chart) _____ 470
Ferns (chart) _____ 482
Palms (chart) _____ 484
Flowering Houseplants (chart) _____ 486
Bromeliads _____ 490
Succulents _____ 492
Terrariums and Dish Gardens _____ 496
Bulbs Indoors _____ 498

Chapter 15
GREENHOUSES _____ 500

Greenhouse Basics _____ 502
Hydroponics: A Soilless Growing Technique _____ 508
Soil for Greenhouse Plants _____ 514
Home Greenhouse Plant Guide (chart) _____ 515

Chapter 16
INSECTS AND DISEASES _____ 522

INDEX _____ 542

chapter 1

THE ABCs OF GOOD GARDENING

Quite simply, gardening is a joy. It occupies your summer hours and winter dreams. The practice of tending a garden can be a full-time preoccupation or an occasional escape to the outdoors. The choices are wide, and they're all yours.

Although it may seem an extravagant claim, gardening is by far the most popular outdoor hobby in the world. It appeals to people of all ages in all places, whether the climate is ideal or not. It provides opportunities to observe closely the ways of nature. It invites you to view, firsthand, the wonders of growth and the excitement of every gardening season. You enjoy blue skies and fresh air, and begin to measure the vagaries of weather against the needs of your garden. Under your husbandry, a packet of annual seeds can grow, sprout to mature plants, flower, and return to seed again. The perennials you plant, once established, will bloom gloriously through a series of summers. Trees and shrubs you select will shape your overall plan, and help you create a private world.

Each successful project will generate new ideas and lively challenges. As your garden matures, the flowers you have grown and the fruits you have harvested will become valued memories for you and your family. Your only obligation is to enjoy the beauty with your friends and to pass on the understanding to all who ask.

Consider Your Climate

With the information from the temperature zone map on the right, you can learn the approximate range of minimum temperatures in all parts of the country, and more particularly in your own area. Use this data to determine the right kinds of plants for your garden.

The climate in your area is a mixture of many different weather patterns: sun, snow, rain, wind, humidity. To be a good gardener, you should know, on an average, how cold the garden gets in winter, how much rainfall it receives each year, and how hot or dry it becomes in a typical summer. You can obtain this general information from your state agricultural school or your county extension agent. In addition, acquaint yourself with the mini-climates in your own neighborhood, based on such things as wind protection gained from a nearby hill, or humidity and cooling offered by a local lake or river.

Then carry the research further by studying the microclimates that characterize your own plot of ground. Land on the south side of your house is bound to be warmer than a constantly shaded area exposed to cold, northwest winds. An area in the full, hot sun is generally drier than a depression along a drainage route.

Watch how the snow piles up in the garden. Drifts supplying valuable extra water may be caused by the shape of the house or a deflection of wind around a high fence or wall. Study the length of tree shadows in winter and summer and use the information to avoid disappointments. All these findings can help you decide what to plant and where to grow it best.

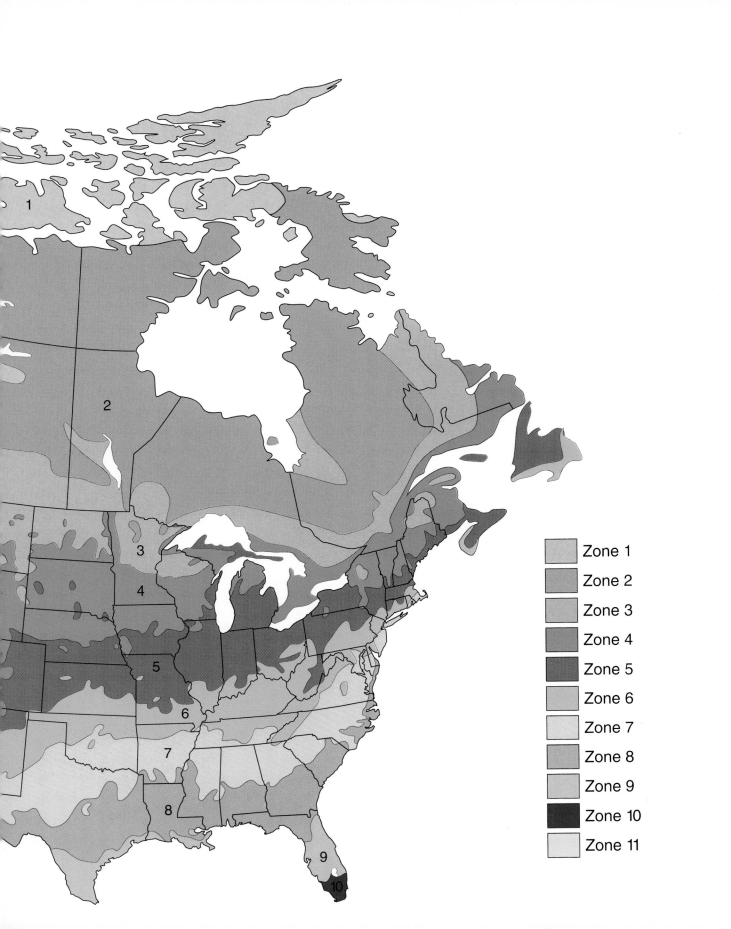

Zone 1
Zone 2
Zone 3
Zone 4
Zone 5
Zone 6
Zone 7
Zone 8
Zone 9
Zone 10
Zone 11

Know Your Soil

Good soil is as important to your garden as a good foundation is to your house. There's one big difference, though. With your soil you don't have to be satisfied with what you have. If you find that you don't have ideal—or even good—garden soil, you can improve it.

Gardening is like most hobbies in that you can get as involved as you like. No one is going to say you must thoroughly understand the soil or how plants grow in order to enjoy your garden. If you're at all serious about gardening, though, there are a few things you should know about your soil.

Most garden publications will tell you an ideal garden soil is deep, friable, fertile, well-drained, and high in organic matter. Don't be disappointed if your soil doesn't fit that description. Few garden soils do.

If you find the soil to be less than ideal, you can either leave it as is or try to improve it. Before you start making changes, find out what you have. And even if you decide not to make changes, getting to know your soil will help you decide what plants will grow best on your lot.

In getting to know your soil, you'll need to understand certain physical and chemical characteristics. Physical characteristics include the soil's composition, texture, structure, depth, and drainage. The main chemical characteristics you'll need to be aware of include the pH and the overall fertility level.

Composition. Soil is composed of four primary materials—sand, clay, silt, and organic matter (humus). The type of soil you have and many of its characteristics are determined by the proportion of

these four materials present.

The composition of your soil is related to soil texture and soil structure. It is important to know something about the composition of the soil if you attempt to adjust the pH or apply chemicals to your garden, because recommendations generally vary according to soil type. Knowing something about your soil's composition will also give you an idea of how well it will hold fertility and how well it will drain.

Although it would take a laboratory analysis to determine the exact proportions of sand, silt, clay, and organic matter in your soil, you can get a good idea what they are by observing the soil when you work it and by feeling its texture.

The two types that probably would give you the most problems are soils with too much clay and soils with too much sand.

A soil high in clay tends to be sticky. It will stick to your shovel when you're working it. And when it's moist, you can easily squeeze a clayey soil into a tight ball.

Soils with too much clay can cause problems for the gardener because they tend to be wet and difficult to work. Clay particles are small and fit closely together, leaving extremely small pores for air and water. On the other hand, your soil needs some clay to give it strength and water-holding capacity.

Soils with a high proportion of sand are nearly the opposite. The particles—and the spaces between them—are much larger, so sandy soils are crumbly in texture. If you try to squeeze a handful of your soil into a ball and it always crumbles apart, you have a sandy soil.

Sandy soils are commonly called light soils—and they're very easy to work. They cause problems for gardeners, though, because water and plant nutrients move through them too quickly.

The term *soil texture* is closely related to soil composition in that it refers to the size of the soil particles. Texture depends on the relative amounts of sand, silt, and clay in the soil and influences porosity, water-holding capacity, drainage, and soil atmosphere.

Soil texture should influence the way you manage your garden. For

If you pick up a handful of your soil and can squeeze it into a tight, sticky mass, your soil is likely high in clay.

A loose, crumbly soil like that above won't hold any shape. This soil has a high sand content and won't retain moisture.

Soil of the proper texture will mold into your hand—yet crumble apart when squeezed.

example, if you have a fine-textured clay or silt soil, you need to be especially careful that you don't work the soil when it is too wet.

The term *soil structure* describes how soil particles are grouped and arranged. Structure also may influence porosity, water-holding capacity, drainage, and soil atmosphere. If soil is crumbly and somewhat porous, but not too lumpy, it has good structure. Adding organic matter (humus-making materials) may improve structure.

Depth. The root zone of plants is wider and deeper than most gardeners realize, so you want a soil that is deep enough to accommodate it. Because roots grow best in topsoil, that soil should be as deep as possible.

Drainage. Soil drainage is important because soil occasionally receives more water than it needs. Plant roots need air as well as water, so if all the soil's pores are filled with water, your plants will suffer. A poorly drained soil often will be too wet and cold for proper plant growth.

Chemical characteristics. Soils have chemical reactions going on all the time, but the only chemical characteristics you need to know about are the pH (the acidity-alkalinity relationship) and the overall level of fertility. The only sure way to determine your soil's pH and fertility is with a soil test. Color, soil texture, and other physical characteristics should not be used to indicate soil fertility.

Soil testing

The only accurate way to determine the levels of various nutrients in your soil—and to find out what percentage of those nutrients will become available to plants during the next growing season—is to take a soil test.

Many gardeners think soil testing only determines the soil's pH, but, through it, you also can find out what nutrients are present. Standard soil tests will tell you the pH of your soil, how much phosphorus and potassium are available, and how much organic matter the soil contains. If you think you might have a problem, tests also are avail-

able that give you a complete report on the other essential elements.

The first step in soil testing is to get a good, representative sample of the soil in your garden. Take samples from different areas by digging to a depth of six to eight inches and taking a thin slice of soil from the edge of the hole. Mix the samples thoroughly to obtain about a half-pint of soil as your final sample.

Remove roots, sticks, or stones from the sample, and keep it in a clean, dry, covered container until it's tested. If you have several kinds of soil in your garden, you may want to take separate samples.

Once you have a sample, your local county extension office can tell you where to send it. Most states operate soil testing services that charge a small fee (perhaps $3 to $5 per sample) for their work.

If you want to get involved yourself, buy a soil testing kit and do your own tests. Remember that your results may not be quite so accurate as those from a standardized laboratory.

The final, and most important, step in soil testing is interpreting the results. The most accurate soil test will do you little good if it's interpreted poorly.

More and more state extension services are developing special interpretations and recommendations for tests of lawn and garden samples. In some cases, the recommendations are even computerized. Those you receive will tell how much lime you should add to adjust the pH and how much phosphorus and potassium you should add to bring these elements up to acceptable levels.

Nitrogen recommendations generally are not based on the soil test, because the element moves through the soil so quickly that the amount of nitrogen changes.

Making changes

Once you know what your soil is like, you're ready to try some improvements. Your changes can be as simple as tilling the soil, or as complex as establishing a complete composting system.

Proper tillage can go a long way toward improving the structure

of your soil. On the other hand, improper tillage can do your garden some harm.

Never till your soil when it's too wet. Take a handful of soil and squeeze it together. If it forms a sticky, compact mess, then it's too wet to be worked. Heavy clay soils that are tilled when they're too wet become hard and lumpy.

Even when moisture content is right, it's possible to overwork your soil. You don't want to work it so finely that it will crust after a rain. You want to break up the clods and level the surface, but not destroy the soil structure.

Soil amendments. If you find it necessary to improve the physical structure of your soil, there are a number of approaches you can use successfully. If you have a heavy clay soil, you might consider adding some sand to it for improved drainage and workability. Or if you have a light sandy soil, you might consider mixing in some clay to improve the texture.

A more common approach to improving your soil's physical characteristics is to add organic matter like compost or peat. Such materials can go a long way toward improving your soil's structure.

Humus sometimes is called a cure-all for every soil weakness. If you add humus to sandy soil, you'll get improved water retention; add it to a clay soil, and the soil will be more friable and easily worked. If you till it deeply into heavy soil, you will get improved drainage. And, if it's added regularly over a period of years, humus will improve the fertility of any soil.

There are several types of humus-producing organic materials available. Among these are manure, compost, peat moss, sewage sludge, sawdust, and straw. If these materials are applied over a period of several years, there always should be enough humus decaying to supply your soil with a certain amount of plant nutrients. However, because none of these materials contains very many plant nutrients, they should not be substituted for fertilizer.

Try to incorporate organic matter into the soil in the fall to give the microorganisms in the soil a chance

to decompose the material in advance of spring planting.

It's also a good idea to incorporate about two pounds of 10-10-10 fertilizer per 100 square feet. The microorganisms that decompose the organic matter get their energy from plant nutrients, so if you don't add the fertilizer, they tie up essential elements during the decomposition process, elements that are then unavailable to plants.

You may see chemical soil amendments on the market whose makers claim they will improve the structure of your soil and increase your yields. Be sure to check carefully before buying such products. Soil scientists have tested many such products, and have found few (if any) that have a significant effect on soils and plant growth.

Fertilizers. The easiest method of improving soil fertility is through the addition of chemical fertilizers. Unfortunately, fertilizers can be expensive, so it makes good sense to apply them only as needed.

Plants need at least 16 elements for healthy growth. Only four of them commonly are applied as fertilizer—nitrogen, phosphorus, potassium, and calcium. Plants also use large amounts of carbon, hydrogen, and oxygen—elements they get from air and water—as well as sulfur and magnesium.

The elements needed in smaller quantities—called *micronutrients*—include iron, manganese, zinc, copper, molybdenum, boron, and chlorine. Although micronutrients are needed in smaller quantities, they're important. These elements are generally present in soils, but in some parts of the country, one or more of them may be deficient.

Your soil's pH. The pH scale is used as an index of your soil's acidity or alkalinity. Plants differ, but most can tolerate a fairly wide range of pH values.

Most garden plants thrive when the pH is between 6 and 7 (close to neutral) and grow reasonably well with a pH between 5.5 and 7.2. If you find your soil has a lower pH (too acid), you will need to add hydrated lime or pulverized limestone to neutralize it. Be sure to follow soil test recommendations in deciding how much to add.

Compost: How to Make and Use It

Compost is the heart and soul of organic gardening. You need not be a strict organic gardener, though, to reap the benefits of composting. The use of compost to improve the physical structure of your soil is a good idea, even if you use chemical fertilizers.

Organic matter often is thought of as a magical substance designed to cure all your soil's problems. Believe it or not, that is close to the truth. Adding organic matter to your garden will improve the structure, water-holding capacity, and aeration of soils containing too much clay, as well as those with too much sand.

Compost is the organic matter most frequently recommended to gardeners. Not only will compost improve your soil's structure, but it also will contribute needed nutrients to the soil.

Basically, compost is nothing more than well-decomposed organic materials. It can include some of the same dead plant materials you ordinarily would spade under in working your garden. By composting them, you simply speed up the decomposition process.

Making compost. There are few set rules to follow in making compost. Your system can be almost as simple or as elaborate as you choose. There are, however, a few general guidelines that will help you make compost with a minimum of problems.

Inside a compost heap many kinds of bacteria and fungi go to work breaking down or decomposing the various materials in the pile.

To do their job, the bacteria need a source of energy and a certain amount of moisture. And depending on the type of bacteria working for you, they may need oxygen.

Aerobic bacteria—those requiring oxygen to live and work—are the most desirable because they get the job done more quickly than anaerobic bacteria—those not requiring oxygen. The anaerobic types, though slower, *will* get the job done, and the heap in which they grow will not require as much of your attention.

The type of bacteria you have depends on how frequently you mix your compost heap. And that, in turn, determines how long it takes to make the compost. The more frequently you turn the heap, the quicker the process of decomposition will be.

Location. You'll want to give careful attention to the location of your compost heap. Choose a fairly level spot with reasonably good drainage. Avoid placing it in a depression where it might become waterlogged during a wet season.

Your location also should be close to a water supply—or at least within reach of your garden hose, so if it becomes too dry, you easily can sprinkle it down.

A shady spot also is preferable because too much sun will dry out your pile too frequently. The heap also should be close to your garden, accessible to a wheelbarrow, and shielded from living areas, if possible.

Type of enclosure. It is not absolutely necessary to have an enclosure around your compost heap, but an enclosure makes the pile much easier to build and maintain. An enclosure also helps to prevent loose materials from blowing around your yard.

The type of bin you build can be simple or elaborate—depending on the construction materials you have to work with.

Bricks, concrete blocks, wire, snow fencing, or wood can all be used. If you use wood, remember that the same bacteria working in the heap will be trying to break down the wood, so use cedar, cypress, or redwood, if possible, because these three resist decay.

You will need a three-sided enclosure with removable slats or boards on the fourth side so you can reach the pile to turn or remove compost. If you build your compost heap alongside a garage or other building, don't use the side of the building as one side of the enclosure. This, too, could decay.

Also remember to build your enclosure so air can get in to nourish the bacteria. If you use concrete blocks, lay them so the holes or air passages are horizontal, rather than vertical. And if you use wood, be sure to leave some space between the boards.

The most common size for compost bins is four by four feet and at least three to four feet high. If you need more room, you'll find two small bins are much easier to manage than one large one—especially when it's time to turn the compost. The largest bin you should consider is about 25 square feet.

The height of the bin is also important. If you build a pile less than three feet high, it will tend to dry out. And if you build it more than four feet high, it will be difficult to turn.

Many gardeners like to have two bins side by side. With this arrangement, they can use material from one bin while material in the other bin is composting. Another use for the second bin is for transferring the material from one side to the other when turning.

Some gardeners prefer to excavate a foot or so below ground level to reduce the height of the pile, but you'll need a well-drained site for this to work.

You won't need to worry about adding either a floor or a cover for the bin because microbes and earthworms coming up from soil beneath the pile are necessary parts of the process. And if your pile is rained on, the shower probably will save you the trouble of hosing it down to add moisture.

Building the pile

Once you have selected the site and built the bin, you're ready to begin building the pile. You can start a compost pile any time, although fall is one of the best times because there is usually a ready supply of compost materials, such as dry leaves and garden refuse, that must be discarded anyway.

What goes in? Almost any plant or animal material can be turned into compost. Some materials—large sticks and branches, whole bones and animal fat, for example—decompose slowly and probably should be avoided.

Leaves, grass clippings, weeds, garden refuse, table scraps, cornstalks, straw, old mulches, sawdust, manure, brewery wastes, seaweed, nutshells, fish wastes, tobacco stems and wastes, wool clippings, corncobs, paper scraps, ashes, feathers, pine needles, peat moss, and even old sod are all materials that qualify for addition to the compost heap.

You should *avoid* diseased vegetable plants or roots, charcoal, and other material that is not biodegradable.

Hard or fibrous materials, like corncobs and stalks, apple pomace, cotton stalks, sugar cane leaves, certain nutshells, wood chips and paper, should be chopped or ground up before they are added to the heap.

To begin the heap, spread a six- to 12-inch layer of material in the pit. Then, add a layer of manure—if you have it—or a layer of fertilizer. Top this with a one-half- to one-inch layer of topsoil or soil-sand mixture, moisten thoroughly, and repeat the layering process until you reach the desired height.

Organic gardening purists will shudder at the thought of adding fertilizer to a compost heap. However, adding a fertilizer high in nitrogen to each layer will feed the bacteria so they do their work more quickly. Adding a complete fertilizer, containing phosphorus and potassium, will produce compost with more balanced fertility.

The amount of fertilizer you'll need to add depends on the organic matter in the layer. For tough ingredients like sawdust, straw, or crushed corncobs, use about two pints of 12-12-12 for each 25 cubic feet. For grass clippings, weeds, and similar materials, you'll want to use about 1½ pints. Add limestone to the heap only if you know your garden soil is too acid.

As you assemble the materials for each layer, try to mix different kinds of materials. Layers consisting of one material, such as grass clippings or leaves, will not decompose properly.

You also might want to consider alternating layers of wet materials —fresh grass clippings, for instance —and dry, weathered materials. The dry layers will absorb some of the excess moisture from the wetter materials—and each will benefit.

Adding layers of soil throughout the pile helps to bring in microbes, absorb odors, and hold the compost pile in place.

Make sure you have enough materials to build your pile at least three feet high. Shallower piles are often more difficult to keep moist and may not reach a high enough internal temperature for proper composting. At the same time, avoid making a pile that is too high to turn easily.

When topping off your pile, consider the climate and the time of year. In dry climates or seasons, cup the top of your pile to catch and hold rain. In rainy seasons or more humid climates, mound the top of the pile to shed rain.

Managing the pile. As long as there is oxygen within the pile, the aerobic bacteria will swiftly decompose the materials. As soon as the supply of oxygen is exhausted, anaerobic bacteria take over. Although they work more slowly, the result is similar. Each time you turn and aerate your compost pile, the aerobic bacteria begin their work anew.

During decomposition, temperatures inside the heap will rise to between 150 and 170 degrees Fahrenheit. Such high temperatures quickly can dry out the compost. If it's allowed to dry, the finished compost will have been burned and will have little value for improving your soil.

The high temperatures aid decomposition, but they also are beneficial because weed seeds, insects, and most disease organisms cannot survive under these conditions.

The bacteria that turn wastes into compost also need moisture to do their work. Ideally, the composting material should be spongy. On the other hand, you don't want it to be soggy. A waterlogged compost pile will block out oxygen and will soon become dominated by the anaerobic bacteria.

About three weeks after you complete it, turn the pile to aerate it. Turn it again two weeks later and you should have compost ready to add to your soil in about three months. If you're in a hurry or willing to devote more effort to it, turn your pile every three days (making sure to keep it moist), and you will have finished compost in about two weeks.

If you're in no hurry, you need only turn the pile every three or four months, and you will have compost in about a year.

Compost is ready to use when it's uniformly dark in color, crumbles readily, and has a clean, woodsy odor. The time required to make it will depend on the materials you started with and how diligent you are in feeding, watering, and turning the pile.

You can apply compost at any time. If it's ready before you're ready to use it, cover it with plastic to keep the nutrients from leaching away.

If you apply some compost to your garden before beginning to plant, spread a one- to three-inch layer over the entire area and work it into the soil. During the growing season, use compost to topdress your plants—being careful not to disturb the roots.

You also can use compost liberally every time you start a new plant. Mix up to one part compost with three parts of the soil in the planting pocket.

Compost also makes an excellent mulch—both in your vegetable garden and around flowers and shrubs—to help your plants get through hot, dry summers. It's very good for making potting soils and starting seeds in flats. Remember, compost will supply some needed nutrients, but it cannot be a substitute for a balanced fertilizer— especially if you have a new garden with poor soil.

COMPOSTING TIPS

In drier climates or seasons, cup the top of your compost pile so it catches whatever rain might fall.

During rainy seasons and in more humid parts of the country, mound the top of the pile to shed rain.

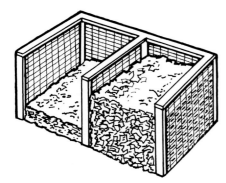

While compost is being made in one bin, store finished compost in the spare for a constant supply.

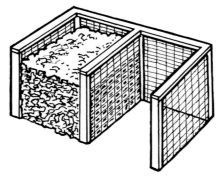

An extra bin comes in handy for turning. Just move compost from one to the other.

Plant Foods: How to Choose & Use

How to choose plant foods depends on the objectives you have for your lawn or garden. If you simply want to keep your plants alive, a yearly application of a complete fertilizer should do the trick. But if you want your plants to do their best, you'll need to do more.

Of the 16 nutrients essential to plant growth and reproduction, only four are likely to be deficient in soils: nitrogen, phosphorus, potassium, and calcium. The first three are included in mixed, commercial fertilizers, whereas calcium is usually sold separately in the form of limestone.

The best way to know how much and in what proportion to add plant nutrients is with a soil test (see page 11). Once a soil test indicates what nutrients you need to add, you can select a fertilizer to correct most of those deficiencies.

As you become more involved in gardening and managing your soil, you will probably hear a good deal about the benefits of one type of fertilizer compared to another. In weighing these arguments, remember that plants can't distinguish between the sources of their nutrients. Plants simply need to have all of the nutrients present in sufficient quantities, in the proper proportions, and in a form they can use.

The key to nutrient value is availability. Fertilizer needs to be reasonably soluble and available to plants soon after application. Soil

NITROGEN
Nitrogen is part of both chlorophyll and protein molecules. It is necessary for new cell formation in all parts of the plant. Nitrogen is more likely to be lacking in comparison to other nutrients. Symptoms of a shortage include yellow-green stunted plants.

POTASH
Potash is essential for strong stems and roots—especially in vegetables. It also is necessary for deep flower color. An acute deficiency will show up in the form of plants with weak stems and a yellowing and browning of leaves at their tips and edges.

PHOSPHORUS
Phosphorus is essential for early growth and development of roots and stems. It stimulates fruit and seed production. A deficiency shows up as a red or purple discoloration of leaves. Because phosphorus is almost immobile in the soil, place it close to roots.

elements such as phosphorus and potassium—though plentiful in the soil—can become fixed to soil particles so they are not available to plants.

Organic plant foods include compost, manure, sewage sludge, bone meal, tankage, blood meal, cottonseed meal, and soybean meal. If you're planning to buy any of these materials, remember that their analysis—in terms of nitrogen, phosphorus, and potash—is low, so the actual nutrients you buy may be more expensive than if you bought them as one of the inorganic fertilizers.

Other characteristics of organic plant foods also should be considered as you make your selection.

With the exception of bone meal, nitrogen is the predominant nutrient in the plant foods. They usually contain less phosphorus and potash. In bone meal, phosphorus predominates. The nutrients in organic plant foods are insoluble and become available only as the material decays in the soil. That makes them slow-acting and long-lasting. And finally, organic fertilizers alone are not balanced sources of the nutrients your garden needs.

Inorganic plant foods are either mined or manufactured and have characteristics that contrast strongly with organic fertilizers. Their nutrients are in soluble form so they are quickly available to plants but are not very long-lasting.

Their solubility can make them caustic to plants. If you apply them in concentrated amounts, be careful to keep them from direct contact with roots and foliage or you might kill the plants. Analysis of chemical fertilizers is relatively high in terms of the nutrients they contain.

The ratio of nutrients contained in fertilizer must be printed directly on the container. The numbers indicate the percentage of nitrogen, phosphorus, and potash, in that order. Thus, a 12-12-12 fertilizer contains 12 percent, by weight, of each nutrient, with the remainder being inert matter.

Because of the different characteristics of organic and inorganic fertilizers, many gardeners find a com-

PLANT	SEASON TO FEED	SPECIAL NOTES
Annuals	Before planting	Spread food before turning soil for bed. Feed again when plants are thinned
Bulbs, tubers	Early spring or fall	Add food to planting pocket, either complete plant food or superphosphate
Evergreens	Early spring	Feed sheared ones again in fall. Use "acid" foods for azaleas, camellias
Fruit trees	Fall or spring	Use supplementary nitrogen in early spring in addition to yearly feeding
Hedges	Spring	Feed sheared hedges again in fall
Houseplants	Any time	Feed sparingly every two or three months except during winter when plants cease active growth
Lawns	Spring and fall	Supply extra nitrogen in fall if grass is damaged by drought or hard use
Perennials	When growth starts	Repeat when flower buds appear
Roses	Spring and summer	Fall feeding may force new growth that will be damaged by cold
Shrubs	Spring or fall	One feeding a year usually sufficient for mature plants
Small fruits	Spring or fall	Two feedings a year preferred for most bramble fruits. Extra summer feeding may increase crop
Trees	Spring	Repeat in fall if tree is weak, or damaged by drought, disease, or insects (see page 111)
Vegetables	Planting time	Side-dress when plants are thinned, or shortly after thinning. Check instructions on specially formulated vegetable foods
Vines	Spring or fall	Feed both spring and fall until plants get well established, then once a year

your plants need the nutrients, how quickly the nutrients become available from the fertilizer you select, and which fertilizer placement will be most beneficial.

The chart at the left summarizes when you should fertilize various types of plants. In determining the proper fertilizer placement, it helps to realize that phosphorus and potassium are fairly immobile once they're placed in the soil. As a result, they need to be placed near the root zone of the plants you're trying to feed. With these two elements especially, it does little good to spread fertilizer on top of the ground and hope it will work its way down to the root zone.

Broadcasting fertilizer with a mechanical spreader is the best way to cover large areas. In your garden, it's best to broadcast fertilizer in the fall or spring, before planting. Then work the fertilizer into the top two or three inches of soil.

Starter solutions are best used when transplanting large plants such as tomatoes. You can buy a commercial preparation or mix your own by dissolving one cup of 5-10-5 or 5-10-10 in three gallons of water. Pour this around the roots as the planting hole is filled until the soil is thoroughly moistened.

Side-dressing is a way to add nutrients needed during the growing season. Spread the fertilizer in a row at least six inches from the base of the plants—letting the band extend eight to 12 inches away from the row.

Deep feeding is usually not necessary to get nutrients down to the roots of trees and shrubs (see page 111). Use a water lance with tree food only for young trees. The majority of a tree's feeder roots— the ones that can use nutrients— are located in the top ten to 12 inches of soil, so deep feeding is not required. Check with your local arborist or county extension office for help analyzing your trees' needs.

Base feeding. For roses and shrubs, begin fertilizing six to 12 inches from the plant, and extend the circle of plant food six to 12 inches beyond the branch tips. Scratch the fertilizer into the soil, being careful not to damage shallow roots.

bination of the two produces the best results. Cost and available supplies may influence your choice.

Fertilizer forms. Liquid plant foods have no particular advantage over the dry forms, except around individual plants or for use as starter solutions. They're also good for accurate application to houseplants and other container-grown plants.

Slow-release fertilizers, like sulphur-coated urea, are relatively new products for home gardeners. They work on the same principle as the "time" capsules you take for your cold—they feed the plants slowly over an extended period. Slow-release fertilizers are especially useful on lawns, because you can apply them at higher rates and

not burn the grass. They also save the time of repeat applications.

A complete fertilizer is simply one containing all three major nutrients. The nutrients in any particular fertilizer may not be in the proper balance or ratio for your particular needs. Look for a fertilizer that contains nitrogen, phosphorus, and potassium in the approximate ratio recommended by the soil test. Then base your rate of application on the recommendations provided by the soil test.

Micronutrients. Some fertilizers contain a small quantity of certain micronutrients. However, because you usually must pay extra for micronutrients in fertilizers, it is best not to apply them unless you

find your plants have serious problems growing, and a soil test shows one or more micronutrients to be in short supply. Because these elements are generally needed in such small amounts, any excess can be toxic to most of the plants.

Limestone should only be applied if a soil test indicates your soil is too acid and you need to raise the pH. Soils with a pH of 6.5 to 7.0 will support the growth of most garden plants. (Do not add limestone without first having a test.)

Applying plant foods

Applying plant foods most effectively requires you to know when

Watering

Conserving water is not only a way to save money; it's become a necessity in some drought-plagued parts of the country. Here are some guidelines to help you get the most from the water you use—and help you save money, too.

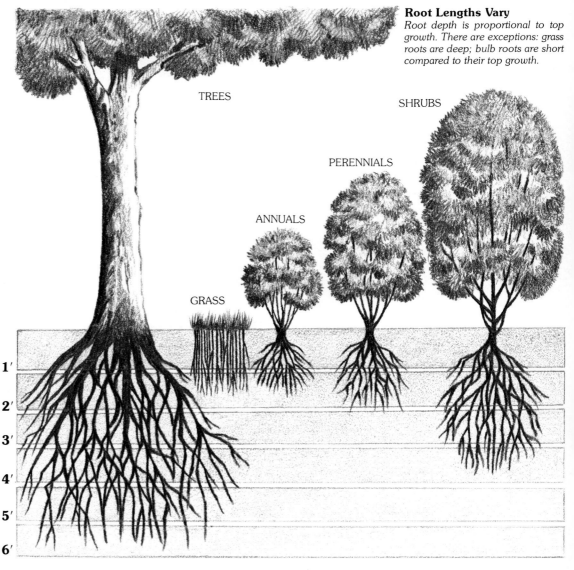

Root Lengths Vary
Root depth is proportional to top growth. There are exceptions: grass roots are deep; bulb roots are short compared to their top growth.

TREES

SHRUBS

PERENNIALS

ANNUALS

GRASS

1'
2'
3'
4'
5'
6'

Water requirements of plants. High temperature and low humidity cause plants to give off (transpire) huge quantities of water into the air, creating a drain on soil reserves. Under these conditions, a large, mature tree releases as much as 200 gallons of water a day. Small plants release much less, but the actual quantity surprises many people.

A block of sweet corn often transpires more than 12 surface inches of water in a season. The average tree, shrub, or flower can grow without regular feeding or cultivation, and even survive several insect attacks. But let it go dry for only a short time, and growth is stunted severely—or the plant dies. Plants require water for every physiologic function, so adequately supply yours with moisture.

How much to water. No rule applies to all plants, but a good one to follow is to supplement rainfall until you've supplied plants with one inch each week. When you water the lawn or garden, mark a one-inch level inside three one-pound coffee cans and space them within an area covered by a sprinkler. If less than one inch of rain falls during the week following the last watering, run the sprinkler until water reaches the one-inch mark. Empty the cans and reset them each time you move the sprinkler.

Deep watering. This saves both time and money. Water applied to only the top inch or two of soil is wasted because it evaporates before the plants can use it. Roots will penetrate deeply into moist soil. Top growth depends on a continuous supply of deep water to promote strong supporting roots—

especially important for trees in windy regions.

Light watering results in shallow root systems. Hot midsummer sun and wind will dry out the surface soil in a few days, leaving the plants high and dry. For this reason, let sprinklers or trickle systems do the watering. Few of us will patiently hold a hose long enough to supply sufficient amounts of water over large areas.

Soil amendments. You can save moisture and improve the structure of any common soil by spading in leaf mold, compost, peat moss, aged sawdust, or other partially decayed organic matter. All act like sponges.

Sandy soil dries out at least three times faster than clay and twice as fast as loam. Adding organic matter improves the tilth of all three. It binds sandy soils for better water retention, and opens up clay and heavy loam soils for better penetration by water and air. Mulches also will save soil moisture.

Water robbers. Weeds in your lawn and garden steal water and plant food from the soil—sometimes more than the plants use themselves. Eliminate them with a hoe or other hand tool when they're small.

Wind is another robber. Prevailing winds injure a garden or lawn by increasing soil water evaporation

and plant transpiration. Avoid much of this moisture loss by establishing windbreaks, such as evergreens or a fence designed to reduce the force of winds.

What plants have priority? Some won't survive unless the soil is reasonably moist at all times. Care for these first if you do not have enough time or water to cover everything. Bluegrass lawns often turn brown in summer heat and drought. Don't worry about your lawn if you have other plants that need water more. This only means the grass is dormant, not dead; it will turn green again when cooler weather and fall rains stimulate new growth.

Drip irrigation

It's possible to have a severe drought and a thriving garden at the same time. The way to do it is called trickle or drip irrigation. It's a system to make a little water go a long way.

The basic principle is simple. Water is delivered in small quantities under low pressure directly to where it does the most good—right to the root zones of the plants.

This water migrates through soil by capillary action. Most air passages in the soil remain open, in contrast to the flooding of furrow irrigation or oversprinkling. Oxygen is always available to roots, and stresses of overwatering are thus eliminated.

Trickle irrigation is a handy way to conserve water. Little is lost to evaporation or runoff, especially if the unit is buried under a layer of mulch. If you don't have a ready source of organic matter for use as a mulch, rolled black plastic will do. The black plastic is especially effective spread under heat-loving crops such as melons, tomatoes, and peppers.

Trickle irrigation systems vary from dealer to dealer, but the one shown consists of half-inch polyethylene header pipe and a roll of thin, tape-like porous tubing.

The header pipe connects to a garden hose and routes water through the garden. It is placed either down the center or along one end of the garden. Small puncture holes are then made with a screwdriver into the header pipe at intervals corresponding to each garden row. Small eight- to ten-inch pieces of rubber connecting hose are then inserted into these holes. The other end of the connecting hose attaches to a length of porous tape.

This tape is rolled out along each vegetable bed and cut to the same length as the row. The end of the tape is then crimped to prevent water loss when the system is in use.

Porous irrigation tape is best placed three to four inches away from the base of the plants. It's often a good idea to plant a double row of vegetables and place the tape down the center of the row. This is especially effective with peas, beans, and peppers.

To water, simply turn on the garden hose for several hours a day. Water will continuously ooze out of the porous tape. The soil should always be kept slightly moist.

Pump only clear, clean water through the system. Dirty water will clog the porous tape.

Most trickle irrigation systems come equipped with a ball valve or pressure emitter to regulate water pressure within the system. Too much water pressure will result in blowouts and split tapes. Low pressure will result in inefficient operation. It's a good idea to keep the system's water pressure somewhere between three and four pounds per square inch.

In the fall, the porous tape and connecting tubes should be cleaned and stored in a dry place. Header pipes can be left intact in the garden over the winter.

1 *Components for a typical trickle irrigation system, such as the one shown in use in the top photo.*

2 *Sections of rubber connecting hose are inserted into puncture holes made with a screwdriver in the header pipe.*

3 *At the other end of the connecting hose, attach a length of porous tape the length of the row it will nurture.*

Mulches

Mulches provide many benefits. A three-inch layer of mulch conserves moisture, keeps the soil cooler for better plant growth, and cuts down on time spent weeding. It blocks the sunlight which weed seedlings need to thrive.

The best and easiest way to conserve soil moisture in flower beds and around trees is by mulching. A two-inch mulch of grass clippings, straw, ground corncobs, or other material can cut water loss due to evaporation from soil as much as 50 percent. Mulching insulates the soil against hot sun and drying winds; it eliminates rain-compacted soil that keeps oxygen from penetrating the root zone.

Mulches not only prevent water loss, they actually can cause moisture to be added to the soil. Moisture in warm air invades the interior of the porous mulch and condenses when the air comes in contact with the cooler soil surface. Research shows that when air temperature is 100 degrees Fahrenheit, a three-inch mulch can keep the soil underneath up to 25 degrees cooler. This not only conserves moisture; it also promotes better root growth and more efficient uptake of water and nutrients. When soil temperature is high, roots stop growing, and plants suffer—even if moisture is plentiful.

Apply mulch in late spring or early summer. Wait until the heavy spring rains are over and the ground has warmed up enough to be tillable.

Mulch also to decrease rapid runoff of rainwater, and to prevent dirt from splashing on both flowers and food crops. As organic mulches decompose, cultivate them into the soil to improve its tilth, then put down a fresh layer of mulch.

Great for acid-loving plants, pine straw helps maintain soil acidity as it breaks down.

Ground corncobs and ½-inch composition edging keep chrysanthemums neat.

Bagasse—the crushed, juiceless remains of sugar cane—provides a fine mulch.

SOME RECOMMENDED MULCHES

KIND OF MULCH	DEPTH	SPECIAL FACTS ABOUT THESE MULCHES
Grass clippings	2 inches	Rate high as a mulch. Spread only ½ inch at a time. Grass clippings will break down very readily in the soil.
Peat	2 inches	Soak well before using. Horticultural peat breaks down readily, tends to scatter. Sphagnum moss is coarser grade. Both are available at most garden supply centers.
Ground corncobs	2-3 inches	Improve soil structure, fertility. Especially good for roses and for other plants needing a medium acid soil. Apply plant food before mulching.
Coarse vermiculite	2 inches	Wet down. Clean, good insulator, fireproof, good for water penetration. Conditions soil when worked in. Doesn't add humus. Use the special horticultural grade only.
Composted leaves	2-3 inches	Partly rotted tree leaves from compost heap. Break down fast enough to add plant food and humus to soil.
Ground tobacco stems	3-4 inches	Desirable color, have some value as insecticide, add some fertility and humus. The odor can be undesirable.
Gravel or flat stones	2 inches	Where plentiful, practical to use as mulch for woody plants. Hold moisture well. Don't add humus or food.
Boards or planks	———	Line up on both sides of vegetable and cut-flower rows. Hold moisture, prevent weeds. Can be stored for re-use.
Black plastic	———	Roll out along vegetable and cut-flower rows. Holds in moisture, controls weeds. Punch holes for drainage.
Cottonseed hulls	2-3 inches	Readily available only in cotton-growing areas. Insulate and help condition soil, but are low on food.
Sawdust	2 inches	Get at local sawmill. Breaks down slowly. Weathered sawdust is the most desirable. Don't mix fresh with soil.
Spanish moss	4 inches	Available only in South, where it can be had cheaply. Tedious to apply neatly. Water penetration good.
Peanut hulls	2-3 inches	Available in the peanut-growing areas. Insulate, condition, and add some fertility to the soil. Blow easily.
Pine needles	2 inches	Gather fallen needles from beneath trees. Make good-looking mulch and effective, but burn rather readily.
Chopped hay	3-4 inches	Use alfalfa hay, chopped slough hay, or salt-marsh hay in areas where they grow. Somewhat of a fire hazard.

Straw or hay makes a good mulch for vegetables.

Redwood sawdust mulch will last a long time.

Cocoa bean hulls conserve moisture extremely well.

chapter 2

LANDSCAPING

No matter where we live, we want a buffer against rush, noise, and too many people, a sheltered spot where we can relax in comfort. Fortunately, this kind of private retreat can be created on your own lot through landscape planning. By using your land wisely, you can expect other benefits, too. It's possible to set aside a place to play, find room for vegetable and flower beds, screen out the view of a hillside neighbor, or make your streetside entry beautiful. In short, you can shape your outdoor space to fit your needs.

Because landscaping is so flexible and works best when individualized, give your plans as much personal attention as possible. Even if you hire a professional designer, you'll need to examine your family's life-style and explain what you want to accomplish. If you do all the planning yourself, list every goal in detail. Think in terms of a total plan where the house and lot are integrated and no space is wasted. When you have a complete design in mind, you can segment the work, doing one section one year and another the next, but still have a unified look when you're finished. It's best to plant key trees and shrubs the first year so they will be growing as you complete other work. Whenever possible, established trees should be incorporated into the new plan rather than removed. In this serene backyard (right), a full-grown weeping willow stands as a focal point in the overall design. Around it, a serpentine grass area subtly creates a stream-like illusion while actual water shimmers in the shallow pool. Here, as in all well-planned designs, you see a skillful blend of plants and structural features. Study the following pages for landscaping principles and structural ideas that you can adapt to your own plan.

Put Your House in Proper Setting

The first impression a home gives is greatly governed by the landscaping out in front. Ideally, the streetside entrance should be simply planned and planted. It should enhance, not overpower, the home's architecture. Walks, too, can add to the design.

A landscaped entry can erase the bareness of a new home or revitalize the looks of an older one. Before the front of this L-shaped home (below) was redesigned, a few random shrubs were spotted by the door and under the windows. The walk took a typical curving course from the driveway.

Now, precast concrete-aggregate squares pave all but the planting areas, and a hurdle fence and lamps define a court within the "L", directing traffic to the front door. A Russian olive tree lightly shades the courtyard and adds height to the design. Two winged euonymus shrubs—one inside the fence, one out—balance each other and lead the eye to the court and doorway. In the summer, petunias furnish low-care color.

Outdoor Living

A well-planned outdoor living area offers privacy, comfort, and convenience; it's a natural extension of indoor living space. Functional structures, such as decks and benches, provide the framework; trees, shrubs, vines, and flowering plants add beauty.

The most livable outdoor decks and patios are hidden from the view of neighbors and secluded by shrubs, small trees, fences, or screens. An eye-high fence creates needed privacy along the sides of the deck (below), and a large specimen tree serves as a natural canopy.

There's comfort here, too. The built-in benches and outdoor furniture invite you to sit and relax; the deck provides a level surface underfoot and dries off quickly after a rain. Hard surfacing of some kind —bricks, paving blocks, flagstones, or concrete—is an essential element of a comfortable living center.

Sliding glass doors link the deck and indoor family kitchen. This arrangement is especially convenient when barbecues and outdoor parties are scheduled.

Gardens– None Too Small

"Miniatures" have long been favorites in art, flowers, even pets. A tiny garden, too, can have greater impact than its large counterpart. Its diminutive size makes the area easier to care for, too. Don't overlook front, back-, or side yards for refreshing compact gardens.

Too little space can limit would-be gardeners, but it need not stop you from creating a restful haven of green or colorful, blossom-filled retreat. Small areas mean lawns (and the resulting upkeep) are nearly out of the question, so pave or deck most of the surface. Leave some spots open for flowering plants, trees, and shrubs, or climbing vines to soften stark lines of constructed privacy screens and fences.

That little courtyard out back can be developed into a focal point for townhouse dwellers. This home (left) has a combination of dogwood, willow oak, rhododendron, daffodils, ivy, tulips, firs, azaleas, and wisteria inviting you outside on a sunny day. A well-screened garden opens a bathroom to a pleasant view and an abundance of light.

Any room can benefit beautifully from an adjacent garden. A previously ignored spot outside a window can become a soothing escape if part of the wall is replaced by French or sliding glass doors and a petite patio constructed.

A sitting garden just off the living or family room (bottom left, opposite) gives season-long changes in blooms and greenery and, at the same time, gracefully disguises a fence separating two homes—both built close to property lines.

A bedroom garden (above) is a charming way to greet the day. Colors, textures, and shapes are coordinated so they extend the room into the outdoors.

A breakfast garden (bottom, right) off the kitchen is a treat for family and guests alike, with delicious smells contributed by both the cooks and gardeners in the family. This yard is only 40 feet wide and 27 feet long. Low-care ferns and evergreens fill the center rectangle, while small planting beds at the ends of the steps hold clumps of annuals. Potted specimen trees and espaliered magnolias add to the overall effect.

All the gardens on these two pages are supplemented by container plants, naturals for small spaces. These pots can be moved around at will to create an ever-changing scene. Use clay pots of varying sizes, make planters of redwood or rough-sawed cedar, or set pots in decorated jardinieres or hanging baskets. Be sure to put large containers on platforms and casters so dragging them around won't be a back-breaking project.

Let your imagination wander beyond the plants shown here. You can even grow vegetables in containers. Miniature vegetables, such as cucumbers and tomatoes, adapt well to pot culture. A standard-size tomato in a large bucket can be an eye-catching, tasty addition.

Making your own plan

Before you start to measure and draw a plan for your dream landscape, such as the one on the facing page, check to see if a plan of the house is already available. Can it be obtained from the builder or architect? If you used a Federal Housing Administration-insured or Veterans Administration-guaranteed loan for your house, the local FHA or VA office may have a plan. Get a copy; it will save you time in developing garden plans that fit your house.

Secure a loan plat. Next, see if there is a loan plat with your deed; if not, it may be on file with the loan company or local office of the FHA.

Get a copy of this, too, because it shows lot lines drawn to scale, location of house on lot, drive, any other paved areas, all structures, easements, and so on—information you can transfer to your own drawing.

When you talk with the builder, architect, or FHA official, also ask whether there is topographical data on file. It may show grades and drainage.

By all means, find out where any underground water or power lines are located. Indicate on your plan, too, the placement of the septic tank and field.

Do you need a surveyor? If your lot is irregularly shaped, if your house has different levels or unusual angles, or if your lot is rough and hilly, you'd be wise to hire a qualified land surveyor. The firm could save you from making costly mistakes.

Their survey will show the exact sizes of both lot and house, indicate exact grades of walks, steps, walls, drives, and the ground itself. And they can locate accurately all trees and other features of the property.

Do-it-yourself surveying. If your lot is relatively small and level, you can easily be your own surveyor. By taking all the measurements yourself, you'll be well acquainted with all the features of your property.

Start with graph paper, such as that shown on the facing page. The one-inch squares are divided into smaller segments to give you ten small squares to the inch. The larger squares will represent ten feet on the ground—the smaller squares will be equivalent to one foot on the ground. After you have established the lot lines and the position of your house on the graph paper, it is a simple matter to measure from the corners of the house to locate and record accurately the various features (trees, walks, slopes) on the plan.

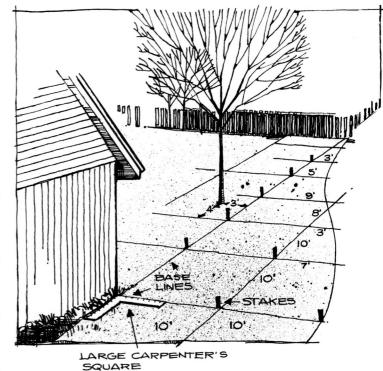

LARGE CARPENTER'S SQUARE

There are graph papers divided into several different numbers of squares, so if you find graphs divided into eight squares per inch, just have the larger squares on the graph represent eight feet on the ground. You may need to tape two graph pages together to get your entire lot drawn on it. Or you can put the backyard on one sheet and the front yard on another.

Take your ground measurements with a flexible 25- or 50-foot tape—one that winds up on a reel. It will come in handy later for laying out your plantings. Use a 12-inch ruler for aiding in the accurate recording of your measurements on the graph paper.

Measure carefully all around the outside of your house. Make a rough sketch as you go. Measuring to the nearest half-foot will do if you find smaller fractions difficult to translate to your lot. Plot all measurements you take on the graph paper and check to see that they agree.

Indicate door and window locations on the diagram; they will help later when you're ready to design plantings in relation to the house.

You are now ready to survey land around the house. Begin by measuring out from the corners of your house and projecting lines with stakes set at ten-foot intervals, as in the sketch above. These will be

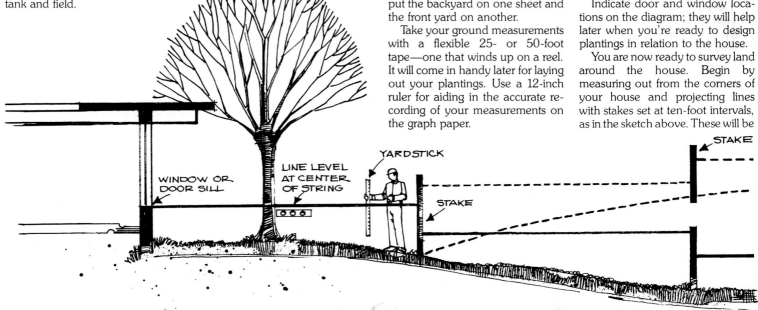

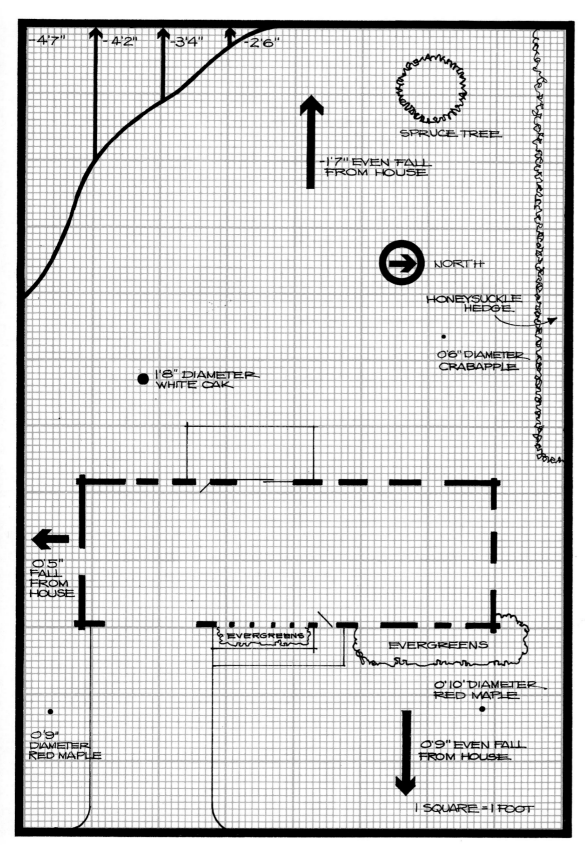

-4'7" -4'2" -3'4" -2'6"

SPRUCE TREE

-1'7" EVEN FALL
FROM HOUSE

NORTH

HONEYSUCKLE
HEDGE

0'6" DIAMETER
CRABAPPLE

1'8" DIAMETER
WHITE OAK

0'5"
FALL
FROM
HOUSE

EVERGREENS

EVERGREENS

0'10' DIAMETER
RED MAPLE

0'9"
DIAMETER
RED MAPLE

0'9" EVEN FALL
FROM HOUSE

1 SQUARE = 1 FOOT

the base lines for your survey.

Next, measure from the base lines at right angles, running out to the points on your property lines, (as illustrated at the top of the opposite page).

If all your property lines are straight, just locate lot corners. If you plot base lines on the graph paper, measure from them to lot corners and draw lot lines onto the plan by connecting the corners.

Curved lot lines. Locate curved lot lines by measuring to a number of points off your base line. Be certain that all your measurements are made at right angles to base lines, from points set along the base line by your stakes.

Next, draw walks, drives, walls, fences, and all other structures on your lot plan. Seeing their relationship in the form of a diagram will help you visualize what you'll want to add or change later.

You also can locate the top and bottom of all terrace slopes by measuring from the base lines (as sketched at the bottom of the facing page). To avoid extra distance by measuring uphill or down on sloping property, use stakes at intervals and stretch a taut cord between them. Check with a level to be certain the cord is always in a horizontal position.

Additional tips on measuring grades are included on the following pages. If your property is sharply sloped, you might be wise to hire a professional surveyor.

Determine what to save. Once your plan includes all the information about existing plants and buildings, it is time to decide what to save, what to move, and what to remove completely. At this stage, even if you've decided not to hire a landscape architect to do the entire job, you still may wish to hire one on a "consultation only" basis. You'll get the most for your money if you do have a plot plan on which you can make notes of his or her professional advice.

If your family includes children, let them participate in making your basic plan and in considering what is to be changed or added. If they feel they have a part in planning, count on them to feel more interested in future care.

Grading Slopes for Correct Drainage

To determine needed changes in grade, you can use either a simple level or a precisely calibrated model, like that used by a builder. Your measurements should be as accurate as possible, but they need not be to the closest fraction of an inch.

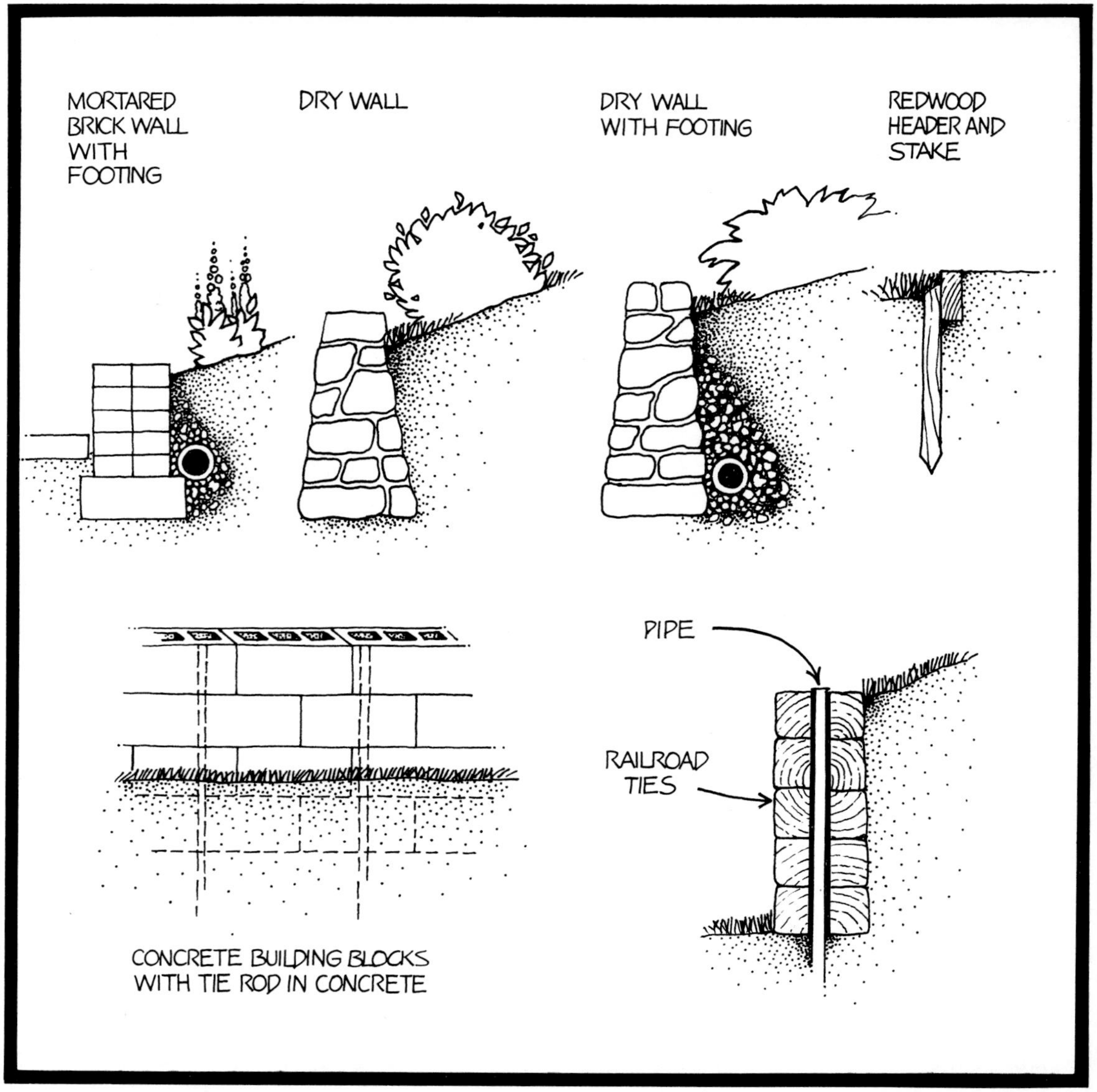

MORTARED BRICK WALL WITH FOOTING

DRY WALL

DRY WALL WITH FOOTING

REDWOOD HEADER AND STAKE

CONCRETE BUILDING BLOCKS WITH TIE ROD IN CONCRETE

PIPE

RAILROAD TIES

You can determine elevation by using a carpenter's level or string level and string. Here's how: tightly stretch the string horizontally, from floor level to any point you wish. Make sure the string is horizontal by holding the carpenter's level along it (or by using a string level). Now measure up or down to that point to find the difference in grade. Add or subtract this from the floor grade of 100,000 feet to figure the relative elevation.

If grade changes are rapid or steep, you may have to stretch string at a higher or lower level in several steps. From this survey, you should be able to tell such factors as whether you need one or two steps, if drainage tile is necessary, and where the grade must be changed.

When you have to change steep slopes, it is generally less expensive and more attractive to use retaining walls than to fill or excavate to achieve a more gentle slope. Walls may be of stone, brick, or concrete block—depending on which best suits the architectural style of your home. Railroad ties also are used widely to solve the problems caused by a steeply sloping lot. In sketches on this and the opposite page, a variety of effective solutions to hillside problems are shown. Retaining walls can enhance your landscape. But if the height needed exceeds four feet, do not attempt to install it yourself. Doing so requires expert knowledge and professional equipment.

If you've noticed a retaining wall leaning forward at an angle from its base, you are probably looking at the work of an amateur unfamiliar with nature's quirks. That person is apparently unaware that when soil is saturated, it exerts strong pressure on any restraining structure. "Weep" holes at intervals in a wall are sometimes able to solve the problem, but, usually, the best long-range solution is to install drainpipes set in a bed of loose aggregate or pebbles, behind and at the foot of the wall. Make sure the drain's end opens where water can run off safely, without eroding surrounding areas.

Pictured above are a number of suggestions for solving drainage problems by using retaining walls.

Easiest for an amateur to install is either a dry rock wall (laid without mortar) or one made with railroad ties. Both let soil water escape through cracks, thus avoiding a buildup of water pressure and its resulting problems.

These and other retaining walls are least troublesome if they're installed at a slightly backward slant—three inches of slant to every vertical foot of wall. Walls that are to remain truly vertical *must* have concrete footings, loose aggregate fill, drainage pipes, or tiles.

If the installation of a wall on your property requires excavating, be sure you plan to set good topsoil to one side; then replace it on top the new grade you have formed. If sod is good, it, too, should be removed with care, rolled up, and re-laid where needed.

If you decide to use "fill" soil to correct a steep slope, you'll get best

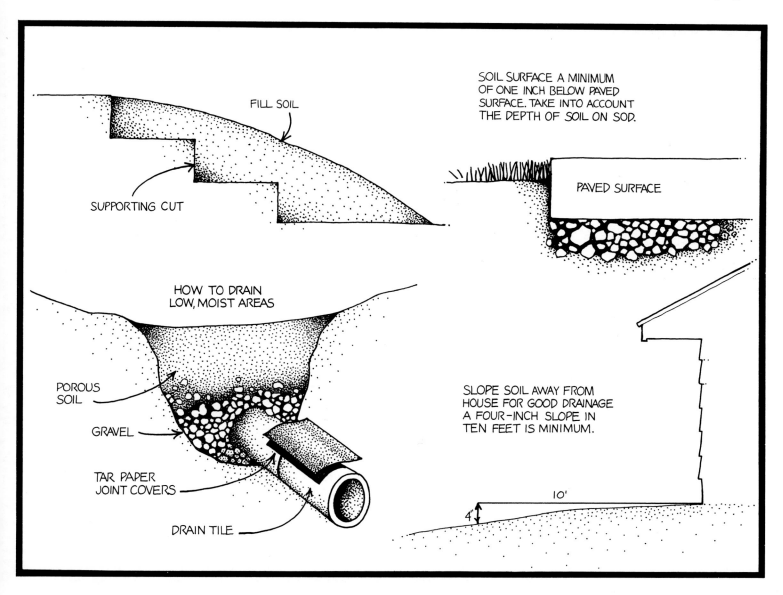

results if you make a series of supporting cuts (as shown in the sketch above, top left). This holds fill soil and makes it less subject to erosion before grass or ground cover becomes well established and able to keep soil in place.

Make sure the area of soil close to the house slopes away from it to get good drainage. A four-inch slope in ten feet is minimum if you are to avoid water seeping into the foundation and basement. The survey you made when you began to plan tells the exact slope. Check to see whether you need to make any changes in grade. A lawn that slopes as much as three feet hori-

zontally to each vertical foot may be mowed with safety.

In all cases where you have used fill to bring an area up to the level required for installing paved surfaces, remember new soil surface must be no less than one inch below a paved surface. Also, consider the depth of soil on adjacent sod.

Diversion gutters provide a good way to drain low, moist areas. Dig a shallow trench six to eight inches wide and deep. Put an inch of gravel in the bottom of the trench, then lay drain tile in place, using tar paper to cover the joints. Now fill with several more inches of gravel before adding porous soil (add peat

moss to soil if it's high in clay) to a level just below the former soil surface. Re-lay the sod you saved when you began the excavation. Such gutters keep moisture away from your house and prevent soil washing away in the rain.

Before the gutter is laid, note where the drainage tile will empty. It should run onto a flat sodded area or harmlessly into a sewer.

Don't overlook the alternatives of using plants to solve problems caused by hillside slopes. Shrubs such as dwarf barberry and creeping juniper are favorites for keeping the slope of a graded terrace from eroding. Combine them with some

spring-flowering bulbs and with low-growing annuals for seasonal color on the slope. A vast array of ground covers can provide additional color and texture while holding soil.

Rock gardens are another good way to treat a hillside. You can change an ugly bank into a major asset this way. Rocks must be secured to the bank by embedding the largest portions, leaving the smaller portions exposed. The process can be a lot of work—but worth it. The soil below must be porous for a garden to work well. See Chapter 11, "Special Gardens," for aid in choosing plants for rock gardens.

Analyzing Your Lot

To help you focus on the next step in developing your landscape plan, we offer a sample house and lot, sketched at right. Arrows indicate how to look at your own property in order to arrive at the best decisions.

Transforming your lot into the landscape you want may seem overwhelming. It takes time but can be enjoyable. The sketch at right helps you start. In the illustration, note all assets, liabilities, and some general problems to consider when developing an overall landscape plan. Consider these features along with your likes and dislikes.

Analysis. Note these factors: direction of winter winds; direction and angle of morning and afternoon sun (who wants a patio that gets hot, late afternoon sun?); unlovely views of the neighbor's garage; a too-narrow drive from the street to garage front entrance; unattractive view of an apartment house located to the northwest of the house; proximity of lot line to neighbor's drive; direct view of the street from the living room; lack of privacy at the rear of house.

Some clear assets are a view of distant hills and an existing oak of an approximately ten-foot diameter shading area at the rear of the house, including the dining and kitchen areas.

Look at your lot plan in these terms and decide its particular assets and liabilities. They may not, of course, be identical to those described above. Make a careful list of

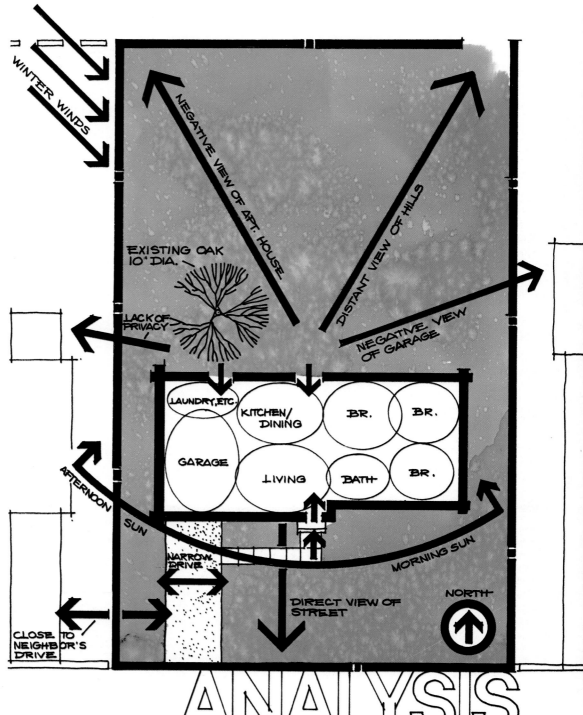

WINTER WINDS

NEGATIVE VIEW OF APT. HOUSE

DISTANT VIEW OF HILLS

EXISTING OAK 10' DIA.

LACK OF PRIVACY

NEGATIVE VIEW OF GARAGE

AFTERNOON SUN

LAUNDRY, ETC.

KITCHEN/DINING

BR.

BR.

GARAGE

LIVING

BATH

BR.

MORNING SUN

NARROW DRIVE

CLOSE TO NEIGHBOR'S DRIVE

DIRECT VIEW OF STREET

NORTH

ANALYSIS

similar points that relate to your own house and surrounding property.

Concept. Compare, now, the sketch at left with the one at right to see what has been done to capitalize on the assets and minimize defects existing before a landscape plan was developed.

Notice that both structural and planting changes have been made. Plantings have accomplished more privacy for the front of the home from the street, as well as from the neighbor's property at left. Plantings also have helped to screen out the view of the neighbor's garage on the right, and of the more distant apartment house to the rear; they also protect against winter winds.

Structural changes have been used to widen the drive, partially to enclose play space, and to provide some separation and enclosure for outdoor living area. Enclosed work and storage space at the rear have been added in a convenient spot.

The shade of the oak tree has been used effectively by putting both play and outdoor living space at the rear of the house. To take advantage of the attractive view of hills, plantings near that edge of the lot have been kept low so they won't cut off the view.

Your good and bad points will be different from those in our plan, but you should find enough similarities to help you take the next step forward and, ultimately, arrive at solutions. And don't forget to accentuate your assets.

Make tentative alterations on the plan of your existing property, using both structural and plant changes to see what solutions you create. There is often a choice of several answers. Don't settle for the first that comes to mind until you have compared it with alternatives.

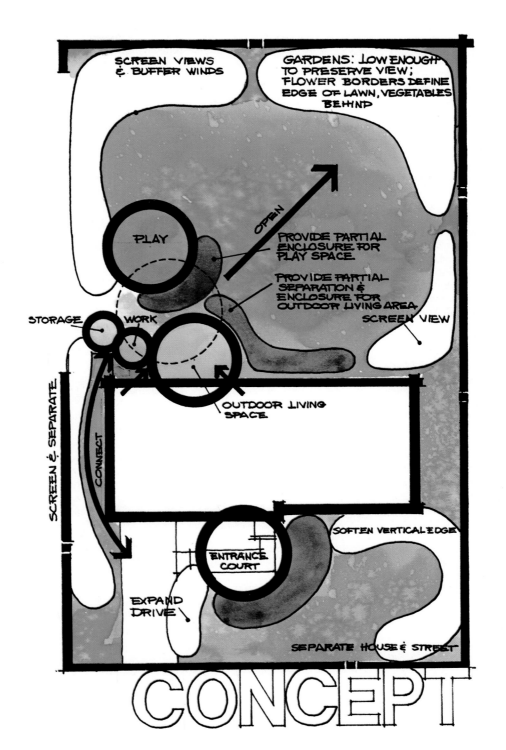

Choosing Plants

Once you've decided where to place the plants, you still need to choose the *right* plants for the right place. You'll want variety in size, texture, color, and growth habit. Be sure the plants will be healthy in the spots where you put them.

Shade trees should receive your attention first. These take time to grow and should be set out as soon as possible, especially if you'll do your landscaping in stages, over a number of years. Trees will grow while you proceed with the lesser elements in the landscape. Plan their placement carefully.

Many state agricultural colleges and county extension offices have informative booklets listing shade trees suited to the soil and climate conditions of your area. They will help you compare growth rates, heights at maturity, density of shade, and other factors.

If there's an arboretum nearby, visit it. You'll see mature trees there, all labeled, that also will help you decide. In addition, visit several nurseries, if possible. Compare prices, and you will discover they're based largely on the diameter of the tree. "Whips," or young unbranched trees, often sold bare-rooted, will cost little, but you'll have a long wait for shade. A tree four inches in diameter will cost a great deal more, but it will provide shade more quickly. And you can speed the growing time, *only after the first year,* by fertilizing around young trees in the fall or spring. (Check page 111 for more information on feeding trees.)

If you buy a good-size tree, let the nursery plant it. The extra money is well spent. Their staff knows how to do least damage to the roots and how to set the tree in place. A reputable nursery also will offer a guarantee usually not given if you do the work yourself.

Trees such as maples, oaks, and beeches can grow to heights of 60 feet or more. Unless your property is large, don't use too many of these shade trees or you will diminish the importance of smaller ornamental trees that also can play an important and colorful role in your plan. Also, you will have a lot with too much shade.

Evergreens, such as pines, firs, and spruces, will not grow so tall as oaks and other large shade trees, nor are they of spreading habit. Their conical form offers interesting contrast. And they remain green during the winter, another point in their favor if they become part of your overall plan.

Young evergreens are commonly sold as "container-grown" plants, and these can safely be planted as a do-it-yourself project. Be sure to consult Chapter 4 on trees before you do any planting yourself. Also, frequently water newly planted trees during the first few years after planting, unless rainfall is heavy.

For all the evergreens—shrubs as well as trees—it's important they go into winter well-watered. Watering during a dry fall is particularly critical to keep them alive.

If you feed evergreens, use only fertilizer formulated for conifers, and only in recommended amounts. It's easy to burn tender roots and cause permanent damage to them.

Ornamentals include a huge selection of trees and shrubs that do not grow much higher than the first story of a house, or, through consistent pruning, can be held at that height. Redbud, dogwood, saucer magnolia, flowering crab, and Japanese maple are but a few on the list, depending on your growing zone and the effect you wish to create. Most need full sun for the best effect and the best color, so keep this in mind as you plan their placement.

Evergreen shrubs deserve a place in your landscape for the contrast they offer to deciduous shrubs and for their year-round green foliage. Several varieties of arborvitae, holly, juniper, yew, and pines, such as mugo, in the correct placement, need little care in return for years of beauty.

Ground covers, lovely lifesavers in spots where shade's too deep for grass or where mowing's difficult, also fill an important role in landscape plans. Among those performing well in shade are vinca, ajuga, English ivy (as far north as New York City), pachysandra, and creeping thymes that send up a spicy scent when you walk on them.

Lawns must be chosen according to area. (Check Chapter 3 on lawns for help.) But no matter what grass seed you use, a lawn is an important element of the landscape because it offers a welcome, smooth contrast to other plants. As a gem gleams against a dark velvet setting, so shrubs, trees, and other plants are more interesting when set against the background supplied by the expanse of your lawn.

Flowers can play a big seasonal part in a landscape plan, but remember, if low maintenance is a major goal, you'll be wise to limit the space given to them.

Filling in your plan. Notice, at the bottom of this page, the key signs used in the sample landscape plan pictured on the opposite page. They are symbols for ground cover, evergreen trees, evergreen shrubs, deciduous shrubs, overstory shade trees, understory ornamentals, deciduous shrubs, lawns, and flowers.

Use a sheet of tissue paper and colored pencils to draw similar symbols on your chart. This makes it easier to visualize the results on your lot. Compare your chart with the plan pictured on the opposite page. Does it have a comparable distribution and mixture of the various plant materials: trees for shade and ornament, evergreen trees and shrubs, deciduous shrubs, ground cover, lawn and flowers? If not, do you want to change your plan—perhaps eliminate some plants?

Beginners tend to overplant simply because it is difficult for them to gauge how much plants are going to grow during the years to come. Go back and check references to see if you've allowed enough space for the growth of shrubs and trees over a ten-year period.

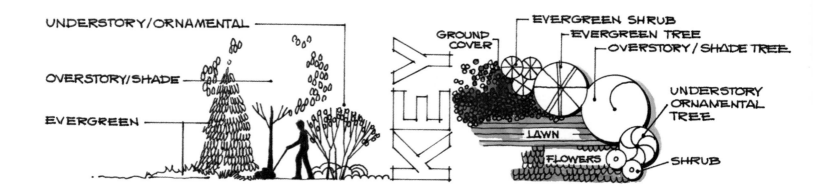

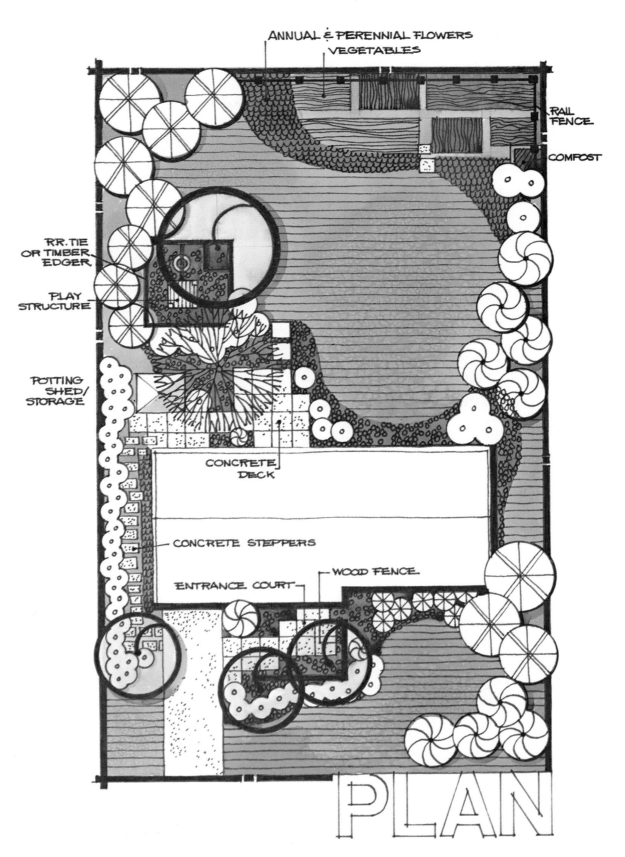

ANNUAL & PERENNIAL FLOWERS
VEGETABLES

RAIL FENCE

COMPOST

R.R. TIE OR TIMBER EDGER

PLAY STRUCTURE

POTTING SHED/ STORAGE

CONCRETE DECK

CONCRETE STEPPERS

WOOD FENCE

ENTRANCE COURT

PLAN

The Master Plan

The sketches on this and the facing page show what the sample landscape plan —described on pages 30 to 33—looks like when some changes are made.

Compare this drawing of the front entrance with the sketch on page 33 to see how the appearance of the front of the house has been dramatized and revitalized through structural changes combined with new plantings.

An ornamental shrub and ground cover in a rectangular planting area have made the front entrance much more attractive. A low, partial fence plus two ornamental trees lend privacy to the area, and two evergreens (extreme right) cut off what was previously an undesirable direct view into living areas from the street in front. The conical form of the evergreens will generally cause less shading than spreading trees and will not unduly darken the living areas. They will remain as a green privacy screen all the year around. The separation be-

tween indoors and out will be less sharp than it was before—another desirable goal because it gives you more living space. If strung with lights, these same trees will make cheery decorations during winter holidays.

In front of the entry fence and the ornamental trees, low-growing deciduous shrubs make a flowing transition between lawn and paved entry area. Flowering quince and dwarf barberry are two possible choices for this spot. If you live in a temperate zone, you may prefer dwarf azaleas that would add an accent of color in the spring. In either

case, an interplanting of bulbs that flower in the spring would be attractive. If you'd like to change your plan so it is similar to this one, take a black-and-white snapshot of the front of your house and have it enlarged to, say, 10x12 inches. Then use tissue paper to sketch the proposed plantings in the appropriate locations indicated on the landscape plan.

If the results are not what you sought, move plantings on the paper until what you see pleases you and your family.

In addition, structural elements may not look as you had hoped they would when you drew the plan on cross-sectioned paper. If so, try changing their location and height until the final product approximates the view you had in mind.

At this stage, even drastic alterations cost nothing but paper and time. Later, they may be expensive or impossible.

In the artist's sketch below, you see the rear of our sample house plan.

Notice several important structural changes. The concrete deck —with access from either the dining room or the kitchen-utility area— provides an attractive outdoor living area for the whole family to enjoy.

A potting shed and storage unit make it easy to put garden tools out of sight when not in use. A partly enclosed play structure with adjacent play area will appeal greatly to the younger members of the family.

And the roof partially covering it— another valuable feature—allows you to use the area even in a light rain.

In installing a paved area, care was taken to leave enough open space around the shade tree at the rear of the house so it receives adequate moisture. If you surround a tree with large areas of paved surface, you are almost certain to lose the tree because vital moisture won't be able to reach its roots.

Remember, also, that if you've done any filling around a tree that you wish to save, you must install a "tree well" that permits the base of the tree to stay at its original soil level. (See page 43 for an illustration.) The well should be at least

twice the diameter of the tree.

Additional plantings include a second shade tree to protect both play area and deck from hot summer sun.

A small planting bed close to the house includes an ornamental tree and some ground cover. (Or you may use flowering plants that do not need full sun.) A grouping of understory ornamental trees (only one shows at lower left in this sketch) wipe out an undesirable view of the neighbor's garage and lend greater privacy to the entire rear area of the property.

Lawn reaching beyond the deck area should be bordered with a

mowing edge for easy maintenance and for separation of lawn from adjacent beds of shrubs and ground cover.

If croquet, volleyball, or badminton are favorite family sports, make sure you have included enough open lawn space. Try not to plant easily damaged shrubs or flowering plants near such areas where they are almost certain to be tramped on as balls or birds are retrieved.

To see if backyard changes suit your family and accommodate your favorite activities, try the technique described earlier. Use an enlarged photo of your property taken from the rear. Lay tissue paper over it and indicate proposed locations of new structures and plants.

Front Entrances

Soften, cool, screen, define. Plants at the front of your home can have many purposes. As it blends with the neighborhood, your landscape arrangement also reflects your personality and your family's style. Trees and shrubs may be selected to create an enchanting view or block a less pleasant one. The blunt lines of house corners, porches, walls, walks, and drives are soothed with natural, flowing lines of well-placed greenery. Splashes of spring and fall color signal "welcome" to friends and passersby. The effects of extremes in temperature are tamed by trees that reduce heat glare and chilly winds.

Favorite landscape plants have balance and grace that outdo any sculpture. Yet almost nothing makes homeowners so nervous as deciding what to plant around the front of the family dwelling. The trees and shrubs set along a foundation are fairly permanent. Because this is true, wise selection is vital; correct choices can spell little maintenance and a pleasing arrangement for years to come.

Plants can contribute to the beauty of your home. They have a multitude of forms, textures, and colors. They also have characteristic lines determined by their trunks, stems, and branches.

But their value is far more than decorative. Some are downright practical, as well. Can they offer a screen for privacy or shade? Are there some that will reduce mainte-nance problems? Can they mark off areas that reflect interests of family members—a garden patch, a play area complete with tire swing, a gracious rose showpiece, or a quiet place to sip lemonade and watch the birds?

The placement of many trees and shrubs can be ecologically sound, too. Plants can affect climate in limited areas. Cooling, parasol-like trees on the sunny side of the house can reduce strain on the air conditioner. Farm families have long known that a windbreak to slow wintry gales assists in conserving heat and restraining drifts. City folks are discovering this, as well, when they plan tree placement.

The color of trees and shrubs can make a yard appear cooler, too. Green and blue-green are cool; red, orange, and yellow are hot, advanc-ing colors. Remember the changing seasons. Will the plants you chose for the focal point remain attractive through most of the year? Take care to select colors that coordinate with your home's paint or siding and with other plants.

Size, like color, can accent or overwhelm. That cute young shrub just under the living room window may one day grow tall and bushy, blocking your view. Set trees where they will frame the house. Select plants that will stay in scale with ar-chitectural features even when full-grown; avoid large plants near the entrance.

With new homes, put one or two fast-growing trees near the corners of the house. Slower-growing trees on other corners and along the back will be stately by the time the speedy ones start to deteriorate.

■ MONOTONOUS, UNIFORM PLANTINGS; SHRUBS WHICH GROW UP TO BLOCK VIEWS FROM WINDOWS; PLANTS WITH SEVERE UPRIGHT FORMS THAT CONFLICT WITH A HOUSE'S HORIZONTAL LINES.

■ PLANT CHOICES WITH LITTLE REGARD FOR THEIR RELATIONSHIPS TO THE HOUSE; PLANTINGS THAT APPEAR SPARSE AND UNDERSIZED.

■ OVERFORMALITY--FORMALLY TRIMMED SHRUBBERY NOT WARRANTED BY STYLE OF HOUSE; TEDIOUS CARE; PLANTS NOT USED TO CREATE THE OUTDOOR SPACES, BUT RATHER AS ORNAMENTS FOR THE HOUSE.

■ DEVELOP THE LANDSCAPE PLAN AROUND IMPORTANT ASPECTS OF THE HOUSE. FOR EXAMPLE, FOCUS LANDSCAPE TREATMENT TOWARD CREATING A SHADED ENTRANCE. IN ALL PLANTINGS, CONSIDER THE SEASONAL QUALITIES OF PLANT MATERIAL: FLOWERS, FALL COLOR, WINTER COLOR, OR FORM.

■ CREATE A NATURAL SETTING FOR THE HOUSE. INFORMAL PLANTINGS CAN SOFTEN ABRUPT BUILDING EDGES ALLOWING THE HOME TO BECOME PART OF THE LANDSCAPE. PLANTINGS WHICH RESEMBLE FIELD OR FOREST MAY ATTRACT BIRDS AND SMALL ANIMALS.

■ EXTEND HORIZONTAL BUILDING LINES AND SOFTEN ABRUPT VERTICAL EDGES BY USING MASSES OF PLANTS AT CORNERS. SUBTLE CHANGES IN THE TYPE AND HEIGHT OF PLANTS PRODUCE AN UNDULATING, APPEALING FRAME FOR THE HOUSE.

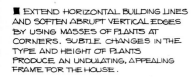

Patio Surfaces

When building a patio, choose surface materials with the exact texture and appearance you want. Your patio options are almost unlimited: concrete or concrete slabs, stone, clay tile, bricks, even wood. Or use a combination.

No matter what patio surface you prefer, you probably can do part or all of the work yourself. Select a surface that gives a "designer's touch" to your overall backyard landscaping.

Concrete. Always a popular choice for patios, concrete is a versatile surface because you can pour it in any shape and then give it a variety of finishes before it hardens. Stamping, scoring, brushing, exposing aggregate, and adding pigment are ways to take away the monotony of smooth concrete.

Concrete slabs. Buy them in a variety of surface textures and colors ready to lay, or make your own by pouring concrete into a form you've constructed from wood or metal. Patio blocks are usually about two inches thick and are laid on a bed of sand, gravel, or packed soil.

Flagstone, slate, bluestone. These are expensive, but beautiful, textured surfacing materials. They're available in earthy colors, such as buff, yellow, reddish-brown, and gray. Installation usually means mortaring them into place in a random, jigsaw-like pattern on a concrete bed.

Brick. Lay bricks on a bed of sand, securing them with additional sand brushed into the joints between bricks. Or set them in mortar on a bed of concrete. Select an interesting pattern for your patio (see sketches) and be sure to use long-wearing SW (Severe Weather) grade brick.

Clay tile. A good choice—but expensive. Use quarry tile or patio tile, choosing from several different sizes, colors, and shapes.

Loose surfaces. Wood chips, bark, pea gravel, pebbles, or crushed rock generally are used in combination with other patio materials. Use them around trees and shrubbery or between slabs in a "stepping-stone" walkway. To prevent weed growth through the loose surface, lay a sheet of polyethylene film or building felt before spreading the aggregate. Contain perimeters with corrugated metal edging or with redwood 2x4s set on edge.

Construction Tips

• Check local building codes and zoning ordinances before you start building your patio. Then, lay out a scaled version of your design on paper, marking the dimensions

carefully. Use the drawing to figure the amount of surfacing materials your new patio will require (a building materials supplier can help determine your needs). Keep the price you're willing to pay in mind as you make your plans—fancy flagstone or slate will be much more expensive to install than other materials, such as concrete or patio blocks.

HERRINGBONE

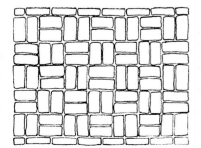

BASKET WEAVE VARIATION

BASKET WEAVE (brick on edge)

BASKET WEAVE (brick laid flat)

• The next step is to stake out your design and prepare the site. Depending on the terrain, you may need to remove terraces or high spots or bring in fill dirt for low areas.

• The surface of a patio is usually even with the surrounding yard or slightly above it. That means you'll have to excavate six to eight inches to accommodate the patio's surface and base. For drainage, a patio adjacent to the house should be sloped one-eighth to one-fourth inch per foot away from the house.

Prepare a two- to four-inch bed of fine gravel or sand before laying the patio. Be sure the bed is free from high or low spots.

If you want to set the surface material in mortar, pour an additional bed of concrete about four inches deep. Let it harden and cure before laying the patio.

Decks

Build a deck to expand the living space of your home. Then, you can move many of your favorite activities outside where you'll enjoy them in the fresh air.

What is a deck? It's an idyllic island for basking in the sun—your very own secluded corner for grabbing some well-deserved outdoor privacy without leaving home. And it's a great place to entertain your family and friends. When remodeling an older home, one of the best ways to increase property value is to add a deck.

You can build a deck to suit almost any terrain or setting. Use it to frame a pleasant view or to solve the landscaping problems posed by an odd-shaped yard. Attach it to your house and use it as a walk-out balcony to expand the second story. Or build a low, freestanding platform around the shady comfort of a big backyard tree. If your yard is on a slope, a deck will give you a much-needed level surface for many activities.

Then embellish your deck with weatherproof furniture and graceful accessories, such as potted plants and colorful outdoor cushions. Or

build in benches for extra seating and add a countertop/grill arrangement for barbecues and parties. If you prefer not to cover the entire deck, construct a small, roofed alcove at one end as a shady dining spot. Outdoor lighting is a plus, too.

Remember, build a deck for both privacy and comfort. You'll enjoy your deck more if you build it away from annoyances such as neighbor children's play area, noisy street traffic, or a loud air conditioner. You might want to use dense shrubs or a constructed privacy fence to further reduce outside distractions.

Also, keep an eye on the sun. The north and east sides of a home are usually cool in the afternoon and evening, so they make good locations for a deck. Depending on climate, a deck facing west or south may get too warm during parts of the day.

Construction Tips

Building a deck is like any home improvement project—you need to plan carefully before beginning. Whether you design the deck yourself or call in a professional to do it for you, consider a few basics before you start.

• Check for restrictions in zoning and building codes. Do local zoning ordinances have a "setback" requirement specifying how far the deck must be removed from your property line? If so, it's a good idea to call in a surveyor before you start building. Also, if there's an easement in your property deed allowing for excavation on your lawn, you may want to avoid building in that area.

• Can you build all or part of the deck yourself? Of course! Most decks—even the more elaborate ones—are suitable projects for the average do-it-yourselfer. If you need help selecting materials, check with an employee at your local building supply outlet. For help with construction, you may want to hire a carpenter.

• To avoid the "added-on" look, be sure your deck blends with the design and color of your home. Decks constructed from garden-grade redwood or cedar can be left with a natural unstained look. With other woods, you'll want to stain or paint.

Where to Plant Trees

Trees offer irreplaceable charm and character to a home. Plant them in poorly chosen locations, though, and they can lose their appeal as they mature. Follow these few easy guidelines when landscaping your property.

Because trees contribute to the enjoyment of your home, their care is important. Failure to locate trees properly when they're young can lead to disappointment years later when growth begins to show a mistake was made. But by then it's usually too late to do much about it without a lot of work.

Each tree variety has its own spacing and growth requirements. That's why it's wise to consult with the staff at a tree nursery before purchasing something new for your lawn.

In general, trees reaching a height of 20 feet or more should be planted at least 15 feet from any structure to keep their roots away from the foundation. Never plant such a tree near utility lines or under a roof overhang. (For more tree selection tips and planting information, see Chapter 4.)

Shade trees. With shade trees, keep in mind the direction and angle of the sun as you plan a location for planting. Before you start digging, select a spot where the tree will provide adequate shade *where you need it.* Locate trees to frame the house, choosing those that will stay in scale with the size of your home and its architectural features.

There are different types of shade trees, each offering unique shading characteristics.

Pyramidal-shaped trees (for example, pin oak, small-leaved linden, and red horse chestnut) are excellent for placement on lawns or along streets. They must be spaced widely to permit light to penetrate beneath them so grass will not be shaded out. Avoid planting them directly in front of windows. Their dense foliage will hide the home and block the view.

Weeping shade trees (such as beech, willow, and European ash) need open spaces, too. Typically, they spread as wide as they are tall. Most city lots only will accommodate smaller weeping shade trees.

Vase-shaped trees (such as red and white oak, sugar maple, and sycamore) grow tall, with top branches spreading somewhat wider than bottom ones. They make wonderful backyard trees where lots of shade is needed. However, too many vase-shaped trees in a small area make lawns difficult to maintain because of lack of sunlight.

Rounded trees, such as red maple, hawthorns, serviceberry, on the other hand, cause few problems for lawns. Their branching makes them suitable for planting along streets. They also make beautiful front lawn specimens.

Columnar trees (gray birch, white poplar, and Lombardy poplar) are tall and slender. They're excellent when planted close together along property lines to screen views and provide a windbreak.

Small flowering trees. Beautiful as ornaments and useful as boundary trees, small trees, such as crab apples and redbuds, also are favorites for planting near walks or patios because their not-too-vigorous root systems will not split the concrete. Plant them at lot corners and with flowering borders—their shade doesn't interfere with the growth of most flowers. Most flowering trees can be placed within eight feet of your house.

Conifers. Before buying one of the many varieties of pine, spruce, fir, cypress, or hemlock, check with the staff at your nursery to see what the shape and size of a mature tree will be. Needle evergreens, such as large pine and spruce, will "outgrow the house" if planted too close. Keep them at least 20 feet in front and 20 feet to the side of your house, so they don't interfere.

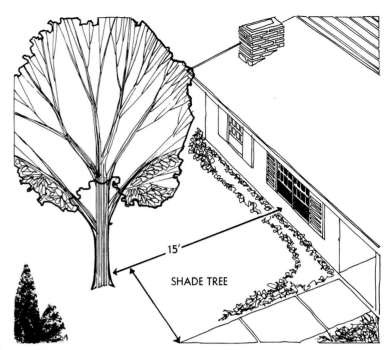

If the height of a tree will exceed 20 feet when mature, plant it at least 15 feet from the house or other buildings. For very large trees, double this spacing. Shade trees should be planted at least ten feet from walks, drives, and patios so their roots won't break up the surfacing.

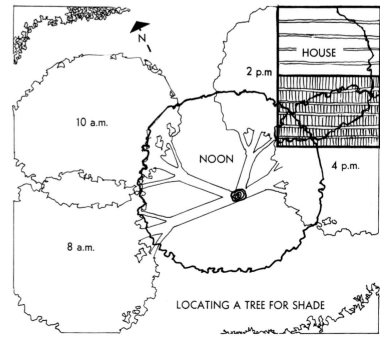

Keep the shade "target" in mind as you locate trees. For afternoon shade in the summer, plant trees ten to 15 feet south and 20 feet west of the target area. If the tree will grow to be large, increase the distance away from the base in both directions. Take care not to plant tall-growing trees under power or telephone lines.

LOCATING A TREE FOR SHADE

FOUNDATION PLANTING

Locate foundation plantings carefully. Be sure you know how large they will be when full-grown. If you're trying to fill a barren area, don't overplant to fill the space. Give shrubs and trees adequate room to grow naturally without crowding. Allow three feet between the house and trunks for most shrubs; spreading junipers should have four feet.

SMALL FLOWERING TREE

Dwarf-type fruit trees and other small flowering trees are ideal for small lots because you can plant them fairly close together without interfering with other gardening. Allow about ten feet between trees (or enough distance so their branches just touch—not entwine—when mature) and at least eight feet from your house.

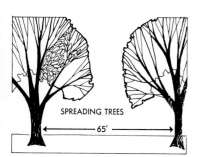

SPREADING TREES

Large trees with wide-spreading branches—for example, linden, silver maple, and sweet gum—need at least 65 feet between trunks. If they're closer than this, their branches eventually will entwine and block out the sun from the lawn or flowers below. Even if branches don't tangle, less-than-ideal spacing can mean trees will have uneven branching.

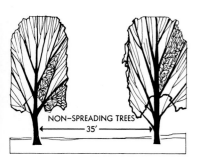

NON-SPREADING TREES

Non-spreading trees under 35 feet high (the hybrid maple, for instance) need 35 feet between trunks to show off their beautiful forms. Non-spreading trees with a narrow shade area, such as Bolleana poplar, don't need as much room allocated to them. For uniform growth among these non-spreaders, be sure to buy grafted stock.

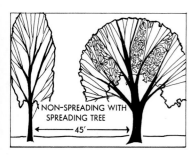

NON-SPREADING WITH SPREADING TREE

Non-spreading trees planted with spreading trees create a problem when the larger ones compete with the smaller for nutrients and light. Unless they're planted 45 feet apart (for example, a pin oak with a silver maple), the smaller tree will grow lopsided. If your landscape plan doesn't permit this much space, consider substituting shrubs for the small tree.

SAVE TREES WHEN CHANGING GRADES

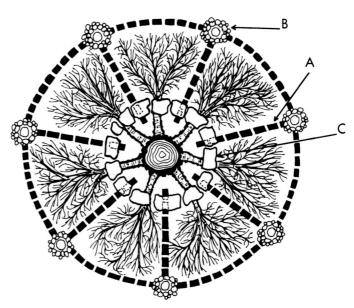

Provide proper drainage and air circulation for tree roots before adding topsoil to level a grade. Otherwise, the tree could suffocate. Spread tree food, then lay drainage tiles in spoke-wheel fashion (A) from trunk to drip line of outer branches. Add six-inch bell tile (B) wherever "spokes" meet perimeter. Use stone for wall (C) around trunk, starting two feet out, up to intended level.

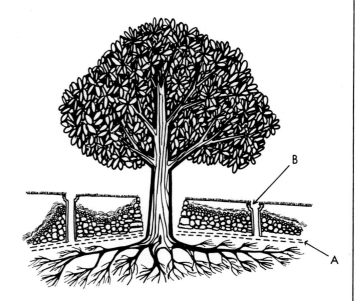

(Side view of above procedure.) Before adding topsoil to level grade, cover ground-tile ducts (A) with coarse material such as rock, gravel, or stone, as shown. Add thin layer of hay, then pile topsoil to desired level. To prevent clogging, cover tile openings in tree well with stones. Cap bell tiles (B) with screen wire.

Over-head Shelter

If the afternoon sun makes your deck or patio a little too hot to handle and you don't have a large shade tree handy, build an overhead canopy to take the heat off.

A structure designed to provide shade is an easy addition to most decks or patios. The procedure: 1) Sink two, four, or more support posts in the ground below the frost line (treat them with penta first) and set in concrete. Make sure they're perpendicular. 2) Attach horizontal beams to the posts and, if necessary, to the house. 3) Install the canopy.

Depending on the amount of shade you want, you can choose from a variety of shelter treatments. For lots of shade, use tightly spaced lattice (lath strips, 1x2s, 2x2s, or the like) or even canvas. For filtered sunlight—enough for many plants—space the roof treatment into a trellis-like effect. Let vining plants climb and spread across the structure.

For a structure that lets in plenty of light, allow beams to be exposed or install a sun screen of widely spaced stringers reaching from beam to beam. Corrugated plastic laid across the beams makes a quick and easy shelter. Pitch the roof slightly so rain and snow don't accumulate on top.

Use your imagination as you design this kind of structure. The construction doesn't have to be only functional; it can also be a dramatic addition to the architectural lines of your home. If the shelter is a canopy for an existing deck, match your materials as closely as possible, or re-stain the deck so it matches the new canopy.

Gaining Privacy with Hedges

Privacy can be much simpler and lovelier than stone walls or a moat around your castle (or modest home). A formal or informal hedge can nicely separate your yard from the sights and sounds of the world around.

Formal (as above) or informal hedges provide a shield from outside annoyances, while blending with other garden features.

Whether in the suburbs with neighbors close to lot lines, in the city with a postage stamp yard, or even in the country where farm buildings loom near the house, hedges can screen out eyesores, offer friendly separation from the folks next door, and join all the elements of your landscape design.

There's nothing new about plants—rather than a fence or wall—for privacy. Excavations indicate that around 4,500 years ago Egyptians grew such natural screens—much like we use today.

A hedge can be any continuous, close planting of trees, shrubs, even tall annual flowers. The plant you select depends on why you want the hedge. Some thorny choices provide a barrier almost as forbidding as a stone wall. Others cleverly distract the eye from an ugly television antenna on the neighbor's house or separate a home auto repair center from the patio.

A plant screen takes more space than a fence or wall, but it also has the advantage of color and texture variations. Some are also good insulators against noise and the lights of oncoming cars. If space is a problem, vines on fences or partitions of wood, brick, or plastic can be used as screens.

Evergreen shrubs provide privacy in winter better than decidu-ous shrubs and trees, but they don't offer the variety of twig and flower color you get with hedge plants such as forsythia and camellia. However, location is important. Deciduous hedges might work just as well around a patio because they're at their leafy best when you're making most use of the patio.

Of the many shrubs available, some make better screens than others because they are denser. Refer to the chart on shrubs (see pages 123 to 150) for more details. Heights will vary from region to region because of environmental conditions and the varieties of shrubs on the market.

Central region shrubs	Height (in feet)
Amur privet	to 15
Common lilac	8-10
Cranberry bush viburnum	8-10
French hybrid lilac	6-10
Japanese barberry	3-4
Japanese quince	5-7
Lynwood forsythia	5-8
Pfitzer juniper	6
Snowball bush (*Viburnum plicatum*)	8-10
Tatarian honeysuckle	to 10
Vanhoutte spirea	5-6
Warty barberry	3-4
Wayfaring tree viburnum	8-10

Southern region shrubs	Height (in feet)
Border privet	to 10
Camellia (*C. japonica*)	3-40
Camellia (*C. sasanqua*)	2-8
Crape myrtle	to 25
Flowering quince	to 5
Gardenia species, varieties	to 6
Hydrangea (*H. macrophylla*)	5
Oleander	to 20
Shrub althaea (*Hibiscus syriacus*)	to 12

Eastern region shrubs	Height (in feet)
Common box	to 25
Common lilac	10-20
Common privet	to 15
Japanese quince	to 10
Lynwood forsythia	8-10
Mock orange	4-8
Rose (*Rosa rugosa*)	to 6
Vanhoutte spirea	to 6
Winged euonymus	to 8

Western region shrubs	Height (in feet)
Abelia	to 6
Bridal-wreath spirea (*S. prunifolia*)	4-8
Camellia (*C. reticulata*)	to 30
Camellia (*C. sasanqua*)	to 30
Darwin barberry	3-10
Dwarf Japanese yew	to 3
Hydrangea (*H. paniculata*)	to 10
Japanese flowering quince	3-6
Japanese holly	4-10
Japanese privet	6-10
Myrtle (*Myrtus communis*)	3-10

Screening your driveway

Cars may be a symbol of our lifestyle, but where we put them offers a challenge to landscape designers. The solution to the problem of off-street parking can be an asset to your home. The plants used can also help protect the car from summer heat and winter wind.

Here are three designs for an 85x60-foot property, each with a different solution. All plans are developed for minimum maintenance. The plants are keyed in the box below.

Right: the parking area cuts out a 24-foot strip from the property but reduces the lawn area to be groomed. Small trees are used here and in the other two plans. The

dogwoods and hawthorns are clouds of white in spring—the broom is yellow. Imperial honey locusts cast a light shade over the parking area. The trees are deciduous but not messy.

Below left: parking space in the design provides enough room for you to swing your car around and head out to the street. Two white flowering crab apples (Katherine) and two pink ones (Hopa) form a spectacular blooming triangle, regardless of the viewing angle. Oregon holly grape has yellow flowers (to supplement the forsythia), followed by turquoise-blue berries.

Below right: an asphalt or gravel parking space is actually an extension of the street. It makes parking easy for a larger number of cars—but check with local au-

thorities to see if you are permitted to do this. Landscaping here calls for more trees—to provide privacy for the house and to screen the car space. The design is well-adapted to a slightly sloping yard.

Don't settle too quickly on plain concrete or asphalt. Even the driveway and off-street parking

area offer a chance for introducing texture, color, and pattern into your landscape. Dark paving retains heat late into a summer evening. Deciduous trees can be the answer to keeping the cars and the area near the house as cool as possible.

Bumpers made from railroad ties or 2x4s can protect plantings.

Small Trees	Height (in feet)
A Cutleaf staghorn sumac	5-10
B Crab apple, Hopa	6-10
C Crab apple, Katherine	6-10
D Dogwood, Chinese	10-12
E Hawthorn 'Autumn Glory'	9-15
F Honey locust 'Imperial'	30-40
G White birch	20-35

KEY

Shrubs	Height (in feet)
H Warminster broom	3-6
I Cranberry cotoneaster	3-4
J Paxistima canbyi	8
K Euonymus fortunei 'acuta'	3-4
L Bigleaf winter creeper	2-4
M Forsythia 'Lynwood'	5-7
N Oregon holly grape	2-4
O Spreading cotoneaster	5-6
P Beautybush	7-8

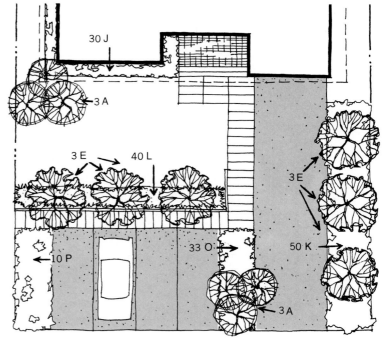

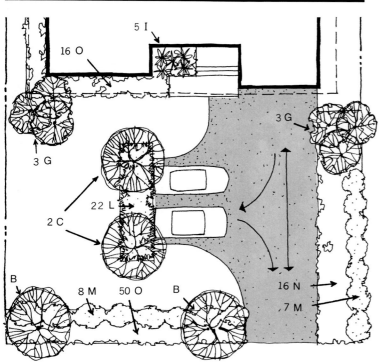

Privacy Fences

Your yard is one of the few places you can go for a little peace and quiet. So, why not screen it from the hustle and clatter of day-to-day living?

Constructing your own privacy fence is relatively easy. And it's a lot less expensive than buying and installing pre-built fence panels.

If you have a deck, extend its design by building your fence from similar materials in order to maintain a more unified landscaping appearance.

Or build a fence with its own character and make it a focal point of the yard. The design possibilities are infinite.

For example, look at the drawings of four designs shown on this page (sketches at right). The first, a herringbone pattern, uses 1x6 boards toenailed to a frame of 4x4 posts and 2x4 rails. The angular pattern is accentuated by half-inch spaces between the boards, which also allow sunlight to filter through.

The board-and-board design (upper right) offers an attractive horizontal line. The 1x8 boards are nailed alternately on both sides of the posts, so the fence looks the same from the neighbor's side. A vertical board-and-board fence (lower left) is another version of the same pattern. For an interesting change in the design, use fence boards of varying widths—either same-width boards in pairs or any combinations you like.

Where a solid screen is not necessary, an open slat design is hard to beat. It breaks the wide-open feeling and allows good flow of air. For this fence variation, space 1x3 boards their own width apart. Secure the boards at the top, bottom, and middle. The simple fence needs less lumber than others do.

A louver fence (lower right) offers both beauty and ventilation. Fence boards—usually 1x6s or 1x8s—are angled and overlapped slightly. The degree of angle determines the degree of privacy.

Or you might try a handsome fence of alternate horizontal and vertical ½x5-inch louvers. Such a fence offers built-in privacy from street and neighbors, while allowing cooling breezes to pass through.

Construction Tips

- A privacy fence usually stands tall, so it needs to be sturdy. *How tall* depends on your preference and the local building codes. Check with a building inspector for regulations, especially if you plan to build a privacy fence that is higher than five feet.

- Also, have a surveyor check property lines. Even after your boundaries have been established, it's a good idea to build the fence six inches or so inside your lot line just

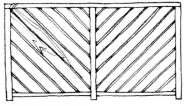

HERRINGBONE

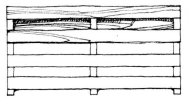

BOARD-AND-BOARD (horizontal)

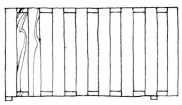

BOARD-AND-BOARD (vertical)

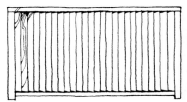

LOUVER

in case there was a faulty survey.

• When choosing materials, keep in mind that redwood and cedar are sturdy choices. Left untreated, they will weather to a soft, driftwood gray. Or you can stain or paint the wood.

The construction of your fence is largely dependent on the sturdiness of the posts you install. Choose posts that are large enough—usually 4x4s, sometimes 6x6s—and plant them firmly in the ground. The best method is to set posts in concrete to a depth exceeding the frost line in your part of the country. Except for redwood or cedar, treat sections of the fence posts that will be below the surface with penta (pentachlorophenol), and be sure each post stands straight. Taper the tops of posts to shed water and help prevent rot.

Set posts far enough apart to keep expenses down but close enough to each other for proper support. Six feet between posts is usually about right. Use galvanized nails. Horizontal rails should joint at posts—never in between.

Gates should be a minimum of three feet wide, with latches and hinges firmly attached to adjoining walls or posts.

Landscaping Ideas

Take that landscaping challenge and blend, disguise, or correct it with a little imagination and a lot of planning. Ideas presented here are only to plant the seed—or construct the screen, arrange the no-weed mulch, or splash with the color of tree blossoms. Eyesores and imperfections often inspire clever design solutions.

design concept—
front of ranch house

- ☐ expands scale of entrance
- ☐ creates sense of enclosure
- ☐ provides elements of interest to make the entrance more exciting

1 redbud
Cercis canadensis 30′
- ☐ flowers: purplish pink in May
- ☐ yellow fall color
- ☐ loose, informal shape
- ☐ defines space in court, provides canopy

2 wood screen
- ☐ gives partial enclosure; extends architecture to unify space

3 wood bench
- ☐ unifies design elements

4 wood edger 2x4 redwood
- ☐ provides crisp edge
- ☐ contains mulch material

5 purpleleaf winter creeper
Euonymus fortunei 'colorata'
- ☐ provides rich green carpet in entrance court
- ☐ mulch: bark, chips, or pea gravel
- ☐ leaves dark, deep purple above; paler beneath in autumn, winter

6 light/sculpture
- ☐ vertical element to add interest, scale, and light to entrance court

7 entrance court
- ☐ provides space for use as well as display
- ☐ different ground textures and patterns to give warmth (exposed aggregate and ground cover)

8 clay pots with annuals
- ☐ provide movable color

9 rhododendron 'P.J.M. Hybrids' 6′
- ☐ large, lavender-pink flowers
- ☐ broad-leaved evergreen—glossy foliag
- ☐ tender without winter mulch

ALTERNATE PLANT
- ☐ compact species of hydrangea

Landscaping as an art form

Texture. Are the leaves rough or smooth? Lacy or fuzzy? Shiny or dull? Textures are important when plants are placed near buildings, because contrasting textures emphasize or minimize architectural lines. Contrasts within groups of plants also can be part of the design. For example, the fine, feathery quality of juniper may be enhanced when placed beside a shiny, broad-leaved evergreen.

Color. Flowering plants can add sparkle to a landscape. But they are best used as accents rather than major components because their blooms are often brief and their foliage seldom striking. Plant them in large clumps.

Fragrance. Scent is one of the garden's most subtle delights. Roses, lilacs, and hyacinths are familiar. A mock orange close to an outdoor sitting area or gardenia bush beneath a bedroom window is a refreshing design inspiration. But don't stop with flowers. Many trees and herbs can be a treat to the nose, as well.

Character. What sets your favorite plants apart from others? These qualities give a plant character. Tamarisk, weeping willow, and columbine are delicate; oaks stately; lindens and aspens sparkling and gay; cedars and yews somber. Mixing plants of different characters can add up to visual chaos. Select plants in keeping with the character of your house, too. Think twice before using a flamboyant, exotic bush (suitable for a modern California ranch house) to frame a Cape Cod.

Harmony. Your landscape design can be a three-part harmony, just like your special tune. In music, it's the pleasing arrangement of notes; around your home, it's a combination of size, role, and eye level (or what you see when you look straight ahead). Large plants, trees for example, fix visual boundaries and provide canopy. Medium-size plants serve as screens while they also outline an area. Small ones, such as ground covers and flowers, supply color, pattern, and texture.

10 *Japanese tree lilac*
Syringa reticulata 30'
☐ creamy white flowers
☐ interesting bark

11 *quaking aspen*
Populus tremuloides 65'
☐ slender upright form
☐ light gray to white bark
☐ gold-yellow brilliant fall color
ALTERNATE PLANTS
☐ river birch
☐ black alder

12 *pachysandra*
Pachysandra terminalis 12''
☐ broad-leaved evergreen (white flower spikes in May)
☐ white berries
☐ dark green and lustrous
ALTERNATE PLANT
☐ periwinkle

13 *wood edger 2x4 redwood*
☐ outlines design

14 *precast concrete steppers*
☐ extend paving from entrance court to rear yard
☐ add interest to blank area

15 *mulch*
☐ pea gravel
☐ keeps area low-care

design concept—
front of colonial house

- ☐ creates warm, inviting entrance court
- ☐ uses plants to create framework for entrance, with lower plants used in a formal design to complement the architecture
- ☐ larger plants provide color and interest

1 sugar maple
Acer saccharum 80′

- ☐ tall, round form
- ☐ yellow-orange fall color

2 dorothea crab apple
Malus 'Dorothea'

- ☐ flowers—crimson to rose
- ☐ fruits—bright yellow
- ☐ dense, rounded habit
- ☐ provides soft transition from building to ground

3 saucer magnolia
Magnolia x soulangiana 25′

- ☐ one of the earliest plants to bloom
- ☐ large tulip-like flowers appear before leaves
- ☐ location of plant gives importance to house entrance
- ☐ annual pruning needed until desired canopy is reached

4 compact burning bush
Euonymus alata 'compacta'

- ☐ brilliant red fall color
- ☐ easy to maintain as formal hedge due to its slow to moderate growth—little trimming needed
- ☐ coarse branching structure with corky ridges on branches
- ☐ softens straight lines of walkway

ALTERNATE PLANTS

- ☐ barberry
- ☐ boxwood

5 purpleleaf winter creeper
Euonymus fortunei 'colorata'

- ☐ broad-leaved evergreen
- ☐ fall and winter color: purple

ALTERNATE PLANT

- ☐ periwinkle for shady situations

6 pagoda dogwood
Cornus alternifolia 15′

- ☐ unique horizontal branching
- ☐ small cream-colored flowers
- ☐ interesting winter branching pattern
- ☐ intended to reach over top of entrance door for shade and accent

7 dwarf Japanese yew
Taxus cuspidata 'nana'

- ☐ formal/traditional dark green
- ☐ evergreen plant
- ☐ easily maintained as a very thick formal hedge
- ☐ used as a continuous line to provide horizontal extension that appears to reduce height of house

ALTERNATE PLANT

- ☐ juniper for hot, exposed locations

8 brick surface

- ☐ entrance court is large enough to be in scale with house
- ☐ traditional theme

9 flower border

- ☐ adds a splash of color to entrance court

10 bigleaf winter creeper
Euonymus fortunei 'vegeta'

- ☐ semievergreen
- ☐ showy pink capsule with orange berrylike fruit
- ☐ used here to break starkness of chimney

ALTERNATE PLANT

- ☐ clematis

design concept— entrance with grade change

☐ provides smooth architectural extension of house entrance to drive

1 cutleaf staghorn sumac
Rhus typhina 'laciniata' 10′

☐ foliage: fine-textured, feathery
☐ fall color: bright orange red
☐ provides interesting textural quality to entrance

ALTERNATE PLANT

☐ smooth sumac

2 creeping juniper
Juniperus horizontalis

3 retaining walls
(railroad tie construction)

☐ provides crisp architectural grade transition from drive to entrance
☐ ties together architectural and natural elements of entrance

4 recess this area from drive to facilitate easy access to and from auto

5 steps

☐ grade transition with railroad ties
☐ steps and earth slope

6 purpleleaf winter creeper
Euonymus fortunei 'colorata'

☐ used here to hold slope
☐ attractive foliage

ALTERNATE PLANTS

☐ periwinkle
☐ creeping juniper

7 radiant crab apple
Malus 'Radiant' 25′

☐ flowers: deep pink, very showy
☐ fruits: bright red
☐ desired canopy obtained by pruning
☐ accents entrance, provides interest, interrupts roof line

ALTERNATE PLANTS

☐ other crab apple varieties

8 bigleaf winter creeper
Euonymus fortunei 'Sarcoxie'

☐ semievergreen
☐ showy pink capsule with orange berrylike fruit
☐ glossy green foliage
☐ will intertwine with ties

9 rhododendron 'P.J.M. Hybrids' 6′

☐ flower: bright lavender pink
☐ broad-leaved evergreen, foliage turns purple in fall
☐ provides splash of color at entrance

ALTERNATE PLANTS

☐ other varieties of rhododendron

10 sargent juniper
Juniperus chinensis 'sargenti'

☐ evergreen
☐ steel blue foliage

11 common witch hazel
Hamamelis virginiana 15′

☐ yellow flowers blooming in late fall
☐ fall color clear yellow
☐ excellent specimen for seasonal interest
☐ provides smooth transition from front to side of house

ALTERNATE PLANT

☐ star magnolia

Landscaping Ideas

Outdoor living areas become your little corner of the world. Backyards and garden corners greet you with soothing lines and cheerful colors, while permitting privacy, low-key entertaining, and easy maintenance. Pay special attention to shapes and hues for a lovely view throughout the year.

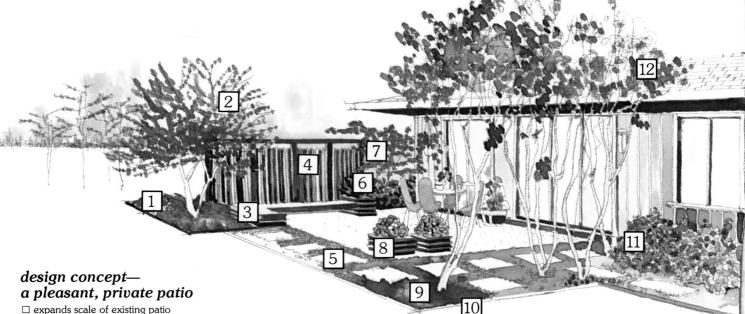

design concept—
a pleasant, private patio

☐ expands scale of existing patio with ground cover and concrete stepping-stones

☐ creates a sense of intimacy and enclosure with privacy screen and plant materials

1 creeping juniper
Juniperus horizontalis 12''

☐ foliage: bluish green to steel blue

☐ maintenance-free, low-growing mat

☐ well suited for hot, dry conditions

2 redbud
Cercis canadensis 30'

☐ branches lined with small pink-purple blossoms in early spring

☐ picturesque character with rounded form

☐ fall color: yellow

3 wood bench

☐ one end serves as planter

☐ unity between bench and planters

4 wood screen

☐ encloses space and adds privacy

☐ provides architectural extension of house

5 precast concrete stepping-stones

6 Mollis azalea

☐ flower: choice of several bright colors

☐ loses leaves in winter

☐ needs protection in cold climates

☐ grows best in well-drained soil, but must be kept moist

7 Japanese maple
Acer palmatum 20'

☐ foliage: green to red, fine-textured

☐ fall color: scarlet

☐ interesting form

☐ sturdy

8 wood planter boxes

☐ give vertical dimension to patio

☐ useful for bright flowers

☐ can be moved for new look or seasonal plant needs

9 purpleleaf winter creeper
Euonymus fortunei 'colorata' 12''

☐ easy to establish and maintain

☐ leaves turn a purple-red in autumn

10 wood edger

☐ maintains edge of planting spaces

11 Anthony Waterer spirea
Spiraea x bumalda

☐ maintains low, rounded form

☐ crimson flowers in flat-topped clusters

12 shadblow serviceberry (juneberry)
Amelanchier canadensis 60'

☐ vertical lines add height to horizontal architecture

☐ light gray bark

☐ fall colors: rich yellow and red

☐ needs little pruning or fertilizing

ALTERNATE PLANTS

☐ amur maple

☐ tatarian maple

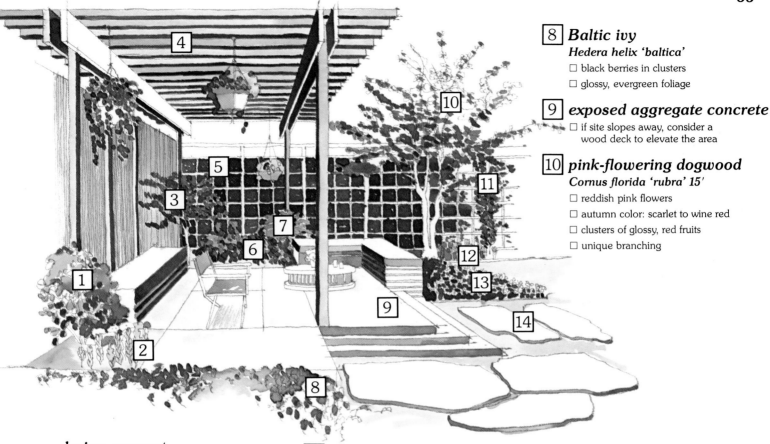

8 *Baltic ivy*
Hedera helix 'baltica'
- [ ] black berries in clusters
- [ ] glossy, evergreen foliage

9 *exposed aggregate concrete*
- [ ] if site slopes away, consider a wood deck to elevate the area

10 *pink-flowering dogwood*
Cornus florida 'rubra' 15'
- [ ] reddish pink flowers
- [ ] autumn color: scarlet to wine red
- [ ] clusters of glossy, red fruits
- [ ] unique branching

design concept—
a secluded garden corner
- [ ] creates a structured garden space with the help of plants

1 *bayberry*
Myrica pensylvanica 6'
- [ ] dull green, semievergreen foliage
- [ ] aromatic leaves
- [ ] wax-gray berries

2 *sedum autumn joy*
Sedum spectabile 'Autumn Joy' 16''
- [ ] flowers in late summer
- [ ] plant retains mushroom-shaped seed head through winter
- [ ] soft, light, moss-green leaves

3 *Japanese maple*
Acer palmatum 20'
- [ ] foliage: green to red, fine-textured
- [ ] adds a sculptural element to garden
- [ ] fall color: scarlet

4 *latticed wood sun screen*
- [ ] gives overhead definition to space
- [ ] provides interesting shadow patterns

5 *lilac: Ludwig Spaeth*
Syringa vulgaris 'Ludwig Spaeth'
- [ ] used as hedge behind lattice
- [ ] deep purple flowers
- [ ] lovely scent
ALTERNATE PLANT
- [ ] Zabeli honeysuckle

6 *Korean azalea*
Rhododendron yedoense 'poukhanense'
- [ ] flower: bright lavender-pink in early spring
- [ ] hardy in North
- [ ] broad-leaved evergreen in South

7 *spreading cotoneaster*
Cotoneaster divaricatus 6'
- [ ] small pink flowers
- [ ] bright red fruit in fall
- [ ] fall color: dull red
- [ ] arching, spreading habit
- [ ] pruned and developed as garden specimen
ALTERNATE PLANT
- [ ] pyracantha

11 *jackman clematis vine*
Clematis x jackmani 12'
- [ ] large violet/purple flowers
- [ ] do best in partial shade
- [ ] prune to ground in dormant season

12 *tulips*
- [ ] a splash of seasonal color
- [ ] plant several varieties for blooms from early spring through early summer

13 *lily-of-the-valley*
Convallaria majalis
- [ ] rich, lustrous foliage
- [ ] prefers shade
- [ ] serves as a spring-flowering ground cover
- [ ] hardy

14 *stepping-stones*
- [ ] expands living space without "solid concrete" look
- [ ] free form fits soft lines of garden space

design concept— a narrow display garden between house and driveway

- ☐ narrow space developed as a summer display garden
- ☐ year-round appeal of area achieved with ground cover and posts

1 Katherine crab apple
Malus 'Katherine' 20'
- ☐ flowers: large, double, pink to white
- ☐ small red fruits
- ☐ used here to terminate garden and to soften corner of house

2 wood posts of varying heights
- ☐ pleasant surprises rising from ground cover
- ☐ discarded telephone poles, railroad ties, or tree rounds—buried in ground at least 1½ feet, deeper for higher posts

3 giant allium
Allium giganteum
- ☐ six- to eight-inch round purple flowers (from bulb) on five- to seven-foot stems
- ☐ a specimen
- ☐ for summer color: geraniums (sun) impatiens or caladiums (shade)

4 purpleleaf winter creeper
Euonymus fortunei 'colorata' 12''
- ☐ carpets areas between display posts
- ☐ semievergreen to evergreen
- ☐ turns purple in fall
ALTERNATE PLANT
- ☐ periwinkle

5 clay tile or crockery
- ☐ larger elements provide scale and balance in the composition

6 clay pots with seasonal flowers—geraniums, petunias, and mums
- ☐ pots of various sizes and styles must harmonize
- ☐ ideal for summering houseplants, if area is shaded
- ☐ use one or two for herbs—pots can later be moved inside

design concept—back door beautification

☐ makes an otherwise dull entrance a pleasant and convenient feature

1 daphne spirea
Spiraea japonica 'alpina' 12″

☐ flowers: light pink masses in spring—intermittent blossoms throughout summer

ALTERNATE PLANTS

☐ creeping juniper 'Blue Rug' (sun)

☐ pachysandra (shade)

2 mulch

☐ bark chunks or gravel

☐ contained by edger or existing walk

3 shelf

☐ adds interest to a plain house

☐ a handsome setting for potted plants

4 Korean spice viburnum
Viburnum carlesi 5′

☐ flowers: pink to white with spicy fragrance

☐ small black berries attract birds

☐ foliage: wine red in autumn

ALTERNATE PLANTS

☐ rhododendron

☐ Japanese quince

5 wood platform

☐ expands feeling of space at entrance

☐ handy for outdoor cooking

6 space frame

☐ an architectural extension of entrance

☐ a place for summer potted plants

☐ firewood storage rack below

7 harbinger European bird cherry (mayday tree)
Prunus padus 'commutata' 30′

☐ blooms in early May

☐ flowers: small, white clusters

☐ for scale and space definition

ALTERNATE PLANTS

☐ pagoda dogwood

☐ Japanese tree lilac

8 back door mini garden

☐ for bright annuals and bulbs

☐ 30-inch water saucer for birds

☐ wood-edger-defined bed

☐ birdhouse in tree above

chapter 3

LAWNS AND GROUND COVERS

We all know the lawn we'd like to have: one that's lush and green, beautifully landscaped, easy to maintain, and free of weeds, disease, bugs, and other pests. The question is, how do you grow a lawn that's mostly trouble-free?

The answer is easier than you think. Lawn care isn't difficult once you've established the type of turf that's right for your climate and location. If problems do crop up from time to time, you can cure them quickly before a lot of damage is done.

Remember, when grass is growing strong, caring for a lawn is more like the relaxing and enjoyable pastime it was meant to be. This chapter will help by taking the mystery out of soil, grass seeds, fertilizers, watering, and mowing. And you can turn to the many handy charts included for exact lawn information and specific gardening advice on almost any lawn topic you need to know about.

You'll even find a section on ground covers—they're a gardener's delight for sidestepping difficult lawn problems such as shady spots, steep slopes, and poor soil conditions. And ground covers are beautiful, too. If you've never experimented with any of these attractive and easily cared for plants, get ready for a pleasant surprise when you do.

In short, all of the basic lawn-care information you need to know is here. Use it as you shape your turf into a masterpiece like the flawless circle of grass (opposite) bounded by an exposed aggregate path and flower borders.

Preparing Soil for a New Lawn

What is soil? It's a mixture of clay, silt, sand, water, organic material, even living organisms. Soil can be good or poor, fine or coarse, heavy or light, but whatever kind of soilbed you have, be sure you prepare it properly before planting your new lawn. Don't skimp on this important first step!

If you have a lawn that needs shaping up, chances are you'll be able to work wonders on it without making a completely new start (see information on how to "Perk Up Your Lawn," pages 66 to 67).

But if your lawn has serious problems, such as areas of poor soil, terraces that are too steep, or unsatisfactory drainage, then redoing the entire lawn probably is in order. Likewise, if you have no lawn at all, follow these steps to prepare a perfect soilbed for planting.

Grading. Initially, your most important job is to make sure that the lawn area is relatively level and drains properly. If the area is small, you can do the job yourself with a shovel and rake. For a larger area, though, call in a professional with specially designed graders to smooth things out. When finished, the lawn should slope away from the house slightly (about one-eighth to one-fourth inch per foot) and be contoured so gentle swales conduct excess rainfall to a lower grade. Watch out for depressions—they'll become waterlogged when it rains. If you have a high water table, it may be wise to install drainage tiles.

For steep slopes that can't be graded (more than 35 degree incline), consider installing a retaining

Just before cultivating, spread the fertilizer with mechanical spreader to broadcast nutrients evenly, according to the manufacturer's package instructions.

Cultivate using a small rotary tiller. Work fertilizer and other nutrients well into the root zone, about four to six inches deep, after removing debris.

The properly cultivated soilbed consists of marble-size aggregates of soil. These lumps hold moisture and seed better than pulverized soil.

wall or plant the slope with a ground cover.

Soil test. Before you cultivate the soil and get ready for seeding, it's a good idea to have your soil tested for fertility and pH. Many garden centers, nurseries, and universities offer this service. Fees will vary. Contact your county extension office for the name and address of the nearest soil test lab. The extension office can also give you instructions for mailing the soil sample.

Adequate levels of phosphorus and potassium are important for vigorous root growth, so you'll want to add these nutrients if the soil test shows they're needed. Also, most grasses grow best when the soil is neutral (pH of 7) or *slightly* acid. If the soil test shows a pH of less than 6, spread enough lime to sufficiently "sweeten" the soil.

Finally, broadcast a balanced fertilizer containing nitrogen (preferably slow-release), phosphorus, and potassium, or a specially formulated lawn food just before cultivation. Follow the manufacturer's package instructions and use a good mechanical spreader.

Cultivation. Cultivating breaks up the soil for seeding and works pre-applied nutrients down to the root zone where they'll do the most good. In small yards, a rotary tiller does the job just fine, but in larger areas, you'll find that plowing or disking with tractor-drawn equipment will save you a lot of time and effort.

Before cultivating, be sure to remove pieces of plaster, brick, cement, and other debris. Then, choose a day when the soil is suitably moist—not wet enough to cake or clod, but not powder dry, either.

Don't over-cultivate. The ideal soilbed is cultivated only until lumps of marble-size soil result. Never pulverize soil until powdery or dust-like, because over-cultivated soil "runs" when wet and cakes hard after it dries. You'll find that a pebbled surface accepts seed and water much better. Seed settles into the cracks and crevices between the lumps of soil where moisture and warmth are retained and germination is quicker.

Ways to start a new lawn

There are several ways to start a new lawn. The right method for you depends on the type of grass you want, how fast you want a lawn, how much money you want to spend, and, most important, where you live.

Lawn experts typically divide turf into two categories: cool-climate grasses (grown primarily in the northern half of the country) and warm-climate grasses (those that succeed only in the South). Northern grasses, such as Kentucky bluegrass, fescues, and perennial ryegrasses, are usually propagated by seed—although using bluegrass sod is another popular way to quickly start up a new lawn. However, sod can be expensive.

In the South, many grasses are planted *vegetatively* with live stems or sections of sod. Vegetative planting works because grass plants have the remarkable ability to sprout from joints or nodes even after being chopped or shredded into fragments. In most cases, stem sections of the plant need not be rooted because root systems will develop from the joints. Most popular southern grasses can be planted vegetatively by sprigging, plugging, or sodding. Common Bermuda grass, centipede, carpet grass, and *Zoysia japonica* may be planted from seed. Whatever method you choose, there are a few guidelines that will help to guarantee the best results.

Sprigging. Grass sprigs are actually pieces of stem taken from sod torn apart. The soil is shaken off, exposing long runners that are usually cut into sections about four inches long.

The best sprigs have both roots and leaves, but bare stolons or rhizomes may be used if they have at least two nodes.

You can buy sprigs packed with moss so they stay moist. They're usually sold by the bushel in large polyethylene bags.

Or you can buy a section of sod and shred your own sprigs. A square yard of sod may yield more than a thousand zoysia or Bermuda sprigs, or at least several hundred of

St. Augustine or centipede. Thus, it's easy to plant a whole lawn from just a few yards of sod. You simply do a little more work.

Before planting the sprigs, prepare a good soilbed (see page 60). Then lightly bury one end of each sprig with soil, covering the lowest joint, but leaving the upper joint exposed. Plant sprigs either in furrows or in a checkerboard fashion on six-to 12-inch centers. After planting, keep sprigs well watered and free from weeds until they are established.

Stolonizing. Actually a method of sprigging, stolonizing is nothing more than broadcasting between five and eight bushels of sprigs per 1,000 square feet. Topdress the sprigs with about a half-inch of soil, roll lightly, and keep moist by watering often with a fine mist while new growth takes hold.

Both sprigging and stolonizing should be done in the early spring to allow a full season's growth before cooler weather sets in.

Sodding. Especially popular in the North, sodding is a good choice whenever you have an area where seeding is difficult (for example, on slopes) or when you want a lawn in a hurry. Bluegrass sod is the best selection, because bluegrass root systems are second to none for weaving a tight, close-knit turf.

The best times to sod are spring and early fall. When buying sod, choose thin, weed-free rolls (no more than three-fourths to one inch thick). Prepare a soilbed free from depressions, mounds, and debris. Before laying the sod, fertilize the soilbed with a plant food high in phosphorus and potassium to promote vigorous root growth. If nitrogen is added, it's wise to use a slow-release, water-insoluble form.

Lay sod by putting one strip against the next. On a slope, lay strips across the hill rather than up and down. Vertical seams should not line up precisely. Follow with a light topdressing of soil to help fill the cracks between strips, and roll the newly sodded area immediately. Water thoroughly and regularly for about two weeks. Thereafter, follow regular lawn care procedures. Wait until the grass is well-established before mowing.

Plugging. Plugs are actually small sections of sod, often circular in shape. In the South, they're often used to establish warm-climate lawns, such as zoysia or Bermuda grass.

You can rent a plugging tool to make plugs from existing turf, and then use the same tool to dig holes in the area where plugs will be planted. Most plugs vary from two to four inches in diameter and are planted about one foot apart. Apply fertilizer after digging holes, but before setting plugs. For planting a new lawn, two-inch plugs are just as good as larger ones. Use the four-inch size for filling in any bare spots that might appear in old lawns.

Once planted, plugs provide centers of growth that eventually fill into complete turf. Plugging is much more economical than sodding, with a square yard of sod yielding around 300 two-inch plugs—enough to plant 40 square yards! But complete fill-in growth is slow.

Seeding. If you live where cool-climate grasses flourish and you don't want to sod your new lawn, then seeding is the alternative. Starting a lawn from seed requires careful attention to soil preparation, planning, and—when it comes to purchasing your seed—smart shopping. Check the charts on the next few pages to help you make your choice.

(continued on page 65)

Sow seeds with a mechanical spreader in the ratio recommended on the seed package. Uniform distribution is important for a thick, smooth lawn.

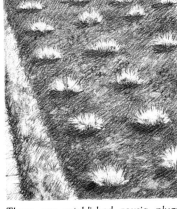

These are established zoysia plugs. Bermuda grass and zoysia plugs spread by aboveground runners (stolons) or underground stems (rhizomes).

Sprigging is perhaps the best way to establish a new lawn vegetatively. Bury individual sprigs one by one so that uppermost nodes show aboveground.

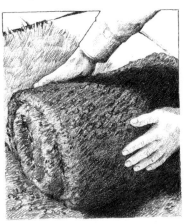

Lay sod soon after you buy or cut it. Alternate end joints, then roll sodded area. Water new sod often until roots take hold and new growth starts.

COOL SEASON GRASSES

Grass	Description	Light	Mowing Ht. (Ins.)	Comments
BENT GRASSES Agrostis sp. **Colonial** A. tenuis **Velvet** A. canina **Creeping** A. stolonifera	Shiny green, thick, fine-textured turf produced by most species.	sun	¾	Fine bents are used mainly by golf greenskeepers. They are not recommended for a home lawn, unless you're willing to spend effort required for regular watering, feeding, spraying, and mowing (with a reel mower). Adapted for use in cool, humid climates. Tolerates light shade.
Redtop A. gigantea	A coarse-textured stemmy form of bent grass. Differs from all other bent grasses in its fine-textured beautiful effect.	sun	1½-2	Tolerates some shade, only in hot summer areas. Adapted to wide range of moist conditions and soils. Persists on dry, coarse soils. Doesn't tolerate much traffic. Under heat stress, it turns brown. Main advantage is as temporary, emergency cover. Not used in top quality lawn seed mixtures.
BLUEGRASSES Poa sp. **Common Kentucky** P. pratensis	Hardy sod-forming perennial grass; dark-green-colored blades with V-shaped leaf tips. Blades upright, fine-textured soft growth. Extensive root system penetrating soil 3 to 4 feet.	sun	1½-2½	Main grass used for lawns in northern half of United States, but will grow in cool mountain altitudes of the South, also. Has upright blade so turf is not dense; however, blends well with other bluegrasses. Appears best in home lawns during spring and fall, as a rule. If summer is hot and dry, it goes dormant; turns green with cooler, moist weather. Susceptible to various diseases depending on conditions. Many new cultivars are being derived from common Kentucky bluegrass.
Windsor	Bright blue-green leaf blades. Plants tend to creep. Low-lying dense turf.	sun	¾-1½	While it can be mowed shorter than Kentucky, because of its low habit, 1½-inch mowing height is better than ¾-inch. Start lawn by seeds, as with all bluegrass. Vigorous, drought- and disease-resistant. A versatile, attractive bluegrass.
Merion Kentucky	Denser, more prostrate growing than Kentucky bluegrass. Attractive blue-green color.	sun	¾-1	Considered an improvement over Kentucky bluegrass, but somewhat slow to germinate. Weak point is its susceptibility to rust disease, but is resistant to leaf spot. Demands extra feeding. Tolerates shade better than Kentucky.
Delta	More erect, stiffer, but not as dense as Kentucky bluegrass.	sun	1½-3	Tolerates drought more than some others; resists most diseases fairly well. Establishes itself and greens up well in spring.
Newport	Dark green color with medium coarse texture, similar to Merion. Similar to Kentucky in growth habit.	sun	1½-3	Requires less fertilizer than Merion. Not as tolerant to low temperatures and drought as some other cultivars. Susceptible to several diseases.
Park	Produces vigorous seedlings. Similar to common bluegrass in growth habit. Medium dark green color. Forms dense sod.	sun	1½-3	Has good drought tolerance and good spring green-up rate. Fairly good resistance to most diseases.
Fylking	Medium-fine textured turf having dark green color. Low growth habit.	sun	1½-2	Good resistance to most diseases. Proves drought resistant and handles low temperatures. Can grow on sandy soils.
Rough-stalk meadow-grass P. trivialis	Shiny apple-green colored turf of high shoot density. Smaller stemmed than common Kentucky.	shade	1½-2	Grow in shade only. Avoid sandy soil. Does not tolerate heat and drought. Adapted to cool, moist situations. Tolerates low temperatures.

Grass	Description	Light	Mowing Ht. (Ins.)	Comments
FESCUES *Festuca sp.* **Coarse, Tall fescues** *F. elatior*	Alta or Kentucky-31 and Goar are all medium-coarse, tall, tough fescues. Leaves are large, medium green and grow in clumps.	light shade	2-2½	Useful mostly for play areas that get rough treatment. Sow as a pure stand and at hearty rate for finer texture. Disease- and drought-resistant.
Fine, Red creeping *F. rubra*	Highlight, Jamestown, Koket, and Ruby are commonly used cultivars. They form a very fine-textured grass, which is medium to dark green color. More and improved cultivars are being released. Chewings fescue is similar to red fescues, except it does not creep and is tufty.	shade	2-2½	Adapts well to shade. Needs little nitrogen. Is drought-resistant and will grow in dry, sandy soils. Used in some lawn grass seed mixtures. Germinates faster than bluegrass, but is compatible with it. More susceptible to disease than coarse fescues.
RYEGRASSES *Lolium sp.* **Annual, Italian** *L. multiflorum*	Large-seeded and germinates rapidly to show green growth in a few days. Blades are coarser than bluegrass.	sun	1½	Useful for quick green cover for a season. Dies out, mostly, in one year. Used for over-seeding Bermuda lawns in South for green cover over winter. Will not live over summer in South or winter in North.
Perennial *L. perenne*	Coarse, rather sparsely set blades have a waxy sheen. Not quite as coarse as annual rye.	sun or light shade	1½	Cultivar such as Citation, Compas, Derby, Game, Manhattan, NK-100, NK-200, Omega, Pennfine, or Yorktown should be used. Many have a fine-textured appearance, almost equal to that of bluegrass. Often sown in mixture with bluegrass. Becomes established quicker than bluegrass or fescue. Doesn't mow as neatly as bluegrass.

SOUTHERN WARM SEASON GRASSES

Grass	Description	Light	Mowing Ht. (Ins.)	Comments
BAHIA GRASS *Paspalum notatum*	Very coarse-textured, fairly open, erect growing and tough. One of widest leaved species. Spreads slowly by stolons and roots as it goes.	sun	2-3	Tolerates partial shade. Turns brown if temperature drops to 30 degrees Fahrenheit. Limited to warm areas where low maintenance desired. Popular varieties in southern coastal region are Argentine and Pensacola. Start by seed or sod. Feed three times a year. Mow often enough to keep wiry seed stalks removed.
BERMUDA GRASS *Cynodon dactylon*	Hybrid forms are the most beautiful to use, provide a dense, fine-textured carpet. U-3 is a medium fine-textured dark green turf with gray cast. Tifdwarf has miniature leaves. Tifgreen is dark green and very fine-textured. Tiflawn is medium fine with dark green leaves. Tifway is medium fine with very dark green leaves. Sunturf is a very fine, dark green grass of high quality. Ormond is fine-textured with blue-green color. Santa Ana is medium-textured with blue-green leaves.	sun	¾-1	Bermuda grasses are vigorous and spread by creeping. Unless contained, they will become a weed by invading flower beds. Propagation is by sprigs, plugs, or sod. Tiflawn cultivar is tough and wear-resistant where traffic is heavy. It's adapted throughout the South. Tifgreen tolerates partial shade throughout the South. U-3 tolerates the cooler regions of the upper South. Tifdwarf requires less frequent mowing than others listed. Tifway keeps its color late into the fall throughout the South. Sunturf, Ormond, and Santa Ana are especially well-adapted to California, being smog- and salt-resistant. Feed Bermuda lawns every two months in deep South, but about four times a year in other regions. Mow common Bermuda lawns higher than hybrids—not less than 1 inch high.

SOUTHERN WARM SEASON GRASSES (continued)

Grass	Description	Light	Mowing Ht. (Ins.)	Comments
CARPET GRASS *Axonopus affinis*	Growth habit similar to centipede grass. Coarse-textured and fairly dense with light green color.	sun	1-2	While it doesn't make a quality turf, it takes hard wear and needs little attention. Adapted to lower South, into upper South. Commonly started by seeds but can be done with sprigs spaced 6 to 12 inches apart. Feed at least once a year. Keep mowed often enough to prevent unsightly seed stalks.
CENTIPEDE GRASS *Eremochloa ophiuroides*	Slow-growing, medium-textured grass that spreads by creeping stems and rooting as they go. Seldom grows to 4 inches tall. Medium green color.	sun	1½	Commonly started by sprigs or plugs spaced 6 to 12 inches apart. Similar to St. Augustine grass, except it will grow into cooler parts of warm humid regions. Not as tolerant to drought as other southern grasses; discolors more readily at low temperatures. Needs little fertilizer and seldom needs mowing. Avoid seashore environment and heavy traffic. Usually propagated by sprigs or plugs, spaced 6 to 12 inches apart; water regularly.
ST. AUGUSTINE GRASS *Stenotaphrum secundatum*	Produces broad, flat stems and coarse but attractive blue-green leaves. Plants establish quickly and spread fairly fast in warm humid regions of lower South. Highly rated variety is Bitter-Blue. Other improved cultivars are available.	sun or light shade	1½-2	Propagates readily by sprigs, plugs, or sod. Space sprigs 6 to 12 inches apart. Stays green all year in the warmer sections of warm humid climates. Loses color during winter in other areas, but can be sprayed with green dye. Maintains good color with occasional feeding. Will grow in sun, but is used widely because it tolerates shade so well—even dense shade. Main problem likely to be encountered is susceptibility to insects and fungus diseases. Helps to de-thatch turf once a year.
ZOYSIA GRASSES *Zoysia sp.* **Manila** *Z. matrella* **Mascarene** *Z. tenuifolia* **Korean or Japanese** *Z. japonica*	Manila grass is similar to the finer Japanese. Mascarene has bright green leaves. Japanese or Korean grass has gray-green leaves which are upright and coarse. Emerald and the hardy Meyer cultivars have fine, dark green blades, not unlike Kentucky bluegrass. Produce thickest of turfs.	sun	¾-1½	Adapted to warm section of approximate southern half of the United States. Most are susceptible to drought. They're used on mild East and West coastal regions for seaside lawns because of tolerance to salt air. Meyer zoysia grows into zone 5. Turns brown after first frost in more northern parts of its limit and greens up in May. Emerald is more cold-resistant than other zoysias and will stay green in frost-free areas of the South. Crabgrass, weeds, and bluegrass are crowded out. Susceptible to brown patch, dollar spot, and various insects. Tolerates some shade. Start by planting sprigs or plugs 6 inches apart in spring. Feed spring and fall. Mow Japanese zoysia 1½ inches, but mascarene and Manila ¾ to 1 inch.

WESTERN GREAT PLAINS DRYLAND GRASSES

Grass	Description	Light	Mowing Ht. (Ins.)	Comments
BLUE GRAMA GRASS *Bouteloua gracilis*	Grayish-green, slightly hairy leaves grow in low tufts, which run together as they enlarge.	sun	2-3	Propagation mainly by sowing seed. More desirable where quality of turf is not important. A low-maintenance grass. Heat- and drought-resistant.
BUFFALO GRASS *Buchloe dactyloides*	Fine-textured, soft, low-growing, grayish-green grass of fairly good density. Distinctive feature is curling of the leaf blades. Turns straw color in high temperatures.	full sun	½-1½	Good where quality lawns are not possible because of drought and alkaline soil in the Great Plains. Does not survive where rainfall is over 25 inches a year. Minimum rainfall is 12 inches. Low maintenance required. Grown from seeds, sprigs, or plugs.

Starting a lawn from seed

The first step is choosing the right seed for your lawn. For example, should you plant bluegrass, one of the fine fescues, a bent grass, or perhaps a perennial ryegrass?

Generally, the best answer is to select a mixture (a combination of species) or a blend (a combination of cultivars of the same species). Most bags of commercial lawn seeds are mixtures. That way, you can have one type of grass that does well under certain conditions, along with one or more other species that thrive in different circumstances. If disease strikes, the damage probably will be limited to just one of the grasses in the mixture. Also, choose your mixture according to the amount of sunlight different areas of your lawn receive. Do you have many shady areas? If so, choose grasses that do better in shade (such as fescue varieties).

Kentucky bluegrass is unbeatable for many lawns. It is beautiful and reasonably easy to maintain. In addition, there are many excellent botanical varieties to select: Arista, Baron, Fylking, Glade, Majestic, Merion, Nugget, Plush, Prato, Sydsport. Mowing height for most bluegrasses ranges from 1½ to 2½ inches, with slightly higher grass required in some situations.

Fescues are well adapted to poorer, sandy soils and can tolerate dry shade, so one of the fine chewings fescues is often included in a lawn seed mixture with bluegrass. Popular fescue varieties include Highlight, Jamestown, Koket, and Ruby. Because of their adaptability to poor soil, fescues seldom need fertilizing. Otherwise, their maintenance requirements are similar to bluegrass, so they make excellent partners.

Tall fescue, on the other hand, is a coarse grass, not usually desirable for fine lawns, but useful in high traffic areas and where other grasses won't grow. If you plant one of the coarse fescues, you take the chance that it might spread to finer surrounding lawns (much to a neighbor's dismay!).

The perennial ryegrasses have made rapid progress in recent years with the discovery of many outstanding new cultivars. Once considered too coarse for fine lawns, today the improved ryegrasses nearly match bluegrass in beauty and ease of maintenance. The real benefit, though, is that they start quickly—sometimes showing a touch of green within a few days after seeding. Among the improved cultivars are Citation, Compas, Derby, Game, Manhattan, NK-100, NK-200, Omega, Pennfine.

Bent grasses grow well only in moist, humid climates, or where they get day-in, day-out care (on a golf course, for example). Close cropping is a must, so bent grasses require frequent mowings. Colonial bent grasses require the least care; creeping bent grasses the most.

Successful planting

Sow bluegrass, fescue, or bent grass in August or September, when there are several weeks of cool weather before freezing. Because perennial ryegrasses grow quickly, you can plant them either in the fall or during the first favorable spring weather when the soil is not too moist.

To be sure of success when seeding a new lawn, choose a high-quality seed mixture containing very little "crop" (weeds). The package should also list the purity of desired cultivars. A good mixture containing mostly bluegrass, some fine fescue, and a portion of perennial ryegrass will be able to contend with most of the weeds your lawn contains. When buying seed, you get what you pay for: a more expensive seed will more than make up for its price by the quality of lawn it produces.

Before planting, prepare the soilbed properly (see instructions on page 60), so the surface is cultivated to marble-size soil clods.

Then, broadcast seeds with a mechanical spreader, following the package instructions for the correct amount of seed per 1,000 square feet. Mix the seeds in the hopper before spreading.

If the soil surface is ideal, seeds will fall into cracks and crevices between the soil aggregates, where they will germinate. When planting on a slope, work across the slope—not up and down—so grass seed will not wash away when you water it or when it rains. Avoid planting seeds too deeply or they may not come up at all. If soil is sandy or powdery, though, roll the lawn just once to firm up the seed.

Mulch will help protect new seedlings and keep them from washing away. Use straw, burlap, nylon mesh, or other suitable materials. Water the newly planted lawn often, but lightly. When new seedlings are about two inches high, they're ready for their first mowing.

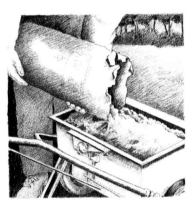

1 *Prepare your soil properly for seed. Add fertilizer and lime before cultivating. See page 60 for instructions.*

2 *A rotary tiller works fertilizer into the soil and helps make the soilbed surface suitable for accepting seed.*

3 *Smooth out high and low spots in the soil before seeding. Remove stones and other debris.*

4 *Choose a high-quality seed and sow it with a mechanical spreader. Stir the seed in the hopper before starting.*

5 *If soil is powdery or sandy, it may be necessary to roll the surface to firm the seed. Roll only once.*

6 *Water seed lightly immediately after seeding. Water often to keep soil moist until new seedlings are established.*

Perk up Your Lawn

Even the best lawns need help from time to time—especially after a tough winter and a long, hot summer. Thin lawns get thinner and bare spots get bigger without action. So, give your lawn a little extra care when it needs it. Your reward is a healthier, greener lawn just a few months later!

Take a few minutes to look closely at your lawn. What do you see? If you notice bare spots, thinning grass, too many weeds, or a buildup of thatch, it's probably time to start thinking about turf renovation. You may even want to rip up the entire lawn and start over, especially if you'd like to replant with one or more different grass species.

The best time to rejuvenate a tired lawn varies with the climate. In the North, autumn is best. Southern lawns, however, should be worked on either in spring or early summer. Start by removing all trash, litter, and fallen leaves from the lawn.

Repairs. If you have bare spots, repair and sow them individually. Cultivate the soil to a depth of four to six inches, working in a helping of balanced fertilizer. Rake the area smooth. Then, spread a quality seed over the area, tamping lightly with a spade to firm up the seeds. Follow with a mulch (straw, burlap, or mesh), and water lightly. Continue to sprinkle the area until new growth is established.

Compacted soil can be a problem, especially in southern zones or where there is exceptionally high traffic. Freezing and thawing in the North help break up compacted soil, but aeration is the answer in warmer climates and for problem areas. Use aeration equipment (a special pitchfork-like tool or a spiked roller), making sure you penetrate the soil deeply and remove the "core" of compacted earth from each spike imprint.

Thatch. Often mistaken for excess grass clippings, thatch is really a decaying accumulation of fibrous leaf sheaths and roots. A certain amount of thatch is beneficial to any lawn: it recycles plant tissues, serves as an organic fertilizer, and helps control the growth of weeds.

However, too heavy a buildup of thatch may harbor insects and disease, as well as prevent water and fertilizers from reaching and penetrating the soil. New grass has difficulty breaking through a thick thatch layer, so it's best to remove the excess before trouble starts.

Thatch removal is easiest with a power turf thinner ("power rake"). Set the blades of the machine deep enough to make small cuts in the soil—you have to cut all the way through thatch accumulations to do any good. Two or more passes may be necessary for a mature lawn. A power rake will kick up a good deal of thatch as it does the job, so rake up the debris and save it for mulch or the compost pile. You'll be surprised at the improved appearance of your dethatched lawn after just a few days.

Over-seeding. A power dethatcher is also an excellent way to prepare a thin lawn for overseeding. And you can improve the quality of your lawn at the same time by introducing better grasses. Set blades of the power rake deep enough to expose the soil so that new seeds will lodge in the scratches. After the soilbed is prepared, select a high-quality seed. One of the bluegrasses mixed with a little fine fescue is a popular choice, but you also might want to consider one of the fast-growing, improved perennial ryegrasses, too. Avoid substandard mixes of seed containing annual rye, tall fescue, or other haygrasses.

Spread seed with a mechanical spreader at a rate of about *half* that used for seeding a new lawn (usually, sow around one to two pounds per 1,000 square feet). Water the new seeding lightly, but thoroughly, until new growth starts; then, water only to prevent soil from becoming dry. Too much watering after the lawn is established encourages weed growth. Mow your lawn only when new growth reaches a height of at least two inches.

Weeds and pests. Time for lawn rejuvenation is also a good time to check your lawn for damage from weeds or other pests. Look for telltale patches of brown or wilted grass—you can use the charts on pages 68 to 74 to identify problems and select a cure. A note of caution: insecticides and herbicides can retard growth of new seed, so apply them only to lawns where grass growth is established.

Starting from scratch. If you decide there's no hope for your existing lawn and you'd like to get a fresh start, then a complete lawn renovation is in order. The first step is to eliminate existing vegetation, by stripping of sod or by using a contact herbicide. (Check local restrictions for the use of herbicides

1 *Clean your lawn of leaves and debris before undertaking any lawn rejuvenation. Mow the grass shorter than usual to prepare for lawn fix-ups.*

2 *Treat bare spots individually. Cultivate exposed soil to a depth of four to six inches, working in fertilizer. Rake smooth and seed, tamping as shown.*

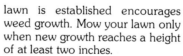

3 *Apply fertilizer to the entire lawn. Wait until new grass has a good start before application. Use the kind with slow-release nitrogen.*

4 *After sowing seed over a scarified lawn, water with a fine spray to avoid washing seeds away. Keep soil moist until new grass is established.*

5 *In northern zones, weed control is effective in the fall. Use recommended weed killers for broadleafs. Apply exactly as the manufacturer suggests.*

before applying.) Before cultivating, allow the herbicide to do its work and then dissipate. Then apply fertilizer, lime if necessary, and till the soil until it's ready for seed (see instructions for soil preparation on page 60).

Cut and roll back sod with a spade to repair low spots in your lawn. Use the same technique to clean an area for a vegetable or flower garden; then, transplant the sod to a bare spot elsewhere in your lawn.

Leveling humps and hollows

Lawn irregularities are annoying but will occur as long as helpful earthworms thrive and seasons pass with freezing and thawing. Such bumps and dips cause few problems. However, higher spots may interfere with mowing and detract from the appearance of your lawn, and low spots get boggy when it rains.

Minor irregularities are eliminated by topdressing low spots with a loose mixture of weed-free topsoil and peat or sand. Apply the soil mixture right onto the grass and smooth it over with the back of a stiff rake. Repeat this process twice yearly until the surface is level.

Deeper depressions call for more drastic action. Slice strips of sod about 20 inches wide, cut underneath with a sharp spade or shovel, and roll the strips back completely to expose the low spot. Fill in the depression with high-quality, weed-free topsoil (ideally, fortify this soil with a little fertilizer rich in phosphorus and potassium). Tamp the new soil firmly before rolling sod back into place. Topdress the replaced sod with about one-fourth inch of soil, and water deeply.

High spots are tricky to repair and require a heavy roller to do the job right. First, use a sharp, flat spade to remove thin wedges of turf from the high spot. Space the slices about ten inches apart, and cut each wedge about six inches deep. Soak the area thoroughly, and then roll the high spot. The pressure of the roller should compress the turf and soilbed enough to seal the spaces left from the removal of soil wedges, thus lowering the hump. If a slight high spot still exists, wait several months and repeat the process.

Lawn care

Once you've established a beautiful lawn, a little care goes a long way toward keeping it lush and healthy. A healthy lawn crowds out weeds.

Mowing. Because grass plants *are* vigorous and fast growing, regular mowings are essential. Mow whenever the grass demands it—a good rule of thumb is never to cut off more grass than you leave. If the recommended height of cut is two inches, mow when the grass is three and one-half inches high. If height of cut is one inch, mow when the grass is just under two inches.

The different species of grass require different mowing heights. See the charts on pages 62 to 64 for recommendations. In shady spots, cut grass less frequently and at a height one-half inch taller than normal. This will help conceal thin growth that's unavoidable where sunlight is sparse.

You have many choices when it comes to mowing equipment. There are advantages and disadvantages to both reel and rotary machines. Generally, though, reel mowers make a cleaner cut and are especially good for low-cut lawns (for example, bent grass turf). Rotary mowers are more maneuverable, more easily lifted and stored. When dull, rotaries tend to fray grass tips rather than cut them, resulting in a brownish tinge when the damaged grass leaves dry out.

Perhaps the most important mower considerations are the size, shape, and quality of your lawn. Choose a mower large enough to handle the job, and then keep the blades sharp and in good repair.

Watering. Light sprinklings do more harm than good on an established lawn, so water deeply. If you want your lawn to remain deep-rooted and healthy, water until the soil is wet to a minimum depth of six inches. Twelve is better yet.

Once watered, lawns hold their moisture for a remarkably long time. More lawns suffer from excessive watering than from drying out. There are several signals when grasses are about to dry out: 1) turf loses resiliency so you can see footprints or mower tracks long after you've crossed the lawn; 2) grass assumes a bluish cast; and 3) growth is substantially slowed. When these warnings appear, it's time to water.

A lawn with fairly heavy soil will require around three hours of watering for moisture to penetrate to the proper depth. But sandy soils don't hold moisture well, so lengthy waterings are of little value.

Fertilizers. Most lawns need a little help if they're to wear and look their best. A good fertilizer—rich in the nutrients all lawns thrive on, such as nitrogen, phosphorus, and potassium—also encourages lawns to fight off weeds. Too much fertilizer, though, can brown or "burn" the grass or simply increase the need to mow it.

Experts agree that one light feeding in the fall and another in the spring are plenty for grasses in most zones. A soil test will tell you if your lawn is lacking essential nutrients, and you can adjust your feedings accordingly. Nutrient levels are printed on the fertilizer bags; so if you're spreading a 12-12-12 combination, it consists of 12 percent nitrogen (N), 12 percent phosphorus (P), and 12 percent potassium (K).

In the spring, fertilize when grass starts to green by applying nutrients in the ratio 2-1-1. For most lawns, four pounds of nitrogen per 1,000 square feet are plenty.

Fertilize in the fall, applying the three key nutrients in a ratio of 1-2-2. This will encourage healthy root and growth during winter. Nitrogen applied before winter should be the water insoluble, slow-release kind.

Most organic fertilizers, such as manure, tankage, sewage sludge, and soybean meal, contain nitrogen as the main nutrient. They are slow acting and long lasting, but not as quickly efficient as chemical fertilizers.

Clippings are good sources of nitrogen when left in the lawn after mowing. They decompose quickly and do not contribute to thatch accumulation. If for some reason, though, you're forced to mow when the grass is much higher than normal, it's a good idea to rake clippings away or to catch them as you mow.

CONTROL OF WEEDS THAT MAY INVADE LAWNS

Name	Comments	Controls
Black medic *Medicago lupulina*	Low-growing annual or biennial with hairy stems. As with many weeds, gains foothold where grass is thin, especially in dry situations. Small, yellowish flowers usually appear from March to late fall.	Thicken turf by feeding, mowing high, and watering to choke out weeds. A good cultural schedule is best defense against all weeds. Apply post-emergent herbicide in early spring and again in fall.
Buttercup, Creeping *Ranunculus repens*	A perennial with trailing stems. Yellow ½-inch flowers bloom June to August. Likes cool, moist areas of Northeast and Northwest.	Dig out small infestations. For larger areas, apply a post-emergent herbicide in spring.
Carpetweed *Aizoaceae* family	Found across the country. Easy to recognize—many narrow stems, small leaves, and tiny white flowers. Forms thick flat mat. Blooms June to November. Self-seeding.	Maintain a thick turf by following a good cultural schedule to choke out weeds. This pest can be killed with post-emergent herbicide.
Chickweed, Common *Stellaria media*	An annual with delicate, creeping stems that tear easily when pulled. Tangled stems root readily under cool, moist conditions. Found across the country. Produces tiny white, starlike flowers from February into December. Self-seeding.	If small infestation, pull weed early, before first seeds form. Use care to get all stems. For large area, apply post-emergent herbicide in spring or fall.
Chickweed, Mouse-ear *Cerastium*	A creeping perennial that forms dense mat-like growth. Tiny white flowers appear from April into October. Prefers moist, cool conditions. Grows in most areas except along Mexican border or in North Dakota.	Difficult to pull, because it entangles in the grass. Control by applying a post-emergent herbicide.
Clover, White *Trifolium repens*	A perennial readily recognized by typical cloverleaf shape and round white blooms. Spreads by creeping along and rooting in. Self-seeding. Leaves will stain clothing when bruised.	Dig out clover as soon as appears. For large area, use post-emergent herbicide.
Crabgrass, Common *Digitaria sanguinalis*	An annual bunch grass found across the country, except in Southwest and southern Florida. Blooms July to October. Doesn't grow in shade—likes moisture and sun. Seeds mature in late summer and early fall.	Follow a good cultural schedule to choke out pest. Mow lawn high during spring to shade germinating seedlings. Apply a pre-emergent control in early spring.
Crabgrass, Silver, also called Goose grass *Eleusine indica*	An annual bunch grass. Likes warm, moist soil. Blooms June to October. Seeds from July through October. Found across country except in Northeast.	If small infestation, dig out. For large area, use a pre-emergent herbicide. After weed appears, apply post-emergent type.

Name	Comments	Controls
Daisy, Oxeye *Chrysanthemum leucanthemum*	A perennial that spreads by underground stems and seeds. Blooms June to August. Found across the country, except in the Dakotas and parts of Wyoming and Montana.	Dig weeds out as soon as appear because they are hard to eradicate. Use strong concentration of a post-emergent but *only* on individual plants.
Dallis grass *Paspalum dilatatum*	A tall perennial bunch grass that grows in moist, warm areas of the East coast, South, some areas of the Southwest, and Oregon coast. Grows from May into fall. Spreads by underground stems. Self-seeding.	If small infestation, dig out. For larger area, apply a post-emergent herbicide. Give two or more treatments, if necessary. Space treatments one week apart.
Dandelion *Taraxacum officinale*	Found across country except in a few areas of deep South. Produces coarse-toothed, long leaves in bunch. Bright yellow blooms, followed by round white seed heads. In cold areas, flowering occurs from March until a freeze; in warm areas, flowering occurs year round.	The entire taproot must be dug out; otherwise, a new plant will grow. Use a post-emergent herbicide in the fall. Spot chemical applicators are available.
Dock, Curly *Rumex crispus*	A perennial with a 1½- to 2-foot taproot. Produces one or more tall stems. Found across the country. Its spikes of whitish flowers appear from June into September.	If small infestation, dig out, being sure to get the entire root. On larger area, apply a post-emergent herbicide. Apply spray into each plant crown.
Garlic, Wild, or Wild onion *Allium canadense*	A perennial weed common in South, many central states, and East and Northwest coasts. Likes wet, clay soils. Blooms May to July. Spreads by bulbs and seeds.	Mow lawn regularly to prevent seed formation. Apply post-emergent herbicide in late fall and early spring.
Geranium, Wild *Geranium masculatum*	An annual that blooms February into June. Most likely a problem in dry, sandy soils on West coast and occasionally in East.	Water the area, then weeds will pull easily. Control with a post-emergent herbicide.
Hawkweed, or Devil's-paintbrush *Hieracium aurantiacum*	A creeping perennial that varies in height. Grows in moist, cool soil in northern half of the U.S. A cluster of red-orange blossoms appears at top of flower stalks in July and August.	If small infestation, dig out. For larger area, use post-emergent herbicide in spring or fall.

CONTROL OF WEEDS THAT MAY INVADE LAWNS (continued)

Name	Comments	Controls
Heal-all, or Self-heal *Prunella vulgaris*	A creeping perennial with clustered leaves. Lilac flowers appear May to fall. Spreads by creeping stems and seeds. Thrives in rich, moist soil, except in North Dakota, parts of South Dakota, Montana, and Wyoming.	If small infestation, dig out. For larger areas, use post-emergent herbicide.
Ivy, Ground *Glechoma hederacea*	A creeping perennial that can quickly invade a lawn. Thrives mainly in damp, shaded areas in the eastern half of the country, except in Florida. Blue flowers appear April to June. Has square stems.	If small infestation, pull out. For larger area, apply post-emergent herbicide in spring or fall.
Knotweed, Prostrate *Polygonum aviculare*	Family of annual weeds that develop a mat of wiry stems and small leaves. Many have clusters of tiny greenish or pinkish flowers from July to September. A stout taproot makes it hard to pull.	To pull, first soak ground deeply. Difficult to eradicate if allowed to mature. Use a post-emergent herbicide.
Lamb's-quarters *Chenopodium album*	Common annual weed. Leaves have white underside. Occurs most in newly seeded lawns or lawns having thin turf. Plumelike whitish flower heads and seeds appear June to October.	Mow lawn closely. Soak soil for easy pulling. For large area, use post-emergent herbicide.
Nettle, Dead *Lamium album*	Creeping annual or biennial that occurs on thin grass in rich, moist soil. Lavender flowers in spring and fall. Spreads by creeping stems and seeds.	Pull if lawn is new. On established lawn with large infestation, control with post-emergent herbicide.
Nimblewill *Muhlenbergia schreberi*	A creeping perennial grass with long narrow stalks. Bears yellowish or light green flower heads. Fine grayish-green leaves. Found in eastern and central part of the country. Spreads by self-seeding and runners.	Easily pulled during growing season. Difficult to eradicate, but solid colonies can be spot-treated with post-emergent. Use care not to kill surrounding grass.
Nut grass, Yellow, also called Nut sedge *Cyperus esculentus*	A perennial in moist, sandy soils. Appears July to September. Spreads by tubers and self-seeding.	Control difficult because of deeply rooted tubers.

Name	Comments	Controls
Pennywort *Hydrocotyle sibthorpioides*	A perennial that thrives in shady, moist areas in southern California, from Massachusetts to Florida, and west to Indiana and Texas. Produces small, round white flower heads July to October. Spreads by seeds and underground stems.	Apply a post-emergent during active growing period.
Plantain, Broad-leaf *Plantago major*	A perennial (sometimes annual) with broad leaves, 3 to 6 inches long and bunched low. Tall, slender stalks bloom June to October. Spreads by seeds.	If small infestation, dig out when soil is moist. For larger area, use a post-emergent herbicide in early spring or fall.
Quack grass, or Couch grass *Agropyron repens*	A vigorous-spreading perennial bunch grass. Forms a dense root structure by rooting at every joint on underground stems. Found across country except in parts of Southwest and deep South.	Cannot be eradicated without killing lawn grasses, too. A black plastic cover extended over a patch will starve all growth. Or apply a post-emergent control; wait three weeks before re-seeding lawn.
Shepherdspurse *Capsella bursa-pastoris*	A persistent annual that forms a circle of low leaves with white flowers on tall stems. Seedpods are shaped like a shepherd's purse.	Fairly easy to pull if soil is moist. For larger area, use a post-emergent herbicide.
Sorrel, Red, also Sheep sorrel *Rumex acetosella*	A perennial that forms a mat-like growth in early summer. Found across the country wherever soil and drainage are poor. Spreads by underground stems and seeds.	Use a post-emergent control in early spring and early fall.
Thistle, Canada *Cirsium arvense*	Thrives in clay soils in the North. Long prickly leaves and lavender flowers. Spreads by seeds and underground roots. Blooms July through October.	Use knife to cut below ground and remove crown from roots. For larger infestation, apply a post-emergent herbicide.
Yarrow, Common, also called Milfoil *Achillea millefolium*	A creeping perennial with very finely divided, soft leaves and white cushiony blooms. Grows in most regions with poor soil, except in the Southwest. Spreads by seeds and underground stems.	Dig weed out as soon as it appears. For larger area, control by a couple of applications of a post-emergent herbicide.

DISEASES OF LAWN GRASSES AND THEIR CONTROL

Disease	Grasses Attacked	Infection Signs and Controls
Brown patch	Bent grasses and St. Augustine grass.	Leaves first turn brown and appear water-soaked, followed by wilting and turning light brown. Rot may set in. Irregular brown spots show in lawn from 1 inch to several feet in diameter during warm, humid conditions. Use only slow-release ureaform nitrogen to feed. Fast-acting nitrogen causes too-soft growth, making grass more disease-susceptible. Water mornings only. In acid soil areas, apply lime. Catch grass clippings when mowing.
Copper spot	Bent grasses, including redtop.	Grass leaves show light tan spots, with darker color around the edges. When spots are dead, they are copper-colored. Spots in lawn are 1 to 2 inches in diameter. Disease appears oftener in acid soils of humid coastal areas. Lime may be needed if soil test shows too much acid. Catch grass clippings when mowing. Feed spring and fall.
Dollar spot	Bent grasses are most susceptible. Kentucky bluegrass, fescue, zoysia, Bermuda, and St. Augustine may be affected.	Dollar spot is so named because the spots are commonly the size of a silver dollar. The spots often run together to form irregular areas, and grass is killed. Most likely to show up in warm, wet weather. Feed spring and fall to help overcome the problem. Catch grass clippings when mowing.
Fairy rings	These fungi don't attack turf directly, but prevent grass roots from taking in water, oxygen, and nutrients.	Mushrooms appear in circles or part circles and can vary from a few inches to about 50 feet in diameter. Strip off dead turf, which may range 3 to 6 inches wide. Grass is often greener inside the area than elsewhere. Sod underneath the mushroom ring is tight and hard. Use a garden root feeder to soak the area deeply. Start about 2 feet out and work toward the ring to keep grass roots alive. Repeat a few times. All infested soil can be taken out and replaced with rich compost before resodding.
Fusarium blight	Kentucky bluegrass, red fescue, and bent grasses.	Most likely to occur in central states and Northeast, especially on lawns exposed to sun. Small tan spots appear in early summer and may come together to make larger areas. Give lawn deep soaking during dry periods—never give frequent light sprinklings. De-thatch and avoid too acid soil by applying lime. Avoid excessive nitrogen feeding.
Gray leaf spot	St. Augustine grass.	Fungus spreads fast during humid, warm, rainy weather. Little brown spots show up on grass blades, spread into long areas having gray centers with purple waterlogged edges. Grass looks scorched. Avoid quick-release nitrogen; use slow-release ureaform.
Grease spot	Kentucky bluegrass, bent grasses, fescues, ryegrasses, Bermuda grass, and St. Augustine grass.	Most noticeable during humid, hot weather, especially on turf growing in poorly drained soil. A white, cottony film appears on the turf surface. Next appear reddish-brown spots, a few inches in diameter and with a greasy look and nearly black borders. In time, the grass dies. Provide good drainage on new lawns to help prevent the problem. Give lawn deep soaking during dry periods. Water mornings only.
Leaf spots and blights	Kentucky bluegrass, Bermuda grass, and fescues.	Small, roundish, gray, brown, or purplish-black spots show up on leaf blades which spread to kill leaves and roots. Most likely to show in wet weather in mid-spring until fall. Catch grass clippings, de-thatch lawn, and use only slow-release nitrogen fertilizer.
Ophiobolus patch	Bluegrasses, bent grasses, fescues, and ryegrasses.	The disease is most common in the Pacific Northwest. May occur in the Northeast. Light reddish-brown patches from a couple of inches to about 2 feet in diameter appear. In time, they turn yellowish-tan when root and foliage die. Have soil tested and follow recommendations. Avoid quick-release fertilizer.
Powdery mildew	Bluegrasses and fescues.	Grayish white, white, or brown mold appears on leaf blades. Often found in areas of low air circulation, shade, and poorly drained soil. Warm, humid days and cool nights favor it. Catch grass clippings. During hot humid weather, avoid over-watering and fertilizing.
Red thread, Pink patch, Corticium	Bluegrasses, fescues, bent grasses, and ryegrasses.	Prevalent along the northern coastal areas. Grass blades stick together with red thread-like growths. Cool moist weather favors its development in spring or fall. Irregular pink patches 2 to 6 inches in diameter. Follow grass maintenance schedule, and apply lawn fertilizer in spring and fall.

Disease	Grasses Attacked	Infection Signs and Controls
Rust	Bluegrasses, ryegrasses, Bermuda grass, zoysia, St. Augustine.	Orange or reddish-brown or black blisters appear on grass leaves, causing plants to wither and die. When the blisters burst, the spores can spread to infect healthy grass. Mow lawn each time it grows ½ inch to remove infected parts, and catch clippings. Promote good growth by regular feeding and watering.
Snow mold	This fungus disease can occur on all grasses in regions where snow is on the ground for some time.	As snow melts in spring, tan or pinkish patches appear on grass from 6 inches to several feet in diameter. Usually worse in wet, shaded areas where snow lingers. Mow lawn shorter than usual on last mowing in fall and catch clippings.
Smut or Stripe	Bluegrasses and bent grass.	This fungus favors cool spring and fall. Grass leaves develop black or gray stripes that rupture to discharge black spores. Like rust spores, they can infect turf in other areas of the lawn. Diseased plants become stunted and turn yellowish-green. Before dying, leaves look shredded and curled. Bluegrass lawn seed blends should be used for seeding a lawn. At least one variety in the blend will be resistant to smut.

NOTE: For chemical control, multipurpose fungicides are available for home lawns because many lawn diseases are difficult for a home gardener to identify. Such formulations are designed to control several specific diseases. In starting a new lawn, work plenty of organic fertilizer into the soil and always follow a good cultural schedule.

COMMON LAWN INSECTS AND THEIR CONTROL

Insect	Description and Trouble Signs	Controls
Ants	Several kinds may occur in lawns. They make nests underground. Around each entrance, a mound of soil particles may smother grass and make lawn unsightly.	Let grass grow taller to hide ant mounds. If ants become too large a problem, Diazinon or carbaryl (Sevin) are effective insecticides that are biodegradable or non-persistent a few days after application. Use chemical only as last resort.
Armyworms	These pests are found in dense groupings feeding on grass to make a somewhat circular area. The caterpillar is up to 1½ inches long with green, tan, or black stripes on its back. Damage occurs springtime through late summer.	Keep lawn healthy by watering and feeding on schedule. Use slow-release ureaform lawn fertilizer. Control pest with Diazinon at first sign of extensive feeding.
Billbugs	Adults are ¼- to ¾-inch long, black or reddish-brown beetles with long snout. They chew holes in stems of grass, depositing eggs in them. Eggs hatch into chunky, legless, ½-inch-long larvae, which puncture stem and crown as they feed. Kill grass in patches; grass blades break off at soil line.	In lawns with a history of billbug damage, treat with Diazinon or carbaryl to control adults in early spring. Or, treat to control larvae in early summer.
Chinch bugs	Adults have black bodies with white wings and reddish legs. Nymphs grow from very small size to ⅛-inch-long adults. They prefer dry, sunny areas. Chinch bugs feed at all stages of their development, leaving large yellowish-to-brown patches	Well-fed lawns discourage the pest. Treat the two generations of this insect in June and August with Diazinon or carbaryl.

COMMON LAWN INSECTS AND THEIR CONTROL (continued)

Insect	Description and Trouble Signs	Controls
Cutworms	Smooth grayish or brownish caterpillars, up to 2 inches long, feed at night after hiding under protective covering during the day. They cut off grass at the soil line and can be a problem from spring until late summer. Grass stems are eaten away at soil surface, leaving small dead spots.	If affected area is small, it can be puddled with water to bring worms to the surface to collect and destroy. Control with carbaryl or Diazinon.
Fiery skippers	Distinguished by yellow, orange, and brown butterflies that hover over the lawn during hot part of the day. Eggs are deposited on grass and hatch into brownish-yellow worms that feed and cause round 1- to 2-inch dead spots. A wide range of grasses is susceptible to the larval activity. These larvae chew grass foliage rather than roots.	As a natural control, a parasite may show up to attack the worms. The evidence will be white cottony masses. Otherwise, apply carbaryl or Diazinon.
Grubs, White	Grubs are the larvae of beetles, including Japanese and June. Larvae are thick, whitish, C-shaped underground worms that vary from ¾ to 1½ inches in length. Grubs eat grass roots, leaving brown, dead patches easily lifted out of the lawn.	In small areas, cut away sections of sod; pick and destroy grubs from underside. In severe infestations, Diazinon may be used for control.
Leafhoppers	These yellow, brown, or green slender, wedge-shaped insects are less than ½ inch long. When you walk on the lawn, they flit away as you pass. Leafhoppers are especially active in lawns on East and West coasts, although they can be found throughout the country. They suck juices from leaves, causing grass to turn white, later yellow, then brown.	Control with Diazinon or carbaryl when leafhoppers are abundant.
Mites	Clover mites show as tiny red specks against white paper. They are found in lawns across the country. Bermuda grass mites are pale green and microscopic; they may occur in Gulf Coast and western lawns. All spider-like mites suck juices from grass leaves. Grass wilts, turns yellow, and dies.	Because overly succulent grass growth attracts mites, avoid heavy fertilization. Control with Diazinon at first sign of infestation.
Mole crickets	Brownish insects live in soil during day and come out at night. Mole crickets are about 1½ inches long and mostly a problem in southern lawns. They cut off underground stems and roots in the day and work on aboveground stems at night. Results leave lawns with areas that appear closely clipped. This pest is at its worst in moist, warm weather.	Control with Diazinon.
Nematodes	Transparent roundworms with whitish or yellowish tint. They are tiny, often microscopic. Their presence may not be realized until a bleached-out area is noticed. Lack of vigor and stunting of lawn may occur. The pests feed mainly on grass roots but some on stem and leaves. Disease may set in because of weakened turf.	To avoid and suppress nematodes, keep turf well-fed and water on schedule. Won't require chemical treatment.
Sod webworms	Tan-colored moths, about ¾ inch long, lay eggs at dusk. Gray or light brown larvae up to 1 inch long feed on bluegrasses and bent grasses, doing most damage during spring to midsummer. Feed on shoots and crowns of grass causing irregular, close-clipped brown patches.	Treat with carbaryl or Diazinon when larvae are present.

NOTE: Your county extension office has current information about recommended insecticides and best time of application. Use a chemical only as a last resort and according to directions on container labels. Proper fertilizing, mowing, and watering are your best defenses against insects, weeds, and disease.

Ground Covers

No matter how hard you try, there are some places your lawn just won't grow. But don't give up—try planting a ground cover instead. There are dozens of hardy varieties to choose from, including ones that do well in deep shade.

Easy to maintain and wonderfully attractive, ground covers are a gardener's delight. They hug and bind the soil—a real benefit to steep slopes—and, once established, practically take care of themselves. You can choose varieties to grow in conditions ranging from deep shade to bright sun, from poor, sandy soil to perfectly prepared garden fare.

Better still, they spread fast to fill in those trouble spots you've always worried about. Do a little research and select the cover that's right for the sun, soil, and climate in your region (pages 78 to 85 offer lots of good ideas). Then, visit your nearby garden center and purchase enough plants to get started (see page 76 for general planting instructions). As soon as your ground cover is fairly well established, the only care it will need is occasional watering, weeding, mulching, and pruning. Ground covers are usually quite resistant to diseases and pests, so they're not major problems.

And here's a good idea: if you need a fast, reliable ground cover to hold the soil in an area where you eventually plan to sow grass seed, plant a temporary annual cover such as sweet alyssum, portulaca, verbenas, petunias, or California poppies. They'll transform the area from bare dirt to attractive, soil-binding cover in just a few weeks.

You'll love the effect low-growing ground covers have on your landscape. Try different shapes and textures as you plant garden-like beds of greenery. Few lawn-keeping ventures are more enjoyable than growing ground covers.

Planting, propagating, and maintaining ground covers

Planting. You can plant ground covering perennials, shrubs, and vines in either spring or fall. Shallow-rooted kinds or those planted on windy, exposed slopes do better when planted in spring, particularly if your winters are harsh.

Deep-rooted plants, though, can handle fall planting easily. In fact, most ground covers can be set out anytime of the growing season, provided they're given adequate water and protection from wind until roots are established.

Prepare the soilbed as you would for planting grass seed (see page 60). Cultivate a good, balanced fertilizer into the soil for most ground covers. *Note:* for some plantings, fertilizer does more harm than good. The alpine ground covers grow naturally in poor soil and a rich diet doesn't suit them. To be safe, check planting instructions for your choice of ground covers before preparing the soil.

When planting, remember that small, single-stemmed root cuttings take longer to establish than those planted in larger bunches. Ground covers normally spread by underground stems or by trailing runners, so—depending on variety—they may be planted anywhere from six inches to five feet apart.

For example, pachysandra can be spaced as far as a foot apart at planting, but covers much faster when set six inches apart or so. Most ground covers that are more prostrate in habit (such as periwinkle or ivy) can be placed at one plant per square foot. Alpine or rock plants are spaced one foot apart.

Shrubs such as cotoneaster, junipers, and euonymus need at least three square feet of space per plant. Vines (except annuals) typically need even wider spacing, with trailing roots spread at least three to five feet apart.

If you plant on a hillside, be sure to make a small depression around each plant to hold water.

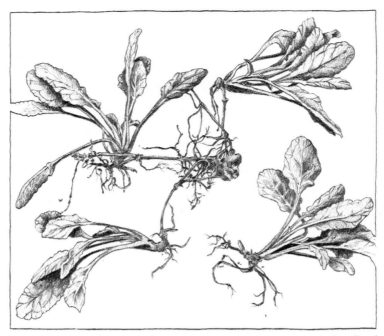

If you want quick coverage, buy a lot of plants and place them close together. But if you have the time and patience, buy fewer and let them multiply in the corner of your garden. Then, divide them and transplant where you want.

Prepare soil for ground covers the same way you get ready for a new lawn. Most ground covers like organic matter—compost or peat—worked into the soil. Later, you might want to apply a second helping of fertilizer to speed growth.

Propagation. Root division is the quickest way to propagate many ground covers. Spring or fall are good times, but it can be done anytime if you're careful.

"Layering" is a natural method to increase many prostrate ground covers, providing your soil is rich enough to promote new root growth. Pin or cover low-to-the-ground trailing stems in one or more places to induce new plants. Year-old growth works best for layering.

Cuttings are another easy way to propagate many of the woody plants. Some, such as pachysandra and ivy cuttings, are started by inserting them in pots of soil, sand, or peat moss.

Many low-growing perennials are started from seed. It's an easy procedure, but new plants require care until they are a fairly good size. Start small seeds in trays or pots, and transplant seedlings when they have four to six leaves. (For more information on starting ground covers from seeds or cuttings, see Chapter 6: Vines.)

Care and maintenance. If you start ground covers out according to the soil, light, and water they need, you'll have little maintenance once a healthy growth is established.

Be sure to mulch between plants, especially after initial planting, to help control weeds and to provide a natural, slow-release fertilizer. A good mulch also protects root systems in the winter, preventing damage. Use peat moss, sawdust, rotted manure, wood chips, oak leaves, pine needles, straw, or ground corncobs.

Even with a layer of mulch, your ground cover will need weeding once in a while. Be especially careful to completely remove deep-rooted weeds such as witch grass, or they'll overrun your prized foliage in no time. Shallow-rooted weeds can be removed by hand after a rain while the soil is moist.

Occasional pruning is a must with most ground covers. Some are so vigorous, they can choke other plants if not trimmed. When purchased, plants may be rangy in appearance, so prune them back for thicker growth and more buds. Plants with long, trailing stems (myrtle, bearberry, ivy, winter creeper) can be cut back halfway with good results. And woody ground covers benefit from pruning with sharp shears several times a year.

Water ground covers in dry weather. On steep hills, build ridges to keep water from running downhill too fast.

Samples of ground covers

Imagine places in your lawn where you can grow colorful patches of ground cover. Surrounding trees, framing flower gardens, accenting shrubs, or cascading over a cobble wall surrounding your patio. There are many possibilities. Few sights are more beautiful than a ground cover's delicate blooms bobbing amidst a sea of leafy green. And so easy! Be adventuresome and try several varieties. Why struggle any longer to grow grass where it's shady, too steep, or just too much work? You'll find a ground cover that's the right answer for any difficult spot!

Bugleweed *Ajuga reptans*

Bearberry *Arctostaphylos uva-ursi*

Sheep fescue *Festuca ovina*

Snow-in-summer *Cerastium tomentosum*

Hall's honeysuckle *Lonicera japonica 'halliana'*

Lily-of-the-valley *Convallaria majalis*

Pachysandra *Pachysandra terminalis*

Periwinkle *Vinca minor*

GROUND COVERS

Name	Zone	Description	Light	Comments
Algerian ivy *Hedera canariensis*	9-10	Three- to five-lobed shiny leaves, 5 to 7 inches across. Variegated cultivar has green and white foliage.	sun or shade	Prefers rich, moist soil. One of most widely used ground covers in warm parts of California and similar climates. Space new plants 18 inches apart.
Baby's-tears, Angel's-tears *Soleirolia soleiroli*	10	Creeping runners give dense cover of shiny ⅛-inch, rounded green leaves.	shade	Best grown in rich, moist soil, in light to deep shade, and in small areas, such as under trees or shrubs. Set new plants 6 to 12 inches apart. Use plenty of compost in soil. Start any time of year and water regularly until well-established.
Baltic ivy *Hedera helix 'baltica'*	5-10	One- to 2-inch-long, dark green, lobed leaves 6 to 8 inches high. Trailing stems root as they spread.	sun or shade	Does best in rich, moist soil. Hardiest of English ivy cultivars. Space new plants 12 inches apart. Fertilize established planting with lawn fertilizer in early spring. Takes two or three years to completely fill area.
Bearberry, Kinnikinick *Arctostaphylos uva-ursi*	2-10	Wide-spreading evergreen shrub 6 to 12 inches tall. Dark green, shiny leaves are an inch long. Bright red berries attract birds.	sun or light shade	Prefers sandy acid soil by seaside or high in mountains. Will grow in windy, dry situations. Set plants 1 to 2 feet apart in early spring or late fall.
Bearberry cotoneaster *Cotoneaster dammeri*	5-10	Small oval, alternate shiny evergreen leaves. Tiny white flowers, masses of red berries.	sun or light shade	Good to cover seashore and rocky spots. Roots well in any soil, but must be well-drained. Use in areas with plenty of room to spread without need of heavy pruning.
Bird's-foot trefoil *Lotus corniculatus*	3-10	Three ½-inch leaflets per leaf stem distinguish this spreading plant. Grows 1 to 2 feet tall. Is evergreen in warmer areas. Yellow pea blooms are followed by claw-like pods.	sun or light shade	Tolerates poor soil, but needs good drainage. Best used to cover large areas. Sow seed at rate of 2 pounds on 50x20-foot area. Or set plants 6 inches apart spring or summer. Mow area as if it were a lawn to keep growth compact and even.
Blue fescue *Festuca ovina 'glauca'*	3-9	Grows 4 to 10 inches high. Makes compact mounds of whitish-blue blades to provide attractive appearance year round.	shade or part sun	Thrives in most soils, but best in poor, fairly dry soil. Tolerates seashore planting and wind-blown exposures. Space plants 6 inches apart for tight appearance and 10 to 12 inches for loose appearance.
Bishop's weed, Goutweed *Aegopodium podagraria 'variegatum'*	3-10	Grows 8 to 10 inches high. Mass of green and white leaves produced with cluster of white flowers in mid-summer. Spreads rapidly by underground stolons. Freeze kills tops in fall with new growth each spring.	shade or part sun	Will grow in almost any soil. Avoid hot sun in windy situations. Best planted in a contained situation where its rampant growth won't crowd other areas. Will grow under most trees and shrubs. Plants may be set in spring or early fall. Set plants 6 to 10 inches apart. Grown mainly for attractive foliage—cut off flower stalks to maintain neat appearance. Easy to lift, separate, and replant from established plantings.
Carmel creeper *Ceanothus griseus 'horizontalis'*	7-10	Lilac-like shrub with small elongated leaves. Grows 18 to 30 inches tall, with wide spread up to 10 to 12 feet. Evergreen with violet-blue, 2-inch flower clusters.	full sun	Grown widely along Pacific coastal areas. Resists salt spray and strong winds. Prefers good drainage and sandy soil. Set nursery plants about 4 feet apart. Discourage weeds by applying a light, weed-free mulch. Pinch back shoots lightly during growing season. For long life, avoid overwatering.
Carpet bugle, Bugleweed *Ajuga reptans*	3-10	Produces deep green, 2- to 4-inch shiny leaves, forming rosettes flat on ground or up to 5 to 6 inches high. Blue flower spikes in spring rise 4 to 6 inches above foliage. Several cultivars with multicolored leaves are now available. Turns bronzy-red in fall.	sun or light shade	Considered one of best low-growing ground covers. While it prefers sunlight or partial sunlight, it can be useful in deeply shaded areas. Prefers moist, enriched soil. The multicolored cultivars are especially useful in such situations as self-contained edging around patios or front entrances. Space plants 6 to 12 inches apart. Keep watered in hot, dry weather. Feed early spring to maintain dense cover. Make sure plants don't smother over winter from wet tree leaves. Cover lightly with brush or evergreen prunings.

Name	Zone	Description	Light	Comments
Chamomile, English, or Roman chamomile *Chamaemelum nobile*	3-10	Fragrant evergreen herb with bright green, fine, fern-like foliage. Grows 3 to 10 inches high. Tiny daisy-like flowers are produced if allowed to grow. Spreads fast by creeping stems.	sun	Deep-rooted so resists drought. Used as lawn substitute where drought is extreme. Can be mowed and walked on. Will tolerate partial shade. Plant divisions in early spring, 4 to 12 inches apart.
Chaparral broom, Coyote brush *Baccharis pilularis*	8-10	Produces gray-green, holly-like leaves. Tiny white flowers in summer. Evergreen shrub that spreads quickly, making dense cover 1 to 2 feet high.	sun	Native to Pacific coast. Grows in any soil and makes an effective deep-rooted plant to hold soil on slopes. Attractive cover all year. Tolerates adversity—drought, heat, wet conditions, salt spray. Buy male plants from nursery —female plants produce unsightly, cottony seeds. Set plants about 4 feet apart—mulch between to inhibit weeds. To get plants well-rooted in first season, water occasionally.
Corsican mint, Creeping mint *Mentha requieni*	6-10	Tiny, creeping plant grows from less than an inch up to about 2 inches high. Spreads quickly, producing a fine cushion of green. When crushed, tiny leaves yield peppermint fragrance. Tiny, pale lavender flowers in late spring.	sun or light shade	With its shallow root system, constant supply of moisture is needed. Plant in garden where it can be appreciated at close range—among stepping-stones, for example. Tolerates some traffic. Provide soil well enriched with moist peat moss or fine compost. Set plants 6 inches apart in early spring. When established, plants can be divided and more new plants set.
Corsican pearlwort, Irish moss *Sagina subulata*	4-10	Produces mossy evergreen matting with ¼-inch leaves. Grows about 4 inches tall. Tiny white flowers in summer. Cultivar 'aurea' has golden leaves. Creeping stems root as they grow.	light shade	Similar to moss sandwort in appearance, but leaves shorter. Suited for filling in vacant spots between stepping-stones and in rock gardens. Likes rich, moist, well-drained soil. Set plants 6 inches apart in spring. Established mats can be divided to plant other spots.
Creeping lilyturf *Liriope spicata*	4-10	Forms mounds of long, ¼-inch-wide grassy leaves. Plants 6 to 12 inches high. Spreads steadily by underground stems. Evergreen, fountain-like effect. Bears lavender-white flowers on tall spikes during summer.	sun or shade	Doesn't tolerate foot traffic. Best suited for borders, beds, under trees, shrubs, or on slopes. Tolerates most soils and drought. Grown widely in the South. Set plants in spring or fall 12 inches apart. For more attractive foliage each year, clip off old leaves in spring when new growth is seen. Old plants can be divided and replanted.
Creeping mahonia, Dwarf holly-grape *Mahonia repens*	5-10	Short, bluish-green evergreen shrub. Leaf size is 3 to 6 inches with two to four pairs of leaflets having holly-like spiny edges. Clusters of yellow blossoms in spring, followed by black, grape-like fruit. Spreads by underground stems.	sun or shade	Grows in many soils. Best in soils high in organic matter. Space nursery plants 1 foot apart in spring. Prevent weeds and hold moisture by maintaining a 2-inch mulch.
Creeping mazus *Mazus reptans*	5-10	One-inch high, fast-growing cover with tiny lavender snapdragon-like flowers.	sun or shade	Stays green in zones 9 and 10, but tops die to ground in other zones in winter. In zone 5, cover with brushy non-packing mulch to protect from winter sun and winds. Grows best in moist soil enriched with organic matter, such as compost or peat. Space plants 1 foot apart in spring.
Creeping phlox, Moss phlox, Ground pink, Moss pink *Phlox subulata*	2-10	Hardy, spreading plants 4 to 6 inches tall. Trailing stems yield thick carpet of needlelike foliage completely blanketed with pink, white, violet, or red flowers in early spring.	sun	A good choice for almost any well-drained soil. Desirable for brilliant color display on slopes, in front of perennial borders, for cascading over walls, or in rock gardens. Rich soil not needed. Space plants 12 to 18 inches apart. After flowering, trim stems back halfway to stimulate new foliage. Easy to divide old plants for other areas.
Creeping speedwell *Veronica repens*	5-10	Shiny, dark green ½- to ¾-inch scalloped-edge green leaves. The spreading plant mat is about 4 inches tall. Clusters of blue, pink, or white flowers in spring.	sun or light shade	Give full sun in zones 5 to 8 and light shade in 9 to 10. Grows best in all areas in moist soil well enriched with organic matter. Space plants early spring 6 to 12 inches apart. Plant in an area where it can be contained and away from lawns.

GROUND COVERS (continued)

Name	Zone	Description	Light	Comments
Creeping thyme *Thymus serpyllum*	3-10	Hardy trailing, evergreen-forming, close-napped green carpet. Tiny ¼-inch leaves are fragrant. Bears flower clusters of red, pink, white, rosy purple in summer.	sun	Adapted for use between stepping-stones and as ground cover. Avoid rich soil—best in poor, dry, well-drained soil. Stands neglect and traffic. Mow, if needed, to keep uniform. Space new plants 6 to 12 inches apart in spring. Easy to divide old plants to start new ones.
Crown vetch *Coronilla varia*	3-10	Single plant spreads out 6 feet or more and 12 to 24 inches or more in height. Compound, fernlike leaves are 6 to 10 inches long. Clusters of attractive pink and white pealike flowers appear in masses in spring, with scattered blooms until early fall.	sun	A hardy vine grown widely on banks along freeways. Once established, it takes care of itself. Tolerates drought. Best used in difficult areas such as ravines, steep slopes. Perhaps best plant to control erosion because strong mat of roots holds soil in place. Also, often selected as a creeping perennial border. Difficult to eliminate and should be used only where it can be contained. On slopes, space plants 3 to 4 feet apart; on level ground, 5 to 6 feet apart. Can start from hulled seeds in early spring or late summer. Bushy new growth can be obtained by cutting back to ground in early spring.
Cypress spurge *Euphorbia cyparissias*	3-9	One foot tall with dense, narrow, gray-green leaves 1 to 2 inches long. Clusters of yellow-orange flower heads in spring. Spreads quickly by stolons to form thick cover. Dies back in fall, but reappears in spring.	sun	Grows in variety of well-drained soils. Good for hot sunny slopes. Grows too thick in moist, rich soil. Space new plants 18 to 24 inches apart in spring. New plants may be started by dividing old plants and replanting.
Dichondra, Lawn leaf *Dichondra micrantha*	10	Grows about 1½ to 2 inches tall; shorter if it gets foot traffic, taller if soil is loose and rich. If above 2 inches, mow to keep it at usual lawn height. Creeping plants produce round, dark green leaves that overlap—¼ to ½ inch in diameter.	sun or shade	Grown widely as grass substitute in parts of California and other areas where lawns will not grow. Can be used in other mild, Bermuda grass areas where temperature doesn't go below 25 degrees. At lower than freezing temperatures dichondra must not be walked on, but it will stand light traffic in warm period. Useful in small areas, too, for decoration. Like Dutch clover, it stains clothing if crushed. Like grass, it can be started by seeding or by setting plugs 6 to 12 inches apart. Dichondra likes uniform moisture. Maintain good color by using a balanced, low-strength fertilizer. Self-seeding.
Evergreen candytuft *Iberis sempervirens*	3	Evergreen shrub grows 8 to 12 inches tall, with 24-inch spread. Dense, glistening, dark green, cushiony. Roots in where stems touch soil. Two-inch white flower clusters cover plants early in spring, with some cultivars flowering at intervals all season.	sun	Handsome in both flower and foliage. Useful to cover ground or soften rocks in small areas. Needs well-drained soil containing organic matter. Adapts to seashore conditions. Space new plants 12 to 18 inches apart. Or, it's easy to start from seed. Shear plants back part way after bloom.
Ferns, New York *Thelypteris noveboracensis* **Hay-scented** *Dennstaedtia punctilobula* **Resurrection** *Polypodium polypodioides*	2 3 7	Produces long, gray-green fronds with many paired, notched leaflets having rusty appearance on underside.	shade	Many kinds. Range 6 to 36 inches tall. They spread by rootstalks underground. Most thrive best in moist soil high in leaf mold or peat. Especially charming in natural settings or on shady side of walls. Ferns die back in fall, reappear in spring. Space plants about 12 inches apart in light shade; larger growing ferns up to 18 inches apart.
Five-leaf akebia *Akebia quinata*	4-10	Large leaves divide into five rounded leaflets, 3 to 5 inches long. Underground runners spread quickly. Fragrant purple flowers bloom in early spring, but are nearly hidden by leaves.	sun or light shade	A good selection where rapid cover is desired. Grows too thick in many areas with moist, rich soil. Should be used only where can be contained because can smother and kill small trees and shrubs. Propagate by seeds, root cuttings, or divisions. Shoots may grow up to 10 feet in one year.
Forget-me-not *Myosotis scorpioides* 'semperflorens'	5-10	Narrow, 1- to 2-inch leaves. Pale blue ¼-inch flowers with pink, yellow, or white centers during spring and summer. Creeping stems grow quickly to provide dense cover. Dies back in winter; reappears in spring.	shade	Grow in moist spots with light shade. Charming in natural setting. Needs rich, moist soil. Takes care of itself. Self-seeding. Space plants 12 inches apart in early spring. Can start new plants by dividing old ones and replanting.

Name	Zone	Description	Light	Comments
Galax, Galaxy, Beetleweed *Galax urceolata*	3-8	Heart-shaped, gleaming evergreen leaves ½ to 5 inches across. Two-foot-tall flower spikes sport many small white blooms in midsummer. Spreads by underground stems. All leaves rise from plant base.	shade	Grows wild in southeast United States, but hardy north of its natural range. Likes shady, cool, and moist situations. Leaves present throughout the year, but turn a bronze color with age. Does well under rhododendrons. Requires soil high in leaf mold or other organic material, such as acid peat moss. Space plants in spring or early fall when foliage has matured. Cut leaves are long lasting—used widely by florists for greenery.
Gazania, Trailing gazania *Gazania ringens*	8-10	Creeping plant with 3- to 6-inch, narrow leaves. Produces 1½- to 2½-inch yellow daisy-like flowers in spring, with scattered flowers rest of season. Flowers love sun, but close on cloudy days. Runners root as they grow out.	sun	Trailing habit makes it suitable to cover banks or cascade over walls, but can serve as cover for flat spots. Plants resist drought, but benefit from watering during extended heat. Tolerates poor soil. Space plants 18 to 24 inches apart. Discard old woody plants every fourth year and use younger plants from the divisions for replanting in early spring. Mulch new planting to control weeds.
Germander, Chamaedrys germander *Teucrium chamaedrys*	5-10	Small shrub to 18 inches tall. Evergreen in milder zones; leaves fall in northern zones. Spreads by underground rootstalks. Leaves about 3 inches long, saw-toothed and hairy. Small rose-colored flowers appear among the dense foliage.	sun	The species responds well to shearing once or twice a year to induce extra branching. Shear to a height of about 10 inches. Prune winter-killed shoots in spring. Likes well-drained soil. Space plants 12 inches apart. The cultivar 'prostratum' grows only 4 to 6 inches tall.
Ginger, Wild *Asarum canadense*	4-10	Two- to 6-inch round, heart-shaped dark green leaves, so thick that weeds don't stand a chance. Spreads by creeping underground stems, sending up 6- to 10-inch leaf stems. In late spring, red-purple flowers can be seen at base when leaves are parted.	sun or light shade	Very good cover for light to deep shade and rich soil. Will grow under taller plants. Space plants about 12 inches apart. For new plants, divide old ones and replant in early spring. Sometimes called 'snakeroot,' the plant can be dried and used as a flavoring.
Ground morning-glory *Convolvulus mauritanicus*	8-10	Evergreen grows 12 to 24 inches tall. Lavender-blue, 2-inch wide, trumpet-shaped blooms stay open all day to provide a colorful cover.	sun or light shade	Performs best in Southwest and on West coast. Useful to cover hot, sunny, dry slopes but is not a thick ground cover. Tolerant of different, well-drained soils. Space plants 24 to 36 inches apart. When plants get scraggly, prune in early spring before growth starts again. Can root from cuttings taken from established plant in spring. Or, start it from seeds.
Hall's honeysuckle *Lonicera japonica* 'halliana'	5-9	Vigorous evergreen to semievergreen, growing 18 to 24 inches tall. Deep green, 3-inch oval leaves. Fragrant white to yellow flowers appear in late spring and summer.	sun or shade	Makes a quick ground cover, but is a weed in parts of eastern states. Grows in any soil and is best adapted as cover for ravines or steep banks. Must be contained by shearing. Space plants 24 to 36 inches apart. Avoid planting if trees or shrubs are in area—vine will climb over them and can kill them as it twines around. Grow new plants by division of roots and replant. Keep under control by annual heading back.
Hottentot fig *Carpobrotus edulis*	10	Thick, grayish-green, 3- to 5-inch leaves on trailing stems form dense 4- to 6-inch-high carpet. About 4-inch bright, daisy-like yellow to rose flowers in spring, followed by fig-shaped fruit.	sun	Thrives only on the West coast. Tolerates sand and grows in various well-drained soils. Useful for small spots in garden for color accent. Used widely, especially in California, as cover on gentle slopes. Good for holding sandy soils in place. Space plants 12 to 18 inches apart for quick coverage. Sections of trailing stems can be used to scatter over prepared soil, covered lightly with soil, and watered to root new plants.
Indian strawberry, Mock strawberry *Duchesnea indica*	5-10	Plants make mat 2 to 3 inches thick. Has three-leaflet, 1- to 3-inch leaves, similar to wild strawberry. Flowers are yellow, about ¾-inch across, followed by ½-inch bright red berries held above the foliage. Fruit is not tasty. Plant is semievergreen.	sun or shade	Runners shoot out quickly and root well to make attractive cover in large areas. Avoid small areas. Thrives in any soil, including shaded areas on seashore or desert. Start from seed. Or, divide old plants in early spring or fall. Space plants 12 to 18 inches apart. Leftover plants can be used in hanging baskets.

GROUND COVERS (continued)

Name	Zone	Description	Light	Comments
Ivy geranium *Pelargonium peltatum*	9-10	Trailing plant with thick, five-lobed, smooth leaves. Two- to 4-inch white, red, pink, and lavender bloom heads. Produces mounds of foliage 36 to 60 inches across.	sun or shade	Grows in light shade or sun in almost any soil, but prefers well-drained, light soil with some organic matter. Blooms year round along coast, but inland only during warm weather. After last frost, cut back in spring to rejuvenate. Replant about every fourth year in Southwest where plants grow quickly. Space rooted plants 12 to 18 inches apart for new cover.
Lantana, Trailing lantana *Lantana montevidensis*	9-10	Evergreen; a trailing shrub in warm climates. Arching 18- to 24-inch-high canes are covered with dark green, 1-inch long, serrated-edge leaves. Many fragrant ¾- to 1-inch clusters of lavender flowers. New varieties have white, yellow, and orange blooms.	sun	Makes colorful cover on sun-drenched slopes. Withstands drought, but does best with occasional watering. Does well in almost any soil. Cuttings taken in early fall can be rooted and set out in spring. Space plants 18 inches apart and plant anytime. Also can be propagated by layering. Cut back plants in spring before new growth starts. This eliminates old wood and stimulates new thick branching and good flowering.
Lamb's-ears, Betony *Stachys byzantina*	3-10	Soft, silvery, woolly-looking, 4- to 6-inch leaves. Plant grows 12 to 18 inches tall and spreads by underground roots to make solid mat of cover. Flower spikes appear in summer with a lot of small, purplish blossoms. Generally grown for attractive leaves.	sun	Hardy plant for hot, well-drained sunny areas. Space plants 12 to 18 inches apart. Needs little water. Grow from seed in spring or divisions of old plants in spring or fall. Remove old foliage in spring, give light feeding, then water.
Leadwort *Ceratostigma plumbaginoides*	6-10	Plants spread quickly by underground stems. Glossy green tops grow 9 to 12 inches tall and produce clusters of ¾-inch cobalt blue flowers that appear in late summer to early fall. Semievergreen. New foliage slow to appear in some areas.	sun or shade	Useful as under-planting for shrubbery and as cover for banks and slopes. Also, useful in small bed near patio, where the colorful flowers can be admired. Leaves are red bronze in fall. Can overrun area if not confined. Prefers well-drained soil enriched with organic matter. Space plants 18 to 24 inches apart. Discourage weeds with mulch between new plants. Easy to grow new plants from little rooted divisions. Shear established planting to ground in early spring to stimulate fresh foliage. Flowers appear at tips of new growth.
Lily-of-the-valley *Convallaria majalis*	2-7	Produces white or pale pink, bell-shaped, fragrant ¼-inch blooms. Broad, pointed leaves about 8 inches long from base—two leaves per plant. Tops freeze back, but reappear each spring. Spread to cover from underground stolons.	shade	Makes dense carpet in shady areas, such as north side of wall or around base of shade trees or shrubs. Will tolerate dense shade, but does best in light shade in moist, organically enriched soil. Space nursery pips 6 to 8 inches apart for quick cover in early spring or fall. Plants can be lifted and divided from established patch to start cover in another area. For better size and quality of plants and flowers, apply a balanced fertilizer in early spring and again after bloom.
Maiden pink, Garden pink *Dianthus deltoides*	2-10	Forms dense evergreen carpet of gray-green, grasslike leaves. Red, pink, or white, spicy fragrant, ¾-inch-diameter flowers grow to 8 inches in late spring.	sun	Recommended as effective heavy-blooming cover for small areas and in full sun. Fine for rock gardens, too. Keep well weeded until the moderate spread fills all bare ground. If weeds are allowed, it's difficult to seed later, as grass and weeds are hard to tell from pinks. Space plants 6 to 8 inches apart. Shear plants back lightly after flowering. New plants are easy to start by dividing old plants or by rooting cuttings.
Max Graf rose *Rosa rugosa X R. wichuraiana*	5-10	Rugged, fast-spreading thorny cultivar. Long, trailing, rooting stems may send up shoots 36 to 48 inches. Glossy rugose leaves and 3-inch-diameter bright pink, white, or reddish-purple blooms with yellow centers—from June on. Develops colorful fruits.	sun	Best used in natural setting. Useful on rugged slopes and banks. Best viewed from a distance. Space plants 24 to 48 inches apart in spring. New plants can be started by cutting off and digging rooted, trailing stem for replanting. Cuttings can be rooted, too. Max Graf can be pruned back for denser growth. The Memorial Rose *(Rosa wichuraiana)* is lower growing and can take partial shade, as well as sun.

Name	Zone	Description	Light	Comments
Mondo grass, Dwarf lilyturf *Ophiopogon japonicus*	8-10	Produces mounds of grasslike foliage about 6 inches tall. Arching leaves are 8 to 12 inches long. Plants bear ¼-inch-diameter lavender flowers on short spikes. Tight clusters of ¼-inch blue berries follow.	shade	Especially valuable as cover in shady areas. It is tough and takes average soil or exposure. Used widely in lower South. Spreads slowly at first, but faster when established. Grows best in moist, organically enriched soil. Space plants 6 to 12 inches apart. Old plants can be divided for new starts.
Moneywort, Creeping jennie, Creeping charlie *Lysimachia nummularia*	2-10	Produces penny-shaped, bright green leaves. Plant spreads fast to form 1-inch-thick carpet. Semievergreen until last of year in colder zones. Bright yellow, 1-inch-diameter flowers appear most of summer.	shade	Useful only when planted where it is contained by pruning or borders. Never plant near lawns, or it can take over. Grows practically anywhere and stands some foot traffic. Thrives in moist to wet spots. Space plants 12 to 18 inches apart. Dig up rooted stems of established plants for new starts.
Moss sandwort, Irish moss, Lazy-man's lawn *Arenaria verna*	2-10	Can be mistaken for moss when not in bloom. Forms a 1- to 2-inch-high, needlelike green foliage. White ⅛-inch flowers appear above mat. Creeping runners spread fast to form slightly mounding appearance.	sun or light shade	Useful in small areas and on slopes. Used frequently between stepping-stones or flagstone. If area is hot, needs light shade. Has shallow roots and needs moist, well-drained soil. Extreme cold weather causes silvery appearance in foliage. Separate existing plants in early spring. Space plants 6 inches apart.
Paxistima *Paxistima canbyi*	5-8	Spreading evergreen with boxwood-like leaves. Grows a foot tall. Green, fine-textured foliage turns bronze in winter. Trailing wiry branches root in, spread slowly. Inconspicuous white flowers in spring.	sun or shade	Does best in acid soil and popular for use in front of rhododendrons or in rock gardens. Will grow in hot areas of zone if grown in shade only. Compact growth in sun zones 5 to 8. Does best in well-drained, moist, and rich soil. Space plants a foot apart in spring and apply mulch to control weeds until plants cover ground. Divide old plants or root cuttings for new plants.
Pachysandra, Japanese spurge *Pachysandra terminalis*	4-9	Forms lush carpet of growth 6 to 8 inches tall. Leaves attractively saw-toothed at edges. Evergreen. White flower heads appear above foliage in spring. Inconspicuous white berries may appear later.	shade	One of the most attractive and widely grown ground covers on level ground or on slopes in light to deep shade. Spreads slowly, but worth waiting for. Useful in beds, borders, dense shade under trees, and narrow spaces. Prefers moist, rich soil. An occasional feeding is desirable when grown under trees or where there is root competition. Needs little care. Space plants 6 to 12 inches apart in spring. New plants can be started from cuttings or divisions from old plants. Cover between young plants with coarse mulch to inhibit weeds. Few weeds can grow in dense foliage of established pachysandra.
Parrot's-beak, Coral-gem *Lotus bertheloti*	9-10	Slender, trailing branches, with hairlike, gray-green leaves spread fast, rooting as they spread. Bloom in early summer with profusion of inch-long, pea-shaped, bright red flowers.	sun	Useful cover for sunny areas. Makes colorful display on slopes or banks. Likes well-drained, hot, dry spots. Resists shade or excessive moisture. Space plants 18 to 24 inches apart. Can be grown from seed, cuttings, or plant division. Prune early in spring to stimulate new growth and for best appearance.
Periwinkle, Creeping myrtle, Common periwinkle *Vinca minor*	4-7	Produces a fine, evergreen trailing carpet. Roots in as it grows. Height about 6 inches. Has glossy, ¾- to 1-inch leaves. Spreads out in all directions. Cover is dotted with 1-inch-diameter, lavender-blue flowers in early spring.	sun or shade	Takes full sun in zones 4 to 7; light to deep shade in all areas. One of the best plants for cover. Does well in most soils. Good for slopes. Little care, except trimming, needed once established. Start from cuttings or divisions. Space plants 12 to 18 inches apart. Makes attractive background for spring-flowering bulbs.
Purple winter creeper *Euonymus fortunei* '*colorata*'	5-10	Evergreen vine trails over ground and roots in as it goes to form an attractive, dense mat about 6 inches high. Deep green, 1-inch oval leaves turn purplish-red in fall and winter.	sun or shade	Spreads rapidly, rooting well to hold soil. Can be used on steep banks; will ramble over rocks. Tolerates full sun or light shade. Space plants 12 to 24 inches apart and use coarse mulch between plants. Propagate mainly by cuttings and division in spring and early fall.

GROUND COVERS (continued)

Name	Zone	Description	Light	Comments
Scotch heather *Calluna vulgaris*	4-10	Bushy little shrubs 4 to 24 inches tall with tiny, needlelike evergreen leaves. Bears a multitude of tiny pink, lavender, purplish, and white bell-like blooms strung along the branches. Keeps flowering from midsummer until fall.	sun or light shade	Does best in highly organic, moist soil. Low-acid soil may limit success in some areas unless soil is amended. Use special fertilizer in early spring. Early spring is also good time for planting in zones 4 to 6; fall planting best for zones 7 to 10. For new plants, divide old ones. Space plants 12 inches apart and mulch between to prevent weeds until established growth fills in. Prune back old plants halfway to encourage uniform, compact growth.
Silver mound artemisia, Satiny wormwood *Artemisia schmidtiana*	3-10	Produces attractive mound of silvery gray, finely cut foliage 1-foot tall. Inconspicuous, tiny yellowish flowers late in summer and early fall. Plants grow together quickly to form cover.	sun	Unusual foliage provides excellent accent. Does well in about any well-drained soil, needs little care, and resists drought. Space plants 12 to 15 inches apart in spring. For new plants, divide old ones in early spring or early fall. If old plants lose neat mound effect, cut back for quick renewal.
Snow-in-summer *Cerastium tomentosum*	2-10	Grows 3 to 6 inches tall and produces tiny, fuzzy silvery-gray leaves. Multitude of ½-inch white flowers appear early summer. Plant grows to 24 inches, with 48-inch spread. Self-sowing.	sun	Does well in any well-drained soil, including desert, mountain, or coastal areas. Its creeping stems spread out quickly and make hardy cover for large area. Good to grow between rocks. Space plants 12 to 24 inches apart. Easy to start new plants by divisions of old plants, by seeds, or by cuttings. When plants get scraggly, cut back to stimulate new, fresh appearance.
Spreading English yew *Taxus baccata 'repandens'*	5-10	Dwarf Japanese form grows about 3 inches tall, with long trailing stems growing out from base of plants. Evergreen needlelike foliage.	sun or shade	Does best in rich, moist, well-drained soil. Space nursery plants 36 to 48 inches apart in spring. Spread a mulch between plants and grow annual flowers between yews until stems fill in spaces.
Spring heath *Erica carnea*	5-10	Evergreen shrub 7 to 15 inches tall, with spread of 24 to 36 inches. Spiky stems are crowded with little dark green leaves. Plant is similar to heather.	sun or light shade	Useful for cover and color on well-drained banks and slopes. Many varieties available in different colors. In mild winter areas (zones 7 to 10), may flower in January and provide color up to four months or more. In zones 5 to 7, blooms in February to May, depending on location. Tolerates many soils, but best in acid soils. Needs full sun in the North; light shade in hot zones 9 to 10. Tolerates seaside salt spray and winds. Space plants 24 to 36 inches apart. Keep watered. Start new plants from divisions of old plants. Cut off faded blooms.
Star jasmine, Confederate jasmine *Trachelospermum jasminoides*	8-10	Luxurious, dense foliage. Cover is 8 to 18 inches high. Glossy evergreen leaves 1½ to 3 inches long. Bears many fragrant 1-inch-diameter white flowers from late winter through early summer—depending on area.	sun or shade	Common ground cover in zones 8 to 10 of South and West. Does best in moist, rich soil. Container-produced plants can be set out anytime, spacing 24 to 36 inches apart. Pinch out all stem tips to stimulate branching.
Stonecrop sedum *Sedum*	3-10	Shallow-rooted creeping runners spread quickly. Many species are only 2 to 3 inches high. Thick, fleshy evergreen or semi-evergreen foliage. Shape, size, and color vary. Popular album species has ¼-inch evergreen leaves, reddish tips in winter.	sun or light shade	Useful grown between rocks, in stony areas, and on difficult slopes or banks. Mossy stonecrop (acre species) is weedy—it can cover an acre quickly with masses of yellow blossoms. Sedums will grow on poor soil and will resist drought and neglect. Needs little winter protection; a light cover of leaves will prevent heaving. Space plants 9 to 12 inches apart. Divide old plants for new ones. For small area, Dragon's Blood is a newer cultivar exhibiting rich red color.
Sweet woodruff *Galium odoratum*	4-10	Distinctive due to eight or nine narrow, pointed leaves arranged like spokes on a wheel on square stems. Grows 6 to 8 inches tall. Leaves are fragrant. Tiny white flowers in clusters appear in spring and early summer.	shade	Useful beneath rhododendrons and high-branched conifer trees. Does best in moist, acid soil that contains plenty of humus. Space plants 10 to 12 inches apart. Divide old plants in early spring or early fall for new starts. Or, start from seeds.

Name	Zone	Description	Light	Comments
Thrift, Sea pink, Common thrift *Armeria maritima*	2-10	Grasslike evergreen with narrow leaves. Six inches tall. During spring and most of summer in cool situations 10-inch flower stems bear ¾-inch clusters of white, pink, rose, or lilac flowers. Intermittent bloom in warm zones.	sun	Billowing cover in rock gardens or beds. Does well in sandy soil, near seashore, or in nearly any well-drained soil in full sun. Division of one large clump yields hundreds of new starts. Space plants 8 to 12 inches apart in early spring or early fall. Mulch between plants. For best appearance, lift, divide, and replant when centers of old plants die. Feed with slow-release fertilizer in early spring; again in early fall.
Trailing African daisy *Osteospermum fruticosum*	9-10	Trailing evergreen with fleshy, gray-green leaves. About 18 inches tall. Produces 3-inch lavender flowers with purple centers mostly from November through March. Scattered flowers rest of year. Long runners root as they creep along.	sun	Popular mainly on West coast. Useful to cover large slopes or level areas for colorful effect. Likes rich soil, but will tolerate some drought. Space plants 24 inches apart. Water occasionally when there's severe drought. Pinch off all tips of young shoots to induce branching. Cut back old plants to keep in bounds.
Trailing ice plant *Mesembryanthemum crystallinum*	9-10	Grows 10 to 12 inches tall with irregular appearance. Thick, succulent, gray-green, three-sided leaves are 2 to 3 inches long. Trailing stems root fast. Masses of 2- to 3-inch brilliant red and pink flowers blanket foliage in spring.	sun	One of several genera which is commonly called ice plant. Popular on West coast for colorful display on slopes or level areas. Grows well in sandy soils. Self-sows. Space plants 18 inches apart anytime. Can take cuttings and plant with first rooting. Water well.
Violet, Sweet *Viola odorata*	4-7	Hardy perennial with deep violet or white flowers, ¾-inch across. Delicate scent. Well-known as a source of perfume. Low-growing plant with simple heart-shaped leaves.	sun or partial shade	Makes attractive cover. However, the dainty-looking plant spreads quickly beyond intended bed. Should be used only where can be contained. Propagate by divisions or runners. Thrives in partial shade and fairly rich soil. Requires good moisture and winter mulching. Blooms early in spring. Suitable for rock gardens.
Virginia creeper, Woodbine, American ivy *Parthenocissus quinquefolia*	3-10	Creeping vine grows quickly, 10 to 12 inches high. Large, five-leaflet leaves. Leaflets 2 to 6 inches long. Turns brilliant red before dropping in fall. Vines root in as they spread. Tiny greenish flowers are followed by clusters of ¼-inch bluish-black berries.	sun or light shade	Native to eastern United States. Will climb trees. Coarse, rampant growth. Useful to cover rocky ground, ravines, or slopes. Needs little or no care when grown in fairly rich, moist soil. Space plants close together—about 36 inches. For thicker covering, new plants can be started from rooted trailer or by seeds in very early spring.
Wild strawberry, Sand strawberry *Fragaria chiloensis*	3-10	Plants spread quickly by runners to provide a shiny cover 6 to 12 inches thick. Dark green leaves are 2 to 3 inches long. White, 1-inch blossoms appear in profusion in spring, followed by red berries.	sun or light shade	An attractive cover that also yields edible fruit. Widely adapted for small or large areas. Moisture is important because root system is shallow. Space plants 12 to 18 inches apart. Remove blooms on new plants so plants will produce runners. In early spring, set mower at 2 inches cutting height and mow off old foliage before new growth starts to encourage fresh foliage. Then feed with a balanced fertilizer.
Wilton carpet juniper *Juniperus horizontalis 'wiltoni'*	2-10	Very hardy, creeping evergreen about 4 inches high. Sends out stems up to 10 feet in all directions, rooting as they go to form dense cover. Needlelike leaves are blue-green.	sun	Full sun is best but will tolerate light shade, especially in zones 9 to 10. Hardy. Retains blue color through winter, making lovely landscape accent. Can tolerate city conditions and dry soil. Space plants 36 inches apart in spring. Apply mulch to control weeds.
Woolly yarrow *Achillea tomentosa*	2-10	Evergreen with silvery green, mat-like growth. Five-inch-long leaves. Six to 12 inches tall. Yellow blossoms spring to fall.	sun	Useful in sandy or rocky areas. Hardy cover plant. Space plants 6 to 12 inches apart in spring. Can be mowed to maintain uniform height.
Yellow-root *Xanthorhiza simplicissima*	4-10	Low-spreading shrub, about 24 inches tall, that does well as a ground cover. Unique, uniform height, with dark green four- to five-leaflet leaves all issuing from rigid yellow stems. Foliage turns orange in fall. Spreads fast by underground stems. Sprays of purplish flowers appear in early spring.	sun or shade	Loves moist, even wet, areas along banks and streams. Useful in wild or natural settings. Plant in soil enriched with peat moss. New plants can be had from old ones by separating and replanting. Set divisions 18 to 24 inches apart.

chapter 4

TREES

Worshipped by ancients, beloved by poets, enshrined by history—trees have been valued through the ages.

Their "roots" are mentioned in early U.S. annals. Many early settlers brought trees with them. Later, our nation welcomed trees from China, Japan, and Korea. The ginkgo, many of the magnolias, Oriental cherries, and crab apples from the Far East are just as familiar to American homeowners as are native trees, such as the flowering dogwood, white fir, and douglas fir.

Fact and folklore combine to make charming tales. Johnny Appleseed went west with two big bags of apple seeds. Reports of that lumberjack of early American logging days, Paul Bunyan, still are repeated and embellished around campfires. And almost as numerous as sites claiming "Washington slept here," are trees linked with the first president—those he planted, saved, chopped down, or stood under.

Other trees, like the Charter Oak that once stood in Connecticut, are tied closely to important moments in our history. Many—such as the Yoshino cherry trees in Washington, D.C., and the General Sherman Bigtree, the largest living tree in the world—have become tourist attractions.

Traditions associated with trees abound: a crown of laurel for the victor; a white spruce, Scotch pine, or Norway spruce for a Christmas tree; two trees for the newlyweds' home (with a tree later planted for each child).

Whether to start a tradition or for a more immediate purpose, you'll find an array of tree varieties available in a catalogue or at the local nursery. When making your selection, think first of what you want the tree to do: add color, provide a privacy screen, shade a play area, soften harsh architectural lines, hold the soil, or attract wildlife. As a bonus, many trees also will have an accompanying tradition or tale.

Selecting a Tree to Fit Your Needs

Trees symbolize stability. Grandparents tell their grandchildren how they, too, played beneath *that* tree. People feel at home when their trees bloom. Analyzing why you want a tree before you buy one may lead to your selection becoming a "family tree."

What do you want from a tree? *Shade* is probably your first request. But also consider your overall landscape design, soil type, and climate.

Often, homeowners not only want shade, they want it *fast*. Fast-growing trees, however, have some drawbacks. The silver maple grows quickly, and its leaves have an attractive, silvery-gray underside. But the silver maple also is called the soft maple. Like many shade trees that grow rapidly, its large limbs can be broken easily by strong winds and ice storms. Because such trees grow quickly, they need a lot of water, sometimes plugging sewer lines as the roots reach out to any available source of moisture. The large roots also lift sidewalks if trees are planted too close to them.

An alternative to trees that grow quickly are those maturing at a more moderate rate. For example, the green ash is a vigorous tree while young, eventually slowing growth to develop a broad crown.

If you want shade in a short time, extra care can help any tree. Fill around the roots with good soil at planting, keep it watered, and guard against pests. With this care, even a slow-growing tree can pro-

duce shade faster than you might expect (see pages 106 to 107).

Trees can also enhance your *landscape design*. Check the chart (see pages 94 to 105) for the height of your choice when it's full-grown. Those small evergreen trees, often sold as shrubs, can grow to be giants if they aren't suited to heavy pruning. Lofty trees often blend with older homes on large lots, but low, ranch-style homes mix well with the horizontal branching of smaller trees.

Small shade trees, such as corkscrew willow (*Salix matsudana 'tortuosa'*), Russian olive, or amur maple, work well on today's pocket-size properties. They protect the house from the elements and cut down the summer temperature indoors. A Japanese maple, for example, can fit into a nine-foot-square area without impeding traffic—and it doesn't require constant pruning to keep it in bounds. Dogwood, redbud, and crab apple are also suitable.

Though not a conspicuous part of your design, the soil around your home helps to determine what will grow and what won't. Marshall's seedless ash (a green ash variety) and the Japanese pagoda tree flourish in dry soils that are hard to keep watered—those with slopes or open southern exposures, for example. Weeping willow, larch, holly, red maple, or sweet gum can thrive in low, wet ground. Sandy soils often demand trees with deep roots, such as quaking aspens (*Populus tremuloides*), pignut hickory (*Carya glabra*), or scarlet oak.

Temperatures limit your selections, too. Wind and cold are a ferocious duo, but some trees—such as white ash, white oak, Scotch pine, and Siberian elm—are hardy enough to survive both.

A special hardiness is required for trees in *urban* areas. The ginkgo has been around for thousands of years but has been able to survive in modern air pollution. Other smog-resistant trees include ash, cedar, and cypress.

Frequently, however, city trees need to be not only tough, but small enough to be planted near overhead power lines. Hawthorns and crab apples fill these needs.

A small space can often present a big problem. Solve it by planting a tree, such as this Japanese maple, scaled to the size of the area and house.

For low, wet ground, you can't find a more graceful Northern tree than the weeping willow. Or you may prefer a larch, holly, red maple, or sweet gum.

Marshall's seedless ash does well in dry soils that are hard to keep watered. The disfiguring seedpods of other ash trees are absent.

Small shade trees, such as the corkscrew willow, are perfect for pocket-size areas. They provide natural air conditioning.

This Russian olive tree brings shade, protection, and charm to an ordinary carport, but stays small so it will never be overpowering.

Honey locust is widely recommended as a substitute for American elms lost to Dutch elm disease. Ask for a thornless, podless variety.

Flowering trees for color, grace

Some trees can be a blooming good deal. They lift sagging winter spirits with their bouquets of color. And they're low-care. The five trees shown on these two pages demand only a minimum of fussing. Water in dry periods, prune to shape, and treat them to feeding once a year.

Those splashes of color won't be automatically dazzling. There's a knack to selecting and placing flowering trees. Select a tree that's different from your neighbors', perhaps one that blooms a little earlier or later with a different shade of yellow, purple, red, white, or pink.

Check the chart (see pages 94 to 105) to make certain temperatures, soil types, even local air pollution are compatible with your choice of flowering tree.

The silk tree (top, right) is no fragile beauty. Feathery foliage and dramatic pincushion flowers make it a great ornamental, but it has practical value, also. In addition to doing well in poor, dry, gravelly soil, the silk tree grows faster than other shade trees.

The purple-leaved plum (center, right) graciously tolerates another adversity: drought. Its ancestry is Persian, but offsprings do well in a variety of soils. From the time delicate flowers appear in April, until the leaves drop in the fall, you can count on color. The tree grows well in shade but takes on its best red-purple hues in the sun. Prune to a single trunk while young, or it will have a shrub shape.

Crab apple trees (bottom, right) dominate the May landscape, producing purple, pink, red, or white blooms. Combine crab apples of different colors for a hillside bouquet. Large masses of flowers extend from the tips of the branches almost to the center of the tree.

Columnar varieties take little space, so they can be planted along property lines. Others are low and spreading or weeping. These forms are natural and need little pruning.

The crape myrtle (*Lagerstroemia indica*, opposite page, top), grown in tree or shrub form, needs pruning to retain a single-trunk growth. The

Long stamens, not petals, make up the showy part of the silk tree flower. Place near rear of yard.

April through fall, the purple-leaved plum is a lovely show. Direct sun needed for deep leaf color.

Crab apples will flourish where other trees won't. Blooms extend from branch tip to tree center.

effort is worth it. Its crinkled blossoms present a long-playing show with a heavy flush of bloom, followed by sporadic blooming the rest of the growing season. It often blooms in the first year. Crape myrtles can tolerate wet or dry summers, as well.

Dogwood (below) is special year round. In spring, fragile-looking blooms layer on horizontal branches. The color comes from white or pink bracts—the real flowers are small and green. Through the summer its foliage isn't marred by insect or disease. In fall, the trees give you a bonus of scarlet leaves and berries. In winter, its horizontal branching is picturesque in an otherwise bleak landscape.

Crape myrtles are abloom later in the season than many other trees. Use as a specimen.

With understated beauty, dogwoods signal the arrival of spring. In fall, they have scarlet leaves.

Autumn colors

As summer ends, the colors that dance in a bonfire take over deciduous trees. Yellows, reds, and oranges mingle. The results are breathtaking with rich bronzes and deep russets. Foliage and fruit hues vary from year to year depending on the weather.

You can count on showy reds every fall, but they turn even more vivid when the days are sunny and the nights cooler than 45 degrees. Trees in hollows will be the first to color because the cold air settles to low spots and works its magic on chemicals in the leaves. Intense afternoon sun strengthens color, so the western sides of trees often carry the most brilliant hues in early autumn—something to remember when deciding where to put new deciduous trees.

The most vibrant colors appear after a warm, dry summer and early autumn rains. But a long rainy season in late fall makes them drab.

There's a subtle sequence in the show of fall color, although most of it happens in September and October. Trees and shrubs usually average two weeks of bright color.

Most of the berries and other fruits prized for their fall color stay bright through the winter—or attract fine-feathered visitors to dine.

1. The clearest yellow under fall skies belongs to the ginkgo—an ancient tree admired today for its trouble-free nature and symmetrical shape. Use it as a lawn specimen. The ginkgo has the strange habit of dropping all its leaves within minutes. No prolonged raking job!

2. Clusters of fruit form on hawthorns in late summer and remain well into winter. Plant a variety of hawthorn when you need a large shrub or compact tree. After the hawthorn's scarlet leaves drop, its berries are especially bright when evergreens provide a lush green backdrop.

3. If reddish brown is your favorite choice in fall color and you have room for only a small tree, plant an amur maple. This hardy tree seldom exceeds 15 feet. It's dense enough to work well as a lot line

hedge or screen. During the summer, you get an extra treat: bright red, winged seeds contrasting with green leaves.

4. Look closely at a vernal witch hazel (*Hamamelis vernalis*) during its golden-glory stage in September. Buds already formed promise an early spring. The unique, ribbon-like flower breaks open in February—even when snow is on the ground. Witch hazel tolerates shade but reaches perfection in a sunny location. It's a hardy choice for most parts of the country.

5. The scarlet finale put on by dogwoods comes late in the extravaganza of fall color, but it's worth the wait. Place the tree near the house so you can applaud the color from inside. If your lot slopes, plant dogwood at the base; the tops of the leaves carry a lot of color. So long as your part of the United States isn't too hot or dry, you'll find a dogwood to suit your landscape.

6. Mass several of the staghorn sumac (*Rhus typhina*) on a slope, along a fence, or at the end of your driveway. The leaves turn an incomparable orange-red in autumn. These, plus the serpentine branches, make the tall sumac interesting in every season. Garden catalogues and nurseries often label them as cutleaf or fernleaf.

7. A sugar maple in full fall color fits the image of the season at its best. The perfectly rounded specimen tree is majestic when its five-lobed outsize leaves turn gold—or gold blended with orange. Familiar as the source of maple sugar, this maple also can be appreciated for its storm-hardiness and minimal demands on the gardener.

8. If you like surprise endings, plant a winged euonymus. One fall it may color pink; in another, red. The turning of the leaves can be early or late, but the show is a hit every fall. *Euonymus alata* grows to nine feet—use it as a tall hedge.

9. Starlike leaves make the sweet gum distinctive in any season. But when they turn a kaleidoscope of red, crimson, yellow, and bronze, followed by wine red in the fall, the effect is doubled. Plant as a specimen. The round brown fruits are a popular addition in autumn flower arrangements.

TREE TREASURY

Trees	Type	Fall Foliage	Shade Density	Height/ Width	Zone	Soil Preference	Comments
ARBORVITAE **Oriental** *Platycladus orientalis*	Coniferous	—	Dense	50' tall	4	Moist, well-drained	Use as specimen tree or hedge.
White cedar *Thuja occidentalis*	Coniferous	—	Dense	50' tall Width varies with variety	2	Moist, well-drained	Use as specimen trees, or shear and use in foundation plantings. Dense, scalelike foliage. Easily damaged in storms.
ASH *Fraxinus* sp. **Green** *F. pennsylvanica* 'lanceolata'	Deciduous	Yellow, purple	Light	60' tall 25' wide	2	Tolerant	Little care. Use as specimen tree. "Marshall's seedless" is popular variety.
White *F. americana*	Deciduous	Yellow, purple	Light	90' tall 45' wide	4	Tolerant	Volunteer seedlings can become a problem.
ALDER *Alnus* sp. **European** *A. glutinosa*	Deciduous	Brown	Medium to light	75' tall 40' wide	4	Tolerant; takes wet conditions	Flower catkins present in winter.
Italian *A. cordata*	Deciduous	Brown	Medium to light	60' tall 25' wide	6	Tolerant; takes wet conditions	Flower catkins present in winter.
BAUHINIA *Bauhinia variegata*	Broad-leaved evergreen	—	Light	20' tall 15' wide	10	Well-drained; slightly acid	Use as specimen tree in small yards. Trees covered with 3- to 4-inch pink, white, or purplish blooms in late winter and early spring. Not hardy in storms.
BEECH *Fagus* sp. **American** *F. grandifolia*	Deciduous	Yellow gold	Dense	40' tall 60' wide	4	Tolerant, but prefers acid soil	Occasional inedible nuts. Lower branches drop off. Shallow root system; must not be disturbed.
European *F. sylvatica*	Deciduous	Yellow gold	Dense	90' tall 50' tall	5	Tolerant, but prefers acid soil	Occasional inedible nuts. Shallow root system; must not be disturbed.
BIRCH *Betula* sp. **Canoe or Paper** *B. papyrifera*	Deciduous	Yellow	Medium to light	90' tall 40' wide	2	Tolerant, but prefers moist areas	Beautiful white bark peels naturally. Grow in clumps of two to four trunks.
Gray *B. populifolia*	Deciduous	Yellow	Medium	25' tall 10' wide	4	Tolerant	Short-lived. Light bark. Not as showy as other varieties.
Weeping *B. pendula*	Deciduous	Yellow	Medium	50' tall 20' wide	2	Tolerant	More prone to borer attack than other birches. Use as specimen tree. Short-lived.
BOX ELDER *Acer negundo*	Deciduous	Yellow brown	Medium	60' tall 30' wide	2	Very tolerant	Drought-, heat-, and cold-resistant. Can become pestiferous. Branches break easily.

Trees	Type	Fall Foliage	Shade Density	Height/ Width	Zone	Soil Preference	Comments
BUCKEYE, OHIO *Aesculus glabra*	Deciduous	Brilliant orange	Medium	30' tall 30' wide	4	Moist, well-drained	Use as specimen tree; 5- to 7-inch greenish-white spike flowers in spring. Round 1- to 2-inch shiny brown inedible nuts in fall. Soot-tolerant.
BUTTERNUT *Juglans cinerea*	Deciduous	Yellow	Medium	80' tall 50' wide	4	Moist, well-drained	Use as specimen tree. Hard-shelled, edible nuts in fall. Often short-lived.
CASTOR ARALIA *Kalopanax pictus*	Deciduous	Red-brown	Medium to dense	80' tall 60' wide	5	Rich, moist	Disease-resistant. Plant for shade; ½-inch, rounded leaves. Black fruits produced in late summer. Young trees sometimes have thorns that disappear with maturity.
CATALPA *Catalpa speciosa*	Deciduous	Brown	Medium to dense	60' tall 35' wide	5	Tolerant	Disease-resistant. Plant for shade. Handsome panicles of white flowers in midsummer, followed by curved cigar- or pencil-like seedpods. Often messy.
CEDAR *Cedrus* sp. **Atlas or Atlantic** *C. atlantica*	Coniferous	—	Medium to dense	60' tall 35' wide	6	Rich, well-drained	Produces 2- by 3-inch cones. Stiff branches often droop slightly. Use as specimen tree. Trees don't do well in close plantings.
Deodar *C. deodara*	Coniferous	—	Medium to dense	100' tall 40' wide	7	Rich, well-drained	Same as above.
CHESTNUT, CHINESE *Castanea mollissima*	Deciduous	Yellow gold	Dense	50' tall 50' wide	5	Rich, well-drained	Use as specimen tree or in open grove. Covered with white flowers in early summer, followed by tasty nuts. Not self-fertile.
CHINABERRY *Melia azedarach*	Deciduous	Yellow brown	Medium to dense	45' tall 30' wide	7	Tolerant	Plant for quick shade. Fast-growing tree with fragrant, 5- to 8-inch, lilac-colored flowers, followed by ½-inch, yellow, inedible berries. Short-lived and easily damaged in storms.
CRAB APPLE *Malus* sp.	Deciduous	Yellow, orange, brown	Light to medium	10'-50' tall 20' wide Average: 15' tall 15' wide	Varies	Rich, well-drained	Grows in almost any climate in U.S. Produces single, double, or semi-double, 1- to 2-inch white or pink flowers in spring followed by ½-inch yellow, green, or red fruits; good in jellies and for birds. Use as specimen tree or in row along drive.

TREE TREASURY (continued)

Trees	Type	Fall Foliage	Shade Density	Height/ Width	Zone	Soil Preference	Comments
CYPRESS, FALSE *Chamaecyparis* sp.	Coniferous	—	Dense	12'-50' tall	4	Well-drained; slightly acid	Use as specimen or foundation trees, depending on variety. Don't plant tall varieties too close to house. Needs pruning regularly.
CYPRESS, ITALIAN *Cupressus sempervirens*	Coniferous	—	Dense	60' tall 3' wide	8	Well-drained; fairly dry	Use in hedges and wind-breaks. Quick-growing, but best where summers are long, hot, and dry. Foliage is bluish-green and scalelike.
DOGWOOD *Cornus* sp. **Flowering** *C. florida*	Deciduous	Orange, brown, red	Light	15'-30' tall	5	Well-drained	Use as specimen trees or ac-cent plants. Best in lightly shaded areas. Have 3- to 5-inch, pink or white, single flowers. Most varieties bear red inedible berries.
Japanese *C. kousa*	Deciduous	Orange, red, brown	Light	20' tall	6	Well-drained	Bear 3- to 5-inch white flow-ers, occasionally tinged with pink. Three-quarter-inch red inedible fruits relished by birds are produced in late summer. Use as specimen.
DOVE TREE *Davidia involucrata*	Deciduous	Yellow brown	Medium	50' tall 40' wide	7	Well-drained	Occasionally produce unusual spring flowers: two large white pendulous bracts surround 1- to 2-inch, yellow, ball-like flower head; whole structure is 9 to 12 inches long. Use as specimen tree. Slow-growing.
ELM *Ulmus* sp. **American** *U. americana*	Deciduous	Yellow brown	Medium	110' tall 40' wide	2	Tolerant	Large, long-lived tree; slightly pendulous branches. Beautiful as specimen tree. Susceptible to Dutch elm disease.
Chinese *U. parvifolia*	Deciduous; evergreen in warm areas	Red, yellow, brown	Medium	50' tall 40' wide	5	Tolerant	Fast-growing, with attractive gray peeling bark on mature trees. Use as specimen tree or screen. Self-sows and can be-come a problem.
Siberian *U. pumila*	Deciduous	Yellow brown	Medium to dense	65' tall 50' wide	4	Tolerant	Fast-growing. Use in screens. Resistant to Dutch elm disease. Easily damaged in storms.
Smooth-leaf *U. carpinifolia*	Deciduous	Yellow brown	Medium to dense	80' tall 70' wide (other varieties smaller)	5	Tolerant	Several varieties. Most fast-growing, disease-resistant. Uni-form growth. Use as lawn spec-imens, street trees, and accents for foundation plantings.

Trees	Type	Fall Foliage	Shade Density	Height/ Width	Zone	Soil Preference	Comments
EUCALYPTUS **Blue gum** *Eucalyptus globulus*	Broad-leaved evergreen	—	Medium to dense	150' tall 50' wide	9	Tolerant	Use in windbreaks. Too large for most gardens. Fast-growing. Easily damaged in storm. Bark peels. Generally messy.
FIG *Ficus carica*	Deciduous; evergreen in warm areas	Yellow	Dense	30' tall 30'-40' wide	7	Tolerant. If soil is too rich, fruit production will be low	Hardy. Fast-growing tree that provides dense shade as well as tasty fruits early in life. Most varieties are self-fruitful, so only one tree needs to be planted. Versatile lawn or yard tree.
FIR, DOUGLAS *Pseudotsuga menziesi*	Coniferous	—	Dense	100' tall	5	Moist, well-drained	Hardy. Fast-growing for a conifer. Can be sheared and used as a hedge or left to grow as impressive lawn specimen. Use in windbreaks and backgrounds. One-inch, bluish-green, soft needles. Attractive.
FIR, WHITE *Abies concolor*	Coniferous	—	Dense	75' tall	4	Moist, well-drained	Hardy. Fast-growing for a conifer. Use as a specimen tree. Often loses lower branches as it matures. Fragrant 2-inch, blue-green needles.
FRINGE TREE *Chionanthus virginicus*	Deciduous	Gold, yellow	Light	30' tall 20' wide	5	Moist, well-drained	Use as lawn tree. After first leaves appear, trees open up with profusion of 6- to 8-inch, fleecy white flower clusters. Slow-growing.
GINKGO **Maidenhair tree** *Ginkgo biloba*	Deciduous	Yellow	Medium to dense	90' tall 40' wide	5	Tolerant	Slow-growing. Insect- and disease-free. Resistant to smog. All leaves fall off at same time in fall. Use as specimen tree only where space permits. Buy non-fruiting forms because fruit produces obnoxious odor.
GOLDEN-CHAIN TREE *Laburnum x watereri*	Deciduous	Yellow brown	Light	30' tall 15' wide	6	Moist, well-drained	Disease-resistant. Trees produce hanging clusters of 1-inch yellow flowers reaching 20 inches in mid-spring. Two-inch brown seedpods form in fall and cling until midwinter.
GOLDEN-RAIN TREE *Koelreuteria paniculata*	Deciduous	Yellow brown	Light to medium	30' tall 15' wide	6	Well-drained	Use as specimen tree. Twelve- to 15-inch clusters of small yellow flowers cover tree in early summer, followed by 2-inch bladderlike seedpods. Soot-tolerant. Easily damaged in storms.

TREE TREASURY (continued)

Trees	Type	Fall Foliage	Shade Density	Height/ Width	Zone	Soil Preference	Comments
GUM, SWEET *Liquidambar styraciflua*	Deciduous	Yellow, red, gold	Medium to dense	70' tall 50' wide	6	Tolerant, but best in moist, well-drained	Fast-growing in moist areas. Disease-resistant and pest-free. Bark is attractive silver gray. Prickly, round seed clusters form on mature trees in fall and cling through part of winter. Plant in wet areas.
HACKBERRY *Celtis occidentalis*	Deciduous	Yellow brown	Medium to dense	75' tall 50' wide	4	Tolerant, but best in moist, well-drained	Good for city planting. Soot-resistant. One-half-inch berries are produced in fall. Warty bark. Common varieties are susceptible to a fungus disease called "witches' broom."
HAWTHORN *Crataegus* sp. **Downy** *C. mollis*	Deciduous	Red gold	Light to medium	25' tall 15' wide	5	Tolerant	Stiff 1-inch thorns. Covered with white flowers in early spring. Pear-shaped red fruit in fall.
Paul's scarlet *C. laevigata 'pauli'*	Deciduous	—	Light to medium	25' tall 10' wide	5	Tolerant	Double white flowers in spring. Scarlet fruits in fall.
Single seed *C. monogyna*	Deciduous	Red gold	Medium to light	30' tall 20' wide	5	Tolerant	Stiff 1-inch thorns; small white flowers followed by ⅜-inch red fruits in fall. Slightly pendulous branches.
HEMLOCK *Tsuga canadensis*	Coniferous	—	Dense	50' tall	2	Moist; slightly acid	Use as specimen tree or shear for hedge and screen. Flat ½-inch, dark green needles. Slightly pendulous branches.
HICKORY **Shagbark** *Carya ovata*	Deciduous	Gold brown	Light to medium	90' tall 50' wide	5	Tolerant	Use as background or specimen tree in large yard. Slate-gray, loosely flaking bark. Tasty, edible nuts on mature trees in fall.
HOLLY *Ilex aquifolium*	Broad-leaved evergreen	—	Dense	70' tall 40' wide	7	Tolerant; well-drained, slightly acid	Sharply pointed green leaves and ½-inch, bright red berries. Some varieties variegated. Use as specimen tree or foundation plant. Easily sheared. Best if both sexes planted.
HONEY LOCUST, THORNLESS *Gleditsia triacanthos*	Deciduous	Yellow	Light to medium	40'-70' (varies with variety)	5	Tolerant	Use in difficult city conditions where hardy tree is needed. Hybrids do not have thorns or seedpods like common honey locust. Foliage is fernlike and delicate. Plant on lawn and other areas where light shade is desired.

Trees	Type	Fall Foliage	Shade Density	Height/ Width	Zone	Soil Preference	Comments
HORNBEAM, EUROPEAN *Carpinus betulus*	Deciduous	Yellow	Medium	40' tall 40' wide	6	Tolerant	Use in hedges or windbreaks. Easily sheared.
HORSE CHESTNUT *Aesculus* sp. **Common** *A. hippocastanum*	Deciduous	Yellow brown	Medium to dense	75' tall 40' wide	3	Moist, well-drained	Twelve- to 15-inch spikes of white flowers in spring, followed by 2- to 3-inch, inedible nuts. Massive when mature. Often messy. Soot-tolerant.
Red *A. x carnea*	Deciduous	Yellow brown	Medium to dense	40' tall 35' wide	4	Moist, well-drained	Five- to 8-inch spikes of red flowers in spring. Soot-tolerant. More hardy and less messy than common horse chestnut.
JAPANESE PAGODA TREE *Sophora japonica*	Deciduous	Red gold	Medium	75' tall 60' wide	5	Moist, well-drained	Pest-, soot-, and disease-resistant. Fast-growing. Ten- to 15-inch clusters of tiny white flowers cover tree.
JUNIPER *Juniperus* sp. **Chinese** *J. chinensis*	Coniferous	—	Dense	50' tall	4	Well-drained	Use as specimen tree. Other varieties come in shrub and ground cover forms. Scalelike, pointed leaves.
Eastern red cedar *J. virginiana*	Coniferous	—	Dense	80' tall	3	Well-drained	Slow-growing. Use as specimen or in windbreaks. One-half-inch blue berries are relished by birds. Scalelike, pointed leaves. Easily sheared.
KATSURA TREE *Cercidiphyllum japonicum*	Deciduous	Yellow orange	Medium to dense	60' tall 40' wide	4	Moist, well-drained	Insect- and disease-free. Gives good shade, but allows air circulation. Use as specimen. Attractive peeling bark.
LARCH, EUROPEAN *Larix decidua*	Deciduous	Yellow	Medium	60' tall	2	Moist; slightly acid.	Needlelike foliage. Cones stay on year round. Use as specimen. Branches slightly pendulous.
LINDEN *Tilia* sp. **American** *T. americana*	Deciduous	Yellow	Medium	70' tall 40' wide	2	Moist, well-drained	Tiny, white panicles in midsummer. Blue berries in late summer and fall. Not soot-tolerant. Use as specimen tree.
Small-leaved European *T. cordata*	Deciduous	Yellow	Medium to dense	70' tall 30' wide	4	Moist, well-drained	Fast, hardy growth. Soot-tolerant. Tiny, fragrant white panicles in midsummer. Blue berries in late summer and fall. Use as specimen tree.

TREE TREASURY *(continued)*

Trees	Type	Fall Foliage	Shade Density	Height/ Width	Zone	Soil Preference	Comments
MAGNOLIA *Magnolia* sp. **Cucumber tree** *M. acuminata*	Deciduous	Brown	Dense	85' tall 30' wide	5	Rich, well-drained	Grow for shade. Inconspicuous flowers and colorful cucumber-shaped seedpods. Branches often skirt ground. Beautiful, fast-growing specimen.
Saucer *M. x soulangiana*	Deciduous	Brown	Light	25' tall 25' wide	6	Moist, well-drained	Use as specimen. Five- to 10-inch white-purple cup-shaped flowers cover tree in early spring before leaves appear. Attractive slate-gray bark.
Southern *M. grandiflora*	Broad-leaved evergreen	—	Medium to dense	90' tall 80' wide	7	Moist, well-drained	Many varieties. Use as shade trees in large yards and street trees in the South. Old leaves replaced every two years. Eight-inch white flowers in spring and summer.
MAPLE *Acer* sp. **Amur** *A. ginnala*	Deciduous	Scarlet	Medium to dense	20' tall 20' wide	2	Tolerant	Can stand cold, heavy winds. Attractive in fall. Winged seeds relished by birds. Use as specimen tree or in hedges and screens.
Japanese *A. palmatum*	Deciduous	Scarlet	Medium to light	20' tall 20' wide (other varieties smaller)	6	Moist, well-drained	Use as specimen and lawn trees. Red or red-green. Foliage finely cut. Often do best if planted in partial shade.
Norway *A. platanoides*	Deciduous	Bright yellow	Dense	90' tall 50' wide	4	Tolerant	Fast-growing. Hardy. Provides deep shade. Shallow root system makes plant growth beneath them almost impossible. Soot-tolerant. Crimson King variety has red leaves.
Paperbark *A. griseum*	Deciduous	Red orange	Medium	25' tall 20' wide	6	Tolerant	Bright fall color and peeling, cinnamon-brown bark.
Red *A. rubrum*	Deciduous	Red orange	Medium	70' tall 50' wide	4	Tolerant, if kept moist	Fast-growing. Attractive red flowers and seeds. Deep green foliage. Occasionally suffer storm damage.
Silver *A. saccharinum*	Deciduous	Yellow orange	Medium	100' tall 80' wide	3	Tolerant, if kept moist	Fast-growing. Finely cut leaves; silver undersides. Branches skirt ground. Roots can damage pavement. Occasionally suffer storm damage.
Sugar *A. saccharum*	Deciduous	Yellow, orange, red	Medium to dense	75' tall 50' wide	3	Moist, well-drained	Grow more slowly than other maples. Not soot-tolerant. Source of maple syrup. Storm-sturdy.

Trees	Type	Fall Foliage	Shade Density	Height/ Width	Zone	Soil Preference	Comments
MONKEY-PUZZLE *Araucaria araucana*	Broad-leaved evergreen	—	Light to medium	80' tall 40' wide	7	Tolerant	Plant for unusual effect.
MOUNTAIN ASH *Sorbus* sp. **European** *S. aucuparia*	Deciduous	Red brown	Light to medium	40' tall 30' wide	3	Well-drained	Use as lawn or specimen tree. Covered with 3- to 5-inch clusters of small white flowers in spring. One-fourth-inch red berries in fall. Treat for borers.
Korean *S. alnifolia*	Deciduous	Orange, scarlet	Light to medium	50' tall 30' wide	5	Well-drained	Use as lawn or street tree. Three-fourths-inch white blossoms followed by ½-inch red berries, relished by birds in fall. Green, fernlike foliage. Low branches often skirt ground.
OAK *Quercus* sp. **Cork** *Q. suber*	Broad-leaved evergreen	—	Medium to dense	60' tall 50' wide	7	Moist, well-drained	Fast-growing. Interesting bark. Source of commercial cork. Use as specimen tree.
Holly *Q. ilex*	Broad-leaved evergreen	—	Medium to dense	60' tall 50' wide	9	Well-drained, loose	Use as specimen tree or shear like hedge. Leaves light green below, darker above. Previous year's foliage drops in spring.
Live *Q. virginiana*	Broad-leaved evergreen	—	Dense	60' tall 100' wide	7	Moist, well-drained	Fast-growing. Easily transplanted. Use as specimen or shade tree. Massive.
Pin *Q. palustris*	Deciduous	Scarlet	Medium	75' tall 40' wide	5	Well-drained; slightly acid	Use as specimen tree. Hardy and storm-sturdy.
Red *Q. rubra*	Deciduous	Red	Medium	75' tall 50' wide	5	Well-drained; slightly acid	Fastest growing oak. Ornamental. Leaves cling to tree well into winter. Soot-resistant.
Scarlet *Q. coccinea*	Deciduous	Scarlet	Medium	75' tall 60' wide	4	Well-drained; slightly acid	Fast-growing. Use as shade or specimen tree. Do not transplant well.
Shingle *Q. imbricaria*	Deciduous	Yellow red	Medium	75' tall 60' wide	5	Well-drained; slightly acid	Use as hedge or windbreak. Easily sheared. Leaves cling to tree into winter.
White *Q. alba*	Deciduous	Violet, purplish-red	Medium to dense	90' tall 80' wide	4	Well-drained; slightly acid	Slow-growing; majestic when mature. Difficult to transplant.
Willow *Q. phellos*	Deciduous	Yellow	Medium	60' tall 40' wide	6	Well-drained; slightly acid	Fast-growing; shallow roots make transplanting easy. Use as specimen tree.
PECAN *Carya illinoinensis*	Deciduous	Yellow	Light to medium	100' tall 75' wide	6	Deep; well-drained	Use as lawn or specimen tree. Edible nuts produced where summers are long.

TREE TREASURY *(continued)*

Trees	Type	Fall Foliage	Shade Density	Height/ Width	Zone	Soil Preference	Comments
PEPPERIDGE Black Tupelo, Sour gum *Nyssa sylvatica*	Deciduous	Scarlet, orange	Medium	70' tall 50' wide	5	Moist, well-drained; slightly acid	Use as specimen tree. Pest- and disease-resistant. One-half-inch inedible black fruits relished by birds in fall. Good for wet area plantings. Do not transplant well.
PINE *Pinus* sp. **Austrian** *P. nigra*	Coniferous	—	Dense	75' tall	4	Well-drained	Five-inch dark green needles in bundles of two. Use as specimen tree or in windbreak. Soot-resistant. Cones are 2 to 3 inches long.
Monterey *P. radiata*	Coniferous	—	Dense	50' tall	7	Well-drained	Four- to 6-inch green needles in bundles of three. Plant as specimen. Most widely planted in southern California.
Ponderosa *P. ponderosa*	Coniferous	—	Medium to dense	100' tall	6	Well-drained	Four- to 6-inch dark green needles in bundles of three. Fast-growing. Large; ideal for specimen plantings in large yards. Attractive brown platelike bark. Smaller variety is available.
Red *P. resinosa*	Coniferous	—	Dense	75' tall	3	Well-drained	Use as specimen tree or in windbreak. Four- to 6-inch dark green, flexible needles in bundles of two. Subject to pine bud moth infestation in some areas.
Scotch *P. sylvestris*	Coniferous	—	Dense	75' tall	3	Well-drained	Fast-growing. Three-inch, blue-green needles in clumps. Red bark on mature trees. Hardy in seashore or city conditions. Drought-resistant.
White *P. strobus*	Coniferous	—	Medium to dense	100' tall	3	Well-drained	Two- to 5-inch light green needles in bundles of five. Mature specimens stately. Easily sheared and shaped.
POPLAR *Populus* sp. **Lombardy** *P. nigra 'italica'*	Deciduous	Yellow	Light	90' tall 15' wide	3	Well-drained	Very fast-growing. Useful for quick screens and windbreaks while other trees reach maturity. Short-lived and susceptible to canker disease.
White *P. alba*	Deciduous	Red brown	Light to medium	60' tall 50' wide	3	Well-drained	Fast-growing. Use as specimen. Leaves have gray, fuzzy undersides. Canker-resistant columnar variety that lives longer is available.

Trees	Type	Fall Foliage	Shade Density	Height/ Width	Zone	Soil Preference	Comments
PRUNUS *Prunus* sp. **Almond** *P. dulcis 'dulcis'*	Deciduous	Yellow	Medium	24' tall 15' wide	7	Moist, well-drained	Use as early flowering specimen tree. One- to 2-inch single flowers cover tree in early spring.
Apricot *P. armeniaca*	Deciduous	Yellow	Medium	30' tall 20' wide	6	Moist, well-drained	Early flowering. Used especially in southern California. Bears tasty fruits.
Cherry, Higan *P. subhirtella*	Deciduous	Yellow	Light to medium	30' tall 30' wide	6	Moist, well-drained	Use as specimen tree. Most popular variety is pendulous weeping cherry. One-inch single pink flowers cover trees in early spring. Some forms bloom again in fall.
Cherry, Oriental *P. serrulata*	Deciduous	Yellow	Light to medium	Most varieties 20'-25' tall 20'-25' wide	6	Moist, well-drained	Use as specimen trees. Many hybrids. One-half- to 2½-inch pink or white single or double flowers cover trees in early spring. Fragrant.
Cherry, Sargent *P. sargenti*	Deciduous	Red	Medium to dense	50' tall 50' wide	5	Moist, well-drained	Use as combination specimen and shade tree. One- to 2-inch single pink flowers cover tree in spring, followed by ½-inch fruits. Attractive bark.
Cherry, Yoshino *P. yedoensis*	Deciduous	Yellow	Light to medium	40' tall 40' wide	6	Moist, well-drained	Use as specimen tree. One-inch white or pink single flowers cover trees in early spring. Famous for Washington, D.C., display.
Peach *P. persica*	Deciduous	Yellow	Light to medium	25' tall 20' wide	6	Moist, well-drained	Use as specimen tree. One- to 2-inch single or double pink or red flowers, followed by tasty fruits. Not insect- and disease-resistant.
Pissard plum *P. cerasifera 'atropurpurea'*	Deciduous	Purple	Light to medium	25' tall 20' wide	4	Moist, well-drained	Use as specimen tree. Fine for small yards. Three-fourths-inch pink flowers cover tree in early spring, followed by purple foliage. Do best in full sun. Need occasional pruning.
REDBUD **Judas tree** *Cercis canadensis*	Deciduous	Yellow	Light to medium	35' tall 30' wide	5	Moist, well-drained	One-half-inch purple-pink blossoms cover tree in early spring. White and pure pink varieties available. Mix with other flowering trees for dramatic effect.
REDWOOD, DAWN *Metasequoia glyptostroboides*	Deciduous	Brown	Medium to dense	100' tall	6	Moist, well-drained	Very fast-growing. Interesting specimen tree in large yards. Needlelike foliage falls off in winter.

TREE TREASURY *(continued)*

Trees	Type	Fall Foliage	Shade Density	Height/ Width	Zone	Soil Preference	Comments
RUSSIAN OLIVE *Elaeagnus angustifolia*	Deciduous	Yellow brown	Medium	20' tall 20' wide	2	Tolerant	Attractive, silver-gray foliage with yellow-green berries in spring. Hardy, pest-resistant and soot-tolerant. Peeling brown bark on mature specimens. Trunk often gnarled.
SERVICEBERRY *Amelanchier* sp. **Shadblow** *A. canadensis*	Deciduous	Yellow, red	Medium	60' tall	4	Moist, well-drained	Trees covered with 1-inch white flowers in spring, followed by edible maroon and purple berries, relished by birds.
Apple *A. x grandiflora*	Deciduous	Yellow, orange	Dense	25' tall	4	Moist, well-drained	Larger white flowers than other serviceberries in spring, followed by edible red to black berries relished by birds.
SILK TREE **Mimosa tree** *Albizia julibrissin*	Deciduous	Yellow	Light	35' tall 25' wide	7	Tolerant	Feathery, fernlike foliage. Covered with pink, powder puff-like flowers throughout the summer. Good near patios or porches and on lawns. Not storm-sturdy. Often more than one trunk.
SMOKE TREE, AMERICAN *Cotinus obovatus*	Deciduous	Scarlet red	Medium	25' tall 20' wide	6	Tolerant	Use as lawn or specimen tree. Excellent fall color.
SPRUCE *Picea* sp. **Colorado** *P. pungens*	Coniferous	—	Dense	100' tall	3	Well-drained	Dark green to pale blue foliage. Use as specimen tree. Mature trees lose lower branches.
White *P. glauca*	Coniferous	—	Dense	75' tall	2	Well-drained	Use as specimen or in windbreak. Dwarf varieties work well in foundation plantings. Black Hills spruce *(P. glauca 'densata')* is a smaller form of white spruce.
SYCAMORE *Platanus* sp. **Buttonwood** *P. occidentalis*	Deciduous	Yellow brown	Medium to dense	100' tall 80' wide	5	Moist, well-drained	Use as shade tree. Large, glossy green leaves. Rounded 1-inch seedpods. Attractive bark, peeling with variegated shades of cream. Sometimes messy. Subject to fungal blight.
London plane tree *P. x acerifolia*	Deciduous	Yellow brown	Medium to dense	100' tall 80' wide	5	Moist, well-drained	Use as shade tree. Soot-tolerant. Resistant to diseases that affect sycamore. Round seedball.

Trees	Type	Fall Foliage	Shade Density	Height/ Width	Zone	Soil Preference	Comments
TREE-OF-HEAVEN *Ailanthus altissima*	Deciduous	Yellow gold	Light to medium	50' tall 50' wide	5	Tolerant	Fast-growing. Insect- and disease-resistant. Male trees have objectionable odor when in flower. Soot-tolerant. Not storm-sturdy. Can become a weed tree.
TULIP TREE Yellow poplar *Liriodendron tulipifera*	Deciduous	Yellow	Dense	100' tall 50' wide	5	Moist, well-drained	Insect- and disease-resistant. Use in wet areas. Massive and impressive if given plenty of space. Two-inch greenish-yellow, tulip-shaped flowers cover tree in spring after leaves unfurl.
WALNUT *Juglans* sp. **Black** *J. nigra*	Deciduous	Yellow	Medium	100' tall 50' wide	5	Well-drained	Slow-growing. Bear 2- to 3-inch tasty nuts in fall. Not good lawn or street tree. Roots give off toxic substance that kills nearby trees. Plant two for better nut production.
English *J. regia*	Deciduous	Yellow	Medium to dense	60' tall 30' wide	6	Well-drained	Slow-growing. Use as specimen tree. Bear 1½- to 2-inch tasty nuts. Plant two for better nut production. Variety 'carpathian' more tolerant to cold temperatures than other varieties.
WILLOW *Salix* sp. **Babylon weeping** *S. babylonica*	Deciduous	Yellow	Medium	40' tall 40' wide	6	Moist, well-drained	Fast-growing. Use as specimen in wet areas. Pendulous branches sweep the ground. Easily storm- and insect-damaged. Need frequent pruning.
White *S. alba*	Deciduous	Yellow	Medium	75' tall 60' wide	2	Moist, well-drained	Fast-growing. More upright than other varieties. Need frequent pruning.
Wisconsin or Niobe weeping *S. x blanda*	Deciduous	Yellow	Medium	40' tall 40' wide	4	Moist, well-drained	Fast-growing. Hybrid. Use as specimen tree. Long pendulous branches. Needs frequent pruning. Not storm-sturdy.
YELLOWWOOD *Cladrastis lutea*	Deciduous	Orange, yellow	Medium to dense	50' tall 40' wide	3	Moist, well-drained	Use as specimen or shade tree. One-inch white flowers in cluster 12 to 15 inches long. Attractive, light gray bark.
ZELKOVA *Zelkova carpinifolia*	Deciduous	Red brown	Medium	75' tall 60' wide	7	Tolerant	Slow-growing. Use as specimen tree. Good replacement for American elm. Drought- and wind-resistant.

How to Plant and Maintain Trees

The reason for selecting a certain tree may be as grand as accenting a new home or as simple as providing a windbreak. But the planting procedure is pretty much the same—whatever the tree, wherever you decide to place it.

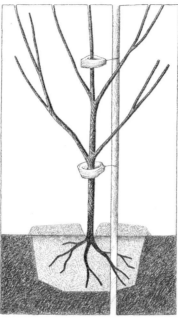

For bare-root trees, dig hole wide enough so roots can spread out naturally. Build mound for roots to rest on.

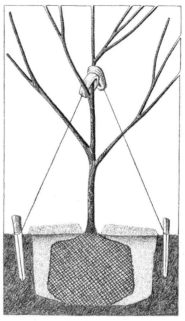

Balled-and-burlapped trees often get off to a faster start than bare-root trees. No need to remove burlap.

A lance is another way to conserve by shooting water to root zone. Mulch will reduce moisture loss even more.

Trees are not only one of the most permanent features of your yard, they also can be the most expensive. It pays to deal with a reputable local nursery or well-known mail order house.

Trees can be bought balled-and-burlapped (B&B), container-

If planting is delayed, "heel in" by digging a trench for tree roots. Cover with loose soil and keep moist.

grown, or bare-root.

Balled-and-burlapped means they have been dug with a ball of soil left around the roots, then wrapped in burlap. B&B or container-grown trees usually get off to a faster start than bare-root trees because fewer roots are disturbed in transplanting. But they usually are more expensive.

When to plant. The time to plant depends, in part, on the site and the kind of tree you select. A slope facing south can be used earlier in the spring than one facing north. Shaded areas are slower to warm up, but this shade can reduce dehydration of roots and leaves during and after planting. And planting can start sooner where soils are loamy and well-drained, not heavy and damp.

Digging and planting in the fall—instead of spring—carry certain advantages. Rainfall is less and soil is often in better working condition. The warm soil and cool air stimulate root growth. However, the new tree then faces the long winter with a limited root system for support. Plant tender trees and most broad-leaved evergreens in the spring.

Heeling in. Unless they have

special care, trees can't survive long out of the ground. If planting is delayed for a few days, keep roots and top moist in a protected location away from sun and wind. Cover the roots with damp peat, burlap, wet leaves, waterproof plastic sheets, or moist newspapers.

If replanting is going to be delayed two or three weeks, "heel in" the plants (see drawing at left). Choose a shady area away from drying winds. Dig a sloping trench large enough to accommodate the roots. Place the roots in the trench and rest the trunk against the sloping side. Cover roots with loose soil and keep them moist. Evergreens should be heeled in upright and placed close together if there are more than one.

Gently remove the heeled in tree from its temporary trench and plant in a permanent setting as soon as possible.

Soil structure. Although trees vary in their tolerance for different soil conditions, most do best in well-drained soils. To test the drainage of the area where the tree is to be placed, dig a hole at least a foot deep and fill it with water. The next day, fill the hole again and see how

long the water remains. If the water is absorbed within 12 hours, then drainage is adequate for planting.

If water remains in the hole for more than 12 hours, the soil probably has the consistency of clay. Mix the soil with sand or organic matter. Drainage can be improved even more by digging the hole where you'll plant the tree a foot deeper than required and filling in this extra space with stones, crushed rock, or gravel.

Do not add fertilizer to the soil replaced in the hole, and do not add peat moss, vermiculite, sand, or pine bark to soils that pass the drainage test.

Medium- to slow-growing trees are often least vulnerable to insects, disease, cold, and storm damage. However, a way to stimulate growth of a problem-resistant tree is to start by digging a big hole—the bigger the better. The poorer the native soil, the bigger the hole should be for faster growth. Break up clods and use the same soil to replace around the tree roots or rootball.

In general, dig the hole at least a foot deeper than the height of the roots and twice as wide as the root span or rootball. If planting on or

Canvas soaker hoses get water where it is needed without washing away topsoil or losing moisture to the air.

Cover the young tree trunk with tree-wrap paper, burlap strips, or aluminum foil to reduce damage from pests.

near the lawn, spread a tarp or plastic over the grass and pile the soil onto the covering. Loosen several inches of soil at the bottom of the hole to facilitate drainage.

For bare-root plants (first drawing, top, opposite page), build a loose mound of soil at least six inches high for the roots to rest on. Make sure the hole is wide enough for the roots to spread out naturally and deep enough so the tree, when planted, is slightly higher than it was before being dug (you'll see a soil stain on the trunk). Press the soil firmly around the roots until the hole is about three-fourths full. Pack lightly to make sure there are no air cavities. Add a bucket or two of water. The tree will settle slightly.

After the water has been absorbed, add soil to fill the hole, but do not do more tamping. Leave a depression around the trunk to catch water. Water the tree deeply. It may take five to ten gallons.

The process is somewhat faster with a balled-and-burlapped tree (second drawing, top, opposite page). Set the ball in a hole at least one foot larger in diameter and six inches deeper than the size of the rootball. Cut the binding around the trunk but leave the burlap in place. It will rot. If the tree rootball is wrapped in a sheet of plastic, gently cut the covering away.

If the tree has been growing in a container, remove it and cut off any outer roots that circle the soil mass.

Fill the hole and water as you would for bare-root trees.

Watering. Water your new tree every two weeks—each week during hot, dry weather—for the first year or two. Allow the soil to dry at the surface before you water again. The amount of water needed is the amount the soil can absorb. Stop watering when water no longer seeps in rapidly.

A water lance (far right, top, opposite page) attached to a garden hose will put moisture into the root zone, instead of losing it to the air. A canvas soaker hose (top, left) puts a lot of water where it's needed without washing away soil or losing water through evaporation. Withhold water when all the leaves drop, but soak the ground once shortly before it freezes for the winter.

Mulching. Reduce moisture loss even more with a layer of mulch two to three inches thick. Use semi-decayed wood chips, pine bark, well-decayed manure, peat moss, or leaf mold.

Keep mulch away from the trunk to reduce damage caused by rodents and decay.

Wrapping and staking. Wrap young tree trunks with special paper from a nursery (second illustration, left), burlap strips, or aluminum foil. This extra step reduces damage from borers, exposure to the sun, the nibbling of rabbits or rodents, and lawn mowers. Hard maples and oaks are particularly sensitive to sunscald.

Staking and tying a tree also protect the trunk, but are most important to keep movement caused by wind from disturbing new roots needed to establish the tree. Support the newly planted tree with a 2x2-inch stake, five or six feet long. Drive it between the roots four to six inches from the trunk and 20 inches into the ground. Attach it to the tree with wire run through pieces of old garden hose (so the wire won't cut into the trunk). Keep the tree staked and wires taut until the tree has become established—one to three years.

Support a balled-and-burlapped or container tree with guy wires. Pound three short, sturdy stakes into the ground at equal distances around the tree and run hose-protected wires from the trunk to each stake. Place guy wires high enough so that leverage from the top does not loosen them. Wires with turnbuckles let you adjust the pull of the wires.

Pruning. Branches and twigs of transplanted trees (except evergreens) must be pruned by about one-third to balance the loss of roots when the tree was dug. Leaves lose moisture as quickly as roots can take it in. If roots are cut without the branches being pruned proportionately, the plant may die of dehydration.

Trimming can help the looks of your new tree, as well as improve chance of survival. See the first illustration below. Black marks show where to make pruning cuts. The second illustration shows how prudent pruning improves the structure of the tree. Start by cutting off any diseased branches, crossing branches that rub, and broken branches. Remove young shoots low on the trunk and one of any two heavy limbs opposite each other.

Evergreens probably won't need pruning because the wrapped rootball protects the roots from injury.

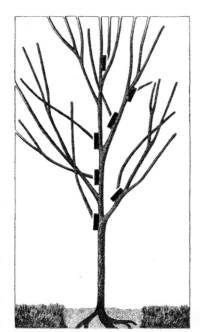

Most deciduous trees must be pruned by about one-third when transplanted. The black marks show where to prune.

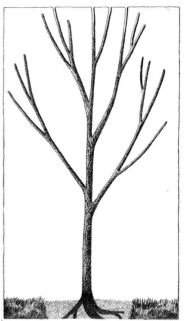

Pruning improves tree structure. A few healthy branches can mean a more vigorous tree than many weak ones.

Pruning and Repairs

Where to prune and how much? Compare the trunk and branches of your trees with the pictures on these two pages.

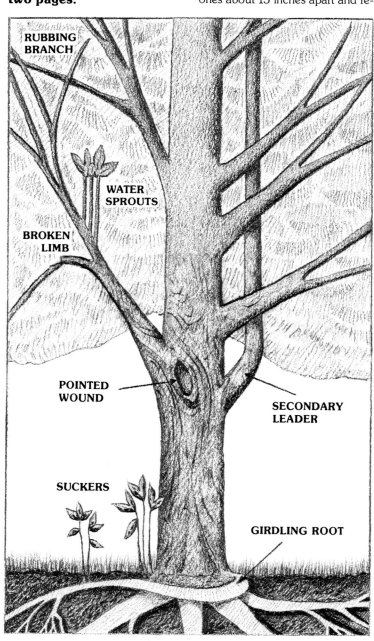

RUBBING BRANCH

WATER SPROUTS

BROKEN LIMB

POINTED WOUND

SECONDARY LEADER

SUCKERS

GIRDLING ROOT

Early spring or late winter—when deciduous trees are free of foliage —are good times to prune trees. At these times, you can see the arrangement of branches and can expect faster healing of large cuts.

First pruning should be done at planting time, as described on page 107, to aid in tree growth. A tree with no main branches (a whip) can be cut to a height of five to six feet. If you set out a tree with branches, select four or five thick, healthy ones about 15 inches apart and re-move the others.

As the tree grows, cut off one or two lower branches each year until "head" (or main branches) is at the height you want. Young trees need leaves to make the food they need for growing, so don't cut off too many branches in one season. Even if they're unsightly or imperfect, the leaves are needed. If the lower branches are growing too fast for the trunk, trim them back for the first several years, rather than cut them off entirely.

After the tree reaches the shape you like, prune only to remove broken or diseased branches and thin occasionally.

Prune branches that might be on a collision course with a building or power line. If branches are cut when small, wounds will heal faster.

Small flowering trees, such as crab apple and dogwood, are pruned much like other trees, although two or three "leaders" should be left untouched. Most flowering trees should be pruned at the end of blossom time.

Reasons for pruning involve the tree's health and your preference. You might want to prune:

• to remove diseased, dead, or broken branches;

• to shape for special purposes—as a shaped specimen or to screen an eyesore, for example;

• to renew old plants;

• to eliminate suckers and wild growth;

• to hold the tree within bounds;

• to produce new fall growth for winter color;

• to ensure production of larger flowers or fruits;

• to aid in transplanting—by compensating root loss.

Keep a few principles in mind. For example, heavy pruning on top causes leaves and branches to grow. Heavy pruning of the roots lessens vegetative growth (leaves), but increases production of flowers and fruit. Heading-back—or cutting back tips—of new growth forces development of lateral branching.

If two branches rub, remove the smaller of the two. A tree should have only one main trunk. A secondary leader is no problem when the tree is small. However, after

branches grow larger and heavier, the V-shaped crotch weakens and the tree may split in high winds or snowstorms. Even a small split offers easy entry for insects.

Remember, the position of branches does not change as the tree matures—a branch that is now a few feet off the ground will always be at about the same height. It won't rise much higher. Low branches on mature trees shade the grass and make mowing difficult.

Probably the main pruning principle concerns your own life and limbs: think about what you can do and what you should leave to professionals with heavy-duty equipment. Large tree limbs and high branches are best left to a professional tree service or arborist. Also, fill small hollows and squirrel holes yourself, but filling larger ones, especially those marked with fungi, will require the help of a professional tree specialist.

An ounce of prevention may keep a branch—or the whole tree—from falling on roof, power line, car, or people. A good many trees may give warnings for years before disaster occurs. Check them—especially those friendly old favorites—for large open wounds, holes caused by insects and bird nests, disease, fungi, dead tops, and patches of dead bark. Look for injured roots. Has there been any excavating near the tree, or has the grade level around it been changed? Nearby construction in the past 15 years can result in tree root damage long after the building is completed.

Tools of the trimming trade range from three basic tools to a shed full of specialized instruments. Home gardeners find pruning shears handy for light pruning and trimming. A saw is needed for larger branches. Hand loppers—long-handled and requiring use of both hands—let you prune higher sprouts and thicker twigs.

After each use, wipe blades clean. Lock the shed door or hang the tools where children can't get them. At the end of the season, oil and clean off any rust. Sharpen blades of square-edge blades and take saws to a commercial saw sharpener.

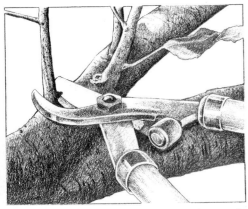

Water sprouts are soft, fast-growing branches usually shooting out from the trunk or large limbs. Although they're small, they tax the strength of the tree. Cut them off flush with the trunk or limb.

Suckers are growths coming from the base of the trunk or from roots. Dig down to where it attaches and make a cut flush with the trunk or root. If any of the sucker remains, pruning only induces more shoots.

Crowded branches never develop to full size. Large branches compete with small, and the small ones become targets for disease and breakage. Remove limbs that contribute least to the shape of the tree.

Low branches shade out grass and hamper lawn mowing. If a tree has several low branches, remove only one or two each season. On mature shade trees, the lowest branch should be at least six feet above the ground.

Closely spaced limbs or one just above the other off a major limb, create a source of weak growth. Remove the smaller of the two or the one that is least needed for the shape of the tree.

Remove broken or injured branches by making a cut as close to the parent limb as possible. Repair soon after damage occurs. Such breaks can peel bark back to the main branch, offering easy entry to insects and disease.

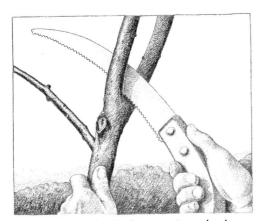

Double or secondary leaders sometimes develop on young trees. They're not a problem when trees are small; but after branches are heavy, the crotch becomes weak and may split in high winds.

Girdling roots are large ones that wrap around the base of the tree. They're not only unsightly; they also gradually cut off the flow of nutrients. Cut root off at origin and remove all that touch the trunk.

Crossed branches or those rubbing against each other create wounds that are constantly open to insects and disease. Remove one offender and trim the wound of the other. Paint wound.

Repair damage on older trees

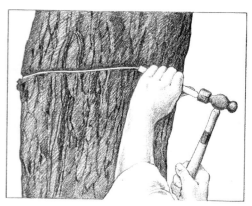

Dead stubs resulting from improper pruning or storm damage should be removed. This stub would eventually decay, permitting entry of insects or disease into the heart of the tree. Trim stub so it's flush with trunk.

This wood shows what can happen when wounds are left unattended. Saprophytic lichens indicate the wood around the wound is already dead. Look closely and you also may see insect holes. Call a professional.

Strangling with a wire—such as for a clothesline or barrier—is one of the surest ways to kill a tree. If the wire is still visible, cut it away with a chisel held at an angle. Remove wire and paint wound.

Prepare your trees for winter's rigors

Large bark wounds will result in the death of the tree unless they heal properly. Carefully trim away jagged edges of wound, leaving ends pointed. Apply a coat of shellac or tree asphalt paint. Paint twice a year.

This wound shows result of proper pruning. Coat twice a year. In a few years, it should be healed completely. Paint only with products made specifically for trees. Other paints and sealers can harm them.

Along with unpacking winter coats and checking the antifreeze, wise home gardeners also prepare their trees for winter. Apply mulches, three to six inches deep, to broad-leaved shrubs and newly planted trees when the ground freezes.

Cold, drying winds are especially damaging to broad-leaved evergreens and also can be a hazard to needled evergreens, such as pine and juniper. Antidesiccant sprays can help reduce the drying. They form a film on leaf surfaces. Spray once in November and again in January or February.

Unless the fall was especially wet, February also is a good time to give evergreens a thorough soaking. Those on the south and west sides of the house are the first to suffer because they are exposed to the sun longer and the frost comes out of the ground faster on those sides. Turn the garden hose on slowly so only a half inch of water spouts up when you hold the hose upright. Or use a water lance to put water to root zone. Let the water run near the evergreen's base for four hours or up to all day—until the soil can't absorb more water.

Snow may look lovely piled on tree branches, but it can kill evergreens and young trees. Bind branches of small trees close together to prevent accumulation. Knock snow off larger ones.

An ice storm calls for a quick survey of damage. Quick-growing trees (such as poplars, willows, elms, and maples) and older ones are susceptible. Trim broken branches so they're flush with the main branch or trunk. If the weather is above freezing, treat the wound with shellac or tree asphalt paint.

Old wounds like this are cozy places for squirrels or for certain birds. But decay has already reached the center of the tree, and the plant will not live much longer without treatment by a professional.

If the hole is still shallow, carefully clean out deadwood and apply tree shellac or asphalt paint to the surface inside. Then fill the hollow almost to the outside rim with a stiff mixture of concrete.

How to cut off a large limb

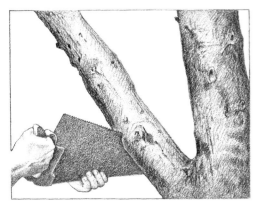

Make first cut on the underside of the limb about 15 inches from trunk. This will keep the bark from tearing when you make final cut. Cut about one-fourth of the way through—or until saw "pinches."

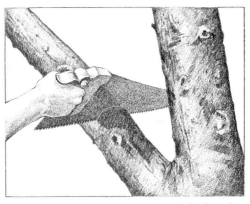

Make the second cut on top side of limb about four inches beyond the first cut. Saw all the way through. When the branch falls, the bark will strip back to the cut on underside of the stub.

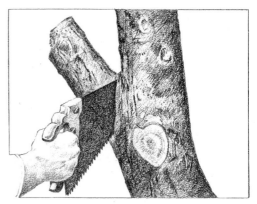

Remove stub or you'll end up with the problem shown at top left, opposite page. Support the stump as you cut, or its weight will strip bark from the trunk. Make sure cut is flush so bark can grow around it.

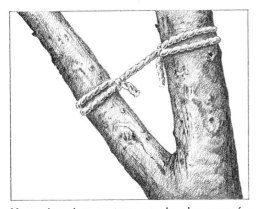

Heavy branches on trees can be dangerous for amateurs. Tie heavy rope around branch and attach securely to trunk or a sturdy higher limb before you saw. If job requires climbing, leave it to a professional.

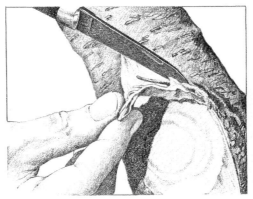

Trim the bark around all wounds until the edges are solidly attached to wood. Final trim should be oval. Wounds shaped in this way heal much faster than round ones.

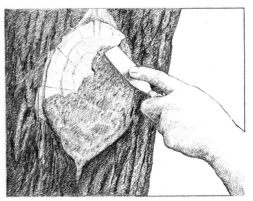

Paint with tree wound dressing to lock out moisture and disinfect. Apply thick substances with putty knife, thin ones with small paintbrush. Redo every spring and fall until wound closes.

Feeding a tree

Tree feeding—or fertilizing—involves the right diet for the right tree at the right time. Benefits can include faster rate of growth, larger and greener leaves, the correction of nutritional deficiencies, and a speedier recovery from diseases (such as verticillium wilt).

But feeding may not be a favor for your trees. Increased rate of growth may be good for young saplings, but more mature trees may be left with weaker wood, and therefore more susceptible to damage from storms and more in need of pruning. The lovely larger leaves can become more subject to disease. And some trees by nature grow slowly. Check on what to expect from your variety (see tree chart, pages 94 to 105).

Inspect conditions at the site: are tree needs on soil texture, drainage, and exposure right? Root and trunk restrictions (such as rocks or a girdling root) or damage from disease and insects may be the "slow-grow" culprits.

Trees have evolved systems that enable them to function and grow well in soils considered nutritionally poor by most U.S. Department of Agriculture standards. Fertilization bypasses these systems and can be unnecessary—even harmful—to the plant.

Consult with your local arborist or county extension office when you're trying to pinpoint your tree's condition. Deep injections aren't necessary because most of the tree's feeder roots (the ones using the nutrients) are in the top ten to 12 inches of soil.

Fertilizer broadcast on the surface works as well as a soil injection. Place plant food where the roots are—under the crown spread of the tree and a few feet beyond.

Except where specific minerals are deficient (see soil test information, page 11), most trees show little response to anything but nitrogen. Don't use more than six pounds nitrogen per 1,000 square feet of surface.

Complete fertilizers (those also containing phosphorus and potassium) in quantities sufficient to supply six pounds of nitrogen per 1,000 square feet are sure to injure grass near the tree if applied on the surface.

chapter 5

SHRUBS

Whether your interest in gardening and yard care is an occasional one or consumes every spare moment, shrubs can be favorite components of your landscape design. Though they require little care, shrubs provide beauty throughout a season or the year around.

The term *shrub* is often used to describe a multi-trunked, woody perennial plant that is shorter than a tree. The definition is imprecise because the list of plants included is vast and varied. (See chart, pages 123 to 150.)

Shrubs fall into three general categories. Narrow-leaved evergreens are called coniferous (having cones). Many are pyramidal in shape. Pines, yews, and junipers belong to this group. Broad-leaved evergreens include the many different rhododendrons, along with the hollies, boxwoods, mahonias, and others. Some are evergreen (keeping leaves year-round) only in the South. Third are the deciduous shrubs (those losing all their leaves once a year). Many are flowering.

Less expensive than trees but more expensive than many annual and perennial flowers, shrubs are ideal in a progressive landscape design—the kind where a little is added each year over three to five seasons. The first year might call for foundation plantings; the second, for privacy screens or hedges. The third year might mean a planting to separate house from street, and the fourth year may be time to enclose the flower garden and add a showy flowering shrub to fill in any bare spots in a border.

Although the eye-catching beauty of a *flowering* shrub may be the perfect choice for some parts of your yard, consider a shrub's other features as well; the shrub may spend most of the year without blooms. Other seasonal rewards are the autumn color, decorative fruit, and colorful bark.

Shrub Shapes and Uses

Dress up or cover up, hide or accent. Multi-talented shrubs may be selected to add finishing touches to a landscape design or to serve as a first budget-minded purchase to brighten the front yard of a new home.

Shrubs are the quick-and-easy answer to many landscaping questions. *Quick* because most shrubs grow rapidly and bloom or spread within the first season after they're planted. *Easy* because many are hardy enough to withstand minimal care and even drought. Yet they are graceful year after year with only occasional pruning.

Where to plant. Informal shrub borders frame a house and separate it from neighbors. A lower planting under windows, with a slightly higher one near the door, em-phasizes the entrance because of the contrast in heights.

Foundation plantings, those around the base of a house, can bring out the best architectural features of your home and make it blend with the surrounding landscape. The basic rule for foundation plantings is to develop strong corner groupings, with accent plantings placed at either side of the doorway. In general, place plants where strong vertical architectural lines meet the ground.

If your house has a high foundation, use large shrubs at the corners, and train one or more vines or es-paliered plants on one of the walls.

Planting for the side of the house should be simple in outline. It need not be continuous—the foundation can show without impairing the basic design.

For the front of the house, plan strong corner groupings that will be attractive for at least three seasons. Choose upright, rounded, or pointed evergreens, such as junipers, yews, and pines. Then supplement them with a special doorway accent, such as a flowering vine—clematis, perhaps. Use short hedges around corner plantings (see top illustration, this page) to unify the house and site and also to form a textured background for a flower bed.

Why plant shrubs. Low-spreading, quickly growing species are useful on slopes where soil erosion could become a concern. Step-up planters with spreading evergreens can change a problem slope into an easy-care area. These slopes next to steps can be hard to keep covered with vegetation. They end up as play areas—bicycle runs in summer and sled runs in winter—but they're also eyesores. Solve the problem by using a retaining wall and fill the area with evergreens, such as yews. Low varieties will not grow tall enough to block light from basement windows, and upright varieties reduce the height of the foundation wall.

Shrubs also can soften the stark, often blank and rigid, look of walls. To make a high wall appear lower, group shrubs of similar height along the wall's base.

Or use the canvas-like blankness

Low and trailing

Medium spreading

Round compact

Horizontal spreading

Upright

of a fence to create an artistic, es-paliered design, such as the fire thorn, or pyracantha (opposite page). Fire thorn berries are fiery orange or red; the branches, thorny and evergreen. Its spring blossoms are a lacy white. Buy fire thorn plants from a local nursery to ensure their hardiness in your area.

What to plant. For an approach to landscape design that will mean less work for you, consider the nat-ural shapes of shrubs available in your part of the country. The shapes of deciduous flowering shrubs are shown (see drawings, right) with common shapes for narrow-leaved evergreens or con-iferous shrubs (left).

For informal borders, use *rounded forms*. Most mature plants in this group will spread up to six feet, so give them plenty of room when you plant to make pruning easier and faster.

Vertical lines characterize *erect* or *upright* forms, making them perfect accents. They can be used as nar-row hedges but need careful prun-ing.

With graceful, fountain-like silhouettes, *arching shrubs* add a restful touch to the garden. Use them for shrub borders or specimen plants—or to highlight the ends of narrow hedges.

Large *spreading* types, with branches extending to provide horizontal lines, accent the architec-tural features of the home, making them useful as foreground plants.

However, for small gardens where you want a variety of plants, choose upright, medium-size plants, and not many sprawlers and spreaders.

These features—along with size and texture—can be used to adjust the proportions of a garden by mak-ing a short one appear longer or a long one shorter. Broad-leaved and bold plants in the front, with small-leaved, delicate ones farther away make the view seem longer. Light and bright colors advance or stand out, and dark colors seem to re-cede. So use light, bright foliage shrubs in the foreground—those with silver, bluish tinges, or yellow. Toward the back, use deeper tones—purples or deep greens—to give the illusion of space.

Arching branches highlight a cor-ner of your yard. In bloom, they're like a bridal bouquet.

Shrub	Height (in feet)	Flower colors
Arnold honeysuckle	8	red
Beautybush	15	pink
Border forsythia	10	yellow
Fountain butterfly bush	12	lilac
Lilac daphne	3	blue
Many-flowered cotoneaster	12	white
Slender deutzia	4	white
Vanhoutte spirea	6	white

Erect forms are fine for blocking a tall eyesore. They're good for small spaces.

Shrub	Height (in feet)	Flower colors
Hibiscus	10	various
Common lilac	20	various
Highbush cranberry	15	white
Lemoine mock orange	6	white
Red-osier dogwood	7	white

Rounded forms may be set where space is not a problem, or be pre-pared to prune often.

Shrub	Height (in feet)	Flower colors
Dwarf winged euonymus	4	white
Flowering quince	6	various
Hydrangea varieties	4-9	various
Kerria	6	yellow
Persian lilac	10	lilac
Tatarian honeysuckle	10	pink-white
Weigela	10	red
Witch hazel	10	yellow

Spreading shrubs can make high walls appear to be lower. Such plants can also be combined with taller ones.

Shrub	Height (in feet)	Flower colors
Japanese quince	3	various
Dwarf ninebark	4	white
Fragrant viburnum	9	white
Morrow honeysuckle	8	white
Spreading cotoneaster	6	pinkish
Sargent crab apple	6	white
Staghorn sumac	20	greenish

Flowering shrubs add splash of color

Like Cinderella, many useful shrubs are once a year transformed into beauties as they don colorful blossoms. With careful and creative planning, gardeners can select several varieties so the blooming sequence extends the season as early and late as possible.

Plan your garden with an eye to the hues and tints of those blooms. Some folks keep to a single color—all orange, red, white, or lavender, for example. Others blend shades within a range—yellow with orange and orange red, perhaps. You'll be happiest massing several of the same kind of shrub and blossom color. One of everything may give a polka-dot effect, causing the eye to jump from one color to the other.

Plant flowering quince if you want brilliant color early in the season; blossoms burst in late April.

Choose a shaggy fringe tree (chionanthus) to extend the blooming season. Expect leaves and flowers early June.

After a bleak winter, flowering shrubs cheerfully reward us in spring. Most flowering shrubs repay a bit of pruning and some fertilizing with lovely foliage and otherwise carefree maintenance.

The flowering quince (top, opposite page) stays in bounds, so little trimming is necessary. Heights vary depending on variety.

The fringe tree—chionanthus—(bottom, opposite page) can reach heights of 25 feet, so it may be treated as a small tree or large shrub—depending on how you prune it.

The raphiolepis (right) is not only loaded with fragrant flowers until late May, but it also resists drought.

The shrub below has several names: potentilla, buttercup shrub, shrubby cinquefoil. It will bloom for ten weeks or more and is not bothered by insects or diseases.

Where the climate is warm, raphiolepis will stay green all year, in sun or shade, in drought or salt air.

Cinquefoil is one of this shrub's names. It needs no pruning and works well in front of taller shrubs.

A living fence screens beautifully

Divide, define, or screen with flowering shrubs. A living fence is twice as friendly as a wooden or masonry barrier, and it'll be much less expensive.

Making your choice. Most flowering shrubs will grow well in any soil where perennials will grow (check charts, pages 123 to 150). Although sunny spots are best for intensive color, daphne, mock orange, snowberry, and witch hazel are a few that do well in shade.

Some beauties, such as Japanese barberry, crape myrtle, hibiscus (or rose-of-sharon), and forsythia can also resist the pollution and other adverse conditions of city life.

Flowering shrubs are not only versatile, they're also lavishly colorful at low prices. Nurseries can keep costs low because most shrubs survive with only a small rootball or bare roots, so maintenance and postage costs can be kept low.

And the purchase may be a wise one. Some, such as certain varieties of lilacs with a dense growth of branches, make notable specimens alone or massed in a group to blot out an eyesore. Or they can be planted in rows and trimmed as an informal hedge.

How soon you want blossoms can help determine the selection. Some, such as Froebel spirea or deutzia, flower soon after being planted. But they have shorter lives than others, such as mock orange, honeysuckle, lilac, or althaea. The longer-lived shrubs may not bloom well for a few years, but once established, they will reward you with years of bouquets.

Combine evergreens with deciduous shrubs so that every season there's a different focal point in the landscape design.

Designing a border. Often this design takes the form of a border —useful in dividing or separating, and beautiful with tasteful combinations of textures, colors, and sizes. Start from the back, selecting the taller shrubs, so they don't overpower your garden when mature. Shrubs seven feet high are good for most borders. The plants will likely

The F.J. Grootendorst rose blooms in June, then periodically until frost; is a dense, thorny beauty.

Hills-of-snow hydrangeas invite cutting when fresh. Blooms can be dried for a winter bouquet, too.

Long-time favorites, lilacs, leaf early and drop leaves late. They do best where winters are cold.

be much smaller when you buy them. The generous spaces between them may bother you for a year, but the shrubs fill in after that. Also, check their mature shapes. Arching shrubs, such as forsythia and spirea, for example, work well in informal hedges with plenty of space but can soon grow over a garden path.

Blooms vary, too. Some impatiently burst out before the leaves to give a solid pattern of undiluted color. Flowering cherries, redbud, many azaleas, and forsythia seem to be gigantic bouquets of pure fluff. Other shrubs clothe themselves with leaves before filling in with less conspicuous blooms.

Combining colors. The wealth of colors available makes choosing a shrub similar to selecting a piece of furniture or clothing. A well-planned landscape design is completed slowly—a few items each season. Harmony and balance are maintained if you're sure flowering shrubs that bloom at the same time complement each other. Bright oranges and magentas don't and actually seem to vibrate when next to each other.

Hot reds and scarlets mix well with the gentler, more quiet pastel pinks. Strong yellows and pinks are a jarring combination. But different shades of yellow and yellow orange are lovely with the yellow green of opening leaves. Red looks best with white and dark green as background colors. Rose pink and yellow pink look best when set off with some white.

Select colors with the background in mind, too. Rosy purples or bluish pinks can look unpleasant in front of a red brick house or a wall with orange or yellow tones. Instead, sparkle the border with white flowers, creamy tones, and pale pastels.

Remember, deep or dark colors recede into the background of dark foliage but stand out with lighter yellow greens. For shady areas or with evergreens as a background, flowers with lighter tones are more effective. Against white or pale-colored walls, and in full sunshine, brilliant and dark flowers are striking. Careful planning of colors can make your landscape a refreshing picture.

The June-blooming kolkwitzia or beautybush grows to a height of 15 feet and width of eight.

Famed as the sunniest sign of spring, forsythia produces its flowers in mid-April. Leaves follow.

Froebel spirea needs little pruning to maintain its height of four feet. It's seldom troubled by insects.

Choosing and Planting a Hedge

Low, high, or in between—the height of your hedge depends on the kind of shrubs you select and the trimming you do. Regular pruning also encourages dense foliage and branching.

Low hedges (one to three feet; see below): Shrubs used for low hedging should be naturally neat, grow slowly, and tolerate regular shearing or pruning. If you want to keep a hedge less than two feet tall, shear-

ing is essential. Begin training your plants the first year after planting to keep them in bounds.

Medium hedges (three to five feet; right, top): This group includes azaleas and many of the yews. If you don't want a formal, sheared effect, an annual or semiannual clipping will keep the plants compact and uniform.

Shrubs of medium height can be used to block out unsightly objects in the backyard, a clothesline or recreational vehicle, for example. Evergreens are a common choice, but deciduous shrubs with dense branching are useful as well.

Tall hedges (four to eight feet; right, below): Tall shrubs make excellent background plantings. As they age, some begin to look like small trees. They may develop bare, multiple trunks and spreading tops, characteristics that make them useful as semi-open partitions and screens. These hedges allow for air circulation and take up less ground than shrubs that have foliage growing low to the ground. They need only touch-up pruning to keep tidy.

Proper placement of your shrubs

Placing shrubs is a little like putting together a jigsaw puzzle—both vertically and horizontally. But this puzzle is a challenge because you need to consider the size of the mature plant. What you see in the nursery may only be a youngster—perhaps a fifth of its mature size.

Shrubs can be fitted together with a little overlap here and there. Up-front plants dress up the edge, while background shrubs complete the picture. For best effect, use at least three of each kind of shrub you select for your landscape.

Shrubs should be set from a property line at least half their expected diameter at maturity. This allows your shrubs to grow to full size without spreading into a neighbor's yard or onto a sidewalk.

Foundation plantings should not be placed directly beneath the drip line of overhanging eaves. The centers of such shrubs are best at least six inches beyond the drip line. This will reduce the danger of ice or snow falling from the roof onto the shrubs and causing damage.

Shrubs can help shady spots be attractive parts of your landscape design. The north wall of the house, near trees or tall shrubs, and near separation walls are places leafy shrubs can fill.

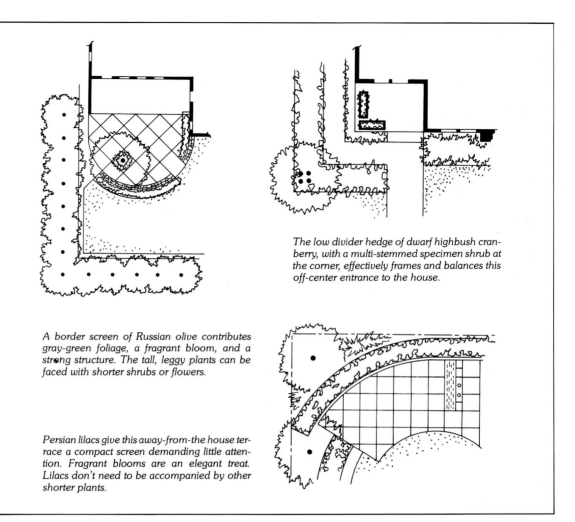

The low divider hedge of dwarf highbush cranberry, with a multi-stemmed specimen shrub at the corner, effectively frames and balances this off-center entrance to the house.

A border screen of Russian olive contributes gray-green foliage, a fragrant bloom, and a strong structure. The tall, leggy plants can be faced with shorter shrubs or flowers.

Persian lilacs give this away-from-the house terrace a compact screen demanding little attention. Fragrant blooms are an elegant treat. Lilacs don't need to be accompanied by other shorter plants.

Thick or thin? Plant for effect

How you plant a hedge depends on the effect you want and how fast you want it. Use the trench method if the hedge will be lined up straight and plants set close together (right illustration). The staggered row (left illustration) is good if there is space for a wider hedge or if you want a screen more quickly.

The staggered row approach can help disguise an unsightly wire mesh fence. Plant a row on each side and soon the fence is covered.

For easy pruning, a formal hedge demands a width almost equal to its height. The actual width of the hedge might be equal to half the height, but you'll want an extra foot or so of space on either side to maneuver around.

For a quick, dense hedge, use the staggered row method. This approach is ideal where you've got space for a wider informal hedge. Mark holes before digging to get even spacing.

If your hedge will be straight and one plant wide, the trench method works well. A trench two spades wide accommodates most young plants. This method permits easy maintenance.

Specimen or mixed?

Combined in a border or rock garden or used alone as a specimen, shrubs attractively planted are an asset to your property. Take careful notice of each plant you'd like to use—its shape, foliage texture, color of blooms and leaves, and size. Then think how the plants would look together and with other parts of their surroundings.

In the border and rock garden (above), the shapes of the evergreens and euonymus blend with the rocks and tulips for spring, an-

nuals for summer, and chrysanthemums for fall to make an overall picture on a sloping lot. On the other hand, the rhododendron (right) stands alone, needing no background or foreground plantings to accompany it. Such dramatic forms accent a front entrance or add a spark of color to a landscape. Choose accents for the most important places only.

Pick plants not only to disguise a fence or screen the view of a busy street, but also consider how well the shrub combines with things around it. Take a tip from nature: mix plants that grow near each other in forests, marshes, or deserts.

DECIDUOUS SHRUBS

Shrubs	Height	Foliage and Flowers	Zone	Exposure and Soil	Comments
ALTHAEA (see hibiscus)					
ARALIA, FIVE-LEAVED *Acanthopanax sieboldianus*	3-6'	Dark green palmate-arranged leaves that turn yellow in the fall. Sharp spires at leaf base.	5	Tolerant of most light and soil conditions.	Use as foliage plant or in hedges. Soot-tolerant.
BARBADOS-PRIDE *Caesalpinia pulcherrima*	10'	Two-inch red flowers in clusters 8 inches long appearing throughout the summer. Foliage is light green and fernlike.	10	Full sun or partial shade. Slightly acid soil.	Use as an informal hedge or border. Showy flowers add color all summer. Clip old flowers for more vigorous blooming.
BARBERRY *Berberis* sp. **Japanese** *B. thunbergi*	5'	Half-inch yellow flowers bordered with red hang on the plant in early spring, followed by bright red oval berries. Foliage is bright green but red-leaved varieties do exist. Twigs are thorny. Dwarf form grows to two feet.	5	Full sun or partial shade. Tolerant of most soil types.	Use in hedges or alone as specimen plants. Easily sheared. Makes an attractive barrier planting. Berries are eaten by birds in winter.
Korean *B. koreana*	4'	Quarter-inch yellow flowers in hanging clusters in spring, followed by bright red berries. Twigs are thorny.	6	Full sun or partial shade. Tolerant of most soil types.	Use in hedges or alone as specimen plants. Easily sheared. Makes an attractive barrier planting.
Mentor *B. x mentorensis*	3'	Quarter-inch yellow flowers hang on the plants in early spring, followed by dark red berries. Twigs are thorny.	7	Full sun or partial shade. Tolerant of most soil types.	More heat, drought-resistant than other varieties. Makes an attractive barrier. An evergreen in zones 6 to 10.
BEAUTYBUSH *Kolkwitzia amabilis*	15'	Half-inch pink or pink and white flowers, followed by unusual brown seedpods that cling until winter. Foliage turns red in the fall. Bark peels attractively.	6	Full sun or partial shade. Moist, well-drained soil.	Use as specimen plants; they look best when grown singly. Needs no pruning or special care. Branches are upright and arching.
BLADDER SENNA *Colutea arborescens*	15'	Small yellowish-red flowers. Bladder-like seedpods follow.	8	Well-drained soil. Full sun.	Very fast growing. Use for quick screens and hedges. Self-sows readily; can become pestiferous.
BLUEBEARD *Caryopteris x clandonensis*	3'	Clusters of small blue flowers that open in the fall.	6	Full sun. Light, well-drained soil.	Use as an accent plant. Prune severely in early spring to promote more vigorous blooming. Easily damaged by cold.
BLUEBERRY, HIGHBUSH *Vaccinium corymbosum*	15'	Small quarter-inch white or pinkish blossoms in late spring, followed by tasty blue-black berries. Leaves turn brilliant scarlet in the fall and twigs stay bright red all winter.	3	Full sun or light shade. Well-drained, acid soil.	Use as individual specimen plants or in informal hedges. Shallow root system is easily damaged by hoeing. Keep mulched. Prune old and dead wood in the spring.
BROOM *Cytisus* sp. **Kew** *C. x kewensis*	1'	Small, yellow, pealike flowers in early spring.	6	Well-drained soil. Full sun.	Quick growing. Use in rock gardens or on slopes. Forms a dense mat that can spread to 6 feet.

DECIDUOUS SHRUBS (continued)

Shrubs	Height	Foliage and Flowers	Zone	Exposure and Soil	Comments
Scotch *C. scoparius*	10'	Pealike flowers in spring. Mixed colors. Dwarf varieties grow to 2 feet.	6	Well-drained soil. Full sun.	Quick growing. Use as specimen plants. Prune after flowering.
Spike *C. nigricans*	6'	Yellow, pealike flowers on spikes. Six to 12 inches long in midsummer.	5	Well-drained soil. Full sun.	Quick growing and hardy. Blooms in all situations.
BUCKEYE Dwarf horse chestnut *Aesculus parviflora*	15'	Half-inch white flowers in spike clusters 10 to 15 inches long in midsummer. Dark green palmately arranged leaves. Leaves turn yellow in the fall.	5	Full sun. Moist, well-drained soil.	Vigorous and attractive. Often forms a dense mound twice as wide as it is tall. Reproduces by underground suckers. Bears shiny brown, inedible nuts.
BUCKTHORN, ALDER *Rhamnus frangula*	12'	Small berries, changing from red to black in the fall. Smooth branches.	3	Full sun or partial shade. Moist, well-drained soil.	Only one variety, Tallhedge, is of any importance. Use it in hedges and screens. Pest-resistant and a vigorous grower. Easily sheared.
BUSH CLOVER *Lespedeza bicolor*	10'	Half-inch light, purple pealike flowers in small clusters opening in midsummer to early fall.	5	Well-drained soil. Full sun.	Plant for useful late summer color. Can be cut to the ground each season without harming flowering.
BUTTERFLY BUSH *Buddleia* sp. **Fountain** *B. alternifolia*	12'	Quarter-inch lilac-colored flowers on long spikes in early summer. Foliage is an attractive gray-green.	6	Well-drained soil. Full sun.	Vigorous and hardy. Use as a specimen plant in large yards. Needs a lot of room to be showy. Prune back after flowering. Branches do not die back in winter.
Orange-eye, Summer lilac *B. davidi*	15'	Half-inch flowers clustered on spikes up to 18 inches long. Foliage is an attractive silver gray.	5	Well-drained soil. Full sun.	Vigorous and hardy. Open and shaggy in appearance. Plants die back to the ground each winter in cold areas.
CHASTE TREE Hemp tree *Vitex agnus-castus*	15' in warm climates; 5' in cooler areas.	Small blue or white flowers packed on spikes 5 to 9 inches tall in midsummer through early fall. Leaves are gray-green and aromatic.	7	Full sun. Well-drained soil.	Hardy and pest-resistant. Upright growth habit. Dies to the ground in winter in cool areas. Requires no summer pruning.
CHOKEBERRY *Aronia* sp. **Black** *A. melanocarpa*	3'	Half-inch white blossoms in spring, followed by purplish-black half-inch berries. Leaves turn red in the fall.	4	Full sun or partial shade. Well-drained soil.	Hardy and pest-resistant. Does better in dry conditions than other varieties. Use in low borders. Berries are inedible.
Purple *A. prunifolia*	12'	Half-inch white or pink blossoms followed by half-inch purple berries. Leaves turn red in the fall.	5	Full sun or partial shade. Well-drained soil.	Hardy and pest-resistant. Upright growth. Use in screens or windbreaks. Berries are inedible.
Red *A. arbutifolia*	12'	Half-inch white or pink blossoms, followed by quarter-inch bright red berries. Leaves turn red in the fall.	6	Full sun or partial shade. Well-drained soil.	Hardy and pest-resistant. Upright growth. Use in a shrub border. Berries are inedible and not attractive to birds.

Shrubs	Height	Foliage and Flowers	Zone	Exposure and Soil	Comments
CINQUEFOIL, SHRUBBY *Potentilla fruticosa*	4'	Half- to 1-inch yellow or white single flowers appear from midsummer until fall.	2	Well-drained soil. Full sun.	Hardy and pest-resistant. Low growing and dense. Use in foundation plantings or in low borders. Requires little pruning. Valued for their long periods of bloom.
COTONEASTER *Cotoneaster* sp. **Cranberry** *C. apiculatus*	4'	Very small red-violet flowers in the spring, followed by half-inch orange-red berries. Shiny green leaves.	5	Full sun or partial shade. Well-drained soil.	Spreading, horizontal branching habit. Use on slopes or in foundation plantings. Can be trained on walls.
Creeping *C. adpressus*	10"	Very small pinkish flowers in the spring, followed by half-inch red berries. Shiny green leaves.	5	Full sun or partial shade. Well-drained soil.	Low-growing roots where branches touch ground. Use on slopes or in rock gardens and walls. Needs no pruning.
Diel's *C. dielsianus*	7'	Small pinkish half-inch flowers in spring, followed by half-inch red berries. Leaves are shiny green, turning red in the fall.	6	Full sun or partial shade. Well-drained soil.	Widely spreading branches. Forms dense mound twice as wide as high.
Early *C. adpressa 'praecox'*	2'	Very small pinkish-red flowers in the spring, followed by half-inch red berries. Shiny green leaves.	5	Full sun or partial shade. Well-drained soil.	Low, mound-shaped plants. Use in rock gardens and foundation plantings.
Many-flowered *C. multiflorus*	12'	Half- to 1-inch white flowers cover the branches in spring, followed by large red berries. Shiny green foliage.	6	Full sun or partial shade. Well-drained soil.	Very showy all seasons. Use as a specimen plant.
Peking *C. acutifolius*	10'	Very small pinkish flowers in the spring, followed by half-inch black berries. Shiny green leaves.	3	Full sun or partial shade. Well-drained soil.	Dense and upright growth. Use in shrub borders, screens, or hedges. Needs no pruning.
Spreading *C. divaricatus*	6'	Small pink-violet flowers in the spring, followed by half-inch red berries. Leaves are shiny green, turning red in the fall.	5	Full sun or partial shade. Well-drained soil.	Widely spreading branches in upright plants. Use in hedge borders or as a specimen plant.
Sungari *C. racemiflorus 'soongoricus'*	8'	Half-inch white flowers in clusters in spring, followed by half-inch red berries. Foliage is gray-green.	4	Full sun or partial shade. Well-drained soil.	Hardy and vigorous. Very showy all seasons. Long arching branches. Use as a specimen plant.
CRAPE MYRTLE *Lagerstroemia indica*	7-20'	One-and-a-half- to 2-inch flowers on clusters 8 to 12 inches long in late summer. White, pink, red, lavender blooms. Leaves turn yellow and red in the fall. Bark peels in an attractive whorled pattern.	7	Full sun. Moist, rich, well-drained soil.	Pest- and disease-resistant. Prune in early spring before flowering. Use in informal hedges or as specimen plants.
DAPHNE *Daphne* sp. **February** *D. mezereum*	4-5'	Small, pinkish, very fragrant flowers in clusters along the stems in early spring, followed by half-inch, red poisonous berries.	5	Full sun or partial shade. Does best in light, sandy soil.	Small and upright in growth habit. Needs some winter protection in cold areas. Keep roots cool in warm weather by mulching. Use as a specimen plant.

DECIDUOUS SHRUBS (continued)

Shrubs	Height	Foliage and Flowers	Zone	Exposure and Soil	Comments
Lilac *D. genkwa*	3'	Half-inch pale blue lilac-like flowers in early spring, followed by small white berries. Blossoms are not as fragrant as February daphne.	5	Full sun or partial shade. Does best in light, sandy soil.	Not always winter hardy. If plant suffers frost damage, trim back to ground level. Use as a specimen plant. Keep roots cool in warm weather by mulching.
DEUTZIA *Deutzia* sp. **Fuzzy** *D. scabra*	7'	Single or double, white or pink flowers completely cover the branches in early spring. Light green foliage. Several varieties with different shades of blooms are available.	6	Full sun or partial shade. Tolerant of most soil types.	Plants are very showy. Use as specimen plant. Prune old wood each year; prune new wood after flowering.
Slender *D. gracilis*	6'	Half- to 1-inch white blossoms completely cover the branches in early spring. Light green foliage.	5	Full sun or partial shade. Tolerant of most soil types.	Use as specimen plants or in beds and borders. Cut branches for early indoor forcing. Prune old wood each year; prune new wood after flowering. Has wide-spreading, arching branches.
DOGWOOD *Cornus* sp. **Cornelian cherry** *C. mas*	20'	Small yellow flowers in 1-inch clusters cover the plant in early spring, followed by half-inch edible red berries. Leaves turn red in the fall. Variety 'Aureo-elegantissima' has variegated leaves. Variety 'Flava' has yellow berries.	5	Full sun or partial shade. Tolerant of most soil types.	Hardy and pest-resistant. Colorful all seasons. Use in hedges, screens, or as specimen plants. Berries make tasty preserves. Flowers earlier than most other shrubs. Cut twigs in late winter for early blooms indoors. Can be trained to tree form.
Japanese *C. kousa*	20'	One- to 2-inch clusters of white flowers in late spring, gradually turning pinkish, followed by reddish, raspberry-like fruits. Leaves turn red in the fall.	5	Full sun or partial shade. Tolerant of most soil types.	Use as a specimen plant. Very showy. Berries are relished by birds.
Red-osier *C. sericea*	7-10'	Two-and-a-half- to 3-inch loose clusters of white flowers borne intermittently from late spring to midsummer, followed by clusters of inedible white berries. Leaves turn red in the fall. Twigs are brilliant red in winter. Variety 'Flaviramea' has brilliant yellow twigs in winter. Variety 'Kelseyi' is dwarf, reaching only 2 feet in height.	2	Full sun or partial shade. Tolerant of most soil types.	Vigorous and hardy. Prefers moist areas. Reproduces by underground stolons, so plant in an area where space is not limited. Use in hedges, screens, or on moist embankments near ponds. Berries are relished by birds.
Tatarian *C. alba*	10'	Two-inch clusters of white blossoms appear in late spring, followed by half-inch bluish-white berries. Leaves turn reddish green in fall. Twigs are vivid red during the winter. Variety 'Sibirica' has coral-red berries.	3	Full sun or partial shade. Tolerant of most soil types.	Hardy and pest-resistant. Grown especially for winter color of the twigs. Use in informal hedges or screens or as specimen plants. Berries are inedible but are relished by birds. Prune before new growth in early spring. Old stems lose color, so for maximum intensity, the shrub should be pruned often. Tolerant of wet areas. Variegated forms are less vigorous.

Shrubs	Height	Foliage and Flowers	Zone	Exposure and Soil	Comments
ELAEAGNUS *Elaeagnus* sp. **Autumn olive** *E. umbellata*	18'	Tiny, yellowish-white, fragrant flowers appear in the spring, followed by scaly, brown, inedible berries that turn red in the fall. Leaves are dark green above and silvery below.	2	Well-drained soil. Full sun.	Vigorous and hardy. Use in hedges and screens. Requires little care.
Cherry *E. multiflora*	6'	Three-quarter-inch fragrant flowers appear in late spring, followed by half- to 1-inch red cherrylike berries. Foliage is dark green above and silvery beneath.	5	Well-drained soil. Full sun.	Vigorous and hardy. Use in hedges and screens. Requires little care. Berries are edible and relished by birds. Soot-resistant.
Silverberry *E. commutata*	10-12'	Tiny, silvery yellow, fragrant flowers appear in the spring, followed by half- to 1-inch silvery, rounded berries. Leaves are silvery on both sides.	2	Well-drained, slightly alkaline soil. Full sun.	Vigorous and hardy. Use in hedges and screens. Requires little care.
ELDERBERRY American, Sweet *Sambucus canadensis*	8'	Eight- to 12-inch clusters of tiny white flowers appear in midsummer, followed by edible blue-black or red berries. Aurea variety has brilliant yellow foliage all summer.	4	Full sun or partial shade. Rich, moist, well-drained soil.	Large, vigorous spreading plant. Use berries in wines and preserves. Fruit is relished by birds. Does best in wet area. Use in out-of-the-way places. Easily pruned.
EUONYMUS *Euonymus* sp. **European spindle tree** *E. europaea*	20'	Inconspicuous flowers in late spring are followed by bright pink seed capsules in the fall, opening to reveal orange seeds. Leaves turn red in fall.	4	Full sun or partial shade. Tolerant of most soil types.	Very hardy and vigorous. Subject to scale infestation.
Strawberry bush *E. americana*	8'	Small, pinkish-purple flowers in spring, followed by pinkish-red, warty fruits that bear bright orange seeds. Leaves turn dark red in the fall.	7	Full sun or partial shade. Tolerant of most soil types.	Very hardy native shrub. Use in hard-to-plant, moist areas.
Winged *E. alata*	8'	Subtle flowers in spring, followed by pinkish-red seed capsules in fall. Leaves turn crimson in fall. Twigs lined with unusual bark ridges. Compacta, a dwarf variety, reaches 4 feet tall.	4	Full sun or partial shade. Tolerant of most soil types.	Very hardy and useful. Use in hedges and screens or as specimen plants. Little pruning required. Very showy throughout the year.
FORSYTHIA *Forsythia* sp. **Arnold dwarf** *F. x intermedia* 'Arnold dwarf'	4'	Small, greenish-yellow flowers appear randomly over the plant in early spring. Foliage is deep green.	5	Full sun or partial shade. Tolerant of most soil types.	Low growing with arching branches that root on contact with soil. Vigorous grower forms dense mat of foliage. Use as ground cover on slopes and other areas where soil stabilization is important.
Border *F. x intermedia*	10'	Two-inch, trumpet-like, yellow-gold flowers in early spring, followed by deep green foliage. Many varieties: Spring glory, Lynwood, Primulina, Spectabilis and Beatrix Farrand.	5	Full sun or partial shade. Tolerant of most soil types.	Vigorous and hardy. Graceful arching branches. Give plenty of space for optimum beauty. Cut twigs in late winter for early indoor bloom. Prune after flowering.

DECIDUOUS SHRUBS (continued)

Shrubs	Height	Foliage and Flowers	Zone	Exposure and Soil	Comments
Korean golden bell, Early forsythia F. ovata	5'	One- to 1½-inch trumpet-like, yellow-gold flowers in early spring, followed by deep green foliage.	5	Full sun or partial shade. Tolerant of most soil types.	Graceful, arching branches. Most cold-hardy of the forsythia group. Blooms before other varieties.
FOTHERGILLA Fothergilla sp. **Alabama** F. monticola	6'	Unusual two-inch white, thimble-like flowers on spikes before leaves appear, followed by deep green leaves that turn yellow to scarlet in fall.	6	Prefers light shade along with moist, well-drained soil.	Use in foundation plantings or as specimen plants.
Large F. major	10'	Unusual 2-inch white, thimble-like flowers, followed by deep green leaves that turn yellow, orange, or red in fall.	5	Prefers light shade and moist, well-drained soil.	Use in foundation plantings or as specimen plants.
FRANKLIN TREE Franklinia alatamaha	10-30'	Two- to 3-inch cup-shaped, fragrant white flowers with yellow centers cover plant in fall, with leaves that turn orange-scarlet at the same time.	6	Full sun. Moist, rich, well-drained, acid soil.	Use alone as specimen plants. Will die back in colder areas. Mound soil around stems in winter for added protection.
HAZELNUT Corylus sp. **European hazelnut, Filbert** C. avellana	25'	Catkins produced in the fall and carried over until spring, followed by 1-inch seed husks that contain edible half-inch nuts. Leaves are large and green except in yellow variety Aurea. Contorta has interesting branches.	5	Tolerant of most light and soil conditions.	Hardy and spreading. Most picturesque during the winter months. Reproduces by suckers. Use in areas where its spreading habit is not a problem.
Purple-leaved C. maxima 'purpurea'	30'	Catkins produced in the fall and carried over until spring, followed by 1-inch seed husks that contain edible half-inch nuts. Leaves are large and purple.	5	Full sun. Tolerant of most soil types.	Hardy and spreading. Holds color all season. Use as specimen plants.
HIBISCUS Rose-of-sharon, Shrub althaea Hibiscus syriacus	6-10' or more	Two- to 4-inch single, double, or semi-double flowers in late summer with light green foliage. Some varieties have variegated leaves. Flower colors include white, pink, red, blue, and violet bicolors.	6	Full sun or partial shade. Moist, well-drained soil.	Soot-resistant. Can be trained to tree form through pruning. Use in hard-to-plant, narrow areas. Plant in hedges, screens, or as specimen plants. Hardy in seashore locations. Young plants will need winter protection in cold areas. Valued for its late blooming color.
HONEYSUCKLE Lonicera sp. **Amur** L. maacki	15'	Small, whitish-yellow, very fragrant flowers in late spring, followed by quarter-inch scarlet, inedible berries held well into winter.	3	Full sun or partial shade. Well-drained soil.	Cold-resistant. Later flowering than other honeysuckle varieties. Upright and not as spreading in growth habit as other varieties. Berries are relished by birds. Plants stay attractive late in the season. Evergreen in warm climate areas. Use in hedges, screens, or as specimen.

Shrubs	Height	Foliage and Flowers	Zone	Exposure and Soil	Comments
Blueleaf *L. korolkowi*	12'	One-inch rose flowers in late spring, followed by red-orange inedible berries later in the season. Foliage is blue-green in color.	5	Full sun or partial shade. Well-drained soil.	Grown primarily for its attractively colored foliage. Spreading so looks best in a large area. Young plants can be difficult to establish. Use as a specimen plant or in a hedge. Berries are relished by birds. Difficult to transplant.
Clavey's dwarf *L. x xylosteoides* 'Clavey's dwarf'	3'	Small, yellow flowers in late spring, followed by tiny red berries later in the season. Foliage is gray-green.	4	Full sun or partial shade. Well-drained soil.	Dense and compact. Use as an excellent hedge plant that can be clipped or unclipped.
Morrow *L. morrowi*	8'	Small, whitish-yellow flowers in late spring, followed by deep red-purple inedible berries. Xanthocarpa variety has yellow fruits.	4	Full or partial shade. Well-drained soil.	Dense, mound-shaped. Berries are relished by birds. Use in hedges, screens, or as specimen plants.
Tatarian *L. tatarica*	10' Dwarf varieties grow to 3'	One-inch fragrant flowers in late spring, followed by quarter-inch red berries later in the season. Colors depend on variety but include scarlet, rose, pink, white, and bicolors. Fruit is yellow on several varieties. Foliage is blue-green.	5	Full sun or partial shade. Well-drained soil.	Pest- and disease-resistant. Very vigorous and showy. Berries are relished by birds. Upright growth. Use in hedges, screens, or as specimen plants. Can get untidy when mature.
Winter, Fragrant *L. fragrantissima*	8'	Tiny, white, very fragrant flowers cover the plant in early spring, followed by quarter-inch inedible red berries.	6	Full sun or partial shade. Well-drained soil.	Flowers earlier than most other woody shrubs. Very spreading and looks best in a large area. Evergreen in warm climate areas. Berries are relished by birds. Use in hedges, screens, or as specimen plants. Cut twigs in late winter for early bloom indoors. Prune after flowering.
HYDRANGEA *Hydrangea sp.* **French** *H. macrophylla*	5-8'	Five- to 10-inch rounded clusters of tiny flowers cover the plant in midsummer. Blue, pink, or white shading is dependent on soil pH. Acid soil produces blue flowers; alkaline soil produces pink flowers.	6-7	Full sun or partial shade. Rich, moist, well-drained soil.	Very showy in flower. Use in foundation plantings or shrub borders. Dies back in cold winter areas. Often used as a houseplant. Prune after flowering.
Hills-of-snow *H. arborescens* 'grandiflora'	4'	Six-inch clusters of tiny white flowers in rounded heads cover plant in midsummer. Large bright green leaves.	4	Full sun or partial shade. Rich, moist, well-drained soil.	Dense and globular in shape. Very showy in flower. Often dies back in cold winter areas. Use in foundation plantings or in low informal hedges. Prune in early spring before new growth.
Peegee *H. paniculata* 'grandiflora'	30'	Twelve-inch pyramidal clusters of flowers cover the plant in midsummer. Blossoms are white, gradually turning to pink or purple and cling well into winter.	4	Full sun or partial shade. Rich, moist, well-drained soil.	Can be trained to tree form. Use as a specimen plant in large yards. Cut flower clusters for dried bouquets. Pruning will increase size by encouraging more vigorous growth.
Oak-leaved *H. quercifolia*	6'	Six-inch conical clusters of tiny white flowers in midsummer. Leaves are shaped somewhat like oak leaves and turn red in the fall.	5	Full sun or partial shade. Rich, moist, well-drained soil.	Showy all seasons. Very spreading; best planted alone as specimen plants. Prune after flowering.

DECIDUOUS SHRUBS (continued)

Shrubs	Height	Foliage and Flowers	Zone	Exposure and Soil	Comments
KERRIA *Kerria japonica*	8'	Two-inch yellow flowers bloom in mid-May. Popular for green twigs in winter.	5	Full sun or partial shade. Tolerant of most soil types but prefers well-drained.	Use as shrub border or specimen. Prune after blooms fade. May suffer winterkill; cut deadwood in early spring.
LILAC *Syringa* sp. **Chinese** *S. x chinensis*	15'	Half-inch red-purple, fragrant flowers on clusters 6 to 8 inches tall appear in late spring. Alba variety has white flowers. Foliage is smaller than most lilacs.	3	Well-drained soil. Full sun.	Upright spreading growth. Cut off dying flowers and seed clusters to promote better growth. Use as specimen plant in large yards. Prune old wood yearly during dormancy. Remove young unwanted suckers when they appear, but leave some to keep plants vigorous.
Common *S. vulgaris*	20'	Half-inch fragrant flowers in clusters 6 to 8 inches long. Flowers can be single or double, depending on variety. Colors include violet, blue, pink, white, yellow, and magenta. Foliage is glossy green. Over 400 varieties available.	4	Well-drained soil. Full sun.	Dense, vigorous, upright growth. Use as a specimen plant or in hedges and screens. Cold-resistant. Cut off dying flowers and seed clusters to promote better growth. Prune old wood yearly during dormancy. Remove young unwanted suckers when they appear, but leave some to keep plants vigorous.
Hungarian *S. josikaea*	12'	Quarter-inch red-purple, fragrant flowers on clusters 4 to 6 inches tall in late spring. Foliage is shiny green.	4	Well-drained soil Full sun.	Valued for its late blooms. Cut off dying flowers and seed clusters to promote better growth. Use as specimen plant in large yards or in screens and hedges. Prune old wood yearly during dormancy. Remove young unwanted suckers when they appear, but be sure to leave some to keep plants vigorous and to replace dead branches.
Late *S. villosa*	10'	Quarter-inch rose to white flowers on 8-inch flower clusters in late spring. Flowers have a different fragrance than other species.	2	Well-drained soil. Full sun.	Cold-resistant and vigorous. Dense and spreading. Use as hedges, screens, or windbreaks. Cut off dying flowers and seed clusters to promote better growth.
Littleleaf *S. microphylla*	6-10'	Quarter-inch red-violet, fragrant flowers on 4-inch-long clusters in late spring. Small glossy green leaves. Superba variety has pink flowers.	4	Well-drained soil. Full sun.	Valued for its broad growth habit —often twice as wide as high. Use as a specimen plant. Cut off dying flowers and seed clusters to promote better growth. Prune old wood yearly during dormancy.
Meyer's *S. meyeri*	6'	Quarter-inch violet, fragrant flowers on clusters 4 inches tall in spring. Foliage is shiny green.	6	Well-drained soil Full sun.	Low, compact growth habit. Use in informal hedges and borders. Cut off dying flowers and seed clusters to promote better growth. Prune old wood yearly during dormancy. Remove suckers when they appear, but leave some to keep plants vigorous. Blooms early in life.

Shrubs	Height	Foliage and Flowers	Zone	Exposure and Soil	Comments
Persian *S. x persica*	6-10'	Quarter-inch violet, fragrant flowers on 3-inch-long clusters in late spring. Small leaves. Alba variety has white flowers.	5	Well-drained soil. Full sun.	Valued for its small size. Use as specimen plant or for accent. Cut off dying flowers and seed clusters to promote better growth. Prune old wood yearly during dormancy.
Preston *S. x prestoniae*	8'	Quarter-inch pink, slightly fragrant flowers on 8-inch flower clusters in late spring.	2	Well-drained soil. Full sun.	Large and dense so is ideal for use in windbreaks and screens. Cut off dying flowers and seed clusters to promote better growth. Prune old wood yearly during dormancy.
MOCK ORANGE *Philadelphus* sp. **Lemoine** *P. x lemoinei*	4-8'	One- to 2-inch single or double fragrant white flowers in early summer.	5	Full sun or partial shade. Moist, rich, well-drained soil.	Use as specimen plant or in shrub border. Needs little pruning, except of deadwood.
Sweet *P. coronarius*	10'	One- to 2-inch single, white, very fragrant flowers in early summer. Foliage turns yellow in fall. Aureus variety has yellow leaves in early spring, turning greenish later in season.	5	Full sun or partial shade. Tolerant of most soil types.	Tolerates drier conditions than most shrubs. Use as specimen plant or in shrub borders. Needs little pruning, except of deadwood.
Virginalis *P. x virginalis*	5-9'	One- to 2-inch single or double fragrant white flowers in early summer. Dwarf varieties grow to 3 feet.	5	Full sun or partial shade. Moist, rich, well-drained soil.	Very showy with delicate flowers. Use as specimen plants or in shrub borders. Needs little pruning, except of deadwood.
NINEBARK *Physocarpus opulifolius*	10'	Quarter-inch white-pinkish flowers in 1- to 2-inch clusters in early spring, followed by greenish-brown seed capsules that cling through midwinter. Luteus variety has yellow foliage. Nanus grows to 4 feet.	2	Full sun or partial shade. Well-drained soil.	Cold hardy. Needs no pruning. Very dense. Use in screens, borders, and windbreaks. Not very showy.
PEARLBUSH *Exochorda* sp. **Pearlbush** *E. racemosa*	10-12'	Strings of white buds open into 2-inch single flowers in mid-spring.	5	Full sun. Tolerant of most soil types.	Use as specimen plant in large yards. More hardy with less flowers than Wilson pearlbush.
The Bride *E. x macrantha*	4'	Strings of white buds open into 2-inch single flowers in mid-spring.	6	Full sun. Tolerant of most soil types.	Use as specimen plant or in low shrub borders.
Wilson *E. giraldi* 'wilsoni'	10'	Strings of white buds open into 1- to 2-inch single flowers in mid-spring.	5	Full sun. Tolerant of most soil types.	Upright growth. Use as specimen plant in large yards. Prune after flowers fade to prevent leggy growth.
PEONY, TREE *Paeonia suffruticosa*	7'	Six- to 12-inch single, semidouble, or double flowers appear in late spring. Many colors and varieties. Foliage is gray-green.	5	Partial shade; can tolerate full sun. Rich, moist, well-drained soil.	Very showy with flashy flowers. Use as specimen plants or in beds. Protect in winter in cold winter areas. Hardier than they look. Occasionally need staking.
PHOTINIA, ORIENTAL *Photinia villosa*	15'	Small white flowers in 1- to 2-inch clusters in late spring, followed by half-inch red berries. Red fall foliage.	5	Full sun or partial shade. Well-drained soil.	Use as an unusual specimen plant. Showy all seasons. Berries are relished by birds.

DECIDUOUS SHRUBS (continued)

Shrubs	Height	Foliage and Flowers	Zone	Exposure and Soil	Comments
POMEGRANATE *Punica granatum*	20'	One- to 4-inch single or double flowers appear in late spring. Single flowered varieties are followed by 2½-inch yellow-red edible fruit in the fall. Both types have leaves that turn yellow in the fall. Colors include white, yellow, and bicolors. Smaller varieties are available.	9	Full sun. Tolerant of most soil types.	Likes hot, dry situations. Use as specimen plants or in informal hedges and screens. Needs little pruning. Prune before new growth in the spring.
PRIVET *Ligustrum* sp. **Amur** *L. amurense*	15'	Quarter-inch white flowers in 1- to 3-inch clusters in early summer, followed by small black berries in the fall. Leathery green foliage.	4	Full sun or partial shade. Tolerant of most soil types.	Quick growing. Cold-resistant and hardy. Very dense. Use in clipped or unclipped hedges or screens. Soot-tolerant.
Border *L. obtusifolium*	9'	Quarter-inch white flowers in 1- to 3-inch clusters in early summer, followed by small black berries in the fall. Leathery green foliage. Regelianum variety or Regal privet grows to 4 feet.	4	Full sun or partial shade. Tolerant of most soil types.	Quick growing and attractive. Very dense with horizontal branches. Use in clipped or unclipped hedges and screens or use as a specimen plant. Berries are relished by birds. Soot-tolerant.
California *L. ovalifolium*	15'	Quarter-inch white flowers in 1- to 3-inch clusters in early summer, followed by small black berries in the fall. Leathery green foliage.	6	Full sun or partial shade. Tolerant of most soil types.	Quick growing and attractive. Very dense. Use in clipped or unclipped hedges and screens or use as a specimen plant. Semievergreen in warm climate areas. Berries are relished by birds. Variegated varieties are not as hardy.
Common *L. vulgare*	15'	Quarter-inch white flowers in 1- to 3-inch clusters in early summer, followed by small black berries in the fall. Leaves are a leathery green.	5	Full sun or partial shade. Tolerant of most soil types.	Subject to blight in many localities. Quick growing, wide, and dense. Use in clipped hedges or as a specimen. Berries are relished by birds.
Ibolium *L. x ibolium*	12'	Quarter-inch white flowers in 1- to 3-inch clusters in early summer, followed by small black berries in the fall. Leathery green foliage.	4	Full sun or partial shade. Tolerant of most soil types.	Quick growing; more attractive than amur privet. Very dense. Use in clipped or unclipped hedges or screens. Soot-tolerant. Berries are relished by birds.
PRUNUS *Prunus* sp. **Beach plum** *P. maritima*	10'	Tiny white, single or double flowers in mid-spring, followed by half- to 1-inch red edible berries.	3	Well-drained soil. Full sun.	Showy. Use fruits raw or in jams and preserves. Cold-resistant. Use in borders or as a specimen.
Dwarf flowering almond *P. glandulosa*	3-5'	One-inch single or double, white or pink flowers appear in mid-spring. No fruits.	4	Well-drained soil. Full sun.	Showy. Use in low borders or as a specimen plant.
Flowering almond *P. triloba*	10'	One-inch double pink flowers appear in mid-spring. No fruits.	3	Well-drained soil. Full sun.	Showy. Use as a specimen plant or in a shrub border.
Nanking cherry *P. tomentosa*	5'	Half-inch whitish-pink flowers appear in early spring, followed by half-inch red edible berries.	3	Well-drained soil. Full sun.	Showy. Use fruits raw or in jams and preserves. Cold-resistant. Use in borders or as a specimen plant.

Shrubs	Height	Foliage and Flowers	Zone	Exposure and Soil	Comments
Purple-leaf sand cherry *P. x cistena*	7'	Half-inch white or pink single flowers appear in mid-spring, followed by blackish-blue tasty berries in the fall. Foliage is reddish-brown all season.	3	Well-drained soil. Full sun.	Use berries in preserves. Berries are relished by birds. Cold-resistant. Use in shrub borders or as a specimen plant.
Sand cherry *P. besseyi*	7'	Half-inch white single flowers appear in mid-spring, followed by tasty blue-black half-inch berries in late summer and fall, often in large quantity.	3	Full sun. Light, well-drained soil.	Use berries in jams and preserves. Berries are relished by birds. Cold-resistant and drought-resistant.
PUSSY WILLOW *Salix* sp. **Goat willow, French** *S. caprea*	25'	Twigs are covered with 1- to 2-inch silver-pink catkins in early spring that gradually turn yellow with pollen. Leaves are light gray-green.	5	Full sun. Moist, well-drained soil.	Quick growing. Use in screens or as specimen plants. Prune after catkins disappear. Cut twigs in late winter for indoor bouquets.
Korean rose gold, Rose gold *S. gracilistyla*	10'	Twigs are covered with 1- to 2-inch rose catkins in early spring that gradually turn yellow with pollen. Foliage is gray-green.	6	Full sun. Moist, well-drained soil.	Quick growing. Bushier and blooms earlier than other pussy willow varieties. Cut twigs in late winter for indoor bouquets. Use in screens, shrub borders, or as a specimen plant. Prune after catkins disappear.
Purple osier, Basket *S. purpurea*	9'	Twigs are covered with 1-inch gray catkins in early spring that gradually turn yellow with pollen. Leaves are gray-green. Twigs are purple in winter. Nana variety grows to 3 feet.	5	Full sun. Moist, well-drained soil.	Quick growing. Use low varieties in borders and beds. Taller varieties in hedges and screens. Valuable for hard-to-plant, wet areas. Prune after catkins disappear.
Pussy willow *S. discolor*	20'	Twigs are covered with 1-inch white catkins in early spring that gradually turn yellow with pollen. Foliage is gray-green.	2	Full sun. Moist, well-drained soil.	Quick growing. Smaller, hardier, and blooms later than goat willow. Cut twigs in late winter for attractive seasonal indoor bouquets. Use in screens or as specimen plants. Prune after fuzzy catkins disappear.
QUINCE *Chaenomeles* sp. **Flowering** *C. speciosa*	6'	One- to 2-inch single or double flowers cluster on branches in mid-spring, followed by 1-inch yellow-green fruits. Pink, red, bicolors, and white flowers, depending on variety.	5	Well-drained soil. Full sun.	Very showy. Use fruits in jellies and jams. Use as specimen plants or borders and hedges.
Japanese *C. japonica*	3-4'	One- to 2-inch reddish-orange single flowers cluster on branches in mid-spring. Alpina variety reaches 15 inches and has orange flowers. No fruit of any consequence.	5	Well-drained soil. Full sun.	Use in low borders and foundation plantings. Little pruning necessary.
REDBUD, Chinese judas tree *Cercis chinensis*	8'	Half- to 1-inch red-purple, pealike flowers cover the branches in mid-spring. Leaves are large and turn yellow in fall.	8	Partial shade. Well-drained soil.	Use as specimen plant, on lawns, or in foundation plantings. Needs no pruning. Requires some wind protection.

DECIDUOUS SHRUBS (continued)

Shrubs	Height	Foliage and Flowers	Zone	Exposure and Soil	Comments
RHODODENDRON, AZALEA *Rhododendron sp.* **Albrecht** *R. albrechti*	5'	(For other rhododendrons, see broad-leaved evergreen shrubs chart, pages 148 to 149.) Two-inch rose-colored blossoms cover plant in spring.	6	Full sun or partial shade. Moist, acid soil.	Hardy and fragrant.
Coast, Dwarf *R. atlanticum*	2'	One-and-a-quarter-inch white, tinged with crimson, blossoms cover plant in spring.	6	Full sun or partial shade. Moist, acid soil.	Hardy and fragrant.
Flame, Yellow *R. calendulaceum*	10'	Two- to 2½-inch orange to scarlet flowers.	5	Full sun or partial shade. Moist, acid soil.	Hardy. Brilliantly colored. Blooms later than other varieties. Holds blossoms for long periods.
Knap Hill *R. 'Knap Hill Hybrid'*	5'	Three-inch flowers in large clusters bloom in early summer. Colors include red, yellow, pink, and white. Leaves turn red or yellow in fall.	5-8	Full sun or partial shade. Moist, acid soil.	Showy. Use as specimen plants or in mass plantings.
Mollis hybrid, Chinese *R. molle*	5'	Two- to 3-inch flowers cover plants in late spring: pink, yellow, salmon, and white.	6	Full sun or partial shade. Moist, acid soil.	Vigorous showy hybrids. Use in beds, foundation plantings, or as accent.
Royal *R. schlippenbachi*	15'	Three-inch freckled, pink flowers in spring. Leaves turn red in fall.	5	Full sun or partial shade. Moist, acid soil.	Tall slender plants. Use in bed and foundation plantings or as accent plants.
Sweet, Smooth *R. arborescens*	10'	Two-inch white or rose-tinged flowers in early summer. Leaves turn scarlet in fall.	5	Full sun or partial shade. Moist, acid soil.	Blooms later than other varieties. Colorful flowers very fragrant.
ROSE ACACIA Moss locust *Robinia hispida*	7'	One- to 2-inch pink flowers on pendulous 2½- to 3-inch clusters appear in early summer, followed by red-brown seedpods. Twigs are covered with red-brown bristles.	6	Well-drained soil. Full sun.	Reproduces by underground stolons and can become pestiferous if not controlled. Prune after flowers fade. Use on hard-to-plant slopes and embankments.
ROSE-OF-SHARON (See hibiscus)					
SIBERIAN PEA TREE *Caragana arborescens*	20'	One-half to 1-inch yellow pealike flowers in late spring, followed by yellow-green seedpods. Pendula variety is a weeping form that is sometimes grafted to top of arborescens.	2	Full sun. Tolerant of most soil types.	Very hardy and vigorous. Use in windbreaks, screens, or tall hedges. Drought and cold-resistant. Use pendulous variety as a specimen plant. Prune after flowers fade.
SPICEBUSH *Lindera benzoin*	6-15'	One-quarter-inch yellow fragrant flowers appear in tiny clusters in early spring, followed by small red berries in fall. Leaves turn golden yellow.	5	Partial shade. Moist, well-drained, acid soil.	Use as specimen plant or in a mixed shrub border. Both sexes are needed to produce berries. Use leaves in tea. Prune after flowers fade.
SPIREA *Spiraea sp.* **Big Nippon** *S. nipponica 'rotundifolia'*	5-8'	Tiny white flowers in flat clusters in late spring. Foliage is attractive blue-green.	5	Full sun or partial shade. Tolerant of most soil types.	Use as specimen plants or in shrub borders. More upright in growth than other varieties. Prune after flowers fade.

Shrubs	Height	Foliage and Flowers	Zone	Exposure and Soil	Comments
Billiard S. x billiardi	6'	Tiny pinkish-red flowers in 8-inch pyramidal spikes in midsummer, often continuing through fall.	5	Full sun or partial shade. Tolerant of most soil types.	Use in shrub borders or in mass plantings. Reproduces quickly by underground stems, forming a dense mound. Prune in early spring while plants are dormant.
Bridal-wreath S. prunifolia	6'	Half-inch double white flowers line branches in mid-spring. Leaves turn red-orange in fall.	5	Full sun or partial shade. Tolerant of most soil types.	A popular spirea. Showy. Long arching branches. Use as a specimen plant or in shrub borders. Prune after flowers fade.
Bumalda S. x bumalda	2'	Tiny pink flowers in flat 4- to 6-inch clusters on spikes in midsummer and often blooming through fall. Froebeli or Froebel, a popular variety, grows slightly taller.	6	Full sun or partial shade. Tolerant of most soil types.	Use in shrub borders, foundation plantings, or rock gardens. Prune in early spring while plants are dormant. If old flowers are kept trimmed, blooming period is often prolonged.
Garland S. x arguta	3-6'	Tiny white flowers in small flat clusters line the branches in mid-spring.	5	Full sun or partial shade. Tolerant of most soil types.	Showy arching branches. Use as a specimen plant or in shrub borders. Dwarf variety in foundation plantings or beds. Prune after flowers fade.
Japanese, Mikado S. japonica 'atrosanguinea'	6'	Tiny red flowers in 2- to 5-inch flat clusters appear in early summer.	6	Full sun or partial shade. Tolerant of most soil types.	Use as specimen plants or in shrub borders. Use low-growing forms in rock gardens and edgings. Prune in early spring while plants are dormant.
Reeves S. cantoniensis	5'	Tiny white flowers in rounded 1- to 2-inch clusters appear in late spring. Leaves turn red-brown in fall.	7	Full sun or partial shade. Tolerant of most soil types.	Showy arching branches. Semi-evergreen in warm climate areas. Use as specimen plants or in shrub borders. Prune after flowers fade.
Thunberg S. thunbergi	5'	Half-inch white flowers in clusters of two to five appear in mid-spring. Leaves turn yellow in fall.	5	Full sun or partial shade. Tolerant of most soil types.	Very showy. Blooms earlier than most other varieties. Use as a specimen plant or in shrub borders. Tends to lose some branches each year in cold winter areas, so pruning is essential for neat appearance and best growth. Prune after flowers fade.
Vanhoutte, Bridal-wreath S. x vanhouttei	6'	Half-inch white flowers in 1- to 2-inch clusters cover branches in late spring. Leaves turn red-orange in fall.	5	Full sun or partial shade. Tolerant of most soil types.	Very hardy and showy. Use as a specimen plant or in a shrub border. Long, arching branches. Most widely grown spirea. Prune after flowers fade.
SPIREA, FALSE Sorbaria sp. **Kashmir** S. aitchisoni	10'	Small white flowers in 8- to 10-inch, spirea-like clusters appear in early to late summer.	6	Partial shade. Tolerant of most soil types if kept moist.	Use as a specimen plant in large yards or in a mass planting. Good on hard-to-plant slopes to hold soil. Cut off fading flowers and heavily prune branches every two to three years.

DECIDUOUS SHRUBS (continued)

Shrubs	Height	Foliage and Flowers	Zone	Exposure and Soil	Comments
Ural *S. sorbifolia*	6'	Small white flowers in 8- to 10-inch, spirea-like clusters appear in early to late summer.	2	Full sun or partial shade. Tolerant of most soil types.	Can become a pest if not pruned often. Use in large yards, in shrub borders, or on slopes.
STEPHA-NANDRA **Lace shrub** *Stephanandra incisa*	8'	Insignificant, tiny whitish flowers in 2-inch clusters appear in early summer. Finely cut leaves are vivid green; turn red-purple in fall. Twigs are dense and contorted.	5	Full sun or partial shade. Tolerant of most soil types if kept moist.	Attractive showy foliage. Use in shrub borders or informal hedges. Dwarf forms in beds, edgings, or in rock gardens. Prune in early spring while plants are dormant.
STEWARTIA *Stewartia* sp. **Showy,** **Mountain** **camellia** *S. ovata 'grandiflora'*	15'	Two- to 4-inch, cup-shaped white blossoms with purple centers appear in midsummer. Foliage turns red-orange in fall. Bark is variegated and peeling on mature shrub.	7	Full sun or partial shade. Rich, moist, acid soil.	Use as specimen plant. Needs little pruning.
Virginia, **Silky camellia** *S. malacodendron*	12'	Two- to 4-inch, cup-shaped white blossoms appear in midsummer. Foliage turns red-orange in fall.	7	Full sun or partial shade. Rich, moist, acid soil.	Use as specimen plant. Needs little pruning.
SUMAC *Rhus* sp. **Fragrant** *R. aromatica*	8'	Inconspicuous yellow flowers in mid-spring, followed by red berrylike fruits in the fall. Foliage turns yellow and red in fall.	3	Full sun. Light, well-drained soil.	Quick growing. Use as a ground cover on hard-to-plant slopes or in foundation plantings. Attractive in fall. Pruning encourages growth.
Shining, **Dwarf** *R. copallina*	20'	Tiny greenish-yellow flowers on 4- to 5-inch spikes, followed by red hairy berrylike fruits. Foliage is lustrous green, turning scarlet in the fall.	5	Full sun. Tolerant of most soil types.	Quick growing. Use as a specimen tree or as a backdrop in a shrub border. Attractive in fall. Pruning will encourage more stems to grow. Plant both sexes to get fruit.
Smooth *R. glabra*	20'	Tiny greenish-yellow flowers on 4- to 8-inch spikes in midsummer, followed by bright red berries. Foliage turns vivid red in the fall. Laciniata variety has lobed leaves.	2	Full sun. Tolerant of most soil types.	Quick growing. Use as a background or screen plant. Can become a pest. Plant both sexes to get fruit. Attractive in the fall. Pruning encourages growth.
Staghorn *R. typhina*	30'	Tiny greenish-yellow flowers on 4- to 8-inch spikes in early summer, followed by bright red berries. Foliage turns vivid red in the fall. Dissecta and Laciniata varieties have lobed leaves. Twigs are fuzzy.	3	Full sun. Tolerant of most soil types.	Quick growing. Use as a background plant in large yards. Spreads by underground runners and can become pestiferous. Plant both sexes to get fruit. Pruning will encourage more stems to grow.
SUMMER-SWEET *Clethra alnifolia*	10'	Tiny white or pink fragrant flowers on 4- to 6-inch spikes in mid- to late summer. Foliage turns yellow in fall.	5	Full sun or partial shade. Tolerant of most soil types if kept moist.	Use in shrub borders or informal hedges. Spreads by underground runners.
SWEET **SHRUB** **Carolina** **allspice** *Calycanthus floridus*	10'	Two-inch, red-brown aromatic flowers appear in late spring. Foliage is dark green, turning yellow in fall.	5	Partial shade, but can tolerate full sun. Rich, moist, well-drained soil.	Use as a specimen plant or in shrub borders. When they open, blossoms smell like fresh strawberries. Leaves and bark are also aromatic.

Shrubs	Height	Foliage and Flowers	Zone	Exposure and Soil	Comments
SYMPHORI-CARPOS *Symphoricarpos* sp. **Chenault coralberry** *S. x chenaulti*	3'	Inconspicuous pink flowers in mid-summer, followed by small red berries, white on one side in fall.	5	Full sun or partial shade. Tolerant of most soil types.	Berries are attractive in fall. Use in shrub borders; use low forms as vigorous ground covers. Gracefully arching branches. Spreads by underground runners. Prune in early spring while plant is dormant.
Indian currant, Coralberry *S. orbiculatus*	7'	Inconspicuous greenish-white flowers in midsummer, followed by small red-violet berries. Leucocarpus variety has white berries.	3	Full sun or partial shade. Tolerant of most soil types.	Berries are attractive in fall. Use on hard-to-plant slopes. Prune in early spring while plant is dormant. Spreads by underground runners.
Snowberry *S. albus* 'laevigatus'	3'	Inconspicuous pink flowers in mid-summer, followed by half-inch white, waxy berries in fall.	3	Full sun or partial shade. Tolerant of most soil types.	Berries are attractive in fall. Use as specimen plants or in hedges and shrub borders. Upright arching branches. Prune in early spring while plant is dormant.
TAMARISK *Tamarix* sp. **Kashgar** *T. hispida*	15'	Tiny pink flowers in long slender clusters appear on twig ends in late summer. Foliage is light green and scalelike, creating a feathery effect.	7	Well-drained soil. Full sun.	Will thrive in dry areas. Use as a specimen plant or in a shrub border. Prune branches back severely in early spring while plants are dormant.
Odessa *T. ramosissima*	18'	Tiny pink flowers in long slender clusters appear on twig ends in late summer. Foliage is light green and scalelike, creating a feathery effect.	5	Well-drained soil. Full sun.	Will thrive in dry areas. Use as a specimen plant or in a shrub border. Prune branches back severely in early spring while plants are dormant.
Small-flowered *T. parviflora*	9'	Tiny pink flowers in long slender clusters appear on twig ends in late summer. Foliage is light green and scalelike, creating a feathery effect.	5	Well-drained soil. Full sun.	Will thrive in dry areas. Use as a specimen plant or in a shrub border. Prune branches back severely in early spring while plants are dormant.
VIBURNUM *Viburnum* sp. **Arrowwood** *V. dentatum*	15'	Tiny white flowers in 1- to 3-inch clusters in early summer, followed by blue berries in fall. Foliage turns red in fall.	3	Full sun or partial shade. Well-drained soil.	Use as a specimen plant or in shrub borders. Berries relished by birds. Little pruning needed.
Burkwood *V. x burkwoodi*	6'	Tiny pink or white fragrant flowers in 2- to 3½-inch clusters appear in late spring, followed by red berries turning black as they mature. Foliage is green above, whitish below, and turns red in the fall.	5	Full sun or partial shade. Well-drained soil.	Use in shrub borders or in foundation plantings. Berries are relished by birds. Little pruning needed.
Black haw *V. prunifolium*	15'	Tiny white flowers in 2- to 5-inch clusters appear in mid- to late spring, followed by bluish-black berries in fall.	3	Full sun or partial shade. Well-drained soil.	Use in shrub backdrops or screens. Berries are relished by birds. Berries tasty in jellies and jams. Can be trained to tree form.

DECIDUOUS SHRUBS (continued)

Shrubs	Height	Foliage and Flowers	Zone	Exposure and Soil	Comments
European cranberry bush *V. opulus*	12'	Tiny white flowers in 2- to 4-inch clusters, surrounded by a margin of half-inch blossoms in late spring, followed by red berries in fall. Foliage of all varieties turns red in fall. Nanum variety grows to 2 feet. Compactum, 5 feet.	3	Full sun or partial shade. Well-drained soil.	Dense and vigorous. Use tall forms in shrub borders or screens. Use low forms in edgings and rock gardens. Roseum, or European, snowball variety is often infected with aphids that scar foliage. Needs little pruning.
Fragrant snowball *V. x carlcephalum*	9'	Small white fragrant flowers in rounded 4- to 5-inch heads, followed by red berries turning black as they mature. Foliage turns red in fall.	5	Full sun or partial shade. Well-drained soil.	Use as a specimen plant or in shrub borders. Berries relished by birds. Little pruning needed.
Fragrant *V. farreri*	10'	Tiny, whitish-pink fragrant flowers in 1- to 3-inch clusters in early spring, followed by red berries. Berries change to black in midsummer. Leaves turn red in fall. The Album variety has white flowers. Nanum reaches only 1½ feet.	6	Full sun or partial shade. Well-drained soil.	Earliest blooming viburnum. Not too cold hardy. Berries not numerous but are relished by birds. Use as a specimen plant or in shrub borders. Little pruning needed.
Highbush cranberry *V. trilobum*	12'	Tiny white flowers in 2- to 3-inch clusters surrounded by a margin of half-inch blossoms in late spring, followed by red cranberry-like fruits in fall. Foliage turns red in fall. Compactum variety grows to 5 feet.	2	Full sun or partial shade. Well-drained soil.	Berries tasty in jams and preserves. Vigorous and hardy. Use in shrub borders or screens. Needs little pruning.
Japanese snowball *V. plicatum*	10'	Tiny white flowers in 2- to 4-inch rounded ball-like clusters in late spring. Leaves turn red in the fall. Tomentosum variety has a ring of half-inch blossoms surrounding each flower cluster.	5	Full sun or partial shade. Well-drained soil.	Use as specimen plant or in a shrub border. Hardier than European snowball. Needs little pruning.
Korean spice *V. carlesi*	5'	Small, pink, fragrant flowers in 2- to 3-inch clusters in mid-spring, followed by small black berries in midsummer. Foliage turns to a red color during the fall. The Compactum variety grows to 2 feet.	5	Full sun or partial shade. Well-drained soil.	Use as a specimen plant or in shrub borders. Berries relished by birds. Needs little pruning.
Linden *V. dilatatum*	10'	Tiny white flowers in 2- to 4-inch clusters in early summer, followed by red berries in fall. Foliage turns red-brown in fall. Xanthocarpum variety has yellow fruit.	5	Full sun or partial shade. Well-drained soil.	Vigorous grower. Use as specimen plant or in screens in large yards. Berries relished by birds. Little pruning needed.
Nannyberry, Sheepberry *V. lentago*	30'	Tiny white flowers in 3- to 5-inch clusters in late spring, followed by black berries. Foliage turns red-purple in the fall.	3	Full sun or partial shade. Tolerant of most soil types.	Use in shrub backgrounds or in screens. Dense, arching branches. Berries are relished by birds. Vigorous and hardy.
Sargent cranberry bush *V. sargenti*	12'	Tiny white flowers in 2- to 3-inch clusters surrounded by a margin of half-inch blossoms during mid-spring and followed by red berries. The Flavum variety has golden yellow berries.	6	Full sun or partial shade. Well-drained soil.	Similar to European cranberry bush. Very vigorous and hardy. Use in shrub borders, screens, or as specimen plants. Berries relished by birds. Needs little pruning.

Shrubs	Height	Foliage and Flowers	Zone	Exposure and Soil	Comments
Siebold *V. sieboldi*	10'	Tiny white flowers in 3- to 5-inch clusters, followed by bright red berries gradually turning black in the fall. Foliage is large, deep green, and turns red in fall.	5	Full sun or partial shade. Well-drained soil.	Very showy all seasons. Vigorous and hardy. Use as specimen plants or in shrub borders. Berries relished by birds. Needs little pruning.
Wayfaring tree *V. lantana*	15'	Tiny white flowers in 2- to 5-inch clusters in mid-spring, followed by berries gradually changing from green to red to black. Foliage turns red in fall.	3	Full sun or partial shade. Tolerant of most soil types.	Use as a specimen plant in large yards or as a shrub backdrop. Berries resemble raisins in winter and are relished by birds. Hardy and drought-resistant.
Withe-rod *V. cassinoides*	12'	Tiny white flowers in flat 3- to 5-inch clusters in early summer, followed by small green berries turning red and then black. Foliage turns red in fall.	4	Full sun or partial shade. Well-drained soil kept moist.	Use in mass plantings or beds. Little pruning needed. Berries are relished by birds.
WEIGELA *Weigela* sp. **Old-fashioned** *W. florida*	8-10'	One-inch pink, trumpetlike flowers cover plant in late spring. Foliage is deep green. Variegata variety has yellowish-white leaf margins. Alba variety has white flowers.	5	Full sun or partial shade. Tolerant of most soil types.	Use as a specimen plant or in shrub borders. Graceful, arching branches. Prune after flowers fade.
Weigela hybrids *W. hybrids*	9-12'	One- to 2-inch trumpetlike flowers cover plant in late spring. Foliage is deep green. Colors range from white, pink, red, and magenta.	6	Full sun or partial shade. Tolerant of most soil types.	Very showy. Graceful, arching branches. Use as a specimen plant or in shrub borders. Occasionally dies back in cold winter areas.
WINTER-BERRY Black alder *Ilex verticillata*	15'	Inconspicuous white flowers in early summer, followed by red berries in fall. Foliage turns yellow in the fall. Chrysocarpa variety has yellow fruit. Nana grows to 3 feet.	4	Full sun or partial shade. Moist, well-drained, slightly acid soil.	Both sexes are needed for fruit production. Use in borders or as a specimen. Fine in hard-to-plant, wet area. Upright growth. Cut winter twigs for Christmas decorations.
WITCH HAZEL *Hamamelis* sp. **'Arnold promise'** *H. x intermedia*	15'	One- to 2-inch ribbonlike yellow flowers cover the plant early in spring. Foliage turns red-brown in fall.	5	Full sun or partial shade. Rich, moist, well-drained soil.	Grown for very early bloom. Use as specimen plants or in shrub borders. Needs little pruning.
Chinese *H. mollis*	30'	One- to 2-inch unusual, yellow ribbonlike, fragrant flowers cover plant in early spring. Foliage turns yellow in fall.	5	Full sun or partial shade. Rich, moist, well-drained soil.	Grown for early bloom and scent. Dense and rounded. Use as specimen plants or in shrub borders. Needs little pruning.
Common *H. virginiana*	15'	Half- to 1-inch yellow, ribbonlike flowers appear in late fall. Foliage turns yellow at same time.	5	Full sun. Rich, moist, well-drained soil.	Grown for late bloom. Use as shrub backdrop. Often open and loose in growth. Soot-tolerant.
Vernal *H. vernalis*	6'	Half-inch yellow, ribbonlike fragrant flowers in late winter or early spring. Blooms open on sunny days only. Foliage is yellow in fall.	5	Full sun or partial shade. Rich, moist, well-drained soil.	Grown for early bloom and scent. Vigorous and dense. Use as specimen plant or in shrub borders. Needs little pruning.

CONIFEROUS SHRUBS (continued)

Shrub	Height	Shape and Foliage	Zone	Soil	Comments
ARBORVITAE, AMERICAN *Thuja occidentalis*	Varieties vary; average 7-10′	Most are compact pyramidals. Green or blue-green, odd scalelike foliage in fan formation.	3	Rich, moist, well-drained soil.	Slow growing. Use as foundation plants or in hedges. Cannot tolerate heat. Prune in early spring before new growth.
CEPHA-LOTAXUS Japanese plum yew *Cephalotaxus harringtonia*	30′	Multi-stemmed; wide spreading. Fastigiata cultivar is columnar in habit. Dark green with 1½-inch needles.	6	Moist, well-drained, acid soil.	Similar to yews but not as dense. Use in hedge or screen. Bears 1-inch, plum-shaped purple-green fruits. Shear in spring before new growth.
CUPRESSO-CYPARIS *Cupressocyparis leylandi*	Variable with shearing. Can become 50′.	Narrow, columnar. Scalelike foliage.	5	Moist, well-drained soil.	Very fast growing. Easily sheared to any dimensions. Hybrid between monterey cypress and nootka cypress. Prune in early spring before new growth.
CRYPTOMERIA Japanese cedar *Cryptomeria japonica 'nana'*	3′	Dwarf variety. Broad, mound-shaped. Dark green, needlelike foliage.	5	Moist, well-drained soil.	Use in foundation plantings. Handsome in patio tubs.
FALSE CYPRESS *Chamaecyparis sp.* **Dwarf hinoki** *C. obtusa 'nana aurea'*	4′	Broad, flattened foliage; scalelike and fan-shaped.	5	Moist, well-drained, slightly acid soil.	Slow growing. Use in rock gardens or around foundations. Prune any time.
Moss sawara *C. pisifera 'squarrosa'*	Variable with shearing. Can become 30′.	Dense, conical. Feathery soft, scalelike foliage.	4	Moist, well-drained, slightly acid soil.	Slow growing. Needs constant pruning. Prune any time.
Plume *C. pisifera 'plumosa'*	Variable with shearing. Up to 100′.	Dense foliage; fluffy, scalelike, and feathery green. Also a gold variety.	4	Moist, well-drained, slightly acid soil.	Slow growing. Use as specimen tree. Can get unsightly when mature. Prune any time.
Thread leaf *C. pisifera 'filifera'*	Variable with shearing. Up to 100′. Average 6-8′.	Dense foliage; long, threadlike, and dark green. Some varieties are yellow.	4	Moist, well-drained, slightly acid soil.	Slow growing. Unusual foundation or specimen plant. Can get unsightly when mature. Prune any time.
JUNIPER *Juniperus sp.* **Creeping, Creeping cedar** *J. horizontalis*	1′	Dense; low spreading. Blue-green or steel-blue needles.	3	Well-drained soil.	Excellent ground cover, especially on sloping areas. Handsome blue berries in the fall. Color intensifies in winter.

Shrub	Height	Shape and Foliage	Zone	Soil	Comments
Dwarf common *J. communis* *'compressa'*	4'	Broadly spreading. Foliage is grayish green with quarter-inch needles.	3	Well-drained soil.	Good foundation plant. Prune any time. Plant in rock gardens.
Hollywood *J. chinensis 'torulosa'*	20'	Broadly conical. Tufted needles and scales.	4	Well-drained soil.	Use as specimen tree. Interesting, twisted branching habit. Do not prune. Also a variegated form.
Japanese garden *J. chinensis* *'procumbens'*	2'	Dense; low spreading. Blue-green, needlelike foliage.	4	Well-drained soil.	Use in foundation plantings or in rock gardens. Prune any time.
Pfitzer *J. chinensis* *'pfitzerana'*	6'	Dense; broad, flat-topped. Feathery, scalelike foliage and needles.	4	Well-drained soil.	Fast growing. Tolerant of partial shade. Needs constant pruning. An excellent foundation plant to go with other plants.
San Jose *J. chinensis 'San Jose'*	1'	Dense; short and spreading. Both needle- and scalelike foliage.	4	Well-drained soil.	Use as an interesting ground cover. Widely planted in southern California. Prune any time.
Savin *J. sabina* *'tamariscifolia'*	2'	Dense; low spreading, flat. Blue-green, needlelike foliage.	3	Well-drained soil.	Branches grow slightly upward. Use in rock gardens, foundation plantings, or along walkways. Prune any time.
Shore *J. conferta*	1'	Dense; low spreading. Quarter-inch green needles.	6	Prefers sandy seashore locations.	Use as ground cover in sandy, hard-to-plant areas. Prune any time.
PINE *Pinus* sp. **Bristle-cone, Hickory** *P. aristata*	10-40'	Variable shape. Dark blue-green needles in clusters of five, 1 to 1¾ inches long.	6	Well-drained soil.	Slow growing. Picturesque branching habit. Use as specimen tree or as an accent. Especially good in patio tubs so can be moved for effect. Prune after spring growth has started.
Dwarf white *P. strobus 'nana'*	6'	Dense; rounded to conical. Soft green needles in bundles of five, 4 inches long.	4	Well-drained soil.	Slow growing. Use in foundation plantings or as a part of rock gardens. Prune after spring growth has started.
Mugo, Mountain *P. mugo*	30'	Dense; rounded, low spreading. Bright green needles in pairs, 1½ to 3 inches long.	4	Well-drained soil.	Slow growing. Use in foundation plantings. Subject to scale infestation. Prune after spring growth has started.
SPRUCE **Dwarf white** *Picea glauca 'conica'*	8'	Dense; pyramidal. Single trunk. Half-inch tufted, light green needles.	5	Well-drained soil.	Slow growing. Use in conjunction with low growing shrubs, or plant as a specimen tree. Needs no pruning.
YEW *Taxus* sp. **Irish** *T. baccata* *'fastigiata'*	15'	Dense; narrow columnar or rounded. Dark green, lustrous 1-inch needles. Also a golden variety.	7	Well-drained, slightly alkaline soil.	Upright picturesque branching. Use in hedges or screens. Fleshy red berries in the fall. Prune after spring growth has started.

CONIFEROUS SHRUBS (continued)

Shrub	Height	Shape and Foliage	Zone	Soil	Comments
Japanese *T. cuspidata*	20'	Shape depends on variety. Green, lustrous 1-inch needles.	5	Well-drained, slightly alkaline soil.	Ideal foundation, hedge, or specimen plants. Easily sheared. Red fleshy berries in the fall. Prune after spring growth has started.
Spreading English *T. baccata 'repandens'*	3'	Dense, low spreading, flat. Green, lustrous 1-inch needles.	6	Well-drained, slightly alkaline soil.	Branches slightly pendulous. Use in foundation plantings or as a ground cover. Bears fall fruit.

BROAD-LEAVED EVERGREEN SHRUBS

Shrub	Height	Foliage and Flowers	Zone	Exposure and Soil	Comments
ABELIA, GLOSSY *Abelia x grandiflora 'Edward Goucher'*	6'	Half- to 1-inch pink flowers in clusters of one to four appear in midsummer and continue until frost. Glossy green leaves turn bronzy in the fall.	6	Full sun or partial shade. Well-drained soil.	Dense and rounded shape. Often dies back in cold winter areas but will quickly resprout in spring. Prune in early spring. Use in border, foundation plantings, or small hedges. Loses leaves in cold winter areas. Hardiest of abelias.
ANDROMEDA *Pieris sp.* **Mountain, Fetterbush** *P. floribunda*	6'	Small, white fragrant flowers in drooping 4-inch clusters of three to five in the early spring. New buds form in midsummer. The shrubs are attractive year-round. Young foliage is bronze.	5	Full sun or partial shade. Well-drained, slightly acid soil.	Very showy. Use in borders or foundation plantings. Needs some protection in cold winter areas. Prune after flowers fade.
Japanese, Lily-of-the-valley bush *P. japonica*	10'	Small, white fragrant flowers in drooping 5-inch clusters of three to five in mid-spring. Foliage is bright green. Young foliage is bronze.	6	Full sun or partial shade. Well-drained, slightly acid soil.	Showy, so makes a good ornamental shrub. Use in borders, foundation plantings, or as specimen plants. Needs some protection in cold winter areas. Prune after flowers fade.
AUCUBA Japanese laurel *Aucuba japonica*	15'	Tiny violet flowers appear on the plant in March, followed by red berries in fall. Foliage is large and variegated with bright yellow markings.	8	Partial or deep shade. Moist, well-drained soil.	Both sexes needed for berry production. Needs little pruning. Use as a foundation plant or in tubs that can be brought indoors during the winter. Smog-resistant so works well in urban areas.
BARBERRY *Berberis sp.* **Black** *B. gagnepaini*	6'	Small yellow flowers cover the plant in late spring, followed by blue-black berries in the fall. Glossy green leaves on stems armed with small—but sharp—thorns.	6	Full sun or partial shade. Moist, well-drained soil.	Dense branching habit. Showy all seasons. Use in hedges or in shrub borders. Needs little pruning.

Shrubs	Height	Foliage and Flowers	Zone	Exposure and Soil	Comments
Chenault *B. x chenaulti*	4'	Tiny yellow clusters of flowers appear in mid-spring, followed by half-inch blue-black berries in the fall. Attractive glossy green, spiny-looking leaves.	7	Full sun or partial shade. Moist, well-drained soil.	Dense branching habit. Use in hedges or in shrub borders. Very effective all seasons. Needs little pruning.
Darwin's *B. darwini*	8'	Yellow-red flowers cover the plant in mid-spring, followed by purple berries in the fall. Glossy green leaves turn green-violet in the fall. Twigs are armed with thorns.	7	Full sun or partial shade. Moist, well-drained soil.	Dense branching habit. Seldom will grow over 5 feet high in home garden. Use in hedges or in shrub borders. Effective all seasons. Needs little pruning to stay looking neat.
Dwarf magellan *B. buxifolia 'nana'*	2'	Glossy green leaves on stems armed with small thorns.	6	Fun sun or partial shade. Moist, well-drained soil.	Dense branching habit. Use in low hedges, in borders, or wherever you want to separate one area from another without blocking a view. Needs little pruning.
Mentor *B. x mentorensis*	3'	Tiny yellow clusters of flowers appear in mid-spring, followed by red berries in the fall. Glossy green leaves on stems armed with small thorns.	6	Full sun or partial shade. Moist, well-drained soil.	Cold- and heat-resistant. Dense branching habit makes it good for screening. Loses some leaves during the winter in cold areas. Use in hedges or shrub borders. Needs little pruning.
Threespine *B. wisleyensis*	4'	Small whitish flowers appear in mid-spring, followed by blue-black berries in the fall. Glossy green leaves on stems armed with long three-parted spines.	6	Full sun or partial shade. Moist, well-drained soil.	Hardy and vigorous. Dense branching habit. Use in hedges or shrub borders. Needs little pruning.
Warty *B. verruculosa*	3'	Small yellow flowers appear in late spring, followed by blue-black berries in the fall that hang on through the winter. Glossy green leaves with white undersides on stems armed with thorns.	6	Full sun or partial shade. Moist, well-drained soil.	Effective all seasons. Dense branching habit. Use in hedges or shrub borders. Needs little pruning.
Wintergreen *B. julianae*	7'	Abundance of tiny yellow clusters of flowers appear in mid-spring, followed by blue-black berries in the fall. Glossy green leaves on stems armed with small thorns.	6	Full sun or partial shade. Moist, well-drained soil.	Effective all seasons. Dense branching habit. Hardy and vigorous. Use in hedges or shrub borders. Needs little pruning.
BOTTLE-BRUSH, CRIMSON *Callistemon citrinus*	25'	Four- to 8-inch, brush-like clusters of long red stamens appear in late winter and continue through the summer.	9	Full sun. Well-drained soil.	Quick growing. Use as specimen plants or in screens. Prune after flowers fade to encourage vigorous growth. Slightly pendulous branches.
BOXWOOD *Buxus* sp. **Common box** *B. sempervirens*	15' Many shorter varieties	Small, glossy green leaves. Argenteo-variegata variety has leaves spotted with white.	6	Full sun or partial shade. Moist, well-drained soil.	Many varieties. Use as specimen plants or in shrub borders. Needs winter protection in cold areas. Easily sheared but demands little pruning to look tidy.

BROAD-LEAVED EVERGREEN SHRUBS (continued)

Shrubs	Height	Foliage and Flowers	Zone	Exposure and Soil	Comments
Littleleaf box *B. microphylla*	3'	Small, glossy green leaves. Compacta and Nana are dwarf cultivars averaging 15 inches.	6	Full sun or partial shade. Moist, well-drained soil.	Easily sheared. Use as hedge plants. Some varieties turn brownish in winter but green up in spring. More cold-hardy than sempervirens varieties.
CAMELLIA *Camellia* sp. **Common** *C. japonica*	45'	Three- to 6-inch, single or double showy flowers appear in mid-fall and continue through the spring. Colors include red, pink, white, and bicolors. Attractive glossy green leaves.	8	Partial shade. Moist, rich, well-drained, acid soil.	Many varieties. Use as specimen plants or in shrub borders. Needs winter protection in cold winter areas. Needs little pruning.
Sasanqua *C. sasanqua*	15'	Two- to 4-inch, single or double showy flowers appear in early fall and continue through midwinter. Colors include white, rose, and pink. Thin, leathery, glossy green leaves.	7	Partial shade. Moist, rich, well-drained, acid soil.	Several varieties. Use as specimen plants or in shrub borders. Valued for early bloom. Needs little pruning.
COTONEASTER *Cotoneaster* sp. **Rock** *C. horizontalis*	3'	Small pink flowers appear in early summer, followed by bright red berries in early fall. Glossy green leaves. In cold winter areas, leaves turn orange in the fall and drop off. Variegata variety has leaves edged with white.	6	Well-drained, slightly alkaline soil kept on the dry side. Full sun.	Flat spreading branches. Use in rock gardens or on hard-to-plant slopes as a ground cover. Prune in early spring before new growth.
Small-leaved *C. microphyllus*	3'	Small white flowers appear in early summer, followed by red berries in the fall. Glossy green leaves.	7	Well-drained, slightly alkaline soil kept on dry side. Full sun.	Flat spreading branches. Use in rock gardens or along walls. Prune in early spring before new growth.
DAPHNE *Daphne* sp. **Burkwood** *D. x burkwoodi*	4'	Half-inch, whitish, fragrant flowers appear in mid-spring, followed by small red berries in midsummer. Leaves are gray-green. Often drops its leaves in early spring in cold winter areas.	6	Partial shade. Moist, well-drained soil.	Dense, mound-like growth habit. Does not like wet soil. Often touchy about growing conditions. Use as specimen plants or in shrub borders. Poisonous if eaten. Needs little pruning
Rose, Garland flower *D. cneorum*	1'	Small, pinkish, fragrant flowers appear in mid-spring. Leaves are gray-green. Alba variety has white flowers. Variegata variety has leaves edged in white.	5	Partial shade. Moist, well-drained soil.	Dense, mat-like growth habit. Does not like wet soil. Needs protection in winter in cold climate areas. Often touchy about growing conditions. Use in beds, borders, or rock gardens. Poisonous if eaten. Needs little pruning.
Winter *D. odora*	4'	Tiny red-violet, fragrant flowers appear in early spring. Foliage is glossy green.	7	Partial shade. Moist, well-drained soil.	Dense, mound-like growth habit. Most fragrant of the daphne species. Needs some protection in winter in cold climates. Often touchy about growing conditions. Use in beds, borders, or as a specimen plant. Poisonous if eaten. Needs little pruning.

Shrubs	Height	Foliage and Flowers	Zone	Exposure and Soil	Comments
ELAEAGNUS, THORNY *Elaeagnus pungens*	15'	Small, white, fragrant flowers in mid-fall, followed by brown, changing to red, berries in the spring. Leaves are green above, silvery beneath. Variegated forms available. Twigs are thorny.	7	Full sun or partial shade. Tolerant of most soil types.	Hardy, vigorous, and pest-free. Use in windbreaks, screens, or hedges. Easily sheared in early spring before new growth.
EUONYMUS *Euonymus* sp. **Big leaf winter creeper** *E. fortunei* 'Sarcoxie'	4'	Tiny, inconspicuous flowers in the spring, followed by pinkish seed capsules that open to reveal orange berries inside.	6	Full sun or partial shade. Tolerant of most soil types.	Will lose leaves in cold winter areas. This rambling shrub can be trained on walls or used as a ground cover. Easily pruned all year. Use in foundation plantings, rock gardens.
Evergreen, Japanese spindle tree *E. japonica*	15'	Tiny flowers in spring, followed by pinkish seed capsules. The capsules open to reveal orange berries inside. Foliage is glossy green. Varieties Albomarginata, Aureomarginata, and Aureovariegata all have leaves marked with white or yellow.	8	Full sun or partial shade. Tolerant of most soil types.	Easily sheared to any dimension. Use in foundation plantings, shrub borders, or as specimen plants. Can be pruned all year long.
Spreading *E. kiautschovica*	10'	Tiny, inconspicuous flowers in the spring, followed by pinkish seed capsules. The capsules open to reveal orange berries inside. Foliage is light glossy green.	7	Full sun or partial shade. Tolerant of most soil types.	Hardier than japonica species in cold winter parts of the country. Easily sheared any time of year. Use in foundation plantings, shrub borders, and as specimen plants.
FATSIA Japanese aralia *Fatsia japonica*	20'	One- to 2-inch, rounded white flowers appear on stalks in clusters in mid-winter, followed by small blue berries. Foliage is large, deeply cut, and glossy green. Variegata variety has leaves edged with yellow.	8	Partial to heavy shade. Rich, moist, well-drained soil.	Use in foundation plantings, shrub borders, tubs, or as specimen plants. Often used as a houseplant in the North. Prune in early spring before new growth.
FIRE THORN *Pyracantha* sp. **Gibbs** *P. atalantioides*	15'	Small white clusters of flowers in the spring, followed by bright scarlet berries in the fall and winter. Twigs are thorny. Aurea variety has gold berries.	7	Full sun. Tolerant of most soil types if kept on the dry side.	Colorful. Berries are relished by birds. Easily sheared any time. Use in borders or as specimen. Loses some leaves in cold winter parts of the country.
Scarlet *P. coccinea*	6'	Small white clusters of flowers appear in the spring, followed by bright scarlet berries in the fall and winter. Twigs are thorny. Varieties Kasan and Pauciflora have orange-red berries.	7	Full sun. Tolerant of most soil types if kept on the dry side.	Colorful. Berries are relished by birds. Easily sheared any time. Use in borders, espalier on a wall, or grow as specimen. Loses some leaves in cold winter parts of the country.
GARDENIA Cape jasmine *Gardenia jasminoides*	6'	Two- to 4-inch, very fragrant, single or double, waxy white flowers appear in mid-spring and continue through the fall. Thick, leathery, glossy dark green leaves.	8	Full sun or partial shade. Rich, moist, acid soil.	Use as specimen plants or in shrub borders and in tubs. Often used as houseplant in North. Plants need protection from excessive heat. Not as hardy as the camellia. Prune in early spring.

BROAD-LEAVED EVERGREEN SHRUBS (continued)

Shrubs	Height	Foliage and Flowers	Zone	Exposure and Soil	Comments
HEATH *Erica* sp. **Cross-leaved** *E. tetralix*	2′	Small, rose-colored flowers in 1- to 3-inch clusters appear in midsummer. Leaves are hairy, gray, and needlelike.	4	Full sun. Moist, well-drained, acid soil.	Use in beds, borders, or rock gardens. More cold-hardy than other varieties. Mulch for best results. Prune in early spring.
Darley *E. x darleyensis*	2′	Small, lilac-colored flowers appear in late fall and continue through spring. Leaves are bright green and needle-like.	6	Full sun. Moist, well-drained, acid soil.	Use in beds, borders, and rock gardens. Prune fading flower heads. More vigorous than other species. Mulch for best results.
Spring *E. carnea*	1′	Small, rose-colored flowers appear in small 1- to 3-inch clusters in early spring. Other varieties are pink, red, and white. Foliage is lustrous green and needlelike.	6	Full sun. Moist, well-drained, acid soil.	Use in beds, borders, and rock gardens. Prune after flowers fade to encourage more vigorous growth. Mulch for best results.
Twisted *E. cinerea*	2′	Small flowers in 2- to 4-inch clusters appear in early summer. Foliage is lustrous green and needlelike. Colors include rose, pink, white, and purple.	6	Full sun. Moist, well-drained, acid soil.	Use in beds, borders, and rock gardens. Not so hardy as other varieties. Mulch for best results. Prune after flowers fade to encourage more vigorous growth.
HEATHER *Calluna vulgaris*	3′	Small, single or double flowers appear in midsummer in 1- to 4-inch clusters. Many varieties. Flower colors include rose, purple, pink, white, and coral. Foliage is green or yellow, changing to bronze in the fall.	5	Full sun. Tolerant of most soil types; prefers slightly acid soil.	Use in beds, foundation plantings, rock gardens, or as a ground cover. Mulch for best results. Prune in early spring before new growth begins.
HIBISCUS, CHINESE *Hibiscus rosa-sinensis*	8′	Three- to 6-inch, single or double flowers appear in midsummer and continue for several months. Colors include white, red, pink, and yellow. Leaves are glossy green and large.	9	Full sun or partial shade. Tolerant of most soil types.	Very showy and quick growing. Needs protection from severe weather. Use as a specimen plant or in screens. Prune in early spring before new growth.
HOLLY *Ilex* sp. **Chinese** *I. cornuta*	9′	Tiny inconspicuous flowers in early summer, followed by bright red berries in the fall and winter. Leaves are glossy green with pointed tips. D'or variety has yellow berries.	7	Full sun or partial shade. Well-drained, slightly acid soil.	Female plant can produce fruit without aid of pollen. Needs little pruning; best done in early spring. Needs protection from severe weather in cold winter areas.
Japanese *I. crenata*	15′	Tiny inconspicuous flowers in early summer, followed by black berries in the fall. Leaves are small and glossy green. Convexa variety has convex leaves that resemble boxwood.	6	Full sun or partial shade. Well-drained, slightly acid soil.	Sexes are separate. Varieties for almost every garden use. Use as specimen plants, in hedges, shrub borders, or screens. Needs protection from severe weather in cold winter areas. Prune in early spring before new growth.
Long-stalk *I. pedunculosa*	15′	Tiny inconspicuous flowers in early summer, followed by bright red, drooping berries. Leaves are glossy green and spineless.	6	Full sun or partial shade. Well-drained, slightly acid soil.	Sexes are separate. More cold resistant than other varieties. Fruit is prominent and attractive. Use as specimen plants or in shrub borders.

Shrubs	Height	Foliage and Flowers	Zone	Exposure and Soil	Comments
HOLLY GRAPE Oregon grape *Mahonia aquifolium*	3'	Small clusters of yellow flowers appear in mid-spring, followed by blue-black grape-like fruits in midsummer. Leaves are glossy green and holly-like. Turns bronze in the fall. Dwarf variety, Compacta, averages 12 inches high.	6	Partial shade. Moist, well-drained soil.	Hardy and attractive. Use in shrub borders, foundation plantings or as a tall ground cover. Reproduces by underground runners. Needs protection from winter winds or foliage will either get unsightly or fall off. Prune in early spring.
LAUREL Cherry, English *Prunus laurocerasus*	18'	Small white flowers in 2- to 5-inch clusters appear in late spring, followed by blue-black berries in the fall. Glossy green leaves.	7	Full sun or partial shade. Moist, well-drained soil.	Quick growing. Use in screens, windbreaks, or hedges. Easily sheared. Use dwarf varieties in foundation plantings. Prune in early spring before new growth.
Sweet bay *Laurus nobilis*	40'	Inconspicuous white flowers appear in early summer, followed by black berries in the fall. Leaves are dark green.	7	Full sun or partial shade. Moist, well-drained soil.	Useful in formal gardens because it is easily sheared and shaped. Leaves are aromatic and used in cooking. Use in small hedges or in tubs. Prune in early spring.
Mountain, Calico bush *Kalmia latifolia*	10'	One-inch cuplike flowers appear in 3- to 6-inch clusters in early summer. Leaves are glossy green. Colors include white, pink, and rose. Variety 'Fuscata' has a purple band on the inside of each flower.	5	Partial shade. Moist, acid soil.	Very hardy and cold-resistant. Use in shrub borders or in mass plantings for effect. Needs little pruning, but it is best done after flowers fade. Clip off developing seed capsules for more vigorous growth.
LEUCOTHOE, DROOPING *Leucothoe fontanesiana*	6'	Small white, lily-of-the-valley type clusters appear along the stems in early summer. Leaves are glossy green and turn bronze in the fall.	5	Partial or deep shade. Moist, well-drained, acid soil.	Use in shrub borders and foundation plantings. Cut old canes off every spring to keep plants vigorous. Leaves drop off in cold winter areas.
MYRTLE *Myrtus communis*	15'	Half- to 1-inch white flowers appear throughout the summer, followed by blue-black berries in the fall. Leaves are deep green and aromatic. Variegata variety has leaves with white margins. Compacta variety averages 3 feet.	9	Full sun or partial shade. Well-drained soil.	Use in hot, dry situations as specimen plants, shrub borders, or hedges. Easily sheared to any dimension. Prune before new growth in the spring.
NANDINA Sacred bamboo *Nandina domestica*	8'	Small white flowers in 4- to 8-inch clusters appear in midsummer, followed by many bright red berries. Alba variety has white berries. Leaves turn red in winter areas.	7	Full sun or partial shade. Rich, moist, well-drained soil.	Cut off old stems in early spring each year. Use in foundation plantings or in shrub borders. Several plants will result in increased berry production.
OLEANDER *Nerium oleander*	20'	Two- to 3-inch, single or double fragrant flowers in early spring continue to bloom throughout the summer. Colors are red, yellow, white, rose, pink. Foliage is narrow and glossy green.	8	Full sun. Rich, moist, well-drained soil.	Tolerant of hot, dry conditions. Soot-resistant. All parts of the plant are poisonous. Can be trained to tree form. Use in tubs, shrub borders, screens, or as specimen plants.

BROAD-LEAVED EVERGREEN SHRUBS (continued)

Shrubs	Height	Foliage and Flowers	Zone	Exposure and Soil	Comments
PHOTINIA *Photinia serrulata*	40'	Small white flowers in clusters 4 to 7 inches wide appear in mid-spring, followed by red berries in the winter. Foliage is bronze when young, later turning glossy green.	7	Full sun or partial shade. Well-drained soil.	Very vigorous and hardy. Keep dry during the summer. Must be pruned back occasionally to prevent legginess. Use in shrub borders, screens, or as specimen plants.
PITTO-SPORUM, JAPANESE *Pittosporum tobira*	18'	Small white fragrant flowers appear in mid-spring. Leaves are leathery and green. Variegata has leaves variegated with white.	8	Full sun or partial shade. Tolerant of most soil types.	Very hardy and pest-resistant. Use in screens, hedges, and shrub borders. Prune after new growth begins and again later in the season.
PRIVET *Ligustrum sp.* **Chinese** *L. sinense*	12'	Small white flowers in 2- to 4-inch clusters appear in midsummer. Foliage is glossy green.	7	Full sun or partial shade. Tolerant of most soil types.	Very hardy and pest-resistant. Slower growing than other varieties. Use in screens, hedges, and shrub borders. Prune after new growth begins and again later in the season.
Glossy *L. lucidum*	30'	Small white flowers in 4- to 8-inch clusters appear in late summer, followed by blue-black berries. Tricolor variety has pale yellow leaf margins that have a pinkish hue when young.	8	Full sun or partial shade. Tolerant of most soil types.	Very hardy and pest-resistant. Use in screens, hedges, and shrub borders. Prune after new growth begins and again later in the season.
Japanese *L. japonicum*	10'	Small white flowers in 3- to 6-inch clusters appear in midsummer, followed occasionally by blue-black berries. Foliage is dark green above, light green below.	7	Full sun or partial shade. Tolerant of most soil types.	Very hardy and pest-resistant. Use in screens, hedges, and shrub borders. Prune after new growth begins and again later in the season.
RAPHIOLEPIS Indian hawthorn *Raphiolepis indica*	5'	Three-and-a-half-inch-long, dark green leaves. Pinkish half-inch flowers in loose clusters in April, followed by clusters of blue-black berries. Rosea cultivar has deep pink blooms.	9	Tolerant of most soil and light conditions.	Slow growing, so pick them flat or upright according to your landscape needs.
RHODODEN-DRON, AZALEAS *Rhododendron sp.*		(For other rhododendrons, see deciduous shrubs chart, page 134).			
Glen Dale *R. 'Glen Dale Hybrid'*	5'	One- to 3-inch, single or double flowers cover the plant in spring. Foliage is glossy green. Many colors. Over 400 varieties.	7	Partial shade. Well-drained, acid soil.	Dense and spreading. Use in beds, foundation plantings, shrub borders, or in mass plantings display. Cut off fading flowers for more vigorous flowering the next year. Keep mulched for best results.
Indica *R. indicum*	6'	Two- to 4-inch clusters of flowers cover the plant in early summer. Foliage is glossy green. Many varieties ranging in color from pink to violet.	6	Partial shade. Well-drained, acid soil.	Dense and spreading. Use in beds, foundation plantings, shrub borders, or in mass plantings for display. Cut off fading flowers for more vigorous flowering the next year. Keep mulched for best results.

Shrubs	Height	Foliage and Flowers	Zone	Exposure and Soil	Comments
Kaempferi Hybrid R. 'Kaempferi Hybrid'	6'	Two- to 3-inch single flowers cover the plant in spring. Foliage is glossy green. All colors. Many varieties.	7	Partial shade. Well-drained, acid soil.	Dense and spreading. Use in beds, foundation plantings, shrub borders, or in mass plantings for colorful display. Cut off fading flowers for more vigorous flowering the next year. Keep mulched for best results.
Kurume R. 'Kurume Hybrid'	3'	Half- to one-inch, single or double flowers in clusters of two to four cover the plant in spring. Foliage is glossy green. Many colors. Almost 50 varieties.	7	Partial shade. Well-drained, acid soil.	Low growing and bushy. Use in beds, foundation plantings, shrub borders, or rock gardens. Cut off fading flowers for more vigorous flowering the next year. Keep mulched for best results.
RHODODEN-DRON, RHO-DODENDRON Rhododendron sp. **Carolina** R. carolinianum	6'	Three-inch clusters of rose-violet flowers cover the plant in mid-spring. Leaves are glossy green above with brown undersides. Album variety has white flowers.	6	Full sun or partial shade. Rich, moist, well-drained, acid soil.	Dense and mound-like. Earlier to bloom than other varieties. Use in beds, foundation plantings, shrub borders, or in mass plantings for display. Cut off fading flowers for more vigorous flowering the next year. May need winter protection in some areas. Leaf edges curl under when cold. Keep mulched for best results.
Catawba R. catawbiense	10'	Four- to 6-inch clusters of lilac-colored flowers often spotted with green in early summer. Leaves are glossy green. Album variety has white flowers. Many hybrid varieties in mixed colors, bicolors, and pastels.	5	Partial shade. Rich, moist, well-drained, acid soil.	Dense and spreading. Very hardy and showy. Best hybrid rhododendron varieties. Use in beds, foundation plantings, shrub borders, or in mass plantings for display. Cut off fading flowers for more vigorous flowering the next year. May need winter protection in some areas. Leaf edges curl under when cold. Keep mulched for best results.
Fortune's R. fortunei	12'	Three- to 4-inch clusters of rose-violet flowers in late spring. Leaves are glossy green. Many hybrid varieties in red and pink shades.	6	Partial shade. Rich, moist, well-drained, acid soil.	Very showy. Use in beds, foundation plantings, shrub borders, or in mass plantings for display. Cut off fading flowers for more vigorous flowering the next year. May need winter protection in some colder areas of the zone. Leaf edges curl under when cold. Keep mulched for best results.
Rosebay, Great laurel R. maximum	15'	Four- to 6-inch clusters of red-violet flowers often spotted with green in late spring. Leaves are glossy green.	4	Partial to deep shade. Well-drained, acid soil.	Not as showy as other varieties. Use as background plants in shrub borders or mass plantings. Cut off fading flowers for more vigorous flowering the next year. Leaf edges curl under when cold. Keep mulched for best results.

BROAD-LEAVED EVERGREEN SHRUBS (continued)

Shrubs	Height	Foliage and Flowers	Zone	Exposure and Soil	Comments
Smirnow *R. smirnowi*	10'	Five- to 6-inch clusters of rose-pink flowers, often frilled, appear in late spring. Leaves are glossy green above with fuzzy white undersides.	6	Partial shade. Well-drained, acid soil.	Hardy. Densely branching. Use in beds, foundation plantings, shrub borders, or in mass plantings for display. Cut off fading flowers for more vigorous flowering the next year. Leaf edges curl under when cold. Keep mulched for best results.
ROSEMARY *Rosmarinus officinalis*	4'	Half- to 1-inch fragrant violet flowers cover the plant in late winter and early spring. Leaves are glossy green with a pleasant aroma. Trailing variety, Prostratus, averages 6 inches high.	7	Full sun. Tolerant of most soil types.	Use in beds, shrub borders, and hedges. Needs little pruning. Keep on the dry side to prevent rapid, spindly growth.
SKIMMIA *Skimmia* sp. **Japanese** *S. japonica*	5'	Tiny, fragrant white flowers in 2- to 4-inch clusters appear in mid-spring, followed by bright red berries that cling through winter.	8	Partial shade. Rich, moist, well-drained soil.	Use in foundation plantings or shrub borders. Plant at least two for maximum berry production. Needs little pruning.
Reeves *S. reevesiana*	6'	Tiny, fragrant white flowers in 1- to 3-inch clusters appear in mid-spring, followed by red berries that cling through winter.	9	Partial shade. Rich, moist, well-drained soil.	Dense and compact. Use in foundation plantings or shrub borders. Plant at least two for maximum berry production. Needs little pruning.
VIBURNUM *Viburnum* sp. **Laurustinus** *V. tinus*	10'	Small pinkish flowers appear in late winter, followed by shiny blue berries in midsummer, gradually turning black. Leaves are glossy green.	7	Partial shade. Well-drained soil, kept dry.	Use in hedges and screens. Berries are relished by birds. Keep plants dry after midsummer to harden new growth. Prune in early spring before new growth.
Leatherleaf *V. rhytidophyllum*	10'	Small yellowish flowers appear in 4- to 8-inch clusters in spring, followed by red berries, gradually turning black in the fall. Leaves are glossy green and crinkled.	6	Partial shade. Rich, moist, well-drained soil.	Use in shrub borders, screens, or as a specimen plant. Berries are relished by birds. Keep mulched for best growth. Plant in a protected location to prevent winter winds from drying leaves. Loses some leaves in cold winter areas. Keep plants dry after midsummer to harden new growth. Prune in early spring before new growth.
Sweet *V. odoratissimum*	20'	Small white fragrant flowers appear in 4- to 8-inch clusters in spring, followed by red berries, gradually turning black in the fall. Leaves are glossy green.	8	Partial shade. Rich, moist, well-drained soil.	Use in shrub borders or screens. Berries are relished by birds. Keep mulched for best growth. Keep plants dry after midsummer to harden new growth. Prune in early spring before new growth.
XYLOSMA, SHINY *Xylosma congestum*	15'	Small yellow-green leaves that are bronzy when young.	8	Full sun or partial shade. Tolerant of most soil types.	Can be trained to tree form. Useful in hot, dry areas. Easily sheared to any dimension. Use in shrub borders or hard-to-plant hot areas.

How to Plant Shrubs

Shrubs are the ideal solution to many landscaping needs. But carefully consider *their* needs—sun or shade, wet or dry soil, pruning requirements, winter protection, and the like.

After you pick a site that's suitable, you're ready to plant. Set shrubs out in either spring or fall.

Bare-root shrubs. Make the planting hole slightly larger than the root area for bare-root shrubs. Keep roots moist until you're ready to set the plant in the ground. Place the shovel handle across the hole to help determine when the plant is at the proper depth. It should be a little deeper than it grew before being moved.

Backfill the hole halfway with the soil, then tamp it lightly around the roots. Fill the planting hole with water. Let the water soak in and then refill the hole with soil.

Balled - and - burlapped or container-grown. Although they are more expensive than bare-root plants, balled-and-burlapped and container-grown shrubs—particularly evergreens—are less disturbed by planting and thus start growing much faster.

Make the width of the hole a foot wider than the ball and about as deep. Loosen tight soil at the bottom of the hole. Then grasp the ball and carefully lower the plant into the hole. Center the

plant and tuck soil under the ball if needed to straighten the plant. Loosen burlap only at the trunk. The burlap will decay rapidly and will not interfere with root development. If the rootball is wrapped in plastic or in an asphalt or cardboard container, carefully cut away the covering after the shrub is positioned in the hole. The staff at the nursery or garden center can help you make slits in a metal container. Remove the *metal* container *before* positioning the plant in the hole. Backfill the hole as for bare-root shrubs, above.

New shrub care. Leave a shallow depression around the trunk to catch water in months ahead. Give the newly planted shrub a thorough soaking with a hose. Water deeply again in a couple of days.

Trim the plant back to one-fourth its original height if it is to be sheared, one-half if informal. Shear evergreens enough to make them uniform. Add mulch around the base to within an inch or two of the trunk.

Moving mature shrubs during summer months

The best time to build a patio, add a much-needed room to the house, or install off-street parking may *not* be the best time to move a shrub. So what do you do with the shrub growing right in the middle of the construction site?

It can be moved safely and with a minimum of shock in the heat of midsummer. In fact, this is a better time than earlier in the season. A shrub lifted in *early* summer will have more tender foliage.

A few days before transplanting, use a sharp spade and sink its blade completely into the ground in a circle around the shrub. A small shrub should have a circle with a 12-inch radius.

(At least 18 inches for larger shrubs.) Some of the roots will be cut in the process, so also trim off the soft, tender tips of all branches.

As a protective step, you may want to spray the shrub with an antidessicant, available at many garden centers. (It is relatively expensive, so you may want to eliminate this step.) Allow the spray to dry before digging the shrub. The thin film will hold moisture in the plant and help to avoid the stress of wilting and loss of roots.

Shape roots and surrounding soil into a ball by undercutting lower roots. When the ball is free and can be rocked to one side, use a wide strip of burlap to wind around the ball and hold the soil during moving. Use nails to hold the burlap to the soil. Fasten top with twine.

The balled-and-burlapped shrub—even a small one—is heavy, so extra help will be needed to get the plant out of the hole. If the shrub is large, slide a board under the ball and weight the free end to raise the plant.

Move the shrub to a shady spot protected from the wind. Spray the burlap with water and cover it with a plastic sheet to keep the roots from drying. Remove plastic before planting.

Planting the mature shrub is nearly the same as planting other balled-and-burlapped shrubs, a process described on this page. Let the burlap remain on the rootball after it's placed in the planting hole, but remove the twine fastening. Fill the hole with soil and water as before.

For the next two weeks, cool the plant daily during hot weather with a light mist from the garden hose. Avoid over-watering the newly transplanted shrub. Once a week is enough.

Euonymus, viburnum, mock orange, and privet shrubs all transplant well in the summer. Evergreens cannot be moved safely until the new spring growth has matured.

Dig the planting hole slightly larger than the root area. Put a tarp or plastic next to the hole, and place soil on it to make refilling and cleanup easier.

Keep a bare-root shrub moist until set in the ground. Plant a little deeper than it grew before being moved. A shovel across the hole helps determine planting depth.

If the plant is in an asphalt or cardboard container, place it in the hole before removing container. Cut away sides.

How to Prune Shrubs

The best time to prune is late winter or early spring before leaves or flowers appear. Early pruning allows you to study branch framework before it is hidden by foliage.

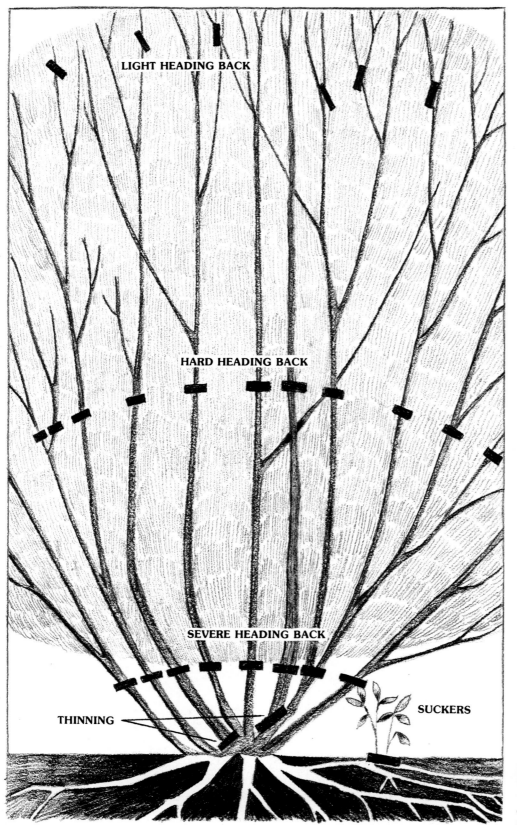

LIGHT HEADING BACK

HARD HEADING BACK

SEVERE HEADING BACK

THINNING

SUCKERS

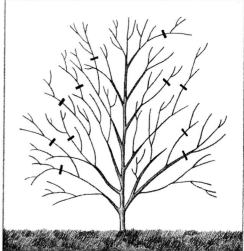

Heading back is the removal of branch tips. Use to reduce size, increase bloom, and control shape of a mature plant. Make cut directly above a strong bud.

Thinning means removal of a limb back to the ground or main branch. Use to control size. Thinning tends to make plants more airy, less dense.

The first step is to remove deadwood. Broken branches and weak, spindly growth also should be trimmed. This protective pruning is all that you need to do—as far as the plant's health is concerned. It may be enough to please the eye, too. Additional trimming should be done only to modify the plant in one of the ways mentioned on this page.

The first flush of spring growth helps pruning scars heal quickly. Trim shrubs a little each year. Annual attention will keep them shapely, sound, and attractive.

Prune shrubs that flower in the spring immediately after blooms have begun to fade. This is called *light heading back*. Remove one-fourth of top growth—about ten to 12 inches—over the crown and sides. Heading stimulates side-branching so the plant grows more compactly.

Shrubs with many twiggy branches benefit from a *hard heading back* or heavy pruning deep into the crown. To keep the plant groomed, remove one-fourth of the branches each year by cutting back half their length.

Some shrubs, such as the hills-of-snow and peegee hydrangeas, as well as the red-osier dogwoods, give peak performance when shrubs are severely headed back almost to the ground each year.

Thinning involves removal of old limbs flush with the base of the shrub. Old shrubs can be rejuvenated with planned thinning; the process will span three years. Cut out about one-third of the oldest canes each year. You'll have a productive plant with all new growth the third year. Remove all stubs that might prevent the shrub from healing completely.

To rejuvenate an old plant: if it is a bushy plant with many limbs growing from the ground, cut out a third of the older branches at soil level each year.

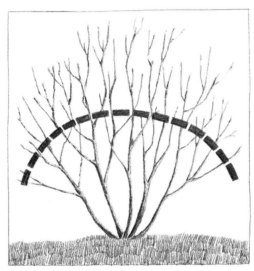

To increase flower size: severe heading back of branches stimulates production of a few strong stems with fewer, but larger, flowers.

To remove suckers: remove suckers unless the new growth is needed to rejuvenate the plant. Dig away soil and cut sucker off where attached to root.

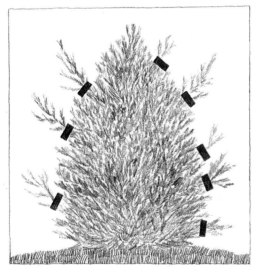

To keep plant symmetrical: fir, spruce, and some junipers are naturally symmetrical. Prune to accentuate natural form. Cut off wayward shoots as they appear.

To keep growth dense: clipping shoots stimulates limbs to produce additional growing points—usually two for one. Use a knife or hand pruners.

To keep plants small: all pruning tends to reduce the size of plants. Either heading or thinning may be used, depending on the shape you want the plant to have.

Special pruning tips: winter-tender shrubs

Winter-tender shrubs, such as abelia, tamarisk, and butterfly bush, kill back to the ground annually in some areas. All three are semi-hardy in temperate climates but need shelter near a wall to avoid permanent damage from cold northwest winds.

Abelia. The grandiflora hybrid is the hardiest abelia and can be grown as far north as New York City. Used as an informal hedge, abelia's graceful

Winter-tender shrubs, such as tamarisk, abelia, and butterfly bush, die back to the ground in some areas. Remove old tops. New sprouts will grow from roots.

Some shrubs, such as hills-of-snow hydrangea, need severe pruning. Cut as desired for bloom. High cuts give more flowers; low give larger flowers.

beauty is retained with only selective thinning.

Prune abelias in April. They develop flowers on new growth. Cut off all growth showing damage that occurred during the winter. Look for crowded stems and cut out a third of them almost to the ground. On mature shrubs, cut out some of the oldest wood to stimulate young wood that flowers well.

If abelia is killed to the ground by a severe winter, cut off all dead branches to near the soil surface. New shoots will grow when the weather warms. In the coldest areas, where killing back is even more severe, the entire shrub should be cut to within several inches of the ground late in the fall and mulched well as soon as ground has a frozen crust.

Buddleia. The alternifolia species or fountain butterfly bush usually doesn't die to the ground like other buddleia. To encourage new growth for next season's bloom, remove some of the oldest canes immediately after flowers have faded in the spring. To keep large plants vigorous, remove up to a third of the oldest canes each year. Leave four- or five-inch stubs with at least two buds.

The *Buddleia davidi* (summer lilac or orange-eye butterfly bush) is another popular butterfly bush. This one does tend to be killed to the ground by most winters, so cut bushes back near to the soil level and allow two buds on each stub. As soon as new shoots have grown a couple of feet, thin out the youngest ones, saving the most vigorous. Then pinch the tips off those shoots remaining. In very cold areas, mound up soil eight or more inches around the base to protect buds near the ground level. Remove the mounds in spring and cut back tops several inches when the danger of frost has passed.

Tamarisk. The ramosissima species develops its flowers on a current season's growth, so prune plants severely to a few inches in early spring, while the plant is dormant. Head back to keep the shrub within the scale of your landscape design and to avoid a bare, open base. Clip flowers off immediately after they bloom.

Pruning evergreens

Pruning evergreens is a more methodical, less creative job than pruning other plants. You can snip and trim a deciduous shrub (knowing you're stimulating growth), but an enthusiastic cut of the wrong evergreen branch could mean a gaping hole in the tree for several years.

Once branches are removed, they are, at best, partially replaced. Only when plants become uneven, scraggly, diseased, injured, or winter-killed, should you approach the shrub with shears or clippers in hand to begin a careful manicure.

Most conifers can be placed in two groups: those pruned after new growth is started—such

as pines, firs, spruces, and hemlocks—and those pruned before new growth—junipers, arborvitae, and yews. Pruning of both types of conifers should be limited to correcting defects and cutting branch tips to insure symmetry and compact growth.

Begin when plants are young, then attend to them regularly—but lightly. One sudden shearing can make evergreens look as if they've had butch haircuts. Avoid cutting out lower branches unless they're dead or diseased. Evergreens look top-heavy if trunks are left bare and they seldom fill in—even after several years. Necessary pruning of lower branches can be camouflaged by ground covers, shorter shrubs that tolerate shade, or annual and perennial flowers.

Pruning of yews and hemlocks usually can be handled with hedge shears. Trim only to reinforce or retain the natural contours of the plant. In most years, you'll need only to cut back new, long shoots. Spruces and firs form natural pyramidal outlines. Remove terminal buds on main branches as soon as they appear. This helps laterals to grow and strengthens weak branches.

Pines probably require the least pruning of all evergreens because they are informal and don't demand shearing to look well-kept. Prune when new growth (called "candles") is most vigorous —before it hardens. Cutting candles on main branches to half their length forces laterals, creating a fuller plant. Junipers make dense, new growth in spring and should be pruned before this time. They require only light trimming, and it should be done in a "shingling" fashion. That is, the top branches of spreading junipers should be trimmed so that they don't overhang the lower branches.

Narrow-leaved evergreens of proper size and shape need only light shearing to keep them neat. To reduce size or retrain, use hand pruners or a knife.

Basic tools for pruning shrubs

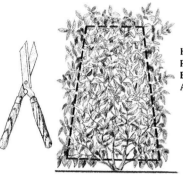

Honeysuckle
Privet
Boxwood
Alpine currant

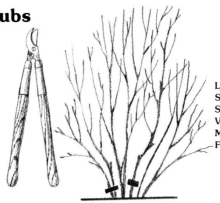

Lilac
Shrub roses
Spirea
Viburnum
Mock orange
Forsythia

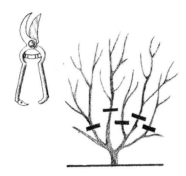

Bush roses
Shrub althaea
Peegee hydrangea
Red-osier dogwood

Above: Formal hedge plants may need several shearings with hedge clippers in a year's time. Clip out-of-place twigs as they appear.

Upper right: Cut out dead, broken, or diseased canes on those shrubs listed by illustration. Use loppers as marked.

Right: Shrubs like these can stand severe pruning with shears. Cut to side branches or buds to stimulate new growth.

Pointers on pruning lilacs

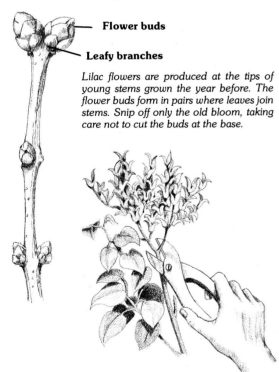

Flower buds

Leafy branches

Lilac flowers are produced at the tips of young stems grown the year before. The flower buds form in pairs where leaves join stems. Snip off only the old bloom, taking care not to cut the buds at the base.

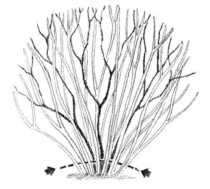

To keep lilacs vigorous or renew an old bush, prune them every few years. Cut a few of the oldest stems (dark in sketch) close to the soil. Remove weak growth. Leave a few vigorous suckers each year.

Clip off seeds when bloom is over. This improves appearance and conserves the plant's energy. Thin out old stems, too. A little pruning each year means the shrub will have both old stems to produce blooms and new stems for strong growth.

When and how to prune all-time favorite shrubs

Althaea *(Hibiscus syriacus* or rose-of-sharon): Needs only light pruning unless you want larger flowers. Then cut back previous season's growth to two buds in winter.

Amur privet: Can be pruned during winter in warm areas, early spring elsewhere. To rejuvenate, cut older woody shoots to ground.

Barberry: Thin and shape as needed in early spring.

Bridal-wreath spirea *(Spiraea prunifolia):* Blossoms appear on last year's wood, so prune after flowers fade in spring. Rejuvenate each year by removing oldest stems.

Chinese hibiscus: In areas where the plant isn't winter-killed to the ground, remove a third of the old wood in early spring.

Cotoneaster: Early spring is the time to remove old shoots and to head back others.

Deutzia: Best pruned after flowering. Head back, remove weak shoots, and thin older ones.

Fire thorn (or pyracantha): Prune to control and shape. In early spring, cut off fruited branches.

Forsythia: Thin out older branches to ground level after spring blooming.

French hydrangea *(Hydrangea macrophylla):* Blossoms bloom on second-year wood, so don't cut unflowered shoots. Wait until after flowering in late spring to clip.

Honeysuckle: Shrubs can be trimmed after spring flowering. Thin out older branches to ground.

Mock orange: Can be headed back and old canes thinned after spring blooms fade.

Mountain laurel: Stands heavy pruning. Clip after spring flowering.

Rhododendrons: Should be cut just above the tiny, leafy branches in winter or spring (in mild climates) or after frost (in harsh). For the largest flowers next year, trim just after blooms die this year.

Weigela: Needs heavy pruning to keep in bounds. Trim back stems that have flowered to unflowered side branches. Cut old wood to ground. Do light pruning in mid-summer.

chapter 6

VINES

Sentimental songs (with lines such as "Tell me why the ivy twines") or daydreams of vine-covered cottages may be romantic, but they limit the potential of versatile vines. Vines can act as earth-hugging ground covers or can extend garden space upward—perhaps somewhat short of Jack's fabulous beanstalk—but high enough to screen an ugly view, provide shade, privacy, or soften a bare chain link fence. When garden space is cramped, the only way to go is up. Vines, such as nasturtium, will wind leisurely skyward, providing a wealth of color as they go. And they demand only minimal care.

For knockout glamour year after year, try wisteria—in violet, blue, purple, pink, red, or white (opposite page). It's hardy and blooms well in all but the coldest climates. For best flowering, shorten the rambling side shoots annually. A woody and vigorous twiner, the wisteria may reach 50 feet. After a few years, it can become so big and heavy it needs a strong support.

Another choice, Henryi clematis, with outsize white flowers measuring six or seven inches across, makes a grand show alone or mixed with shorter beauties. The clematis grows elegantly in a smidgen of soil in front of a divider screen. It's used mostly to provide graceful and colorful decoration, rather than dense shading. Other delightful decorators are fire thorn (a bonus of bright berries) and English ivy (a rich, dark background for other flowers). To cover, try five-leaf akebia, star jasmine, Boston or Japanese ivy, or winter creeper.

How they climb, when they can be planted, what special needs they have—all make a big difference when you're deciding where to put which vine. This chapter will help you find a vine you can support.

How to Select a Vine

Vines can wreath a trellis, scale a fence, prevent soil erosion, brighten a drab corner, and much more. They take up little ground space when they have a support to twine around or climb. There's a vast array of annuals and perennials available.

Versatile vines are functional, lovely, and easy to grow. Some grow so quickly they become pests if they're not pruned regularly or contained with borders. Others become so heavy with blooms or fruit they need sturdy support.

Like shrubs, their rapid, lush growth makes vines a valuable part of your landscape design. But although shrubs grow quickly, vines grow more quickly—both vertically (if provided a support) or horizontally (if permitted to sprawl as a ground cover).

Vines can also be the least expensive feature in your yard. A pinch of seeds or a few small plants can fill spaces or disguise eyesores in a single season. Vines make attractive stand-ins, adding a finished look to your yard until slower growing trees or shrubs fill out.

Consider the vine. Selection depends on soil, light, space, and temperature needs as well as on your preferences. (See chart on pages 163 to 169 for hints.)

Vines have three basic habits: twining, climbing by tendrils or leaf stalks, and climbing by disks or small roots. Check pages 160 and 161 to find out which vines will twine or wind on their own and which must be tied in order to cover a trellis or arbor.

Some so-called vines are really shrubs with long, supple branches that can be tied into place. Rambler roses (see Chapter 10) are one example.

Perennial vines, like trees, can be evergreen or deciduous (losing their leaves). Use evergreen vines to shield north walls in winter. Try deciduous vines to shade west walls from summer sun; they also allow sunlight to reach walls during the winter, when you need warmth.

Consider the use. Choose vines with your landscape design in mind. Supports, such as fences, trellises, and arbors, are parts of the design. Be sure the support harmonizes with the architectural plan of your home. Then, select the vine.

Plain supports—free of complicated designs or bright colors—are inconspicuous, thus permitting the plants and house to blend without distraction. Strings, dowels, and hooks attached to fences or walls can also be used as simple supports. Wire is sturdier than string, but in direct sun, it can heat up and kill young shoots.

The charts on pages 163 to 169 indicate strengths—heat or shade tolerance, for example, of the

Semi-shrubby vines, such as winter creeper, are good for framing doorways where space is limited. They cling to wall by sturdy rootlets and need pruning once a year.

Vines, such as grapes, gourds, and beans, can screen unsightly views or serve as backdrops for flowers. Simple supports won't detract from plain, bold leaves.

Evergreen and dense vines, such as English ivy, do well on north walls. They need little care. Prune to keep them away from windows. Don't use on wood siding.

climbers, twiners, and creepers. You'll find some weaknesses mentioned, too. A few vines can tolerate direct sun—bittersweet, honeysuckle, actinidia, trumpet creeper, wisteria. However, both bittersweet and honeysuckle, for example, though useful as heat-tolerant vines, quickly become a pest when treated as a ground cover if they're not pruned or contained by a driveway or wall. Otherwise, they can engulf shrubs and trees.

Where space is cramped or narrow, vines often are the answer. Many give a full, textured effect without needing much ground space. Whether you have a tiny planting pocket or a wide open space to fill, remember the texture of the vine's foliage. Bold wisteria or gourds shade the house or garden from hot afternoon sun; clematis or cardinal climber daintily accent an entrance. Often vines are richest in either flowers or foliage. Try mixing two kinds of vines, one for blooms, one for leaves.

Vines vary in density of foliage, too. Some provide a solid cover; others are more open. The lighter vines can be used as decorative patterns to break up the blankness of a wall or fence or to add color to a mesh fence.

Vines with fragrant blooms accent patios, porches, or windows. But vines with fruits that fall or attract flies should be placed farther from the house.

Coral vine, silver-lace vine, and other lacy vines informally accent a doorway. Clip to keep thick. They grow faster than winter creeper but need support.

A leafy frame, provided here by twining vines, can be duplicated with clematis, honeysuckle, black-eyed susan, or any good trellis vine. Nip back from window.

Deciduous and airy, Boston ivy gives good autumn color before leaves fall. It is a dependable vine for walls, grows well in partial shade, and is winter-hardy.

Don't limit a retaining wall treatment to free-growing vines. Here, English ivy is trained to formal pattern with wires. It needs less care than a hedge.

How to Train a Vine

First, decide what you want a vine to do—shade, screen, brighten with color. Then pick the type of vine and support to fit the setting. This page shows how to direct your plants upward using plain and simple devices.

Your garden's social climbers and clinging vines have characteristics that determine how they should be supported and trained. Vines that cling with adhesive disks and root-like holdfasts, for example, attach to wooden walls and damage the wood. Use chicken wire or chain link fencing instead to keep vine and wall separated.

Many fast-growing vines grow sparsely at the bottom, then branch out with foliage near the top. Avoid this stringy appearance by winding the leggy part around a support near the ground or by running it back and forth parallel to the ground until the lower part of the support is filled in. Lateral shoots then grow upward for a full look.

Chicken wire is an inexpensive way to hold vines. Thread a rod through the wire and support it from hooks in eaves or rafters. It keeps vines from wood siding.

Chain link fencing makes a durable trellis that will be quickly covered by tendril vines, such as clematis. Train the vine horizontally first, then vertically.

Design your own simple wood trellis from straight bamboo sticks fastened with small plant ties of plastic- or paper-covered wire.

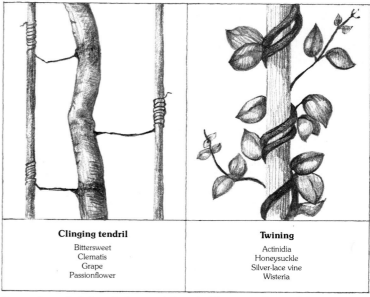

Clinging tendril	Twining
Bittersweet	Actinidia
Clematis	Honeysuckle
Grape	Silver-lace vine
Passionflower	Wisteria

Some vines climb by winding tendrils or leaflike appendages. Others climb by twining their stems around any slender support—string, wire, stake, or trellis.

How to Start a Vine

Perennial vines are often sold in pots, but you can grow your own. Best planting times are early spring or autumn. Most annual vines can be easily grown from seed—indoors or out, depending on days to maturation.

Perennial vines. Easy-care, hardy perennials reward you year after year with blooms or lush foliage. The plants are usually sold in containers through garden centers or mail order catalogues.

To "do it yourself" when starting perennial vines, root stem cuttings in water or a nonorganic rooting medium. Water-grown roots are more brittle and easy to break in potting than those started in nonorganic material, such as perlite or vermiculite.

Use a sharp knife to take a section four to six inches long from a mature vine. Cut just below a point where leaf joins stem; roots develop best there. Remove lower leaves so the bottom inch or two of the cutting is bare. Fill a clean clay pot with evenly moistened vermiculite, perlite, or sand and insert stem end. Water and keep in a cool, light place. Roots appear in three to six weeks.

If cuttings tend to wilt, enclose the pot and stem in a plastic bag. Use a rubber band to hold the bag in place. It's easily removed when the pot needs moisture.

Whether the young vine is homegrown or purchased, transplant it outdoors following the same procedure. Dig and break up clods to a depth of eight to ten inches. Add peat or another amendment if the soil is clayey. Carefully knock the plant out of its container and set it in the hole.

Fill the hole, firm soil lightly, and water. Tie the main stem to a stake, or tape it to a wall. Apply plant food after new growth appears.

Shrub or climbing roses, often treated as vines, are available in bare-root, container-grown, or balled-and-burlapped form. (See Chapter 5, "Shrubs," for planting hints.)

Annual vines. Indoors or out—where to start seeds for annual vines depends on how long they take to mature. Information on the seed packet should tell you this. Count back from the first expected frost in your zone to figure when the seeds should be planted. If maturation takes a long time, brighten winter days by pressing seeds barely under moist soil in little pots and paper cups or into peat pellets. Later, when the danger of frost is past, harden the seedlings by moving them outdoors for several hours a day before setting them into the ground.

If you're in a warm zone or if the vine matures quickly, the seeds can be sown directly into the ground.

Use a sharp knife to take a cutting four to six inches long. Cut just below point where leaf joins stem; roots develop best there. Remove lower leaves.

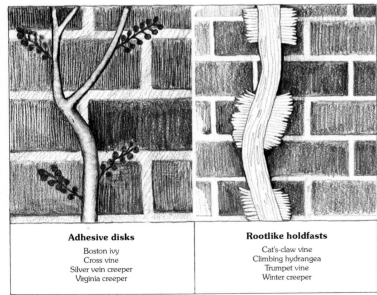

Adhesive disks

Boston ivy
Cross vine
Silver vein creeper
Virginia creeper

Rootlike holdfasts

Cat's-claw vine
Climbing hydrangea
Trumpet vine
Winter creeper

The adhesive disks, or suction cups, attach to a smooth surface. Rootlike holdfasts attach to dry crevices. To hold on, they grow longer.

Fill pot with evenly moistened vermiculite, perlite, or sand. Insert bare stem ends. After about three weeks, remove a cutting to check for roots.

Annual Vines

Transform a "ho-hum" corner of your yard to "wow!" with annual vines. Their life cycles are just a season long, so let your imagination run free from year to year. Annuals make blooming summer fillers.

Annual vines with a lengthy growing season must be started indoors, so sturdy little seedlings can be hardened, then popped into prepared soil when it's free of frost. Plants that mature quickly can be sown directly in your border, garden, or special spot. Don't sow seeds too close together; thinning can damage the roots of remaining plants if the roots are entwined.

After several sets of leaves appear, pinch back tops to force side branching. To extend blooming, clip off flowers as soon as they fade.

Beautify a trellis with the button-bright flowers of the black-eyed susan.

Climbing garden nasturtiums clamber over walls, fences, and slopes along steps.

Grow sweet peas for cutting.

Cathedral bells demand lots of space.

Morning-glories are favorites.

Moonflowers open at night.

Cardinal climbers have showy flowers and leaves to provide color all summer.

ANNUAL VINES

Vine	Fruit and Flower Habit	Comments
BALLOON VINE *Cardiospermum halicacabum*	Inconspicuous white flowers. Balloon-shaped seedpods.	Ideal for screens or trellises. Needs sun. An annual in the North; perennial in the Southeast. Easily grown from seeds, but self-sows in mild zones.
BALSAM APPLE *Momordica balsamina*	Three-inch orange, gourd-like fruit and 1- to 4-inch yellow blossoms.	Large dark green foliage good for screening and fences. Warty fruit produced only in areas with long hot summers; bursts open at maturity. Needs rich, moist soil. A high-climbing vine that clings by tendrils. Needs sun.
BALSAM PEAR *Momordica charantia*	One- to 8-inch gourd-like fruit and small yellow blossoms.	(See balsam apple.) More ornamental than balsam apple because has larger, deeply lobed leaves and grows up to 30 feet long in one season. Fruit is red inside. Vine makes quick-growing cover for screens and porches. Needs sun.
BLACK-EYED SUSAN *Thunbergia alata*	Yellow, orange, or white daisy-like blossoms with purple throats. Blooms throughout the summer.	A twining vine that is also good for ground cover or in hanging baskets. Will grow in sun or shade but requires ample moisture. Temperatures below 50° Fahrenheit may kill. Needs a long growing season.
CANARY-BIRD FLOWER *Tropaeolum peregrinum*	Small feathery yellow flowers in summer.	Thrives in poor soil but needs moisture. Also needs some shade. Prefers cool nights. Grows quickly up to 10 feet long to cover a trellis.
CARDINAL CLIMBER *Ipomoea x multifida*	Two-inch crimson, morning-glory-like flowers all summer.	Deeply lobed leaves. Can grow up to 20 feet long in full sun or partial shade. Needs well-drained sandy soil. A twining vine.
CATHEDRAL BELLS **Cup-and-saucer vine** *Cobaea scandens*	Purple bell-shaped flowers are 2 inches across. Blooms in spring and summer last for six months.	Popular ornamental in the South. Grows rapidly. Clings by tendrils. Can take some shade.
CHINESE FORGET-ME-NOT *Cynoglossum amabile*	Small pale blue blossoms in late spring.	Good for border plantings. Will grow in sun or shade and in wet or dry soil. Best where summers are hot and dry. Grows quickly from seed so need not be started indoors. Make consecutive plantings for continuous bloom. Plants often self-sow and can become a nuisance.
CRIMSON STAR-GLORY *Mina lobata*	Crimson, morning-glory-like flowers. Somewhat larger than scarlet star-glories (see page 164).	Has deeply lobed leaves. When bloom opens, changes from crimson to creamy yellow and orange. Can climb to 20 feet. Twines. Good in sun or some shade.
CYPRESS VINE *Ipomoea quamoclit*	Star-shaped red or white flowers all summer.	Has delicate foliage so does not provide good shade. Is attractive on trellis. Grows to 20 feet long. Takes full sun or partial shade.
FLAME FLOWER *Tropaeolum speciosum*	Scarlet flowers in summer.	(See canary-bird flower.) Showy bloom. Grows quickly from seed so seeds can be planted outdoors.
HYACINTH BEAN *Dolichos lablab*	Purple or white pealike flowers in summer.	Grows rapidly up to 15 to 30 feet. In colder zones, plant in a warm sunny place. Good for climbing a fence or trellis. Many cultivars available. Sometimes called Indian or Egyptian bean.

ANNUAL VINES (continued)

Vine	Fruit and Flower Habit	Comments
JAPANESE HOP VINE *Humulus japonicus*	Fruit resembles hops used in beer-making. Variegatus cultivar has leaves splashed with white.	Will twine on almost anything. Grown for its lush green foliage. Good for screens, porches, and fences. Prefers sun and ample moisture. Can become a pest because it will self-seed.
MARBLE VINE *Diplocyclos palmatus*	Marble-size green fruits change to amber with white stripes in summer.	Good for screening purposes. Grows quickly. Climbs by tendrils. Grow as an ornamental or arbor vine. Leaves are three- to five-lobed. Prefers sun.
MAURANDIA *Asarina barclaiana*	Three-inch white, lilac, or purple flowers in late summer.	A showy vine. Use as a hedge or screen, or plant in a hanging basket. Needs full sun. A perennial in warm zones; an annual in cool.
MOONFLOWER *Ipomoea alba*	Fragrant white flowers that open at dusk and close by noon the next day.	Ideal for screening purposes. Grows rapidly. Prefers full sun. Large heart-shaped leaves. If soil is too rich or fertile, the vine will produce leaves but not blooms.
MORNING-GLORY *Ipomoea purpurea*	Purple, blue, scarlet, pink, or white flowers usually blooming from dawn to noon. Thrive in sunny spot.	Very popular annual vine. Flowers profusely. Good for hedges or screens. Leaves are oval- or heart-shaped. Grows easily in almost any soil. Has become a weed in many states.
NASTURTIUM, GARDEN *Tropaeolum majus*	Brilliantly colored fragrant flowers in summer.	Vining varieties good for covering trellises, fences, tree stumps, and screens. Will grow in poor soil and little sun. Thrives on neglect. Seedlings not easily transplanted; sow seed outdoors after last frost.
ORANGE CLOCK VINE *Thunbergia gregori*	Large orange daisy-like blossoms in summer.	(See black-eyed susan.) Good for flower boxes and as ground cover. Will cover a trellis quickly. Popular in California and the South. Grows in sun or shade.
PERIWINKLE, VARIEGATED *Vinca major 'variegata'*	Small lilac or blue flowers in summer.	Makes an excellent ground cover or trailing vine in the South. Not hardy in the North. Leaves are variegated with creamy white. Good in a hanging basket. Not fussy about soil but prefers shade. Is a perennial but acts like an annual because blooms well in first season and is not tolerant of frost.
SCARLET STAR-GLORY *Ipomoea coccinea*	Trumpet-shaped scarlet flowers with yellow throats resemble morning-glory. Blooms all summer.	Provides good shade. Has arrow-shaped leaves. Likes sun.
SCARLET RUNNER BEAN *Phaseolus coccineus*	Red flowers resembling sweet pea blossoms. Foot-long seedpods.	Tall, twining. Good for covering walls or trellis. Needs support, full sun, and ample moisture. Plant in well-drained soil. Fast-growing. Prefers sun.
SWEET PEA *Lathyrus odoratus*	Fragrant small flowers. Many colors. Blooms all summer.	Very popular. Use for screening, as a border, or for cut flowers. Needs cool temperatures, ample moisture, fertilizer. Prepare ground in fall; plant in spring. Climbs to 6 feet. Hundreds of varieties. Prefers sun.
WHITE DUTCH RUNNER BEAN *Phaseolus coccineus 'albus'*	White flowers resemble sweet pea blossoms.	(See scarlet runner bean entry for advice.) Can climb to 8 feet, but dwarf varieties are available. Plant seeds outside in sunny spot after danger of frost has passed.
WILD CUCUMBER *Echinocystis lobata*	Small greenish-white flowers in summer; long seedpods in fall.	Quick-growing. Needs support. Good for arbors and fences. Prefers full sun. Climbs by tendrils.

Perennial Vines

Perennial vines produce spectacular flowers year after year. Most are winter-hardy in climates where temperatures drop far below zero. Tops may die back, but new growth comes back strongly.

Perennial vines need little more care than an annual pruning. Rampant growers, such as the actinidia, can be pruned heavily to maintain shape. Trim vines while wood is still dormant.

Some of the ivies are slowpokes, adding only a few inches a year. Trim at the ends to encourage dense growth.

Profusely flowering vines, such as the violet trumpet vine and clematis, should be pruned after blooming to give next year's flowers maximum time to develop.

Bougainvillea and fuchsia do well in warm climates and protected areas.

Cat's-claw thrives even in poor soil.

Passionflower has intricate detail.

This red trumpet vine blows its own horn. Moraea and petunias complete the setting.

Trumpet vine provides shade, privacy, beauty. Base takes a foot of growing space.

PERENNIAL VINES

Vine	Zone	Fruit and Flower Habit	Comments
ACTINIDIA *Actinidia* sp.			All will grow in shade.
Bower A. arguta	5	Flowers not ornamental—small, greenish-white. One-inch berries are edible.	Twining vine with dense foliage; ideal for screening purposes. Grows rapidly.
Chinese gooseberry A. chinensis	8	White or yellow fragrant flowers in early summer.	Flowers appear on previous year's wood; leave plenty when pruning if flowers are desired. Good twining vine. Grows rapidly.
BITTERSWEET *Celastrus* sp.			All make good ground covers and grow in sun or shade.
American C. scandens	4	Inconspicuous flowers. Yellow capsules crack open in fall to show red berry inside.	Extremely hardy twining vine. Works well on sunny wall or fence. So vigorous can kill other plants if not kept in bounds.
Oriental C. orbiculatus	5	Inconspicuous flowers. Red and yellow berries in clusters along side of twigs.	One of the best twining vines. Grows rapidly. Rounded leaves.
BLOOD-TRUMPET *Distictis buccinatoria*	9	Red flowers all year in some areas, summer and fall in others.	Popular, vigorous vine. Climbs by tendrils and rootlets. Excellent for a screen. Evergreen. Prefers sun or light shade.
BOUGAINVILLEA *Bougainvillea* hybrids	9	Large clusters of white, red, orange, or purple flowers.	Climbs by twining. Evergreen vine. Grows best in full sun in the South.
CAPE PLUMBAGO *Plumbago auriculata*	9	Small light blue flowers all summer.	Actually a climbing shrub. Needs full sun.
CAROLINA JESSAMINE **Evening trumpet flower** *Gelsemium sempervirens*	7	Fragrant yellow flowers all summer.	Evergreen twining shrub. Requires support. Good ground cover or bank planting. Full sun. New vines can be started from cuttings or from seeds.
CAT'S-CLAW VINE *Macfadyena unguis-cati*	8	Yellow flowers in early spring.	Prune often to promote foliage growth. Climbs by tendrils with claws. Evergreen. Grows rapidly in sun or light shade.
CLEMATIS *Clematis* sp.			All will grow in shade.
Armand C. armandi	7	White flowers in spring.	Blooms on previous year's wood; prune after flowering. Evergreen or semievergreen.
Big-petal C. macropetala	6	Large blue flowers with many sepals in spring.	Prune after flowering.
Curly C. crispa	6	Long purple, bell-shaped flowers all summer.	Blooms on current year's wood.
Duchess of Edinburgh C. florida hybrid 'Duchess of Edinburgh'	6	Pure white double flowers resemble gardenias.	Blooms on previous year's wood.
Durand C. x durandi	6	Dark blue flowers with white, midsummer; seed heads in fall.	Dies to ground in winter.
Fragrant tube C. heracleifolia 'davidiana'	4-5	Fragrant blue flowers in late summer.	Does well in full sun or partial shade.

Vine	Zone	Fruit and Flower Habit	Comments
Golden *C. tangutica*	5	Large bright yellow flowers in late spring; seed heads in early fall.	Soft, gray-green leaves form good background for masses of flowers. Needs full sun. Blooms are long-lasting.
Henryi *C. henryi*	5	Pale flesh-colored to ivory blooms, up to 7 inches across.	A showy climbing vine. Does best in light, loamy, well-drained soil.
Jackmani *C. x jackmani*	6	Large purple flowers in mid-summer; seed heads in fall.	Popular hybrids. Blooms on current year's wood.
Jouin *C. x jouiniana*	5	White or purple flowers in mid-summer; seed heads in fall.	Vigorous climber.
Nelly Moser *C. patens* hybrid 'Nelly Moser'	6	Pale mauve petals; profuse bloom.	Popular hybrid.
Pink anemone *C. montana 'Rubens'*	6	Red or pink flowers in late spring; seed heads in summer.	Long-lasting flowers bloom on previous year's wood. New foliage is bronze-colored. Grows rapidly.
Scarlet *C. texensis*	6	Many bright scarlet flowers in midsummer; seed heads in fall.	Excellent ornamental native. Grows rapidly. Evergreen or semievergreen.
Solitary *C. integrifolia*	6	Small white, blue, or purple flowers in midsummer.	A non-twining, bush-form clematis. Flowers bloom at tips of stems. Grows in sun or shade.
Sweet autumn *C. paniculata*	5	Many fragrant white flowers in late summer; seed heads in fall.	One of easiest vines to grow. Has dense foliage. Resistant to insects or disease. Evergreen or semievergreen. Good for a bank or slope.
Traveler's joy *C. vitalba*	5	Small white flowers in late summer; large seed heads in fall.	Vigorous species with dense foliage. Good for a bank or slope.
Virgin's bower *C. virginiana*	5	Small white flowers in late summer; seed heads in fall.	Native; good for a wildflower garden. Grows rapidly. Withstands wet soil.
CORAL VINE Queen's-wreath *Antigonon leptopus*	9	Pink flowers from late summer to fall.	Withstands hot, dry conditions. Climbs by tendrils. Heart-shaped leaves. Plant in sunny spot.
CREEPER *Parthenocissus* sp.			
Heterophylla *P. heterophylla*	10	Flowers of no ornamental significance.	Grows rapidly. Clings by tendrils. Withstands dry soil. Good in sun or shade.
Silver vein *P. henryana*	7	Blue berries in fall.	Variegated foliage with purple undersides. Prefers shade. Clings by tendrils. Good ground cover.
Virginia creeper, Woodbine *P. quinquefolia*	4	Dark blue berries in fall.	Ideal for covering brick or stone walls, for bank plantings, or as a ground cover. Turns bright scarlet in the fall. Clings by tendrils. Grows rapidly. Withstands dry soil in sunny or shady place.
CREEPING FIG *Ficus pumila*	9	Yellowish, pear-shaped inedible figs.	Excellent for walls. Foliage is small but dense. Evergreen. Grows rapidly. Withstands dry soil and some shade.
CROSS VINE *Bignonia capreolata*	6	Orange-red flowers in late spring.	Vigorous vine; excellent for screen. Climbs by adhesive disks. Evergreen or semievergreen. Grows in sun or part shade.
FIVE-LEAF AKEBIA *Akebia quinata*	5	Clusters of purple flowers in late spring.	Vigorously twining vine; easily trained to supports. Can become a pest if not confined. Will grow in shade. Prefers well-drained soil. Good for a bank or slope or as a ground cover. Semi-evergreen.

PERENNIAL VINES (continued)

Vine	Zone	Fruit and Flower Habit	Comments
FLAME VINE **Orange-trumpet** *Pyrostegia venusta*	9	Three-inch-long orange, mauve, magenta, or red tubular flowers in dense clusters. Blooms midwinter and summer.	Tall woody vine. A climbing evergreen shrub. Easy to grow in full sun. Dwarf varieties available.
GRAPE *Vitis* sp.			All will grow in shade. All good for bank plantings.
Amur *V. amurensis*	5	Black grapes in fall.	Turns purplish-crimson in fall. Vigorous and hardy.
Glory vine *V. coignetiae*	5	Fruit clusters to 8 inches long.	Grows vigorously. Has large leaves that turn red in fall. Ideal for a screen. Clings by tendrils.
River-bank *V. riparia*	3	Inconspicuous but fragrant flowers. Purple or black grapes in fall.	Lustrous foliage. Hardy. Clings by tendrils.
GREENBRIER, COMMON **Horse brier** *Smilax rotundifolia*	5	Black berries in fall.	Dense, vigorous, twining vine. Good for bank planting to hold soil. Withstands wet soil as well. Sometimes thorny. Thrives in sun or light shade.
HONEYSUCKLE *Lonicera* sp.			All will grow in shade.
Chinese woodbine *L. tragophylla*	6	Bright yellow flowers all summer; red berries in fall.	Prefers limestone soil and shade. Twines.
Everblooming *L. heckrotti*	4	Trumpet-shaped flowers in summer; purple outside, yellow inside.	One of the best climbing honeysuckles. Blooms all summer.
Hall's Japanese *L. japonica 'halliana'*	5	Fragrant white flowers in late spring; black berries in fall.	Popular. Grows in almost any soil in sun or shade. Good ground cover. Turns bronze in fall. Semievergreen to evergreen. Grows rapidly.
Henry *L. henryi*	6	Red, purple, or yellow flowers in early summer; black berries in fall.	Good ground cover. Semievergreen in the North; evergreen in the South. Twines.
Sweet, **Italian woodbine** *L. caprifolium*	6	Small fragrant ivory flowers in late spring; orange-red berries in late summer.	Leaves bluish-green underneath. Twines up to 20 feet.
Trumpet *L. sempervirens*	4	Orange-scarlet flowers all summer; red berries in fall.	Hardy honeysuckle. Grows rapidly. Withstands dry soil. Semievergreen to evergreen.
HYDRANGEA, CLIMBING *Hydrangea anomala 'petiolaris'*	5	Large clusters of white flowers in early summer.	One of the best climbing vines. Clings by rootlets to brick and stone. Will grow in shade but bloom best in sun. Prune in fall or early spring.
IVY **Algerian** *Hedera canariensis*	8	Black berries in fall.	Fast-grower. Thick, dark green leaves. Evergreen. Will grow in shade.
Boston, **Japanese creeper** *Parthenocissus tricuspidata*	5	Dark blue berries in fall.	Clings to stonework. Ideal for city conditions. Turns scarlet in fall. Grows rapidly. Withstands dry soil and sun or shade.
English *Hedera helix*	6	Black berries in fall.	Dozens of varieties. Clings to walls and stone. Evergreen. Grows rapidly. Will grow in shade. Good for bank plantings or as a ground cover.

Vine	Zone	Fruit and Flower Habit	Comments
JASMINE **Common white** *Jasminum officinale*	7	Fragrant white flowers in summer.	Popular vine. Blooms all summer; ideal for trellises or arbors. Semievergreen. Prefers sun or light shade.
Japanese *Jasminum mesnyi*	8	Small yellow flowers in spring and summer.	Not a climber. Beautiful, but not as hardy as other jasmines. Prefers sun or light shade.
Star *Trachelospermum jasminoides*	9	Small fragrant white flowers from early spring to midsummer.	Needs moist soil and shade. Grows rapidly. Evergreen. Good twining vine. Will grow in shade. Withstands wet soil.
Yellow star *Trachelospermum asiaticum*	8	Fragrant ivory flowers from early spring to midsummer.	Hardy jasmines. Withstands wet soil. Evergreen. Prefers sun or light shade.
MATRIMONY VINE, COMMON *Lycium halimifolium*	5	Small light purple flowers in early summer; orange to red berries in fall.	Actually a rambling shrub, this plant is ideal for poor soil conditions. It spreads rapidly and may become a nuisance if not pruned. Good for planting a bank. Likes sun.
PASSIONFLOWER *Passiflora caerulea*	8	Petals white or pinkish. Corona is purple. Flowers summer to fall.	Beautiful vines—popular in southern gardens. Climbs by tendrils. Pest-resistant. Some varieties hardy to sheltered Midwest conditions. Prefers sun.
PEPPER VINE *Ampelopsis arborea*	7	Pea-size purple berries.	Semievergreen. Popular in Southeast. Needs support. Grows rapidly. Good ground cover. Withstands dry soil, sun, and shade.
RAMBLER ROSE *Rosa* sp.	4	Large clusters of red, pink, and white flowers in late spring.	Needs support. Prune old canes immediately after flowering. Must be protected in the North in winter. Good for bank plantings in sun.
SCARLET KADSURA *Kadsura japonica*	7	Small ivory flowers all summer; scarlet berries in fall.	Good evergreen twining shrub for a bank or slope. Leaves turn reddish-green in fall. Thrives in sun or light shade.
SILVER LACE *Polygonum auberti*	4	White or greenish flowers in panicles in late summer.	Vigorous twining vine. Dense foliage. Withstands dry soil. Plant in sunny place.
SKY VINE **Bengal clock vine** *Thunbergia grandiflora*	8	Blue on white tubular flowers in pendulous clusters. Blooms in mid-spring.	Popular on arbors and porches. Evergreen vine. Best in sun or light shade.
TRUMPET VINE *Campsis* sp.			All cling by rootlike holdfasts and grow rapidly. Prefer sun.
Chinese trumpet creeper *C. grandiflora*	8	Scarlet flowers in midsummer.	Flowers are large and showy. Needs support.
Trumpet vine *C. radicans*	5	Orange, yellow, and scarlet flowers in midsummer.	Will cling to stone or brick but may need extra support because of its weight. Withstands dry and wet soil.
WINTER CREEPER *Euonymus fortunei*	6	Vegeta variety bears orange berries.	Clings well to walls and stone. Evergreen. Tolerant of sun or shade.
WISTERIA *Wisteria* sp.			All are good twining vines. Hardy in North.
Chinese *W. sinensis*	5	Blue or purple flowers in dense clusters in spring.	Popular vine. Grows rapidly in sun or light shade. Makes beautiful specimen.
Japanese *W. floribunda*	5	Violet, pink, red, or white flowers in racemes in spring.	The flowers bloom from top to bottom of the racemes. Many varieties available. Grows rapidly in sun. Compound leaves.

chapter 7

PERENNIALS AND BIENNIALS

Perennials are our most faithful garden friends and the backbone of most borders. Year after year, they return to fill gardens with lovely flowers and a variety of foliage textures and shades of green. They give a garden a sense of permanence and continuity, filling their allotted areas with little fuss or bother for the gardener. The heights and widths of the taller perennials, such as the peony, hosta, and veronica, give vertical dimension and mass against which interplantings of annuals and bedding plants display their colorful blooms. Perennials are more expensive than annuals, but when the cost is spread out over their years of service, they are actually bargains.

Although not so permanent as perennials, the biennials also deserve a special role in your garden scheme. Biennials are so named because their seed planted in the spring or fall of one year will not produce blooms until the following year. This delay in bloom irritates some gardeners, but once the cycle is started, the time seems immaterial. Many biennials reseed themselves, so they become almost as dependable as the perennials. Some of our great garden beauties are biennials: Canterbury-bells, common foxglove, and Iceland poppy, to name only a few.

Color abounds in the mixed annual-perennial garden along a stone path (opposite). Large blocks of the same kind of plants, often a dozen or more, make bold, interlocking masses of color. Included here are sweet williams, calendulas, pinks, yellow and white violas, and coralbells.

Constant Color

A flower border that's abloom from end to end, and from spring to frost, doesn't just happen. It's the result of careful planning so each plant presents its colors at a specific time and place.

The outstanding results of careful planning are beautifully illustrated in the garden pictured here. In the spring view (above), the border is liberally splashed with the bright flowers of early-season plants. The summer scene (opposite) is equally bright with bloom, but the color comes from plants whose flowers take over just as soon as the spring colors start to fade. And, throughout the growing season, there are different focal points of attention.

A strictly perennial border is difficult to plan, because each perennial blooms for a relatively short period, often just a week or two. That's why annuals are usually

planted among perennials to keep the color going throughout the season. Interplanting is a big reason for the success of this garden. Perennials are generously distributed throughout the border, with blocks of annuals and biennials planted between them. In spring (opposite), the main contributors are gay calendulas, snapdragons, English daisies, Iceland poppies, and blue forget-me-nots. Delphiniums are just starting to show color in the background.

During the summer, more yellows and golds are seen. Accents of blue and white make the colors flow evenly throughout the area. The sedum in the foreground is just ready to bloom, while rudbeckias, campanulas, asters, petunias, marigolds, ageratums, and zinnias fill in the background. When they have finished blooming, the perennials' foliage furnishes background texture and color to the border.

With a little experience and study, this strategy of getting color during each season comes naturally. When the foliage of spring bulbs fades, fill their areas with young annual plants. Then turn areas formerly filled with cool-season bedding plants, such as violas, over to tender bulbs or more annuals for warm weather.

How to Propagate Perennials

Beat the price of buying plants by starting many of your perennials from seeds, cuttings, or root divisions. Homegrown elegance!

Increasing your supply of perennials is usually a simple operation, once you know the process for each type of plant. Some perennials must be propagated from root cuttings, some come readily from seed, many start from stem cuttings, and others are increased by division of the plant's crown. Check the "ABCs" section (starting on page 186) to see how to propagate specific plants.

Take root cuttings when the plant is in active growth, usually in the spring. (Early fall is best for the Oriental poppy.) Lift the plant, wash soil from the roots, and cut the fleshiest roots into three-inch sections; plant these horizontally with a half-inch cover of soil. Replant the parent plant.

Plant perennial seed in either spring or late summer (in sufficient time so the young plants are sturdy enough to make it through the first winter). Plant and care for the seedlings as you do annual seedlings by keeping them watered and lightly fed.

Stem cuttings quickly result in healthy young plants. Take two- to three-inch cuttings, and strip off all but a few leaves at the tip (see drawings at right). Insert the stem end an inch or so into a bed of moist vermiculite, and cover with a plastic sheet. Set the flat where it gets bright light but no direct sun. In two weeks, the cuttings will probably be well rooted and ready to be set in the border.

Dividing the crown of a plant is sometimes a big job, but you end up with several good-size plants.

Lift the plant and wash soil from the roots. With some plants, you can pull sections of the crown free, but most require a sharp knife for cutting through the fleshy crown.

If you have space, start a little nursery where you can keep all your young perennial plants in one spot until they are big enough to set out in the border. Feed lightly the first year so you get firm, sturdy growth. If fed too heavily, the growth will be lush, but weak.

A cold frame is a valuable unit for most plants. It is especially helpful for starting perennials and biennials from seed and for overwintering young plants from cuttings or plants that are of borderline hardiness. The cold frame pictured (below, right) is typical. The slant-topped frame has a removable glass or plastic top and shallow headroom for the plants. Usually, the front wall is eight inches high, and the rear wall measures 12 to 14 inches high.

Seedlings can be transplanted from peat pots into larger pots.

Young plants in flats or individual pots are placed in the frame in early spring for protection from cold snaps. This hardens off seedlings for their move into the garden borders; moving them from a greenhouse or windowsill directly into the garden can shock the plant.

In late fall, before the plants go completely dormant, dig perennial and biennial seedlings and place in the cold frame.

To start a new plant, take a two-inch chrysanthemum cutting. The cut is made just below a leaf on the stem.

After rooting in moist vermiculite for several weeks, the cutting is ready to be moved to a pot for further growth.

PERENNIALS FOR SPECIAL CONDITIONS

Poor Soil
Ageratum, Hardy
Baby's-breath
Candytuft
Catnip *(Nepeta cataria)*
Cerastium
Cranesbill geranium
Daylily
Globe thistle
Hibiscus
Leadwort
Moss phlox *(Phlox
    subulata)*
Oenothera
Sedum (most kinds)
Swamp saxifrage *(Saxifraga
    pensylvanica)*
Thyme
Verbascum
Virginia bluebells
Yarrow

Wet Soil
Astilbe
Bee balm
Bergenia *(Bergenia* sp.*)*
Blue flag *(Iris versicolor)*
Ferns (most)
Forget-me-not
Galax *(Galax urceolata)*
Globeflower
Helenium
Heliotrope *(Valeriana
    officinalis)*
Japanese iris
Lobelia
Loosestrife
Lungwort
Marsh marigold *(Caltha* sp.*)*
Swamp milkweed *(Asclepias
    incarnata)*
Swamp rose mallow *(Hibiscus
    moscheutos)*
Swamp saxifrage
Sweet woodruff *(Galium
    odoratum)*
Vinca minor
Viola

Violet *(Viola sororia)*
Wild ginger *(Asarum* sp.*)*
Yellow flag *(Iris pseudacorus)*

Dry Soil
Anthemis
Baby's-breath
Baptisia
Butterfly weed
Coreopsis
Gaillardia
Helianthus
Heliopsis
Hosta
Liatris
Maltese-cross
    (Lychnis chalcedonica)
Moss pink *(Dianthus* sp.*)*
Oriental poppy
Rock cress *(Arabis* sp.*)*
Rudbeckia
Sedum
Spurge, Flowering
Statice *(Limonium* sp.*)*
Sweet william
Yarrow
Yucca

Long-lived
Aster, Hardy
Astilbe
Balloon flower
Baptisia
Bleeding-heart
Campanula
Daylily
Gas plant
Hosta
Iris
Monkshood
Peony
Phlox
Veronica
Yucca

Shade Tolerant
Anemone, Japanese
    (Anemone hupehensis)

Astilbe
Balloon flower
Bee balm
Bleeding-heart
Candytuft
Columbine
Coralbells
Gas plant
Helleborus niger
Hosta
Hypericum
Jacob's-ladder
Lily-of-the-valley
    (Convallaria sp.*)*
Lobelia
Loosestrife
Maltese-cross
Penstemon
Physostegia
Primrose
Spiderwort
    (Tradescantia sp.*)*
Swamp rose mallow
Thalictrum
Virginia bluebells

Beautifully Foliaged
Astilbe
Baneberry *(Actaea* sp.*)*
Bellwort *(Uvularia* sp.*)*
Bleeding-heart
Bloodroot
    (Sanguinaria sp.*)*
Burnet *(Sanguisorba* sp.*)*
Gas plant
Goutweed or Bishop's weed
    (Aegopodium podagraria)
Hosta
Iris
Lily-of-the-valley
Moss phlox
Peony
Perennial pea *(Lathyrus* sp.*)*
Solomon's-seal
    (Polygonatum sp.*)*
Spurge, Mountain
Stachys
Violet

Perennial Basics

Perennials are stalwart actors that perform well with average care. But with a little extra attention, they will reward you with bountiful bloom. Here's how to give perennials a push toward perfection.

Preparing soil

A perennial grows in the same spot for many years, or even a lifetime. Preparing soil in the bed is the first important step toward getting a plant of top-notch quality. Invest a little extra time at the beginning, and you'll be rewarded with flowers year after year.

As early in the spring as the ground can be worked, turn the soil the full depth of the spade. Work the topsoil toward the bottom; this is where the perennials' roots will be getting most of their nourishment. Rake the ground level, and cover with two to four inches of organic matter: well-rotted cow manure, compost, peat moss, or a combination of them. Blend this into the soil of the bed with a garden spade or spading fork.

It's nearly impossible to add too much organic matter. This material lightens heavy clay soil, improves the tilth of good soil, and increases the water- and nutrient-holding capacity of sandy soils, so don't be afraid to add large quantities. A compost heap is the least expensive source of organic matter; keep one going in your garden. (For information on making a compost pile, see pages 12 and 13.)

Planting

It's difficult to list general tips about planting perennials, because each is unique in some way. However, here are some steps to help ensure success for most.

First, set newly purchased or divided plants at the proper depth—the same level they grew the previous season. You will be able to see marks of the original depth on the dormant stems. Next, provide adequate space for roots so they're not crowded. Dig a hole several inches larger in diameter than the spread of the roots, and space the roots in all directions so they get established quickly. *Hint:* build a low cone of earth at the bottom of the hole, and stretch the roots out over the cone. Then, gradually sprinkle in the soil. Water well and add more soil to bring the level even with the surrounding ground.

Remember that your main goal in transplanting—whether you have a new plant or one obtained through division of an older plant—is to avoid shocking the plant excessively. Don't let roots dry out or break off; they're the plant's lifeline to food, moisture, and good health.

The space you leave between perennials varies with their size at maturity. All will be healthier with a little breathing space. Circulation of air reduces the risks of mold and mildew. Also, proper spacing eliminates excessive competition for soil moisture and nutrients, so your plants can grow to full size. (For help in deciding how much space they need, check the recommended spacing for specific plants starting on page 181.)

Group three or more of one kind of plant together. The overall effect of a border is enhanced when there are repeat groupings of plants at several intervals.

On short stakes, label the locations of newly planted perennials, especially if you're planting in the fall. Some plants are late to emerge in the spring, and it is easy to forget their locations or which plant is which. However, labels in a border may become lost, so keep a permanent record of all your plants. One of the best ways is to maintain a master plan. Record the locations of all plants on it, the year and month they were planted, and the places you obtained them; this information can come in handy in years to come. Keep the master plan in the house. It can be easily lost or damaged in the garden. You may want to make a working copy for use outside.

The first year is the most critical for any perennial. Keep a close eye on foliage for signs of wilting and damage caused by insects or diseases. Keep the soil moist, but don't overwater. Avoid the temptation to overfeed, too. Your plants will be much stronger if they are fed just enough to make normal yearly growth. If fertilized too much, the growth will be rank, weak, and less able to withstand winter damage.

Tall-growing perennials, such as delphinium, lupine, and foxglove, need to be staked. Don't wait until the plants have toppled to give them support. Put the stakes in early, and keep growth tied to them. If transplanting tall plants (such as hostas) in mid-season when they have large, heavy leaves, tie the foliage to a stake to keep the leaves

Turn the soil deeply in perennial borders. A spading fork or spade is excellent for this task. Blend in organic matter to loosen the soil.

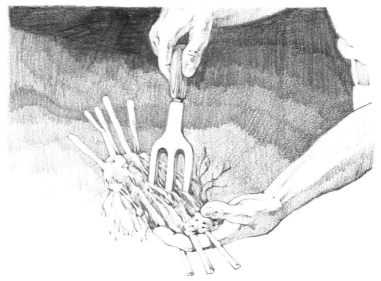

When dividing perennials, wash all the soil from the roots, and pull divisions free, or use a garden hand fork to pry sections from the main crown.

To keep winter mulch in place, stretch sections of chicken wire over the mulched area. Bricks or stones at the corners will keep the wire flat.

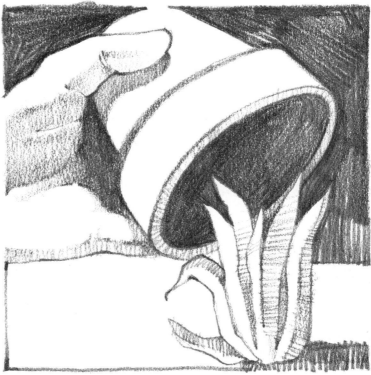

A flowerpot covering the fall growth of a plant protects it during the winter. Spread winter mulch over the pot to help insulate the enclosure.

off the ground and to steady the plant while the roots take hold.

Dividing

Perennials benefit from being divided every few years. Fresh new soil for their roots and a vigorous new start for the plant generally result in a much stronger, better-blooming plant. Even if you don't want more plants, divide old clumps occasionally.

Some perennials can be separated by cutting or gently pulling off sections of the crown. Use a hand fork (pictured opposite) or a sharp knife for tuberous or woody roots. Don't make too many divisions from one plant, and be sure each has enough roots to sustain growth.

When dividing a perennial, wash all or most of the soil away from the roots so you can see where you're cutting. Direct a stream of water into the root area to get the soil out. Keep as many roots attached to each division as possible, but trim away any damaged roots. If any part looks dead or diseased, trim all the way back to clean, white tissue.

Winter protection

After the first killing frost—usually preceded by several light frosts that nip the tops of plants but do not kill the foliage back to the ground—it's time to prepare the perennial border for winter. First, cut and remove dead stalks, trimming stems to within four inches of the ground.

When the beds have been cleared of all dead foliage and weeds, apply a winter mulch of straw or peat moss. This can be held down by sections of chicken wire or branches (as illustrated above). Some plants, such as the poppy and madonna lily, put up a small tuft of growth in the fall that needs extra protection. A flowerpot covering it (above, right) will keep mulch from flattening the leaves. Or loop two wires to hold heavy cloth or paper above the foliage (right).

If fall rains have been light, deeply water the perennials.

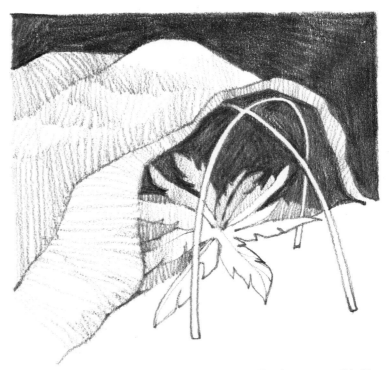

Build a winter tent over the late foliage of a poppy. Two bent wires will hold a protective layer of heavy fabric or paper above the winter growth.

How to Plan Perennial Borders

A successful perennial border should have that carefully planned, unplanned look. It's possible when plants are arranged informally and spaced to show off their best. There's more involved than filling the bed with short and tall plants.

Most perennials bloom for just a few weeks, so you must also consider foliage textures, blending of colors, and distribution of color across the bed throughout the season. If all the flowers bloom at the same time, the border is drab much of the year; choosing plants for season-long color is your most important task. The best way to keep borders bright all season is to in-

PARTIAL-SHADE PERENNIAL BORDER

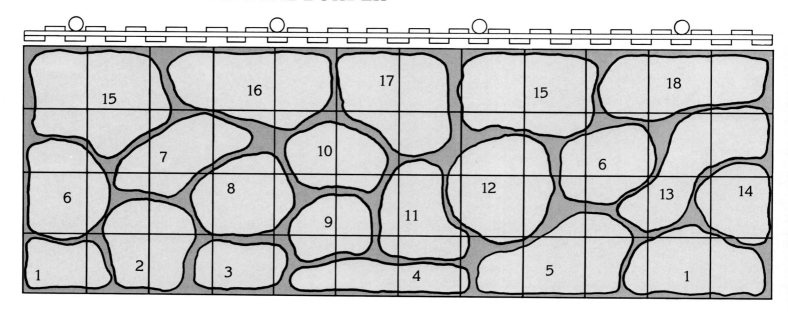

Front-of-the-border

1. Species tulip (8);
   Wax begonia later (3)
2. *Hosta decorata* (3)
3. Dwarf fern (3)
4. Mixed crocus (24);
   Dwarf impatiens later (5)
5. Wild ginger (3)

Mid-border

6. Astilbe (3)
7. Daffodil (10)
8. Tulip (10);
   Tall impatiens later (4)
9. Hosta, Kabitan (3)
10. Bleeding-heart (1)
11. Daffodil (12)
12. *Hosta fortunei 'albomarginata'* (3)
13. Tulip (12); Tall impatiens later
14. *Hosta lancifolia* (1)

Back-of-the-border

15. Lady fern (*Athyrium filix-femina*) (3)
16. Monarda (3)
17. *Hosta sieboldiana* (1)
18. Loosestrife (3)

Note: "Partial shade" here means the location receives morning and perhaps late afternoon sun but not midday sun. If shade is not too dense, daylilies are an excellent choice for back-of-the-border plantings; they will not bloom so heavily as in full sun but will perform adequately. Other plants that should be in every shade border are the caladium and coleus. Their bright foliage is invaluable for season-long color.

The number after each item refers to the quantity of plants or bulbs to set out.

clude annuals in your plan, as we have done here. Get early color by planting spring-flowering bulbs in the areas where the annuals are to be planted later.

The spring-flowering bulbs can be planted close to perennials with arching stems, such as peonies and mums. The perennial foliage covers the yellowing bulb foliage in late spring. To emphasize the informal nature of the border, plan areas of plants, rather than single plants scattered throughout; usually three to five plants of a variety grouped together will make a good showing.

And don't set the plants in rows. Plant them in the shape of a triangle or in no particular shape at all. Of course, some plants that grow large, such as peonies, should be planted singly. The depth of your flower border is important, too, if you have access for tending it from just one side. A depth of four feet as shown on the plans (below) is ideal. With this size, there's enough space for tapering the heights of plants from the front to the back of the border and to work from one side. The borders here are 12 feet long, but if you want yours longer or shorter, simply repeat or decrease plant groupings to fit the desired length of your bed. Space plants so your border looks full but not crowded. Each plant or grouping should have room to display its flowers naturally, without a squeezed-in look. In both plans, the lists of plants are only suggestions. For each one, there are many more that would work equally well. Or, if you wish, include some of your old favorites.

SUNNY PERENNIAL BORDER

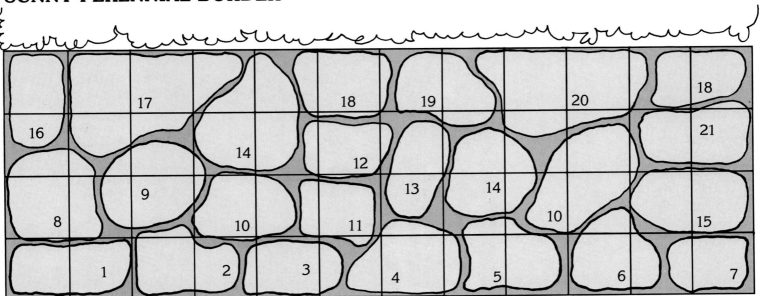

1 Square = 1 Ft.

Front-of-the-border

1. Species tulip (8);
   Dwarf zinnia later (8)
2. Basket-of-gold alyssum (3)
3. Crocus (12);
   Petunias later (4)
4. Silver Mound artemisia (3)
5. English daisy (5)
6. Creeping phlox (3)
7. Daffodil (8);
   Dwarf marigold later (5)
8. Daffodil (10);
   Tall marigold later (8)

Mid-border

9. Peony (1)
10. Tulip (10);
    Tall zinnia later (8)
11. Cushion mum (1)
12. Phlox (3)
13. Yarrow (3)
14. Daylily (3)
15. Aster (2)

Back-of-the-border

16. Solidago (3)
17. Delphinium (6)
18. Lily, Imperial strain (3)
19. Rudbeckia (4)
20. Hollyhock (8)
21. Globe thistle (3)

Note: Our plans are shown as rectangles but can easily be adapted to any shape you prefer. By simply expanding some planting areas or adding plants, you can widen any section to get an undulating edge. If you want a wider border, put a flagstone or patio-block walk along the rear of the border, which will allow you to work on the border from the back. This will also keep the soil from being walked on and packed.

Check the "ABCs of Perennials" (starting on page 186) for suggestions on the plants to substitute.

Plan by height and shape of plants

Before you lift a spade or trowel to set out the first plant, determine what plants you want and where to plant them. This requires planning and, ideally, a master plan for your garden. After determining the locations and sizes of your borders, the most enjoyable part is at hand: choosing the plants and placing them on the plan.

Several characteristics of the plants must be considered. Their heights place them either to the front, middle, or back of the border, and their widths are important in their spacing. Give them room to spread to their full extent, so they don't look too crowded. The blending of flower colors and their distribution throughout the bed at various seasons are important. Also, foliage textures and colors affect the look of the planting.

To help you plan your borders, a garden showing several ideas is pictured at right. Its small size (24x24 feet) makes it adaptable to many garden situations. The drawing shows a courtyard garden just outside the back door of a home. This garden gets full sun all day long, but the plants shown would do nicely with anything more than a half day of sunlight. Perennials are given specific locations on the plan, but the areas in between are left flexible for planting spring-flowering bulbs. The bulb areas are planted to annuals as soon as the bulb foliage fades in late spring.

Shrubs, spaced around the periphery of the low fence (both inside and out), give shape to the garden, and all but the boxwood contribute flowers in season. Containers on the deck flank the access to the garden with flowers.

TREES AND SHRUBS

AA. Cut-leaf beech tree
BB. Red Jade crab apple
CC. P.J.M. rhododendron
DD. Korean boxwood
EE. *Euonymus alata*
FF. Azalea mollis
   (*Rhododendron molle*)
GG. *Viburnum rhytidophyllum*
HH. *Viburnum carlesi*
II. Yew (*Taxus cuspidata 'nana'*)

PLANTS IN SUMMER GARDEN

1. Sweet alyssum**
2. *Campanula carpatica*****
3. Artemisia****
4. American Eagle lily***
5. Verbena**
6. Dragon's Blood sedum****
7. Basket-of-gold alyssum****
8. Petite Harmony marigold*
9. Feverfew*
10. Crimson Topper snapdragon**
11. Nicotiana**
12. Blue Mink ageratum**
13. Nasturtium*
14. Shasta daisy****
15. Diamond Jubilee marigold*
16. California poppy*
17. Purple Beauty phlox****
18. Forget-me-not*
19. Lobelia*
20. English daisy**
21. Perennial sweet pea****
22. Mariner petunia**
23. Rudbeckia*
24. Orange Jubilee marigold*
25. Aster****
26. Cleome*
27. Coral Satin petunia**
28. Zinnias: Envy and Purple
    Giant*
29. Yellow Climax marigold*
30. Glacier petunia**
31. Yellow Spoon
    chrysanthemum****
32. Gaillardia*
33. Redskin dwarf dahlia*
34. Rose Parade petunia**
35. Purple basil**
36. Dill**
37. Golden Chalice lily***
38. Geranium**
39. Portulaca*

*From seed sown in late spring
**Bedding plants set out in early summer
***Bulbs planted in the fall
****Perennials—plant roots fall or spring

PERENNIAL DESCRIPTIONS AND PREFERRED LOCATIONS

Name	Colors	Time of Bloom	Height in Inches	Spacing in Inches	Comments
ERECT					
Daylily	Yellow, red, orange, rose-pink, mahogany	Late spring to fall	18-60	24-30	Adapt for naturalizing or for flower border. Winter mulch is not needed. Endures partial shade.
Delphinium	Blue, white, violet, pink, purple	Early summer-early fall	18-96	20—small 30—large	Use for accent in border. Stake and tie tall kinds. Cut flower spikes before seeds set to encourage more bloom in the fall.
Iris, tall bearded	White, blue, red, pink, yellow, others	Spring	18-48	8-10	Bearded iris need full sun, well-drained soil. Divide and transplant every fourth year. Set rhizome shallow; cover with light layer of soil.
Liatris	Rose, purple, white, bluish purple, pink	Late summer	18-72	14-24	Endures partial shade. Good for accent in the border. In contrast to other spike flowers, order of bloom is from the top down.
Loosestrife	Purple, pink	Summer	24-48	12-24	Prefers a moist, shady situation. The long flower spikes give accent in the border.
Poker plant	Orange, scarlet, yellow, orange, white	Midsummer-fall	36-60	18-24	Excellent accent plant. Prefers light soil, plenty of water. Hardy except in colder areas where they should be mulched heavily.
Salvia	Blue, purple, white	Summer-fall	24-48	18-20	Produces erect spikes. Encourage late bloom by cutting the old spikes back to top of foliage.
Yucca	White	Summer	36-72	36-48	Evergreen. Dramatic accent plant. Permanent; needs no transplanting.
BUSH					
Ageratum, Hardy	White, blue, violet	Fall	24-36	15-30	Useful in borders and for naturalizing. Grows in sun or shade. Fluffy flowers grow in clusters.
Aster, Hardy	Lavender, mauve, pink	Fall	12-48	10-30	Endures partial shade. To cause branching of tall kinds, pinch out tips of shoots when bush reaches 12 inches. Stake tall varieties.
Bleeding-heart	Pink, red, ivory	Spring	12-24	15-24	Endures partial shade. Cut tops of the tall kinds when foliage turns yellow after bloom.
Chrysanthemum	Yellow, red, white, pink, bronze	Fall	12-36	15-24	Give full sun. Divide and transplant every other spring. Best results are from rooted stem cuttings.
Coreopsis	Yellow	Summer-fall	16-30	10-18	Use for mass effect and cut flowers.
Gaillardia	Yellow, red-orange	Summer	12-30	12-18	Use for mass effect in the border. For cut flowers, pick when blooms are slightly cup-shaped.
Gas plant	White, rose-pink	Summer	24-36	20-30	Hardy. Plant for permanence. Unlike most perennials, it doesn't have to be divided.
Heliopsis	Yellow	Summer	36-60	20-24	Grows in full sun. Endures dry situations.
Oriental poppy	White, pink, red, orange, salmon, mahogany	Spring	10-36	18-24	Plant or transplant in early fall. Roots can be divided or cut into 2-inch lengths to start new plants.

PERENNIAL DESCRIPTIONS (continued)

Name	Colors	Time of Bloom	Height in Inches	Spacing in Inches	Comments
Peony	White, red, pink, rose, cream	Spring	36-48	36-48	Seldom needs to be divided; fall is best time. Plant so buds are only 1 inch below soil surface. Needs full sun. Grows well in most soil types that are well drained.
Phlox	Salmon, red, white, pink, red-orange, purple	Summer-fall	6-48	12-18	Replant every third year. Does best in fertile soil with plenty of moisture; a mulch helps. Do not allow seeds to set.
Shasta daisy	White	Spring-summer	24-36	12-20	Endures partial shade. Excellent cut flower. Divide and transplant every other spring.
CUSHION Bishop's weed (*Aegopodium podagraria*)	White and green foliage	Summer	12	7-10	Good ground cover; spreads by underground stems. Useful for edging if it's confined. It does best in shade.
Moss phlox (*Phlox subulata*)	White, pink, blue, rose, red	Early spring	6	6-12	Useful in rock wall, rock gardens, and on banks. Creeps or spreads widely.
Silver Mound artemisia	Cream	Late summer	12-18	10-15	Valuable for use in rock walls and in borders. Grown for its beautiful foliage. Can thrive in poor and dry soil.
Viola	Yellow, white, pink, purple, blue, bicolors	Early spring	6	10-12	There are two major groups within the genus: sweet (*Viola odorata*) and tufted (*V. cornuta*). Both like organically enriched soil and do well in rock and wildflower gardens.

How to plan and produce constant bloom

A major triumph of gardening is filling your borders with bright flowers from spring to frost. This isn't easy to do when using only perennials, so sprinkle annuals liberally throughout the plantings of perennials to back up the seasonal blooms of the permanent plantings. You can select different annuals each year.

When planning a border, the idea is to let plants take turns producing their show of flowers. This is where planning is important—assigning each perennial to a spot where it will provide a particular color at a specific period during the season. In this way, you will have color from one end of the border to the other all season long—from the first spring-flowering bulb to the last chrysanthemum in late fall.

A good sequence of perennials for the backbone planting of your borders might be tulips, iris, peonies, phlox, daylilies, and chrysanthemums. Use these key plants generously in big groups or drifts throughout the border. Then select one or more secondary flowers to serve as fillers to supplement the seasonal bloomers. Some good plants to use as fillers are wild blue phlox at tulip time; daisies and sweet rockets (*Hesperis matronalis*) with the iris; loosestrife and gaillardia along with the phlox. Annuals, such as marigolds, zinnias, and alyssum, take over the filler spots in early summer and continue until late fall.

Border plantings are staggered in height from the low growers at the front to the tallest varieties at the back. To achieve this informal tapering from the front edge on back, without abrupt changes in height, make your borders at least four feet deep; six feet is better, if you have working access from the back. The deeper the bed, the more gently you can taper the heights of the plants.

The border pictured (opposite) is six feet deep. Note how the plants gracefully ascend in height from the front to back. And color is splashed liberally along the entire length of the bed.

For deep borders, you can put a few stepping-stones throughout the plantings so you can weed and tend to the plants' needs without walking through the bed and destroying the texture of the soil.

Choose a color scheme for your borders, too. If you like bright, splashy colors, use a lot of reds, bright yellows, blues, and purples, with a few whites thrown in for contrast. If you prefer a softer look, work with pinks, blues, and the pale yellows; sprinkle white flowers liberally throughout. Some striking gardens depend solely on white flowers; they are especially effective in the evening.

Don't overlook the effects brightly foliaged plants can have in a color scheme. Even different shades of green can be delightful. In sunny spots, use joseph's-coat (*Amaranthus tricolor*) and dusty-miller. For shady areas, rely on coleus, caladium, and the variegated hostas. One beauty of these brightly foliaged plants is that their colors last from late spring until frost.

Summer bulbs can play a big part in your color parade, too. Both tall and bedding dahlias give extended seasons of bloom; gladiolus add their midsummer spikes of color, and tuberoses present fragrant flowers along middle of the border.

Starting with Perennials

Perennials should be the main ingredient in any garden. They come up each spring to fill their allotted spaces with bloom. Most need little extra attention once they're planted.

With so many colors and shapes of perennials available, it is often difficult to choose the ones to include in your garden. The task requires some study first and then a search for those plants that will fill your needs and wants. Among the best ways to learn about perennials are reading books and garden magazines, visiting garden centers and public or private gardens, and ordering garden catalogues from nurseries specializing in perennials.

Perennials are not prohibitively expensive, unless you decide to plant an entire garden in one sea-

CHOOSE PERENNIALS BY HEIGHT

Front-of-the-border (Dwarf to 15 inches)	Mid-border (15 to 30 inches)	Back-of-the-border (Over 30 inches)
Anemone (Anemone canadensis)	Allium (bulb)	Anchusa (Dropmore variety)
Artemisia, Silver Mound	Astilbe	Aster, Hardy
Aster, Hardy (dwarf michaelmas varieties)	Baby's-breath (Gypsophila paniculata)	Baptisia
Baby's-breath (Gypsophila repens)	Balloon flower	Daylily
Bellflower (Campanula carpatica)	Bee balm	Delphinium (species varieties)
Brunnera	Bleeding-heart	Foxglove* (some varieties)
Candytuft	Butterfly weed	Globe thistle
Chrysanthemum (cushion varieties)	Chrysanthemum (many varieties)	Helenium
Crocus (bulb)	Columbine	Helianthus
Dianthus	Coralbells	Heliopsis
Dwarf iris varieties	Coreopsis	Hibiscus
English daisy*	Delphinium	Hollyhock*
Feverfew	Foxglove*	Hosta
Flax	Gaillardia	Iris (spuria and Japanese)
Geranium, Cranesbill	Gas plant	Liatris
Grape hyacinth (bulb)	Hosta (Hosta lancifolia types)	Lilies (bulbs, many hybrid varieties)
Hyacinth (bulb)	Iris	Lupine
Lavender	Lilies (many varieties)	Phlox (Phlox paniculata)
Leadwort (dwarf)	Lobelia	Rudbeckia
Narcissus (miniature varieties; bulbs)	Loosestrife	Solidago
Painted daisy	Peony	Thermopsis
Phlox (Phlox subulata)	Phlox	Verbascum
Potentilla	Poppy	Yarrow (Coronation Gold variety)
Primrose	Rudbeckia	Yucca
Salvia (Salvia azurea)	Shasta daisy	
Stokesia	Spiderwort (Tradescantia sp.)	
Tulip (botanical varieties; bulb)	Tulips	
Veronica (some varieties)	Virginia bluebells	
Viola*		
*Biennial		

son. Most gardeners build their collections of perennials slowly over the years, investing a few dollars each year. Each plant can be better appreciated when acquired in this way. Trading plants with fellow gardeners is a great way to fill areas of your borders, too.

Consider the money spent on perennials as a colorful, lovely investment in your property and personal pleasure. Keep in mind that plants you set out will fill that spot for many years, so the initial investment, when spread out over the years, may make the price of even an expensive plant ultimately add up to just pennies a year.

Eventually, most gardeners find a particular plant they like more than the others and collect as many varieties of it as they can find: daylilies, hostas, lilies, dahlias, and iris are popular specialties.

Your perennial's first year is its most important, because it is establishing its root system. Plant it well and keep a close eye on its needs. In the following years, all you'll need to do is feed and water it occasionally. Perennials become like old friends—they visit each year.

APPROXIMATE BLOOM DATES

| **Spring** | **Summer** | **Fall** |
February through early May	*Mid-May through August*	*Late August to frost*
Ajuga	Astilbe	*Anemone hupehensis*
Anchusa	Baby's-breath	Aster, Hardy
Anemone canadensis	Balloon flower	Candytuft (Autumn Snow variety)
Artemisia, Silver Mound	Bellflower	Chrysanthemum
Basket-of-gold alyssum	Bee balm	Daylilies (late-season varieties)
Bleeding-heart	Butterfly weed	*Helleborus niger* (Christmas rose)
Buttercup	Columbine	Hosta *(Hosta tardiflora)*
Candytuft	Coreopsis	Sedum
Crocus (bulb)	Coralbells	Spiderwort *(Tradescantia* variety Blue Stone)
Dianthus *(Dianthus* x *allwoodi)*	Daylily	
Doronicum	Delphinium	
Dwarf iris	Gaillardia	
Geum	Gas plant	**Note:** Many of the "summer" perennials will continue to bloom until frost if dead flowers are regularly removed and the plant is not allowed to go to seed earlier in the season. A few of the early varieties, such as viola, may have a second season of bloom if the fall is cool and the moisture supply is sufficient.
Grape hyacinth (bulb)	Globe thistle	
Hepatica	Helenium	
Hyacinth (bulb)	Heliopsis	
Phlox subulata	Iris	
Poppy *(Papaver burseri)*	Liatris	
Scilla siberica (bulb)	Lilies (bulb)	
Tulip (botanical varieties; bulb)	Lobelia	
Viola	Loosestrife	
Virginia bluebells	Peony	
	Phlox	
	Poppy	
	Rudbeckia	
	Salvia *(Salvia azurea)*	
	Shasta daisy	
	Spiderwort *(Tradescantia* sp.)	
	Thermopsis	
	Veronica	
	Yarrow	

ABCs of Perennials

When you plant a perennial, you're making a long-lasting investment in color. But before you plant, be sure to check this section for information on season of bloom, zonal hardiness, height of plant at maturity, preferences for sun or shade, soil type, color or colors available, and special cultural information about each species.

ADONIS
Also called spring adonis
Adonis vernalis

ZONE: 3
HEIGHT: 12 inches
BLOOM TIME: March to April
An early bloomer, adonis is often the first plant in the perennial border to show color. Its feathery green foliage and bright yellow blossoms are always welcome after a long colorless winter.

Adonis grows well in a sunny location and tolerates most soil types, but for best results, the plants need a constant supply of moisture. Use adonis in rock gardens and along the front of the border where its early color can be best appreciated. It is especially useful planted in a mass or mixed with wildflowers.

Adonis can be propagated from seeds sown during the spring and fall. Or mature plants can be divided in late spring or fall.

AGERATUM, HARDY
Also called mist flower
Eupatorium coelestinum

ZONE: 3
HEIGHT: 24 to 36 inches
BLOOM TIME: August to September
Hardy ageratum is valuable for late summer color in the perennial border. Its numerous flowers are bright blue.

Hardy ageratum requires little attention and does best in a slightly shaded location. Plants grow in clumps and are extra showy in mass plantings. To propagate, take root cuttings in early spring.

ALUMROOT (See coralbells)

ALYSSUM
Also called basket-of-gold alyssum
Aurinia saxatilis

ZONE: 3
HEIGHT: 12 to 15 inches
BLOOM TIME: Early spring
Often confused with the annual flower, sweet alyssum, basket-of-gold alyssum is grown primarily for its brilliant golden blossoms. Its low-growing nature makes it useful in rock gardens and on slopes. The plants require no special care and grow well in both sunny and partially sunny locations.

Start plants from seeds sown outdoors in the spring or in the fall, with the seedlings overwintered in a cold frame. For quicker results, take stem cuttings any time during the summer.

A. *saxatilis* 'citrina' provides more color than other varieties; A. *saxatilis* 'compacta' has similar growth habits but is somewhat shorter.

ALKANET (See anchusa)

ANCHUSA
Also called alkanet
Anchusa azurea

ZONE: 3
HEIGHT: One to four feet
BLOOM TIME: All summer
Anchusa grows best in a slightly shady location where it is protected from summer heat. Plants require no special care but will respond generously to extra attention. Remove dead flower clusters as they appear to keep the plant blooming all summer long.

Anchusa is available in several varieties, which range in height up to the four-foot-tall A. *azurea*. All varieties are deep blue. To propagate, take root cuttings in spring or fall, or let the last crop of flowers mature and reseed themselves. In the early spring, transplant the new seedlings.

ANTHEMIS
Also called golden marguerite
Anthemis tinctoria

ZONE: 3
HEIGHT: 30 to 36 inches
BLOOM TIME: June to frost
No matter what kind of soil your garden has, anthemis will bloom profusely all summer. All

it needs to produce its disklike yellow or white flowers is a sunny location. Foliage is finely cut and aromatic.

Plant seeds outdoors in the spring, or divide the rootstock of mature plants. Spring-sown plants will often blossom their first summer. Anthemis makes an excellent mid-border plant.

AQUILEGIA (See columbine)

ARMERIA (See thrift)

ARTEMISIA
Also called dusty-miller
Artemisia sp.

ZONE: 3
HEIGHT: Varies with variety
BLOOM TIME: Spring through summer
This family consists of two major plant groups—wormwood and southernwood. Both are grown for their attractive gray-green foliage and delicate scent. Southernwood has lemon-, camphor-, and citrus-scented varieties. Start plants of both groups from root divisions or stem cuttings. Wormwood can be grown from seeds sown in a sunny location in late fall or early spring.

Use *A. ludoviciana 'albula'* (Silver-King) for a background in your garden and for wreath-making. Use *A. schmidtiana 'nana'* (Silver Mound) for edging your flower garden. Use in front- or mid-border locations.

ASTER, HARDY
Also called michaelmas daisy
Aster sp.

ZONE: 4
HEIGHT: To 48 inches
BLOOM TIME: Late summer to fall
Asters are a sure bet if you want a showcase of color in late summer and fall. Asters thrive in almost any soil type, so long as they are in a sunny location. Taller varieties may need staking in windy areas.

Divide plants in the early spring every three or four years, being sure to remove the woody center portions of the plant. To encourage bushiness, pinch back tall varieties in mid-June. Although perennial asters can be started from seed, most will not come true because of hybridization.

Some of the most popular varieties are *A. novae-angliae* 'Harrington's Pink' and *A. novi-belgi* 'Sailor Boy' (violet). Dwarf varieties include: Persian Rose, Melba (pink),

Blue Bouquet, Snow Cushion (white), and Beechwood Challenger (red).

ASTER, STOKES'
(See stokesia)

ASTILBE
Also called false spirea
Astilbe x arendsi

ZONE: 4
HEIGHT: 15 to 30 inches
BLOOM TIME: June to July
Available in white, pink, red, and salmon, astilbe puts on a good show even in shady gardens. Large, feathery flower heads are borne on attractive, finely cut foliage throughout most of the summer. Astilbe thrives on almost any soil type and demands little attention.

Start plants in early spring from seed or by division. For best growth, keep plants well watered and fed. A two- to three-inch layer of mulch around the base of the plant will keep roots cool and moist.

AVENS (See geum)

BABY'S-BREATH
Gypsophila paniculata

ZONE: 3
HEIGHT: Four feet
BLOOM TIME: June to July
Few planting combinations can equal the display of a mass planting of baby's-breath. Baby's-breath grows best in alkaline soil and needs a sunny location to produce its many airy sprays of double white or pink flowers.

In early spring, sow seeds where the plants are expected to stand. Baby's-breath seedlings are nearly impossible to transplant once they have started growing. Divide established clumps every few years, and start new plants from root cuttings.

There is also a creeping variety of baby's-breath *(G. repens)* that grows only a few inches tall. These plants come in both pink and white forms, and they are especially suitable for rock gardens.

BACHELOR'S-BUTTON (See centaurea)

BALLOON FLOWER
Platycodon grandiflorus

BALLOON FLOWER
(continued)

ZONE: 3
HEIGHT: 20 inches
BLOOM TIME: July to August
An old favorite that no perennial border should be without is the balloon flower. Its star-shaped blue, pink, or white flowers, borne on gracefully arching stems, add a touch of elegance to the garden. Balloon flowers need a sunny, well-drained location.

Start plants in the early spring from seeds or by root starts, spacing the plants 15 inches apart. Plants take several years to get established, but once they get well rooted, they will bloom yearly for almost a lifetime. Balloon flowers are ideal plants for mid-border sites.

BAPTISIA

Also called blue or false indigo

Baptisia australis

ZONE: 3
HEIGHT: Four to five feet
BLOOM TIME: June
A hardy perennial that produces plenty of lupine-like flowers in tall, terminal spikes, baptisia is a good candidate for back-of-the-border locations. It is native to North America and grows well in naturalized situations.

Plant baptisia where it will get the benefit of full sun, although partial shade is acceptable. It's not fussy about soil conditions and will continue to thrive even during periods of drought. In windy areas, flower stalks may need to be staked. Baptisia grows rapidly and will quickly spread over a large area. On problem slopes, it's an effective ground cover.

Start new plants from seed in the early spring or from root divisions of established clumps. Baptisia is also available in yellow and white flowering varieties. *B. tinctoria* is the yellow flowering form, and *B. alba* is the white flowering form.

BASKET-OF-GOLD ALYSSUM
(See alyssum)

BEE BALM

Also called bergamot
Monarda didyma

ZONE: 4
HEIGHT: Two to three feet

BLOOM TIME: July to August
Quick-growing and attractive, bee balm is perfect for a mid- to back-of-the-border location. Clusters of white, pink, red, or purple tubular flowers form on tall stalks each summer. Plants are hardy and withstand drought and destructive insect attack. Clumps increase rapidly and need to be divided every year or so to be kept within bounds. Plant bee balm in a sunny or partially sunny location, and keep plants mulched for optimum growth.

Bee balm is attractive to both bees and hummingbirds.

BELLFLOWER
(See campanula)

BERGAMOT
(See bee balm)

BETONY
(See stachys)

BLANKET FLOWER
(See gaillardia)

BLEEDING-HEART

Dicentra spectabilis

ZONE: 4
HEIGHT: 24 inches
BLOOM TIME: Early spring
Every year this old-fashioned favorite brightens the perennial border with graceful stems of pink, heart-shaped flowers. For best results, buy nursery stock and space plants about 24 inches apart. Bleeding-heart needs a moist, partially shady location. It's especially useful planted in bulb gardens where its finely cut foliage makes an excellent background for early flowering bulbs.

In mid- to late summer, most bleeding-hearts will die to the ground, leaving space for annual flowers. Be sure to mark the plant's location so the roots are not harmed by cultivation; established bleeding-hearts should be disturbed as little as possible.

Other shorter varieties, some with different shapes of hearts, have recently been developed. But they are not as reliably hardy as the old-fashioned variety.

BLUE MARGUERITE
(See felicia)

BLUET, MOUNTAIN
(See centaurea)

BRUNNERA
**Also called
Siberian forget-me-not
and Siberian bugloss**
Brunnera macrophylla

ZONE: 4
HEIGHT: 18 inches
BLOOM TIME: May

Occasionally listed as *Anchusa myosotidi-flora,* brunnera closely resembles the perennial forget-me-not, or *Anchusa azurea.* But it appears earlier and, therefore, makes a good addition to the bulb garden.

Sow seeds in late fall and transplant the seedlings to the planting bed as soon as possible in the spring. Because plants are only half-hardy in cold weather locations, let the plant set seed each fall, just in case it is killed by winter temperatures.

BUGLOSS, SIBERIAN
(See brunnera)

BUTTERCUP
Ranunculus sp.

ZONE: 4
HEIGHT: 18 inches
BLOOM TIME: May

Buttercup is often used to describe any one of a number of flowering plants in the enormous ranunculus family. Many are wildflowers that are indispensable in rock gardens or naturalistic gardens.

One particularly good variety is *R. acris.* It has double yellow flowers on slender stems that often reach 18 inches tall. Plants have finely cut foliage and creep along the ground by runners. For a special effect, mingle acris between a planting of blue bearded iris and bleeding-hearts.

R. amplexicaulis grows to only 12 inches tall and is popular in rock gardens. The flowers are white with yellow centers.

BUTTERFLY WEED
Asclepias tuberosa

ZONE: 4
HEIGHT: Two to three feet
BLOOM TIME: Summer

A close relative of the milkweed, butterfly weed has none of its cousin's bad habits. Plants rarely spread and can tolerate any soil type so long as they are planted in a sunny location. Relatively insect- and disease-resistant, butterfly weed is covered with umbels of bright orange flowers all summer long. After the plants have finished blooming, they are covered by the attractive seedpods characteristic of the milkweed family.

Butterfly weed can be started from seed, but best results are obtained by purchasing nursery-started plants. Plants develop a long taproot that makes transplanting difficult, so be sure to plant butterfly weed where it is to remain in the garden. Because plants are slow to emerge in the spring, mark the growing location so the plants are not disturbed by early spring cultivation.

CAMPANULA
Also called bellflower or Canterbury-bells
Campanula sp.

ZONE: 3
HEIGHT: Eight to 36 inches
BLOOM TIME: June

A common plant in almost every perennial garden, campanula comes in an almost limitless array of varieties. Plants thrive in both sunny and partially sunny locations and in almost any soil type.

Plant bellflowers in early spring in mid- to back-of-the-border locations. To keep the plants vigorous, divide them every three or four years. Pinch off flowers as they fade to prolong the blooming season and to prevent the plants from spreading through the garden. All campanula should have winter protection. Plants should be lifted, divided, and replanted every two or three years to ensure hardiness. Do this after blooms end.

C. carpatica makes an excellent edging plant. It sends up blue blossoms all summer long and is hardy to Zone 3. One variety, *C. carpatica 'alba',* has the same growth habit but bears white flowers. *C. glomerata* has both blue and white varieties and will grow to 20 inches tall. These bloom during June and July and make ideal mixed border plants. They multiply generously in Zone 4 southward.

C. persicifolia, or peach-leaved bellflower, is popular for its white or blue nodding flowers on three-foot stems. Some July-flowering varieties have double flowers. Set plants of this variety ten to 12 inches apart. Hardy to Zone 3.

C. lactiflora varieties are generally not hardy north of Zone 5. They are partially shade tolerant and have blue flowers.

CANDYTUFT
Also called iberis
Iberis sempervirens

ZONE: 3
HEIGHT: Four to eight inches
BLOOM TIME: May

In warm climates, perennial candytuft stays green all winter. In cold areas, the plants often die back to the ground. Because of its low-growing nature and its ability to grow in almost any sunny location, candytuft makes a useful and attractive edging plant in front of perennial borders or along walkways.

Start plants from seeds sown in the fall. Or divide established clumps in early spring, spacing them about 15 inches apart. Small white flowers appearing in May often turn a light shade of lilac as they mature. One variety, Autumn Snow, blooms a second time in the fall, then stays in bloom until frost. It grows to seven inches tall. Variety Pygmy, which only reaches four inches, is easily propagated by divisions or seeds. Or use cuttings taken in the spring, rooted in vermiculite, and then planted. Use candytuft as an underplanting with May-flowering tulips. Two other commonly grown varieties are Little Gem and Snowflake.

CANTERBURY-BELLS
(See campanula)

CARDINAL FLOWER
(See lobelia)

CAROLINA LUPINE
(See thermopsis)

CATANANCHE
(See cupid's-dart)

CATCHFLY
(See lychnis)

CENTAUREA
Also called mountain bluet, cornflower, or perennial bachelor's-button
Centaurea montana

ZONE: 4
HEIGHT: Two feet
BLOOM TIME: All summer

Most members of the centaurea family are annuals, including *C. cyanus,* which is also called bachelor's-button. Of the perennial varieties, *C. montana* is one of the most popular. *C. montana* has fuzzy, silver-gray leaves and bright blue flowers. For optimum growth, plant centaurea in a sunny location.

Start plants from seeds sown in the early spring, or divide established plants every second or third year. They are excellent additions to middle-of-the-border plantings. Plants self-sow readily and can become a pest in some locations. They are long lasting and make good cut flowers.

CENTRANTHUS
(See jupiter's-beard)

CERASTIUM
Also called snow-in-summer
Cerastium tomentosum

ZONE: 2
HEIGHT: Six inches
BLOOM TIME: Summer

Cerastium is the perfect plant for steep slopes, sandy areas, or rock gardens where its quick-spreading nature and silvery foliage can be used to advantage. The many tiny, star-shaped white flowers give the plant its common name, snow-in-summer. Start cerastium from seed sown in late spring. Or take stem cuttings or divide established clumps after the plants have finished flowering.

Space clumps about ten inches apart. Don't plan on the planting area being used for other plants at another time; once established, cerastium is almost impossible to eradicate.

CERATOSTIGMA
(See leadwort)

CHINESE-LANTERN
Physalis alkekengi

ZONE: 3
HEIGHT: Two feet
BLOOM TIME: July to August

Grown primarily for its bright red, two-inch calyxes, chinese-lantern is not recommended for a mixed perennial border because of its spreading habits. Start plants from seeds sown in the spring or by division of an established clump.

Chinese-lantern grows under adverse conditions and can be used to brighten up waste places where other perennials won't grow. Calyxes are commonly cut after they turn red for use in dried arrangements.

CHRISTMAS ROSE
(See helleborus)

CHRYSANTHEMUMS
(See pages 192 to 193)

CINQUEFOIL
(See potentilla)

COLUMBINE
Aquilegia sp.

ZONE: 3
HEIGHT: 20 to 30 inches
BLOOM TIME: June

There are few places in the garden where the columbine doesn't seem at home. Try it in the perennial border, rock garden, wildflower garden, or mingled among late-flowering tulips. The columbine is actually a native wildflower that produces arching sprays of red, white, blue, pink, or yellow crown-shaped flowers.

Plant columbine in a sunny location where it will get full to partial sun. Mature plants are difficult to divide; best results are gained by planting seeds. To ensure perennial quality, cut all spent blooms before they start to make seed. When the flowering period has ended, cut foliage back to about four inches.

A. caerulea, or Rocky Mountain columbine, is one of the loveliest of columbines. It has long spurs and blooms on one- to two-foot stems.

CONEFLOWER
(See rudbeckia)

CORALBELLS
Also called alumroot
Heuchera sanguinea

ZONE: 3
HEIGHT: 18 inches
BLOOM TIME: June to September

Mounded foliage and tall, blooming spikes of small, bell-shaped flowers are the trademark of the coralbells. Coral or pink are the most commonly available colors, but plants with white, red, or chartreuse blossoms are becoming more popular. Coralbells are an important addition to the perennial border

where they add color all season.

Propagate from spring-sown seeds, or divide established clumps in the spring or fall. Plant coralbells in a sunny or partially sunny location that will stay moist even during the intense heat of midsummer. Smaller, new plants often form around the base of the mother plants and make it easy to increase your supply. Replant, spacing young plants about 12 inches apart.

COREOPSIS
Also called
perennial tickseed
Coreopsis sp.

ZONE: 4
HEIGHT: 16 to 30 inches
BLOOM TIME: June to frost

A dependable bloomer, coreopsis makes its presence known in the perennial border with yellow, single or semidouble, daisy-like flowers. Plants can be started from seed sown in late summer and overwintered in a cold frame. Or root divisions of established clumps can be taken in early spring. Coreopsis requires a sunny location but will thrive in most any type of soil. Space young plants about ten inches apart.

CORNFLOWER
(See centaurea)

CRANESBILL GERANIUM
(See geranium)

CUPID'S-DART
Also called catananche
Catananche caerulea

ZONE: 4
HEIGHT: 15 to 18 inches
BLOOM TIME: July to September

A heavy bloomer, cupid's-dart is easily started from seeds sown in the garden after the soil warms. Plants require a sunny location and cannot tolerate overly wet soil. Cupid's-dart has feathery foliage and comes in either a blue or white flowering variety. The plants are excellent used at mid-border for a constant supply of summer color. Flowers dry easily and make good additions to dried bouquets.

If you have an established clump of cupid's-dart, divide plants in the spring. One commonly grown dependable variety is Blue Giant. It rarely needs dividing.

Most popular perennials

CHRYSANTHEMUMS

Chrysanthemums have come a long way from the ancient gardens of China and Japan to the football games of today. And they've been greatly improved along the way. They vary from the 12-inch-tall cushion type to the three-foot giants. Plant all varieties in a sunny, well-drained location.

Start new plants from seeds, root divisions, and stem cuttings. Or buy started plants in midsummer. In cold climates, cover the plant during the winter with leaves or straw. To encourage flowering before hard frost, choose varieties grown locally. Pink flowering Fortune (above) teams with the bright yellow Rustic mum.

With good growing conditions, Golden Treasure produces seven-inch flowers. It's a popular corsage.

If a mature plant needs dividing, wait until it's three inches tall in the spring. Dig up and pull apart, selecting sturdy shoots.

Space transplanted shoots one foot apart. Cut or pinch off 3/4 inch from the top of new divisions. Prune when plant is six inches tall.

For bushy, heavily budded plants, fertilize every ten days. Use a two-inch-thick mulch to keep roots cool and conserve ground moisture.

Potomac is a single-flowered variety that grows two feet tall, with five- to seven-inch bloom.

Most popular perennials

DAYLILIES

Every morning new buds on daylilies open to offer stars of color in the garden. Although individual flowers last only a day, each plant blooms for two weeks or more. If you set out an early, a mid-season, and a late variety, you'll have a trio that will flower in succession all summer long.

You can grow daylilies wherever you live. They aren't fussy about soil, they're seldom bothered by insects or disease, and they'll bloom in filtered shade as well as full sun. Plant in fall, feed each spring, and water deeply during dry spells. Varieties range in height from 18-inch miniatures to five-foot towering beauties.

Distant Shore is a good choice for sunny spots in your perennial border or for a mass planting.

Carey Quinn

Kindly Light

Daylily culture

Set out root divisions to start new daylilies. Get divisions from a gardening friend who is separating plants, or buy nursery-grown starts.

For each division, dig a hole 12 to 14 inches in diameter and about 12 inches deep. Firm a cone of blended soil in the center of the hole, and radiate roots around it. Add the rest of the soil around the roots and water well, but do not tamp the soil again.

Divide plants every four or five years; do the job any time after flowering and before frost. Lift the entire clump, cut it into six or eight root sections, and cut off the tops. Replant, spacing new plants 24 to 30 inches apart. Daylilies will quickly fill in the area.

Winnetka

DAISY, BLUE
(See felicia)

DAYLILIES
(See pages 194 to 195)

DELPHINIUM

Delphinium sp.

ZONE: 3
HEIGHT: To eight feet
BLOOM TIME: June and again in autumn

Spring is the time to plant delphiniums. Start with sturdy nursery plants for the impressive hybrid varieties, such as the famous Round Table series of Pacific Coast Hybrids, or the English Blackmore and Langdon Hybrids. Flowers come in yellow, white, blue, pink, or lavender. If you start from seed, sow indoors or in a cold frame in early spring.

Delphiniums require a sunny location but often will not prosper in areas where summers are hot and dry. Plants are also heavy feeders, so before you set any new plants out in the garden, be sure to spread a two-inch layer of well-rotted manure or compost over the garden bed. After this has been tilled under, spread 5-10-5 fertilizer in proportions recommended on the package. Thoroughly spade in an additional two inches of compost or manure, and soak the entire bed. When soil has dried enough to be workable, you're ready to set out new plants.

Space plants about two feet apart to ensure enough ventilation around the plants for vigorous growth. Set crown at soil level—not below. Water well after planting.

Plants do best in an alkaline soil, so mixing in some lime is often a good idea. Keep plants moist at all times.

As bloom stalks develop, set stakes in place, and be ready to fasten bloom stems to them well ahead of the time buds begin to open. If not staked, most delphiniums will topple over in the slightest wind. Most varieties will bloom again later in the summer if the bloom stalk is clipped off as soon as it has finished blooming.

Delphiniums can add a lot of color and charm to the perennial border, but they often show to best advantage planted in a bed of their own. Or plant daylilies or campanulas in front of them. Divide established clumps after the plants get too thick and air circulation is blocked. Plants do not all bloom at once, so bloom periods will overlap.

To keep plants strong and blooming well, add manure or compost to soil every year, in late fall or early spring.

DIANTHUS
Also called pink
Dianthus sp.

ZONE: 3 to 7
HEIGHT: Three to 24 inches
BLOOM TIME: Summer

The dianthus, or pink family includes both annual and perennial varieties familiar to every home gardener. Carnations (*D. caryophyllus*) and sweet williams (*D. barbatus*) are two of the most popular, but several alpine species of pinks are also commonly grown.

One of the best of the alpine varieties is *D. alpinus*. This plant rarely gets over four inches tall and is a perfect candidate for rock or wall gardens. Another species, *D. x allwoodi*, is available in a large mixture of colors and has sweetly fragrant flowers. It, too, is a good addition to the rock or wall garden. Plants are intolerant of hot, dry weather.

Pinks enjoy a sunny exposure and well-drained soil. Slightly alkaline or neutral soil is best. Start plants from seed sown in the garden after all danger of frost has passed. Or make stem cuttings of varieties you especially like, replanting them in the garden after they take root. After clumps become established, divide them every few years in the early spring. Flowers are available in pink, white, red, or bicolor.

DICENTRA
(See bleeding-heart)

DICTAMNUS
(See gas plant)

DORONICUM
Also called leopard's-bane
Doronicum cordatum

ZONE: 4
HEIGHT: 24 inches
BLOOM TIME: Spring

Valued for its bright yellow, daisy-like blossoms, doronicum is a lovely addition to front or mid-border locations. Plants grow in both sunny or partially sunny locations and prefer a rich, fertile soil.

Foliage of most varieties has a tendency to die down during midsummer, so locations should be marked to avoid damaging the root system during cultivation. Root systems are shallow, and the plants will be more tenacious during drought if they are mulched.

One of the hardiest varieties of doronicum

available is *D. cordatum* 'Madam Mason.' It demands no special type of soil and will sometimes put on a second show of bloom if first blooms are promptly cut off as they fade. This variety usually holds its foliage throughout the summer months.

To ensure plant hardiness, clumps should be divided every two or three years after the plants have finished flowering.

DRAGONHEAD
(See physostegia)

DROPWORT
(See meadowsweet)

DUSTY-MILLER
(See artemisia)

ECHINOPS
(See globe thistle)

EUPATORIUM
(See ageratum)

EUPHORBIA
(See spurge)

FALSE DRAGONHEAD
(See physostegia)

FALSE SPIREA
(See astilbe)

FALSE SUNFLOWER
(See helenium)

FELICIA
Also called blue marguerite and blue daisy
Felicia amelloides

ZONE: 5
HEIGHT: One to three feet
BLOOM TIME: Early summer to frost
Valued for its sky-blue flowers on long wiry stems, felicia is best treated as an annual in areas with cold winters. Plants are generous

bloomers, with blossoms that often reach an inch in diameter. Flowers are excellent additions to cut arrangements and are quickly replaced on the parent plant.

Plant in a sunny location. After the main bloom period ends in midsummer, cut the entire plant back to a height of four to six inches. This should induce new growth and another bloom period late in the summer. Start plants from cuttings taken from established plants, or sow a new crop of seeds each spring. Plants will occasionally self-sow.

FEVERFEW
Chrysanthemum parthenium

ZONE: 3
HEIGHT: To 30 inches
BLOOM TIME: Summer
Often listed as matricaria in garden catalogues, this old-fashioned perennial produces masses of inch-wide, cream-colored flowers every summer. It's a good plant to mix with the brighter perennials. Foliage and flower are both scented and make good additions to a fresh cut bouquet. Feverfew is tolerant of most light and soil conditions but will not grow in deep shade. Start plants from divisions of established plants, or buy nursery stock. As the clumps increase in size, lift, divide, and replant every three or four years. To keep the plants in blooming condition, cut off flowers as they fade.

FILIPENDULA
(See meadowsweet)

FLAX
Linum sp.

ZONE: 3
HEIGHT: 12 to 18 inches
BLOOM TIME: Summer
Flax is an often overlooked candidate for the perennial garden. There are both blue and yellow varieties that ask for little more than a sunny spot in the garden. Although most cultivated types are of medium height, the dwarf form, *L. perenne 'alpinum',* is suited to the rock garden because of its small blue flowers in the spring. Another commonly grown flax is *L. flavum,* which blooms profusely all summer on five-inch stems, with feathery foliage and showy yellow flowers. The Heavenly Blue variety produces bright blue flowers on 12- to 18-inch stems, with new flushes of bloom every few weeks.

Some varieties of flax are only half-hardy in cold climates, so it's a good idea to start a new

FLAX
(continued)

crop each spring from seed just in case established plants are winterkilled. Plants started from seeds often will not blossom until their second summer.

Divide established clumps every few years, spacing the young divisions at least eight to ten inches apart.

FLEABANE
Erigeron sp.

ZONE: 3
HEIGHT: Ten to 36 inches
BLOOM TIME: Summer
Fleabane is an undemanding, daisy-like flower that does well in almost any location. Flowers come in pink, lavender, white, orange, or blue. Plants will often bloom all summer.

Plants are easily started from seed or by division. Space divisions eight to ten inches apart. Taller varieties lend themselves well to the mixed perennial border. Shorter varieties are often some of the best plants for edgings or rock gardens. Members of the family that are good subjects for mixed flower borders include: *E. coulteri,* or mountain daisy, bearing white or lavender blooms in midsummer; *E. aurantiacus,* which produces orange blooms and grows ten inches high; and *E. speciosus,* showy or Oregon fleabane with rose, lilac, or white blooms, resembling hardy asters.

FORGET-ME-NOT, SIBERIAN
(See brunnera)

GAILLARDIA
Also called blanket flower
Gaillardia aristata

ZONE: 3
HEIGHT: 12 to 30 inches
BLOOM TIME: Summer
Grown primarily for its attractive two-toned flowers in shades of gold, red, and brown, gaillardia is often best when planted in mass. It also adds a lot of sharp color to mid-border locations. Gaillardia is a half-hardy perennial that will often die back during the winter. Plants are easily started from seed.

Gaillardia makes excellent cut flowers. The stems are so long that the plants will often

need staking in the garden. They enjoy full sun and require a well-drained soil. Gaillardia will tolerate quite sandy soil and seaside conditions.

Divide established plants every few years to keep them vigorous. An annual variety is also available.

Hybrid *(G. x grandiflora)* perennials that make fine border plants include Burgundy, with wine-red bloom that can be as large as three inches across and reach 30 inches in height; Monarch strain, which comes in a range of colors; and Yellow Queen. *G. x grandiflora* 'Goblin', a dwarf variety, is only eight to 12 inches tall, with dark red flowers bordered with yellow.

GAS PLANT
Dictamnus sp.

ZONE: 3
HEIGHT: 24 to 36 inches
BLOOM TIME: Summer
No perennial border is complete without several specimens of gas plants. These old-fashioned favorites bloom faithfully every year for generations. Requiring no special care, gas plants quickly form bushy plants three feet high and three feet in diameter. Plants get their name from the fact that on a hot night when no breezes are stirring, you can often produce a small burst of flame by holding a lighted match over the blooms.

Gas plants can be started from seed, but they will not bloom until their third summer. It's often quicker and easier to purchase nursery stock. Space plants about three feet apart, preferably in a sunny, well-drained location. Back-of-the-border locations are ideal.

Gas plants are long-lived and almost impossible to transplant once they are established, so be sure to plant them where they are to remain. Mature plants will bloom in June and July, but the foliage stays green all summer. Late-blooming bearded iris and spuria iris are enhanced if planted close to clumps of gas plants. When bruised, leaves and stems emit a pleasant fragrance similar to lemons.

D. albus grows about 30 inches tall with spikes of white flowers in June and July. *D. albus* 'rubra' puts out pink blooms but resembles the white variety in every other way. Both are also good used as long-lasting cut flowers.

GAY-FEATHER
(See liatris)

GENTIAN
Gentiana sp.

ZONE: 4
HEIGHT: Four to 18 inches
BLOOM TIME: July to September

Gentians are more often seen in the rock garden than in the perennial border. These plants are descended from mountain wildflowers; they still exhibit a low-growing nature and dislike of hot weather, both characteristics of alpine natives.

Gentians occasionally take a year or longer to start from seed, so purchase nursery stock for best results. Most seed-sown stock will not bloom for at least three years. In areas where summers are hot and long, forget the plant altogether. But in areas where the gentian will grow, there is no more beautiful blue-flowering perennial.

Plant in a lightly shaded location with well-drained soil. *G. andrewsi*, also called the bottle gentian, is one of the most widely grown members of the family. Flowers appear in June and July and are a deep purplish-blue. *G. saponaria* is also fairly widely cultivated. It has blue flowers borne on solitary stems eight to 18 inches in height.

Gentians are also commonly found growing wild in the deciduous forests of North America. These plants must not be dug, because, as in the case of the fringed gentian, they are endangered species and are protected by law.

GERANIUM
Also called
cranesbill geranium
Geranium sp.

ZONE: 4
HEIGHT: Dwarf to ten inches
BLOOM TIME: Early spring

Often confused with the genus *Pelargonium* (also commonly called geranium), cranesbill geranium is a hardy perennial that forms mounds of color throughout the summer. Varieties come in pink, red, or purple, and all are primarily used as edging plants for the perennial border.

Geraniums require no special care and will bloom heavily in full sun or partial shade. They do well in poor soil. In fact, a soil too fertile can result in spindly growth. Foliage is deeply cut and attractive. Smaller forms are good candidates for rock and wall gardens.

Once established, mature clumps need only be divided every fourth or fifth year in the early spring. New plants are best spaced about 12 inches apart. One popular variety, *G. himalayense*, produces purplish flowers

on ten-inch stems and continues to bloom from May to August. *G. sanguineum*, a European native, is generous with its red-purple flowers, also from May to August. *G. cinereum 'splendens'* and *G. dalmaticum* are both reliable dwarf forms. A taller variety, *G. ibericum*, easily grows 18 inches tall. It produces quantities of purple flowers and has deeply lobed leaves.

GERBERA
Also called transvaal daisy
Gerbera jamesoni

ZONE: 8
HEIGHT: 18 inches
BLOOM TIME: Summer

Easily grown in Zone 8 and southward, gerberas also make good greenhouse plants in the North. Plants take at least a year to blossom from seed, so purchase nursery stock or take stem cuttings from mature plants. Set roots so crown is at soil level or just above, and plant in late fall. If you sow seeds, be sure the fuzzy end of the seed is slightly above the soil's surface.

Gerbera is easily recognized by its basal rosette of leaves, with wiry two-foot stems, topped off with daisy-like cream, pink, yellow, rose, orange-red, or violet flowers. Flowers make good additions to cut bouquets.

Divide plants every three or four years, being sure to space plants 12 inches apart.

GEUM
Also called avens
Geum sp.

ZONE: 5
HEIGHT: To two feet
BLOOM TIME: Summer

Although they are somewhat tender to extreme heat or cold, geums will produce plenty of yellow, orange, or scarlet flowers when conditions are to their liking. Plant in full sun in soil high in organic matter. Mulch to help keep the roots moist during hot midsummer weather.

Seed-sown plants will often not mature for at least three years, so purchase nursery stock. Space plants 12 to 18 inches apart. Clumps increase in size slowly; division is seldom needed. In areas with cold winters, mulch the plants more heavily.

The variety *G. quellyon* 'Lady Stratheden' has yellow, double flowers on two-foot stems, but the plant is not hardy north of Zone 6. *G. quellyon* 'Mrs. Bradshaw', Zone 6, has bright red flowers on two-foot stems. Both varieties bloom in June and July.

GLOBEFLOWER
Trollius europaeus

ZONE: 3
HEIGHT: 30 inches
BLOOM TIME: May to June
The moisture-loving globeflower will grow any place its roots can stay moist all summer. Before planting, spade in plenty of compost or organic matter to increase the ability of the soil to retain water. Globeflower will often burn out in a sunny location, so for best results, put it in a spot that will be shaded during the hottest part of the day. Plants are easily started from seeds, but they will not mature for at least one season. For quick results, buy nursery stock. Space plants eight to ten inches apart.

Globeflowers are preferred not only for their ball-like yellow or orange flowers, but also for their finely cut, lacy foliage.

GLOBE THISTLE
Echinops exaltatus

ZONE: 4
HEIGHT: Four feet
BLOOM TIME: July to September
Globe thistle makes an attractive and unusual back-of-the-border plant. Its white, woolly foliage and metallic-blue flowers are good accents against darker plants in front. Start new plants from seeds in early spring or from root divisions. Plants will grow in almost any soil and in either sun or partial shade.

Use flowers in dried arrangements. Taplow Blue variety is a perfect companion for late-flowering yellow daylilies.

GOLDENROD
(See solidago)

GREEK VALERIAN
(See jacob's-ladder)

GYPSOPHILA
(See baby's-breath)

HELENIUM
Also called false sunflower or sneezeweed
Helenium autumnale

ZONE: 3
HEIGHT: Three to four feet

BLOOM TIME: Late summer
A late bloomer, helenium is valuable in the garden border for fall color when few other plants are in bloom. Taller varieties have a tendency to get rangy, but smaller types rarely need to be staked. Helenium is tolerant of temperature extremes and soil types, although it will grow better in rich, organic soil. Flowers vary from yellow and red to bronze and are daisy-like in shape.

Because plants grow so vigorously, they benefit from being lifted, divided, and replanted in early spring every other year. Plant in a sunny location. Start new plants in early spring from seeds, division, or root cuttings.

Use plants in back-of-the-border locations or alone as a small hedge. Flowers are a good choice for fresh cut flower arrangements.

HELIANTHUS
Also called
perennial sunflower
Helianthus decapetalus 'multiflorus'

ZONE: 4
HEIGHT: Three feet
BLOOM TIME: July to frost
Well suited to any sunny dry spot in your garden, helianthus blooms resemble small sunflowers. (It's a relative of the annual sunflower.) Although they're drought-resistant, these plants will produce masses of bloom if watered and fed regularly. Flowers range from pale yellow to deep orange.

Start plants from seeds in the spring after the weather warms, or plant root divisions. Plants grown from seeds will not produce flowers until the following year. The *H. decapetalus 'multiflorus'* variety will produce double flowers. Use helianthus in back-of-the-border locations; plants spread rapidly and are often better planted alone.

HELIOPSIS
Also called oxeye
Heliopsis helianthoides

ZONE: 3
HEIGHT: To five feet
BLOOM TIME: Summer
A bright spot in any garden, heliopsis produces masses of two- to three-inch, orange-yellow flowers every year. Its importance in bringing color to the garden when few other plants are in bloom cannot be underrated. Heliopsis is hardy in almost any location, though without irrigation it does not stand up well to drought. Plants need full sun. They are storm-resistant and won't topple over in high winds. Use heliopsis in mid- and back-of-

the-border locations. One variety of heliopsis, Pitcherana, deserves much more attention than it often gets; it is a dwarf that rarely grows over three feet tall. This variety is well suited to the perennial border and also valuable as a source of cut flowers. It tolerates drought and even does well in dry places.

Similar to Pitcherana is Scabra, sporting deep yellow flowers with dark centers. Blooms measure up to three inches across, appear from July until frost, and are good both as cut flowers and in dried arrangements. The mature plant will grow three feet tall.

HELLEBORUS
Also called Christmas rose,
Helleborus niger;
or **lenten rose,** *H. orientalis*

ZONE: 4
HEIGHT: 12 inches
BLOOM TIME: Late fall to spring
Christmas and lenten roses are unusual because they bloom during the winter. Christmas rose can bloom any time from December to April, often opening its blossoms through bare spots in the snow. Lenten rose will bloom a little later, usually between March and May. Both plants thrive in a partially shady location with a rich, woodsy soil. Flowers are borne on slender 12- to 15-inch stalks. Colors include purple, white, pink, and green.

In areas where falls are long, cool, and wet, the plants will often bloom in the fall, but if killing frost comes early, plants must be protected from winter. (A discarded storm window turned into a cold frame-like structure, with bricks to support it, works well.) Mulch with several inches of straw. Plants are touchy about being transplanted, so plant seeds in the early fall where plants are to remain.

HEMEROCALLIS
(See daylilies, pages 194 to 195)

HOSTAS
(See pages 202 to 203)

HYPERICUM
Also called St.-John's-wort
Hypericum patulum

ZONE: 5
HEIGHT: Two to three feet

BLOOM TIME: May to August
Bright yellow flowers and green shiny foliage are the calling cards of many hypericum varieties. Although most are considered shrubs, a few species make excellent additions to the perennial border. All species tolerate a variety of soils, including sand. One variety, *H. forresti* 'Hidcote,' produces yellow two-inch flowers with evergreen foliage, if it's grown in warm climates. Some varieties will survive in Zone 4, if they are given good winter protection. Start new plants in the spring from stem cuttings, divisions, or nursery transplants.

IBERIS
(See candytuft)

ICELAND POPPY
Papaver nudicaule

ZONES: 2 to 5
HEIGHT: 12 inches
BLOOM TIME: May to June
If you live in an area with long, dry, and hot summers, you might as well forget Iceland poppies. These plants have their origin in arctic areas and are most effective planted where summers are fairly cool. They can also be grown as a winter annual in the South. Iceland poppies have slightly fragrant crepe paperlike petals, and blooms can get up to three inches across.

To start new plants, sow seeds in early spring. You'll get some flowers the first season, but most plants won't bloom abundantly until their second season. In southern areas, treat plants as annuals. Sow seed in the early fall for bloom in late winter and early spring. Iceland poppies are perfect accent plants for spring-flowering bulbs.

INDIGO, BLUE
(See baptisia)

IRIS
(See pages 204 to 205)

JACOB'S-LADDER
Also called Greek valerian
Polemonium caeruleum

ZONE: 4
HEIGHT: To two feet
BLOOM TIME: Spring
Often considered a wildflower, jacob's-ladder can offer bright blue color to either bulb gar-

Most popular perennials
HOSTAS

Hostas are some of the most exciting and useful plants the home gardener can grow. Formerly, there were only a dozen or so kinds commonly available, but now you can choose from over 300 different varieties. Several new varieties are introduced each year.

Hostas range in size from four-inch miniatures to three-foot giants. Leaf textures vary from smooth and shiny to heavily quilted or soft and lustrous. Leaf shapes are also varied: long and narrow, wide and bluntly pointed, or almost round. Hostas produce showy spikes of either white or blue flowers with both early- and late-flowering varieties.

Hosta plantaginea *is a large member of the family. It produces fragrant August flowers.*

Shade-loving hostas

Hostas, also known as plantain lily or funkia, are hardy to Zone 3 and look lush without fuss. Grow them by planting seeds or started crowns. Seeds are slow to develop into sizable plants, so your best bet is to buy crowns for early spring or fall planting.

Although hostas like rich, moist soil, they survive hot dry spells and perform adequately in poor garden soils. For best growth, plant them in a partially shady location. The clumps will increase in size each year and are easy to divide once they become established.

Use hostas as a ground cover under shade trees, as edgings for walkways and driveways, and in separate beds of several varieties planted to make pleasing contrasts of size, leaf shape, and hue.

As with most recently introduced varieties of plants, many of the new hostas have hefty price tags, but there are plenty of less expensive, more common, varieties that will give you a full range of leaf colors and sizes. Hostas make a good garden investment. They last a lifetime and increase fairly rapidly.

Hosta Francis Williams *has handsome foliage.*

Most popular perennials

IRIS

If you want to start a new garden or just brighten up an old one, plant iris. These easy-to-grow perennials are available in seven major classifications: bulbous, tall bearded, dwarf bearded, Dutch, spuria, Japanese, and Siberian—all of which come in an array of colors, sizes, and varieties. Lengthen the bloom period by mixing the early-blooming bearded and Siberian with the later-blooming spuria and Japanese.

Plant Siberian iris for low-maintenance color.

For moist garden locations, try Norma, a Japanese iris.

Tall bearded iris are sure to be your garden favorites.

The Japanese iris, Gay Galliant, is always eye-catching.

Choose iris

Dutch iris are grown from bulbs and are hardy to Zone 5. They are commonly available in yellow, blue, violet, white, and bicolors. Plant them three inches deep and four inches apart.

Spuria iris are perhaps the hardiest and often grow to heights of 36 to 50 inches. Plant them in a sunny, well-drained location, rich in organic matter. Spurias usually bloom about the time the tall bearded irises are beginning to fade.

Dwarf bearded iris rarely grow over 12 inches tall and are ideal for the rock garden or border. They are available in a wide range of colors; many are sweetly scented. Plant in spring or fall.

Tall bearded iris are some of the most magnificent plants in the perennial border. They are available in an almost limitless array of colors and are winter hardy to Zones 3 and 4, if they are given some protection. Bearded iris are grown from fleshy roots called rhizomes. Plant the rhizomes in the fall just barely below the surface of the soil. If planted too deep, there will be no bloom. Bearded iris are also susceptible to excess moisture, so be sure your planting bed is well drained. Lift, divide, and replant every four or five years.

Japanese iris enjoy wet conditions and will often grow four or five feet tall. They also require a slightly acid soil. Many will produce June flowers eight to 12 inches in diameter.

Siberian iris bloom at the same time as the tall bearded group, but the flowers are more long lasting. Siberian iris require a rich, moist soil but, once established, demand less care than other iris types. Plant Siberian iris in the spring or fall, spacing new plants three or four inches apart. Division is rarely needed.

The bulbous iris varieties are generally small in nature, only growing six to eight inches tall. For more information on bulbous iris, see page 285.

JACOB'S-LADDER
(continued)

dens or shrub borders. Foliage is attractive and fernlike. Jacob's-ladder is especially nice planted with narcissus, and it thrives in any shady or partially shady, cool area.

The plant is tolerant of most soils and should be kept moist at all times. A relative, *P. reptans*—sometimes called by the common name of bluebell—grows to two feet tall and bears clusters of drooping blue flowers. Culture is the same as for jacob's-ladder. There is also a white-flowering variety.

To get new plants, divide established clumps, or let the plants self-sow. In a few years, they can carpet an area. If they get too thick, cut out unwanted plants.

JUPITER'S-BEARD
Also called red valerian
Centranthus ruber

ZONE: 4
HEIGHT: Three feet
BLOOM TIME: Summer
A surefire mid- or back-of-the-border bloomer, jupiter's-beard produces flat clusters of rose or white flowers every summer. Once planted in a sunny or partially sunny location, these plants take off and rarely need any attention. Flowers are sweet scented and long lasting; they're excellent used in fresh cut arrangements. Plants grow in almost any garden soil.

Start new plants by dividing established clumps in early spring, or dig young seedlings around the mother plants. Jupiter's-beard self-sows readily and may have to be controlled to keep it from taking over the garden. *C. ruber 'albus,'* the white form of this plant, has the same growth habits, except that it does not produce as much seed. Space new plants 18 to 20 inches apart.

KNIPHOFIA
(See poker plant)

LAMB'S-EARS
(See stachys)

LAVENDER
Lavandula angustifolia

ZONE: 5
HEIGHT: 15 to 30 inches
BLOOM TIME: Mid- to late summer

Lavender is one of the most fragrant plants in the border or herb garden. There are three commonly grown varieties: English or true lavender, often used in potpourris and sachets, is the showiest and produces the most aromatic flowers; spike lavender produces larger, more fragrant leaves; and French lavender, slightly less popular, is grown primarily as a bath scent.

Start seeds of all varieties indoors, ten to 12 weeks before last expected frost. Germination and survival rates are low, so be sure to sow extra seeds or plant divisions. After all danger of frost has passed, plant seedlings outdoors in a sunny location. Harvest fresh leaves and flower heads before they open. Hang cut stems upside down in a shady, well-ventilated area until dry.

In cold climates, mulch the lavender plants with two or three inches of leaves or straw for winter protection.

LAVENDER COTTON
(See santolina)

LEADWORT
Also called plumbago
Ceratostigma plumbaginoides

ZONE: 6
HEIGHT: One foot
BLOOM TIME: August to September
The shiny foliage and bright blue, phlox-like blossoms make leadwort an asset in any garden. It is particularly useful in rock gardens or as a ground cover. Or use it as an edging plant in front of the flower or shrub border. Plant leadwort in a well-drained location that gets full to partial shade. Very hot locations are unsuitable.

If the plants are grown in Zone 6, they need several inches of mulch for winter protection. Leadwort is slow to emerge in the spring, so be careful not to cut into it during early spring cultivation. In the fall, foliage turns an attractive bronze color.

To start new plants, divide established clumps or take stem cuttings in midsummer. Set plants one to two feet apart. Plants spread rapidly by underground roots and will quickly carpet an area.

LENTEN ROSE
(See helleborus)

LEOPARD'S-BANE
(See doronicum)

LIATRIS

Also called gay-feather

Liatris sp.

ZONE: 3
HEIGHT: 18 to 72 inches
BLOOM TIME: Summer to autumn

Although often overlooked and underrated, liatris can add valuable, long-lasting color to most any perennial border. Plants are available with rose, purple, or white flowers borne on tall, spiky stems. An unusual highlight of the plant is its habit of opening its flowers from the top down, instead of from the bottom up as many other plants do.

Plant liatris in any sunny or partially sunny location. They enjoy a light, almost sandy soil but will thrive in nearly any type. Do not plant them where they may be damaged by standing water. Flowers are good for cutting and drying. To start new plants, divide established clumps, or start seeds in the spring for blooming plants the following year. Divide mature plants every three or four years to keep them healthy. Liatris is especially nice in massed plantings.

L. pycnostachya has purple flowers on four-foot stems in July and August. *L. scariosa* 'White Spire' has white flowers on 40-inch stems, blooming in August and continuing well into September. Kobold, a variety of the dwarf *L. spicata 'montana,'* grows only 18 to 24 inches tall. Its red-purple bloom begins in July and continues into September.

LINUM

(See flax)

LOBELIA

Also called cardinal flower

Lobelia cardinalis

ZONE: 2
HEIGHT: 24 to 30 inches
BLOOM TIME: Late summer to early fall

If you've got a shady spot in your garden, lobelia is the plant for you. It thrives in a moist, cool location—preferably a woodland setting—and will easily send up spires of bright red flowers. Lobelia is best planted in groups with divisions or cuttings set six inches apart.

Lobelia is a perfect back-of-the-border candidate, blooming from June to September. Another perennial lobelia, *L. spicata,* is similar in growth habit to *L. cardinalis* but has blue flowers and is less hardy. It grows well in Zone 4. Give it winter protection in colder areas. To start new plants, sow seeds in early spring, or take root divisions.

LOOSESTRIFE

Lythrum sp.

ZONE: 3
HEIGHT: To four feet
BLOOM TIME: June to September

Loosestrife is a good choice for moist, mid- to back-of-the-border locations. It will develop spires of pink, purple, or red flowers from June right up to fall. Loosestrife does well in almost any soil and exposure. In hot dry areas, a thick mulch to retain moisture will often lengthen the bloom period.

To ensure the perennial nature of any lythrum variety, plants should be lifted, divided, and replanted every three or four years. Space plants three feet apart when making original plantings or when replanting divisions of old plants. Early spring is the best time to move old plants or new stock. Water new transplants thoroughly.

Morden Gleam, as close to red as you will find among lythrums, is a popular *L. virgatum* variety that often reaches four feet in height. Morden Pink flourishes in sunny locations and quickly forms a clump three or four feet across and four feet tall. Both varieties are best planted singly in the shrub border or planted in small groups of two or three plants.

LUNGWORT

Pulmonaria sp.

ZONE: 3
HEIGHT: Ten to 15 inches
BLOOM TIME: April to May

Lungwort is one of the best perennials for shady, moist locations where its low-growing stature can be appreciated best. It can be teamed with wildflowers or mingled with bulbs. Flowers appear in small clusters above the plant, first appearing pink and gradually darkening into blue or purple.

New plants can be started from seeds in late fall or early spring, but you'll have better results planting divisions from established clumps in late summer or by purchasing nursery stock. Plants quickly reproduce and can easily carpet an area in several years. Unlike many other spring-flowering plants, the lungwort's foliage remains visible and attractive all summer long. Space plants about ten inches apart.

LUPINE

Lupinus sp.

ZONES: 4 to 7
HEIGHT: Three to five feet
BLOOM TIME: Spring through summer in

LUPINE

(continued)

temperate climates

Although there are many native varieties of lupine, the only strain lending itself well to the home garden is the group called Russell hybrids. These varieties are commonly available in blue, pink, red, yellow, purple, and bicolors. Foliage is deeply cut and attractive.

Lupines can be started from seed, but they will not bloom for at least two years. It is best to buy started plants from a nursery for early spring planting. Where summers are long and hot, lupines will not prosper. Because of their tall, stately manner, lupines are best planted as a mass in back-of-the-border locations. In windy areas, some staking might be necessary to keep them upright.

LYCHNIS

Also called catchfly
or Maltese-cross
Lychnis sp.

ZONE: 3
HEIGHT: 12 to 36 inches
BLOOM TIME: May through July

If you need bright color in the garden, lychnis is the plant to grow. Its big heads of vivid red flowers are surefire favorites for mid- or front-of-the-border locations, depending upon the variety you buy.

Lychnis needs full sun and a well-drained location. If soil is poorly drained, plants will be short-lived. Lychnis is easily propagated from seeds in late fall or early spring. Plants started in the fall will often bloom the same season they are planted. For quicker results, set out divisions from established clumps in early spring.

Foot-high *L. x haageana* hybrids produce blooms that can get as wide as two inches across. They're available in salmon, orange, and red and are perfect for front-of-the-border locations.

The species *L. chalcedonica*, known as scarlet Maltese-cross, is good in back-of-the-border locations where it often reaches three feet tall.

Lychnis needs to be divided every three or four years. Space new plants 18 inches apart.

LYTHRUM

(See loosestrife)

MALTESE-CROSS

(See lychnis)

MARGUERITE, BLUE

(See felicia)

MARGUERITE, GOLDEN

(See anthemis)

MEADOW RUE

(See thalictrum)

MEADOWSWEET

Also called dropwort
Filipendula vulgaris

ZONE: 4
HEIGHT: 18 inches
BLOOM TIME: July to August

Meadowsweet is a favorite for almost any garden situation. It enjoys being naturalized in wet, woodsy gardens but will grow just as well in a perennial border. Use meadowsweet in front- to mid-border locations where its late bloom period can be appreciated best. This flower comes into blossom after the spring perennials die back but well before the fall species start to open.

Although meadowsweet prefers a moist, partially shady location, it can be grown in full sun and poor dry soil—but growth will not be so lush. Flower clusters of double white petals, with a pink blush, grow in beautiful large sprays. Foliage is attractive and finely cut, growing in basal rosettes.

Start new plants from seeds (check catalogues specializing in wildflowers) or from divisions taken in early spring. Plants multiply quickly and will easily naturalize an area.

MERTENSIA

(See Virginia bluebells)

MICHAELMAS DAISY

(See aster)

MIST FLOWER

(See ageratum)

MONARDA

(See bee balm)

MONKSHOOD
Aconitum sp.

ZONE: 3
HEIGHT: Three to five feet
BLOOM TIME: July to September
Monkshood is one of your best choices for a low-maintenance border. It produces abundant spikes of blue, yellow, white, or purple blossoms every year; spreads slowly; and rarely needs staking or special treatment. Plant monkshood in a sunny or partially sunny location where the soil does not dry out. However, overly wet soils can hurt plants. All parts of the monkshood are poisonous, so plant them well away from small children's play areas.

Start new plants from seed sown in late summer, with seedlings set into a cold frame for the winter. Move young plants to the garden when frost danger has passed. Monkshood started in the fall usually blooms the second season.

A. carmichaeli (formerly known as *A. wilsoni*) grows to five feet tall and puts up big spikes of rich blue flowers.

MULLEIN
(See verbascum)

OBEDIENCE
(See physostegia)

OENOTHERA
Also called sundrops and evening primrose
Oenothera sp.

ZONE: 3 or 4 (depending on variety)
HEIGHT: 12 to 18 inches
BLOOM TIME: June through August
Few plants are more suited to the rock garden or front-of-the-border location than oenotheras. They thrive in full sun and light sandy soil, easily producing masses of open, cup-shaped, golden yellow flowers. A side-dressing of well-rotted manure each spring will encourage better growth. New plants can be started from seed, but you'll have better luck with nursery stock or divisions from established clumps. Transplant in early spring, spacing new plants about eight inches apart.

O. tetragona 'Highlight' is perhaps the most popular and is hardy to Zone 3. *O. fruticosa* and *O. missourensis* are somewhat less hardy—only to Zone 4. Individual blossoms of *O. missourensis* often measure a generous four inches across.

OXEYE
(See heliopsis)

PAINTED DAISY
Also called pyrethrum
Chrysanthemum coccineum

ZONE: 4
HEIGHT: 14 to 24 inches
BLOOM TIME: June to July
Painted daisies are unusual for members of the chrysanthemum family because they bloom early in the season instead of during the fall. Painted daisies produce masses of single or double white, pink, and red flowers on graceful stems, perfect for mid-border locations. Foliage is finely cut and attractive. Painted daisies do best where they can get full sun and rich, moist soil. If soil is poor, spade a heavy dose of well-rotted manure or compost into the ground before you plant.

To propagate, sow seed in the early spring in a protected bed. Or buy nursery stock root divisions. Space new plants about ten inches apart. In two or three years, as plants get crowded, divide in late summer. For optimum growth, keep plants well watered during times of drought.

PAPAVER (See poppy, pages 216 to 217)

PENSTEMON
Penstemon sp.

ZONES: 3 to 5 (depending on variety)
HEIGHT: 12 to 20 inches
BLOOM TIME: June to July
Penstemon produces spikes of red, rose, blue, or purple flowers, perfect for front-of-the-border plantings. Plants need a sunny or partially sunny location and will often bloom right through the hottest part of summer, if they are kept moist. Don't let water stand about the roots, though, or they may rot.

Start new plants from seeds in the early spring or from stem cuttings or divisions of established clumps. Space new plants about ten inches apart.

One recommended variety, *P. hartwegi* x *P. cobaea*, has ruby-colored bloom on 18- to 24-inch stems. It thrives to Zone 5. *P. newberryi* only reaches 12 inches in height, with rose-purple flowers in mid-June. If pruned back after flowering, this variety will often bloom again in the fall. It's hardy to Zone 5. Rose Elf is an especially hardy variety that grows as far north as Zone 3.

Most popular perennials

PEONIES

Planted properly, peonies will bloom faithfully every spring, even if neglected entirely. The flowering season begins about the time tulips open and ends six to eight weeks later. Tree peonies (above) open earliest, at least two weeks before the others. Peonies appear in all colors except blue. Extend the bloom time with a selection of early, mid-season, and late-blooming varieties. All except the tree peony are herbaceous, dying to the ground each fall.

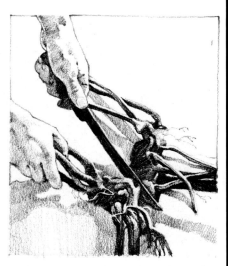

Golden Glow, an early single-flowering variety.

Peonies may be left undisturbed indefinitely. But for more plants, lift and divide the bush types once every six to ten years. The best time for division is September in the North and October in the South.

To divide the plants, loosen the soil all the way around them with a spade, then lift the entire clump by prying under the root mass. After removing the clump, cut back all the stems to a height of four inches.

Wash soil off roots with a strong jet of water, but avoid injury to the fragile pink buds or "eyes." Cut away any damaged roots. Separate root sections carefully with a sharp knife so that each new division has five to eight eyes. (Divisions with fewer eyes may mean waiting a few years for the plant to become established enough to produce significant bloom.) Be sure to keep the root sections moist and protected from direct sunlight at all times.

For bright spring color along a walk, wall, or driveway, plant Festiva Maxima.

Space divisions three feet apart, and plant them so the eyes are 1 ½ to two inches below ground level. A spade handle helps measure. Deeper planting may result in few blooms. Shallower planting risks winterkill. Be careful not to damage the eyes as you fill the hole with soil and tamp it firm. Water thoroughly, and, if rain is lacking, water weekly until the ground freezes.

Most popular perennials
PHLOX

For fragrance, trusses (or clusters) of long-lasting bloom, and ease of culture, fill in with the hardy perennial phlox. Phlox varieties are available in tones of pink, blue, violet, and white.

They range in size from six-inch dwarfs to four-foot standards. Use the dwarf varieties in a rock garden or as edging plants. Taller varieties are ideal in mixed perennial borders where their tall graceful stems add plenty of backup color. Perennial phlox are easily cultivated; they grow best in a sunny location where their roots will remain partially shaded. Phlox prefer a rich, moist soil for optimum growth and color.

For deep blue flowers, try Millstream Jupiter.

Variety Fair One has delicately scalloped red-pink petals.

Pink Princess blooms heavily from early July right up until frost. It's a hardy variety in any garden.

Phlox culture

Plant phlox in the early spring, starting new plants from root divisions of established clumps or from nursery stock. Or take stem cuttings in midsummer and overwinter them in a cold frame for springtime planting. Seed-started plants will often revert to the original lavender color and should be avoided.

Space phlox plants about one foot apart in the garden—dwarf varieties a little closer. If the plants are crowded and air circulation is poor, they will be subject to an unsightly mold on the foliage. As the plants mature, keep them thinned out so that each supports no more than four or five main stalks. Divide roots every three years, and clip off flower heads before they go to seed. In colder areas, add several inches of mulch for winter protection.

PEONIES (See pages 210 to 211)

PHLOX (See pages 212 to 213)

PHYSALIS
(See Chinese-lantern)

PHYSOSTEGIA
**Also called false
dragonhead or obedience**
Physostegia sp.

ZONE: 3
HEIGHT: To 2½ feet
BLOOM TIME: July to September
The common wildflower, *Physostegia virginiana,* has been hybridized and is a good addition to perennial borders if you don't mind its spreading habit. Flowers are attractive in either white or pink and are borne on tall spikes or branching racemes. To those unacquainted with it, physostegia can easily be confused with foxglove.

New plants can be started by sowing seeds in the early spring or by dividing established clumps. Space new plants about 12 inches apart, and divide them again in two or three years when they become crowded. Divide in either spring or fall.

Plants are easy to grow in any type of soil, but for maximum growth, give them a spot where they can get full sun. Most varieties can be used in mid-border locations or can be naturalized in a woodland setting.

PINCUSHION FLOWER
(See scabiosa)

PINK
(See dianthus)

PLANTAIN LILY
(See hostas, pages 202 to 203)

PLATYCODON
(See balloon flower)

PLUMBAGO
(See leadwort)

POLEMONIUM
(See jacob's-ladder)

POKER PLANT
Also called torch lily
Kniphofia sp.

ZONE: 5
HEIGHT: Three to five feet (depending on variety)
BLOOM TIME: Midsummer through fall
Although most poker plants are not reliably hardy in northern areas, many of the new hybrid forms can be carried over the winter if they are given several inches of mulch. Plants are impressive, bearing tall cigar-shaped spikes. Flowers are available in white, vivid yellow, red, and several pastel shades.

Use poker plants singly as specimen plants or in small groupings in back-of-the-border locations. Choose a site that gets full sun but is protected from heavy winds. Soil should be fertile and well drained. When the bloom period ends, cut away the flower spikes. In the fall, cut the entire plant to an inch or so above the ground. In the spring, plants will develop new foliage.

Use nursery stock because poker plants are slow growers and seed-started plants take too long to develop. Mature plants need to be divided at least every five years. Space new plants about 18 inches apart.

POPPIES, ORIENTAL
(See pages 216 to 217)

POTENTILLA
Also called cinquefoil
Potentilla sp.

ZONES: 4 to 5
HEIGHT: Three to 18 inches
BLOOM TIME: June to frost
Often thought of as a low-growing shrub, potentilla is also invaluable as a bright edging plant for either flower border or walkway. These natives of northern North America produce clusters of five-petaled, bright yellow, cerise, or orange blooms right up to the arrival of cold weather. Plants are hardy and will grow in most areas of the country.

Start new plants from seeds or root divisions set out in the spring. Plant them in a sunny location. To ensure good drainage, mix some sand into the soil before planting.

P. aurea puts on a big show of color with a profusion of yellow flowers in May and June. It's hardy to Zone 4 and rarely gets over three inches tall. *P. nepalensis 'willmottiae'* reaches one foot in height and has cerise-colored blossoms hardy to Zone 4. *P. tabernaemontani* forms a low-growing mat.

PRIMROSE

Primula sp.

ZONES: 3 to 5 (depending on variety)
HEIGHT: To 12 inches
BLOOM TIME: Early spring
Primroses form one of the largest families of popular garden plants. Unfortunately, the majority of species are not suitable to the climatic extremes of hot and cold common over most of North America. Primroses need a shady spot where the temperature remains relatively cool, even during the summer. They also need to be kept moist in a rich soil.

New plants can be started from seed or from root divisions taken from established plants. Space new plants four to six inches apart. Many species will make excellent greenhouse plants.

One group of primrose, the polyanthus *(P. x polyantha)*, is perhaps the most popular backyard group because of its relatively hardy nature and large blossoms borne on nine- to 12-inch stems. Flowers vary from brilliant pinks to reds, yellows, scarlets, purples, and whites. Hardy to Zone 3.

P. vulgaris, the true English primrose, has creamy-yellow flowers with a deeper yellow eye, on four- to five-inch stems. It's well suited to the rock garden or for use as an edging plant in the shady border. *P. denticulata* produces bloom in the lavender-to-purple range and often reaches 12 inches in height. Hardy to Zone 4. Watch all primroses for red spider attack.

PRIMROSE, EVENING

(See oenothera)

PYRETHRUM

(See painted daisy)

RUDBECKIA

Also called coneflower
Rudbeckia sp.

ZONE: 3
HEIGHT: To 30 inches
BLOOM TIME: July until frost
Rudbeckia species bear yellow or orange flowers, have a conical-shaped core, and will

often last for a decade or more. Two varieties are of special interest: *R. laciniata* 'Goldquelle' and *R. fulgida* 'Goldsturm.' Unlike other rudbeckia species, these two are compact in form and are free-flowering. Goldquelle is double-flowered with gold-colored blossoms. Both have deep black centers.

Plant rudbeckia 18 inches apart in a sunny location. It is tolerant of almost any soil type. Plants are especially desirable in areas where summer droughts are common, although they will need some watering. Rudbeckias are resistant to disease and insects.

Fall is the best time to divide established clumps that have grown too large.

SAGE (See salvia)

ST.-JOHN'S-WORT

(See hypericum)

SALVIA

Also called sage
Salvia sp.

ZONE: 4
HEIGHT: To four feet
BLOOM TIME: Summer to autumn
Often thought of as only an annual flower, salvia has several varieties that are strictly perennials. Perennial salvia is most commonly available in blue or blue-violet, but the scarlet form, commonly grown as an annual, will also be perennial in warm climates. Salvia is the perfect plant for mid- or back-of-the-border locations. It grows in full sun and in any type of soil. Flowers appear on tall spikes that come on strong in July, continuing right up until frost. Keep fading flowers pinched to encourage continuous bloom.

New plants are best started from division of older clumps or from started nursery stock. Space new plants about ten inches apart. If conditions are to their liking, salvia will spread quickly and need to be divided again in three or four years.

Where winters are cold, mulch salvia with two to three inches of leaves and straw after the first frost for winter protection.

S. x superba 'East Friesland' produces 18-inch flower spikes in June and continues to bloom all summer. Flowers are violet-blue and are excellent used as cut flowers.

Pitcher's sage *(S. azurea 'grandiflora')* has gentian blue flowers on a shrubby plant that often gets three feet tall. In Zone 4, this plant will need some winter protection.

Most popular perennials
ORIENTAL POPPIES

If you want breathtaking color for your yard, plant some Oriental poppies. They range from ten inches to three feet high, and they come in a rainbow of colors. Poppies put on their biggest show through May and June. After that, their foliage dies down. In late summer and early fall, the plants renew growth to get a head start on spring.

Try White Queen mixed with brighter varieties.

Plant Glowing Ember for eye-catching color.

One of the hardiest poppy varieties, Dubloon, puts on a big show of color with a minimum of care.

Poppy culture

The best time to plant poppies is during August and September while the plants are dormant. When you receive your poppy roots from the nursery, don't be discouraged by their long stringy appearance. Properly planted, these roots will quickly mature into vividly colored, large-blooming plants. If any of the root tips are broken, plant them along with the mother plant; even small pieces of poppy roots are quick to grow and produce flowers. Space new poppies about two feet apart, and mulch them with several inches of leaves or straw to help keep the soil moist and maintain an even temperature.

Plant poppies in a garden location where they will get at least six to eight hours of sunlight a day. Almost any type of soil will do so long as it is well drained and relatively fertile. Dig a hole about a foot deep, and mix in some well-rotted compost or manure. Hold the scaly crown of the plant even with the surface of the soil, and gradually fill the hole with soil. Then water the plant thoroughly, and firm the area around the base of the plants with your hands.

Poppies prefer to grow undisturbed, but if you want new plants, divide large mature specimens. After the plant becomes dormant, cut the soil in a circle around it, and then lift up the entire plant with a spade or shovel. Always be sure to dig deep enough, so you don't damage the long, brittle roots. After removing the clump, break it apart with your fingers to make three or four smaller clumps.

Where winters are cold, poppies should be protected with a thick mulch. Or add two wire hoops over the plants at right angles to each other, and top with a canopy of burlap. To keep the burlap from blowing away, bury the edges under a layer of soil and stones. In early spring, carefully remove the mulch, burlap, and wire hoops.

SANTOLINA
Also called lavender cotton

Santolina chamaecyparissus

ZONE: 6
HEIGHT: To two feet
BLOOM SEASON: June to July

Grown primarily for its attractive foliage, lavender cotton is a good foil for other more brightly colored flowers in the perennial border. Most varieties have a fragrance reminiscent of lavender. Santolina can be used as an edging plant, a hedge plant, or alone in rock gardens. Plants produce small spikes of inconspicuous yellow flowers in June and July. Prune old flowers as they fade.

Santolinas aren't winter-hardy north of Zone 6, but some northern gardeners grow plants in pots and keep them in a cold frame for the winter. They also can be overwintered as a houseplant on a sunny windowsill.

Start new plants from root divisions or stem cuttings in either spring or fall. Space plants about six inches apart in a sunny location with sandy soil. Recommended santolinas include: *S. chamaecyparissus 'nana',* which will reach a height of eight inches but should be kept pruned to six when used as a miniature hedge of silvery gray; *S. neapolitana,* also silver-leaved with graceful pendulous branches; and *S. virens,* with dark evergreen foliage, which will tolerate poor soil and hot summer sun.

SCABIOSA
Also called pincushion flower

Scabiosa sp.

ZONE: 5
HEIGHT: To 30 inches
BLOOM TIME: Summer

Scabiosas, or pincushion flowers, are noted for their long, graceful white stamens that protrude above a pincushion-like blue or white bloom. Scabiosas look good mingled among other plants in the mixed border or grown in small clumps of their own.

Plants need a sunny location but are not fussy about soil conditions. Start new plants from seeds or root divisions. If started from seed, scabiosa can be sown in either spring or fall. Plants started in fall should be overwintered in a cold frame and will often bloom the next season. Plants started in spring will usually not bloom until the following summer. Keep new plants spaced about 15 inches apart.

Scabiosas are available in both dwarf and standard sizes, the dwarfs growing to an ultimate height of 18 inches and the standards

growing to two feet or more if they are given good care.

Divide plants in the spring if they become crowded. For best results, dig away the younger plants from around the base of the parent plant, rather than dig the entire clump.

Keep spent flowers clipped to encourage continuous bloom. Clipped flowers make excellent additions to fresh cut bouquets. Foliage is silvery-gray and attractive.

SEA PINK
(See thrift)

SEA THRIFT
(See thrift)

SEDUM
Also called stonecrop

Sedum sp.

ZONE: 3
HEIGHT: Four to 24 inches
BLOOM TIME: Spring to late summer

Commonly thought of as only a rock or wall garden plant, sedums make first-rate ground covers and edging plants. All varieties are fleshy-leaved and can withstand long periods of drought. Sedums bloom in the summer with small clusters of red, pink, cream, white, orange, yellow, or rust-brown flowers. They need an exposed sunny location but will grow in almost any type of soil.

Start new plants in the spring from root divisions, spacing them 12 to 15 inches apart. In no time at all, they will completely carpet an area.

S. kamtschaticum is one of the best edging sedums, shooting up large clusters of bright orange flowers from July to the first frost. Leaves are a rich, dark green that turns reddish gold in the fall. Mature height is only four inches. Variety *S. kamtschaticum 'variegatum'* has the same characteristics of the previous variety, but the leaves are striped with a large band of white.

A hardy, golden-yellow bloomer is the *S. kamtschaticum 'floriferum.'* Never growing to more than six inches, the plant is excellent used as a border edging or in a rock garden. Plants bloom during July and August.

S. telephium 'Indian Chief', a plant growing ten to 14 inches tall, has gray-green foliage, with each stem topped in early autumn by an umbel of copper-colored bloom. Plants often produce ten or more flower stalks per plant. Use in perennial borders.

S. maximum 'atropurpureum', or mahogany plant, has rich brown foliage and

creamy-rose blooms appearing in August. Mature plants can reach 24 inches in height.

S. sieboldi has thick, silver-gray leaves and bright pink blooms every September. Plants are nine inches tall. *S. sieboldi 'variegatum'* has leaves splashed with cream. *S. spectabile* 'Meteor' grows to 18 inches. Foliage is gray-green, with flowers appearing in umbels of red in summer.

SHASTA DAISY

Chrysanthemum maximum (or *C.* x *superbum*)

ZONE: 4
HEIGHT: Two to three feet
BLOOM TIME: Early summer
If you want a standout flower that looks good indoors in bouquets as well as in the garden, try growing some shasta daisies. These single or double, mostly white flowers grow easily from seeds or root divisions. They are not, however, reliably hardy and will need winter protection in Zone 4.

Shasta daisies should be spaced about a foot apart. Use a thick mulch to retain soil moisture. If soil is poor, work in well-rotted manure or compost before you plant. Full sun is best; double varieties can withstand a little more shade than the single varieties.

SNEEZEWEED

(See helenium)

SNOW-IN-SUMMER

(See cerastium)

SOLIDAGO

Also called hybrid goldenrod
Solidago sp.

ZONE: 3
HEIGHT: To three feet
BLOOM TIME: August to September
When you mention goldenrod to a gardener in the United States, you may get something less than an enthusiastic response. The plant has been blamed for causing hay fever, but it is ragweed pollen—its timetable coinciding closely with goldenrod's—that is the chief villain.

Goldenrod is actually quite harmless and can prove to be one of the most showy plants in the perennial border. In Britain, goldenrod is revered as a stately and worthwhile plant. It is frequently mingled with patches of hardy asters for a show-stopping fall color display. Few other combinations are so colorful in a back-of-the-border location as these two

plants at the height of bloom.

Goldenrod is easily started from root divisions of established clumps or from nursery stock. Space new plants about 12 to 15 inches apart. For best results, a sunny location is desirable. Few plants are so tolerant of different soil types or so insect- and disease-resistant as goldenrod. Once given a foothold these plants will need to be divided only every three or four years.

Solidago hybrid Golden Mosa is a strong branching plant with tapered blooms of deep yellow-gold. It grows to three feet tall. The foliage gradually turns a light shade of yellow as the growing season draws to a close. Hardy and drought resistant.

SPEEDWELL

(See veronica)

SPRING ADONIS

(See adonis)

SPURGE

Euphorbia sp.

ZONE: 4
HEIGHT: 12 to 15 inches
BLOOM TIME: April to May
If you want a low-maintenance perennial that thrives even in hot, dry, sunny locations, try growing some spurge. Related to the poinsettia, these plants have attractive foliage and small yellow flowers in tight clusters. Many varieties are commonly grown in rock and wall gardens, but planted alone, they can substitute as an attractive ground cover. Or try spurge as an accent plant in a mixed border.

In the fall, start spurge from root divisions of established plants. Or buy nursery stock. Space plants eight to ten inches apart in a sunny location. Most species are not fussy about soil conditions and can even tolerate partial shade.

E. epithymoides, sometimes called milkwort (all plants of this genus have a sticky, milky fluid in their veins), is bushy in form, grows 12 to 15 inches tall, and puts out yellow bracts of bloom in May. Plants spread rapidly but are easily controlled by pulling out the young plants. In the fall, blooms turn a rosy-bronze color.

E. myrsinites, myrtle euphorbia, is a prostrate plant that has stiff, blue-green foliage growing in spiral whorls about the stems, with small heads of yellow flowers appearing in April and May. Plants make a good ground cover in hot, dry, and sunny areas.

STACHYS
Also called
lamb's-ears or betony
Stachys sp.

ZONE: 4
HEIGHT: Eight to 12 inches
BLOOM TIME: Summer

Often seen in old-fashioned gardens, stachys is again increasing in popularity because of its hardiness, ease of care, and effective contrast of color and texture in the mixed perennial flower border. Most varieties have soft, furry, silver-gray foliage: hence the name, lamb's-ears.

Start new plants from root divisions in early spring. If you have no access to established plants, most mail-order nurseries have several varieties for spring planting. Space new plants about a foot apart. Flowers are inconspicuous and reddish in color.

S. byzantina has silvery leaves and an ultimate height of 12 inches. Leaves are six to eight inches long. Red flowers appear about 12 inches above the attractive gray foliage in midsummer.

STOKESIA
Also called stokes' aster
Stokesia laevis

ZONE: 5
HEIGHT: 12 to 15 inches
BLOOM TIME: July into September

Stokesia is a valuable plant for the perennial border because of its later summer bloom period when few other plants are in flower. They are easy to grow, asking only for a sunny, well-drained location with about 12 inches of space left between plants. New plants are best started from root divisions taken in either fall or early spring.

Plants grow quickly and often need to be divided every fourth or fifth year. To look their best, stokes' aster should be planted individually or in small clumps intermingled among the front and mid-border plants.

One of the most common varieties, Blue Danube, has light blue flowers that can occasionally get up to five inches in diameter. Its mature height is about 15 inches.

Silver Moon stokesia is a hybrid form of Blue Danube and produces large white flowers tinged with blue-lavender in the center.

STONECROP (See sedum)

SUNDROPS (See oenothera)

SUNFLOWER, PERENNIAL
(See helianthus)

THALICTRUM
Also called meadow rue
Thalictrum sp.

ZONE: 3
HEIGHT: Three to four feet
BLOOM TIME: June to July

Often considered a wildflower, meadow rue has several domesticated forms of particular interest to the home gardener. Their graceful, airy foliage and delicate yellow, white, or lavender flowers are perfect mixed with other flowers such as daylilies.

The only meadow rue species that is widely sold by nurseries is *T. minus*. It blooms in July, with fragrant heads of green-tinged yellow flowers.

Other species are more often available as seeds that should be sown in late summer. After the plants are up and growing, overwinter them in a cold frame, and set them in the garden in early spring; most will bloom that season. Spring-sown seed will not produce blooming plants until the following growing season.

T. polygamum, tall meadow rue, grows to seven feet high and bears white flowers from July onward. It needs winter protection north of Zone 4.

T. rochebrunianum, lavender mist meadow rue, is only three feet tall and bears lavender bloom with yellow stamens all summer long.

T. speciosissimum, dusty meadow rue, has yellow bloom heads in summer. It's hardy from Zone 5 southward, and the plants grow to a height of four feet.

THERMOPSIS
Also called Carolina lupine
Thermopsis caroliniana

ZONE: 3
HEIGHT: Three to four feet
BLOOM TIME: June to July

Thermopsis is one of the most pleasant all-around plants for the perennial border. Its graceful spikes of yellow, pealike flowers and finely cut, dark green foliage make it a striking addition to any garden location. Thermopsis is hardy even in areas where the summers are long and hot. Plants multiply steadily over the years, gradually forming clumps up to four feet in diameter. Plus, they are virtually insect and disease free.

Start new plants from root divisions of established clumps or from started nursery stock in either early spring or fall. Seeds should be started in early fall. Space all new plants about 18 inches apart. For best growth, keep plants mulched.

THRIFT
Also called sea thrift, sea pink, and armeria
Armeria maritima

ZONE: 3
HEIGHT: Dwarf
BLOOM TIME: May to July
A good choice for rock gardens or edgings, thrift quickly forms tidy mounds of attractive foliage. Mature plants bear abundantly all summer long in lilac, red, pink, or white.

Plant thrift in an area that gets full sun most of the day, spacing new plants about eight to ten inches apart. Transplanting can be done in either spring or fall. Start new plants from root divisions or nursery stock.

A variety of *A. maritima* with white flowers sends up five-inch bloom stems in the form of tufts of long, narrow leaves. Laucheana types grow six inches tall and flower in May and June. Foliage is evergreen.

TICKSEED
(See coreopsis)

TORCH LILY
(See poker plant)

TRANSVAAL DAISY
(See gerbera)

TROLLIUS
(See globeflower)

VALERIAN, RED
(See jupiter's-beard)

VERBASCUM
Also called mullein
Verbascum sp.

ZONE: 5
HEIGHT: 30 inches
BLOOM TIME: June to October
Once thought of only as a roadside weed, verbascum is now available in several varieties and species that are excellent choices for hot, dry, and sunny spaces requiring tall backup color. They have furry, gray foliage and produce spikes of yellow, white, pink, or salmon flowers from mid- to late summer. Mature plants do not spread or become weedy in the garden and can be started easily from root division or seeds.

Mullein does have a tendency to be biennial in nature, but plants will usually self-sow. *V. phoeniceum* comes in mixed colors—white, pink, salmon, and violet—blooming from June until October. It grows three to six feet tall, depending on the site, and is hardy from Zone 6 southward.

VERONICA
Also called speedwell
Veronica sp.

ZONE: 3
HEIGHT: Six to 36 inches
BLOOM TIME: June to September
This large genus includes both shrub and perennial species, but shrub forms are hardy only in the warmest zones of the country.

Among the perennial plants, there is a good range of sizes, suiting some for use in rock gardens or as low edgings for borders and others for placement at mid- or back-of-the-border locations. Most varieties have blue flowers, but pink and white are also available.

Plant veronica in a sunny, well-drained location, and divide established clumps every four or five years. Keep faded flowers cut off to encourage a longer season of bloom. Veronica shows to best advantage planted in small groupings in the perennial border or planted in mass.

V. alpina 'alba' has white flowers that will continue to blossom all summer long if faded ones are kept picked. Plants grow to only six inches tall and are excellent when used in rock gardens.

V. spicata 'Barcarolle' has spikes of rose-pink flowers from June until August and will reach ten inches tall.

V. latifolia 'Crater Lake Blue' is a good early summer bloomer that produces spikes of blue flowers on sturdy 18-inch stems.

V. incana 'rosea' has rose-pink flowers.

VIOLA
Viola sp.

ZONES: 3 to 5 (depending on variety)
HEIGHT: Four to six inches
BLOOM TIME: Early spring
Close relatives of pansies, violas have slightly smaller flowers and are much more perennial

VIOLA
(continued)

in habit. There are two major groups within the genus: sweet *(V. odorata)* and tufted *(V. cornuta)*. Both need good garden loam that has been enriched with leaf mold, well-rotted manure, or compost.

Soil should stay moist most of the time—but never wet. In areas where summers are long and hot, most violas will not prosper and will need to be replanted each spring or fall.

To start new plants from seed, sow in late summer, transplanting seedlings to a cold frame for the winter. Then set the seedlings into the garden as early as the ground can be worked. Space plants ten to 12 inches apart. Or if you don't have a cold frame, mulch the planting bed over the winter.

Spring-sown seed will often produce blooming plants the same fall. Most varieties rarely get more than six inches tall and can be used as an edging, border plant, or small planting pocket. Flowers are available in blue, purple, pink, white, and bicolors.

Several *V. odorata* varieties are good choices. Rosina produces generous amounts of fragrant pink blossoms on eight-inch stems. It's hardy to Zone 3. Red Giant has red-violet flowers and quickly develops into a sizable clump. It's hardy to Zone 4. Royal Robe has violet-blue flowers on six-inch stems and is somewhat more tolerant of sunny conditions. It grows six inches tall and is hardy to Zone 4.

In the *V. cornuta* group, the variety Catherine Sharp is a desirable plant. It produces generous amounts of bloom over a long time, and plants rapidly increase in size. By the second year, a clump may reach 24 inches in diameter. Catherine Sharp is hardy to Zone 3. Keep faded flowers clipped.

VIRGINIA BLUEBELLS
Also called mertensia
Mertensia virginica

ZONE: 3
HEIGHT: 18 to 24 inches
BLOOM TIME: Early spring
Virginia bluebells are one of the most delightful flowers to plant in the informal border. It can also be naturalized by itself or in combination with other wildflowers. Bluebells produce nodding bracts of sky-blue, trumpet-shaped flowers in early spring.

Bluebells prefer a semi-shady location, well supplied with leaf mold or compost. Plants spread rapidly and can quickly carpet an area.

Start from seeds or from nursery stock.

Because bluebells die down in midsummer, plant them in spots where other plants, such as ferns, can take over and fill in.

YARROW
Achillea sp.

ZONE: 3
HEIGHT: Six to 36 inches
BLOOM TIME: June to September
Most varieties of yarrow are on the tall side—two to three feet—though there are also low-growing varieties with flowers borne on four- to six-inch stems. The taller varieties are good additions to the mixed border, planted singly or in small groupings. Smaller varieties do well in rock or wall gardens.

Yarrow flowers come in either white, red, or yellow with handsome fernlike foliage. The size of the blossoms varies with variety, but most form flat clusters of small flowers on stems held above the plants. Plant yarrow in a sunny, dry location. They're not fussy about soil.

A. ageratifolia, a low-growing variety, is well suited to use in rock gardens or as an edging plant. Single, daisy-like blooms appear on four- to six-inch stems in June and continue until September.

A. filipendulina 'Coronation Gold' grows to three feet tall and is one of the best varieties for dried flowers. Plants bloom golden-yellow from June to August. Start new plants from root divisions or nursery stock.

A. filipendulina 'Moonshine' has pale yellow flowers on 24-inch stems. It has silver-gray foliage and blooms from June until September with good growing conditions.

A. millefolium 'Fire King' has rose-red flowers on 24-inch stems. Foliage is silver.

YUCCA
Yucca sp.

ZONE: 4
HEIGHT: Three to six feet
BLOOM TIME: Summer
Even if you live in the North, give your garden a tropical flavor with one of several varieties of yucca. These striking plants have stiff, sword-shaped leaves and breathtaking stalks of bloom that often reach six feet in height. The flowers are creamy-white and cup-shaped, somewhat resembling large lilies-of-the-valley. Many are heavily scented.

Plant yucca in any location that remains relatively dry. They need full sun but are not fussy about soil conditions. Start new plants from seeds, root divisions, or offsets. Space young plants about three or four feet apart.

ABCs of BIENNIALS

Taking two years to bloom, biennials produce spectacular flowers that are worth an extra season's wait. They'll produce foliage the first year, flowers and seeds the second year. Some biennials die after the second year, but others reseed themselves and are almost as dependable as perennials. Plant in the summer in a flat or a cold frame. Leave in the cold frame all winter in areas of severe cold, and transplant in the spring.

CANTERBURY-BELLS

Campanula medium

ZONE: 4
HEIGHT: Eight to 24 inches, depending on variety
BLOOM TIME: May to July
For show-stopping color in the mixed flower border, be sure to plant Canterbury-bells. These attractive plants produce quantities of cuplike, three-inch-deep flowers. They bloom in long showy spikes from late spring through July. Some varieties are even framed by saucer-like petals three to four inches across. Colors include blue, rose, white, yellow, and pastels. Plant either single- or double-flowering varieties. Canterbury-bells look their best when planted in a middle-of-the-border location.

To start new plants, sow seed in August and September. Transplant the young seedlings to a cold frame for the winter. If you don't have a cold frame, try mulching the plants with several inches of leaves or straw. Later, when all danger of frost has passed, set the young plants into the garden.

Canterbury-bells do best in a sunny fertile location. Do not allow plants to become overly dry.

Carpathaian harebell *(Campanula carpatica)* grows only eight inches tall and produces brilliant blue flowers all summer. It's hardy to Zone 3 and a good choice for rock garden or edge. Variety White Star is a white-flower form. *C. rotundifolia*, or common harebells, is a compact blue-flower variety

that will grow to 12 or 15 inches tall. It blooms from June to August and is tolerant of partial shade. *C. rotundifolia 'olympica'* is slightly more compact and filled with flowers.

Perhaps the most common variety, *C. glomerata*, often reaches 18 inches tall, blooming heavily in May and June. Flowers are violet-blue with white pistils. Some plants may develop as many as 20 to 24 flower stalks.

ENGLISH DAISY

Bellis perennis

ZONE: 4
HEIGHT: Four to eight inches
BLOOM TIME: May to August
Popular in rock gardens or as edging plants, English daisies produce masses of aster-like blooms all summer. Colors include rose, lavender, red, and white. Plants are compact and attractive with flower heads up to two inches across. English daisy needs a sunny location and rich, moist soil. In areas with long, hot, dry summers, these plants will not grow normally.

Start plants from seeds sown in the fall, with seedlings overwintered in a cold frame. Transplant to the garden in early spring for flowers that season. If seed is sown directly in the garden early in the spring, some plants may bloom the first year. For continuous bloom, start new plants each year.

If not contained, the English daisy can easily become a weed in lawns on both the East and West coasts.

Several cultivated varieties are available, including Dresden China, Tuberosa, Giant Rose, Montrosa, and Snow Ball.

FORGET-ME-NOT, ALPINE

Myosotis sylvatica

ZONE: 3
HEIGHT: Eight to 24 inches, depending on variety
BLOOM TIME: Early spring
Planted with spring-flowering bulbs, alpine forget-me-not creates an almost unforgettable sight. Its low-growing nature and sky-blue flowers easily team with the subtle colors of fresh spring bulbs. Myosotis is a good choice if your planting bed stays moist, cool, and shaded from the direct rays of the sun. If planted in hot spots, it quickly goes to seed and disappears.

Myosotis plants spread quickly and make a good ground cover in the rock garden. Flower colors include blue, white, and pink. In the

FORGET-ME-NOT, ALPINE
(continued)

right location, these flowers will continue to appear from early spring to late August.

Plant alpine forget-me-not in the fall and overwinter it in a cold frame. Or plant it early in the season for blossoms six to eight weeks later. If your soil is poor, be sure to enrich it with plenty of compost or leaf mold before planting time. Set plants about a foot apart.

If myosotis is left undisturbed for a time, it will start seedling plants. These can be transferred to a cold frame or a protected area for the winter. Transplant into the garden as soon as the ground is workable.

The alpine forget-me-not may be listed as *M. alpestris* in catalogues.

FOXGLOVE
Digitalis purpurea

ZONE: 4
HEIGHT: Three to six feet
BLOOM TIME: June to July
Foxglove is one of the graceful verticals effective in combination with plants of more bushy growth habit in your flowering border. Most varieties are four to six feet tall, although one variety, Foxy, forms a bushy plant only three feet tall at maturity.

Flowers are available in white, cream, yellow, rose, red, and lavender. The Giant Rusty variety, however, produces rusty-red flowers with bearded lips. All varieties have darker spotting on the inner surfaces of the individual flowers.

Foxglove flowers are thimble-shaped and closely packed on tall, wiry spikes. In windy areas, these spikes may need to be staked to prevent breaking.

Plant foxglove in a sunny or partially sunny location where it won't burn out in midsummer. Almost any soil type is acceptable. Start new plants from seeds sown in the garden any time after the middle of July. They will then bloom the following season. In cold climates, be sure to mulch the seedlings with several inches of leaves and straw for winter protection.

Foxglove, which is native to Europe, is commonly sold in a mixture that includes all of the colors available. The Gloxiniiflora variety has one outsize flower on top, with the remainder of flowers on the spire smaller in size.

Foxglove leaves are poisonous, with the leaves acting as heart stimulants.

HOLLYHOCK
Alcea rosea

ZONE: 3
HEIGHT: Four to eight feet
BLOOM TIME: July to September
Hollyhock is often considered a perennial because it self-sows readily. Its graceful, tall growth habit makes it especially useful in back-of-the-border situations, along walks and fences, or in front of unsightly buildings and other eyesores.

Flowers are available in both single and double forms. The Chater's Double strain is perhaps the most popular, with double, four-inch flowers on spikes that can get six feet tall. Colors include red, pink, rose, and yellow.

Start hollyhocks from seed during July and early August. Sow them in their permanent garden location, or start them in a special seedbed, moving them to a cold frame for the winter. Most will bloom readily the following season. Some new annual varieties will bloom the same season they are planted if they get an early start indoors. Be sure you plant all varieties of hollyhock in a sunny location with well-drained soil.

Hollyhock is susceptible to several pests and diseases. Caterpillars of the painted lady butterfly eat the leaves and can become destructive. Japanese beetles and tarnished plant bugs occasionally are pests. Hollyhocks can also suffer from rust; symptoms are orange-colored spots all over the plants. Rust spores can overwinter on the roots, and new infections can develop. (See Chapter 16, "Insects and Diseases," for suggestions.)

HONESTY
Lunaria annua

ZONE: 4
HEIGHT: To 3 feet
BLOOM TIME: June to July
Grown primarily for its flattened, silvery, two-inch-round seedpods, lunaria is a must for the gardener who enjoys dried arrangements. Plants produce attractive white or blue flowers in midsummer, but their coin-like seed capsules are their most striking feature.

Lunaria does well in a partially shady location, away from the direct rays of the midsummer sun. Almost any soil type will do. Start seeds in late summer in a protected area. Plants will bloom the following season and form seedpods. In milder climates, early seeding will result in blossoms the same season. Reseeding is often not necessary because plants frequently self-sow.

Sometimes called the dollar plant because of its fruits, this biennial is easily grown. Because it self-sows readily, your main chore with the plant is pulling the unwanted extras in the spring.

To dry, cut lunaria when the fruits are mature. Remove the coverings over the fruits, and hang the branches to dry in a cool, airy place. When dry, they're ready to use in arrangements.

PANSY

Viola tricolor

ZONE: 4
HEIGHT: Eight inches
BLOOM TIME: Spring to fall

Popular for their charming "faces" in purple, blue, white, yellow, and bicolors, pansies are often best purchased as started seedlings in the spring and treated as an annual flower. Seeds are small and slow to develop, but if you have the patience, you can sow the seeds in August, overwinter the young seedlings in a cold frame, and set them into the garden in the early spring.

New plants can also be started in late summer from stem cuttings of established stock. Root cuttings in vermiculite.

Pansies will not thrive through long, hot summers. To avoid burned-out plants, set the pansies in a partially shady area. A mulch added at planting time will also help keep the roots cool.

Keep faded flowers pinched off to encourage continuous blooming. This may mean daily picking. Good varieties include Coronation Gold, Aplenglow (red), Imperial Blue, and Sunny Boy (yellow).

The size of the flowers varies with the different varieties. To encourage larger blooms, allow only four or five flower stalks to develop per plant.

Pansies are great for edging flower beds or borders. Also plant them in rock gardens and around spring-flowering bulbs. Use fresh-cut pansies in spring bouquets and in floral arrangements.

SWEET WILLIAM

Dianthus barbatus

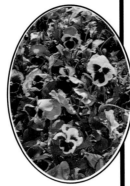

ZONE: 4
HEIGHT: Five to 20 inches, depending on variety
BLOOM TIME: May to July

Large clusters of small, flattened, purple, red, rose, white, or bicolor flowers make the sweet william a good addition to the mixed border or rock garden. Some varieties are double flowered. Sweet william, a popular old-fashioned plant, can be purchased as a started plant and treated as an annual. Or treat it as a biennial, sowing your own seeds in late summer and wintering them in a cold frame. In early spring, move the plants into permanent places in the garden.

Most sweet williams readily self-sow, and in many gardens, these attractive plants will seem perennial. Sweet william does not grow well in acid soil, so lime should be added if a soil test indicates it's needed.

Plants enjoy full sun and a well-drained location for best growth. Good dwarf varieties include Roundabout and Wee Willie. Taller sweet william varieties include Crimson Beauty, Pink Beauty, Pure White, and Scarlet Beauty.

Plant a variety of colors and sizes of sweet william in the front or middle of your border garden for beautiful blooms. Many different varieties are available.

WALLFLOWER

Cheiranthus cheiri

ZONE: 3
HEIGHT: 18 to 24 inches
BLOOM TIME: Early spring

Better known in England than in the United States, showy, fragrant wallflowers are unsurpassed for early yellow color in the garden. They are also available in russet and mahogany shades. In many areas, their bloom period corresponds perfectly with the spring-flowering bulbs.

Wallflowers are named for their popularity as inhabitants of British fence walls, not for any shy, retreating characteristics. They are actually perennials, but you'll be happiest with them when you treat them as biennials and re-sow regularly.

Sow seeds in early summer, pinching the seedlings back if they start to look leggy. In the fall, move the seedlings to a cold frame or protected location. Then, as the soil begins to warm in the spring, transplant them into the garden.

Wallflowers do best in a light, slightly alkaline soil. Add some limestone to the garden at planting time if a soil test reveals that your soil is on the acid side. Wallflowers also need a sunny location but one where they will not burn out in the early summer sun. Morning sun is ideal for them.

For yearly bloom, start new seeds each summer. In milder climates, little or no winter protection will be needed, and the plants can be left in the garden where they are to bloom.

Wallflowers grow most easily along the northern part of the Eastern seaboard and in the Pacific Northwest where they benefit from the moist air from the sea.

chapter 8

ANNUALS

Easy, instant color: this is the beauty and attractiveness of growing annuals. In the strictest definition, an annual is a plant that grows, flowers, sets seed, and dies—all in the same year. The term also has been loosely expanded to include those tender perennials that live over the winter in only the warmest of areas. Either way, annuals grow from seed to flower in a surprisingly short time, producing color all summer long. You can paint it soft or paint it bold, in any range of colors you choose, from frost to frost.

Annuals provide you and your garden with an overflowing oasis of beauty for a modest price. Their rewards are quick, bringing a new look to your landscape in a few weeks. No major investment is required to spruce up the outside of the house. Children in your family? There are few things so satisfying as teaching youngsters the mysteries of nature and watching the delighted grins as their annual seeds pop from the soil, grow, and burst into bloom.

Growing annuals allows you the freedom of changing your mind and your color scheme every growing season. Experiencing the changes and advances in the horticultural world by trying new varieties is as close at hand as a seed packet or flat of seedlings. And nothing is more invigorating than being surrounded by the freshness of flowers in the garden or in the home. Most annuals also boast the virtue of "plant and forget," rarely needing more care than an occasional drink of water. Annuals may be grown from seed started indoors in late winter or planted directly into the ground. Or purchase them in flats at a local outlet. No matter what growing conditions you have—hot or cool, sun or shade, wet or dry—there are annual flowers for you to enjoy.

Uses for Annual Flowers

Colors, shapes, sizes—an incredible range of combinations is available in annual flowers. Widespread, too, are the uses to which annuals can be put; they play various garden roles—both major and minor—quickly and easily.

Massed

A wonderful sense of extravagance abounds in the mass planting of one variety of flower. If you prefer the bold, then mass planting is for you. Such a grouping focuses on a favorite, gives authority to a design, and makes for low care.

Plants may be massed in a single row to separate the lawn from the taller flowers or to bring unity to a mixed shrub border. Massed in a wide bed, annuals add a dominant force to the landscape.

Produce a strong impact by choosing plants that are round and squat. Mounds, low to medium in height and snuggled close, hog the sunlight and leave little room for weeds. The annuals also quickly fill the beds, making them better able to combat heavy winds and rain.

Petunias remain high on the list of most popular flowers. They are joined by calendulas, coleus, marigolds, zinnias, and geraniums. For a sunny spot where resistance to heat is essential, try amaranth, celosia, four-o'clocks, or gaillardia. If shade is a problem, select begonias, impatiens, or ageratum; all will grow well in low light.

For a mass of flashy flowers, choose sweet alyssum, arctotis (African daisy), dahlias, poppies, scabiosa, or lantana. The newer varieties of nicotiana, although not so fragrant, have flowers that remain open all day.

Shining like disks of spun gold in hot, sunny places are massed Ballerina Yellow California poppies.

Tall-growing, no-care salvia makes a colorful property divider that grows in sun or partial shade.

Hedged and edged

For a tidy finish to a flower border, pick one of the dwarf and compact annuals that bloom continuously; they make ideal edging plants. Also, use colorful plants to mark a boundary between the border and the lawn or garden path. Along driveways, patios, or brick walks, an edging of annuals freshly softens the harsh and straight lines.

Any number of annuals makes good candidates for trim, forming lovely mounds of foliage always dotted with attractive flowers. As the plants at the back of the border grow tall and leggy, they will be camouflaged by the delicate bloomers up front.

For a touch of blue, try lobelia, ageratum, or myosotis; if it's red you like, plant begonias or sweet williams. Shades of violet jump out when nierembergias or pansies line up. For mixed bouquets, verbena, dahlias, or midget zinnias will do the trick. Dwarf marigolds reflect the sun's golden rays, as do calendulas and calliopsis.

To keep grass and gravel out of the flower beds, put another edging in front of the live one; make this one of metal, brick, and wood.

Flower hedges don't have to say, "Keep out," except to wind and noise. Plant them to outline the front lawn or divide the children's play area from your garden retreat. Compactness is the clue when choosing hedges; salvia is good, as are tithonia, four-o'clocks, or burning bush (which has no flowers but, perhaps more unique, turns brilliant scarlet in the autumn).

For cutting

Whether you're a serious flower arranger or a person who just likes to cheer up a room with gay blossoms, you will reap rewards from a cutting garden. If you don't have room for a separate cutting garden (see Chapter 11, "Special Gardens"), let your beds and borders double for snipping. Choose annuals with long stems and large, long-lasting blooms for bouquets. Top-notch are snapdragons, calendulas, calliopsis, cosmos, dahlias, gaillardia, zinnias, marigolds, and mums.

Color—pure and wonderful—is the calendula Orange Gem.

Delicate myosotis (forget-me-not) fills bare spots quickly.

They won't be sorry being cut; in fact, they'll be happier, blooming all the more.

For fragrance

When you choose annuals for porch or patio, under the window or at a corner you often pass, why not pick flowers that fill the air with fragrance? Although many folks may literally turn up their noses over the not-so-lovely scent of marigolds, nasturtiums, and chrysanthemums, few can resist the delicate sweet scent of petunias, dianthus, candytuft, sweet pea, sweet alyssum, mignonette, heliotrope, or stocks.

Enjoy your deck in the evening? Then lace it with old-fashioned nicotiana or four-o'clocks. Add some herbs for an unforgettable combination, as well as a tasty addition to favorite recipes.

Tucked into rocks

Gardeners often equate rock gardening with midget evergreens, hardy alpines, and juicy succulents. These aren't the only plants you can use, however, because many annuals also have a place in a rock garden. They are, in fact, an asset to it, for they assure color until frost, well past the usual flush of blooms these slopes display. Annuals are especially valuable to fill in crevices until the permanent plants take hold, to add a spot of color, or to fill bare spots quickly.

The requirements are simple: low growing, creeping, or spreading into a carpet. Sweet alyssum, lobelia, cornflower (or bachelor's-buttons), pansies, linaria, phlox, cuphea, torenia, sweet william, nierembergia, Swan River daisy, portulaca, verbena, ageratum, or ice plant all fit the description. Enliven an old-fashioned dry rock wall with color, using some of these same annuals. Because watering will be a problem, pick the ones known to be drought resistant.

Some annuals (myosotis, stock, dianthus) like full sun and cool soil. This can be a problem in hot areas; ease it by shading the roots with a large rock or a decorative mulch, such as wood chips.

Topper snapdragons produce a steady supply of spires along a fence, edged by mounds of yellow cushion mums.

Shaded

Dark and uninteresting corners of the garden can be made to glow with bright color by choosing the right annuals for those often gloomy spots. One of the best flowers for this purpose is impatiens. Vinca, coleus, begonias, torenia, and nicotiana also grow where other plants give up. For shady borders, pick dainty lobelia or perky pansies. The cooling shade from trees overhead can be made as pretty as it is refreshing.

Mixed in a border

Take four or five different annuals, combine them, break them into irregular swatches, drift them, and swirl them, and you have a mixed border. There is a certain informal gaiety to the palette of colors and the jumble of textures joined in such a mixture.

The basic aim of this type of planting is continuous and overlapping color, so pick long-blooming annuals with care. At the back of borders stand the tall growers, giving height to the arrangement while hiding fences, structures, and unpleasant views; they also offer privacy and shelter. Work down to the lowest edgers, picking plants of intermediate height for the middle ground.

Keep your eyes open to color, ever mindful of not using too much or too little. To keep the patchwork look out of your curves of flowers, always plan for several of each grouped together. What might have been a drab garden color scheme can be given some snap by bordering the house, lawn, fence, or shrubs with a rainbow of summer flowers.

The mixed border needn't be an unchanging scene. Start with color from bulbs in spring, and let the border peak in different parts of the border throughout the season with bloom from favorite perennials, such as iris, poppies, daylilies, peonies, phlox, and mums. You don't need an acre of land to capture this colorful and carefree look, a patch as small as a few square feet is all that is necessary to add another dimension to the garden scene. A mixed blessing of annuals can be effective even in tiny places—ringing the base of the flagpole (with three colors of petunias echoing the furls above), accenting a mailbox, decorating an outside light, brightening the back step, or disguising an old stump.

Before you get down to making a final decision on the site for your mixed border, laying it out, preparing the soil and planting it, stop everything for just a few minutes. Go back into the house and look out the windows, or stand on the porch or patio. If it's possible, set the border where it will look lovely on all sides—even when viewed from indoors. Imagine watching petals glisten in the morning dew or relaxing at twilight watching the flowers reflect the brilliance of the sunset. Now, go ahead and enjoy preparing your mixed border.

Layered

Clothing fashion designers aren't the only ones to claim the layered look. Planting a mixed border so it will have a layered look is like planting an imaginary flight of stairs. Start at ground level, whether lawn or garden path, and build up the bed in stages as it goes back. The layered look can end against a fence, a wall of the house, or the deck of the porch or patio. Use an evergreen ground cover, such as juniper or euonymus, to give year-round color, and add interest by setting annuals between the plants when the season permits.

If the layered look ends at a spot where a planter can be set, tumbling over with bright cascades of flowers, this will help it all the more. Should the ground slope as well, planting will be easier; otherwise, plant in increasing heights, so each layer will billow out and attractively hide the bare lower stems of the layer behind it.

An ideal site for this kind of planting is the front or back door of the house. There's no more cheery way to show off your hospitality than with an inviting bed of favorite flowers. Dress up a rear entry in the same way, and have flowers close enough to snip a few blooms when you want them.

No rainbow can rival the pure, intense red and gold tones of mixed gaillardia, zinnias, and dahlias.

Here's the layered look, a building up from the lawn to the porch with verbena, marigolds, and juniper.

Problem-Solving Flowers

Besides their beauty in flower beds, borders, or bouquets, annuals provide quick, inexpensive, and simple answers to many a landscaping question or need—all inside a few packets of seed.

Borders of mixed annuals around the house will dress it up, while expressing your personality. Highly traveled areas, such as the spot around the garage corner or a route to the patio, merit special attention and should be spotted with annuals, even if only a few. Your friends will do a double take and share in the luxury as they pass by.

If your land slopes away too quickly for easy planting, modify the angle with intermediate terraces and a graceful flow of steps. Use railroad ties, timbers, or rocks to reshape and retain the earth, and fill in the pockets with low-growing shrubs and enhancing annuals. An alternative is planting a strong ground cover that will prevent erosion and then bring life and beauty to the slope by adding colorful blooms.

Often there's a block of land between the driveway and the entry to the house that suffers from a case of the blahs. Bring it to life with a few shrubs, a few rocks, and a mix of your favorite annuals. A narrow strip between the driveway and the property line can be made a wall of vibrant color with a pattern of annual flowers.

Take attention from eyesores, such as sheds and trash storage areas, by hiding them behind flowers. And perk up a delicious but unattractive vegetable garden by edging it with annuals or mixing flowers among the rows.

Brighten up this green corner with mixed colors of ageratum, petunias, marigolds, zinnias, and more.

For drying

Just because autumn leaves have fallen and winter's dreary days have set in, there's no reason to be without tints and hues from the garden. How do you make your home bright and cheery in the face of freezing weather? With the use of colorful dried flowers. Sometimes known as everlastings, flowers suitable for drying have a straw-like texture and hold their shape and color all winter without care or water.

The list of flowers that can be treated as everlastings includes: celosia, statice, strawflowers, bells-of-Ireland, ammobium, and globe amaranth. Flower stems should be cut before the blooms are fully open, tied together, and hung upside down in a dark, airy place for two or three weeks. (For more on drying flowers, see Chapter 11, "Special Gardens.")

For climbing and vining

Climbing annuals, the garden's quick-change artists, can swiftly grow large enough to screen out an unpleasant view, shade a bald plot, enliven a dull corner, or create a secluded nest.

Annual vines grow so rapidly that it's unnecessary to do anything but sow the seeds right into the prepared ground. When you do this, be sure the trellis, netting, or other support is already in place so the roots won't be disturbed later on.

Enjoy the beauty of the red, white, or blue morning-glories as they clothe a harsh wall or soften an unattractive fence. The gay nasturtium is happiest in the poorest of soils, rambling over old tree stumps or down bare, rocky slopes. Watch the flowers of the cardinal climber (*Ipomoea x multifida*) change colors from green to purple blue as it matures. Or try planting sweet peas as soon as the ground can be worked for bouquets of blossoms before hot weather arrives.

Part of the appeal of annual vines is not their instant action, but their short lifetime. Pruning is rarely necessary, and if you decide to paint the house or fence or to let in more sun, just rip them down.

A vivid assortment of zinnias, dahlias, statice, and gaillardia are for looking, cutting, and drying.

Capture the informal and carefree look of wildflowers with California poppies, myosotis, and phlox.

A tiny garden friend sits at the corner of a terrace flat, inviting all to enjoy his mixed bed of begonias, pansies, geraniums, and other flowers.

Terrace flats

Low retaining walls of wood, brick, or stone can contain a terrace garden and serve a good purpose by directing traffic to other parts of the garden or doubling as casual seats. Raised beds are easier to work: you bend and stoop less. In fact, you can even sit down while picking flowers or pulling weeds. Watering, too, becomes a simpler task.

Raised terrace flats are almost a must where the water table is high and the drainage slow. Elevating flower beds gets the roots out of the dampness.

But there are other good reasons for building terrace flats. The soil mixture can be improved and tailored to your needs. Grass and tree roots cannot become invaders of the flower garden. In addition, the annuals are better protected from traffic—pets, athletic children or adults, and lawn mowers.

Low walls and raised beds strengthen the garden design and are most desirable in a flat garden, because they provide a variety of heights. Set a terrace flat against a high wall or the blank side of the house. The terrace relieves the monotony of such expanses and makes them appear lower.

Cookouts and flowers go hand in hand when a raised terrace is set on the paved patio and filled to overflowing with gay annuals.

If you're short of brick or stone, pile chunks of broken sidewalk concrete to make a rough wall, cascading petunias along the top and filling in the crevices with succulents. Wooden railroad ties, too, make an excellent siding for your terrace flat. Fill it with any annual that grows well in a massed bed, and you'll have closer-to-the-eye color all season long. To extend the bloom year, use bulbs in spring and add mums for fall.

This grandstand of mixed color, Sensation cosmos and perennial golden marguerites, blooms with abandon along a fence line.

Nostalgic mixes

Old-fashioned? Yes. Charming? Definitely. There is an excitement in the random appearance of mixed old-fashioned flowers, and necessary care is minimal. You can create this beauty in any planting pocket that receives at least six hours of sun a day. This big splash is inexpensive and can be obtained from seeds or from seedlings purchased in flats— ready to explode with color.

Plant taller zinnias, marigolds, and a few cosmos toward the rear as a backdrop, with snapdragons and petunias midway, and pansies and ageratum up front. Use sweet williams, dahlias, violas, marigolds, and petunias for bright color all summer. For a red-gold mix, try dianthus, marigolds, asters, rudbeckias, and calendulas. Mix statice here and there for garden color and later drying. Focus on two or three colors or a soft mix of pastels.

Informality is the key to making the garden reminiscent of your grandparents'. Mix the clumps so they seem haphazard and not like an army on parade. If you grow your old-fashioned garden from seeds and buy one of the packaged mixes, you can expect to get tall and short plants in a crazy quilt pattern. To establish focus with such a blend, deliberately place other tall plants in the background, or use shrubbery for accent.

Mix the bold and the wispy in your old-fashioned border. At the far back, use spikes of hollyhock or larkspur for tall color, softened by the thin-stemmed delicacy of California or Iceland poppies. In front of giant sunflower plants, mingle some gaillardia, myosotis (forget-me-nots), and dwarf phlox with a carpet of lobelia. Informal doesn't mean total neglect, so be sure to water occasionally and remove faded flowers.

Annuals— Portable Color

Growing annuals in portable planters reflects the mobility and changeability of today's world. Around your home, they are a perfect way to spruce up the outdoors to fit your needs.

Annuals in containers broaden the opportunities for using color and flowers in the garden. Tubs of petunias, pansies, or impatiens dotted beside garden paths invite you to stroll along. On steps leading to the front or back door, pots of brightly blooming flowers say, "Welcome and come in."

Your view from the inside out can be as pretty as your neighbors', when you dress up your windows with boxes of annuals. Remember that large boxes loaded with soil are heavy, so be sure they are securely fastened to the house. If you fill the box with individual pots of annuals, it will be lighter; you will also be able to quickly and easily change the plants should something go awry, or if you want a change of scene.

Patios, decks, and terraces have become popular spots for relaxing and entertaining on warm summer days and evenings. Movable planters allow you to make as much use of these outdoor living areas for your plants, as for your family and friends. Perch pots of annuals on the deck's railing or floor to bring it to life; if the crowd becomes heavy and you need the extra space for sitting, simply move the pots and put them back again the next day.

To enjoy patio planters even more, choose white or pastel annuals, such as ageratum Summer Snow or geranium Showgirl, because darker flowers become lost in the foliage after the sun sets.

Celosia Red Fox is well named—it's carmine, fluffy, and clever in adapting to dependable container growing.

Bricked and paved areas around swimming pools are often filled with lounge chairs, tables, and gaily colored umbrellas—but no living things. Bring beauty right to the water's edge by using tubs overflowing with the perky annual flowers of summer.

Or, if you garden without a garden, high above city streets on roof tops, terraces, or balconies, annuals in portable planters are your answer for summer color. Wrought iron railings can be laced with flowers from vining morning-glories or nasturtiums. They can also spill over to the floor below, as well as soften harsh brick walls.

The popularity today of condominiums, townhouses, apartments, and mobile homes means you have limited space to be a gardener. But you can seemingly multiply those precious square inches by doing your gardening out of the ground in containers.

Annuals for movable planters should be chosen from one of the many lower-growing, compact, and bushy varieties available. Pick out your favorites, and then give them a special place up front to show them off. Let several types keep company in the same container, with a trailer, such as vinca, spilling over the foreground or around the rim. Lay out your mini garden just as you would plan a border, with taller plants behind the lower-growing ones.

If you have the space, grow extra pots of annuals in an out-of-the-way place. Should one of your display plants suddenly take a turn for the worse or need rejuvenation, it can easily be replaced by a fresh, crisp splash of color.

Containers can be of any shape—round, square, hexagonal, rectangular. They must be large enough to give growing room to the roots and have a hole so they drain properly. Good planters are made of plastic, clay, concrete, ceramic, or a weather-resistant wood, such as cypress, redwood, or cedar. Let your imagination go wild: plant up old tubs, kettles, or sawed-off barrels. Large containers will be extremely heavy when planted, so make them easy to move by using casters or a dolly.

Five-inch blooms of the Snow Cloud petunia fill the sunny outdoors with a flair all their own.

A spot for a hanging basket can be filled with gaily colored annuals to enjoy all summer. Move the basket indoors when winter chills the air, and you'll have a living bouquet of annual flowers. These airborne creations enhance their surroundings and beautify outdoor living areas. Let the flowers of begonias, lobelia, impatiens, sweet alyssum, coleus, geraniums, petunias, trailing lantanas, or nasturtiums gracefully cascade from portable planters high in the sky.

Baskets can be suspended from anything sturdy. Hold them in place with wire, rope, metal, or chain hangers. Rival the wonders of Babylon with annual color descending from lampposts, tree limbs, overhangs, patio roofs, or brackets attached to walls, fences, or posts. All your hanging gardens will need are proper light, some protection from high wind, and an easy reach from the garden hose for daily watering.

What you use for your hangings is limited only by your ingenuity and the strength of the support. Baskets and basket-like containers can be made of wood, tree fern fiber, mesh, pottery, clay, plastic, or wire with sphagnum moss. Just make sure they drain well.

You can be a purist and plant your basket with the same variety and same color of annual. Or try combinations, such as begonias with pansies and lobelia, or marigolds with petunias, geraniums, and dwarf zinnias. Add foliage plants to make the blooms stand out.

Annuals in containers

One of the nicest things about growing annuals in containers is that they are easy to reach. If a plant needs work, remove it; do the necessary pruning, pinching, or grooming; and put it back when the job is done. The easy care can't be beat.

For a more interesting effect, use several pots of the same color but of different sizes, to give a graded or tiered look. Choose flower colors, too, that blend harmoniously with each other, so all your planters can be switched around, grouped, and regrouped. Plan on a pot or two of plants with gray or silver foliage, to act as a buffer between bright colors. Growing annuals in containers lets you rearrange the garden at will, changing the look of the landscape as quickly and as often as you change your mind.

Potted plants are one of the easiest accents the gardener knows.

Use them brimming with bright begonias or impatiens to lighten up a dark, shaded spot in the shrub border or along a wall of the tool shed. Match their colors to the shades in nearby flower borders or to the siding on the house. Bring color to a predominantly green shrubbery planting or vegetable garden by letting golden marigolds or calendulas soak up the sun.

Strategically placed, portable planters can screen out unsightly views or divert attention from faltering flowers. Place them where you want your visitors to wander and take a closer look, leading them away from eyesores or newly planted beds that are not ready to make their debut.

Should the annual you chose for your portable garden become larger than expected, it's easy to give it more room to spill over the edges of its container without crowding neighbors. This is an often impossible task if it's at home in the ground and must be cut back.

The wooden boxes (below) are practical as well as attractive. They may be left as they are or picked up and moved side-by-side as a barrier on the edge of the terrace. Line them up where there is no soil, along the driveway, for instance, and you can grow flowers without flower beds. If you start with a good basic design of square or rectangular shapes, the boxes can be interlocked in a zigzag fashion or grouped around a central point. If you design your own, raise them slightly off the ground, so air will freely circulate beneath.

Growing annuals in containers can cut down on your gardening chores. Setting a few planters in prominent positions can give the illusion of many. With all the virtues of movable gardening, though, there are drawbacks: standing out the way they do, your flowers will need to be "picture perfect." For this reason, you may have to do more primping with potted annuals than with those summering in flower beds. But because most containers will be somewhere between ankle and eye level in height, stretching, reaching, and climbing are not big problems.

The amount of sun shining on your container garden each day helps you choose your flowers. If, however, you want to grow sun worshipers and your patio is often shaded, move potted plants to sunny spots during the day and return them to their home at night. If possible, keep containers out of the heat of midday rays and drying winds. Because they're exposed on all sides, they will wilt all the more quickly.

If your portable planters receive uneven sun and the annuals start growing in one direction to reach for light, rotate the planters every few days so the flowers will grow straight and even.

Annuals in containers need more watering than do the same plants growing in the ground. Not only are all sides of the container subject to hot sun and drying winds, but there is also no deep supply of soil to hold water for the roots. Most annuals are also shallow rooted, so the moisture supply for the plants can quickly dwindle. Watch planters carefully and water when the soil starts to dry out, never letting it become bone-dry. Be generous with the hose, letting it run slowly until water drains from the bottom of the container.

Frequent watering means frequent fertilizing is necessary, because valuable nutrients leach away fast. Use a water soluble plant food once a month (following directions on the label) or every other week at half strength.

A packaged potting mix or a homemade combination of one equal part each of garden soil, peat, and perlite or vermiculite will be a perfect medium for your blooms. The additional bonus of container growing is that it lets you tailor the medium to the needs of your plants: dry for celosia, poor for nasturtium, moist for coleus. Be sure plants grouped together have similar needs. Whatever you grow, good drainage is important.

A trio of flower-filled boxes is enjoyed indoors and out. Petunias were started plants; nasturtiums, seed-sown.

This combination of white and double pink petunias is as cooling and refreshing as a plate of cherry vanilla ice cream on a summer's day.

As the season mellows, marigolds replace fading poppies, while calendulas and snapdragons take over from other perennials.

Annuals in Your Border

Beautiful borders must be planned in advance, with a seer's eye to the final pattern and effect. Whether you are a novice or an old pro, you'll find it helpful to sketch the border on paper first. Note colors and bloom times.

Start the color season with plantings of spring bulbs, such as crocus, hyacinths, tulips, daffodils, or clumps of one of the many "minor" bulbs—small in size but big in impact. Without this early color, beds will be bare and unattractive when they could delight with a hint of spring.

Follow the bulb bloom with color from early perennials, such as iris, poppies, peonies, evening primrose, or yarrow. By the time the annuals mature in early summer, they will be large enough to hide fading bulb foliage and take over the spotlight from the passing perennials. The annuals are on their own, although it never hurts to mix in a favorite long-blooming perennial.

The primary goal in planning an annual border should be harmony—harmony of color, size, texture, and design. The key to a happy combination of plants is a compatible variety of them; the result is a glorious flow, rather than a disjointed collection of forms and colors.

Unless your preferences or the architecture of your house dictate a formal garden, an informal approach is usually more pleasing to the eye, and care takes less time. Border edges may be straight or in flowing curves, and the plants within them should be uneven clumps or drifts rather than a stiff arrangement of rows.

Borders may back against a fence or the house or may stand freely along the driveway or in the center of the lawn. Wherever yours will be, blend it with the house and the rest of the property, so it contributes to the beauty of the entire scene.

To relieve monotony, mix plants of different shapes. A carpeting lobelia can be backed up with a mound of impatiens and an upright rudbeckia. In addition to plant shapes, also think of mixing flower forms. Blend the daisy-like shapes of gaillardia, spikes of larkspur, cactus zinnias, bells of petunias, pansy faces, stars of nicotiana, plumes of celosia, and lollipops of cornflowers. Contrast the boldness of sunflowers or marigolds with the daintiness of gypsophila, ageratum, or forget-me-not (myosotis).

Drama is created with color, so open your eyes when choosing your scheme. A border can be monochromatic, with various shades and tints of one dominant color, but often is more appealing when one or two colors predominate, backed up by one or two complements.

Some think nature knows no clashes, but if you have ever seen salmon- and fuchsia-colored impatiens in the same bed, you'd know there are exceptions. Don't be afraid, however, to be bold; borders of red salvia with white petunias or gold marigolds with bronze gazanias are most effective.

So your color scheme will not look like a patchwork quilt, plant at least three of one variety per clump. Repeat favorites or accent plants, so the eye will move along smoothly, but be careful they're not overdone. Have a steady succession in mind, or your border may look haphazardly planned.

Interest in annuals doesn't stop with flower color or form, however. There's a whole world just in foliage, so mix their sizes, colors, and shapes. A few annuals can be added to your border just because of their unique foliage, be they the splotched coleus or the silvery dusty-miller.

The plan below is a general guide to laying out an annual border. It may be switched around at will to please your fancy or fit your needs. Should your border be a shaded one, substitute coleus, impatiens, anchusa, feverfew, lobelia, or nicotiana. Areas with poor soil don't have to be without flowers; California poppy, celosia, calliopsis, gaillardia, and nasturtium will thrive in them.

Heat and little rainfall or irrigation are not appreciated by many plants, but cornflower, cleome, cosmos, gaillardia, portulaca, rudbeckia, and salvia don't seem to mind. If, on the other hand, soil is moist much of the time, use nemesia, monkey flowers (*Mimulus cupreus),* myosotis, nicotiana, or sweet peas.

The size of an annual border can be as long as you want it to be but should only be as deep as your arms can reach. You should be able to tend the flowers at the back without stepping on those in front. If you can place the border where it can be reached from two sides, then it can be twice as wide.

A flower border with a house or fence behind it should have the tallest plants in the rear, working down in two or three stages to a low edger in front. When the border stands where it can be viewed from two or more sides, the tallest flowers should be centered and scaled down to the edges.

Finally, proper spacing between plants is necessary for a full but uncrowded look. Set mounded plants as far apart as their height at maturity; erect or linear growers, half the distance.

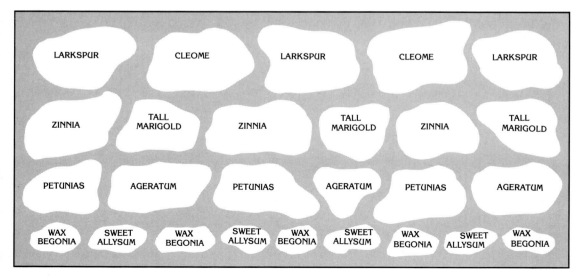

Adapt this plan each year. Change the background plants to cosmos, hollyhock, or amaranth; the intermediate choices to arctotis, calliopsis, geranium, mignonette, celosia, or nigella; the bordering types to browallia, candytuft, pink, nasturtium, pansy, portulaca, or vinca. Let your imagination be your guide—the choices are personal and almost endless.

Getting Ready for Annuals

Plan ahead for summer color by starting many annuals indoors on a windowsill or under lights. Others mature quickly and are easy to grow; plant them directly into the ground.

Containers for seedlings started indoors may be makeshift, such as a cut-down milk container. Or, for consistently better results, use one of the many devices made just for the purpose, such as peat pots or plastic flats. Special seed starters consist of pot and medium, all in one.

The germinating medium should be sterile and well drained. It may be purchased ready-to-use or made at home with peat or milled sphagnum moss and fine perlite or vermiculite in a 50-50 ratio. Don't use soil from the garden, and don't re-use the germinating medium because both may not be sterile. Garden soil contains fungi, causing baby plants to rot at ground level.

If the container is made of peat or fiber, it must be wetted thoroughly before use, or it will act as a wick and pull moisture from the sowing medium. Place the flats or pots in water until they have absorbed all the moisture they can. After the container is completely moistened, place a layer of stones, gravel, old panty hose, or newspaper in the bottom to ensure good drainage.

Fill the container with a premoistened medium to within a quarter inch of the top. The easiest way to wet the material is to place it in a saucepan or plastic bag with water. The medium is difficult to moisten evenly if you place it into the container first.

Has this ever happened to you? Your seedlings are growing strong and healthy and suddenly keel over and die. This is probably "damping off." Sterile milled sphagnum moss (or another planting medium) and proper spacing of seedlings will assist in keeping "damping off" under control. (For more information, see Chapter 16, "Insects and Diseases.")

Most annuals should be started indoors six to eight weeks before the last predicted spring frost in your area. Begonia, coleus, dianthus, impatiens, geranium, lobelia, pansy, petunia, salvia, and snapdragon will take longer.

Seeds may be sowed directly from the package, from a piece of creased paper, or with the fingers. Sow in straight rows and not too thickly. Seedlings will need room for growth, water, light, and air circulation, plus they will transplant easier if properly spaced.

Tiny fine seeds should not be covered but instead are just pressed into the sowing medium. Others are set in so they are planted as deep as they are thick.

Write the name of the plant and the date on a label. You may think you have a good memory, but it is easy to get plants mixed up.

Place the seed flat in a plastic bag, or cover it with a pane of glass to keep the humidity high. This will lessen the need to water. (Watering may dislodge the seeds before they sprout.)

Place the flat in good light but not full sun until seeds germinate. Gentle heat underneath the flat from a heating cable or the top of the refrigerator can give a helpful boost. When you see signs of life, remove the plastic bag or glass, and move the seedlings into full sun.

Watch the medium and keep it lightly moist at all times. Be careful when watering tiny, new seedlings because it is easy to drown or disrupt them. Use a fine mist or spray, or water from the bottom. Once a week when watering, add a soluble fertilizer at one-fourth the recommended rate, to ensure steady growth.

After two sets of true leaves have developed, transplant seedlings grown in flats to individual peat pots. Wet peat pots and medium

For the greatest ease, start your annuals in one-step containers and media. They look like flat cakes until they are placed in water, when they swell to pot size. Plant two or three seeds per pot. After germination, cut off all but the strongest.

Pots should be lined up in a tray of moist peat or vermiculite. Turn the tray regularly if the annuals are growing in a sunny windowsill. No fertilizing is necessary; the medium has enough food until the seedlings can be moved outside.

first, and, handling the transplants by their leaves only, lift them from the flat and transfer them to their new home.

If you have a fluorescent light fixture, use it to germinate seeds and grow stocky plants. Keep the light on for 24 hours a day until seeds germinate, cutting back to 12 to 14 hours after they poke through the medium.

Moving out

Before moving seedlings grown indoors to their summer position in the ground (after danger of frost has passed), they must get used to their new environment. This is known as "hardening off." Move seedlings outdoors for increasing periods of time on mild days, bringing them indoors at night, gradually working up to leaving them outside permanently. Plan on ten to 14 days to harden off annuals.

When you're ready to make the final move, water the transplants and the ground thoroughly. Remove plants from the flats or pots carefully to keep root damage to a minimum. If annuals are in peat pots, be sure the entire peat pot is covered with the soil. Pack the soil so it is in contact with the pot.

The date to set plants into the garden depends on the last expected frost in your area. This information is on many seed packets or weather maps and is available from the county extension office.

Seeding outdoors

Plant easy-to-grow and quick-to-bloom seeds (such as marigold, zinnia, and nasturtium) directly into the ground when it has warmed up to stay.

The first step in sowing seed outdoors is preparing the soil so it is loose, well-drained, and fertile. Spade the soil to a depth of at least eight inches, breaking up large clumps and removing stones and debris.

Mix in organic matter, such as peat moss, leaf mold, or compost, to enrich and condition the soil. Also, check the pH with a soil test, and adjust the level to as close to neutral (7.0) as possible using lime

or sulfur. Mix in a quick-acting, dry fertilizer, such as 5-10-5, at the rate of two to three pounds per 100 square feet.

Rake the seedbed level and to a fine texture. Now you're ready to sow. First, water the soil well. Flowers for a cutting or formal garden should be sowed in straight rows, while others may be scattered randomly. For straight sowing, make shallow furrows with a trowel, finger, or yardstick to the proper planting depth. Sow the seeds evenly or thinly by tapping them from the packet or by spacing them by hand. After sowing, pinch the soil together and firm.

Proper sowing depth is critical to good germination. If it's too shallow, the seeds may dry out; too deep, and the young seedlings may not make it to the surface. Fine seeds are best started indoors, but they can be grown outdoors if left uncovered and treated with extra care. Firm the seeds into the soil with a board. Then mist gently. Larger seeds are planted to a depth of two to three times their thickness.

Your main task for the next week or two until the seeds germinate is to keep the seedbed constantly moist but never soggy. Water with a fine spray every day, if necessary. The seedbed must never be allowed to dry out.

On a hot, windswept location, some shading is beneficial. Or cover the bed temporarily with a thin cheesecloth. This will slow evaporation and keep the seedlings from starting life with a sunburn.

Keep the area weeded, because weeds will compete with the seedlings for food and water and will cut down on good air circulation, inviting disease. Remove weeds carefully, so you don't disturb the seedlings' roots. Water well after weeding in case the roots have been jolted. Seeds planted in rows will make the annuals easy to distinguish from unwanted invaders of the garden.

Gardeners' aids—seed tapes, for instance—are available for the more popular annuals. They cut down on waste and help in spacing the plants properly, but you pay for the convenience. Lay the tape down as instructed on the package, and

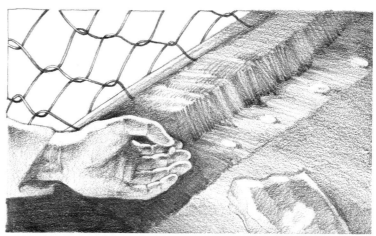

Sow large seeds by hand in a shallow trough to a depth of two to three times the width of the seed. For climbing vines or tall plants that will need support, install a trellis or stakes when you sow the seed.

Scatter fine seeds over a lightly raked seedbed. Do not cover, but press into contact with the soil using a board. Mist lightly; a heavy deluge from the garden hose will wash the seeds away.

cut to the desired length. The tape will dissolve, exposing the seeds in it to the soil.

Another important aid for outdoor sowing is a calendar. Some seeds (sweet peas, California poppy, and others) can be sown as soon as the soil is workable in the spring. Others will have to wait until the danger of frost has passed. (Check the planting instructions for your favorite annuals on the chart, pages 258 to 267.) To check if soil can be worked, take a handful of it and squeeze it into a ball. Drop it onto the ground, and if it doesn't break up, the soil is still too wet. Wait a few

days and try again. If you work soil too soon, the texture will be ruined for the season.

Seeds of hardy annuals may be sown in the fall; in the North, they will germinate in spring, ready to grow with the first warm days. Along the Sun Belt, they will germinate in fall, live over the winter, and produce early long-stemmed flowers. Among these hardy annuals are cornflowers, larkspur, California poppy, sweet alyssum, nemophila, nigella, and annual phlox. Seeds sown in fall should be planted slightly deeper than when planted in spring.

There's little waiting when you buy flats of started annuals. Make sure plants have healthy foliage.

Flats of color

If you're too late or too impatient to grow flowers from seeds, purchase started flats of annuals for summer color. They can transform a dismal backyard almost overnight, and they're available in a wide array of colors and varieties. Although it's probably less expensive to start annuals from seed, you'll get a lot from your investment in started seedlings. For one thing, you'll be rewarded with at least one extra month of color.

Each spring, most nurseries and garden centers stock a wide and often mind-boggling selection of annual varieties. To be sure you get what your planting scheme calls for, read the plant label before buying. It will tell you the variety name, bloom color, and mature height of your seedlings. Choose plants, keeping sun or shade conditions in mind. Measure the area before shopping so you will know how many plants to buy.

If you can't plant your new annuals right away, keep them in a slightly shaded spot, and water daily if it doesn't rain. There is very little medium around the roots, so it will dry out quickly.

Although plants in bloom are lovely, all-green plants are just as good and often bloom better later; check for lots of buds.

Thinning

If you sow your own seeds outdoors, they will probably need to be thinned by the time they have two sets of leaves.

Thinning involves the sacrifice of some plants for the benefit of others and should be done whenever quality is desired over quantity.

Thin plants so the remaining ones will be separated by the distance indicated on the seed packet. If you don't want to discard good plants, transplant them to another part of the garden. The survival rate varies with the kind of flower.

Planting

Before you put your seedlings in the ground, remove them from their containers unless you are planting peat pots. Turn the flat upside down and let the plants slip out. If they don't, tap the bottom of the flat with a trowel.

Dig a hole slightly larger than the rootball, and slip the plant into well-prepared soil. Space low annuals four to six inches apart; taller ones, 12 to 15 inches.

Before planting, water both the ground and the seedlings. If possible, plant on a cloudy day so the heat of the sun won't wilt them. Water heavily to eliminate air spaces around the roots.

Weeding; mulching

Keep the garden free of weeds, not only for the sake of plants' health, but also for their appearance. The best—and simplest—preventive is a good mulch, which not only limits the growth of weeds, but also keeps the ground cool, conserves moisture, and is a neat finishing touch. Try bark, wood chips, straw, hulls, or black plastic.

Feeding

To keep your plants in top shape and full color, give them a monthly feeding of either a dry 5-10-5 or a solution of soluble fertilizer. A slow-release fertilizer makes the task easier. You feed only once, at the start of the growing season, and the food is released throughout the summer as needed. No other food should be used with slow-release fertilizer.

Supports

Plants such as larkspur, hollyhock, and standard snapdragon are so tall or weak they will not stand straight on their own. For these, use a metal, wood, or bamboo stake next to the plant. Tie the flower to the stake. Vining plants, such as morning-glories, need a wooden trellis or a netting fastened between two posts; don't worry about tying them—they climb unaided. Avoid growing vines on wires because wires get hot in the sun and can burn tendrils and new growth.

To get exhibition-size flowers on long-stemmed plants, remove all but the central flower bud with tweezers, a toothpick, or your fingertips.

Watering

If it does not rain, water most annuals deeply once a week. Thoroughly sprinkle the entire bed, not just the plants, or dry soil nearby will pull water away.

Shallow watering only leads to poor root systems that stay near the surface of the soil. These cause the plants to dry out too quickly. If the weather is extremely hot or your soil is sandy, you may need to water more often. However frequently you water, never apply less than one inch of water at a time.

To know when your sprinkler has delivered one inch of water, use a rain gauge, or place an open coffee can halfway between the sprinkler and the farthest point the water reaches. If you time how long it takes to collect one inch of water in the can, you'll know how long to run the sprinkler the next time. (For advice on soaker hoses and trickle irrigation, see Chapter 1, "The ABCs of Good Gardening.")

If possible, water in the morning on days with a sunny forecast, so the foliage will not stay wet too long.

Pinching back

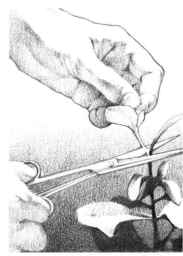

Single-stemmed annuals, such as some varieties of chrysanthemums, dahlias, and snapdragons, benefit from pinching when young to make them stockier and bushier. Either remove the center with your fingertips, or cut it out with scissors.

Trim tall and leggy plants by removing three or four sets of upper leaves just above a leaf axil. Do this when plants are six inches tall, unless they are varieties that branch on their own. Don't worry; you're not killing the seedlings. Pinching not only makes bushier plants, it also causes more flowering.

Multiplication

To get more mileage out of certain plants, grow them in the garden during the summer and indoors during the winter. The best way to do this is to root cuttings that you clip in midsummer. You'll not only have plants to enjoy indoors during cold months, you'll have sizable starts for next spring. The easiest plants to manage in this dual role are coleus, wax begonia, geranium, and impatiens. Take only as many cuttings as you can handle indoors.

Cut about four inches of stem just below a leaf axil. Remove the lower leaves, and insert the cutting into a peat and perlite mix or coarse sand. It is possible to root cuttings in water, but a later transfer to the growing medium might be tricky, because roots will be delicate.

After the cuttings are stuck in the rooting medium, water well, and place the container in a tightly closed plastic bag. Place in good light but not direct sun. In about ten days, check for rooting by gently pulling on the cutting. When you feel resistance, the cutting is rooted. Pot it up, using a rich, porous potting soil in a three-inch pot. Move to bright light, and water whenever the soil surface dries.

Taking cuttings in midsummer also benefits the plant. The snipping will reshape overgrown or sprawling plants and will ensure a fall flush of bloom for many plants.

Although it is possible to dig plants out of the garden and bring them inside for the winter, you'll have better luck carrying them over by cuttings. Plants dug from the garden are often leggy, one-sided, or in a soil riddled with insects and disease. (The pests then often will spread to your pampered houseplants.) Leaves will fall when the annuals first move in, leaving behind an even leggier plant.

Hanging Baskets

There's a special pleasure in growing plants overhead. They can enclose you in a canopy of flowers, giving you high color while not stealing precious outdoor living space.

Blue Perfection viola, Vodka fibrous begonia, and Carpet of Snow alyssum blossom with color overhead.

Baskets can hang from anything high enough and strong enough to hold them. A wide roof overhang, an arbor, a pergola, a pretty gazebo, a tree limb—these are but a few of the possible supports for an over-head garden.

All you need is a handful of screw eyes or large cup hooks fastened to a beam or other solid wood, a few sturdy wire baskets, and some lightweight chain or rope to use for hanging. Sphagnum moss, light-weight perlite, or vermiculite mixed with a standard potting mix will make the pot burden lighter. Do not use soil only, because it is too heavy; the lighter the burden, the better.

If your climate is humid most of the time, plants will grow well in moss-lined baskets. Where humid-ity is low, be sure to spray the bas-kets each day. In extremely dry situ-ations, grow the plants in plastic or clay pots with saucers that will retain more moisture.

Plants in hanging pots need more attention than those growing in the garden. However, this is not a prob-lem if you have all your hanging baskets concentrated in one place within easy reach of the garden hose. Annuals in balls of sphagnum moss will dry out faster than annu-als in clay or plastic pots, so they need to be watered more often. Metal extenders that fit the garden hose make watering a snap.

Use only compact bushy varieties of annuals in sphagnum moss balls if you wish to retain the ball-like ap-pearance of the planter. Otherwise, trailers will do fine, as they do in traditional hanging baskets.

Perfect plants include the Cascade series of petunias; Sky, Pink, Red, Royal, or White are all beauties. Mingle together tiny zinnias of the Buttons, Thumbelina, or Lilliput strains for a rainbow of colors, or try a miniature zinnia variety, Linearis, with golden flowers atop long, thin leaves. Or do a basket with nothing but verbena in a bright color mix—Regalia or the red, white, and blue Spirit of '76 for a cheery, patriotic splash.

Mix and match ageratum Blue Blazer and Summer Snow with any of the Glamour hybrid begonias. Compact plants of the Blue Bells variety of browallia are smothered in blue or white bell-shaped flowers all summer. Plant ivy or scented geraniums by themselves, and the self-branching Carefree or Sprinter variety of geranium with Sapphire or Blue Cascade lobelia. Dwarf marigolds shine in tones of gold or bronze and mix well with white candytuft and nierembergia Purple Robe.

Start semi-trailing Gleam varieties of nasturtium from seed planted in a dry soil and sunny location for blooms in six weeks. And for spheres of color, plant pansies with Rosie O'Day or Carpet of Snow sweet alyssum.

Bring some houseplants outside for a summer vacation under the eaves. Ferns, Swedish ivy, and wandering Jew do well in a sheltered corner with half-light, as do baskets of nephthytis, philodendron, and airplane plant. Coleus and begonias will come back to life outdoors before they have to be moved inside in the fall.

If your houseplants are not in hanging baskets already and you don't want to transplant them, drill three holes in the rims of their saucers, and use chain to hang the saucers and pots together. Rope hangers can be slipped over pot and plant to make it into a hanger, as can nylon monofilament hangers, which are so thin and transparent they give the plants the illusion of hanging in midair.

Bright blooms of color can come to foliage houseplants by adding seeds or seedlings to the pot in spring. These can be pulled in fall when the plants come inside and the flowers start to fade. Double-check the houseplants for any hitchhiking insects.

To keep your baskets looking their best, keep faded flowers picked off, feed with liquid fertilizer twice each month, and hang them where they will be out of the wind.

The sunshine of begonias and alyssum contrasts with pansies.

1 *To start a hanging basket, assemble a wire basket frame, a bag of sphagnum moss, potting mix, and flats of seedlings—pansies, alyssum, and wax begonias, for example. Presoak the moss overnight (if possible) to make it easier to work with, drain off the excess water, and shape the moss into flat cakes. Dry moss is brittle, hard to shape, and difficult to wet when in place.*

2 *After the surplus water has been squeezed out and the moss cakes shaped, gradually line the interior of the hanging basket frame with moss layers. Be sure to work the moss completely around the wire to disguise it. Thicken the moss lining on the inside of the basket until you have a quart-size cavity in the center. Recheck the lining, and add to thin spots.*

3 *Finish the basket with a cushion of moss around the wire rim. After the moss is in place, trim away any excess moss hanging from the sides and bottom of the basket. Then carefully fill the cavity to the top with a good planting mix, shaking it into nooks and crannies as you go. Rap the basket when full until the planting mixture settles to one inch below the rim.*

4 *To plant the baskets, shake all the soil away from the roots of the plants, and tuck them into depressions you make in the moss with your fingers. Space the annuals about four inches apart between the wires. Plant the entire basket in this manner, including the top and bottom. Add more plants if any spots look sparse. Water well, and hang the basket with chains.*

Strawberry Jars

Perk up a plain patio or porch with colorful annual flowers planted in a pocketed strawberry jar. The result: stacks of bloom. Strawberry jars are available in an assortment of sizes; they fit with almost any landscape scheme.

Summer-long color bursts from your strawberry jar when you plant it with trailing lobelia.

Plant a cascading bouquet

Sometimes the pocketed strawberry jar is still used as a container for strawberry plants and their luscious fruit. But more and more gardeners are using terra-cotta strawberry jars to display many other kinds of plants, including petunias, lobelia, succulents, ageratum, dwarf marigolds, and herbs. In fact, any cascading or semitrailing plant is a candidate. A delicate scent is a bonus treat with many you might choose.

Gardening in strawberry jars is simple— mostly a matter of selecting plants that harmonize well with the red clay of the jars. Trailers and small bouquet-shaped annuals fit best in the tiny compartments. They're generally preferred to larger plants that would soon become so big they would overwhelm and hide their interesting containers.

Award-winning annuals. Pristine candytuft or sweet alyssum makes a pleasing contrast to the earthen tones of the strawberry jar. In a cool, moist, and somewhat shaded place, pocket nemophila or nemesia in the openings. A mix of pansies and violas, peeking out in all directions, is a cheerful sight. The most popular flowers for dappled sunshine, impatiens and begonias, also lend themselves to strawberry jar treatment. For a different touch of violet, try nierembergia Purple Robe. Or forget the flowers, and liven up the jar with the finely cut, fernlike, silver-white foliage of dusty-miller.

If you garden where summers are not too hot, flashy colored fuchsia makes a particularly spectacular display. If, on the other hand, temperatures soar where you live, your strawberry jar is ideal for showing off a succulent collection, a gathering of cactus, or a rainbow of portulaca. Keep their soil sandy, and water only lightly.

Your strawberry jar can become a gay ornament almost immediately if you select flats of seedlings already in bud. If you grow your own annuals from seeds, be sure to give them a good head start indoors.

To keep your strawberry jar looking fresh, never let the medium in it dry out completely, and keep faded flowers picked off as they appear. If allowed to go to seed, plants in your jar will stop producing their happy blooms.

Once filled to the top with soil, a large strawberry jar is extremely heavy. To make the jar more mobile, set it on a platform on casters. Then, you can move the jar around as the need arises. Regardless of its size, a strawberry jar should be rotated a quarter turn every two or three days so all the plants receive equal light.

Strawberry jars can find a home wherever you would use other container plantings. For a special effect, mix jars of various sizes, or make your own strawberry barrel by drilling two-inch holes in a barrel.

Savory strawberries. If you remain a stubborn traditionalist and stick with strawberries, try both the June and everbearing varieties in your jar. Surecrop and Catskill are outstanding in the first category; Ozark Beauty and Superfection, in the second. Then there are also French or Alpine wild strawberries, which are perfect in jars because they produce no runners, yet still produce delicious fruits. Avoid the climbing strawberries whose runners are best tied to a trellis, not cascading from a jar.

Because strawberries are prone to disease, you'll have better results with a sterile, soilless potting mix that is rich, light textured, and well drained. Strawberries prefer full sun, although the wild type will be happy in woodland-like half shade.

Plant the jar following the same method as for annuals, with the crown of the plants nearly level with the vertical soil surface. Apply a balanced fertilizer, such as 10-10-10, about six weeks after planting.

When autumn leaves start to fall, move the jar to a protected spot, such as a garage, basement, or tool shed, where the soil won't freeze. Mulch each pocket and the top with pine branches or straw. Bring the jar back out in spring after frost has left the air. In spring, topdress with well-rotted cow manure or other fertilizer. For good-looking plants, replant the jar every two years, or use everbearing types.

Whether filled with strawberries or flowers, a large strawberry jar should have a central core of sand, gravel, or screening mesh, so water will readily reach the bottom plants.

1 *To plant a strawberry jar, first spread a thick layer of gravel or shards (broken clay crockery) across the bottom for drainage. Cover it with a circle of screening mesh or a layer of discarded panty hose. Then, a little at a time, add rich potting soil to the jar and the pockets until the level reaches one inch below the top. Be sure to firm the soil to eliminate air spaces, but don't pack.*

2 *After the jar is filled, add the plant seedlings in groups of two or three to each pocket opening. Simply make a small hole with your finger for each plant, and tuck it in. It's easier to plant a jar from the bottom up, turning the jar as each section is completed. With larger jars, some gardeners plant each pocket as the soil is layered in, making it easier to spread out the roots.*

3 *After all the side pockets are filled, plant the top of the jar. Be sure to save enough plants to fill out the top evenly, spacing them tightly for a full effect. When all the plants are in place, water the entire jar thoroughly. To prevent the soil from washing out of the pockets when you are watering, run the water down the inside of the pot. Keep the jar lightly moist for best color.*

Favorite annuals

MARIGOLDS

Marigolds are a flower family we Americans can truly call our own. The conquistadors discovered the blooms growing in Mexico and returned to Europe with them. "Mary's Gold" soon spread across the continent and into Asia, developing into several forms as it traveled—from the squat French marigold, all the way up to the tall African type. A great number of the new marigolds gardeners plant today are hybrids, results of years of research, which have developed new flower forms and plant sizes. These "mules" do not produce usable seeds but instead put all their vigor into riots of sturdy blooms, adaptable to many situations.

Burpee's Golden Nugget hybrid blooms the earliest and never quits.

The first hybrid marigold ever sold (1939) is still available and popular.

Burgundy Ripple—dwarf and single—has an intriguing two-color face and a high, velvety center.

Marvelous marigolds

Whatever role needs to be filled in your garden, there's a marigold cast for it. Plants stretch from a few inches to a stately four feet. They can find their way into edgings, borders, rock gardens, fillings, plantings, and backgrounds.

Colors range from deep maroon and red through bright orange, gold, creamy yellow, and white. There are single and double flowers; dwarfs and giants; and blooms that mimic carnations, mums, daisies, and powder puffs.

In some marigold varieties, the strong characteristic odor has been bred out, so they are more desirable as cut flowers. Some gardeners, though, swear by the scented types to keep pests away from the rose or vegetable garden.

Although most marigolds bloom from seed in a few short weeks, the taller types should be given an early start indoors because they need more time to mature.

Favorite annuals
PETUNIAS

Sun-loving, fragrant, and free-flowering, the petunia in its many shapes, colors, and patterns is a consistent favorite in gardens everywhere. Actually, it's a tender perennial, so it can live over winters in mild areas. In most places, petunias are best treated as annuals. They're available in both bush and cascading varieties. Distinctive types are the large-flowered grandifloras and the smaller-flowered multifloras that boast more blooms per plant. Newer hybrids are vigorous; uniform in color, height, and habit; and have a long season of bloom.

Each flower of Salmon Bouquet is like a nosegay of pink and salmon.

Pretty petunias are practical, too

Petunias come in both single, bell-shaped flowers and double, fluffy, round balls of many petals that look like carnations. Colors are pastels and deeper tones of red, blue, or purple, plus sparkling white and shades of yellow. Flowers are found in solids and stripes, often bordered or splotched with white, with petal edges that wave, ruffle, or fringe.

Petunias aren't known for their qualities as cut flowers, but several tucked into a mixed old-fashioned bouquet add a graceful note. They are luxurious in their other uses for borders, beds, window boxes, planters, groupings of terra-cotta pots, and hanging baskets.

The double-flowering types are a little more difficult to grow than the single-flowered ones. The singles will grow in poor soil with indifferent watering. Good drainage is a must for either type. Both will also benefit from a monthly feeding. Petunias must be started from purchased plants or seeds given a head start indoors in midwinter.

Color-packed pots of petunias brighten a summer porch.

Razzle Dazzle's white star is truly dazzling against the red or blue.

Favorite annuals
ZINNIAS

Hot weather and zinnias go together. These annuals bloom best once the temperature is consistently high. If planted too early, they will stand still until the thermometer begins to climb. There's a color, size, and type for every spot in the garden. Miniatures—such as Tom Thumb, Thumbelina, Cupid, and Sprite—are suitable for edging a border. The kings of this family, the Zenith, Mammoth Dahlia, and California Giants, may grow three feet tall, with flower heads six to seven inches across. They make an attractive temporary hedge.

Lively describes the giant mixed zinnia.

The large quills of Zenith Torch mix and match.

Zinnia selections

Flower forms of the zinnia include singles, doubles, pompon, cactus flowered (with quilled rays), and crested types (with a cushion center surrounded by broad rays). In the full sunshine, colors of white, pink, yellow, orange, violet, and darker shades of red and bronze glow from early morning into night, from midsummer until frost. Many blooms are two-toned; some are banded with darker shades.

Zinnias are easy to care for and thrive in any soil. In humid or foggy areas or with overhead watering (as from a sprinkler or hose) late in the day, mildew can become a problem; zinnias should be soaked at the roots—the foliage should not get wet.

Besides their uses in beds, borders, rock gardens, window boxes, and planters, zinnias are some of the best annuals to grow for cut flower arrangements. Their long stems and long-lasting qualities make them perfect for bouquets and arrangements.

Seeds may be started indoors or will grow successfully planted directly into the ground.

Warm tones grace Bouquet Hybrid. Its large, double, informally shaped blooms create a shaggy effect.

Tipped petals create the sparkle of Whirligig.

Favorite annuals
GERANIUMS

The versatile geranium, with single- and double-flowering varieties, fills beds and pots with heads of white, pink, red, or salmon. The easy-care *Pelargonium* species has been a garden favorite for centuries, with hybridizing creating new dwarf and micro-mini forms, in addition to the common types that grow to several feet. Foliage is heart shaped, often zoned or banded, and scalloped; many leaves fill the air with the scent of mint, nuts, or fruit. For hanging baskets and tubs, choose a generously vining type, such as the ivy geranium.

Mrs. Kingsley smells like a touch of mint.

This one is scented like its name—Almond.

Two for one—scented leaves and pretty blooms.

In tiny places, plant the dwarf zonal geranium, Cook's Light Pink Comet.

Grow a geranium

Geraniums are at home in the full sun yet will tolerate light shade where temperatures skyrocket. Soil must never be allowed to dry out but must be well drained, because geraniums do not tolerate water-soaked roots. Feed regularly, and keep faded flowers picked off for top-quality blooming.

Geraniums were traditionally grown from cuttings; but recent work has increased the number of varieties grown from seed. They need an early start indoors.

Petite blooms of Lemon Crispum, Prince Rupert.

ANNUAL FLOWERS

Name	Description	Soil and Light	Planting	Comments
ACROCLINIUM *Helipterum*	Two - to 3-inch blossoms on 1-foot stems. White, beige, and pink. Resemble asters or daisies.	Full sun. Well-drained soil. Can take dry spots.	Sow seed outdoors after frost danger passes.	Difficult to transplant. Cut whole stem and dry for flower arrangements.
AGERATUM **Flossflower** *Ageratum*	Long-lasting, fuzzy, quarter- to half-inch blossoms on plants 3 to 6 inches tall. (A few reach 2 feet.) Blue, white, and pink. Varieties: Summer Snow, Blue Mink, Royal Blazer.	Full sun. Will tolerate some shade. Tolerant of all soil conditions.	Start 6 to 8 weeks early indoors, or buy transplants. May be replanted in late summer in mild areas.	Use plants for edgings, borders, rock gardens, or pots.
ALYSSUM, SWEET *Lobularia maritima*	Fragrant, small-petaled blossoms on compact plants 2 to 6 inches tall. White, rose, and blue. Varieties: Rosie O'Day, Violet Queen, Royal Carpet, Carpet of Snow, Sweet.	Full sun. Will tolerate some shade. Tolerant of all soil conditions.	Sow seed outdoors as soon as ground can be worked, or buy transplants. Often self-sows.	Use for edgings, borders, rock gardens, hanging baskets, and window boxes. In warm climates, will bloom all year. Trim to encourage new growth.
AMARANTH **Love-lies-bleeding,** **Tassel flower** *Amaranthus*	Long, red, tassel-like flowers on plants 3 to 6 feet tall. Colorful leaves on some varieties. Varieties: Illumination, Early Splendor, Molten Fire, Love-Lies-Bleeding.	Full sun. Tolerant of all soil conditions.	Start seeds indoors 6 weeks early, or plant outside after all frost danger passes.	Easily transplanted. Likes long, hot growing season. Use as a background plant in a mass planting or against a wall. Drought resistant.
AMMOBIUM **Winged everlasting** *Ammobium*	One- to 2-inch-wide white flowers with large yellow centers on 2-foot-high, unusual stems with raised ridges.	Full sun. Does best in light, sandy soil.	Sow indoors 6 to 8 weeks early or outside after frost danger passes.	Easily transplanted. Cut for use in dried bouquets.
ARCTOTIS **African daisy** *Arctotis*	Daisy-like flowers, about 3 inches in diameter, on stems to 2 feet tall. Mixed colors; some bicolors.	Full sun. Prefers a light, sandy soil.	Sow indoors 6 weeks early or outside after frost danger. In mild climates, sow in late summer for continued color.	Thrives on hot days and cool nights. Drought resistant. Grow where they will receive reflected heat from a wall or walk. Flowers close at night. Cut long stems for flower arrangements.
ASTER **China aster** *Callistephus chinensis*	Blossoms vary from 1 to 5 inches across. Height, color, and flower shape vary with hybrid. Sizes from 8 inches to 3 feet tall.	Sunny or lightly shaded location. Rich, well-drained soil.	Start seeds indoors, 6 to 8 weeks early, or plant outside after frost danger.	Mix with other plants. Tall varieties can be leggy. Have shallow roots and do best when mulched. Late summer bloomer —end of July. Susceptible to fungus diseases. Heavy feeder. Rotate to a new location each year.
BEGONIA *Begonia cucullata*	Everblooming single and double varieties on shrubby plants 6 to 8 inches tall. White, pink, red.	Almost any light condition. Blooms well in shady areas. Loose, rich soil.	Start indoors 4 to 6 months in advance, or buy plants.	Plants do not compete well with other annuals, so mass them alone. Use as a pot plant year round. Take new cuttings from houseplants in early spring for your own bedding supply.
BELLS-OF-IRELAND **Shellflower** *Moluccella laevis*	Bell-shaped, green calyxes surrounding tiny white flowers on 2-foot stems.	Full sun. Rich, well-drained soil kept moist.	Sow seed after frost danger is well past, again in August in warm areas. Occasionally self-sows.	Cut for winter bouquets when flowers are in bloom, remove leaves, tie together, and hang in cool, dry place. Remove small flowers from inside when dry.

Name	Description	Soil and Light	Planting	Comments
BLUE LACE FLOWER *Trachymene*	Two- to 3-inch, pale blue umbel (or umbrella-shaped) flowers on slender branching stalks, 1 to 2 feet long.	Full sun. Well-drained soil.	Sow .seed indoors, 4 to 6 weeks before last frost date is due.	Cut for arrangements. Plants don't do well where nights are hot. Flowers are short-lived, so make continuous sowings.
BROWALLIA Amethyst *Browallia* sp.	Petunia-like blossoms. Size varies. Heavily borne on dense plants. Blue, white, violet. Varieties: Blue Bells Improved, Silver Bells, Velvet Blue.	Full sun or partial shade. Tolerant of all soil types kept moist.	Sow indoors 4 to 6 weeks early, or buy transplants.	At end of season, cut back plants and put in pots on a sunny windowsill for winter blooms.
BURNING BUSH *Kochia*	Dense, globe-like, light green, finely cut foliage plants that reach 3 feet in height. Foliage turns bright red in fall. Variety: Childsi.	Full sun. Tolerant of all soil types kept dry.	Start early indoors, or sow in the garden after the soil warms dependably in spring. Self-sows in mild areas.	Use plants to make temporary hedges. Try in tubs and in hot, windy areas.
CALIFORNIA POPPY *Eschscholzia*	Single- and double-flowered, cup-shaped, long-stemmed flowers with lacy foliage on 1- to 2-foot stems.	Full sun or partial shade. Light, well-drained soil.	Scatter seed outdoors as soon as ground can be worked. Often self-sows.	Try planting in areas where other annuals won't do well, or in tubs and pots. Likes cool weather.
CALLIOPSIS *Coreopsis* sp.	Tall and dwarf varieties: tall to 3 feet, dwarf to 12 inches. Blooms often two-toned, 1 to 2 inches across. Finely cut, foliage on wire-thin stems.	Tolerant of all light and soil conditions.	Sow seed outdoors as soon as ground can be worked. Self-sows in many areas.	Use tall plants for backdrops; dwarf varieties for border plant. Easy to grow. A perennial variety is also available.
CANDYTUFT *Iberis*	Hyacinth-shaped, white flowers on 10- to 15-inch spikes. A globe-shaped variety available in both dwarf and taller forms. Globes come in a variety of colors. Varieties: Umbellata Dwarf Fairy, Hyacinth Flowered Iceberg.	Full sun. Some shade in hot climates. Almost any loose soil.	Sow as soon as ground can be worked. Sow seed every 2 weeks for constant bloom. Sow in fall in mild areas for winter color.	After first flush of bloom, trim plants back to stimulate flowering. Grow for early cut flowers. Hyacinth-shaped flowers are heavily perfumed.
CANTERBURY-BELLS *Campanula*	Two-inch urn- or bell-shaped flowers on stems 2 feet tall. Mixed colors. Some varieties have a bell inside a bell.	Full sun. Rich, moist soil.	Sow 4 to 6 weeks early indoors or plant the seeds outdoors as soon as ground can be worked. Occasionally self-sows.	Some varieties are biennial. Blooms in six months. Likes cool weather.
CARNATION *Dianthus*	Double flowers, 2 to 3 inches across. Florist types borne on wiry stems 16 to 24 inches high; bush forms are 12 to 14 inches high. Bicolors, whites, yellows, reds.	Full sun. Light soil kept moist.	Sow indoors 10 weeks before last frost. Will last several years in mild climate.	Use bush varieties as bedding and edge plants. Keep cutting both types for continuous bloom.
CASTOR BEAN *Ricinus*	Tropical, green, large palm-leaf plants grow to 10 feet. Leaves are 1 to 3 feet long. Young leaves are red-brown on some varieties.	Full sun. Rich, moist soil.	Sow 6 to 8 weeks early indoors, and set outdoors after weather is warm.	Use as a background plant. Seeds are poisonous, so clip off before maturity. In warm climate, can survive several years.

ANNUAL FLOWERS (continued)

Name	Description	Soil and Light	Planting	Comments
CELOSIA **Cockscomb** *Celosia*	Striking flowers 2 to 12 inches in width; shaped like tall plumes or close, fanlike clusters. Plants are 1½ to 2 feet tall. Mixed colors, some intense. Dwarf forms to 8 inches tall.	Full sun. Cannot grow in partial shade. Tolerant of all soil types.	Start 6 to 8 weeks early indoors; sow outdoors after frost danger, or buy bedding plants.	Use dwarf varieties for edgings or borders; tall varieties for mass plantings. Flowers keep color after harvest; good in dried bouquets. Drought tolerant.
CHRYSANTHEMUM *Chrysanthemum* sp.	Two- to 3-inch, single and double, daisy-like flowers on 2 foot stems. Colors vary. Dwarf varieties to 10 inches with 1-inch flowers. Varieties: Golden Raindrops, Palvdosum.	Full sun, but will tolerate some shade. Rich, moist soil.	Plant seeds outdoors when ground can be worked.	Use as edging and background plants. Cut for fresh bouquets.
CLEOME **Spider plant** *Cleome spinosa*	Flower clusters, 7 to 9 inches across, with trailing stamens. Stems 3 to 6 feet tall. Pink, rose, or white. Varieties: Ruby Queen, Helen Campbell, Rose Queen.	Full sun. Rich soil kept on the dry side.	Plant seeds outdoors after frost danger passes.	Unusual seedpods useful in dried arrangements. Use as a screen plant or patio tub plant.
COLEUS *Coleus*	Foliage plants with occasional white or blue spike flowers. Six inches to 2 feet tall. Leaves in almost endless colors and mixtures.	Indirect light or shaded area in rich, well-drained soil.	Sow seeds outdoors when ground is warm, or buy transplants.	Use as an edging plant, or in pots as accents. Easily carried over winter as a pot plant from cuttings. Pinch to keep bushy.
CONVOLVULUS **Dwarf** **morning-glory** *Convolvulus*	Trumpetlike, 2-inch flowers on mounds 1 foot tall and 1½ feet wide. All colors have a white center.	Sunny location in almost any soil type kept on dry side.	Start 4 to 6 weeks early indoors, or outdoors after frost. Chip thick seed for quicker germination.	Use in edgings, borders, or hanging baskets. Unlike regular morning-glory flowers, these stay open all day.
CORNFLOWER **Bachelor's-button** *Centaurea* **(See also dusty-miller and sweet-sultan)**	Two-inch, fine-petaled, zinnia-like flowers on stems 1 to 3 feet tall. Many colors. Varieties: Blue Boy, Pinkie, Snowman, Jubilee Gem.	Sunny location. Do best in well-drained soil.	Sow outdoors in early spring. Sow in the fall about 4 weeks before frost for blossoms before summer heat. Sow in late summer in warm climates.	Use smaller varieties in rock gardens and borders; taller ones for cut flowers.
COSMOS *Cosmos*	Three to 4-inch, daisy-like, single and semidouble flowers. Feathery fern-like foliage forms a shrub-like plant 4 to 6 feet tall. Mixed colors. Varieties: Dazzler, Radiance.	Sunny location. Is shade tolerant. Light soils, partially dry.	Start outdoors after frost danger passes. Often self-sowing.	Use as a background plant or temporary hedge. Cut flowers for fresh arrangements.
CUPHEA **Cigar flower** *Cuphea*	Small, three-quarter-inch, tubular flowers on compact 1 foot plants. Red, lavender, pink, purple, rose—all with black and white tips.	Sun or light shade in average soil.	Start in midwinter, and harden plants in a cold frame or a cool room in spring.	Use as a bedding plant in edgings and rock gardens. Most widely used as a houseplant. Overwinter cuttings taken in the fall on a sunny windowsill.
CYNOGLOSSUM **Chinese** **forget-me-not** *Cynoglossum*	Small, quarter-inch, blue, white, or pink flowers resembling true forget-me-nots, on stems 1½ to 2 feet tall.	Sun or shade. Tolerant of all soil types.	Sow outdoors after frost danger. In warmer climates, may live through winter. Self-sows.	Use in bed backdrops. Plants can become like a weed.

Name	Description	Soil and Light	Planting	Comments
DAHLBERG DAISY *Dyssodia tenuiloba*	Small, half-inch, daisy-like flowers on 8- to 12-inch plants.	Full sun. Does best in light, sandy soil.	Sow 8 to 10 weeks early indoors, or outside as soon as ground can be worked.	Use in beds, borders, or rock gardens. Heat and drought resistant.
DAHLIA *Dahlia*	Single, double, and semidouble, 2- to 3-inch flowers on plants 12 to 20 inches tall. A few tall varieties, 3 to 5 feet in height with 4- to 5-inch flowers, but most taller varieties are grown as perennials.	Full sun. Rich, well-drained soil kept moist.	Start seeds 6 to 8 weeks early indoors, and set outside after frost danger.	Use dwarf varieties as bedding plants. Taller varieties often need to be staked. Cut flowers of all varieties for fresh arrangements.
DIMORPHOTHECA **Cape daisy** *Dimorphotheca*	Three- to 4-inch, daisy-like blossoms on plants 1 foot tall. White, yellow, salmon, rose, bicolors. All shaded blue on underside.	Well - drained soil kept dry. Full sun.	Start 5 weeks early indoors, or sow outdoors after frost danger. In warm climates, sow in fall.	Colorful. Flowers close up at night. Thrives on heat.
DUSTY-MILLER *Centaurea* sp. **(See also cornflower and sweet-sultan)**	Silvery white, fernlike foliage on plants 12 to 15 inches tall. Flowers are small and insignificant.	Full sun. Well-drained soil.	Best to buy transplants.	Use in edges, borders, and rock gardens. Provides good color contrast and variety.
EUPHORBIA **Snow-on-the-mountain** *Euphorbia* sp.	Large, broad foliage with white margins and some totally white leaves. Grows to 2 feet tall. Flowers small.	Full sun. Can handle poor soil conditions.	Sow seeds in early spring when soil can be worked.	Stems contain a poisonous, milky juice that should be kept out of eyes, mouth, and cuts.
EVERLASTING **(See strawflower)**				
FEVERFEW **Matricaria** *Chrysanthemum parthenium*	One- to 2-inch, chrysanthemum-like flowers on 2-foot stalks. Dwarf varieties reach 10 inches. Yellow, gold, white. Varieties: Golden Ball, Snowball.	Sun or partial shade in hot areas. Do best in rich, well-drained soil.	Sow 4 to 6 weeks early indoors, or sow outside after frost. May overwinter in warm areas.	Cut flowers for fresh arrangements. Often used by florists.
FLAX *Linum* sp.	Two-inch single flowers on grasslike stems, 18 to 24 inches tall. Red, blue, violet, pink, or white.	Full sun. Well-drained soil.	Plant seeds outdoors in early spring or fall in warm climates. Sow every 3 to 4 weeks for continuous bloom.	Difficult to transplant. Use in beds or borders.
FOUR-O'CLOCK **Marvel-of-Peru** *Mirabilis*	One-inch, trumpetlike flowers on shrubs 2 to 3 feet tall with dense foliage. Red, pink, white, salmon, yellow, bicolor.	Full sun. Well-drained soil.	Sow seeds outside after soil warms up. Often self-sows.	Blooms in midsummer. Opens late in the day. Provides color in late summer and fall. Hardy. Treat as a perennial in warm areas.
FOXGLOVE **Digitalis** *Digitalis*	Two- to 3-inch-long, bell-shaped flowers on spikes, 2½ to 6 feet tall. Pink, purple, rose, white, or yellow—with darker mottling inside. Varieties: Foxy, Excelsior.	Full or partial shade in rich, well-drained soil kept moist.	Start the seeds 6 to 8 weeks early indoors; set out when soil can be worked. Often self-sows.	After first flowering, cut main spike to encourage more blooming. If heavily mulched, can often be overwintered to a second season.

ANNUAL FLOWERS (continued)

Name	Description	Soil and Light	Planting	Comments
GAILLARDIA **Blanket flower** *Gaillardia sp.*	Two-inch, daisy-like flowers, single and double varieties to 18 inches tall. Dwarf forms to 14 inches. Reds, yellows, creams, and bicolors. Varieties: Tetia Fiesta, Lollipops.	Full sun. Almost any garden soil. Takes dry conditions and heat.	Sow seed indoors 4 weeks before frost goes out of ground.	Use plants in window boxes and other hot areas. Cut for fresh flower arrangements.
GAZANIA *Gazania*	Four-inch, daisy-like flowers, 6 to 12 inches tall. Cream, red, bronze, orange, yellow, pink—with contrasting centers.	Full sun. Sandy, light soil kept dry is best.	Start seeds indoors 5 weeks early.	Use in hot areas. Can take tough conditions. Flowers close at night and on cloudy days.
GERANIUM *Pelargonium*	Versatile group with both single- and double-flowering varieties. Range from 4-inch miniatures to 5-foot "trees." Scented, with leaves smelling like mint, nuts, rose, lemon, and apple. Some varieties are vines with ivy-shaped foliage. White, pink, red, and bicolor. Varieties: Sprinter, Carefree, Colorcade.	Full sun, but can take partial shade. Well-drained soil.	Sow seed indoors 10 to 12 weeks early, or buy transplants.	Use all varieties as bedding, as well as pot plants. Use ivy varieties and scented types in hanging baskets and patio tubs. Overwinter cuttings on a sunny windowsill. Treat as a perennial in warm areas. Use hairpins to fasten stems of ivy geraniums to the soil, encouraging growth close to ground.
GLOBE AMARANTH *Gomphrena*	Three-quarter-inch, clover-like blossoms on plants 12 to 18 inches tall. White, red, pink.	Full sun. Tolerant of all soil types.	Sow seeds indoors 4 to 6 weeks early, or outside after frost danger.	Use in fresh and dried arrangements. Plant in beds, borders, or window boxes. Drought resistant.
GODETIA **Satin flower,** **Farewell-to-spring,** **Rocky Mountain** **garland** *Clarkia*	Cultivated variety has 2- to 5-inch, cup-shaped, double flowers along stems 1½ to 2 feet tall. Wild variety (Rocky Mountain garland) has single 2-inch flowers. Pink, rose, salmon, bicolor.	Sun or partial shade. Light, well-drained soil kept on dry side.	Sow seed outdoors as soon as soil can be worked. Sow seed in fall in mild climate.	Use plants in borders and flower arrangements.
GYPSOPHILA **Baby's-breath** *Gypsophila*	Quarter-inch, rounded flowers on branched stems 15 to 24 inches. White or pink. Foliage is finely cut. Varieties: Covent Garden White, Rose.	Full sun. Does best in poorer soils.	Plant early outdoors. Sow seeds every 3 to 4 weeks for a continuous supply.	Provides a light, airy contrast in the garden. Cut for fresh arrangements.
HELIOTROPE *Heliotropium*	Large, 6- to 12-inch, lilac-like clusters of small, heavily perfumed flowers on plants 1 to 2 feet tall.	Full sun or light shade. Rich, well-drained soil.	Sow seeds midwinter indoors, or buy transplants.	Use plants in borders, patio tubs, or window boxes. Overwinter cuttings as houseplants.
HOLLYHOCK *Alcea rosea*	Varieties include single, double, semi-double, and frilled flowers, 3 to 4 inches in diameter on stalks 24 inches to 6 feet high. Mixed colors. Varieties: Silver Puff, Majorette.	Full sun. Tolerant of a variety of soil conditions.	Sow 8 weeks early indoors; place outside after night temperatures warm. Shelter from wind.	Use plants along fences or buildings, or in back row of flower beds. Some will overwinter one season in mild areas.
ICE PLANT *Mesembryanthemum*	Three-quarter- to 3-inch, daisy-like flowers on 6-inch stems. Silver-flecked foliage. Pink, white, yellow, lavender.	Full sun. Prefer light, sandy soil.	Start 6 to 8 weeks early indoors, or sow outdoors after frost danger.	Use on dry, rocky banks or in rock gardens and window boxes.

Name	Description	Soil and Light	Planting	Comments
IMPATIENS **Garden balsam** *Impatiens* sp.	One- to 1½-inch, cup-shaped flowers on small, mounded plants 6 to 8 inches in diameter. Petals are sky blue with white centers.	Sun or partial shade in warm areas. Prefer light well-drained soil.	Sow seeds as soon as ground can be worked. In warm areas, sow seed in the fall.	Use as a ground cover, bedding, or edging plant. Try mixing with flowering bulbs.
JOB'S-TEARS *Coix*	Ornamental grass, 2 to 2½ feet tall, with large gray, bead-like seeds.	Full sun. All soil types.	Sow 4 to 6 weeks early indoors or outside after frost danger.	Use in dried arrangements. Beads are easily strung.
LANTANA *Lantana*	One- to 2-inch clusters of small flowers on bushy plants, 2½ to 3 feet tall. Dwarf varieties reach 18 inches. Also a trailing form. Yellow, pink, orange, white, red, bicolors.	Full sun. Rich, well-drained soil.	Start seeds mid-winter indoors, or take cuttings from older plants kept indoors.	Use tall varieties in beds or tubs; dwarf varieties in rock gardens or edgings; trailing varieties in hanging baskets. Overwinter as a pot plant from cuttings.
LARKSPUR *Consolida* sp.	Single and double flowers borne on spikes 1 to 4 feet tall. Lacy green foliage. Blue, rose, salmon, pink, white. Varieties: Dark Blue Spire, White King, Pink Perfection.	Full sun, but need some shade in hot areas. Light well-drained, fertile soil.	Sow in early spring outdoors. In milder areas, sow in the fall. Sow at 3-week intervals for continuous bloom.	Cut flowers for fresh arrangements. Use plants along fences and walls.
LINARIA **Baby snapdragon** *Linaria*	Small, snapdragon-like flowers on 12-inch stems. Finely cut foliage. Bicolors with reds, yellows, and lavenders. Variety: Fairy Bouquet.	Full sun. Tolerant of all soil conditions.	Scatter seeds in the fall or early spring outdoors. Not heat resistant.	Use in rock gardens and borders. Mass plantings best.
LOBELIA *Lobelia erinus*	Quarter- to half-inch-wide flowers, on small plants rarely over 6 inches tall. Trailing varieties vine up to 2 feet. Blue, white, and pink. Varieties: Bright Eyes, Sapphire.	Sun, but need some shade in hot areas. Not heat resistant. Moist, but well-drained soil.	Sow seed indoors 6 to 8 weeks early, or buy transplants.	Use plants for edgings, borders, ground covers; trailing varieties in hanging baskets and pots. Cut back after first flush of bloom for new blossoms.
LUPINE *Lupinus*	Small, 1- to 2-inch, clustered flowers on spikes 1 to 3 feet tall. Blue, pink, lavender, yellow, white, bicolors.	Full sun, but shade in warm areas. Not heat resistant. Rich, moist, but well-drained soil.	Sow seed early outdoors. In mild climate, sow again in the fall.	Cut flowers for fresh arrangements. Trim off old flower spikes to encourage new growth.
MARIGOLD *Tagetes*	Double, 3- to 5-inch blossoms on plants 2 to 3 feet tall. Foliage is finely cut—often with a pungent scent. Dwarf varieties have single or double blossoms, 1 to 2 inches across. Cream, yellows, and reds.	Full sun. Almost any rich, well-drained soil.	Start seeds indoors 6 to 8 weeks before last frost date or outdoors after frost danger. Or buy transplants.	Use dwarf varieties in borders, edges, or tubs. Mix tall varieties with other flowers or plant in mass.
MIGNONETTE *Reseda*	Small, drab-looking flowers on 6- to 12-inch spikes. Plants 1 to 1½ feet tall. Blossoms are greenish-brown.	Partial shade, where summers are hot. All soil types, if kept moist.	Sow outside after frost danger, repeating every 3 weeks for continuous blooms. Sow in fall in mild climates.	Plants have a strong, pleasant odor, so place them near the house.

ANNUAL FLOWERS (continued)

Name	Description	Soil and Light	Planting	Comments
MYOSOTIS **Woodland forget-me-not** *Myosotis*	Small, open, one-half to 1-inch flowers on compact plants 8 to 12 inches tall. Blue, white, pink.	Sun or shade. Keep cool. Well-drained soil.	Plant in early spring; fall in warm climate. Self-sows.	Use in beds, borders, and edgings.
NASTURTIUM *Tropaeolum*	Two-inch, single and double blossoms on plants 8 to 15 inches tall. Climbing variety reaches 6 feet. Shiny, rounded, green leaves. Mixed colors and bicolors.	Full sun. Likes sandy soil, but will grow almost anywhere, if soil is kept dry.	Plant seed outside after frost danger.	Will flower more abundantly in poorer soils. Use leaves as tasty, colorful additions to salads. This annual seems to thrive on neglect.
NEMESIA *Nemesia*	Small, three-quarter-inch blossoms on 2- to 3-foot spikes. Compact plants 10 inches tall. Mixed bright colors.	Full sun or partial shade in warm areas. All soil types, if kept moist.	Sow seed in spring after frost danger. In milder areas, sow in early spring or late fall.	After first flush of bloom, cut back to activate more blooming. Plants fold up in hot weather.
NEMOPHILA **Baby-blue-eyes** *Nemophila*	One- to 1½-inch, cup-shaped flowers on small, mounded plants 6 to 8 inches in diameter. Petals are sky blue with white centers.	Sun, but need partial shade in warm areas. Light, well drained soil.	Sow seeds as soon as ground can be worked. In warm climate, sow seed in the fall.	Use as ground cover or edging plant, or with flowering bulbs.
NICOTIANA **Ornamental tobacco** *Nicotiana* sp.	Tube-shaped blossoms, 2 inches in diameter on plants 1 to 3 feet tall. Large basal leaves. Crimson, rose, lavender, pink, white.	Full sun; some shade in warm areas. Tolerant of all soil types. Heat resistant.	Start 6 to 8 weeks early indoors. Seed is slow to germinate. In mild climates, sow outside.	Use with border plants. All varieties are heavily perfumed.
NIEREMBERGIA **Blue cupflower,** **Purple robe** *Nierembergia*	One-inch, cup-shaped, bright purple flowers on 6-inch-tall plants that form a dense, spreading mound.	Full sun. Rich, well-drained soil kept moist.	Start plants early indoors, or buy transplants.	Use plants in rock garden and edging.
NIGELLA **Fennel flower, Love-in-a-mist** *Nigella*	One-and-a-half-inch, open blossoms on plants 1 foot tall. Fine, fernlike foliage. Blue, white, rose, pink, purple.	Full sun. Tolerant of all soil types.	Sow seeds outside in the early spring. In mild areas, can be sown in fall.	Use cut flowers in fresh arrangement. Attractive seedpods form later in the season.
PANSY *Viola* sp.	One-and-a-half- to 3-inch overlapping flowers on low, spreading plants, 8 inches tall. Wide range of colors. Noted for the dark, central, face-like markings on the petals.	Full sun but will need partial shade in hot areas. Rich, moist, but well-drained soil.	Sow indoors 10 to 12 weeks early to get blooms in late spring. Or buy transplants. Sow midsummer for plants that can be overwintered for early spring bloom.	Use as edging plants or in bulb and rock gardens. Keep cutting flowers to stimulate growth. Pinch back young plants to encourage branching.
PERIWINKLE **(See vinca)**				
PETUNIA *Petunia*	Many shapes, sizes, and colors on plants 1 to 2 feet tall. Singles, doubles, semidoubles. Common garden petunia *(P. x hybrida)* has blossoms 2 to 3 inches across.	Full sun to partial shade. Rich, well-drained soil kept moist.	Sow seed indoors 6 to 10 weeks before last frost, and set out plants after frost danger. Or buy transplants.	Use as border plants or in pots and tubs. Try cascade varieties in hanging baskets. Pinch back plants after first blooms to encourage branching.

Name	Description	Soil and Light	Planting	Comments
PHLOX *Phlox*	One- to 1½-inch blossoms clustered on plants to 15 inches tall. Dwarf varieties reach 8 inches. White, red, pink, blue. Varieties: Blue Beauty, Crimson Beauty, Pink Beauty.	Full sun; can take light shade. Can take almost any well-drained soil.	Sow seeds indoors 4 to 6 weeks early, or sow directly outside after frost danger passes.	Use plants in borders, window boxes, and rock gardens. Keep old flowers clipped off to stimulate new growth.
PINCUSHION FLOWER (See scabiosa)				
PINK *Dianthus* sp.	One- to 2-inch, single, double, and frilled flowers on plants 8 to 12 inches tall. Reds, white, bicolors. Varieties: Bravo, Queen of Hearts, Hybrid, China Doll, Baby Doll.	Full sun. Light soil kept moist.	Sow 6 to 8 weeks early indoors, or sow outside after frost danger. May survive winter.	Use as edging plants. After first flush of bloom, cut back to encourage new flowering. Some are fragrant.
POPPY *Papaver* sp.	Two- to 5-inch, silky, crepe paperlike, cup-shaped flowers on 1½- to 3-foot stalks. White, red, pastels, bicolors. Varieties: Iceland, Shirley, Oriental.	Full sun. Tolerant of all soil conditions.	Sow late fall or early spring outdoors. In warm climates, blooms all winter. Seedlings do not transplant well. Mix seeds with sand when planting for better spacing.	Use in mass plantings. Make good cut flowers if harvested when buds just begin to split open.
PORTULACA Moss rose, Sun plant *Portulaca*	Single and double, 1-inch blossoms on creeping plants that reach 7 inches tall. Foliage is dark green and needlelike. White, red, rose, yellow-orange, lavender flowers.	Full sun. Almost any well-drained soil.	Sow 6 weeks early indoors, or outside after frost danger passes. Mix seed with sand before planting for better spacing. Often self-sow.	Use these hardy plants in problem areas, beds, rock gardens, or out-of-the-way nooks.
ROCKY MOUNTAIN GARLAND (See godetia)				
QUAKING GRASS *Briza*	Pendulous, arrowhead-shaped seed clusters on grass stems 15 to 20 inches tall. Smaller varieties reach 12 inches.	Full sun. Tolerant of all soil types.	Sow seed outdoors as soon as ground can be worked.	Use in fresh and dried arrangements. Cut stems before seedpods ripen. Drought resistant.
RUDBECKIA Gloriosa daisy *Rudbeckia* sp.	Large, single, daisy-like flowers on stalks 18 to 24 inches tall. Flowers have brown centers with yellow, orange, or bronze petals.	Full sun, but can tolerate partial shade. Well-drained soil.	Sow seed in late fall or early spring outdoors. Plants often self-sow.	Trim back flowers to encourage new growth. Cut flowers for fresh arrangements.
SALPIGLOSSIS Velvet flower, Painted-tongue *Salpiglossis*	Two- to 3-inch, velvety, petunia-like flowers on plants 2 to 3 feet tall. Purple, pink, yellow, orange, red. All are intricately veined with contrasting colors. Varieties: Emperor, Bolero, Splash.	Full sun. Rich, well-drained soil kept moist for young plants and dry for older ones.	Sow seeds thinly outdoors after frost danger. Plants do not transplant well. Most need protection from the wind.	Use plants as back-of-border specimens. Pinch tops of young plants to encourage branching. Cut flowers for fresh arrangements.

266

ANNUAL FLOWERS (continued)

Name	Description	Soil and Light	Planting	Comments
SALVIA **Scarlet sage** *Salvia* sp.	One- to 2-inch, tubular flowers clustered on spikes. Plants 14 to 20 inches tall; dwarf varieties 12 inches. Deep scarlet, pink, blue, white.	Full sun or partial shade. Rich, well-drained soil.	Start 6 to 10 weeks early indoors, or buy transplants.	Use plants in beds, borders, and patio tubs. Bright colors can be almost overpowering.
SCABIOSA **Pincushion flower** *Scabiosa*	Three-inch flower heads on plants 2 to 3 feet tall; dwarf varieties 14 inches. Blossoms are covered with long, silvery stamens. White, blue, rose, lavender.	Full sun. Rich, well-drained soil kept moist.	Sow indoors 8 weeks early, or outside after frost danger. In warm climate, sow in the fall.	Use in mixed beds or planted in mass. Flowers are long-lasting in cut bouquets. Keep cutting for continuous bloom.
SCHIZANTHUS **Poor-man's orchid, Butterfly flower** *Schizanthus*	One- to 2-inch, open-faced blossoms. Plants 1½ to 2 feet tall. Foliage is delicate and fernlike. Bicolors: pink, red, yellow, white, and purple.	Full sun, or some shade best. Moist, rich, well-drained soil.	Indoors 8 weeks early, or outside when warm. In warm climate, sow in the fall.	Use plant in window boxes or beds. Enjoys cool weather; does not flourish where summers are hot. Good greenhouse plant.
SNAPDRAGON *Antirrhinum*	One- to 3-inch, tubular flowers heavily clustered on spikes. Plants 6 inches to 3 feet tall. Mixed colors. An open-faced variety is available.	Full sun. Rich, well-drained soil.	Sow seeds 6 to 8 weeks early indoors, or buy transplants.	Use dwarf varieties in rock gardens or borders. Try tall varieties in bed backgrounds. Pinching will stimulate growth.
STATICE *Limonium*	Three-quarter-inch blossoms borne on bare 16- to 20-inch, angular stems, rising from a basal rosette of leaves. Blue, lavender, rose, white flowers.	Full sun. Almost any well-drained soil.	Sow 6 to 8 weeks early inside, or outside after frost danger.	Use flowers in dried bouquets. Blossoms hold color well. If seeds encased in husk, break before planting.
STOCK *Matthiola* sp.	Small, many-petaled flowers on spikes. Plants 1 to 2 feet tall. Common color is deep blue, but rose, white, and pink also available.	Full sun; partial shade in hot areas. Moist but well-drained soil.	Start 6 weeks early inside, or outside as soon as ground is worked. In warm climate, sow in fall.	Use in beds. Cut the heavily scented flowers for fresh arrangements.
STRAWFLOWER **Everlasting** *Helichrysum*	Two- to 3-inch, daisy-like, double flowers on 2-foot stalks. Red, salmon, purple, yellow, white.	Full sun. Tolerant of all soil types kept dry.	Sow inside 6 to 8 weeks early, or outside when soil warms.	Use in both fresh and dried bouquets. Dried flowers hold color well.
SUNFLOWER *Helianthus*	Three- to 14-inch, daisy-like blossoms on plants 2 to 10 feet. Yellow, orange, mahogany, bicolors. Varieties: Teddy Bear, Sungold, Mammoth, Red.	Tolerant of all soil types kept moist. Full sun.	Sow seed outdoors after frost danger passes.	Use tall varieties as temporary screens. Try smaller varieties in beds. Grow large varieties for tasty seeds.
SWAN RIVER DAISY *Brachycome*	One- to 2-inch, daisy-like blossoms on short slender stalks up to a foot tall. Blue, rose, white, violet.	Full sun. Rich, well-drained soil.	Sow seed after frost danger passes.	Use in borders, rock gardens, or pots. Does best in cooler areas of the country.
SWEET PEA *Lathyrus odoratus*	One- to 2-inch, bonnet-shaped flowers on climbing plants 20 to 30 inches tall. A dwarf bush type will reach 15 inches tall. All colors (except yellow), plus bicolors. Petals of different varieties may be ruffled or plain.	Full sun or partial shade. Rich, well-drained soil kept moist.	Sow outside as soon as soil can be worked. In warm climate, plant in fall; mulch. Vining types need early support.	Soak seeds. Use an inoculant of nitrogen-fixing bacteria coated on the seeds before planting. Use plant in beds or window boxes. Enjoys cool weather; does not flourish where summers are hot.

Name	Description	Soil and Light	Planting	Comments
SWEET-SULTAN (See also corn-flower and dusty-miller) *Centaurea*	Two- to 3-inch, thistlelike flowers reaching 2 to 3 feet. Foliage is finely cut. Lilac, purple, white, rose, yellow flowers.	Full sun. Tolerant of all soil types.	Sow in late fall or early spring. Sow 3 weeks later for continuous blooms.	Use flowers in mixed beds. Cut flowers for fresh arrangements.
SWEET WILLIAM *Dianthus*	Small, compact plants 4 inches to 2 feet tall with flat, closely packed flowers. Bicolors, reds, whites. Varieties: Wee Willie, Red Monarch, Summer Beauty.	Full sun. Light soil kept moist.	Sow 6 to 8 weeks early inside, or buy transplants. Bloom a second summer in mild climates.	Use as a border and rock garden plant.
TAHOKA DAISY *Machaeranthera*	Two- to 2½-inch, daisy-like flowers on bushy, 20-inch plants with attractive fernlike foliage. Petals are blue-violet surrounding yellow centers.	Full sun or partial shade. Drought resistant. All soil types.	Sow seeds inside 6 to 8 weeks early, or outdoors after frost danger passes.	Cut flowers for long-lasting, fresh arrangements.
TITHONIA Mexican sunflower *Tithonia*	Three- to 4-inch, sunflower-like blossoms on 4-foot-tall plants. Orange-red flowers with light centers.	Drought resistant. All soil types. Full sun.	Sow 4 to 6 weeks early inside, or outside after frost danger.	Use bushy plants as temporary hedges. Grows quickly in hot weather.
TORENIA Wishbone flower *Torenia*	One- to 2-inch tubular flowers with flattened lips. Plants 1 foot tall. Stamens cross to give wishbone effect. Dark blue blotches on the lips; light blue on the throat; yellow center.	Partial shade or full sun in cool areas. Rich, moist, well-drained soil.	Sow seeds 8 to 10 weeks early inside, or sow outside after frost danger.	Use in rock gardens and edgings. Cuttings overwinter on a sunny windowsill.
VERBENA Vervain *Verbena*	Flat clusters of small flowers 2 to 3 inches wide on plants 6 to 10 inches high but spreading up to 2 feet wide. Many bicolor with white centers.	Full sun. Rich, well - drained soil, kept moist. Heat resistant.	Sow seeds 10 to 12 weeks early inside, or buy transplants.	Use as fragrant ground cover or edging and in window boxes or rock gardens. In warm climates, will act as perennials.
VINCA Periwinkle *Vinca* sp.	One-and-a-half-inch, single, phlox-like blossoms on rounded, bushy plants 1 to 2 feet tall. Rose, pink, white, bicolors.	Full sun; partial shade in hot areas. Well-drained soil.	Sow seeds 12 to 15 weeks early inside, or buy transplants.	Use as a border plant or in pots and tubs. In warm climates, treat plants as perennials.
VIOLA Violet *Viola* sp.	Small, 1- to 1½-inch, pansy-like flowers on compact, 8-inch plants. Blue, yellow, red, white, apricot, and purple.	Full sun, but need shade in hot areas. Rich, moist, well-drained soil.	Sow inside 10 to 12 weeks early for blooms in late spring. Plants started midsummer can be overwintered for spring bloom.	Use in edges and rock gardens. Plants flower longer than pansies, a relative.
XERANTHEMUM *Xeranthemum*	One- to 1½-inch, silky, daisy-like flowers. Stems 2½ to 3 feet tall. Pink, red, rose, purple.	Full sun. Tolerant of all soil types.	Sow seeds outdoors after frost danger.	Use in fresh and dry arrangements.
ZINNIA *Zinnia*	Dahlia-like blossoms 4 to 7 inches across on plants 2 to 3 feet tall; rounded, pointed or cactus-type petals. Round blossoms 1 to 2 inches across on plants 6 to 12 inches tall. Mixed colors and bicolors.	Full sun. Tolerant of all soil types.	Start seeds 6 to 8 weeks early indoors, or outside after frost danger.	Use dwarf varieties in borders, rock gardens, or window boxes. Try tall varieties in mixed beds or planted alone.

chapter 9

BULBS

Nondescript, drab, generally ugly—bulbs and bulb-like roots are like well-wrapped packages. They don't look like much, but they travel well. From those plain brown lumps come lovely—always colorful—surprises. Their unexciting but functional packaging enabled such plants to withstand rigors of early travel from Japan, Turkey, Mexico, Russia, and other corners of the globe to Europe and the New World.

This group of travelers included not only true bulbs, but also corms, rhizomes, tubers, and tuberous roots. The differences among them are probably less important than the similarities they share. When dormant, the bulb holds the life of a whole plant. It is a self-contained storehouse that helps the plant to survive for months without soil or moisture. Nutrients are gathered from the leaves and packed into the bulb as support for the plant when it begins to grow again.

But there are differences. True bulbs, such as daffodils and tulips, have a flower bud within them surrounded by layers of food supply. Corms, such as crocus and gladiolus, are a solid mass of stored food, with roots growing from a baseplate and with small buds on top. Tubers are a round, food-storing part of the stem, and the flower develops within them after planting. Tuberous roots producing the dahlia and tuberous begonia are a food-storing part of the root. Rhizomes (for plants such as the calla lily) are, like tubers, stem tissue but are long and sometimes form a "V."

Some are hardy—able to stay in the ground all winter; others are tender and must be dug up and stored when temperatures drop. But, whether true bulb, corm, rhizome, tuber, or tuberous root, all produce flowers or lovely foliage year after year with a minimum of care.

Sunny, Hardy Bulbs

With a burst of color that brightens any winter day, some bulbs flower through the last of the snow. With planning, you can have bulbs blooming periodically from spring into November. Try them massed as a single color (opposite page), or mixed (right).

Whether you select a darwin or species tulip, exuberant crocus, stately hyacinth, glorious glory-of-the-snow, or some other bulb-like flower, knowing a bit about your favorite bulbs will help you put the right one in the right place. Be sure you know when the bulb will bloom and whether it prefers sun or shade. Is it hardy enough to be left in the ground through the winter, or is it tender enough that it must be dug up and stored? (See the latter half of this chapter for information on tender bulbs.)

No matter where you put the plants, keep scale and color in mind. Tall *Allium giganteum* might look silly standing in a small pot or towering over ground-hugging flowers, for example. And a cluster of kaufmanniana tulips wouldn't provide transition between a ground cover and flowering crab apple tree (but darwin tulips might).

A little paper work before you order bulbs will pay off for years, and a few notes through the seasons will keep you an enthusiast. Record flowering dates, plants that go together well (in your garden and in those of other gardeners), and the performance of plants. Write down areas that could be brightened with a bulb flower. Then, depending on the time of year when you need a spot or sweep of color, you can plant one or more of these.

Very early: Crocus (especially *Crocus korolkowi),* glory-of-the-snow (chionodoxa), *Anemone blanda,* puschkinia, eranthis (winter aconite), galanthus (snowdrop), and *Iris reticulata.*

Early: Squill, grape hyacinth, species tulips (kaufmanniana and fosterana), single early tulips, hyacinths, and dwarf daffodils.

Mid-spring: Daffodils *(Narcissus jonquilla),* tulips (greigi, mendel, cottage, triumph, and darwin hybrid), and fritillaria.

Late spring: Tulips (darwin, lily-flowered, parrot, and double late).

The allium family dramatically fills in a flowering border during that "difficult age," when tulips and other traditional features fade. Alliums are showstoppers of tiny, star-shaped flowers massed in rounded heads that measure up to a foot across, depending on variety.

The season is delicately extended with petite, front-of-the-border flowers. The sternbergia, fall crocus, and colchicum still bloom as autumn leaves fall and provide the last outdoor flower color until spring.

Using clumps of color or a massed planting of hardy spring-flowering bulbs is, by far, the most spectacular way to display them—even if there are no more than 20 to 30 bulbs in the mass. It heightens the impact to use one variety and color in a group.

Because they're early, such clumps can be used to dazzle those gaps in your yard usually shaded by deciduous trees and shrubs. By the time they leaf out, the bulbs will have finished their show. The deep green of evergreens provides a good backdrop for early blooms.

Bulbs in borders prove the usefulness of such plants. Feature bulbs during the early spring—through the first three months of the border; not much else blooms until summer. Mixed judiciously with annuals, biennials, and perennials, the border can be a low-care showpiece that focuses on different points as the weeks pass. Some pruning, replanting to replace spent bulbs, and dividing overcrowded growth are all that's necessary over the years. As you plan, remember

that the smaller the bloom, the larger the number of bulbs you'll need. Two dozen daffodils may be enough to make a full drift, but you may easily need three or four times that many of the small galanthus bulbs.

Put those bulb flowers with long leaves behind perennials. The perennials' flowers and leaves will grow up and cover the aging bulb plant foliage after the tulips, daffodils, alliums, and other bulb plants yellow with age.

Early bulbs can be accompanied by almost-as-early perennials (see "Perennials and Biennials," Chapter 7), which tend to be low enough to act as a ground cover even for the midget bulbs. Or use the perennials' leaves as a foreground for the elegant red fosterana tulip and for single or double early tulips.

Take care to separate vibrant colors from each other, using white or creamy flowers, delicate leaves of hostas, ground covers, creeping evergreens, or the foliage of a plant flowering later.

When planning and combining

colors, first decide where to put the tulips. Start at the back with the tallest plants, then those of medium height, and finally the shortest. Catalogues will give heights and blooming times. Start with white or the lightest color in the center of the border, and gradually move to either edge with medium and darker colors. Fill in with low underplantings or ground covers if the front row leaves a gap between bloom and the ground.

If planning and paper work don't appeal to you, keep one hint in mind: plant bulbs in drifts and patches of similar colors and varieties, rather than mixing them. A calculated mix—such as tall daffodils and grape hyacinths—is attractive, but save the third and fourth kind of bulb for another clump.

The formal garden is making a comeback. One reason is the interest and willingness of some garden enthusiasts to work regularly in the garden. A well-ordered plan can also be pleasing. Hyacinths and tulips are spectacular bedding plants in a single color or a geometric design. Sometimes a contrasting plant, such as white pansies or daisies with deep purple hyacinths, is striking.

Naturalizing is the opposite of a formal bed. With this technique, you try to make the bulbs look as if they were growing wild. If planted where the foliage won't be mowed and where drainage is good, grape hyacinths, daffodils, and crocus won't need to be bothered for years—although the plants will appreciate an occasional fertilizing. The unsophisticated way to space the bulbs is simply to take a handful and toss them gently, then plant them where they land.

Rock gardens, though appearing "natural," take a bit more planning. Smaller bulbs, such as squills, crocus, eranthis, oxalis, *Iris reticulata,* species tulips, grape hyacinths, and galanthus work well, because the depth of the soil may not be sufficient for larger bulbs. The bulbs should have at least a foot of good topsoil and about the same depth of porous subsoil. Shallower areas can be planted with a ground cover.

Leading Types of Tulips

For up to six weeks of tiptoeing through tulips, choose from several classes of them. The hardy species tulips are the earliest to bloom and look like relatives that grow wild in other parts of the world. They flower for more years than do other tulips.

Catalogues often indicate the officially designated tulip class names. Classes vary in appearance and bloom sequence.

Early. 1) Single early. 2) Double early.

Mid-season. 3) Mendel (up to 20 inches tall). 4) Triumph (up to 20 inches tall; sturdier than mendel). 5) Darwin hybrid (cross of darwins with wild species).

Late or May-flowering. 6) Darwin (tall; lower part of flower in rectangular outline). 7) Lily-flowered (pointed, curved petals). 8) Cottage (also called single late; flower often egg-shaped). 9) Rembrandt (brown, bronze, red, black, pink, or purple stripes). 10) Parrot (lacy, curled petals). 11) Double late (peony-flowered).

Species. 12) Kaufmanniana. 13) Fosterana. 14) Greigi. 15) Other species.

Kaufmanniana

Kaufmannianas are early blooming, with long, narrow petals that open wide to make them look like water lilies. Only four to six inches high, they do best when planted eight inches deep and six inches apart where they won't be disturbed. Some retain a single pure color. The yellow and watermelon rose-colored kaufmannianas (at right), separated by puschkinias, show the advantages of massing bulbs in rock garden or border.

Fosterana

This dazzler looks much the same whether growing in U.S. gardens or growing wild on Turkish slopes. Years of hybridizing haven't been able to improve on its bright colors, large flower, and vigorous growth. Foliage is sometimes mottled or striped.

Bloom times of varieties differ. Early ones open while the kaufmanniana is still fresh and go well with hyacinths and trumpet narcissus in a border. Or group them in a rock garden. Late varieties come about two weeks after. Early fosterana stands over 15 inches high and grows best in a somewhat sheltered area. Later varieties average a foot high. Fosterana species tulips grow well in varied soils. Plant bulbs eight inches deep, six inches apart.

Greigi

Greigi hybrid tulips have long-lasting flowers. Although they bloom with other mid-season tulips, greigi rival the fosterana hybrids for generous size of flower. Some are a bright scarlet or sport a wealth of yellow gold. Others are bicolors, such as variety shown at left. Sturdy stems lift the bloom eight to 15 inches, depending on variety. Gray-green leaves striped with red, brown, or purple are ornamental.

The greigi, like other species tulips, do better in soil less rich than the other classes require. They tolerate heat better, too.

Leading Types of Tulips

(continued)

Lily-flowered

These elegant golden stars (left) belong to a variety of the lily-flowered class of tulips. They bloom just as April bows out. Glossy flowers are borne on firm stems of about 20 inches.

The long, pointed petals come in yellow, white, or bicolors. They contrast well with the dark and more rounded darwin and cottage tulips. Set lily-flowered tulips where the sun hits them; it will make them seem even brighter.

These unusual tulips hold center stage in the garden, but they also are attractive mixed with other flowers or used alone as a cut flower arrangement for the table or sideboard.

Darwin hybrid

Darwin hybrids, the largest tulips, are the offspring of noteworthy parents. They combine the wild fosterana's bright shades and outsize petals with the darwin's tall stems (over two feet high). Darwin hybrids have strong stiff stems, so this tulip doesn't have to be protected. Flowers, though, last longer when planted in a light shade. Set them six inches apart, eight inches deep. They bloom earlier than the darwins and come in a rainbow of colors, including the fine red varieties, along with the brilliant yellows. This class is dramatic when massed in a single color and variety. You'll be pleased by the number of years the bulbs will bloom.

Parrot

Parrot tulips (in the lower part of the picture, left) are deeply notched and frilled to give them a fluttering, birdlike appearance. Parrot tulips, unrivaled in the garden, are long-lasting when cut for indoor color.

They are strays or mutations of other more sedate classes, so, except for their almost bizarre petals and open faces, parrots are similar to other tulip classes. They bring the rich colors of their forebears but are sometimes streaked with green. The large heads can be top-heavy, so try to find a protected corner for them. They may be mixed carefully with other flowers (colors are often bold) or massed alone. Plant eight inches deep, six inches apart.

Cottage

Cottage tulips, along with parrot tulips, signal the end of the tulip season, with their big, extravagantly bright flowers. The cottage tulip (upper left) has generous yellow-feathered-with-red blooms.

This large class of tulips comes in so many colors and shapes that you'll have no trouble fitting some into your border. Blooms are most attractive when the cottage tulips are nodding in the sunny end of the border or in a bright clump. They last longer, though, in light shade.

Leading Types of Tulips
(continued)

Mendel; triumph

Mendels and triumphs are tulips with a purpose. They were developed to fill the pause between the early and late tulips. Set them eight inches deep, five inches apart. Mix their bulbs with cottage and darwin bulbs to begin the season of tall tulip bloom even earlier. In Zone 5, they open in late April and early May. The foliage ages early enough for you to plant annuals or perennials in the same spots.

If you feel foiled by a half-shady, half-sunny spot that would be perfect for tulips, plant the shady part with triumphs and the sunny with darwins or cottages. The midseason bulbs in the shady spot will bloom the same time as the later ones in the sun.

Doubles—early and late

The early doubles glimmer with the daffodils. Near the first of April, they venture forth with their cheerfully colored, peony-like flowers on stems somewhat shorter than those of many tulips. The late doubles arrive throughout the main season, along with the familiar cottage, lily-flowered, darwin, and parrot tulips.

Doubles are best viewed from a slight distance. Up close you might see them as single, awkward, heavy blooms. Set in a mass away from the house, they look like an exquisite splash of white, scarlet, or rose. Or mix them for a showy effect. Their look is lush in yellow (such as those shown at right) combined with red.

Plant early and late doubles eight inches deep, six inches apart.

Early singles

Set these petite sparklers along the front of your flower border for refreshing April color. A grouping of at least a dozen can be mixed among perennials, where they supply a bright spot to the border for weeks before the first tall, stately tulips and other flowers bloom. The perennials then disguise the yellowing foliage after the blooms fade.

The early singles are shorter (stems are about ten inches long) and less showy than the May tulips. They are hardier than darwins and rembrandts, so they can be planted in less-sheltered positions.

Fragrant early single varieties are available. Check favorite catalogues and garden centers for suggestions.

Other Species of Tulips

"Other" hardly seems a glamorous way to describe the vast and unusual array of tulips coming under the heading of "Other Species" in bulb catalogues. Some bloom early; some arrive late. All are wild tulips or hybrids of them. They tend to be hardy when conditions are right, and they're perfect for rock gardens.

Horned tulip

Horned tulip (also called acuminata) comes to us—without changes—from Turkey. Its crinkled, long, skinny petals make the horned tulip look like a colorful spider. Exotic red and yellow blooms open in May and work well in flower arrangements.

Tarda

Tarda comes on brightly with the mid-season daffodils. White-tipped petals give the blooms an almost iridescent quality. This is probably the best tulip for rock gardens. Or you can plant it in other dry and sunny spots. Nestle it in a nook—sheltered from winter's winds—to be sure of early bloom next spring.

Chrysantha (left)

The chrysantha tulip stands eight inches tall and appears in March. Its ancestors are from Afghanistan, but you'll enjoy its effect clustered near the foundation of your all-American home. The chrysantha is tinted red (with yellow border) on the outside and solid yellow on the inside.

Whittalli (right)

Whittalli tulips bring favorite autumn colors to you late in April. From an almost black center, the petals shade out to a delightful golden orange. This species tulip needs no pampering and thrives under ordinary conditions.

Eichleri

Eichleri, about eight inches tall, glows in late March with its bright red flowers. The bell-shaped blooms have a beige shading and black base (ringed with yellow) beneath.

Daffodils

Bright, nodding blooms are often called either daffodil or narcissus. It's easy to decide which to use. Narcissus is the botanical or scientific name of the whole genus, but the narcissus is also a short-cupped member of the family. Daffodil is the common name for the tribe but also refers to those flowers with long trumpets.

Yellow hoop petticoat

Split cup

Even before the sun brightens late winter and early spring skies, there is sunshine on the ground when daffodils bloom. Varieties of daffodils can be found that flower with the crocus and continue in succession until tulips provide a rainbow of color.

Divisions. The delight of that first daffodil can be extended for weeks with a little planning (bulb catalogue in hand). As tulips are divided into classes, narcissus are separated into divisions. The trumpet division, for example, has the trumpet or corona as long as the outer petals, one flower to a stem.

Another division is called large-cupped. This one has a cup a third or more the length of the outer petals. Members of the doubles division, with their extra petals, are fluffy and showy. Some varieties (opposite page) have long petals of creamy white and a center of lemon and bright orange-red. The triandrus division has up to six flowers on a stem with narrow rushlike foliage. Many triandrus selections are good in the rock garden.

The cyclamineus division has wavy-lipped coronas, petals that curve back, and gracefully drooping heads. The jonquilla division (or jonquils) has a fine scent and long, narrow leaves and stems. The species or wild narcissus are offspring of those growing freely in nature.

Where to put narcissus. Daffodils may be grown in either full or partial sun. Because they go through much of their growth before many trees have foliage, daffodils may be used under large trees, especially if the tree leafs out late. Daffodils make good companions for other plants. If you grow them in rows along driveways, sidewalks, or walls, mix them with iris for late spring, phlox for midsummer, and mums for fall, to hide aging foliage. Or try annuals, such as nasturtiums, zinnias, portulaca, petunias, or marigolds, for a yearly change.

Wherever they go, make sure the earliest varieties, such as *Narcissus cyclamineus,* are planted in sheltered spots. This protection may allow them to bloom a week earlier than if they were exposed.

How to naturalize. Daffodils are able to compete with low grass and may be planted here and there in an unorganized way to look as though they are growing wild in the lawn. However, as with tulips, the foliage must be allowed to mature before being mowed down.

A money-saving tip: use a mix of narcissus for naturalizing. Many catalogues offer such a grouping. To get the casual effect, take a handful of the bulbs and toss them gently. Plant them where they land.

Narcissus' needs. Daffodils need well-drained soil. Soil that is too tight or in low areas with poor drainage may promote bulb rot. If the foliage in spring is streaked with yellow or if it dies prematurely, bulb rot might be the problem. Dig out such bulbs. If you can see rot at the base, discard the bulbs and dig out any nearby to prevent spread. If you don't find rot, the bulbs may be stored in a dry place for replanting in fall.

Early September (in the North) and October are best times for planting. If you're planting later, apply a heavy mulch to postpone hard freezing of the ground, so roots have a longer time to develop. For best effect, plant at least six of a variety to a group.

Unless bulbs are to be naturalized, excavate the planting area to a depth of four or five inches, and turn the soil in the bottom of the hole a full spade's depth. If the soil is heavy, add sand and vermiculite or perlite to loosen it. Dig individual holes eight inches deep from soil surface, six inches apart. Firm the soil in the bottom of these holes with your fist before putting one bulb in each hole. If the soil is poor, add liberal amounts of organic matter, as well as a small amount of high-phosphorus fertilizer. Don't fertilize again until after the leaves have emerged in the spring.

Cover the bulbs, and replace the excavated soil to make the soil surface level with the bed. Water well at planting time and then every week or so until winter arrives.

After the flowers fade and leaves yellow in the spring, the foliage must be left intact to build up the strength of the bulbs for next year's cheerful nodding bloom.

Hyacinths

With the delicate scent reminiscent of yesteryear, hyacinths formally define edges of flower beds and borders. In addition to shades of rose pink, white, and yellow, hyacinths provide distinctive blues, a color their popular planting companions—tulips and daffodils—don't have. In fact, one of the most appealing planting arrangements includes a blue variety, backed up by yellow tulips or daffodils.

White, pink, and blue varieties of hyacinths are pleasing in old-fashioned and modern gardens.

Dutch, common, or garden hyacinth—no matter what you use as the everyday name for *Hyacinthus orientalis,* this species is the most popular of the hyacinth brood. Followed by a multitude of varieties and hybrids, *H. orientalis* is known for its full, compact spike of small flowers. It may grow as tall as 15 inches.

One variety, *H. orientalis 'albulus'* or Roman hyacinth, is a fragrant bulb easily forced to bloom indoors in the midst of winter. Smaller and with looser blooms than the parent group, the Roman hyacinth is hardy outdoors only in the South.

Uses of hyacinths are perhaps less numerous than for other spring bulbs. But, because the odor is so refreshing, you'll want to plant them at the front of borders and near the house or walk.

The hyacinth is less hardy than other bulbs and must be well-protected in winter. It fails to produce vigorous blooms after about three years.

Plant enough bulbs to *fill* any areas you designate for hyacinths. Because of their upright growth, they don't wave around as much as long-stem flowers, and a loose planting can look sparse and spotty. Clumps of hyacinths work well as accents in the perennial border. Placed in front of taller iris, hyacinths appear to be growing from the same leaves. And they bring a touch of sky blue and yellow sunshine to sunny or semi-shady spots between lawn and dark green shrubs or at the corners of foundation plantings.

How to plant hyacinths is similar to the method used for tulips. They may be planted from September to December, depending on the time of hard freeze in your zone. September and October are generally best to allow them time to de-velop a root system before the ground hardens. But there's no plus in early planting, because the bulbs will put out roots only after the air temperature drops to about 40 degrees Fahrenheit. Moisture will be needed to help the bulbs develop strong roots before hard freezing.

Take care to plant in soil that drains rapidly—even after extensive rains. Hyacinths cannot tolerate wet or heavy soils. Plant six inches apart in circles or straight lines and eight inches deep. In good soils, do not add fertilizer. Hyacinths are sensitive to rot in rich soils.

Hyacinths grow well (and last longer) in partial shade. However, you will probably get more perfect blooms in a spot with both full sun and natural protection against strong spring winds. As with other bulb plants, hyacinth foliage must be left for a month or so after bloom; the foliage helps produce food for the next season.

Bulb care

After foliage dies, the next steps depend on where you live and the work you're willing to do. Hyacinths won't bloom as many years if you leave the bulbs in the ground over the winter. A heavy mulch will help, or dig the bulbs up for dry summer storage.

Brush the soil off them, and place in a cool, shaded place for replanting in the fall. Lift the bulbs, too, if you want to replant the area completely with bedding plants after the hyacinth foliage ripens.

Left: Exhibition hyacinths make an outstanding, sweet-smelling addition to the early spring border.

Grape hyacinth

Although not a hyacinth at all, the six-inch grape hyacinth *(Muscari* sp.), seen from a distance, seems to be a miniature version of one. These hardy little bulbs (below) thrive in sun or shade and do best in well-drained soil. Plant four inches deep. There is also a white variety. Grape hyacinth blooms in midspring and is a good choice for naturalizing or for rock gardens.

Hardy Favorites Begin the Season

Hyacinths, tulips, and daffodils may be the bulbs everyone can identify. But make your spring an early and uncommon one with some pint-size members of the bulb family. They're big on color.

Anemone blanda, *or windflower, does best planted in clumps of 12 of the same color.*

Crocus—spring

Species crocus, *Crocus chrysanthus, C. tomasinianus*
ZONE: 4

Across winter-weary parts of the country, nothing starts telephones jingling like the sight of the first crocus. Species crocus are earliest and can push through leftover snow a full two weeks ahead of the hybrids. Flowers last a little over a week, so mix species and hybrids for the longest possible color in those drab days of late winter.

Sturdy little crocus will grow in almost any soil, almost anywhere in your landscape, in any part of the country. Plant the corms about four inches deep and close together—only a couple of inches apart.

Crocus can be left undisturbed for years but will multiply rapidly, so thin them every three years. Because they're so early, spring-flowering crocus are a natural for naturalizing. The blooms will be spent and foliage ripened about the time your conscience nags you into mowing the lawn.

Eranthis

Eranthis hyemalis
ZONE: 4

Eranthis, or winter aconite, appears in February on stems barely taller than mushrooms. Its dainty golden blossoms are shaped like buttercups and settle on a cushion of dark green leaves.

Plant eranthis tubers in late summer. Soak them in moist sand or warm water a few hours before planting. The tubers do best set four inches deep, three or four inches apart, in fairly well-drained soil. They like light shade but do well in full sun. Water eranthis while it is actively growing.

Galanthus

Galanthus sp.
ZONE: 4

By being the first bulb to bloom in very early spring, galanthus shows more courage than even chionodoxa. This characteristic makes it effective planted in a woodland setting, in rock gardens, or at the base of deciduous trees where it blooms and fades before trees leaf out. Also called snowdrop, galanthus' bell-shaped blooms appear even before the frost leaves the ground.

More than many bulbs, snowdrops do well in a clay soil. In the fall, plant them four inches deep and three inches apart in a shady spot. They will spread by self-seeding. If you divide them, do so just after flowering, without disturbing the roots. Keep moist until reestablished. Snowdrops are short-lived in the South.

Iris reticulata

Iris reticulata
ZONE: 4

The *Iris reticulata* is a member of the vast iris tribe. This is a bulbous iris; other members of the group grow from rhizomes or tubers. It's reasonably perennial in Zone 4 with a mulch for winter protection. Standing only four to six inches tall, the reticulata is used best at the front of a mixed border or in a rock garden.

Variety Joyce has large flowers for its class. The pale blue falls are blotched with orange and blue uprights. Another variety is deep purple with an orange blotch. A pale blue variety has white markings on the dark blue falls.

Reticulata iris needs an alkaline soil; if yours is on the acidic side, dust with lime after the blooming period ends. Plant four inches deep, three inches apart.

Siberian squill

Scilla siberica
ZONE: 4

Siberian squill grows quantities of starry blue, nodding bells in short racemes to subtly announce the arrival of spring. Naturalize these five-inch-high gems in grassy areas, beneath shrubs, or along the edge of a flower border. If left undisturbed, squills self-sow and multiply rapidly to give a larger display each year. Squills may be used to form a brilliant carpet to cover an entire bed or garden.

Plant squill bulbs not over four inches deep and about three inches apart in either the sun or partial shade. White and pink varieties are available. Petite squills have prices to match their size—small.

Anemone blanda

Anemone blanda
ZONE: 6

Anemone blanda (top, opposite page) blooms with the earliest narcissus. Other varieties of the blanda come in shades of pink, rose, and deep blue. Use in rock gardens, along a garden path, or in front of shrub plantings.

They like rich, well-drained soil and some shade. Soak tuberous roots in water overnight. Most varieties are not hardy north of Zone 6. Plant them in early fall about four inches deep and two inches apart.

Sometimes called windflower or Greek anemone, the little flower seldom grows over eight inches tall.

Chionodoxa

Chionodoxa luciliae
ZONE: 5

Glory-of-the-snow, or chionodoxa, depends on winter's rain and snow for spring moisture to bring out the best in its blue, star-shaped flowers. Even if you live in regions that suffer extended drought through the summer, you can count on this little plant to be one of the first bloomers in spring, peeking through melting snow.

Only an average of six inches high, chionodoxa grows from an extremely hardy bulb—good for planting in a border, at the base of deciduous trees, or around shrubbery. Its bright blue color combines well with daffodils and other pastel bulb flowers.

Almost any soil will provide enough nutrients for its early growth, but avoid planting on the north side of buildings because it prefers full sunlight. Plant in the fall about four inches deep, three inches apart. Glory-of-the-snow won't be glamorous until a year or two after planting.

When they become so crowded that flowering decreases, lift and replant after foliage ripens and turns yellow. Hardy through Zone 5. Glory-of-the-snow does best where winters are cold.

Puschkinia

Puschkinia scilloides
ZONE: 4

The *Puschkinia scilloides* is also called striped squill. Its creamy white flowers are touched with blue, and it blooms in March and April on graceful stems up to a foot long.

Try it in rock gardens or naturalized in a grassy area. Plant bulbs four inches apart and about that deep. Put them in shade or sun—wherever they can be left undisturbed for several years.

Early spring crocus is a natural for naturalizing in your lawn.

Chionodoxa, or glory-of-the-snow, prefers full sun and cold winters.

Hardy Favorites to Extend the Season

From April through autumn, there are still more bulbs to come. Try some lovely eccentrics you'll never confuse with other common flowers. The nodding crown-imperial fritillaria or the lollipop-like *Allium giganteum* will stop passersby.

Crown-imperial fritillaria is over two feet tall, topped with leafy crown.

Allium giganteum has a four-inch globe of tightly clustered florets.

Fritillaria
Fritillaria imperialis, F. meleagris
ZONE: 5

There are at least 70 species of fritillaria available, but the two best for the home gardening hobbyist are *F. imperialis* (appearing mid-season) and *F. meleagris* (early).

The crown-imperial (*F. imperialis*, left) grows to over two feet. The drooping, bell-shaped flowers of red, orange, yellow, or bronze have an unpleasant scent.

The *F. meleagris* has several common names—snake's-head fritillaria, checkered lily, guinea-hen tulip; a look at the mottled petals tells you all are good descriptions. They come in combinations of purple with white and stand a foot tall. Try them naturalized in grass, under large trees, or in a rock garden.

Plant *F. meleagris* about four inches deep (deeper if the soil is sandy), with four to five inches between them. The larger, taller *F. imperialis* are best ten or more inches apart and nine inches deep. They'll appreciate a slightly acid soil, mulching in the fall, and water in dry weather.

Oxalis
Oxalis sp.
ZONE: 6

Oxalis, or wood sorrel, is a large and varied family. Members grow best—almost year round—in the South and are often found as a greenhouse plant in the North.

With clover-like leaves, blooms are small and yellow, white, pink, or purple, depending on time of year. These lovely rascals are so vigorous they can invade other plants if not contained or grown in baskets. Or plant them in a large open area.

Plant oxalis in the fall only three inches deep. Set them in a sunny to partially shady spot six inches apart.

Allium
Allium giganteum
ZONE: 4
A. moly
ZONE: 3

Actually related to the onion, the allium is as lovely in flower arrangements as it is in the garden. These arrangements can be dried, too. Unbothered by most insects and diseases, the allium has few special needs. It can even be planted spring or fall.

The giant onion, or *A. giganteum,* stands a lofty four feet high, with a magnificent flower ball at least four inches across. Plant bulbs in a sunny, well-drained spot about eight inches deep, six inches apart.

The shorter lily leek or *A. moly* has a looser mass of little flowers in yellow. It does just fine in shady spots. Plant four inches deep, three inches apart. Lily leek works well for naturalizing.

Colchicum
Colchicum autumnale
ZONE: 4

The colchicum is versatile, but you'll get better results if you plant the corms in a cool, moist location shaded from direct sunlight. No special planting needs: dig a hole and cover corms with fine soil.

Colchicums are available in both single- and double-flowered varieties. Try them in flower beds or rock gardens, and under shrubs. For a natural look, try them in a lawn or under trees in a wooded setting.

Colchicums start growing in midwinter, slowly sending up their coarse, grasslike foliage while other plants are still dormant. Later, as the weather warms up, the foliage thickens and continues to grow until early July when hot summer weather makes the plants go dormant.

Then in the fall, the plants burst forth with a profusion of five- to nine-inch flower stalks that bloom until cold weather forces them to become dormant again.

Colchicum varieties go dormant in July but bloom in the fall for a final burst of color before winter.

Crocus—fall
Crocus sp.
ZONE: 4

A crocus looks similar to a colchicum, but they're not related. Their growth habit and life cycle are much the same, though. As with the colchicum, fall crocus goes dormant twice in a year—once in the heat of July and again in the cold of December's wintry blasts.

To plant fall crocus, dig a hole and cover the bulbs with fine soil. If you're planting in a lawn, replace the sod plug and break it up slightly, so the bulbs can grow through; at the same time, you avoid lots of little bare spots in the lawn.

To naturalize, simply toss a handful of bulbs across the ground, and plant them where they land. Don't worry if the bulbs look a little sparse. Crocus quickly reproduces and can carpet the area in only a few years.

Fall crocus are available in a large selection of colors. Most popular include orange-scarlet, bright red, white, blue, and lavender.

Sternbergia
Sternbergia lutea
ZONE: 7

Late August into October is treated to the rich, golden-yellow *Sternbergia lutea.* Looking much like a substantial crocus, egg-shaped sternbergia has a fine satin sheen. Blooms are about two inches across and two inches high. Foliage is a foot long.

In midsummer, plant bulbs five inches deep in a protected but sunny spot with good drainage. Set them three inches apart. *S. lutea,* or fall daffodil, does well in rock gardens and hot dry areas.

Hardy Bulb Know-How

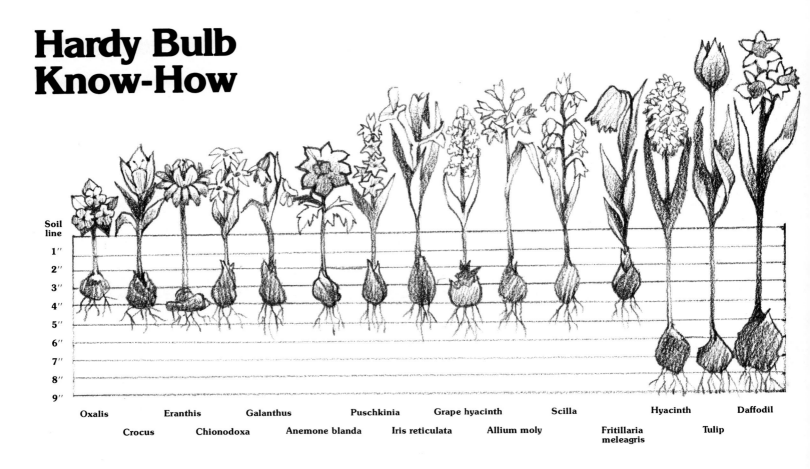

Soil line · 1″ · 2″ · 3″ · 4″ · 5″ · 6″ · 7″ · 8″ · 9″

Oxalis   Eranthis   Galanthus   Puschkinia   Grape hyacinth   Scilla   Hyacinth   Daffodil

Crocus   Chionodoxa   Anemone blanda   Iris reticulata   Allium moly   Fritillaria meleagris   Tulip

---

In autumn, prepare for a brightly colored spring by planting hardy bulbs. The planning starts when you decide what to put where and then order the tulips, daffodils, hyacinths, or dozens of tiny species bulbs. If bulbs are to thrive, a good location and good soil preparation are important.

While bargains abound in many phases of gardening, there are few discount bulbs. The cheap bulbs may disappoint you and produce few or no blooms. The savings come when your care makes top-quality bulbs flower for years.

The first inexpensive tools to use are pencil and paper. Draw a diagram of where you'll plant and how many bulbs will be needed. As you order the bulbs, note the varieties and colors on the diagram. Because minor bulbs are so small, plan for plenty. Use no fewer than two dozen of each. Four dozen will sparkle even more when they freshen a gray, almost-spring day. Galanthus, grape hyacinths, and crocus multiply over the years.

Bulb quality depends not only on size, but also on firmness, weight, and covering. Even if a bulb is large, it may be light and spongy or have cut, bruised outer scales. If you buy at a garden supply center, do your own spot checks. Examine bulbs carefully; squeeze them, check heftiness, and look for the larger sizes.

If any time elapses between purchase and planting of bulbs, be sure to store them in a dry, dark, cool place—temperature not over 50 degrees Fahrenheit. If you plant on a warm, sunny day, never leave bulbs in the sun. Even a short time under such conditions will noticeably reduce the size of blooms.

When to plant

Plant in the fall anytime before deep frost hardens the ground. This may be as early as September in the extremely cold parts of the country or as late as Thanksgiving in the Middle South. In areas with frigid winters, some kinds of bulbs planted late may have smaller flowers or weaker plants.

Soon after bulbs are planted, they begin to develop roots. Some bulbs, such as grape hyacinth and daffodil, may develop a little top growth in the fall. This does not harm the bulbs nor interfere with flowering because the flower buds remain low in the bulb. Leaves produced in the fall may brown or be killed back by severe winter weather, but portions low in the ground will survive and start new growth in the spring.

Where to plant

For most hardy bulbs, the perfect planting site is an area naturally covered by light shade during the warmest part of the day. When this is provided, blooms will last better and retain a deep color. Afternoon shade helps prolong the life of the flowers and keeps the bulbs cooler. Plant under tall trees; much of the bulb growth takes place in spring before leaves are fully developed and while shade is still light. In the heavy shade of buildings, low-branching trees, or shrubs, though, food production by the bulb plant will be reduced and poor flowering in future years can be the expected result.

Under large trees, shallow tree roots often compete with the bulb roots for food and water. To make sure bulbs develop well in late spring, keep them moist. They often cannot benefit from light rains or dews when planted under trees where tree roots are using large amounts of water.

Sunlight and plants go together, but hardy bulbs actually prefer slight shade. In the case of the "pink" daffodils, the shade is desirable because it brings out this trumpet color.

Bulbs in a bed facing south will flower earlier in the season than those in one on the north. A bed sheltered by a house foundation, where soil tends to be warmer, is likely to flower earlier than one set farther away.

Bulbs as annuals

In the deep South and other areas that escape freezing weather, give tulips and hyacinths an artificial winter. In these warm climates, the bulbs must be dug and refrigerated each year. Leave the tulips and hyacinths in place until after blooming and after the foliage has died down. Precool the bulbs by storing them in the bottom of your refrigerator at 40 to 50 degrees Fahrenheit for six to 12 weeks. Or purchase new bulbs that have already had this special cold treatment.

Even where the weather is not so warm year round, there may be situations when you want only a single season of bloom from the tulips, hyacinths, or other bulbs; perhaps you plan to build a garage over the bulb bed. Or you may prefer to replant bulbs yearly, as you might do with annuals, so that different color combinations and arrangements may be used each year.

If bulbs will later be dug out and discarded after one season of flowering, they may be planted in areas not normally well-suited for perennial treatment. They may even be planted in heavily shaded areas; extensive soil preparation is not necessary.

Soils for bulbs

Whether bulbs are for one year or many, drainage is still a critical element. Lack of it results in poor root growth and development of bulb rots. Daffodils can be naturalized in fairly moist places, so long as the ground isn't waterlogged.

In areas such as beds, clumps, and borders, take time to improve the drainage of soil high in clay. Add sand, peat, or vermiculite to a depth of 12 inches (or a full spade depth). If soil is too sandy, work in rich peat or compost. The actual depth for planting bulbs varies according to the variety and the soil—deeper in light, sandy soil, but more shallow in heavy clay. If the soil is well-drained, try planting most tulips at a ten-inch depth, rather than the usual eight. An added benefit: after foliage dies, you can plant late annuals right over the tulips. The tulips will last longer when planted at a little greater depth.

To plant a clump of bulbs, dig a hole nine to 12 inches deep, and replace loose soil until the depth is correct for your bulbs. Mix in fertilizer. (See information on fertilizer, this page.) Set each bulb point up, and press gently into the loose soil below the base.

For a bed of several types of bulbs, outline the area for each group with the end of a rake handle. Space tulips and other big bulbs fairly close (five or six inches) to make a splashy color effect. Wide spacing weakens their impact. Put all bulbs in place, inside outlines, before you plant. Set the bulb firmly in place. Then cover with soil.

Fertilizer

For bulb beds, spade in a fertilizer high in phosphorus, calcium, and magnesium as you plant. Or work bone meal into the soil at the bottom of the hole or bed. Topdress with balanced fertilizer after blooming. Although bulbs contain their first season's food supply, fertilizing is recommended to foster future growth. Plant food will help bulbs root faster. Compost will give them an extra boost, too. When you plant, label clumps with both variety name and color. This will pre-

vent digging in the wrong place if you plant other flowers to bloom after the bulb foliage has died. It will also help you locate various types when it's time to divide old clumps.

Pests

Field mice and chipmunks are a menace to newly planted bulbs in some areas. To reduce the danger, don't plant bulbs next to garden walls or house foundations where the little animals make runs. And before planting in the fall, clean beds of all garden waste that could make ideal nests for mice.

The only sure way to protect newly planted bulbs against mice and chipmunks is to place the bulbs in baskets fashioned from hardware cloth, their tops left open. But this technique is too time-consuming and expensive except in smaller gardens.

Other pests? Quality bulbs are subject to few insects or diseases. But if a plant should show signs of disease, such as misshapen foliage, lift and destroy the entire plant, so the disease will not spread.

Water; mulch

Drought is one pest you can battle. Water the bulbs after planting to settle the soil and give them a good start, and water beds liberally during dry spells. Try to keep water from getting on the leaves. Supplement rainfall when necessary; give beds the equivalent of one inch of water a week.

When there's talk of water for the garden, mulch is sure to be mentioned, too. A three- or four-inch layer of good mulch, such as cocoa bean hulls, straw, wood chips, compost, or ground corncobs, will conserve soil moisture, keep down weeds, prevent extreme temperature fluctuation during the winter, and enrich the soil as the mulch breaks down.

Applying several inches of mulch over perennial beds that include spring-flowering bulbs is a wise precaution anywhere but is vital in areas where sudden thaws and freezes might cause the ground to heave, damaging bulbs and roots. The best materials are those that let

rain and melting snow come through easily, keeping moisture levels adequate. Because the arrival of spring varies widely from area to area—and even from week to week within the same area in different years—the safest way to decide when to remove mulch is to make frequent checks as the weather begins to warm. Usually, when bulb foliage is two inches above soil, it's time to take off the mulch.

After-bloom care

After the first season's bloom, future flowers depend on the care you give the bulbs. Primarily, it's a matter of growing a good crop of foliage, because the leaves provide food for the bulb. Leaves should not be cut or mowed off until they have ripened. With tulips, when foliage is cut with the flowers or otherwise not allowed to ripen, the result is no bloom the following year. Bulbs treated this way often send up a single leaf but no flowers.

When tulips finish flowering, pick off the developing seed capsules. If you don't, the plants will direct their energy to ripening seed, rather than to storing food for future flowers. Flower stems may be left standing. Continue to water plants until the foliage turns yellow.

Sometimes other activities, particularly construction around the home, threaten to interfere with your hardy bulbs' proper aging and food production. If you can't wait until the foliage yellows to move bulbs, dig the entire plants with roots intact. Either replant them temporarily (by digging a shallow trench, laying the plants in at a slant with foliage sticking out, covering the bulbs and roots with soil, and keeping soil moist), or sort the plants and set them into their new permanent place immediately.

Even though you plant fine bulbs and give them good care, you will find that hybrid bulbs tend to throw smaller blooms after a few years and finally disappear, except, perhaps, for a few shoots of foliage. Species or botanicals, however, are more nearly perennial by nature. This group of tulips includes the fosterana, the greigi, and the kaufmanniana.

Hardy Lilies

Make room for hardy lilies in your flower border and you'll have glorious color all summer. By selecting varieties according to when they flower, you can have a progression of bloom from June to September.

There are hardy lilies to fit any sunny spot in your garden. Check out tall or short ones, with solid or blended flower colors. All varieties need sunlight, preferably until about 2 p.m.

The most important consideration in selecting a spot for lilies is drainage: lilies won't tolerate soggy conditions. Planting on a gentle slope is ideal. If your chosen site is level, plant in hills or raised beds for best results.

Set out madonna lilies *(Lilium candidum)* or nankeen lilies *(L. x testaceum)* in late August or early September. All other hardy lilies go in a month or so later.

Except for the madonnas and the Turk's-cap lilies *(L. martagon),* bulbs should be planted about eight inches deep, measuring from the base of the lily bulb. Madonnas are planted one inch below surface and should put up top growth before frost if they are to bloom the following season. Plant Turk's-cap lilies about two inches deep.

Plant all the hardy lilies soon after they arrive, because they are never truly dormant. Add a handful of bone meal to the bottom of each bulb hole and a two- to three-inch layer of straw as mulch over the top.

Cutting individual lilies to float in bowls won't harm next year's bulb strength, but don't cut long stems of many in your border. Lilies need stems and leaves to build up strength for next year's blooms.

Care and feeding

Hardy lilies (left) bloom for years with few disease control or care problems so long as they're planted in sunny, well-drained spots. Each hybrid bulb produces eight to a dozen flowers up to eight inches across on a lofty six-foot stem. Remove blooms as soon as they start to turn brown or seedpods will develop fully.

Flowering in August, this and other hardy lilies can be lifted when the leaves turn yellow. Although you can move them in the spring, fall is better; there's less danger of harming new shoots or roots at that season.

Lilies appreciate a feeding of bone meal once or twice a year. Carefully work it into the soil around the plants.

Color combinations

Design a color scheme for your plantings to gain the most dramatic effect. Orange and yellow lilies (right) complement each other. They increase abundantly and flower with the Japanese iris. Lilies and iris are compatible, because both need rich, well-drained soil.

Ranging from two to six feet tall, lilies' delicate stems may need to be tied to stakes for support, even in protected areas.

Thin green bamboo stakes will be cleverly disguised when lilies are grown in front of evergreen shrubs, hedges, or trees. Plant at least three bulbs in a group.

Tender Bulbs

Unlike the hardy bulbs, tender bulbs must be dug and stored for the winter in all but the mildest parts of the U.S. The fall activity makes a lovely excuse for you to be outdoors in the brisk air, as birds and winter-dreading Northerners head south.

For generations, gardeners have included digging and storing tender bulbs, such as the dahlia, gladiolus, and caladium, as a fall clean-up job. The benefits come each spring: whether new or replanted, tender bulbs give peak performance the same season. Plant after the weather is dependably warm. They will bloom and flourish in the heat of summer when other flowers lag.

For success the first year, buy bulbs that are healthy. Results in future years depend on you. Apply a complete fertilizer at planting time and a side-dressing when blooms appear. This encourages a good growth of foliage to feed next year's bulb.

Although tender bulbs have much in common, they require different care. Tips for the most popular ones are included in the remainder of this chapter.

Dahlias

Dabble in dahlias if you want sure-fire color from midsummer to frost. Types vary from the dwarfs used for edging (see facing page) through larger single, anemone, peony, cactus, water lily, colarette, ball, and pompon types. Some are sturdy six-footers. They even make good temporary hedges if you stick to one variety.

Bushy, dwarf dahlias start easily from seed. Sow indoors in sterile soil, three seeds to a pot, four weeks

Cheerful two- to three-inch, ball-type dahlias come in many colors.

Water lily

Colarette

Cactus

before the frost-free date in your area. Cut off all but the strongest seedling in a pot. Transplant the fat little tuber outdoors in a sunny, well-drained spot when the soil is warm. Or sow seeds directly in the garden. Thin seedlings to 18 inches apart. The dwarfs (one to two feet tall) need no staking.

Buy tubers to start larger dahlias. Set a 1x2 stake next to each at planting time. If you wait, you may damage roots. Make each planting pocket four inches deep and two

feet apart for intermediate-size miniatures and pompons, four feet for tall varieties. Set tuber with the crown (from which buds grow) by the stake. Cover tuber with only an inch of soil. Fill in later as shoot grows. Make a shallow basin around the plant to catch water. Use a low-nitrogen fertilizer formulated for bulbs. Mulch to keep roots cool and the ground moist and free of weeds.

In the fall after a light frost, cut plants back to six-inch stems. Dig

tubers carefully, hose off dirt, and cut away any broken roots. Let the tubers dry in the shade for a week before storing them. Place the tubers (they'll still be somewhat moist) in ordinary cartons with dry sawdust, vermiculite, or sphagnum moss. Label each clump. Store at 35 to 45 degrees Fahrenheit. Add more sawdust if roots start to shrivel.

Wait until spring to divide; each dahlia tuber will need at least one bud or "eye."

Starting standard dahlias from tubers

Before planting a tuber, push a stake in the ground to support the stem. Make holes four inches deep, set tubers horizontally, and fill holes as dahlias grow.

Allow only one shoot to grow per tuber. When it has two pairs of leaves, pinch out the tip. The stem will need tying to keep plant upright.

As each stem matures, cut off side flower buds so only a large central bloom is produced. Dahlias make magnificent cut flowers.

Fancy-leaved caladiums splatter mixtures of red, pink, white, and green in a colorful border.

Caladiums like warmth and moisture. They require shade, except in the early morning and late afternoon.

Caladiums

Color-splashed leaves, not flowers, make caladiums popular with gardeners. Choose from leaf markings that are crimson, rose, pink, cool greens, or practically translucent whites. The tropical-looking plants brighten shady corners of the garden, or they can be used in planters on the patio. In frost-free areas of the country, leave them outdoors all year. In colder parts, the tubers must be dug and stored over the winter.

Start the tubers indoors in March. (Although they can be planted outdoors in the late spring, you'll lose fewer plants by starting them early inside.) Plant tubers one inch deep in wooden flats of half peat and half perlite. Space tubers one inch apart, round side up. Cover lightly with mix, water, drape with clear plastic, and place in a warm spot.

Transplant from flats to four-inch pots when tubers sprout roots. Firm a loose potting mix around the plants, allowing a half inch at the top of the pots for water. Put them in a bright, warm spot. Transfer outdoors when all danger of frost is past and night temperatures reach about 55 degrees Fahrenheit. Tubers planted too early may rot.

Plant the tubers one inch deep, one foot apart in well-drained soil rich in organic matter. For best show, use several plants of the same color together. Caladiums may be grown in full shade but will have more intense color in a little sun. They thrive in warm temperatures and high humidity. Feed once a month.

Water caladiums frequently, and treat foliage to a misting on hot days. Caladium flowers aren't flashy. They are interesting because they resemble the blooms of their relatives, the calla and the jack-in-the-pulpit.

To prepare for storage, stop watering three weeks before the first expected frost date. Tubers are sensitive to frost, so dig them in early fall while the weather is still warm. Let them dry for a week in a warm, dry place. Store in vermiculite, sawdust, or perlite at 60 to 80 degrees Fahrenheit.

Buy hard, round tubers in March or April, and start them indoors. Plant them—round side down—in a flat of barely moist vermiculite, sand, and sphagnum moss.

Dig plants in fall. Dry tubers about two weeks. Remove soil and stems. Store in peat, sand, vermiculite, or sphagnum moss. Leave potted tubers in pots, but bring them inside.

soil that's fertile and constantly moist, yet never soggy. Protect them from winds that might break their brittle stems.

Staking the plants early may save some breakage. Water frequently to keep surface roots moist. The foliage also benefits from frequent misting.

Fertilize every other week with one-fourth teaspoon of 5-10-10 fertilizer for peak growth. Keep plant food at least six inches from stem.

Dig begonias about the time of the first frost. Leave stem and dry foliage attached. Set them in a sunny spot for several days. If stems detach easily, remove them; otherwise, store the whole plant. Pack in vermiculite, sawdust, sphagnum moss, or sand. Store at 45 to 60 degrees Fahrenheit. Keep packing material dry unless tubers shrivel. Then sprinkle with water.

Shade-loving tuberous begonias, such as this picotee, seem iridescent.

Tuberous begonia

Beguiling tuberous begonias are midsummer favorites. They have spectacular flowers, both singles and doubles, ranging from two inches to eight inches across. Flower colors are solid red, pink, yellow, orange, and white, except in the picotee class where margin colors are deeper. Shapes are varied, resembling a rosebud, camellia, narcissus, or carnation.

The upright type of tuberous begonia can be chosen for pots, edgings, and borders, while trailing types are ideal in hanging baskets. Plant begonia tubers indoors in March or April. Keep them warm (at least 65 degrees Fahrenheit) in bright light, but avoid burning sun. When roots develop (usually in three weeks), replant the tubers one inch below the surface of potting soil in a larger pot.

Transplant outdoors after danger of frost is past. Tuberous begonias like shade or partial shade along the north side of the house or under high-branched trees. They prefer

Begonias put on a colorful show with a variety of flower forms—ruffled, rose, picotee, and carnation.

For beginners or experts, the gladiolus is one of the top favorite hobby flowers.

Gladiolus

The sophisticated gladiolus is actually no snob. It grows well in many places—clumps or rows—and need not be started indoors.

Begin planting the bulb-like corms in spring as early as the ground can be worked. Count on 65 to 100 days from time of planting to bloom. Stretch the flowering season over several months by planting some corms every two weeks until the middle of July. Each planting of glads will bloom for about two weeks. Some varieties are called "earlies" or "fast-maturing" in catalogues. They should be planted first and last.

You can choose varieties in almost any color but true blue. Some are ruffled. Many have contrasting eyes. Or try novel miniatures.

Glads prefer sandy loam (slightly acid is best) but grow in almost any soil unless it is soggy. They like full sunshine. Dig ground deeply. If it's poor, work in a complete fertilizer. Large corms, whose heavy blooms will need bracing, should be planted six inches deep. Set them five inches apart in the clump or border, or six inches apart in rows with 20-inch spacing between rows.

Through the summer, cultivate. Mulch to keep roots cool. A side-dressing of plant food, plus ample water applied at flowering time, helps produce a good growth of foliage to feed next year's corm.

Flowers can be cut when the lowest buds start to open. Always let at least four leaves remain behind on the stalk.

Dig glads six to eight weeks after last blooms fade and foliage matures. Late bloomers may still be green until after the first frost, so wait until then to dig. Cut tops to within a few inches of the corm. Place each variety in a separate box or porous sack. Cure in a well-ventilated place for two or three weeks at 75 to 80 degrees Fahrenheit. Before placing the corms in winter storage, dust them lightly with an all-purpose garden or rose dust, and break off the tops.

Corms can be stored in old nylon hose or onion bags hung in a place that stays near 35 to 45 degrees.

Plant glads in rows or clumps of four, eight, or more. For clumps (as above), plant about four inches deep and six inches apart, depending on size of corms. They like full sun and well-drained soil.

Staking may be necessary to keep the tall varieties of glads from falling over. Use inconspicuous stakes, such as bamboo, with string to support the plants. Add more support by working soil up around base of plants.

All tender bulbs appreciate mulching to keep them cool through warm weather. Cover the ground with leaf mold, grass clippings, wood chips, or other organic matter to lessen the need for weeding and to conserve moisture.

All-American pink and salmon glads are real beauties. They're perfect at the back of a border.

Calla lily

Call upon a calla lily (*Zantedeschia* sp.) to clearly but delicately accent a corner of your flower border. The calla has a reputation as an indoor plant but deserves more recognition as a tender outdoor bloomer, happy in full sun or light shade.

Start the rhizomes indoors in mid-spring, then transplant them outside when the soil warms. They'll fill the garden with upright yellow, pink, or white flowers in May and June. Or the rhizomes can be planted outside three inches deep; blooms are slightly delayed if they aren't started early. Give the calla rich soil, liquid fertilizer every two weeks, and lots of water.

Dig the rhizomes after frost. Let them dry in the shade for a few days, then pack in boxes and cover with vermiculite, sawdust, or sphagnum moss. Keep the packing medium dry: calla lily rhizomes are prone to rot. Store at 45 to 55 degrees Fahrenheit.

Gloriosa lily

True to its name, the gloriosa lily is a glorious climber of exotic red and yellow. The flowers of the *Gloriosa rothschildiana* start in midsummer. Although they're lovely in cut flower arrangements, beware of the pollen: it stains clothing.

At planting time, provide a trellis for this lily. Chicken wire four feet high works well. The lilies cling by tendrils.

Plant the gloriosa lilies in a sunny but sheltered spot, setting the long tubers horizontally and about four inches deep.

Dig tubers in the fall before frost. Take care not to dig into new tubers that doubled to form a "V" during the summer. Store in vermiculite in a cool, dry place.

Canna lily

With bronze or green foliage, and apricot, orange, white, red, pink, or yellow flowers, the canna lily is a winsome candidate for your yard or border.

As you plant newly purchased rhizomes or divide last year's, make certain each has at least two eyes. Lay the rhizomes horizontally in the planting hole, with the growing points just an inch below the surface of the ground. Set dwarf types a foot apart; talls, two feet apart.

Dig canna rhizomes before the fall frost and store them as is; leave at least 14 inches of tops attached, and don't clean or divide. Cure them for a couple of weeks in a warm room, dust with a fungicide, and store with the stem down. Packing material is optional, but roots must be kept dry and at 45 to 50 degrees Fahrenheit.

Spider lily

Also known as ismene, basket flower, or Peruvian daffodil, the spider lily *(Hymenocallis narcissiflora)* is a fast-growing, unusual addition to your flower border.

Spider lily is frost-tender, so wait until mid-spring to plant. Set bulbs with tips three inches below the surface. Space 12 inches apart. Buds sometimes form a week after planting, and fragrant flowers on two-foot stems come within six weeks.

After flowering ends, feed and water so plants can develop bulbs and offsets for next year's blooms.

Dig bulbs before frost, then dry in a warm place for a week. Clean away soil, then store bulbs at 60 degrees Fahrenheit. Spider lily is hardy in the South.

Other Favorite Tender Bulbs

Acidanthera

Pleasing to the nose, as well as the eyes, acidanthera adds fragrance to your garden. This plant sends up creamy flowers with dark centers two months after the corms are planted. Each two-foot stem holds four or more buds that open one flower at a time.

Pick a sunny spot, then plant the corms about two inches deep and five inches apart. In mild climates, leave corms in the ground over the winter. In cold areas, dig in fall and store in vermiculite at 35 to 45 degrees Fahrenheit.

Pineapple lily

With a topknot resembling the Hawaiian favorite, pineapple lily *(Eucomis comosa)* puts out spikes of cream and green flowers less than two months after planting. Spikes reach 18 inches long; foliage, 20 inches.

In areas with freezing weather, dig bulbs before frost and store in sacks of vermiculite in a cool, frost-free spot.

Ranunculus

The perfect double flowers of the *Ranunculus asiaticus* bloom during early summer in many colors. On stems reaching 18 inches high, the flowers nod for nearly four months. They demand plenty of sun and a well-drained but not continually dry location.

The stiff, dry tubers may need to soak in warm water for several hours before being planted. Start them indoors in a greenhouse. Or set them outdoors at a two-inch depth when the danger of frost has passed. Either way, the side with the claws should be placed down.

Dig the ranunculus in the fall after foliage dies back. Store through the winter in peat or perlite at 50 to 55 degrees Fahrenheit.

Montbretias

Montbretias *(Tritonia* sp.) go on a blooming spree from August until frost. Each of the strong, 22-inch stems holds ten to 12 buds that flower successively. Plant at least a dozen of these corms in a group. Select varieties with orange, yellow, or scarlet flowers, or plant some of each; the colors are compatible.

Set corms four inches deep and four inches apart in a sunny place. Work a balanced plant food into the soil at planting time, and keep the plants well watered.

In cold areas, dig the corms in the fall and let them cure in a warm place for two weeks. Store like glads (see page 296) at 35 to 45 degrees Fahrenheit.

Snake palm

Snake palm or devil's-tongue *(Amorphophallus rivieri,* above) features divided leaves. A true palm *(Chamaedorea* sp.) stands at its right. In containers or garden, the snake palm likes rich soil. As October approaches, withhold water gradually. Store at 50 degrees.

Agapanthus

Agapanthus africanus (or lily-of-the-Nile) is popular grown in tubs or mixed with other plants. You'll get a burst of midsummer color in sun or light shade. The flowers reach 20 inches tall.

Plant agapanthuses two inches deep in rich, moist soil. They will need lots of water. Fertilize once a month.

If the ground doesn't freeze in your area, agapanthuses can be left in the ground year round. In cold areas, lift them in fall, and store in a cool, dry place. If they're grown in a tub, withhold water as frost approaches, let them dry out, and store in the tub in a cool, dry place until spring rolls around.

Bulbs in Pots Outdoors

Whether you crave color on your balcony, weary of planning a border to hide aging foliage, or want to fill gaps in your landscape, bulbs in pots solve many outdoor problems. Their needs are few: a spongy material for roots, regular watering, good drainage, and nutrients (see Chapter 14, "Houseplants," on forcing bulbs).

Although bulbs in pots demand little, the joys and uses of container gardening are numerous. Because the containers are portable, you can arrange plantings to suit your needs and blank spots. Best of all, plants in pots tend to be healthier. The good ventilation can keep insect populations down. In addition, weeds are the exception, rather than the rule. Turn the pots occasionally to encourage symmetrical growth.

Strong winds can be a problem. Weight plants with extra sand mixed in the soil, or set them out in heavy-duty containers, so a friendly breeze won't knock them over. Or weight pots with plenty of crushed rock in the bottom (which will also help drainage). Sometimes tying several containers together is all that is needed.

Check the bulbs each day to see if they need moisture. Wind and sunshine mean a constant need for water. The cramped root system simply can't keep up with the moisture rapidly transpiring from the leaves.

Mass for color

A multitude of potted trumpet daffodils gives a pure color impact around this garden fountain. Equally grand on patios, steps, and townhouse courtyards, the daffodil is unsurpassable. It produces large flowers of deep golden yellow. These bulbs can be started indoors, then moved outdoors when the spring weather settles dependably. After the bulbs finish blooming, pots of other plants can take over the job. The bulbs then are moved to a less conspicuous location to yellow in privacy.

Bulbs on display

Line up your colorful calla lilies. A useful bench can be put together over the weekend and enjoyed on the patio, deck, or indoors for years. Use 2x2s for the legs and two 2x6 planks for the top. Cut half holes in each 2x6 with a saber saw to form holes for the pots to fit rim-deep.

After the first frost of fall, store the calla rhizomes as suggested on page 298. Unless winters are mild, store the bench in a garage, basement or tool shed.

chapter 10

ROSES

Nothing can say so much—or leave someone so speechless—as a gift of roses. Whether bought from a florist or homegrown, roses say "I love you" and "I'm sorry"; "Good luck!" and "Congratulations."

For hundreds of years, poets and scholars have been able to describe the rose only in superlatives. Yet these beauties—from the aristocratic hybrid tea to the gentle old garden rose—mingle well with bulb, annual, and perennial flowers. This has long been the case. Ancient historical accounts are filled with references to gardens containing roses. They are said to have bloomed in the Garden of Eden, ancient Persia, and the Hanging Gardens of Babylon. Christians chose roses to represent the Trinity, and the white rose for the Virgin Mary.

Roses have symbolized both peace and war. Soldiers throughout history have fought under banners adorned with the rose. England's War of the Roses started in 1455 as the result of a feud between the House of Lancaster (symbolized by a red rose, *Rosa gallica*) and the House of York (with its white rose, *R. alba*). A red and white rose memorialized the settlement.

The budwood of the hybrid Peace rose came to the U.S. from France on the last plane before the fall of France in 1940. Bouquets of this rose were presented to delegates at the first United Nations conference in San Francisco—the day a truce was signed in Europe.

The simple repetition of petaled shapes has for centuries lent its form to fashion, interior design, and architecture. The most popular bloom adorning silver, china, and wallpaper is the rose pattern. Four states, the District of Columbia, and England have all chosen this beauty as their official flower.

Roses demand somewhat more attention than do many other flowers, trees, shrubs, and vines. They're for the person who loves gardening (whether on a large or small basis), but they repay the affection with elegance.

Planting Roses

Dreams of rose-filled summers start as soon as plant catalogues appear. Soon after, garden centers stock bare-root and container-grown bushes.

Whether you order your rose bushes from a catalogue or select them from a garden center is up to you. With the catalogue, you're more assured of getting the variety you want. With the garden center, you can procrastinate a bit into the season, but the selection might be less because the owner may not have your taste in roses.

If you pick out the bushes yourself, note where they are displayed. A shaded spot outside or a cool room are safest; roots may be dangerously dry if the plants are in full sun.

Ordering by mail is not without risk, though. The rose bushes may arrive before you are ready to plant. For a few days' wait, put them in a moderately cold place, and keep roots moist by wetting and then wrapping them in damp newspaper or plastic. If several days will pass, bury the entire plant (canes and roots) in a trench in a cool, shaded spot.

Think carefully about where to put your rose bushes. Their final home should receive at least six hours of full sun a day, preferably in the morning. They'll do best where they'll get light shade in the afternoon. When possible, don't plant them where their roots will compete with roots from trees and shrubs.

Roses need a well-drained spot, so if soil is heavy or clayey, add perlite, vermiculite, or coarse sand. Terracing or raised beds help, too.

Bare-root roses can be planted in late winter in warm areas. If temperatures don't fall below zero degrees Fahrenheit, planting may be done in early spring or late fall. Where the temperature drops lower, plant only in spring.

Roses appreciate a slightly acid soil—6.0 to 6.5. A soil test will tell if sulfur is needed to make it more acidic or if lime is needed to lower the acidity. Mix superphosphate into the soil for healthy root growth.

In most climates, two feet between hybrid teas, grandifloras, or floribundas will be just right. Shrub and old garden roses are best spaced four to six feet apart, depending on their size.

Planting a container-grown rose is not too different from the bareroot method (see illustrations below). Dig the planting hole slightly larger than the container.

If the container is asphalt, cut it along the seam with shears or knife. If it's metal, ask the nursery staff to slice the sides for you. Slide the bush out of the container gently and into the hole.

Loosen the name tag so the wire doesn't cut into the bush. Keep a record of all varieties you plant.

Before planting, remove wrapping, trim root tips, and soak bare-root roses in a bucket of water or mud for six to 24 hours. Make the planting hole at least 18 inches deep and wide.

Rose roots do not require severe pruning before planting. However, all broken or damaged roots should be cut back to healthy tissue. Use hand pruners to make clean cuts.

Make a mound in the hole and firm it. Spread roots around the mound. For a container-grown plant, cut away the container and set so the bud union is slightly above ground level.

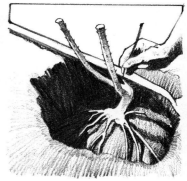

Use a yardstick, broom handle, or shovel handle as a guide for planting depth. In warm areas, the bud union can be about an inch above ground; in cold, it will need to be protected.

Steady the bush at the proper level. Add soil beneath the plant, if needed to bring it higher. Fill the hole about two-thirds full, and firm by using your hands or by stepping on it lightly.

Fill the hole around the plant with water, and allow all of it to soak in. Jiggle stem slightly to get rid of any air pockets. Fill the hole to the top with soil mixed with organic matter.

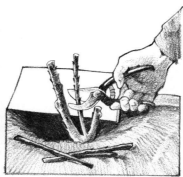

Prune canes back by about a third. Remove all thin, weak, or dead ones. Make cuts slightly above strong outside buds. The result usually is a stronger bush and larger blooms.

Shovel loose soil over the plants about two-thirds of the way up. Leave it in place until new growth is one or two inches long, then wash mound away. Add a mulch.

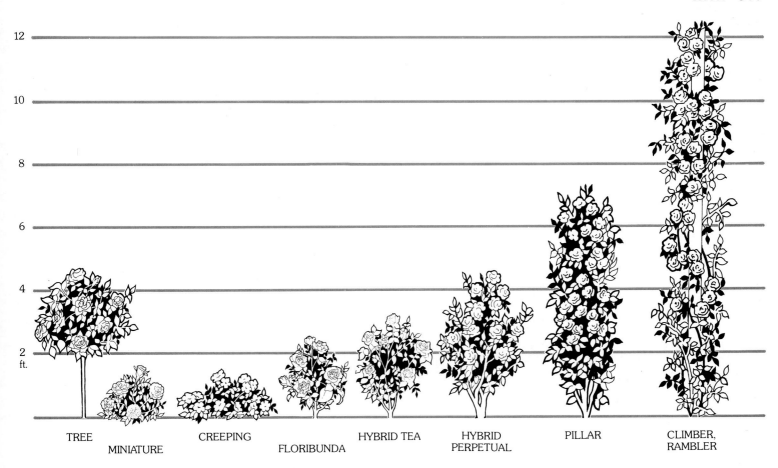

12

10

8

6

4

2
ft.

TREE

MINIATURE

CREEPING

FLORIBUNDA

HYBRID TEA

HYBRID
PERPETUAL

PILLAR

CLIMBER,
RAMBLER

Rose types

From the miniatures that can grow daintily in teacups to the climbers gorgeously framing the entire arbor you stroll through, rose plants range from a tiny three inches to more than 20 feet at maturity.

Shrub roses vary from ground covers to hedges and screens. They're hardy to a variety of growing conditions and tolerant of neglect. You'll find them among both old garden and modern kinds of roses. Among the most notable of the shrub-like roses is the eglanteria. It has a large, dense, thorny habit of growth and will grow eight to 12 feet high. Shrub roses have yellow, copper, pink, or red single or semidouble flowers that appear in the spring.

The hybrid moyesi and hybrid rugosa are large (reaching six feet in height), hardy, disease-resistant shrub roses. The musks will grow in

less sun than other roses, with blooms all season in large clusters. They, too, are tall and disease resistant.

Climbing roses reach skyward with only a little help from you. Tie them to supports, and their pliable canes will stretch far overhead or for distances along a fence. Some are sports (or mutations) of hybrid teas, grandifloras, floribundas, and polyanthas. The smaller, stiffer ones are called pillar roses, and huge rampant growers, with small flowers, are called ramblers.

The casual, flowing lines of the climbing roses have more formal counterparts, the tree roses. Often called "standards," tree roses result from grafting of a strong sturdy stem onto a vigorous rootstock. Onto the stem is budded a hybrid tea, floribunda, grandiflora, miniature, or even a climber. Many have trunks three feet tall. They are perfect to accent a flower bed, en-

trance, or patio. The trunk must be supported by a stake and, because the bark is sensitive to sunlight, wrapped in burlap while young. Tree roses must be heavily protected during the winter in all but the mildest climates.

Miniatures match the elegance of tree roses but on a tiny scale. You will be so smitten by the delicate leaves, buds, and plant, you may become a collector. Their names reveal the fondness of those who developed them: Baby Darling, Cuddles, Baby Betsy McCall, Littlest Angel, Scarlet Gem, and Pixie Rose are a few. Miniature roses vary from three to 18 inches and work well as edgings, in pots, and for rock gardens.

Large and small roses come in an almost bewildering array of colors—pure and blended; flower forms—singles, doubles, and more; plant forms—tiny to large; and hardiness.

Portable beauty— roses in containers

Roses in containers can brighten any spot. Shorter hybrid teas, floribundas, polyanthas, and miniatures look better as movable roses than do tall hybrid teas or grandifloras. Their flowers occur in clusters, making them look like longlasting bouquets. Tree roses—full size or miniature—are also perfect.

Containers must be at least 18 inches across and deep. When filled with soil, all will be heavy, so mount them on casters.

They'll need at least six hours of sun each day. They may also need moisture each day; water before they get bone-dry. Use either a packaged soilless potting mix or your own mix of equal parts garden loam, sand, and peat moss or vermiculite. Before winter, move the planters indoors or to an unheated porch, garage, or basement.

Care of Roses

Shakespeare may be right: A rose by any other name still smells as sweet. But a rose not cared for properly may not be healthy enough to have much scent at all. Rose plants can survive with minimal care—only water is absolutely necessary—but to obtain the bloom that inspires poets, treat your roses to mulching, pruning, fertilizer, and winter protection.

Select a healthy rose bush, plant it correctly, and you're well on your way to a sweet-smelling summer. To get all the way to lustrous leaves and perfect flowers, pamper your plants a little.

Watering roses in the home garden can be accomplished several ways: soaker hoses, overhead sprinklers, garden hose, or watering can. The method you choose depends largely on the number of plants you have, the time you want to spend, and the money you're willing to invest. Soaker hoses conserve water because water trickles from tiny holes punctured along its length. Early in the spring, lay the hose next to a row of bushes where you want it to stay all season. Place a mulch over the soaker hose, and turn the water on to a slow trickle whenever moisture is needed.

Overhead sprinklers keep foliage clean and wash off various insects. However, much moisture is lost to evaporation. This type of watering is best done in the morning, because wet leaves are prone to disease if they don't dry off quickly.

Single rose bushes can be watered by hand, using hose, wand, or watering can. Plants need to be watered deeply, so any of these processes will take time.

Check the soil around bushes at least once a week. Sandy soils will drain quickly and need moisture more often than do clayey soils. The equivalent of one inch of rain should be supplied to the roses each week. Mulched gardens will need less water than unmulched ones. Whenever you water, water deeply; light sprinklings do more harm than good.

Fertilizer applied three times a year helps ensure sturdy plants and maximum bloom. A balanced fertilizer, such as 5-10-5 or a prepared rose food, will provide the nitrogen (for growth and green leaves), phosphorus (for root growth and handsome flowers), and potash (for overall plant vigor). Feed right after pruning in early spring, while the plants are in bud, and about two months before the first frost date in your area. Or simply fertilize once a month during the growing and blooming seasons.

Read directions on the label each time you apply fertilizer. Gently work it into the top of the soil, and water well. Newly planted bushes should not be fed until they bloom. Slow-release fertilizers may be used for the second feeding and provide nutrients only while the soil is warm, thus eliminating the need for further feeding that season. Remember to push any mulch aside, scratch fertilizer into the soil, and replace mulch.

Soluble or liquid fertilizers are a boon if you have a lot of bushes. Mix the food with fungicide or insecticide sprays, and apply them with a proportioning sprayer. For a few bushes, use the watering can. Don't apply liquid fertilizer to rose leaves when temperatures are over 90 degrees Fahrenheit.

Mulch is a versatile, valuable garden aid. It can be a layer of nearly any material spread on top of the soil to keep it cool, conserve moisture, eliminate weeding, and, in some cases, enrich the soil as it decomposes. Mulches available locally are generally least expensive: wood chips, chopped oak leaves, pine needles, sawdust, or cocoa bean shells. Grass clippings often mat down. Straw or hay work well but may contain weed seeds. Apply extra nitrogen to mulched plants.

Trimming roses at the right moment means bigger blooms and vigorous plants. In addition to pruning in early spring (see pages 310 and 311), use pruners for removing suckers (those canes emerging from the roots). Suckers sap the energy of the main bush on plants with a bud union. Others—miniature, old garden, and shrub roses—are grown on their own roots, so they're revitalized by the new sucker growth.

For larger bloom, remove all but a single bud on a stem. You may find a cluster of tiny buds near the tip of the stem or buds down the stem. Gently remove them with a pinch of your fingernails. For a full floribunda spray, remove the central bud as soon as it appears. Do this early in the blooming period or the stem will have a big scar.

After first blooms fade, remove them quickly on most rose plants. Cut the stem down to the first leaf with five leaflets. Many kinds of roses will bloom again. Shrub, old garden, and climbing roses bloom only once, so they don't have to be "deadheaded" (have spent flowers removed). To keep climbers in bloom longer, prune them as soon as their first flush of flowers is finished. Cut the lateral canes back, leaving two five-leaflet leaves on each. A new stem, topped with a bloom, will grow from each leaf axil.

Attractive hips of red or orange will remain on shrubs and climbers when petals fall; the hips are a tasty treat for birds. Prune branches back after the roses go dormant in the fall.

During the first mild weather of late winter, remove loose mulch to allow frozen ground to thaw and dry. Take away the protective soil mounds when leaf buds start to make their first growth. Take special care not to damage any tender, new sprouts.

Cut deadwood back to living, green stems. In the North, you may have to prune to ground level in some years. If there is live tissue above the bud union, plants will send up new shoots. Check for egg cases of insects that may have overwintered in your bushes.

Start a feeding program with your everblooming roses from the time of new growth. One-time bloomers need only one feeding—in early spring or late fall. Apply food at the drip line of bushes. Apply a dormant spray of lime sulfur for insect and disease control.

Regular, once-a-week watering is a must for optimum growth and bloom. Before feeding with either a dry or a liquid food, soak soil well. Water again afterward if you use a granular rose food. Roses will need extra water during hot weather.

Spread a two-inch mulch between bushes in early spring to prevent drying of soil. Do not let mulch come into contact with the canes. Mulch will keep the soil cooler in summer and keep soil from splattering on leaves during rainstorms.

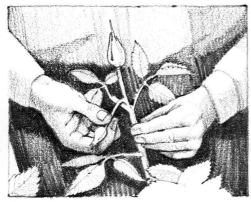

To ensure largest blooms on hybrid teas, break off all side buds on stems while they are small. (If you wait, there'll be a big black scar on the stem.) Use a pinching, twisting motion to remove buds. The result of disbudding is a bloom perfect for a vase.

Whether cutting flowers to use indoors or to remove spent blossoms, make cut above first strong, five-leaflet leaf. At least two good leaves should be left on remaining stem to maintain vigor. Don't overdo the trimming, or the rose is weakened.

In the coldest parts of the country, plastic-foam cones can be used to protect bushes. Wait until the ground is frozen to put the cone on—usually late November or early December. Most roses will have to be pruned severely to fit under the cover.

Winter care

Roses may be nationwide favorites, but caring for them during the winter is strictly a local affair. In areas with cold weather (where temperatures drop below 20 degrees Fahrenheit), bundle up those bushes for survival.

An occasional dip below 20 degrees won't harm the roses, but the mix of cold temperatures, drying winds, and fluctuations in temperature can cause dieback. Much of the damage can be pruned away in the spring with nary a scar.

Rose catalogues will list which plants are tender. As a rule of thumb, consider most of the yellow, pastel pink, and white roses fragile enough to warrant protection.

Classes of roses vary in their hardiness, though. Hybrid teas, grandifloras, and floribundas will need pampering in frosty zones. For years, the most satisfactory protection has been a mound of soil over the canes. Bring soil in from another part of the garden rather than scraping the ground around the rose bushes; the feeder roots in the top part of the soil won't tolerate exposure. Make the mound about 20 inches high.

Or make a cylinder of wire mesh around each bush, and gently stuff them with leaves. Don't use leaves that mat down, however. Oak leaves are perfect; maple leaves must be avoided. Some roses, particularly the miniatures, make the process even easier; these are tough plants and need little protection. Simply rake the leaves into a pile over the bushes. Shrub, old-fashioned, and polyantha roses tolerate frigid temperatures, too. A deep layer of snow keeps roses snug and safe all winter.

Reserve use of plastic-foam cones for the coldest parts of the country (Zone 5 and north) and for the most tender roses. A bright, sunny day in January can turn the plastic-foam protection into a hothouse and induce tender growth that may die when the temperatures drop again.

Old garden rose climbers are among the sturdiest roses, but the more modern climbing varieties need special care where temperatures hover around zero. It's easiest to lower canes to the ground and cover them with leaves or soil.

Part of the charm of container-grown tree roses is their versatility, but they need care to get through winter months. Stop fertilizing tree roses about two months before expected dormancy. In most parts of the country and for most varieties, dormancy sets in around October.

Soil temperature is the critical element for potted roses. The plant must be stored where the soil temperature will consistently stay below 40 degrees Fahrenheit but above 25 degrees. Air temperature might fluctuate, but soil temperature must be kept above the magic 25 degrees. In some parts of the country, the temperature requirements might be met simply by moving the plant to a shady spot. In the North, the container and plant will have to be moved to an unheated garage or shed. In unattached, unheated buildings, protect the roots with a little mulch. Surround the rootball with a 12-inch layer of straw, with the top encircled by the chicken-wire cylinder and stuffed with leaves. In states as far north as Minnesota, potted tree roses should be moved to a storm cellar or laid in a trench (where water won't accumulate) lined with straw and covered with 12 inches of more straw and at least six inches of soil.

Remove the winter protection before new growth starts in the spring. Young shoots are tender and can't withstand rough treatment. Wash the soil mound away from the top of the plant with a gentle spray from the garden hose, and scrape the rest with a trowel. A mulch can be added immediately.

Pruning

The idea of removing parts of a plant—some of them perfectly healthy—to make the rest grow stronger, bigger, and thicker may be hard to accept. When the plant is as regal as a rose, beginning gardeners may be especially nervous to make the cuts.

Although good-looking, your new rose plant likely won't be a showpiece the first season after planting. Still, it will need to be pruned lightly—particularly to remove weak, dead, or diseased wood.

When to start. Immediately begin shaping the youngster to the form you want it to take in years to come, and trim off vigorously growing new branches that reach too far beyond the space you've allocated for the plant. As the rose becomes established, old canes may be removed when new ones grow to replace them.

When to prune. Another beguiling early spring beauty, the forsythia shrub, will tell you when to prune roses. The time this yellow bloomer is at its peak is the time to tend to the roses. In most places, this will coincide with the appearance of buds on the rose bush. Don't wait until the buds have burst into bright green leaves, because then the sap is flowing actively. Somewhere between midwinter (in the South) and mid-spring (in the North) is the proper time.

Although your pruning day may be a warm and sunny one, pull on a pair of heavy gloves and a shirt with long sleeves. Even the youngest or smallest roses can surprise you with a nasty scratch from plentiful thorns. Resist wearing favorite clothing, too; old woody thorns can produce a snag in almost anything —fabrics such as nylon are particularly susceptible.

What to use. Most of the tools you use for trimming shrubs and other light pruning can do double-duty by keeping rose bushes shapely. Curved-edged pruning shears will likely see the most action in your rose garden. Curved-edged ones are better for these plants than the straight-edged, anvil type. Anvil-type shears tend to crush the tender stems instead of making a flat, smooth cut. But they come in handy (although not a necessity) in removing deadwood.

Loppers, the long-handled lopping shears, are good for heavy-duty work on older garden, shrub, and climbing roses' thick branches. A pruning saw is a tool many veterans wouldn't be without; it's great for cutting out thick canes— particularly those too thick or at the wrong angle to handle with loppers.

Pruning shears will likely be the first to lose their sharp cutting edge because you'll use them most. When that happens, have them sharpened or get a new blade. Mashed, torn twigs resulting from dull blades and a frustrated gardener heal slowly and are an invitation to insects and diseases. The mangled twigs die back to healthy wood, leaving unsightly stubs sticking out. Clean, oil, and store shears after your annual pruning. After this, you'll likely need them only to cut blooms for the house and trim away faded roses.

Are borers a problem in your area? If you're not sure, call a local garden center or the extension office. To restrict the spread of borers, apply a grafting wax, pruning compound, or orange shellac to cuts over a half inch in diameter. All the substances are available at most garden centers. You may see white glue recommended as a sealant, too; this works fine until the first rain, then washes away.

Tips for rose types. Hybrid teas, floribundas, and grandifloras do well when a third to a half of the bush height and width is removed each year (see bottom of page for additional pruning hints). Or trim grandifloras to a height of 18 to 24 inches, and hybrid teas and floribundas to 12 to 18 inches tall. Keep function in mind, too: for example, floribundas used as a hedge should keep more height and canes than those used as accent plants. Most large varieties can be pruned each year to keep them suited to a less-than-ample space.

The first step to pruning is probably overcoming your resistance to cut into what seems to be a healthy bush. Remove the wire cage and leaf protection or the plastic-foam cone. Prune all dead canes flush with the bump (or bud union) near the ground. Also trim weak, broken, crossing, or diseased canes to where the pith is white and healthy. Take care not to tear the bark.

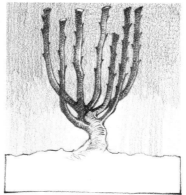

Air circulation and maximum strength are the goals of additional pruning. Cut out branches that are smaller in diameter than your little finger, along with those growing into the center of the bush. Also remove any larger canes growing from the center of the bush; this will let sunshine in and air through the center of the plant. Good circulation helps reduce diseases.

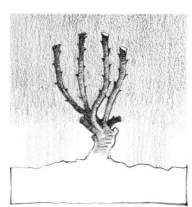

Don't stop yet. Although you may have a pile of cuttings beside you and only healthy canes left, cut out all but three or four of the strongest, spread evenly around the bush. Trim all others down to the bud union. Leave no stubs high on the remaining canes or any stubs near the bud union. They're tempting to insects and diseases. Apply a sealing compound.

Although pruning stimulates growth, severe pruning to within six inches of the ground won't produce larger blooms; disbudding (see page 309) will. However, if black spot disease was a problem last year, cut lower on the canes than usual to get more spores that may have overwintered. Bag cuttings for garbage pickup or burn them.

Weather. Old Man Winter and Mother Nature may not give you total control over pruning heights. In climates where winters are severe, part of the rose plant—even those well protected—will suffer winterkill to part or all of the plant above ground. Even if the root system survives to produce gorgeous blooms year after year, the dead portions will need to be removed for the plant's appearance and to stimulate fresh growth.

Hybrid perpetual, shrub, and old garden roses should have only the oldest canes removed each year. Snip out weak or dead wood, and trim them to keep the shape you want; otherwise, they're fine without further assistance. Prune hybrid perpetuals to no less than 18 inches.

Polyanthas, like shrub roses, should be left as full and natural as space permits. In your early spring pruning, cut out the oldest canes on

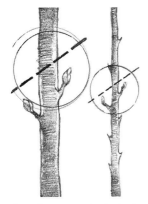

Trim branches a quarter inch above a bud, but not closer, or the bud may not survive. Don't leave too much cane above, either, or the cane will die back. Prune to outward facing buds, when possible, so leaves will tend to grow toward the outside of the bush and leave the center of the bush open and the plant shapely. Slant cuts so water will run off easily and not invite disease.

the bush, and prune to about half their former height. These beauties are sturdy, too, so you'll seldom find much winter damage.

Specialized pruning. Miniature and tree rose hobbyists are prepared for more primping and more decisions. Because tree roses are often viewed up close, they must be kept symmetrical. Prune canes to 12 inches and leave them evenly spaced around the plant.

Miniatures are pruned according to where you put them. Tiny, container-grown accents are trimmed as low as three inches. Low hedges or edging are pruned to about eight inches. Miniatures benefit from an annual once-over, so remove weak, diseased, dead, or crossing canes. Also, remove canes to open the center of the plant to the sun and circulation. Leave up to six new canes on miniatures.

Health tips. Pruning can benefit the strength and health of your roses, so take one extra precaution to avoid spreading disease as you work: after each cut, even on the same plant, dip the pruning shears in a solution of equal parts of household bleach and water. Mix another bucket of the solution two weeks later to carry with you as you stroll by your roses again with shears in hand. A late spring frost may have caused additional dieback, or what once looked like a healthy cane may prove to be sickly as leaves start to unfurl. Just snip it off to a good bud.

Roses seldom die for want of a pruning, but they may get tall and rangy with few flowers. Pruning is needed to control the size and shape of a plant and keep it healthy, vigorous, and blooming. Make sure shears are sharp.

Climbing roses are pruned both early in the spring and after they bloom. Most of them produce flowers on last year's wood or canes, so they don't need to be pruned as severely as hybrid teas, floribundas, or grandifloras. Trim dead branches or broken ones along with overcrowded ones. Pruning more than this in early spring, only results in cutting away the flower buds. However, this is a good time of year to groom the area beneath the plant, applying a mulch to keep weeds down or raking debris away so spring bulbs can grow.

As bloom time ends, bring the shears out again and remove one or two of the oldest canes. Replacement branches need the space to develop properly. Thin dense growth and smaller twigs growing from the major cane. Trim any canes that reach beyond their designated space.

A rose plant grows where it is cut, so prune it back somewhat farther than what you want its final size to be. To get best bloom, train canes horizontally along a fence, and fasten them several places with plant ties, twine, or rags.

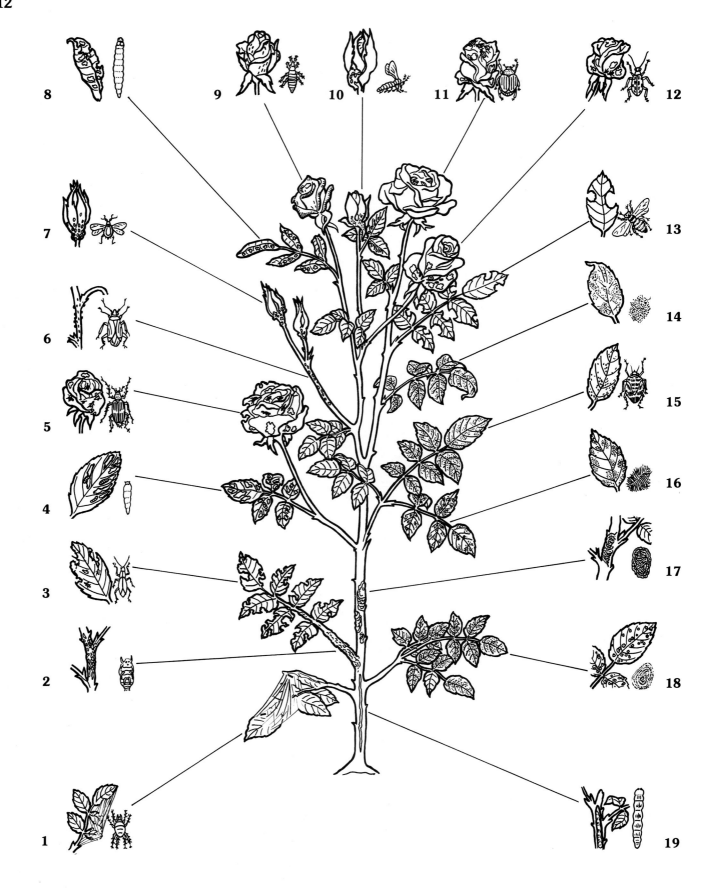

Protect Against Insects, Disease

Strolls among your roses do more than lift your spirits; you'll catch tiny invaders before they do much harm. Healthy plants, a spraying or dusting program, and regular inspections for new problems keep insects and disease in bounds.

1. Red spider mites. Although technically not insects, these tiny pests can work havoc on your roses. They consume plant juices, causing leaves to turn bronze or dull red, wither, and fall. Plants may be stunted. Webs may appear around leaves and twigs. To prevent them, gather and burn dead leaves; mites overwinter in debris to reinfest plants in summer.

If you catch them early, they can often be washed off with water hosed or misted on. They tend to increase rapidly during hot weather, so you may have to resort to a rose miticide applied every three days to kill new mites until the infestation is over.

2. Rose scale. Shady, humid locations are favorite spots for these gray or white scalelike insects. The scales encrust the stems, sucking sap from branches, so plants eventually wilt and die. Cut off infested parts and burn them. The eggs can live through the winter, so make a thorough check in the spring. Apply a dormant lime sulfur spray in early spring. Use a rose insecticide, labeled for use with rose scale, particularly in late spring when the crawlers are hatching.

3. Fuller rose beetle. These crawling, gray-brown beetles are about a quarter inch long but do most of their damage in the larval stage. The beetles leave a black excrement on the leaves. Check your local garden center for an insecticide labeled for use against them.

4. Roseslug. These small, soft, yellow-green, caterpillar-like pests can quickly skeletonize foliage—leaving only a frame of veins. They can also bore into new shoots and the pith of pruned canes, so be sure to seal newly cut ends of canes.

5. Rose chafer. With a preference for light-colored flowers, the rose chafer feeds on buds, open flowers, and leaves in early summer. It's a quarter to a half inch long, iridescent gray-brown, and spiny legged. If the infestation is light, handpick the insects. If numbers appear to be growing, apply an insecticide labeled for use against them.

6. Tarnished plant bug. Their name is descriptive: these insects are a brassy, green to brown, mottled color. They can distort flowers and wilt stem tips. The insect lays eggs along the stem and punctures the plant tissues. It can also carry diseases.

7. Aphids. These greenish-yellow, black, red, green, or brown aphids (also called plant lice) suck juices from tender shoots and buds. They cluster on bud stems and secrete a sticky, disease-prone substance called honeydew. Aphids are easy to control with soapy water.

8. Leafrollers. These are lively, greenish caterpillars that roll themselves up in the foliage and eat through it from the inside out in spring. Or they tie together several leaves and destroy the bud; this "prunes" the cane tip. Handpick the leaves or crush them to kill hidden caterpillars. Or use an insecticide labeled for use against them.

9. Thrips. Only about a sixteenth of an inch long, these tiny insects can do damage beyond what their size might suggest. Because of them, buds fail to open or they produce distorted, discolored, and brown flowers. Thrips favor white and pastel roses, but will bother others, too. Remove infested buds. Check insecticide label to make sure it will control thrips.

10. Rose midge. You may only barely see this minute maggot that attacks buds and young shoots and causes them to suddenly turn black. Cut affected portions off and use a commercial insecticide.

11. Japanese beetles. They are shiny copper and green and develop from white grubs that feed on grass roots. They cluster in groups, destroying flowers and skeletonizing leaves. The Japanese beetle seems to prefer roses of lighter colors and increase in midsummer. Handpick them or spray with an insecticide labeled for use against them. The grubs can be controlled with a soil insecticide.

12. Spotted cucumber beetle. With a yen not only for vegetable garden crops, but also for your flowers, this versatile beetle feeds on rose blooms. It's yellow-green, a quarter to a half inch long, and has black spots on its back. The cucumber beetle also carries bacterial diseases. Read insecticide label to make sure the one you select controls spotted cucumber beetles.

13. Leaf-cutting bee. The bees disfigure foliage with their neat circles "cut" from the margins, and their larvae bore into ends of the pruned stems. To control, wax stem ends after you prune. Cut off stunted stem tips. Use a commercial insecticide.

14. Mildew. This fungus disease occurs most often when days are warm, nights cool, and air circulation poor. It appears as grayish-white patches on leaves, flower buds, and young shoots. The leaves will curl and become distorted in severe cases. Most climbers and ramblers are susceptible. Plant resistant varieties. Use a commercial fungicide.

15. Harlequin bugs. Rose growers in the South—from California to Virginia—may be plagued by this brightly colored pest. Leaves get calico markings and branches turn brown. Bugs and egg masses can be removed by hand. For larger infestations, use an insecticide listing harlequin bugs on the label.

16. Black spot. Black spots with fringed margins show first on leaves in early summer. Leaves turn yellow and drop early. Plants can become defoliated, weakened, and more susceptible to winter injury.

Blooming is reduced. The disease is spread by splashing water; to assist in control, run sprinklers only in the morning so water dries off quickly. When rain is forecast, apply spray or dust labeled for control of black spot. In selecting new plants, choose resistant varieties. Keep roses healthy to help them fight the disease. Pick off spotted leaves.

17. Rose canker. This fungus disease usually enters through wounds and causes canes to turn brown, purple, or white. No growth starts above them. Often the wood dies back from pruning cuts. Prune to below the canker in early spring, and apply a spray of dormant oil.

18. Rust. The orange spots are a problem along the Pacific coast because of the wet, mild weather. Hybrid teas and climbing roses are susceptible. Use a commercial spray.

19. Cane borer. Tunneling into canes and under bark, cane borers kill shoots by hollowing out the pith. Wilting of the top of the plant indicates the borer's presence. Cut off infested shoots and kill borers. Seal canes after pruning. Use an insecticide labeled for use against cane borers.

When you've handpicked insects and judiciously pruned diseased portions of your favorite rose bushes, and the pests are still getting ahead of you, you may decide to take action with a chemical product. If you have only a few plants, a hand sprayer, similar to the kind used for misting indoor plants, does a good, uniform job with insecticides. For more bushes, try a proportioning sprayer that attaches to the end of a garden hose.

Generally, you need not apply insecticides until you notice the insects. For diseases, the approach is a preventive one. Spray or dust every ten days or so, even if you don't see any problems. By the time you notice a disease on your plant, it may be too late to control it. Rather than spray twice, combine insecticides and fungicides (if you need both) in the same spray, or buy one of the combination sprays at a garden center.

Systemic pesticides are absorbed into the plant through the soil and need to be applied less often.

Plant the shimmering pink floribunda, Fabergé, beside steps. It has a compact oval shape, few thorns, and flowers on top.

Uses of Roses

Uses of roses range as wide as the flowers' colors, shapes, and varieties. You'll find both showplace and hidden corners around your home enhanced by the rose—any spot with at least six hours of sun a day and within reach of the garden hose.

What is it that makes a rose so breathtaking and alluring? The splash of pure color, the fragrance, the glossy foliage, the history or legend associated with it, the memory of other rose gardens? It's probably some of each, and you can make even the smallest area spectacular with the right rose.

Use roses to emphasize or camouflage; their arrangement is limited only by your imagination. Formal beds blend best with period architecture; informal beds help soften the sometimes harsh lines of modern architecture. Allow the beds to follow the lines of the house—curving, if needed, to break rigidity.

Three rows of roses will give a full look to the bed yet are not too deep to tend easily. If space isn't generous enough to permit this, an accent or border is still lovely. To keep the colors from appearing spotty, plant varieties in pairs or trios.

If possible, keep them away from the foundation of the house because the soil there is often dry. Eaves and overhangs prevent rainwater from hitting them, so plan to supplement natural moisture.

Interspersed with other plants is one effective way to use roses if you don't have the space or interest for a formal rose garden. Shrub roses form the perfect backdrop for lower-growing plants in the border near your home. Try them and floribundas, instead of other more commonly used flowering material, for a long colorful season.

For long-lasting colors in even the narrowest areas, mix roses with annuals and perennials of various heights.

Include roses in the perennial border to extend the bloom time. Low-growing floribundas or miniature roses are sensational finishing touches as edgings to perennial shrub borders. Or mingle roses with bright annuals; by changing the annuals each year, you get the effect of a whole new scene.

Many of the bulbs make good companions for roses. Lilies, for example, like the same growing conditions and, with proper selection, will bloom all summer in many complementary colors. Gladiolus, dahlia, canna lily, freesia, and other tender bulbs provide a variety of bloom colors and foliage textures, along with filling in bare spots.

Tall growers for the back of the border, such as delphinium, hollyhock, or cosmos, will stand out even more with roses of contrasting colors set in front of them. Miniature roses or ground-hugging annuals can blanket the area between and in front of the roses. If slopes or large areas around your home are carpeted with evergreen ground covers, mix roses with them to break up the single color and add a change in textures.

Along steps to the house or from one level of the garden to another, rose bushes will call attention to the change in height better than a sign saying, "Watch your step." If the ground is level around the steps, plant taller roses at the rear and shorter ones at the front. If the ground slopes with the steps, choose roses of the same height to create a wave of color.

Fences and roses combine delightfully. The fence provides support for tall roses, while roses will make a useful fence lovely. Brighten a dark retaining wall by planting climbers or ramblers atop and letting them hang over. Train them down, and keep them in place by pegging the canes to the wall. For summer-long color, choose one of the everblooming varieties.

Belinda, a musk rose, flowers repeatedly, almost hiding the fence.

Medallion and Sonoma (pink) encourage strolling along the walk.

More uses for roses

High, wide, handsome, and colorful—roses can grow in any direction you need them.

Flanking an entry, while adding emphasis to the vertical lines, climbers can cover eaves and outline windows or doors. At the same time, they add color to the outside of the home and soften hard corners. Such tall beauties need annuals, perennials, or shrubs planted beneath. Or switch and add rose bushes at the foot of vines, such as clematis. Low-growing roses are also a good choice in front of other climbers, such as thunbergia or morning-glory.

Along a walk, roses can be planted straight for a formal, sophisticated look, or curved for a relaxed, informal one. Set the bushes far enough back from the edge of the beds so they do not entangle passersby; two feet is a good rule of thumb for most roses. Use one variety, or choose two whose colors complement each other. In a border, where shrubs are planted at least two deep, the plants may be of the same height. Or place a low-grower along the walk, backed up by one that grows taller.

Pocket gardens prove you don't need a lot of room to create beauty. Around a light post, at an often-passed corner, or any other place with a few square feet of soil is a place for a rose and contrasting annuals. But plan the area as carefully as you would a large border. Fill in around plants with mulch to make your garden weed-free.

Bewitched, a hybrid tea, teams with yellow marigolds to prove pocket gardens can be delightful.

A yellow climbing rose, Golden Showers, and evergreen shrubs invitingly frame the entryway. Or try tree roses for a more formal look.

Line a driveway with Sunsprite, a floribunda.

A rose arbor is the perfect solution to a sun-filled garden—breezy and romantic.

Hedge rose Red Glory is a friendly privacy screen, as beautiful on one side as on the other.

The versatile rose

In pots, in a narrow strip along a driveway, as a pretty privacy screen, on an arbor, and more—roses have innumerable uses.

Containers allow roses to be portable. Choose varieties that grow compactly and containers with drainage holes.

A narrow strip of land between driveway and fence is often perfect for roses. Espalier climbers along the fence, or plant tall tree roses in pots. Lower-growing roses can be placed in front and the bed edged with miniatures or annuals. The spot where the driveway swings into the street is ideal for white or other light-colored roses to make the area more visible.

Privacy screens can be lovely on both sides when you choose a thick hedge rose. Roses for screens should be planted closer together than normal to ensure dense, heavily flowered growth.

Rose arbors add a bit of shade to a sunny garden—both by the climbers and the lath shelter. Cautious gardeners cover the lathing with hardware cloth to protect the blooms from wind, rain, or hail.

Grow roses in containers and you can have color wherever you want it. Floribunda Accent shines around a garden sundial.

Austrian Copper, a five-foot species shrub, is hardy to 20 degrees below zero (Fahrenheit) and has opened the rose season for almost 400 years.

Old Garden Roses

Hardy, low maintenance, long-lived—old garden roses are useful flowering veterans. They also have kept the unique qualities that made them popular in our grandparents' garden and long before.

The term "old garden rose" includes any roses whose class predated the introduction of hybrid teas in 1867. To the home gardener, the term means the best of the gracious and the practical. Singles and doubles alike generally demand less pampering than their more modern relatives. Their colors range from the subdued, matronly violets to the near-risque oranges. Classes and favorite varieties differ in their virtues.

Albas, with clusters of medium-sized, fragrant, pink or white flowers, are tall, dense, and disease resistant. They bloom only once a year but are worth the wait. Alba variety Königin von Dänemark, flesh pink with darker center, has peachy color bud. Maiden's Blush is a pale pink variety, fading to white.

Bourbons, unlike albas, reward you with blooms throughout the season. Plants are moderately hardy, vigorous, and have fragrant double flowers. Try rich pink bourbon variety La Reine Victoria; the color deepens with age. Souvenir de la Malmaison is flesh pink with rosy center, and the white Variegata di Bologna is striped with purplish-red.

Centifolia sounds much more glamorous than its common name (cabbage rose) but—with overlapped petals—the English name is descriptive. It may also be found listed as Provence rose. Some in this class, such as Crested Moss, are hardy to 20 degrees below zero

The hardy Eglantine has long, arching canes, lavish with single pink flowers.

Rosa soulieana, a species rose, serves beautifully as ground cover or climber.

Fahrenheit and bloom once a year—usually in June. The 100-petaled blooms are found in deep pink through white; branches are arching and slender; leaves are wrinkled. The centifolia Rose de Meaux is red or white; Petite de Hollande is rose-pink.

Chinas are not so hardy as other old garden roses, doing best in areas with mild winters. Foliage is almost evergreen and blooms appear intermittently throughout the season. Flowers tend to be small and of pink and red hues. Top pink varieties are Hermosa and Old Blush. The Green Rose is a highly unusual china variety and is, indeed, green.

Damask roses have long been famed for their fragrance. But, except for the autumn damasks, they bloom only once. Flowers are medium to large on drooping or arching branches. The plants are extremely hardy and disease resistant. Damask variety Celsiana is pale pink, fading to warm blush color, while Madam Hardy is white. Rose de Rescht is a bright fuchsia to deep pink damask; it blooms over a long season.

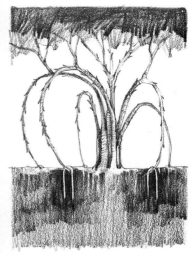
A sprawling shrub rose can be made to look full by pegging its canes. Arch the canes or branches to the ground, and fasten them to the soil with a hoop of heavy wire. Push the wire far enough into the soil so the cane can't spring away. Eventually, the canes will root at the point where they touch the ground and new growth will start from the top of arches. Old canes that show little life should be removed.

Reine des Violettes, a hybrid perpetual, is famed for its changing color—from pastel pink and magenta to a smoky blue.

Old garden roses—

The sweetbrier rose or wild rose, eglanteria, still glimmers in gardens today. Hybrids are hardy plants up to 12 feet high, with small single or semidouble blooms of pink. Colorful hips make these varieties lovely even after petals fall. A special plus: leaves have an apple scent. The Lady Penzance variety is a coppery-pink with yellow centers, and Lord Penzance is a fawn pink color with lemon-yellow tinting.

Gallica, the French rose, is the oldest class of roses known. It's a class of contrasts: flowers may be heavily scented or have no scent at all; they may be single or double; plants may look spindly but are actually hardy. Gallicas bloom once in spring. Reds with purple tones are the Cardinal de Richelieu and the Charles de Mills. Camaieux is white, striped with rosy-purple; the Rosa Mundi is pink, red, and white striped.

Hybrid foetida is often combined with other species for a brilliant yellow, modern hybrid offspring. The term foetida refers to the offensive scent found in the species, but Harison's Yellow—popular since pioneer days—is fragrant. This early-flowering beauty grows to six feet high.

Hybrid perpetual is an old garden rose class that provides a transition between the old and modern rose. Single or double roses bloom throughout the season. The plants are tall, vigorous, and hardy. Shades of pink or rose are found in the Baroness Rothschild, Mrs. John Laing, and Paul Neyron varieties. Frau Karl Druschki is snow white, touched with pink. Roger Lambelin is maroon, edged in white.

Hybrid rugosa is rugged; a number of this rose's varieties are well known. The parent, *Rosa rugosa*, contributes its hardiness, disease resistance, large size, and easy care to the carnation-like F.J. Grootendorst and the superior ground cover, Max Graf.

Hybrid spinosissima varieties are valued for their bloom. The hybrids are mostly modern additions to the shrub border. Try golden yellow Fruhlingsgold or the blush-pink Stanwell Perpetual.

Crested Moss is a hardy rose with double blooms. Buds are enclosed by fringed sepals and look like hats.

An everblooming, climbing tea rose, Sombreuil, is hardy in the South.

The Rosa rugosa 'maxima' *blooms repeatedly.*

Old garden roses—

More old garden roses are available. With mosslike, hairy glands covering the sepals, stem, and leaves, moss roses produce a wonderful scent. Moss roses are sports of centifolias, and most are about seven feet tall. Flowers are large, double, and globular, blooming later in the spring than most roses. Some bloom only once; others flower intermittently throughout the summer and early fall. Favorites include: Alfred de Dalmas, Common Moss, Crested Moss, Gloire des Mousseux, and Salet, all in shades of pink, rose, and salmon.

Noisettes make glorious climbers if you live in a mild climate. This class of old garden rose produces clusters of blooms throughout the summer in a variety of colors. For a golden yellow, try Marechal Niel.

Portland roses, although often not winter-hardy, are a sturdy, erect bush in warmer areas. Flowers, such as the Jacques Cartier with light pink blossoms, are fragrant and worth the effort.

Species roses are the natives, the wild roses. Some, such as Austrian Copper (*Rosa foetida 'bicolor'*), bloom but once— opening the rose season with a flourish. Others, such as Chestnut Rose (*Rosa roxburghi*) in a medium pink, flower repeatedly.

Tea roses are translucent, pastel contributors to the modern hybrid tea roses. The name comes from fresh-tea-leaf fragrance. They're graceful but tender. You'll like Catherine Mermet, soft pink with lilac edges, and Maman Cochet, soft pink with yellow base.

Souvenir de la Malmaison, a bourbon, produces flowers in cycles.

Alfred de Dalmas, a moss rose, grows only two to three feet high.

Early American settlers took the Harison's Yellow rose, a hybrid foetida, with them wherever they went. Blooms are semidouble and fragrant.

Modern Roses

When the subject is roses, modern means after 1867. Hybrid teas, floribundas, and grandifloras are the favorite classes. Hybridizing and special development have brought out their best features.

Hybrid tea

With long pointed buds, high-centered blooms, unforgettable fragrance, and a vast range of colors—clear or blended—it's no wonder that hybrid tea rose varieties are famous. They combine the everblooming quality of old tea roses with the hardiness of hybrid perpetuals.

Alone or by the dozen, the hybrid tea is the perfect flower for a vase. As a bud or combined in an attractive arrangement, these roses have superior features as cut flowers. Hybrid tea varieties are also popular grafted onto sturdy long stems as tree roses.

If protected during the winter, most hybrid tea varieties are hardy up to Zone 5. Provide protection if temperatures drop persistently below 20 degrees Fahrenheit during the winter.

Top hybrid teas

The perfection of roses is wrapped up in the hybrid teas. Many varieties have long stems and high blooms. They're effective as specimens.

American Heritage—a creamy yellow, tickled with pink

Antigua—golden apricot

Apollo—medium yellow

Bewitched—pink

Big Ben—dark, velvety red

Blue Moon—lilac blue

Candy Stripe—streaked pink and white

Carla—pink petals, salmon undertones

Century Two—a pale pink, slightly darker on outside of petals

Perfume Delight is all its name implies. Color stays pure even when the flower is picked.

Charlotte Armstrong—deep pink to light red

Chicago Peace—shades of yellow, bronze, and deep pink

Christian Dior—cherry red

Chrysler Imperial—classic red

Color Magic—changes colors from ivory to pink, coral, and rose

Columbus Queen—masses of pink petals, darker on reverse side

Command Performance—has a star shape; orange-red

Confidence—pearly light pink, shaded in peach and yellow

Crimson Glory—deep velvety red

Dainty Bess—rose pink

Diamond Jubilee—buff yellow to apricot

Double Delight—white, edged in red

Duet—pink; deep pink reverse

Eclipse—golden yellow

Eiffel Tower—medium pink

Electron—glowing pink

First Love—pearly pink

First Prize—ivory pink center, deeper pink outside

Fragrant Cloud—orange-red

Friendship—flesh-colored

Garden Party—white

Granada—red, gold, yellow, pink mix

Grand Slam—red

Gypsy—dark, orange-red petals

Heirloom—magenta, lightens to lilac with age

Helen Traubel—apricot-pink

Irish Gold—medium yellow, often tinged with pink

Isabel de Ortiz—deep pink, silver reverse

Jadis—rose-pink

John F. Kennedy—dazzling white

Kordes' Perfecta—a creamy white, tipped with crimson

Lady X—pale, pinkish-lavender

Lemon Spice—lemon yellow

Matterhorn—ivory white petals from yellow tinted buds

Medallion—light apricot

Michelle Meilland—creamy pink, shaded salmon centers

Mirandy—deep red

Miss All-American Beauty—dark pink (almost red)

Mister Lincoln—dark red

Mojave—desert red, apricot, and orange

Neue Revue—white, edged in red; fragrant but thorny

Oklahoma—dark red (almost black)

Oldtimer—yellow-bronze

Oregold—deep gold

Papa Meilland—dark crimson

Paradise—silvery mauve, shaded to pink at center; red edges

Pascali—creamy white

Peace—light to golden yellow, pink edges

Peer Gynt—golden yellow, with a touch of red on edges as it ages

Perfume Delight—old rose

Pharaoh—brilliant red

Pink Peace—deep, dusty pink; lovely, but not a copy of the famous Peace rose

Portrait—blend of pinks, ivory

Pristine—white with pink picotee

Promise—clear, dawn-pink

Proud Land—brilliant red

Red Devil—red; silver reverse

Red Lion—cherry red

Red Masterpiece—deep red

Rose Gaujard—cherry red with reverse of pale pink and white

Royal Highness—pale pink

Rubaiyat—rose-red

Seashell—luminous shades of peach, shrimp pink, and coral

Silver Lining—silvery pink with darker pink edges

Snowfire—scarlet; white reverse

South Seas—soft salmon to coral pink

Spellbinder—ivory buds open to blush pink, deepen to rose-red

Sterling Silver—lavender

Summer Sunshine—yellow

Sunset Jubilee—coppery pink with tints of light yellow

Susan Massu—light yellow, tipped with blush of light pink

Sutter's Gold—orange and rust-red buds open to golden orange with scarlet veining

Swarthmore—cherry pink to dusty rose, edged in gray

Tiffany—pink with yellow base

Toro—dark red

Tropicana—fluorescent, coral-orange

White Knight—pure white

White Masterpiece—pure white

Wini Edmunds—strawberry with straw-yellow reverse

Yankee Doodle—light yellow, flushed with apricot and salmon; a good specimen plant

Medium-pink, urn-shaped buds spiral open to high-centered Jadis blooms.

The Better Homes and Gardens hybrid tea has a yellow reverse on pink.

Plant several bushes of First Edition, a floribunda, for a splash of color.

Cathedral's ruffled petals shimmer as coppery peach buds open to scarlet-orange.

Bon Bon is a petite, 2½-foot tall rose that makes a compact hedge.

Floribundas

The best floribunda hybrids bear large clusters of flowers from June to frost. This makes them well suited for mass plantings and landscaping.

Because they have so many flowers and are constantly in bloom, they have many uses. Floribundas make fine foregrounds for beds of hybrid teas and make gorgeous low, flowering hedges to separate your yard from the neighbors'. They're most handsome when many of one kind and color are planted together.

You'll find so many colors and flower sizes that the challenge will be selecting a favorite variety. They come in single and double flowers. Choose the one you admire most and the one that would fit the color scheme and design of your home and garden.

Choose floribundas instead of other kinds of roses when you're more interested in show and durability than individual blooms; although a floribunda rose is good-looking, it is looser and seldom has the size or perfect form of the hybrid tea when viewed close up.

These plants are the result of crossing hybrid teas with hardy, dwarf-size polyantha roses and have the best features of both parents. They are hardier, lower-growing, and bushier than most hybrid teas. And they're relatively free of disease.

Planting, care, and winter protection of floribunda roses are the same as for hybrid teas.

Polyanthas, the small-cluster-flowered forerunners of today's floribundas, are often listed with them in catalogues. Heights are from 18 to 24 inches.

Try polyanthas for bedding, low hedges, and front-of-the-border plantings. Although many have been replaced in the rose garden by their larger, flashier offspring (the floribundas), several polyanthas are worth including in your garden (see listing on opposite page).

Polyanthas' blooms range up to two inches across and put on a colorful display.

Favorite floribundas

Accent—bright crimson red

Anabell—orange-salmon

Angel Face—deep lavender

Apache Tears—white with scarlet edges

Apricot Nectar—creamy apricot with touches of pink and gold

Bahia—orange-red with golden yellow reverse

Betty Prior—carmine pink

Bon Bon—rose-pink with silvery reverse; blooms all summer

Cathedral—vibrant orange with touches of yellow

Charisma—orange and gold

City of Belfast—orange-red

Else Poulsen—bright rose

Europeana—dark crimson

Evening Star—pure white

Fabergé—warm peach-pink; can stand partial shade

Fashion—coral and peach-pink

Fire King—orange to scarlet

First Edition—bright coral

Gene Boerner—medium pink; petite replicas of perfect hybrid teas

Ginger—coral-orange

Iceberg—glistening white

Ivory Fashion—ivory white

Little Darling—blend of yellow and soft pink

Matador—orange-gold blend

Orangeade—bright orange

Picnic—coral with yellow base and a tinge of pink

Redgold—gold, edged in red

Rose Parade—shrimp pink

Sarabande—orange-red

Saratoga—white

Sea Pearl—pearly pink diffused with peach and yellow

Spanish Sun—golden yellow

Spartan—orange to coral

Sunsprite—sunny yellow; early-blooming; disease-resistant

Tamango—velvety crimson

Vogue—cherry-coral

Woburn Abbey—orange tints, shaded with red and gold

Pretty polyanthas

Cecile Brunner—a dainty light-pink-on-yellow sweetheart rose

China Doll—bright pink

Margo Koster—salmon

The Fairy—light pink; a good choice for gardens demanding low maintenance

Bahia shows its prizewinning style with exuberant displays of ruffled orange-pink flowers.

Grandiflora

Grandifloras have been awarded proud names by their developers—names such as Queen Elizabeth, Montezuma, Comanche, Scarlet Knight.

This class of rose has famed parents: the floribunda and the hybrid tea. From the hybrid tea, it inherits flower form and long cutting stems; from the floribunda, it receives hardiness, continuous flowering, and clusters of blooms.

Grandiflora is one of the newest classes of roses and was developed in the 1950s for the rose Queen Elizabeth. This variety is still one of the best you can grow if you have a sunny location for it.

Grandiflora bushes are taller than those of most floribundas, so they are good to use at the back of a rose bed or as a screen. Allow 24 inches between the bushes; for hedges, plant them closer. There's no lovelier way to hide an eyesore, such as garbage pails, than with several of the same variety of grandiflora.

Plant and tend them as you would hybrid teas and floribundas. Growth is robust, foliage healthy, and bloom profuse. Grandifloras are excellent roses for beginners and hobbyists alike.

Grow them as far north as Zone 5. Although they are hardy, the grandiflora will suffer less winterkill when provided with some protection in areas where temperatures consistently drop below 20 degrees.

Pick a grandiflora

Aquarius—blended pinks
Arizona—orange, gold, pink
Camelot—coral-pink
Carrousel—dark red
Comanche—red to orange
John S. Armstrong—vivid dark red
Montezuma—rose-salmon and terra-cotta
Mount Shasta—pure white
Olé—orange-red
Pink Parfait—pastel pink
Queen Elizabeth—dawn pink to radiant carmine
Scarlet Knight—velvety crimson to scarlet
Sonia—coral side of pink

Montezuma ranks as an all-time rose classic. This rose-salmon grandiflora is prized for fully double blooms.

Cherry-Vanilla is upright in habit and has semi-glossy leaves.

Keep cut roses fresh, bright

Although roses are special outdoors, few gardeners can resist bringing some indoors. A few precautions will keep them fresh for as long as possible.

Wait until late afternoon and carry a bucket of lukewarm water with you. Cut the stems at an angle, and set the flowers into the bucket with water up to their necks.

Pass up flowers that are too open, have falling or wilted petals, seem off-color, or have very dark leaves. Be sure at least two healthy five-leaflet leaves remain on the stem to help the plant maintain its strength and vigor. Don't take any more leaves than necessary if you want your bush to keep producing new bloom.

After you've finished gathering the roses, trim the stem ends again, and remove any torn or shredded leaves. Thorns can be removed, too, without any harm to the flower. Place bucket, water, and roses in a cool, dark spot or in the refrigerator for several hours or overnight before you arrange the flowers for an accent anywhere in the house.

The two biggest enemies to cut flowers are bacteria and high temperature. To avoid a buildup of bacteria, change the water every day and remove all leaves below the water surface. Rotting leaves encourage the growth of bacteria. The water added should be at room temperature.

If possible, keep the flowers in a cool spot away from bright sun but also away from the air conditioner's breeze. At night, move the flowers to a chilly enclosed porch or the refrigerator. The effort can give you an extra day or two with the roses.

To lengthen the life of the cut roses, add a floral preservative (from the florist) or a drop of bleach. Add no more than a quarter teaspoon of bleach for a large vase.

To revive roses that wilted during cutting or those going limp in an arrangement, cut off the base of the stem at a slant, and scrape along the stem at several spots until the green underbark shows. Next, place the roses in water so hot you can just stand to hold your hand in it, and leave roses there until the water cools. Finally, put them into cool water up to the flower head for an hour. Then rearrange.

Queen Elizabeth graciously lends its ruffly pink to small pocket gardens.

Comanche, in red, combines with the yellow hybrid tea, Golden Prince.

Climbing Roses

If you're truly romantic and poetic, set an arbor in your garden and drape it with climbing roses. Or turn a common tool shed into a rose-covered cottage with a trellis of long-caned roses clambering high and across the roof. Although these roses must be tied to their support because they do not have tendrils, you'll like the results.

Enjoy the abundant beauty of tall climbing roses. They include sports or mutations of other rose classes, such as hybrid teas, grandifloras, floribundas, and polyanthas. The difference is their long pliable canes lift blooms high, if provided support. The climbing sports have flowers identical to their parents, but the bushes are not so hardy. Check catalogues for climbers in your favorite varieties. Those roses listed on the opposite page are climbers only, not sports of others.

Climbers need good air circulation to stay healthy. When you use a trellis, space it at least two feet from any solid structure. This not only cuts down on disease, it also gives you freedom to prune and spray.

Climbers grow little from the base of the plant, so don't remove whole canes or you'll rob yourself of next year's bloom. After flowers fade, cut clusters off below the bottom flower, leaving two or three leaves on short stems attached to the main branch. In the spring, cut out all deadwood and the oldest canes.

Most climbers will withstand temperatures around 20 degrees Fahrenheit. However, if your area's thermometer dips below zero, take climbers off their supports, lay the canes on the ground, peg them down, and cover with oak leaves or soil. In early spring, remove the protection and tie the climbers back up.

Like many true old-fashioned climbing roses, this delicate pink beauty is not hardy north of the Mason-Dixon line.

Talisman is an easily trained variety; a good choice for arbor, fence, or trellis.

New Dawn glimmers as a pale pink, flowering repeatedly. Buds open fast.

Paul's Scarlet Climber has vigorous bright scarlet, weather-resistant flowers, but it usually blooms only once. Plants can grow to 20 feet tall.

Piñata has large, yellow blooms, diffused with orange and red. The plant repeats consistently and can stand alone as a shrub.

Red Fountain has arching canes filled with sprays of velvety, ruffled, double, dark red blooms. They train well but are strong enough to be left without staking.

Rhonda produces clusters of large, double, salmon-pink flowers.

Royal Gold, though tender, has yellow flowers that won't fade.

Royal Sunset, with hybrid tea-shaped flowers, is a tender climber. Color is a deep apricot that fades to light peach in summer heat.

Talisman has medium-size, yellow-bronze, flat flowers with a strong fragrance. It's easily trained to an arbor or trellis.

Tempo, vigorous and disease-resistant, has large, double, early blooming flowers.

White Dawn, with gardenia-like, hardy, semidouble flowers, is everblooming, fragrant, and white.

Ramblers, primarily offspring of the *Rosa wichuraiana* and *R. multi-flora,* are huge, fast growers. In years past, they were the popular climbers but have lost out to newer varieties. Most popular in far northern latitudes.

Good climbers

Famous rose varieties have produced long-caned mutations that make lovely climbers. This list, though, includes climbers only.

Aloha is a climbing hybrid tea, not a sport of a bush rose. Petals are rose-pink on one side, deeper on the other. They form a cup-shaped flower that appears recurrently.

America is slow to climb, easy to train. It is coral pink, opening from salmon buds. Flowers are large, pointed, and spice scented.

Blaze blooms heavily in early summer and continues throughout the season. Semidouble flowers are bright scarlet and slightly fragrant. They form in large clusters.

Coral Dawn has color befitting its name.

Don Juan, with its dark velvety red blooms and stiff stems, makes a good pillar rose. Tips freeze in cold winters but snap back fast.

Dr. J.H. Nicolas does well on pillar or trellis. Medium rose-pink flowers are large and globular.

Golden Showers has stems so strong and stiff it can stand unsupported. Daffodil yellow flowers are semidouble and fragrant.

Handel plays a medley of wavy, frilled, double, white flowers edged in rose-pink or red.

High Noon shines with bright yellow flowers, tinted with red. The loose, double, cupped blooms appear throughout the summer on this hybrid tea.

Joseph's Coat opens into yellow blooms that pass through stages of orange and scarlet as they age. The small fluffy flowers are showy all season long on this vigorous—though tender to cold weather—pillar rose.

With full sun, climbers offer beautiful old-fashioned blooms.

Miniature roses

With a delicacy that evokes sighs from viewers, miniature roses are also known for their sturdiness and versatility. Recent breeding has produced new varieties by crossing the fairy rose (*Rosa chinensis 'minima,'* or *R. rouletti*) with both polyanthas and floribundas. These varieties, though small, are just as hardy and colorful as their taller cousins.

Like their relatives, miniatures are exquisite contributors to landscape designs. Try a low hedge of them to separate the patio from the lawn or to frame the pathway to the front door. Or use them in a downright practical way as a hardy ground cover on an otherwise bare, unsightly, hard-to-plant slope.

Miniatures make hobbyists of the casual gardener when used another way. Try a few miniature varieties in containers and suddenly you're a collector, studying the specialized catalogues and corresponding with other smitten fans.

Start new miniatures in four-inch pots, gradually working them into larger pots as they grow. Dress up windows with boxes of miniatures. Rather than plant the roses directly into a soil-filled window box, fill the box with individual flowerpots of minis. In that way, the roses can be easily moved indoors in winter or replaced quickly if something goes awry.

If you have a spot to hang a basket, fill it with miniature roses for a continuous display of summer color. The best varieties for baskets are Red Cascade, Green Ice, and Sugar Elf. Let their flowers cascade from lampposts, tree limbs, gutters, overhangs, and brackets attached to fences or house.

Don't forget that roses in containers outdoors will need watering more often than if they were in the ground. A plastic pot often works best because it's better at keeping soil moist than the terra-cotta pots. Check them daily, and, when dry, water until the water runs out the bottom of the container. A mulch at the top of the planter will help keep the roses moist.

Whether indoors or out, soil must be well drained. Use a packed soil-less potting mix, or mix your own with equal parts of loam, sand, and peat moss or vermiculite.

Inside, miniatures need a lot of light, too. A south window is best. Or keep them under high-intensity, fluorescent lights ten to 14 hours a day. Set them on a tray of pebbles with water to keep humidity high.

Outdoors, miniatures tolerate a little more shade than their larger cousins and are happy in the dappled shade of an ornamental tree. But don't plant them too close to the tree; they might lose out to tree roots in their search for water.

Prune the minis according to their use. Near a hedge, you could trim only enough to keep them tidy; indoors, in a teacup or other decorative device, you might keep them at about three inches.

Baby Betsy McCall—light pink with touch of cream at base

Baby Darling—apricot

Baby Masquerade—changes from yellow to orange and red as it opens

Beauty Secret—medium red

Bo-peep—soft pink

Chipper—coral-pink

Cinderella—dainty white with hint of pale, dawn-pink

Cuddles—coral-pink

Dwarfking—dark red

Easter Morning—ivory white

Gloriglo—fluorescent orange with white reverse

Gold Coin—yellow

Green Ice—apricot buds open to white blooms

Hula Girl—orange-yellow

Janna—white with pinkish-red edges

Jeanie Williams—red and yellow bicolor

Jeanne Lajoie—medium pink

Kathy—rich red

Kathy Robinson—pink with buff reverse

Lavender Lace—lilac

Littlest Angel—medium yellow

Magic Carrousel—white with red edges

Mary Adair—apricot

Mary Marshall—coral-orange with yellow base

Over the Rainbow—red and gold blend

Pixie Rose—deep rose-pink

Cinderella is a delicate choice for both indoor and outdoor culture.

Judy Fischer is a perfect flower for tabletop displays.

Red Cascade—dark red
Rosmarin—blend of pinks
Scarlet Gem—orange-red
Seabreeze—medium pink
Sheri Anne—orange-red; yellow base
Simplex—white
Starina—orange-red
Top Secret—deep red
Toy Clown—white with red edges

Tree roses

Tree roses bring height and accent to the landscape. Use them as a formal specimen, or underplant them with floribundas or annuals for a more informal look.

Tree roses are effective lining a walk. They are also good in that narrow strip of land between driveway and fence.

But tree roses may not be suitable for the weekend gardener seeking only low-maintenance plants for year-round use.

Give them the same soil mix as for miniatures. Because they are much larger with proportionately larger pots, consider setting them on platforms with casters so they can be easily moved.

The best fertilizer for movable roses is water soluble. Feed once a month, following label directions, or for more even growth, every other week at half strength.

When winter comes, move the planters indoors or into an unheated porch, garage, or basement.

Tree roses are actually several roses combined. A strong grower is grafted onto a root understock. And onto the stem is budded any bush rose—hybrid tea, floribunda, grandiflora, polyantha, miniature, and even climbers.

When planting, place a stake next to the trunk, and use soft ties to secure the trunk to it in three places. The stake should extend into the head. Wrap the young tree's trunk with burlap or purchased tree wrap. If hot summer weather is fast approaching, cover the canes with moist sphagnum moss, or pop a plastic bag over the tree's head to prevent canes from drying out and to help them sprout quickly. Remove any coverings as soon as the buds break into leaf.

Any spot needing an air of distinction is a possibility for tree roses; they can be the crowning glory.

chapter 11

SPECIAL GARDENS

Before throwing your hands up in despair over a problem spot in your landscape (or maybe the problem is your entire landscape), try turning the problem into a special garden. Overly dry slopes or corners can become desert gardens featuring cactus and other succulents. Continuously moist ones are perfect for gentle, informal wildflower collections. Tall, billowing grasses make elegant additions to borders separating your yard from the one next door; or use pampas, plume grass, or arundo as textured foliage accents. A steep slope—whether in sunshine or shade—can be transformed into a tapestry of color and, at the same time, hold the soil during rainstorms.

For a gracious touch in even the smallest spaces, add a water garden—either in a tub above ground or in an excavated pool. When the water is surrounded by certain plants, you'll find yourself making lots of little friends—so long as you stay quiet; a wildlife garden and mini-size bird sanctuary can bring you hours of pleasure. If your tastes lean toward the gourmet or toward the fresh and natural, add plantings of herbs—as plain or fancy as you like. Or do you crave lovely flowers but don't have the space for a big flower garden? A few square yards near the garage are sufficient to keep you supplied with cut flowers, with the accent on tall straight stems and full blooms rather than an eye-catching display outdoors. No yard at all? A craving for color where there isn't soil? Container gardening is for you. From the time of the pharaohs, plants have been grown in places where they probably wouldn't grow without help from a gardener. You, too, can solve problems beautifully.

Why mow your lawn? For a month in summer, oxeye daisies put on a display, then turn it over to clover, queen-anne's-lace, mustard, and wild asters.

Wild-flowers

Awakening as the soil warms, wildflowers announce the arrival of a new season. Enjoy their beauty from early spring to autumn.

The secret of a successful wildflower garden is working with nature to select the correct plants for your environment. Choose several kinds of flowers so you have blooms all summer and in autumn, besides early spring. Include foliage plants that will complement the flowers and berries, and add a variety of shapes and textures. Ferns work well in shady, moist areas. Mayapple and jack-in-the-pulpit make interesting ground covers.

Wildflowers are often split into two groups—sun-lovers and shade-lovers. Almost all of the spring-blooming species will adapt to an area receiving filtered light.

Buy wildflower roots or bulbs from a nursery or catalogue to avoid endangering rare species. Or, get wildflower starts from friends. Wildflower hobbyists generally are willing to share extras when they divide their plantings—especially if you will trade for part of one of your favorites. Otherwise, take only from condemned property or from a construction site. If you gather roadside seeds, do not take all of your supply from one area.

Propagate your own plants, raising them from cuttings or seeds. Set out spring-blooming wildflowers in the fall and summer- and fall-blooming plants in the summer or fall. For best effect, plant in clumps or drifts. Avoid rows.

Select plants that will flourish in the environment you have, or change the environment to meet the plants' needs. To know what plants will flourish on your property, study your area's characteristics. Find out what grew originally on your property. Also study the slope of the land, prevailing winds, aver-age amount of rainfall per year, general level of humidity, and the water drainage patterns. After analyzing each, you'll have a good idea of the wildflowers able to grow. Study existing vegetation, too.

If you must change the environment to grow the wildflowers you want, create the right conditions—shade, soil, and moisture—before you purchase your plants. The closer you come to creating the conditions the plants prefer when growing naturally, the better they will do. The amount of sunlight and wind is controlled by trees and shrubs, for example.

The soil structure and chemical composition often dictate what plants will flourish. Moisture depends on rainfall, surface contours, and soil type. You may find it necessary to water wildflowers native to moist habitats more often than you water other plants.

Usually, you won't need special soils; a typical garden loam is fine for all but desert species (see pages 368 and 369). Wildflowers won't grow in close-packed or compacted soils, though, because the roots will suffocate. Add leaf mold to compacted soil. Also, establish paths of wood chips or gravel in your garden so foot traffic won't pack the soil around the plants.

After your garden is planted, don't cultivate with a hoe, but do all the weeding by hand. Cover the bare earth around the plants with a leaf mulch until existing vegetation takes over. Don't use a chemical fertilizer or a weed killer on your wildflower garden.

As the growing season comes to an end, protect the plants against winter with a four- to five-inch layer of leaves. Then remove leaves in spring after danger of frost passes; a few may be left to enrich the soil when they rot.

Come May and June, the brightest blues under the sky belong to members of the iris family—the blue-eyed grasses.

WILDFLOWERS

Name	Description	Soil and Light	Propagation	Comments
ALUMROOT *Heuchera*	Tiny blossoms on stems 16 to 36 inches tall. White, red, purplish. Blooms from May to August.	Shady location. Well-drained, dry soil.	Seeds or division.	Leaves mottled when young.
ANEMONE, RUE *Anemonella*	Delicate blossoms on stems 5 to 9 inches tall. White and pink. Blooms from March to June.	Shady location. Well-drained, dry soil.	Seeds or division.	Divide after plant has died back in the fall.
ARBUTUS, TRAILING *Epigaea*	Tubular white and pink blossoms from March to May. Plants are 3 inches high.	Partial shade. Well-drained, dry soil.	Seeds, stem cuttings, or stem layering.	Keep well mulched. Bears white berries.
BANEBERRY *Actaea*	Small, white blossoms in April and May. Later, red or white berries on 2-foot high plants.	Shade. Well-drained, dry soil.	Seeds or division.	Sow seeds in the fall.
BEE BALM *Monarda*	Large, red blossoms on 2-foot high plants from June to September.	Shade. Well-drained, moist, acid soil.	Seeds, stem cuttings, or division.	Will adapt to partially sunny location.
BELLWORT *Uvularia*	Pale yellow blossoms on graceful 4- to 12-inch plants from April to June.	Shade. Well-drained, moist soil.	Seeds or division.	Fleshy, winged seed capsules.
BISHOP'S-CAP *Mitella*	Tiny, white flowers from April to June on 6- to 12-inch plants.	Shade. Well-drained, moist soil.	Seeds or division.	Keep well mulched.
BLACK-EYED SUSAN *Rudbeckia hirta*	Flat, daisy-like flowers on 2-foot high wiry stems; yellow petals with brown centers. Blooms in July and August.	Sunny. Well-drained soil.	Seeds, but often self-sows.	Often grown as biennial.
BLOODROOT *Sanguinaria*	Large leaved, with single white flowers in April and May on plants 8 to 10 inches high.	Shade. Well-drained, dry soil.	Seeds or division.	One leaf for each flower. Leaves form thick mat.
BLUEBELLS *Mertensia*	Two-foot tall stems with blue flowers in April and May.	Sun or partial shade. Well-drained, moist soil.	Seeds or division.	Plants disappear during the summer.
BUTTERCUP Crowfoot *Ranunculus*	Small, yellow flowers from April to August on plants 6 to 24 inches high.	Shade or partial shade. Tolerant of most soil types.	Seeds or division.	Can become like a weed.
BUTTERFLY WEED *Asclepias tuberosa*	Clusters of small, red-orange flowers in July and August on plants 2 feet high.	Sunny. Well-drained, dry soil.	Seeds or root cuttings.	Brilliant color.
CARDINAL FLOWER *Lobelia cardinalis*	Clusters of tubular, red flowers from July to September on plants 2 to 3 feet tall.	Partial shade. Well-drained, moist, acid soil.	Offsets, divisions, stem cuttings, or seeds; often self-sows.	Keep well mulched.
CINQUEFOIL *Potentilla*	Tiny, yellow flowers from June to August on 3- to 6-inch plants that turn red in fall.	Shade. Well-drained, dry, acid soil.	Seeds, division, or stem cuttings.	Good ground cover.

Name	Description	Soil and Light	Propagation	Comments
COLUMBINE, WILD *Aquilegia*	Finely cut, pendulous, yellow and red flowers from April through July on 1- to 2-foot plants.	Shade. Well-drained, dry, slightly acid soil.	Seeds, but often self-sows.	Showy.
CONEFLOWER, PRAIRIE *Ratibida*	Large, yellow flowers from June to August on plants up to 6 feet tall.	Sunny. Well-drained, dry soil.	Seeds or division.	Graceful and showy.
CONEFLOWER, PURPLE *Echinacea*	Large, single, purple flowers from June to October on plants 3 to 4 feet tall.	Sunny. Well-drained, dry soil.	Seeds or division.	Tall and impressive.
DOG-TOOTH VIOLET **Adder's-tongue,** **Trout lily** *Erythronium*	Solitary white flowers in April and May on plants 6 inches tall.	Shade. Well-drained, moist soil.	Offsets or seeds.	Forms a dense mat. Leaves are mottled with brown.
DUTCHMAN'S-BREECHES *Dicentra cucullaria*	Unusually shaped, white flowers in April and May, clustered on stems of plants 6 to 12 inches high.	Shade. Well-drained, dry soil.	Division or seeds.	Spreads into clumps. Disappears after flowering.
EVENING PRIMROSE *Oenothera*	Pale yellow, fragrant flowers in July and August on plants 2 to 4 feet tall.	Sunny. Well drained, dry soil.	Seeds.	Flowers open only at night. Treat as a biennial.
FLAG, BLUE *Iris* sp.	Large, purple blossoms in May and June on plants 2 to 3 feet tall.	Sunny. Moist to wet, slightly acid soil.	Division or seeds, but often self-sows.	Forms a dense colony.
FOAMFLOWER **False miterwort** *Tiarella*	Small, white flowers cluster on plants 6 to 12 inches high.	Shade. Well-drained, moist soil.	Division or seeds.	Effective in mass.
FORGET-ME-NOT *Myosotis*	Pale blue flowers with yellow centers on 6-inch plants. Blooms all summer long if conditions are right.	Sunny. Well-drained, moist to wet soil.	Division or seeds.	Keep moist.
GENTIAN, CLOSED **Blue gentian** *Gentiana andrewsi*	Tubular, violet flowers in August and September on plants 1 foot tall.	Sun or partial shade. Well-drained, moist to wet, slightly acid soil.	Division or seeds.	Flowers remain closed.
GERANIUM, WILD *Geranium maculatum*	Large, red-violet flowers in clusters on plants 2 feet tall.	Shade. Well-drained, moist soil.	Division or seeds.	Effective in mass.
GINGER, WILD *Asarum*	Inconspicuous, tubular, violet-brown flowers in April and May. Blooms appear at the base of plants that will grow to 4 to 8 inches tall.	Shade. Well-drained, moist soil.	Division or rhizome cuttings.	Interesting ground cover.
HEPATICA *Hepatica*	Rose, white, or blue flowers from April to May on 6-inch plants.	Shade. Well-drained, dry, slightly acid soil.	Division or seeds, but often self-sows.	Valued for early color. Showy.

WILDFLOWERS (continued)

Name	Description	Soil and Light	Propagation	Comments
JACK-IN-THE-PULPIT *Arisaema triphyllum*	Unusual, vase-shaped, greenish-brown flowers from April to June on plants 2 feet tall. Red berries follow later in the season.	Shade. Well-drained, moist soil.	Seeds, but often self-sows.	Showy and attractive.
JACOB'S-LADDER Greek valerian *Polemonium*	Small clusters of blue flowers on 3-foot plants in June and July.	Shade. Well-drained, moist soil.	Division or seeds.	Fine border plant.
LADY-SLIPPER, YELLOW *Cypripedium calceolus*	Yellow flowers (often veined in blue) bloom in May on plants to 30 inches tall.	Shade. Well-drained, moist soil.	Division.	Showy. Give an annual topdressing of compost.
LOBELIA, BLUE *Lobelia siphilitica*	Tiny, blue flowers from August to October on terminal clusters of plants 2 to 3 feet tall.	Sun or partial shade. Well-drained, moist soil.	Division, offsets, stem cuttings, or seeds.	Valuable for late summer color.
MALLOW, ROSE *Hibiscus*	Large, red, pink, or white flowers from July to September on plants 6 feet tall.	Sunny. Well-drained, moist soil.	Division, stem cuttings, or seeds.	Use as a background plant.
MARIGOLD, MARSH *Caltha*	Small clusters of brilliant yellow flowers in April and May on plants 2 feet tall.	Sunny. Moist to wet soil.	Division.	Plants disappear in summer.
MAYAPPLE Mandrake *Podophyllum*	Single, white, daisy-like flower in April and May on 12- to 18-inch plants.	Partial to full shade. Well-drained, moist soil.	Division or seeds.	Rapid spreader. Good, quick ground cover.
MEADOW RUE, EARLY *Thalictrum dioicum*	Inconspicuous, greenish or violet flowers in April and May on 2-foot plants.	Shade. Well-drained, moist soil.	Division or seeds.	Handsome, dainty foliage.
MEADOW RUE, TALL *Thalictrum polygamum*	Large clusters of white flowers from August to September on plants to 10 feet tall.	Sunny. Well-drained, moist to wet soil.	Division, stem cuttings, or seeds.	Use as background plant.
PARTRIDGEBERRY *Mitchella*	Small, white flowers in June and July on plants to 6 inches tall. Small red berries follow later in the season.	Shade. Well-drained, moist, acid soil	Stem cuttings or seeds.	Effective ground cover.
PASQUEFLOWER *Anemone sp.*	Large, purple flowers in March and April on plants 16 inches tall.	Sunny. Well-drained, dry soil.	Seeds or root cuttings.	Early and attractive.
PHLOX, BLUE *Phlox divaricata*	Clusters of pale blue flowers in April and May on stems 6 to 15 inches tall. Small leaves appear opposite each other on the stem.	Partial shade. Well-drained, dry soil.	Division or stem cuttings.	Often forms large clumps.
POPPY, CALIFORNIA *Eschscholzia*	Brilliant orange, cuplike flowers from April to June on plants 10 to 20 inches tall.	Sunny. Well-drained, dry soil.	Seeds.	Vigorous and hardy.

Name	Description	Soil and Light	Propagation	Comments
PRAIRIE ROSE *Rosa setigera*	Pink flowers from May to July in small clusters. Branches grow up to 15 feet long.	Sunny. Well-drained, dry soil.	Seeds or stem layering.	Branches are thornless.
SAND VERBENA *Abronia*	Small, pink, yellow, or lilac flowers from May to September on low plants.	Sunny. Well-drained, dry soil.	Seeds.	Trailing stems creep along the ground.
SHOOTING-STAR *Dodecatheon*	Small, attractive, red-violet flowers in May and June in clusters on foot-long stalks.	Light shade. Well-drained, moist soil.	Division, root cuttings, or seeds.	Plant disappears in summer.
SNAKEROOT *Cimicifuga*	Tiny, white blossoms in spike clusters from July to September on plants up to 8 feet tall.	Shade. Well-drained, moist soil.	Division or seeds.	Dried plants work well in fall arrangements.
SOLOMON'S-SEAL *Polygonatum*	Inconspicuous, greenish-white, bell-shaped flowers appear in May and June under the leaves on plants 1 to 2 feet tall. Bluish-black berries follow.	Shade. Well-drained, dry, slightly acid soil.	Division or seeds, but often self-sows.	Good ground cover in shady areas.
SPIDERWORT *Tradescantia*	Blue or white flowers in small terminal clusters on 1 to 2 foot, grasslike plants. Has blooms from June to August.	Sun or partial shade. Well-drained, moist soil.	Division, stem cuttings, or seeds.	Vigorous and quick growing.
SPRING-BEAUTY *Claytonia*	Delicate, pinkish-white blossoms from March to May on plants 4 to 6 inches tall.	Shade. Well-drained, dry soil.	Division or seeds, but often self-sows.	Good ground cover in shady areas.
SUNFLOWER, SAWTOOTH *Helianthus giganteus*	Large, yellow blossoms with brown centers in clusters on plants 10 feet tall. Has flowers from July to October.	Sunny. Well-drained soil.	Division or seeds.	Showy background plant.
TOOTHWORT *Dentaria*	Tiny, pinkish-white flowers in April and May in small clusters on plants 6 to 12 inches tall.	Shade. Well-drained, moist soil.	Division or seeds.	Valued for early spring color.
TRILLIUM *Trillium*	White or purple blossoms from April to June. The erect stems are about a foot long.	Shade. Well-drained, moist soil.	Division or seeds.	Effective in mass. Showy.
TURTLEHEAD *Chelone*	White or pink flowers line stem like snapdragons from July to September on plants 3 feet tall.	Shade. Well-drained, moist soil.	Division, stem cuttings, or seeds.	Interesting and handsome.
VIOLET *Viola sp.*	Flowers from April to June on small 6- to 8-inch plants.	Shade. Well-drained, moist soil.	Division or seeds, but often self-sows.	Can become like a weed.
WOOD ASTER, BLUE *Aster cordifolius*	Small, light purple flowers that bloom as open clusters in August and September. Plants grow up to 4 feet tall.	Partial to full shade. Well-drained, moist soil.	Division.	Good background plants.
WOOD ASTER, WHITE *Aster divaricatus*	Small, whitish-purple blossoms appear in flat clusters on 15-inch plants in August and September.	Partial shade. Well-drained, moist soil.	Division, but often self-sows.	Effective in mass. Vigorous and attractive.

FERNS

Name	Height in Inches	Soil and Light	Comments
Beech *Thelypteris hexagonoptera*	8-16	Shade. Well-drained, dry soil.	Striking, triangular leaves that are wider than they are long. Easy to grow, forming a dense mat.
Bracken *Pteridium*	16-32	Shade. Well-drained, moist or dry soil.	Large, coarse fern. Good for background planting.
Christmas *Polystichum acrostichoides*	12-30	Shade. Well-drained, moist soil.	Excellent for cutting. Can take some sun.
Cinnamon *Osmunda cinnamomea*	30-60	Shade. Well-drained, damp, acid soil.	Eight-inch-wide fronds turn to a cinnamon brown.
Ground cedar *Lycopodium sp.*	2-4	Shade. Well-drained, dry soil.	Dainty and fernlike. Good for poor, open forest soils.
Ground pine *Lycopodium sp.*	5-8	Shade. Well-drained, dry soil.	Looks like small tree. Not really a fern but is similar.
Hay-scented *Dennstaedtia punctilobula*	16-36	Shade. Tolerant of most well-drained soil conditions.	Lacelike fronds. Quick-spreading ground cover; useful on slopes.
Interrupted *Osmunda claytoniana*	24-48	Shade. Well-drained, damp, acid soil.	Graceful, large fronds in clusters. Grows slowly.
Lady, Northern *Athyrium filix-femina*	16-32	Shade. Well-drained, dry soil.	Finely toothed fronds.
Maidenhair *Adiantum*	10-20	Shade. Well-drained, moist soil.	Lacy fronds on black, wiry stems.
Male *Dryopteris filix-mas*	12-30	Shade. Well-drained, moist, gravelly soil.	Try them massed under trees.
New York *Thelypteris noveboracensis*	12-24	Shade. Well-drained, dry, slightly acid soil.	Quick-spreading ground cover. Formerly called *Dryopteris noveboracensis*.
Ostrich *Matteuccia*	24-60	Shade. Well-drained, moist to wet soil.	One of the tallest and most stately ferns. Plume-like fronds. Use in backgrounds.
Polypody *Polypodium*	4-36	Open shade. Well-drained, dry, gravelly soil.	Forms great mats over rocks and steep banks. Evergreen.
Rattlesnake *Botrychium virginianum*	8-24	Shade. Well-drained, moist soil.	Dainty fronds. Attracts snails.
Royal *Osmunda regalis*	Up to 72	Open shade. Well-drained, moist to wet, acid soil.	Tall, dramatic clumps.
Sensitive *Onoclea sensibilis*	24-54	Open shade to partial sun. Well-drained, moist to wet soil.	Handsome, showy fern. Delicate, bronzy-pink foliage.
Spleenwort, Ebony *Asplenium platyneuron*	6-15	Shade. Well-drained, dry soil.	Extremely hardy evergreen species. Plant between rocks.
Spleenwort, Maidenhair *Asplenium trichomanes*	3-6	Shade. Well-drained, dry soil mixed with limestone chips.	Will thrive in any rock cleft, if given foothold.
Walking *Camptosorus rhizophyllus*	4-12	Shade. Well-drained, dry soil.	Delicate. Best suited to rock garden. Reproduces from leaf tips. Attracts slugs.
Wood, Evergreen *Dryopteris sp.*	12-24	Shade. Well-drained, dry soil.	Deep green, thick fronds.

Wild-flowers in the Shade

Many wildflowers grow prettily in shady places similar to their woodland homes. They can be problem-solvers, too, by occupying spots where few other plants thrive.

Snakeroot adapts well to an informal, shaded garden. Backed up by yellow daylilies, the plant adds height to a border.

An easy plant to grow, jack-in-the-pulpit *(Arisaema)* is a hardy species. Plant it in a sheltered, shady spot protected from drying winds.

Trillium blooms in spring with a three-petaled, waxy flower measuring about two inches across. Start it in soil rich in organic matter. Trillium is perfect with other low-light favorites, such as hostas, violets, or begonias.

Snakeroot *(Cimicifuga)* is best at the back of your garden because it often grows to eight feet tall.

Hepatica, named for its liver-shaped leaves, blooms on the first warm days. Hepaticas like to be planted in a woodsy setting but need some sun while blossoming.

Bloodroot *(Sanguinaria)* spreads quickly into clumps. Blooms are white; sap is blood-red.

Dutchman's-breeches *(Dicentra)* have three to 12 white flowers that look like wide "breeches" on each plant. The plant prefers a rich, woods-like soil.

To add decorative foliage, try ferns. Most grow best in the shade. Depending on variety, ferns will grow under semi-dry or moist conditions.

Maidenhair fern *(Adiantum)* prefers a mulched, woodsy soil. This fern will spread gradually as a filler between other shady plants.

Ostrich fern *(Matteuccia),* if planted along the banks of a stream or in a wet, marshy spot, will help control erosion.

Shooting-star looks like a delicate meteorite. Give it a shady, moist spot.

When large-flowered trillium blooms, you know spring has arrived.

You're planting pure gold when you set out a clump of marsh marigolds.

In a large area or small, many early-season wildflowers bloom in the shade. To get them established around your home, start with roots from a wildflower nursery. Be sure to select places you won't mow, because the plants need time not only to bloom but also to die down undisturbed.

Violets can be naturalized as companion plants if you don't mind the violet foilage in the grass throughout the summer months. Many wildflowers make good mixers, too: try bluebells among your tulips or other spring bulbs.

Once established, most wildflowers reward you year after year without prompting. Marsh marigolds (right) repeat their cheerful show year after year, once you get them settled in a moist, partially shaded location. For drier spots, try the creeping buttercup.

Although not spectacular in size and color, wildflowers for shady spots deserve a close look. Their subtlety is their charm.

Dutchman's-breeches and hepaticas claim this shady nook with their lacy foliage. They're tiny but breathtaking.

Wild-flowers in Sunny Spots

Carpet a corner with sun-loving wildflowers and you'll be rewarded with a pageant of color as one species after another comes to bloom. To ensure a good stand, sow new seed yearly

Sow packaged mixed wildflower seeds from a commercial grower for a variety of continuous blooms all summer long. You'll find you can transform an everyday lawn into a blossoming pasture-lawn with wildflowers, and you can retire your lawn mower, too.

California poppies *(Eschscholzia)* open when the sun strikes them and close when the sun sets. The bright yellow to deep orange blooms are offset by feathery blue-green foliage.

Butterfly weed *(Asclepias)* catches the attention of butterflies and is a good candidate for pasture-lawns. On a smaller scale, it mixes well with non-native annuals and perennials in a flower border. This plant thrives in sunny, dry places.

Purple coneflowers *(Echinacea)* have stiff branching stems with solitary flowers. The flowers resemble black-eyed susans in shape, except that the petals curve backward. The three- to four-inch purple-red flowers have a prickly, rising dome for the flower head.

Forget-me-nots *(Myosotis)*, praised through poetry and folklore, grow well at the edge of a brook or pool and in other moist locations. They're a pale blue.

Marsh marigolds *(Caltha)*, too, like it damp. They grow best along the banks of streams, or as their name implies, in swampy areas.

Living up to its name, the brilliant orange butterfly weed will attract a host of colorful insects.

The well-known black-eyed susan spreads quickly.

Queen-anne's-lace takes over with no attention from you.

In this rock garden, yellow sea dahlia (Coreopsis maritima) *rises above clumps of baby blue-eyes* (Nemophila menziesi), *poppies, and blue* Phacelia viscida.

Fancy Grasses

Swaying fronds of tall, ornamental grasses add graceful elegance to your landscape design. Lofty ones can act as finely textured screens, and short ones fill bare spots in a flower border or edge a walk. Many do double duty. Dried, they add a wispy look to winter bouquets for any room in the house.

No shrub or flower can add the touch ornamental grasses can. Blue oats peek above a bed of heath.

Gardening with ornamental grasses may be just the touch needed to give your backyard the finished look, make it different from any in the neighborhood, and keep maintenance to a minimum. At the same time, you can be growing your own material for a dried winter arrangement to put on the mantel, buffet, or table.

For greatest effect, clump two or more plants of one species near a similar-size group of another. Repeat these clumps periodically at intervals for balance and a variety of textures.

A wispy filler, *Helictotrichon sempervirens* or blue oats (above) lends distinction to an entry planting in a bed of spring heath, with a bright pot of petunias nearby. The arching foliage and unusual color also make it an excellent choice for front-of-the-border placement with almost any combination of annual or perennial flowers. Or use it as a cheery sidewalk edging.

The dramatic grouping at the edge of a patio (opposite page, top) is just one of the shows grasses can put on around your home. Three varieties team effectively in that arrangement: at the back is tall *Spartina pectinata,* often called cordgrass; the tasseled specimen in the center is annual fountain grass, or *Pennisetum setaceum;* around the edges are tufts of the bluish *Festuca ovina,* or sheep fescue.

Sheep fescue by itself can also make a wonderfully work-free ground cover. The silvery blue tufts have ornamental value—with practical value as a bonus. The ten-inch wiry clumps grow in sun or shade equally well but don't tolerate traffic with the resilience of many other ground covers. Sheep fescue is a good choice in Zone 3 southward.

Towers of *Miscanthus sinensis,* a winter-hardy perennial grass, provide eye-level privacy for loungers and sunbathers on the patio. It grows up to six feet high. A variegated form of this species, commonly called zebra grass, is also available for use in the garden.

Another perennial ornamental grass to consider is *Erianthus ravennae,* or plume grass. It sends up 12-foot-high plumes from three-foot plants. Bamboo-like *Arundo donax* (also called giant reed), six to eight feet tall, is hardy in the South and makes a good potted plant in the North, if you have a suitable spot to overwinter it indoors. *Carex morrowi 'variegata,'* a sedge, is another perennial possibility; it's just a foot high and has striped foliage.

Don't overlook the outstanding grasses that can be grown annually from seeds. Try bold pampas grass *(Cortaderia)*—a half-hardy perennial usually grown as an annual. Its silky plumes wave ten feet high. Cut and dry them to add a natural, comfortable look to a corner indoors where live foliage plants don't survive because of low light. Pampas grass seems to fall in and out of favor with interior designers; no matter, this natural material is inexpensive. Use them any way you want indoors.

Outdoors, add a decorator's touch with the popular edging plant, liriope. Blooming in summer, its flowers resemble grape hyacinth. This ground cover is fine for the shade. Set the young plants nine inches apart in a spot protected from foot traffic. Liriope is a good choice in Zone 5 and any place south.

Or try quaking grass *(Briza).* It forms bushy plants just a foot tall and has cone-shaped seed heads that tremble in a breeze. For something different, plant job's-tears *(Coix lacryma-jobi).* It sets pearly-white seeds that can be dried and strung for beads. Other annuals good for long-lasting mixed bouquets are foxtail millet *(Setaria italica),* cloud grass *(Agrostis nebulosa),* and squirreltail grass *(Hordeum jubatum).*

Seldom-used ornamental grasses deserve attention as dramatic landscape accents—and for other uses limited only by your imagination. However, take care to keep ornamental grasses under control. Some are self-seeding, so pick seed heads when mature to keep plants confined.

Tall cordgrass, tasseled fountain grass in the middle, and bluish sheep fescue make a delightful grassy trio.

For sunbathing or tea-sipping, there's no place like the backyard. Miscanthus sinensis *fills in the screen.*

Attract Wildlife to Your Garden

Plant a special garden and soon special friends will come calling. A wildlife garden brings a new dimension to your backyard. The trees and shrubs that attract birds and furry little animals are lovely, too.

This stone-basin birdbath nestles among rock garden plants and blooming alpine species.

When you have a wildlife garden, you're a part of the soothing but always busy world of nature. Keep your bird feeder supplied with seeds in the winter and add bits of string in the spring and you'll have visitors darting in and out of the yard. But when you have the plants they love, too, they are more likely to set up housekeeping or call even more often. If you can boast wildlife visitors, the sweet scent of flowers, and the beauty of berried trees and shrubs, you'll have the most pleasing, alive garden ever.

But the advantages don't stop with the aesthetics. Consider birds, for example. As natural controllers of insects, their ability is unequaled. Fledglings more than double their own weight in insects eaten daily during summer months. A single flicker can consume thousands of ants a day.

Four basic needs are shared by birds and other wildlife: food, water, shelter from weather and enemies, and a safe home. The natural hollow in a rock (above) set among rock garden plants and blooming alpine species makes a perfect birdbath. The inverted lid of a garbage can or a snow saucer sunk in the ground can serve equally well as an inviting watering and bathing place for birds.

If you have dogs or cats, you'll soon find out that wildlife view them as marauders. But they often can coexist with some help from you. When pets share the same yard with wild visitors, be careful to plant "escape" shrubs close to bird-baths, and set feeders away from overhanging limbs or beams from which your usually docile tabby can stalk.

Some wildlife get a bit greedy so that other visitors are driven away. Squirrels, for example, appreciate a drink at a birdbath. To keep squirrels welcome, provide ground-level feeders for them and swinging or pole-supported feeders for birds. Without this plan, squirrels will raid the bird feeders. If you're trying to grow vegetables, screen the crops with wire-mesh and lath boxes or cages so squirrels don't overeat.

Even a more formal birdbath is a watering stop for squirrels.

Honeysuckle fruits are choice food for robins, sapsuckers, and waxwings.

Berries for birds

Bird-pleasing berries are borne by colorful trees and shrubs that make charming additions to your yard. Many of these heavily fruiting trees and shrubs bloom beautifully in the spring or early summer, so you get a colorful bonus in addition to the birds that come to dine later.

When planning your landscape to attract birds, include shrubs such as flowering quince, abelia, boxwood, holly, privet, mock orange, yew, and rugosa rose. Plant trees such as horse chestnut, serviceberry, redbud, eastern wahoo *(Euonymus atropurpurea)*, hawthorn, and sweet gum. For bird fare during summer months, you might also include Virginia creeper, chokeberry, barberry, dogwood, honeysuckle, hackberry, red mulberry *(Morus rubra)*, and elderberry.

Huckleberry fruits *(Gaylussacia* sp.) are choice food for robins, sapsuckers, waxwings, and bluebirds. The fruits appear in abundance on tall handsome plants that form an excellent privacy screen for outdoor living areas. With little or no care, they'll give you a perennial supply of food for your fine-feathered visitors.

Perhaps the most brilliant fruit in late summer (and into the winter months) is produced by the mountain ash. It also has handsome foliage and is well suited to small properties. This ash does best in full sun. The red-orange fruit clusters attract robins, bluebirds, cedar waxwings, finches, grosbeaks, woodpeckers, catbirds, grouse, and Baltimore orioles.

Annual and perennial flowers can provide food throughout the summer and fall. The seeds of sunflowers, marigolds, and zinnias are popular with the birds. Check with local nurseries, bird societies, and the county extension office for regional advice.

If you really appreciate birds, provide food supplies for the hardy ones spending the winter in your area. They'll go for such fruiting plants as bittersweet, hawthorn, euonymus, holly, juniper, buckthorn, sumac, and hemlock.

To prevent birds from damaging those fruits you're going to use, protect trees with netting. Also, plant berried shrubs to give birds a free meal. Your fruit trees won't look quite so alluring. Tempt birds away from strawberries, blackberries, raspberries, and cherries by dotting mulberry, serviceberry, and elderberries around your yard. Virginia creeper could divert them from grapes. You'll probably suffer some losses, but these other attractions should reduce them. Keep feeder trays filled with an assortment of seeds, grains, nutmeats, and some grit, such as sand or crushed shells. A separate hanging of suet will keep bird traffic brisk. Place such treats well away from your garden.

Birds vary in their preferences. Although many birds like to augment their insect diets with your vegetables, berries, and other fruits, wrens are, first and foremost, insect-eaters. They have a preference for leafhoppers, plant lice, scale insects, whiteflies, and even the tiniest insect eggs. Install a wren house to encourage a pair to set up housekeeping in your area.

Cotoneasters line their branches with stem-hugging fruits that are delightful prizes for many kinds of birds.

Planning a "Wild" Garden

In nature, plants that grow in a certain area result from a network of causes—the climate, soil, topography, and more. The plants will attract certain birds and animals. In your yard, you are the one to evaluate the conditions, select the plants, and place them to attract little creatures to your "wild" garden.

Planning a garden with wildlife in mind differs from most other kinds of landscaping because all the trees and shrubs have two purposes. They either provide food in the form of fruit, seeds, or berries, or are exceptionally well suited as nesting sites or shelter. Of course, many of the fruiting species are ornamental at flowering time, too, so you aren't completely sacrificing beauty in the bargain.

If you stagger the planting over several years, put the trees in the ground the first season. They grow slowly and should be given priority in your garden.

As a rule, shrubs give the effect you want sooner than trees. Put them in the planting plan the first season, if budget permits, or at least by the second season. For example, you might start by planting a *Symphoricarpos albus* (or snowberry) in the spring. You'll find it a useful shrub because it's small and grows in partial shade. The snowberry's white, grape-like fruits are a good lure for jays, grosbeaks, juncos, and finches. Later, you might add a mountain ash tree. It grows to medium size and is excellent for city lots.

Cotoneasters come in many sizes and shapes. Their fruits are appreciated by many kinds of birds, including robins and waxwings. The tall, spreading varieties of cotoneasters make a tight green hedge; medium sizes are for foundation plantings; and low, spreading forms are great for naturalizing.

While waiting for plants to mature, set out feeders and provide water. In fact, many wildlife enthusiasts continue to provide food even after their trees and shrubs are mature. One reason is that they have a better opportunity to view visiting birds and animals at a well-placed feeder. Also, even a carefully planned set of trees and shrubs won't produce food crops constantly. Supplemental feeding is in order.

Many specialists feed birds all year, believing that summer birds will maintain their high ratio of animal (insect) food versus plant food, regardless of ready availability. Feeder food draws flocks, and the birds complete their meals with a dessert of garden insects.

On the plan (opposite), you'll notice brush and rock piles. Devices such as these are valuable for shelter. Bolster this effect by relaxing a little when cleaning your garden. Don't rake under dense stands of shrubs and trees. A small length of rotting log could harbor a friendly toad. During the night, toads eat just about any pest that moves—cutworms, slugs, and potato beetles. One toad can devour up to 15,000 insects in a garden season. Provide a shallow container of water to encourage toads to remain in your garden.

Also include an open area, like the grassy section in the plan. Robins and other birds find grass a gold mine of worms after a summer rain. You will also want to keep an area open for your own enjoyment and to better see your wildlife visitors.

KEY for right page

1. **Flowering dogwood** *is a large shrub or small tree with fruit favored by 36 species of birds. The plant's flowers are ornamental. Native on East Coast and in the South; use red-osier dogwood elsewhere.*

2. **Highbush cranberry viburnum** *is a tall, upright shrub with showy white flowers and glossy red fruit. It grows quickly bearing fruit the second year.*

3. **White oak,** *a grand shade tree that produces acorns enjoyed by squirrels, blue jays, thrashers, and flickers, is a good nest site.*

4. **Elderberries** *are decorative small trees that produce fruit tasty in pies and jams. The 30 species of birds that like elderberries will give you competition on the harvesting.*

5. **Wild species** *of grapes will attract birds when fruit is ripe. Other vines providing cover are bittersweet and Virginia creeper.*

6. **Brush piles** *of twigs and small limbs provide protection from predators, as well as nest sites. When set near watering/bathing spots, birds and small animals can use the shelter as a place to escape when frightened.*

7. **Winterberry** *attracts 22 species of birds, along with some animals. These big shrubs often serve as nest sites, too.*

8. **White pines** *are large trees that work well as winter windbreaks, screens, and nest sites. Cardinals, chickadees, and crossbills are just a few of the species of birds that use white pine seeds for food.*

9. **Blackberries** *permitted to naturalize into a thorny tangle become nest sites and escape areas. Berries are popular as food for birds.*

10. **A shallow pool** *of water is essential for birds and other animals. Unless you want fish, make the pool only a few inches deep, with a rough-finished or rocky surface. Sweep it out often and add fresh water, or install a recirculating pump.*

11. **A rock pile** *becomes protection for toads and other tiny creatures.*

12. **Crab apples** *are small, ornamental trees that produce bird-pleasing fruits. Don't get one of the sterile varieties, such as Spring Snow. They don't set fruits.*

13. **Hawthorn** *is a petite, domed tree with clustered flowers and red fruits. It provides choice sites for nests.*

14. **Viburnum or nannyberry** *attracts blue jays, robins, bluebirds, waxwings, and many other songbirds.*

15. **Honeysuckle**—*a tall variety, not a dwarf—does well along a fence. It will take shade of the surrounding trees and shrubs.*

16. **Red maples** *are dense trees with tops for nesting but serve as only a fair food source for birds.*

17. **A beech tree** *supplies nest sites. Big birds, such as flickers, grosbeaks, and woodpeckers, like the nuts; squirrels love them, also.*

18. **Autumn olive elaeagnus** *is good for shelter, escape, and food. Let it grow in shrub form; do not prune heavily.*

19. **Sumac,** *an interesting tall shrub that produces conical clusters of red fruits, pleases 17 birds. Plants sucker freely and can become a pest.*

20. **White spruce** *is a native evergreen that gives good winter cover.*

Cedar posts laid horizontally edge informal planting beds.

Herb Gardens

Herbs display nature's beauty and magic. Yet, they demand little care, spread naturally, and have unique fragrances. Their leaves, stems, blossoms, roots, and stalks are used for the fragrance and for flavoring you'll love.

Herbs offer a wide range of choices. Whether sweet or sour, subtle or strong, they can be planted formally or informally.

Formal arrangements, or traditional herb plantings, date back a long time. The Roman nobility's idea of luxury was a well-ordered garden gracing the entrances to their homes. A simple, traditional design consists of two three-foot paths crossing at their midpoints. The four square herb beds may be bordered with brick or stones.

Another popular design is the wagon wheel. Bricks or stones are sunk into the ground to form the "spokes" and "rim." Herbs are planted in the wedge segments.

Appearance is important in the traditional herb garden. Keep the walks trimmed and use mulches to combat weeds and retain moisture.

Informal arrangements, such as a sea of spearmint crowding a lawn or walkway, give a refreshing scent when the mint is trampled underfoot or clipped with the lawn mower. Creeping thyme and chamomile offer the same results.

Plant a small garden near your kitchen door. A seven- by 12-foot plot can accommodate as many as ten varieties of herbs. The plot should be in full sun and the soil well drained. Plant your favorites, such as chives, thyme, sage, parsley, basil, rosemary, and mint.

Or, plant a triangle garden. If the sides are about 14 feet long, the garden can hold six or seven differ-

If yard space is limited, plant in pots. These fiber pots are lightweight.

Camphor-scented southernwood makes tending summer squash a delight.

ent kinds of herbs. Plant taller mints at the back of the garden. Next, four or five sage plants, then equal amounts of parsley and summer savory. Set chives along the front leg of the triangle and a plant or two of thyme in the corners.

Plant annual cooking herbs among your vegetables. However, plant perennials along the edges of your vegetable garden because it will be tilled each year. Grow parsley and basil as a border around the vegetables. Sow dill and coriander between tomatoes, cabbage, and broccoli. Herbs often distract or repel pests from your vegetables.

Herbs in containers are handy if you are short on space. Push flue tiles into the ground to make attractive planters and keep the herbs in bounds. Or set out plants in individual clay pots. Indoors, place potted herbs in a sunny window receiving four to six hours of light per day, or grow them under artificial lights. Mist plants occasionally and water regularly.

Use herbs fresh in salads or brew them in teas. Or dry them for fall arrangements, potpourris, or sachets. Several herbs can be frozen. Tie tarragon, chives, parsley, dill foliage, and basil in bunches; then blanch or steam for a minute. Cool, seal in plastic bags, and freeze.

Plant a variety of mints, lemon verbena, balm, thyme, sage, comfrey, and chamomile for traditional teas. Making herbal tea is simple. Use one tablespoon of fresh leaves (or one teaspoon of dried leaves) for each cup of water. Pour boiling water over the leaves, and cover the teapot to let it steep. After three to five minutes, strain and serve.

A potpourri is a fragrant blend of dried flowers and spices. To make one, you will need many dried rose petals and a mix of dried garden herbs. Herbs to consider include: sage, lemon verbena, rosemary, rose geranium, thyme, mint, basil, chamomile, and caraway. From your spice rack, add cinnamon, allspice, mace, cloves, or nutmeg. Orrisroot is a scent preservative that must be added and can be purchased at most pharmacies. Cure the potpourri in a covered container for five to six weeks, stirring it every few days.

The simplest traditional design has two three-foot paths crossing. According to the ancients, this cross frightens evil spirits.

ABCs of Herbs

Through the ages, gardeners have grown herbs. Reasons have varied—and still do. In other times, some herbs were thought to have magical powers. Try your hand at growing herbs for flavorings, teas, a potpourri, and dried arrangements.

ANISE
Pimpinella anisum

Use leaves to spice up salads or act as a garnish. This annual grows to two feet tall.
Planting: Plant in a sunny location when all danger of frost has passed in the spring. Sow the seeds where the anise is to remain; the seedlings do not transplant well.
Harvest: When the flower clusters turn gray-brown, clip them into a paper bag. Store the dried seeds in airtight containers.

ARTEMISIA
Artemisia sp.

You'll find two major perennial groups in this family—wormwood and southernwood. Height will vary with the variety. Both are grown for their attractive gray-green foliage and delicate scent. Southernwood has lemon-, camphor-, and citrus-scented varieties.
Planting: Start either group of plants from root divisions or stem cuttings. Wormwood also can be grown from seeds sown in a sunny location in late fall or early spring. In cold climate areas, mulch with two to three inches of leaves or straw for winter protection.
Harvest: Cut back the plants in the fall. Use the dried stems whole in decorative arrangements.

BASIL, SWEET
Ocimum basilicum

Grow this annual herb for its fragrant leaves and as a tasty addition to stews, roasts, and casseroles.
Planting: Start seeds six to eight weeks early indoors, or sow directly outside after all danger of frost has passed. Keep plants pinched

back for continuous growth.
Harvest: Snip the leaves off the stem before flower buds open. Spread in a well-ventilated, shady area until dry. Store in airtight containers out of direct sunlight.

BAY
Laurus nobilis

In ancient times, bay (also called laurel) was made into garlands for victors.
Planting: Buy small bay plants from a nursery. Put them in a sunny area with well-drained soil and in tubs or pots. Bay will grow three to six feet tall. If you live in the northern part of the country, move plants indoors during the winter.
Harvest: To dry the leaves, hang branches in a dark room where the temperature doesn't exceed 70 degrees Fahrenheit. Store in airtight containers.

BORAGE
Borago officinalis

Plants produce starlike, blue and white flowers in early summer and continue until fall. Blossoms are attractive to bees, too.
Planting: Sow seeds in a sunny location in early spring.
Harvest: Pick young leaves as needed. This annual will grow to 18 inches tall.

CARAWAY
Carum carvi

Caraway seeds give a gourmet—and tasty—touch to your baking and candy making.
Planting: Sow seeds in a sunny location in late fall or early spring. Caraway is a biennial that grows to eight inches tall the first year and to 24 inches the second year.
Harvest: After flower clusters turn brown, clip their seed heads into a paper bag, and shake them so seeds come loose.

CATNIP
Nepeta cataria

Use fresh or dry catnip for tea.
Planting: Set out seeds or divisions in sun or partial shade in fall or early spring. Plants are perennial, spread rapidly, and grow to three feet tall.
Harvest: Pinch leaves off and spread in a shady, well-ventilated area until dry to the touch. Store dried leaves in an airtight container out of bright light.

CHERVIL

Anthriscus cerefolium

Wake up dozens of recipes—from beans to yogurt—with the tart taste of chervil.
Planting: Sow seeds in a sunny location in late fall or early spring. Do not plant them deeply; light is needed for germination. Pinch plants for continuous growth. They'll grow to two feet tall.
Harvest: Clip whole plants before flowering, and hang them upside down in a shady location. Store dried leaves in airtight containers in a dark room or cupboard.

CHIVES

Allium schoenoprasum

Grow chives near the back door so you can snip some and add them to your dinner. Dried leaves lose freshness quickly.
Planting: In early spring, plant seeds or divisions in a sunny place. Pinch back to encourage vigorous growth. Use leaves fresh or frozen.
Harvest: Pot a few bulbs in late summer and leave outdoors under mulch until frost. Then, bring the pot inside and place in a sunny windowsill for a harvest all winter.

COMFREY

Symphytum officinale

Use fresh young leaves in salads and tea.
Planting: Plant in a sunny or partially shady location with a slightly alkaline pH.
Harvest: Pick comfrey before it flowers. Dry leaves and roots. Store in airtight containers.

CORIANDER

Coriandrum sativum

Recipes for fruit salad, pickles, and stew have a special taste with coriander.
Planting: After danger of frost has passed, plant seeds in a sunny location where the coriander is to remain. This annual grows to 30 inches tall.
Harvest: When the flower clusters turn brown, clip the seeds into a paper bag. Coriander often reseeds itself.

CRESS, GARDEN

Lepidium sativum

Garden cress, a garnish, should not be confused with watercress, a member of the nasturtium family. Also called peppergrass, its

curled-leaf varieties are most flavorful.
Planting: Sow seeds in the spring as soon as ground can be worked. Make sowings every week for a longer harvest. Garden cress, an annual, also can be grown indoors.
Harvest: Leaves can be harvested as early as ten days after planting.

DILL

Anethum graveolens

Dill is decorative as well as a key ingredient for favorite pickles. It's also good with cooked vegetables.
Planting: Sow in a sunny location after danger of frost has passed.
Harvest: Pinch off leaves in early summer, and dry them in a cool, airy place. Seal dried leaves in an airtight container. Clip flower heads, when brown, into a paper bag. Store seeds in an airtight container.

FENNEL

Foeniculum vulgare

Actually an annual, fennel acts like a perennial plant in warm-climate areas.
Planting: Plant seeds or transplants in full sun after danger of frost has passed.
Harvest: Use fresh leaves as needed. When the flower heads have turned brown, clip entire seed heads into a paper bag.

GARLIC

Allium sativum

The bulb of the garlic adds its strong flavor and scent to favorite foods.
Planting: Plant garlic cloves in a sunny location in the early spring. In the late summer, when the tops begin to turn yellow, bend them over with the back of a rake.
Harvesting: Dig bulbs when foliage turns brown. Store bulbs in a net bag, or braid tops to form a rope. Hang in a cool, dark, well-ventilated area.

GERANIUM, SCENTED

Pelargonium sp.

Scented varieties divide into six categories: rose, lemon, mint, fruit, spice, and pungent.
Planting: Scented geraniums are annuals in cold winter areas and perennials in warm climates. Start seed ten to 12 weeks early indoors, or buy transplants. Plant them in a

GERANIUM, SCENTED (continued)

sunny location after danger of frost has passed. Scented geraniums often are grown in containers and hanging baskets.
Harvest: Snip fresh leaves as needed. Clip leaves in the fall and dry in a well-ventilated, shady area. Store in airtight containers; or use in nosegays, potpourris, and sachets. Pot cuttings in late summer, and bring indoors for year-round use.

HOREHOUND
Marrubium vulgare

Use horehound leaves for tea or syrup. This perennial grows from one to three feet tall.
Planting: Horehound can be propagated from seeds, cuttings, or divisions. Start from seed in the spring or fall or from cuttings, spring through summer; or divide large plants in spring. Horehound does well in poor, dry soil.
Harvest: Cut back June through September to avoid burrlike blossoms. To dry leaves, hang them in a warm location, then seal in an airtight container. Pot plants for winter.

LAVENDER
Lavandula sp.

You'll find three kinds: English is showiest and produces the most fragrant flowers; spike lavender produces larger, fragrant leaves; and French is used as a bath fragrance.
Planting: Start all varieties indoors ten to 12 weeks early. Lavender seeds have low germination rates, so plant many. Set outdoors after danger of frost has passed.
Harvest: Clip fresh leaves as needed and flower heads before they open. Mulch in cold climates.

LEMON BALM
Melissa officinalis

This perennial grows to two feet tall. Lemon balm makes a refreshing addition to chicken, fish, or lamb.
Planting: Sow seeds indoors ten to 12 weeks early, or directly outdoors in a sunny or partially shady location after all danger of frost has passed. Do not cover seeds completely with soil; light is needed for their germination.
Harvest: Snip fresh leaves for tea and as an ingredient for other recipes.

LEMON VERBENA
Aloysia triphylla

The leaves have a fresh lemon scent and may be used in potpourris or drinks, or added to stuffing.
Planting: After frost danger passes, set cuttings or seedlings two feet apart in a sunny, well-drained area. Lemon verbena is a deciduous perennial and is often planted in containers, where it will grow to six feet. The plant drops its leaves in winter or when brought indoors.
Harvest: Dry the leaves in trays in the shade. Store in an airtight container.

MARJORAM
Origanum majorana

Snip fresh leaves as needed.
Planting: Sow seeds eight to ten weeks early indoors. Set seedlings in sunny garden spot after all frost danger passes. When blossoms fade, cut the plant back several inches to encourage new growth. Marjoram is an annual in cold areas; perennial in warm.
Harvest: Hang the plants in a warm, well-ventilated area until dry. Strip off leaves and store in an airtight container.

MINT
Mentha sp.

Popular mint varieties are apple mint, orange mint, spearmint, and black peppermint. Mint plants spread and can become like a weed.
Planting: Plant seeds or root divisions early in the spring. Divide mint plants every few years.
Harvest: Clip fresh leaves any time. To dry, cut back stems to the second set of leaves just before the plants flower. Hang stems in a well-ventilated, shady area; then store in airtight containers.

OREGANO
Origanum vulgare

Wild marjoram is another name for this perennial. It will grow to a foot tall.
Planting: Sow seeds in mottled or partial shade after frost danger has passed. Pinch back plants to encourage bushiness.
Harvest: Clip leaves as oregano begins to flower. Dry in a sunny, well-ventilated spot. Store in airtight containers. In the fall, cover plants with two or three inches of straw or leaf mulch to keep them from winter-killing in cold climates.

PARSLEY
Petroselinum crispum

Pot up young plants in late summer for wintertime harvest.
Planting: Sow seeds outdoors in late fall or early spring.
Harvest: Cut fresh sprigs as needed. To freeze, wash thoroughly first. Dry the whole plant, crumble the leaves, and store in airtight containers.

ROSEMARY
Rosmarinus officinalis

Rosemary, a perennial, reaches four feet in warm climates. It will not survive the winter in cold climates.
Planting: Start seeds indoors in midwinter, or plant stem cuttings.
Harvest: Snip fresh leaves as needed. To dry, cut the plant back by half while in bloom. Dry in a shady, well-ventilated area, and store in airtight containers. In cold climates, pot up stem cuttings in late summer for use during the winter.

SAGE
Salvia officinalis

Although sage can be grown from seeds, you will get faster results from root divisions.
Planting: Sow seeds outdoors in early spring. Or plant root divisions or stem cuttings. Trim plants to encourage bushiness.
Harvest: Clip fresh leaves as needed. To dry, cut the stem tips when flower buds begin to form; spread the tips in a shady area. Cover this perennial with mulch in winter.

SUMMER SAVORY
Satureja hortensis

Savory, an annual, grows to 18 inches tall.
Planting: In early spring, sow seeds outdoors in a sunny location.
Harvest: Clip fresh leaves as needed. To dry, cut the whole plant before flowering. Hang in a shady area. Store in airtight containers.

SWEET CICELY
Myrrhis odorata

Sweet cicely prefers shady, moist, rich soil.
Planting: This perennial grows best from self-sown seeds, because the plant needs to freeze and thaw to complete its growth cycle. Transplant seedlings in spring.

Harvest: The green leaves or green seeds are anise-flavored. Use roots raw or cooked.

SWEET WOODRUFF
Galium odoratum

Leaves are valued for making "May wine."
Planting: Seeds have a long germination period. It's better to make stem cuttings or root divisions in the spring or fall. The perennial grows to only eight inches and likes shady, moist, acid soil. It spreads rapidly and requires pruning.
Harvest: Snip leaves while the plant is in bloom. Dry in a shady, well-ventilated place.

TANSY
Tanacetum vulgare

Use with beef, fish, lamb, pork, or omelets. Some people find tansy too bitter.
Planting: Divide established plants in early spring and set two feet apart. Roots are invasive, so put in bottomless containers.
Harvest: Dry flowers for use in arrangements.

TARRAGON
Artemisia dracunculus

Pot up plants in late summer for use during the winter. Choose the French variety for taste preferred in food dishes.
Planting: Plant stem cuttings or transplants in a sunny location in early spring. Divide established plants every few years. Keep plants mulched to avoid damaging the dense, shallow root system with hoeing.
Harvest: Snip fresh leaves as needed. To dry, cut the plants back to four inches in early summer and early fall. Store cuttings in airtight containers when dry. Cover the perennials with more mulch for the winter in cold climates.

THYME
Thymus vulgaris

Bees are attracted to thyme, a perennial.
Planting: Sow seeds four to six weeks early indoors or outdoors after all frost danger passes. Or plant stem cuttings or root divisions in a sunny location.
Harvest: Clip fresh leaves as needed. To dry, cut plants back to two inches before flowering. Spread cuttings in a shady, well-ventilated area. Store in airtight containers away from bright light. In cold climates, add mulch for winter.

Rock Gardens

Eroding slopes, inclines too steep to mow, grade changes, a slant from house to walk or driveway—many landscaping problems are solved with a rock garden. To avoid a helter-skelter look, start with a rough sketch of where the rocks and plants will go.

Plants teamed with rocks are often the best answer when a bank has to be held in place against erosion. Also, up-to-date architecture often features the creation of sharp grade changes; when the change is nearly vertical, a low wall may be required. A dry stone wall (where materials are loosely piled instead of mortared together) may be the answer for a grade change from terrace to street, for example. The resulting planting pockets between the rocks are perfect locations for favorite rock garden plants.

Be prepared. Although the results may have a casual and informal look, rock gardens will take planning and hard work to establish. And not all your effort will be visible. About a third of each large boulder will be hidden in the side of your "hill." But once the work is done, it is low-care and can be admired for years.

Careful planning is the essential first step in establishing a good rock garden. Before you cut into the bank, you must know what type and size of rock you'll be using. Plot where rocks will go and where you want interesting undulations in the slope. Plan, too, where major plantings will be.

Just two or three huge boulders are sufficient for a large rock garden. ("Huge" means about three feet in width, length, diameter, or all three.) If the boulders are being hauled in from the countryside or

A rock garden near an entrance looks like a dry creek bed, with river rocks leading down from the driveway.

a nursery, have them dropped as close as possible to their assigned location in the garden. This will simplify the backbreaking job of moving the heavy boulders.

Best rocks are those that look at home in your setting: those naturally found in your area or some that harmonize with rocks used in your house or patio paving. All the rocks should be of the same general kind, rather than a geological collection. Weathered rocks are preferred.

Lightweight porous rocks, such as limestone, are ideal. They absorb moisture and act as a buffer during dry spells. Nonporous rocks, such as granite, can cause rapid drying of surrounding soil because they don't absorb moisture. Avoid novelty rocks that call attention to themselves and overshadow the plants. Also, avoid all soft and scaly rocks, shale, and unweathered sandstone. For a small area, avoid heavy labor by using easy-to-handle synthetic and volcanic rock.

For the best effect, try to keep the design as informal as possible. The rocks themselves should look as if they were embedded there a century ago, and the plants as if they volunteered to grow without any assistance from a gardener. Vary shapes and sizes of stones, but avoid geometrical arrangements.

When the major boulders are in place, fill the voids between them with soil mix. Start with a base of garden loam and make it more absorbent by adding perlite, vermiculite, or peat moss—about a fourth the volume. Rich soil isn't necessary and may even make the dwarf plants grow too big for their assigned places.

Plants for your garden can include annuals, dwarf evergreens, perennials, hardy bulbs, and succulents. For year-round stability and beauty, you'll want a planting of shrubs. Dwarf mugo pine, cotoneaster, and creeping juniper can fill the bill. Perennials, such as artemisia and sedum, also can be part of the permanent plantings. Then blanket the remaining areas between stones with colorful bedding and foliage plants you set out each spring. For showy color, assign three to a dozen adjoining planting

For summer color, try petunias, geraniums, fibrous begonias, marigolds, dusty-miller, and sedum.

pockets to a dazzling plant, such as red moss phlox. It will soon grow into one bold mass.

To provide a long season of bloom, include pockets of spring-flowering bulbs in your plans. As their foliage dies down in late spring, fill in their spots with bedding annuals. For color in the fall, plant a few cushion mums.

As a rule of thumb in selecting plants, use those that are known to grow well in your neighborhood. This can cut down on replacements.

Cover the soil around plants and stones with mulching material—redwood bark is a good choice. The mulch will keep down weeds. Rock gardens are easily maintained, but they cannot fend for themselves. If weeds do peek through, pull them out by hand. The dwarf plants usually planted in rock gardens generally don't compete well with weeds.

Primroses, tulips, daffodils, and rhododendrons give a spring glow.

A rock garden is a beautiful way to hold a slope. With careful planning, you can stagger plants so the garden is colorful from spring to fall.

Putting rocks into place

For a natural effect, embed at least the bottom third of boulders in your rock garden. Slant flat rocks back into the soil to divert water to plant roots. If rocks are placed in a horizontal position, slanted forward, or placed so upper rocks overhang lower, water will run off them instead of soaking in.

Set the rocks into the slope to form a series of small plateaus and planting pockets. A long slope should be handled as a series of ledges. Start construction at the bottom of the slope, and use both large and small stones to avoid the look of even ridges.

Rock walls should not be absolutely vertical; the face should slant back slightly, with bottom stones larger than top. A slant of two inches for every foot in height is sufficient. Form planting pockets by breaking stones at an angle to form V-shaped spaces. Rock walls are built like masonry walls, except mortar is replaced by soil.

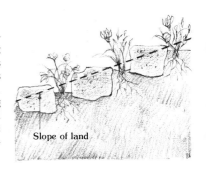

Slope of land

Flowering plants for rock gardens in sun

Alyssum
Evergreen candytuft
Pink saponaria
 (*Saponaria ocymoides*)
Dalmatian bellflower
 (*Campanula portenschlagiana*)
Siebold sedum
Moss phlox
 (*Phlox subulata*)
Thyme
Dwarf columbine
Pink
Creeping veronica

Small rosettes and tufts for sunny exposure

Blue fescue
Dwarf thrift
Dwarf pink
Hen-and-chickens
 (*Sempervivum
 soboliferum*)
Woolly yarrow
Ajuga
Dwarf iris

Sedum, cerastium, and cranesbill fill planting pockets.

Plants for shade

Bleeding-heart
Fern
Phlox
Hepatica
Forget-me-not
 (*Myosotis* sp.)
Caladium
Primrose
Tuberous begonia
Bloodroot
 (*Sanguinaria* sp.)
Hosta
Lily-of-the-valley

These start easily from seed sown among rocks

Kenilworth ivy
Bleeding-heart
Blue phlox
Fairy linaria
Iceland poppy
Spanish poppy

Good dwarf annual flowers

Dahlberg daisy
Pygmy marigold

Sanvitalia
Sweet alyssum
Portulaca
Fairy linaria

Spreading plants for large banks

Lavender
Catnip
Cerastium
Moss phlox
Sun rose
 (*Helianthemum* sp.)
Woolly veronica
Hardy verbena
Silver Mound
 artemisia

Annuals suitable for low walls and banks

Dahlberg daisy
Ageratum
Torenia
Fairy linaria
Pygmy marigold
Siberian wallflower
Nierembergia
Lychnis
 (*Haageana* hybrids)

Small bulbs

Crocus, Cloth-of-gold
 (*Crocus angustifolius*)
Grape hyacinth
Chionodoxa (or glory-of-the-snow)
Siberian squill
Galanthus
Kaufmanniana tulip
Eranthis (or winter aconite)

Dwarf shrubs

Alberta spruce
Canby pachistima
Dwarf alpine willow
Dwarf Japanese yew
Garland flower
 (*Daphne cneorum*)
Hypericum
Rhododendron—dwarf
 species and hybrids
Sand myrtle
 (*Leiophyllum* sp.)
Scotch heather
 (*Calluna vulgaris*)
Teucrium

Hints for rock walls

Plan your rock wall carefully and you'll have not only a unique way of displaying plants but also a useful means of preventing erosion.

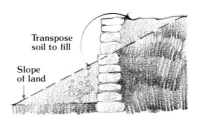

To get more use from a sloping lawn, level it with a retaining wall (above). If the wall is mortared, concentrate on spreading plants set behind it to soften the hard line across the top. Pinks, cerastium, and alyssum are possibilities.

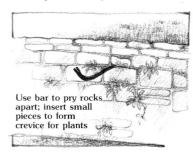

To replace or add plants to an almost vertical wall, spread roots flat, and wrap in wet sphagnum moss. Use a bar to pry rocks apart, and wedge small stones in to make

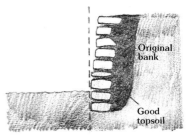

a crevice for plants. Make a downward slanting hole, and slide the wrapped roots into the crevice on a flat trowel, spatula, or pancake turner. Fill in soil around roots.

Think first of stability when building a new wall. Slant the face back slightly. Ram good soil mix between stones. If possible, plant the perennials as you build.

Shady Gardens

Cool shady spots—so welcome on blistering days—are gardening challenges. Light is a requirement for any plant, but some can get by on less than others. Try the shade-loving plants described on these pages.

A location in semi-shade suits lots of plants. Try fibrous begonias, cyclamen, Japanese maple, ferns.

Many plants tolerate shade but bloom sparingly without more sun. Others prefer shade and won't grow or bloom as well in full sun. You'll have many plants from which to choose for non-sunny spots.

This shade is created in many ways—a nearby apartment house, the spot between the garage and house, a patio on the north side. You can create lush settings for protected patios or decks by filling adjacent planting areas with shade plants or massing potted plants. If you're willing to rotate container-grown plants into the sun for a few hours each day, your choices are almost limitless. Suggestions here feature plants that tolerate shade permanently. Most of these plants get only indirect light, but this is great for ferns and for ivies draping the walls. Potted plants could include a pink camellia, blue lobelia, fatsia, caladium, and impatiens.

A shaded front walk can extend a special welcome when bordered with flowers. Combine alyssum and fibrous begonias for a white-on-white effect. Plants soon will grow to good size if planted in loose, rich soil and fed lightly each month.

In the narrow space at the side of the house (as shown at right), planting beds and planters in the paving make room for several plants, including fibrous begonias, cyclamen, ivy, privet hedge, ferns, and a Japanese maple. Container-grown plants (here, azaleas) provide color.

A shady border in spring can feature the fascinating early growth of ferns: they uncurl! Mix them with arched spikes of bleeding-heart and the bright colors of bulbs. A low mound of wild ginger will soon form a compact carpet. Large leaves of hosta will provide dramatic contrast to the surrounding lacy foliage.

You'll find advantages to developing a restful haven of plants in that shady stretch or corner. It's far more pleasant to tend to a garden out of the blazing sun. And you may find yourself with fewer gardening chores: plants in the shade require less water, and their flowers almost always last longer.

You're not limited to any one type of plant. Shade-loving plants can be found among annuals, hardy perennials, hardy bulbs, tender bulbs, ground covers, vines, evergreens, deciduous flowering shrubs, and small trees. (Check charts in the chapters covering each kind of plant.)

Perennials for shade. For a refreshing lift year after year, plant several of these perennials.

• Astilbe, sometimes called false spirea, has fernlike leaves and spires of white, pink, or red fluffy flowers on two- to three-foot plants.

• Bee balm is a fragrant plant. The scarlet, lavender, pink, or white blooms appear in late summer.

• Bishop's weed, or goutweed, *(Aegopodium podagraria)* makes a delightful ground cover when planted with ferns and hostas. It's a vigorous creeping perennial and should be contained. The variegated type is generally the best to plant, because the green-leaved variety is more invasive.

• Bleeding-heart, with its pink, heart-shaped flowers, flourishes in spring. The foliage dies down in summer. Everblooming, dwarf varieties are available, also.

• Carpet bugle, bugleweed, ajuga—all are names for the ground cover *Ajuga reptans.* Its six-inch-high spikes of blue flowers are showy in the spring.

• *Helleborus niger,* or Christmas rose, isn't really a rose, but it's a choice plant that has beautiful flowers at a surprising time of the year. Its leaves are large (ten inches across), evergreen, and divided like fingers. Time to plant is early spring or early autumn. Choose a protected place shaded in summer but with winter sun. Soil should be deeply prepared, with humus worked into it. Water well all year. Similar, but spring-blooming, is the *Helleborus orientalis,* or lenten rose.

• Columbine's airy blossoms come in white, yellow, pink, red, or blue. The plants grow up to three feet tall.

• Coralbells have tiny pink bells on two-foot stems. The plant is decorative even when not in bloom because of its neat tufts of leaves.

• Hostas have leaves varying from thumbnail to platter size and from glossy smooth to heavily quilted—depending on variety. These elegant but hardy plants are best known for their leaves, yet also have spikes of white or blue flowers.

• Primroses merit a spot in the shady garden. There are many types. All sport rich, green foliage—crinkled or sometimes ruffled—and two-tone flower blendings of red, yellow, pink, white, and purple.

This 15x15-foot area offers in miniature all you could want in a garden. The emphasis is on container-grown plants.

Other shade-loving perennials include: hardy ageratum, anchusa, gentian, globeflower, jacob's-ladder, leadwort, lobelia, lungwort, and meadowsweet.

Annuals for shade. For variety, select different annuals each year. They come in a wide assortment of bloom and foliage colors.

• Coleus plants are pretty from the moment they are set out. They are available at garden centers.

• Impatiens' blossoms are small, but their effect is great because of their prolific blooming habit. The mounds of glossy green foliage are all but covered with evenly spaced flowers that range through shades of red, orange, pink, and purple to the purest of whites.

Other favorite annuals that thrive in less-than-sunny spots include: begonias, calliopsis, cynoglossum, mignonette, and torenia.

Wildflowers also are topnotch candidates for shady spots. (See pages 346 and 347.)

Tall Aloe striata *contrasts with the sharp-toothed aloe next to it and low-growing succulents with rounded leaves.*

Desert Gardens

Lots of heat and little water may seem to be certain disaster for a garden, but careful selection of plants that love such desert-like conditions can mean an exotic view instead of a barren wasteland.

Combine cactus and other succulents with hardy annuals and perennials tolerant of dry soils. You'll have an exquisite arrangement of fleshy foliage and colorful blooms. Cactus and other succulents have long been popular among plant collectors and hobbyists for indoor and greenhouse gardening. Now enthusiasts are finding those plants suitable for outdoor use, too. Especially in the Southwest, where the climatic conditions are favorable for the growth of most succulents, these plants provide beauty year round.

Winter care. In cold climates, tender types can be placed in the garden during summers, either in sun or partial shade. Before frosts come, these plants must be brought indoors to a well-lighted window. Or plant them directly in the soil and, in the fall, snap off the offsets to make houseplants. After the offsets have roots, reduce water. Two waterings per month are needed.

Culture. In general, cactus and other succulents require a medium-rich, well-drained soil and as much sunlight as possible. Rock gardens and rock walls are good locations for many cactus and other succulents.

For once, rocky ground or a slope are gardening advantages; otherwise, mix in sizable amounts of sand and pebbles to get the soil to drain more quickly. Feed with a high phosphorus fertilizer once a year—in early spring when new growth begins. Provide iron if plants yellow. Water only when weather produces drought-like conditions.

The wide variety of plants within this group means you can find a cactus or other succulent compatible with your climate, landscape, and other plantings. Besides the familiar spike and barrel shapes covered with spines, there are many shrubs and ground covers.

Pick a plant. Best-known cold-hardy kinds that survive winter temperatures in the North are sedums and sempervivums.

Sedums (sometimes called stonecrop and live-forever) come in both trailing and upright varieties. Some are evergreen; others, deciduous. Flowers, though not the main attraction, are pretty. Trailing sedums are often planted in crevices in rock walls or used as a ground cover. Upright sorts can be used to edge perennial borders. All sedums propagate easily; leafy stems produce roots when placed in moist soil.

Sempervivums (often called hen-and-chickens) are rosette in form and evergreen in foliage. As big rosettes mature, they send up flower stalks, then die; but many small plants carry on.

A more striking succulent is the vertical *Aloe striata,* (opposite page), with smooth-edged, spear-like leaves. The orange to red blooms are long lasting.

The *Aloe brevifolia* (below) is a spiny, well-shaped specimen. The cluster of thick, sharp leaves send out flower stalks 20 inches high with red flowers throughout the year.

Although fewer cactus thrive in cooler zones, the flat, round, *Opuntia fragilis* is one of the cactus hardy through Zone 4.

Aeonium arboreum, *three feet high, has rosettes of leaves and yellow blooms.*

Aloe brevifolia *is three inches high.*

This low-care planting emphasizes a variety of sizes, textures, and colors.

Dazzling fillers

Check with a local nursery for the best cactus and other succulents for your area. Then fill in between with the annuals and perennials listed below.

Perennials
Baby's-breath
Baptisia
Butterfly weed
Coreopsis
Felicia
Flax
Gaillardia
Heath aster
   (*Aster ericoides*)
Liatris
Lychnis
Phlox
   (*Phlox subulata*)
Rock cress
   (*Arabis* sp.)
Rudbeckia
Spurge
Yarrow
Yucca

Annuals
Amaranth
Ammobium
Arctotis
Aster
Browallia
Celosia
Cleome
Cornflower
Cosmos
Dusty-miller
Feverfew
Four-o'clock
Gaillardia
Gypsophila
Ice plant
Poppy
Portulaca
Rudbeckia
Salvia
Star-of-Texas
   (*Xanthisma texana*)
Sunflower
Zinnia

Water Gardens

Water lilies, lotus, and other aquatics may be legends along the Nile and in the Orient, but they'll grow equally well in a tub on your patio or small pool in your yard. The introduction to this chapter (page 337) features a planting pocket around a minute pool made from a 2x3-foot washtub. Slabs of rock and plants outline the edges.

Any watertight container can be transformed into a tiny garden pool. Preformed plastic or fiber glass pools are available, or use a PVC (polyvinyl chloride) pool liner. A wooden tub or half barrel can be set above or into the ground. The picture (at right) and the drawing (below, left illustration) show both approaches.

Exquisite water plants grow in soil-filled containers submerged in water. If you're using a single large plant in a big tub, plant directly in the bottom of the container and fill tub with water. Pools should be at least one foot deep. If the pool is deeper, use bricks or rocks to prop the containers up to the correct planting level.

At planting time, fill the container with garden loam. Incorporate slow-release fertilizer at the rate suggested on the package. Add clay to the mix for lotus.

Plant hardy water lilies in late spring. Press soil firmly about tuber, so crown of plant is above the soil line. Top the soil with a layer of sand. The surface of the sand should be six to eight inches below the surface of the water. In late fall, store hardy water lily tubers in a cool spot in the basement. If you try tropical water lilies, treat them as annuals.

Lotus tubers are planted horizontally, so the growing tip extends above the soil. Cover the rest of the tuber with a shallow layer of soil and a sprinkling of sand. Cover the growing tip with two to four inches of water. After the plant becomes established, increase water to ten inches. Store tubers in a cool basement over winter.

A dripstone, combined with an underground waterline, gives the effect of a musical, natural spring. The dripstone (see drawing, far right) extends far enough forward to form a sound chamber. Water lilies dislike running water, so use other plants around the pool edges.

An underground waterline funnels the water to your garden pool. Before starting, check local building codes. Buy enough half- or three-quarter-inch plastic pipe to run from the sill cock to the shutoff valve in the garden area and add

several feet—enough to run sill cock to about six inches below ground. Also buy a single or multiple control valve, two elbow connections, pipe adapters for the control valve, a two-foot length of three-quarter-inch galvanized pipe (threaded at both ends), a sill cock assembly, a saddle tee, drain valve, and pipe joint compound.

Perk up your patio with a wooden tub full of exotic—but hardy—water plants.

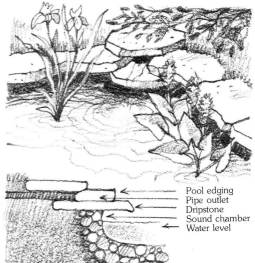

Pool edging
Pipe outlet
Dripstone
Sound chamber
Water level

How to install an underground waterline

1. Make sure you turn off the water at the main entrance valve to your home.
2. Remove the existing sill cock with adjustable

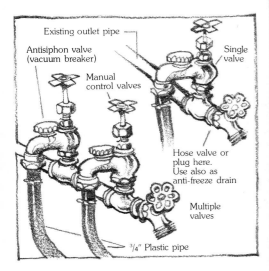

pipe wrench. Uncoil the plastic pipe and stretch it out in the sun. The sun will warm the plastic, making it easier to handle.

3. Attach the control valve to the existing outlet pipe. If the sill cock is of the freezeless type, it will extend inside your house about a foot, so you will have to add a piece of pipe to replace the length lost because of removal of the sill cock assembly.

Apply joint compound to the male threads only to seal the pipe joint. Use a tee fitting to connect valve and sill cock (as shown above). An antisiphon valve or vacuum breaker prevents the water from the system from flowing back into the water systems in your house. The vac-

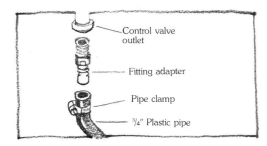

uum breaker should be at least seven inches above the level of the ground outside.

4. Connect the plastic pipe to the control valve, using a fitting adapter and a pipe clamp. Use pipe joint compound on the male threads of the adapter. The pipe is positioned on the adapter and is secured with the screw-type clamp.

5. Stretch out the plastic pipe and turn on the

Combine wood and water with a deck next to a sunken fiber glass pool.

water at the main entrance valve to test the system. Then turn the water off again.

6. At the garden outlet point, assemble the short length of galvanized pipe—sill cock on one end, adapter on the other—to connect the galvanized pipe to the plastic pipe. Then install a drain valve in the plastic pipe; for this, you'll need a saddle tee and drain valve. Place loose gravel around the valve. Bury this end of the system several inches below the rest of the pipe for adequate drainage.

Use joint compound at the connections and a hose clamp where the plastic pipe joins the metal elbow.

7. Turn on the water and check the system.
8. Sink the pipe by digging a V-shaped trench, about six inches deep, along its length. Save the grass sod and reinsert it over the pipe.

Mark the position of the drain valve. In the fall in climates where freezing could be a problem,

shut the water off at the house-end of the system, and dig down the few inches to the valve; drain the system.

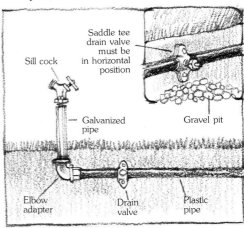

WATER PLANTS

Name	Type of Plant	Height in Inches	Description	Comments
Arrow arum *Peltandra virginica*	Moist soil	24-36	Cultivated for bold foliage, mass effect.	Best at edge of pool large enough to cope with a fast-spreading mass.
Arrowhead *Sagittaria latifolia*	Shallow water	12-24	Hardy. White flowers in summer.	Will also grow in boggy soil at edge of pool.
Bogbean *Menyanthes trifoliata*	Shallow water	10	White, fragrant, fringed flowers in spring and summer.	Best in mud (or submerged container) covered with less than 6 inches of water.
Bulrush *Scirpus sp.*	Shallow water	36-108	Grasslike leaves; chocolate-colored flowers in summer.	Invasive. Plant where it is easy to control.
Cardinal flower *Lobelia cardinalis*	Marsh or shallow water	24	Hardy. Fire-red spikes July to September.	For border or shallow running water.
Cattail *Typha latifolia*	Shallow water	18-48	Swordlike blades; dark brown spikes.	Effective bordering pool. To restrain, plant in tubs, and sink 2 to 4 inches in water.
Cinnamon fern *Osmunda cinnamomea*	Moist soil	36-60	Tall fronds in circular masses. Hardy, with tropical look.	Use in partial shade at pool edge as a background for plants in water.
Eel grass *Vallisneria spiralis*	Submerged	24	Ends of slender leaves float on surface. Fine oxygenator for fish.	Not cold hardy. Plant in pots and submerge.
Elephant's-ear *Colocasia esculenta* 'antiquorum'	Moist soil	18-36	Exotic leaves. For reflective value and framing the pool.	Plant tubers as close to water as possible. The more moisture plants receive, the bigger the leaves. Sometimes called taro.
Floating-heart *Nymphoides peltata*	Deep water	3-4	Round, pad-like leaves; yellow flowers in midsummer.	Rapid spreader. Plant in container (set one foot deep) away from water lilies.
Flowering rush *Butomus umbellatus*	Shallow water	36-48	Pink flowers July to September. Hardy.	Grow in submerged pot. Divide and repot each year or plant won't flower.
Forget-me-not *Myosotis scorpioides*	Marsh or shallow water	24	Clear blue flowers bloom May to October.	Needs only an inch of water. Also grows in any ground that stays wet or swampy.
Goatsbeard *Aruncus dioicus*	Moist soil	48-72	Delicate foliage; showy white flowers in June. Hardy.	For pool border as background. Delicacy contrasts well with heaviness of other plants. Needs a shady location.
Golden-club *Orontium aquaticum*	Shallow water	12-18	Tiny yellow flowers in spring; floating or aerial leaves.	Thrives planted to depth of 8 inches.
Grass pink orchid *Calopogon tuberosus*	Moist soil	12-18	Hardy. Rare, native. Fragrant pink blooms.	On conservation list in many states. Needs acid soil and shade.
Horsetail *Equisetum hyemale*	Moist soil or shallow water	12-48	Rushlike, ridged, leafless stems.	Grow at pool's edge (or in pots submerged nearly to rim). Needs partial shade.
Leopard plant *Ligularia tussilaginea* 'aureo-maculata'	Moist soil	12-18	Green leaves spotted yellow. Showy.	Ideal for lighting up a shady area.
Lotus *Nelumbo sp.*	Shallow water	24-36	Pink flowers; shield-like leaves rise 2 to 3 feet above water.	Hardy if roots don't freeze. Plant in containers of soil, then submerge in water.
Marsh marigold *Caltha palustris*	Marsh or shallow water	15	Buttercup-like flowers appear April through June. Hardy.	Lovely at edge of pool to reflect in water. Succeeds in moist soil.
Meadow beauty *Rhexia virginica*	Moist soil	12-24	Rosy-purple flowers in summer.	Provides good color among moist rocks, such as near a waterfall or rock border.

Name	Type of Plant	Height in Inches	Description	Comments
Ostrich fern *Matteuccia pensylvanica*	Moist soil	72-108	Bold leaves give massive effect. Hardy.	Can grow in full shade.
Paper plant *Cyperus papyrus*	Marsh or shallow water	48-72	Threadlike leaves; triangular stems.	For large ponds. For smaller ponds, try *C. alternifolius.*
Pickerel weed *Pontederia cordata*	Shallow water	24	Dark green foliage; violet-blue spikes bloom spring to fall.	Depth of water shouldn't exceed a foot. Best at edge of pool in about 3 inches of water.
Rabbitear iris *Iris laevigata*	Shallow water	24	Blue or white flowers in June and July. Looks somewhat like Japanese iris.	Tolerates water year round so is preferred over Japanese iris in continuously wet spots.
Swamp pink *Helonias bullata*	Moist soil	12-24	Leaves in basal rosette; fragrant pink flowers in spring.	Does best in boggy, acid soil.
Sweet flag *Acorus calamus*	Shallow water	6-36	Yellow-green blades; club-like green spikes.	Use in water at edge of pool or in moist soil around outside.
Tartarian dogwood *Cornus alba*	Moist soil	72	Lovely red stems; dingy white flowers.	Prune random stems of this shrub before new growth begins in spring.
Water arum *Calla palustris*	Moist soil	12	Flowers white inside, green outside in late spring.	Does best in mud at edge of pool. Provides good transition to plantings on dry land.
Water canna *Thalia dealbata*	Shallow water	36-48	Large blue-green leaves; purple flowers in summer.	Not cold hardy. Plant in containers and overwinter indoors as a houseplant.
Water chestnut *Trapa natans*	Floating	2-4	Feathery leaves below water and solid rosette above; small white flowers; edible seeds.	Propagation by seeds that drop to the bottom of the pool and overwinter there.
Watercress *Nasturtium officinale*	Shallow water	4-6	Hardy. Edible, bright green foliage.	Thrives in sun or shade and in cold running water.
Water hyacinth *Eichhornia crassipes*	Floating	9	Glossy green leaves; violet flowers.	Tender. Spreads like a weed in the South. Available only in states where supplies already exist.
Water lettuce *Pistia stratiotes*	Floating	2	Forms rosettes of fluted blue-green leaves.	Good in hot places with partial shade. Can be kept in place by letting roots take hold in a pot of soil.
Water lily *Nymphaea odorata*	Deep water	3-5	Many species, many colors. Spring through summer bloom.	Plant in container of rich soil. Submerge, with 6 to 12 inches of water above the container. Divide every few years.
Water milfoil *Myriophyllum aquaticum*	Submerged	6-18	Feathery leaves; flowers not showy.	Good oxygenator. Will need replacing periodically because fish eat it.
Water plantain *Alisma plantago-aquatica*	Deep or shallow water	12-36	Heart-shaped, plantain-like leaves; white flowers through the summer.	Blooms best in shallow water. Leaves narrower in deep water. Invasive.
Waterweed *Elodea canadensis*	Submerged	24-36	Dense whorls of leaves. Oxygenates water for goldfish.	Can be weedy if pool has soil bottom. To control, plant in container and sink in water.
Yellow flag *Iris pseudacorus*	Moist soil	30	Yellow flowers in spring.	For double pleasure, plant at border so plants reflect in the water. This can be a very showy flower.

Container Gardening

Postage-stamp yards, decks, balconies, and apartments are all prime candidates for container gardening. Many flowering annuals, bulbs, roses, vegetables, and even small fruit trees and shrubs do well. You'll find more tips on container growing in chapters devoted to specific groups of plants

Frequent waterings are a must for container plants. These strawberries thrive in flat-backed buckets along a wall.

Well-drained soil, sunlight to fit their needs, protection from overly playful breezes, fertilizer, and lots of moisture—container-grown plants have needs similar to almost any plants, but you are in charge of how much they receive and when their needs are met. Enhance their beauty by mixing and moving them around.

Remember to keep larger plants in the background and flowering varieties in a spot where the light is right. Almost all container plants should be turned occasionally to encourage symmetrical growth.

Remember, though, that strong winds can present a problem. If plants are not properly weighted with sand mixed with the soil or set in heavy containers, breezes can knock them over. Many plants, such as fuchsias, cannot tolerate the drying effects of wind.

Compared with those who can afford to scatter plants with wild abandon, container growers have to use their wits to get the most from less. For example, think of your outdoor space as having a vertical dimension (see opposite page), as well as a horizontal one.

Try displaying plants one above the other on a wall, either in hanging baskets, planters flattened on one side, or pots on shelves. Not only do you take advantage of the entire plant, but you dramatically increase your total growing room, as well.

Chances are, there will be a hot spot on your balcony, deck, or terrace that just can't seem to get out of the sun. Perfect for this are sun lovers, such as brightly tufted geraniums, a marvelous selection of roses, a vast array of flowering shrubs, or enough kinds of vege-

tables to make delightful, delicious salads all summer (see below).

Sun and heat can play some mean tricks, though; without ventilation and adequate watering, the sunny spot can turn into a micro-desert that will dry up even the hardiest of plants. Be sure containers are placed on bricks or pieces of wood to aid the circulation of air and be sure the soil is well drained. Check the surface of the soil frequently, and water when it feels dry to the touch. In midsummer, when hot days are the rule, daily waterings may be necessary.

Wine barrels—cut in half—had holes drilled in the base for drainage. They hold lettuce, kohlrabi, and Swiss chard.

A miniature kumquat tree provides pleasing background texture, as well as mottled shade, for geraniums and primroses.

A stately maple thrives in a container backed by a lacy screen.

edging plants, such as sweet alyssum, lobelia, and dwarf marigolds, about three to five inches apart; taller plants, such as petunias, celosia, and coleus, about four to six inches apart. Keep annuals with a tendency to get leggy, such as petunias and coleus, pinched back.

To get the best bulb blooms, remember good drainage. If the soil is waterlogged, bulbs may rot and succumb to disease.

Whether grown for their evergreen foliage or spectacular blossoms, shrubs can provide instant landscaping for a terrace, patio, backyard, or deck. Be sure to buy them to stay in scale with their containers and surroundings. Extra tall types, such as lilacs, are too large to thrive for long in containers. But medium-size, small, and low-growing shrubs, such as deutzia, cinquefoil, or the ever-popular hills-of-snow hydrangea, are ideal.

After you buy the plant, place it in a container as soon as possible. Fill the bottom of the tub with drainage material (broken pot fragments or gravel), and cover with several inches of coarse peat moss. Be sure your soil mix is adequately moistened. If you're using a clay pot, soak it in water first, so dry clay won't pull all the moisture from the soil. If you're planting a bare-root tree or shrub, fill the pot about halfway with soil formed into a little mound. Spread the roots around the mound and cover with additional soil. Water well.

Roses need six to eight hours of sunlight a day but seem to like partial shade during the midday hours. An inch of peat moss over the drainage material in their containers keeps the soil from filtering downward and possibly obstructing the free flow of water.

For the owner of a deck or balcony, vines are perfect for disguising pillars, poles, and other supports. Or a brick wall, exposed to the searing rays of the sun, can be transformed into a cool bower of gracefully climbing grape, wisteria, honeysuckle, or a spectacular rose, each grown in its own container.

Your favorite kinds of plants and the light conditions available can be brought together in a charming compromise. Many trees, shrubs, walls, buildings, and dividers cast restful, dappled shade just right for such sun-sensitive plants as fuchsia, coleus, impatiens, or tuberous begonia. Where deep shade prevails, use the delicate fronds of the various ferns and the trailing vines of the ivies.

Sometimes plants can be lifted out of the shade and into window boxes. Combine plants—flowering and foliage—that complement each other. For soil, buy a lightweight potting mix, or make your own with soil, peat moss, and perlite. Cover the bottom of the box with broken clay pot fragments, and add a layer of coarse peat moss or nylon netting. Then fill with soil. A handful of slow-release fertilizer mixed with the soil will keep the plants healthy. Moisten the soil thoroughly and set out the plants. Or put plants in separate pots and set the pots in the box. This way you can change pots as needed.

Annuals grow well in window boxes or a variety of other containers. Buy seedlings or start your own. When grown in pots or raised beds, most annuals will look best if planted close together. Space low

Hexagonal planters provide a natural, yet tailored, look to plants.

An arrangement of darwin, triumph, lily-flowered, early double, cottage, and early single tulips wait with a variety of daffodils to adorn your table.

Flowers for Cutting

The beauty of a main border can be marred by snipping flowers for floral arrangements and bouquets. But both a beautiful border and a house full of flowers are possible by growing a cutting garden.

A cutting garden is a plot of land set aside for the purpose of growing flowers for indoor bouquets only. If well planned, this garden will supply cut flowers for floral arrangements from early spring through late fall.

Grow a cutting garden in a sunny—but secluded—spot. Such a specialty is not grown for beauty outdoors but for the beauty of indoor arrangements. For example, set it behind a border, where the coming and going of blooms will not be noticed. Or plant it in your vegetable garden, because the culture of many glorious annuals is similiar to that of vegetables.

Include perennials, biennials, and annuals in your cutting garden, but set the perennials apart from the biennials and annuals so the perennials' root systems will not be disturbed. Plant short-season annuals and tender bulbs every three weeks for a succession of blooms. And select varieties that bloom at different times.

The flowers will grow best in rows running north and south. Developing to perfection, the flowers here may be picked often without a thought of causing gaps in a more visible border.

Little work is one of the charms of the cutting garden: prepare the soil, plant the garden, and keep control of the weeds.

Her Grace, a triumph tulip, is regal.

But be sure to prepare the soil well. Each year in the fall, add a compost mixture to the soil, and spade it in so the ground will be easier to work in the spring.

Through the growing season, hoe the garden regularly to control weeds. Or, after the flowers have sprouted, add mulch to keep weeds down.

There's no need to remove yellowing foliage from plants; the garden's only purpose is to raise cut flowers, not provide beauty outdoors. But you may want to remove the flower heads after they fade to prolong the flowering period. That way the plant will not waste energy on flowers past the right stage for displaying. Picking the spent flower heads will encourage the plant to produce another crop of blooms.

To make access to the flowers easier, make a path through the garden. A path can be just bare earth you walk on to pack down. This is simple to dig up if the garden is to be used later for another purpose. Or lay concrete slabs; they can be removed at the end of each season.

With extra planning, it's possible to grow two cutting gardens on the same plot of land within a year's time. In fall, plant a spring cutting garden; months later it is fresh with spring-blooming tulips and daffodils in a painter's palette full of colors. Later, you might dig up the bulbs and plant a summer cutting garden, complete with annuals blooming into autumn. Mingle vegetable plants among the flowering plants.

For year-after-year blooms, plant perennials in a spot all their own.

Tulips and daffodils grow profusely each spring if planted correctly. Plant the bulbs in good garden loam with thorough drainage. In the fall, work the soil and enrich with organic matter before planting the bulbs.

As with other plants, set bulbs in rows running east and west so they will receive the full benefits of the sun. (See Chapter 9, "Bulbs," for planting information.) Choose varieties that will complement the colors of your interior decor.

After the plants are through blooming, the foliage will turn yellow and die back.

If you've decided to go to the extra effort of planting a summer garden in the same spot, the spring-flowering bulbs will have to be dug up before all of the foliage has died back. However, this aging process is necessary for the strength of next year's bulbs. Dig a trench in another area and place the maturing tulip and daffodil bulbs there—dug intact with foliage—so the plants will die back naturally, completing the process of storing nutrients.

The spring garden diagrammed (at right) is five feet wide and 12 feet long. There are no paths in the garden because the flowers can be reached easily for cutting.

Several different classes of tulips are included in this spring cutting garden. Early double and early single tulips both flower in April in most parts of the country. Triumph and mendel tulips are mid-season bloomers. Darwin, lily-flowered, and cottage tulips all bloom about a month later. Choose varieties and colors in each of these classes that will complement one another in an arrangement for the table or sideboard. Twenty bulbs of each variety were planted in this garden.

For a sunny display of daffodils, plant double narcissus, large cupped narcissus, bicolor trumpets, yellow trumpets, pink daffodils, and white trumpets. With the help of a good bulb catalogue, choose varieties that bloom at different times throughout the spring.

SPRING GARDEN PLAN

DAFFODILS	TULIPS
Large cupped	Darwin
Double narcissus	Triumph
Bicolor trumpets	Lily-flowered
Yellow trumpets	Early double
Large cupped	Cottage
Pink daffodils	Early single
Winter trumpets	Mendel
Large cupped	Darwin

Spring cutting garden 5 ft. x 12 ft.

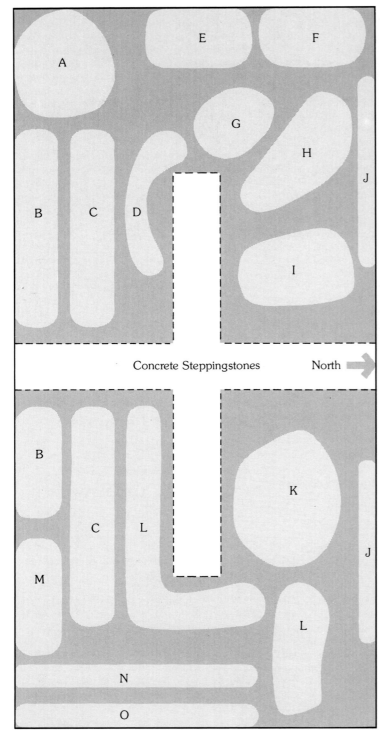

Concrete Steppingstones   North →

Summer cutting garden 7 ft. x 14 ft.

A. Zucchini
B. Geranium
C. Chrysanthemum
D. Scabiosa
E. Ammobium
F. Pepper
G. Xeranthemum
H. Marigold
I. Statice
J. Nasturtium on trellis
K. Tetra zinnia
L. Dwarf dahlia
M. Telstar petunia
N. Beet
O. Carrot

Summer and fall flowers bloom with vegetables. Fertile soil is a must.

Summer Cutting Garden

As spring warms into summer, plant a cutting garden with summer- and autumn-blooming beauties. Many kinds of annuals can be chosen. Select plants that will flower at different times throughout the summer.

Because the planting and culture of annuals are similar to vegetables, several kinds of vegetables also can be grown in your cutting garden. Peppers, zucchini, beets, and carrots will all grow well. Or, plant your cutting garden in the vegetable garden and eliminate preparing a separate plot of land.

Flowers bloom much sooner when seedlings are set out, rather than when seeds are sown directly into the garden. Start your own plants in early spring by sowing seeds indoors in a flat. Or purchase bedding plants from a good garden center. Dwarf dahlias and petunias should be sown in seedbeds or flats in early spring for a May planting date in the cutting garden. Plant only sturdy, healthy seedlings.

The summer garden (at left) is plotted creatively, much like a perennial flower border. (Straight rows work as well.) The path is optional and is made of concrete steppingstones so the annuals could be better reached for cutting and so weeding would be easier.

Many annuals make excellent dried flowers for fall arrangements. Dry statice, ammobium, and xeranthemum for long-lasting bouquets.

Chrysanthemums bloom until frost.

Handling Cut Flowers

Delight a friend and please your family with flowers from your own garden. Whether an artistically planned arrangement or a simple, single bloom in a bud vase, flowers brighten any room.

A little know-how about handling cut flowers will keep them glowing in a fresh floral arrangement. Flowers remain alive after cutting, so they need proper treatment and care to help them take up and retain water. They need a constant water supply to transport food and to keep the stems stiff.

Gathering freshly cut flowers in a basket may sound lovely, but if you handle cut flowers this way, they will lose water quickly and wilt. As a result, the flowers will have a short life. To gather flowers correctly, carry a pail of tepid water to the garden. Use lukewarm water, instead of cool, because the plants are stimulated by warmth and

slowed by coolness.

Cut flower stems at an angle and plunge them into the pail of water, deep enough to almost reach the flower heads. If putting several kinds of blooms in one pail, wrap each kind in sheets of newspaper first to keep them separated.

If you're cutting only a few stems

and bringing them indoors immediately, it isn't necessary to carry water with you to the garden. Instead, cut the stems and carry the flowers with their heads down. This will keep the stems straight and prevent the flower heads from breaking off.

Resnip each stem at an angle underwater before placing the stems in a pail of tepid water. Place the pail in a cool spot out of direct sunlight, and let stand until the water reaches room temperature. This may take several hours or even overnight. This step, which should

be done before arranging the flowers, is called conditioning.

It is best to pick flowers in the early morning or the late evening, when the temperature is coolest. Also, avoid flowers that have been marred by insects, diseases, or weather. The damage will detract from the beauty of your arrangement.

To add to the good looks and life of your bouquet, be careful to pick flowers that are at the perfect stage for cutting. Avoid buds that are too tight, as they will never fully open. Also avoid flowers that are at full bloom, because their life expectancy after picking will be short. For flowers that bloom in clusters, cut them when half of the blooms are open.

For stems that are thick or woody, make a one- to two-inch slit with scissors or a sharp knife from the base of the stem upwards. This will help the stem take in enough water for the blooms to keep supplied with moisture. Otherwise, moisture will not be available and

the flowers and foliage will wilt even more quickly.

Poppies, dahlias, and other garden flowers with hollow stems (or stems that secrete a milky substance when cut) need to be seared with a flame immediately after cutting. (See drawing below.) The burner from your chafing dish will do nicely. An old candle works just as well, however. Carry the candle or other means of producing a flame with you into the garden, and sear stems as you go. If the stems are recut when arranging the flowers, resear the stem.

Flowers whose stems have been seared still need conditioning by being plunged into a pail of lukewarm water and left there for several hours or overnight.

After tulips and roses are picked, their buds and flowers open in a hurry. To slow the process, gently hold the blooms shut with florist's tape until the fresh arrangement is put on display.

Always use clean containers for floral arrangements. Clip off all foliage that will be under the water level in the finished arrangement. Leaves in the water disintegrate rapidly, give the water a foul smell, and shorten the life of the cut flowers.

Heavy-headed flowers (such as the large mums at right) often bend by the flower head, nearly breaking off. To temporarily improve the situation, insert a toothpick pointed at both ends through the bloom into the stem. Such blooms are not long lasting.

If you want to use garden lilies in a centerpiece, snip off the pollen-bearing stems of each bloom before you make the arrangement. Otherwise, bits of stamen are apt to drop off and stain the flowers—and

the tablecloth below. These stains are hard to remove.

Fully opened chrysanthemums help make floral arrangements beautiful, but their petals drop off easily. To keep the petals on, hold the stems upside down and drip candle wax carefully around the calyx. The calyx is the outer circle of green under the petals.

In combining flowers, you'll find an arrangement is most effective when it has been designed to suit a specific setting. The size, shape, and color of a flower composition should fit into its surroundings and be displayed in a container complementing both flowers and decor. On a small table, a dainty arrangement is appealing and attention-getting. A tall vase requires height in the arrangement, and a shallow bowl will display a short flower arrangement well. Coordinating the colors of flowers to colors of room furnishings increases the importance of both. For example, yellow snapdragons and mums will pick up the yellows, golds, and similar shades in upholstery.

Place your finished floral arrangement away from drafts. Air circulating from fans or air conditioners will soon dry it out. Keep the flowers out of direct sunlight, too, as this will cause dehydration.

Dried Flowers

As winter whistles around corners and paints the landscape gray, you can have a souvenir of summer with a bright or subdued arrangement of dried flowers—many grown in your own garden. Some keep a sweet scent.

Unlike your favorite snip-and-display fresh flowers, a dried arrangement is a longer project.

Collect and dry flowers during the summer and fall. Gather blooms from flower gardens, herb gardens, ditches, roadsides, and creek banks. By winter, you'll have a supply of preserved materials.

Use any of several drying methods—all are easy. Select the method that best suits you: silica gel, borax, air drying, pressing, or glycerin.

Pick healthy flowers at various stages of development. This adds a natural look to your arrangements.

Silica gel

Using silica gel to dry flowers is called desiccant drying. A desiccant absorbs moisture, and, with flowers, the silica gel takes moisture from the plants.

Actually, silica gel isn't a gel at all, just tiny blue crystals. It is available at craft stores and is reusable. (To reuse, simply heat it for one hour in a 250 degree Fahrenheit oven. This will restore the crystals to full potency.)

A metal container with a tight lid, such as a cookie tin or a coffee can, is needed for this technique. Put one to two inches of silica gel in the bottom of the container. Place the flowers, with their stems cut to about one inch, face up in the drying medium. Do not let flower petals touch or overlap. Gently sprinkle another inch of the silica gel crystals over the flowers in the container.

Place the cover tightly on the tin, and put the container in a dark, dry place for the required amount of time (see chart, opposite page). When the flowers are dry, the petals should feel papery and brittle.

To remove the flowers from the container, slowly pour off the silica gel, while cupping your hand under the flower head. Gently shake off the drying compound, and remove any excess granules with a soft artist's brush.

When drying delphiniums, larkspur, rosebuds, other buds, snapdragons, lilacs, and leaves, lay them in a horizontal position in the silica gel.

For flowers that work well in silica gel, see the chart. Dark red flowers turn black in the process. Other colors are preserved beautifully.

This potpourri mix is attractively concealed beneath dried camellias, pansies, alyssum, rue, and more.

Store the dried flowers in airtight boxes, such as plastic shoe boxes, until ready for use. To keep the flowers in good condition, place the stems in dry floral foam. This will keep them from being damaged. To keep dried plant material in top condition, especially over prolonged periods or when excessive humidity may be a problem, add three or four tablespoons of silica gel to the storage container.

A petal that has fallen from a flower can be repaired easily. Place a dab of white glue on the end of the petal, and rejoin the petal to the flower center using a pair of tweezers.

Borax

Use ordinary household borax in the same manner as silica gel. Directions are the same, except the flower should be placed face down, and the lid should be left off while the flowers dry. Borax is a less expensive method than silica gel, but it takes twice the amount of time. Also, borax doesn't preserve flower color quite as well.

Air drying

Air drying is easy. Start by gathering flowers at midday when blooms are at their best. Don't pick flowers after a heavy rain or when they're covered with dew, because mildew can form and cause the flowers to rot.

Strip all leaves and foliage from the stems. Gather the stems together in a bunch and bind with elastic ties. Hang the bunches of flowers upside down in a dark, dry, well-ventilated room. The air drying process takes two to three weeks.

Pressing

A thick telephone book is perfect for pressing flowers. At one-inch intervals throughout the book, place a layer of newspaper with a layer of facial tissue on top. Put a flower on the facial tissue, and cover with another layer of facial tissue and newspaper. If the facial tissue is omitted, the ink from the newspaper or phone book may be picked up by the flowers. Use the same thickness of materials on each page

DRIED FLOWER AND FOLIAGE TIME CHART

Drying Method	Time	Plants
Silica gel	2 to 3 days	Coralbells, lantana, miniature rose, myosotis, viola
	3 to 4 days	Dwarf dahlia, dwarf marigold, feverfew, larkspur, pansy, small zinnia, tea rose
	4 to 5 days	Buttercup, delphinium, hydrangea, large zinnia, peony, shasta daisy
	5 to 6 days	Aster, calendula, large dahlia, lilac, marigold, snapdragon
Borax	Double above drying times	Any recommended for silica gel
Pressing	3 to 4 weeks	Buttercup, daisy, delphinium, dusty-miller, fern, hydrangea florets, lobelia, pansy, sweet alyssum, verbena, viola
Air drying	2 to 3 weeks	Annual statice, artemisia, bells-of-Ireland, blue salvia, celosia, Chinese-lantern, delphinium, glove amaranth, heather, honesty, larkspur, peegee hydrangea, strawflower, yarrow
		Field flowers: dock, goldenrod, pampas grass, teasel, tansy
Glycerin	1 to 2 weeks	Foliage: aspidistra, beech, crab apple, eucalyptus, holly, laurel, oak, peony, pyracantha, sycamore, yew

for even drying. With a weight (more books or a brick, perhaps) on the telephone book, store for three to four weeks in a dark, dry place.

The flattened flowers won't make three-dimensional arrangements but can be used to make a picture. Buds, stems, and leaves also can be pressed to complete an attractive picture. Use tweezers and white glue to anchor the flowers to the background material. Let the picture dry overnight. Then insert it in a frame and cover with glass. Tape the back of the picture to the frame, so the picture is airtight and will stay dust-free.

Glycerin

Foliage, such as peony, oak, and beech leaves, will be more supple and usable if treated with glycerin. Glycerin preserves foliage so it will last indefinitely. Before mid-August, gather all foliage to be treated because it will still be tender then.

A solution of one part glycerin and two parts hot water should be mixed in a jar. Shake well. Scrape or pound the ends of the young

branches, and place in two to three inches of the solution. Let stand for one to two weeks; much of the solution will be absorbed. The leaves should feel pliable and change colors to dark greens or soft shades of brown and rust.

Include the glycerinized foliage in dried arrangements and fresh floral arrangements; water will not damage the material.

The glycerin solution may be used repeatedly. Keep it stored in a tightly covered jar.

Dried arrangements

Dried plants can be added to both formal and casual arrangements. If flower and leaf stems are short, lengthen them with florist's tape and wire. Combine the blooms with glycerinized foliage in an arrangement in a container filled with florist's foam.

Insert foliage first, using it as a guide for height and outline. Place larger and darker flowers in the lower center section. Fill in the arrangement with more flowers, making sure some of them extend be-

low the rim of the container on the outside. Then place your completed creation in a spot out of direct sunlight.

For a carefree touch, try stalks of wheat, milkweed pods, cattail, and several sprays of curved bittersweet in a tall vase. Choose a vase of a neutral hue to bring out the autumn colors in the dried materials. (Soaring stems of pussy willow, which appear early each spring, will last through the year.) This type of arrangement is particularly at home in an entrance hall, in a corner of a room, or beside a fireplace.

If you use branches of bittersweet or mock bittersweet berries, remember that they are poisonous and should be displayed well out of the reach of children or pets.

Lavender pillows

Lavender pillows are simple to make and retain their fragrant scent for several months. Simply remove the lavender flowers from the stalks and combine with powdered orris-root. Stuff dainty pillows with the mixture. Use the pillows in closets, trunks, or dresser drawers.

chapter 12

VEGETABLES

There are many reasons people start a vegetable garden. Some enjoy working outdoors; some want the satisfaction of raising their own food. Others garden to keep physically active and save on their grocery bills. Still others garden just for fun. Whatever your reason for starting a garden, you'll soon realize that gardening is easy, enjoyable, and a great learning experience for both children and adults. A vegetable garden quickly becomes more than just something to tinker with; it becomes a way of life.

When you raise food crops, you become acutely aware of the sun, rain, and most of all, the life-giving soil. You work with these natural elements and sometimes battle them to produce nutritious vegetables for your table. Success brings an age-old satisfaction that goes back to the days when there were no supermarkets to use. Growing your own food is the best way possible to get a sense of season, of the natural cycles of the earth. The rhythm of sowing, growing, and harvesting can be just as valuable to your well-being as the vitamin- and mineral-rich harvest you eat, freeze, or can.

There aren't any mysteries to good gardening—all you need to know are some simple basics. After that, you'll probably learn more from firsthand experience than from a whole library devoted specifically to vegetable gardening. You're bound to have some occasional disappointments, but, on the whole, your many successes will surprise even you. And best of all, you'll get full-size, well-formed, tasty vegetables you'll be proud to feed your family and friends.

Planning Your Garden

Good planning is essential for a successful harvest. You'll save a lot of time and disappointment later on if you have a workable plan for your garden prepared well in advance of planting.

The first step to good garden planning is finding an acceptable site. Few backyards are perfect, but you'll have better luck if you place your garden in a spot where it will receive at least six to eight hours of sunlight a day. The site should be well-drained and close enough to the house for easy maintenance. A slight slope is also preferable.

Fertile soil is another feature to look for when selecting a garden spot. But don't give up in despair if the soil in your backyard seems tougher than cement. Even the worst soil is easily improved by adding manure, leaves, compost, old straw—anything to increase its organic content.

Then, after you select your garden site, make a list of what vegetables you want to grow, and study their spacing and cultural requirements. This way you'll know approximately how much garden space you'll need to dig. Or, to be more accurate, sketch the entire garden on paper, with the vegetables correctly spaced according to seed packet instructions.

If your yard is too small to accommodate all your favorite crops, eliminate some from your list. Squeezing too many vegetables into an area may become unproductive and messy.

When you are sketching the garden plan, always be sure the vegetable rows run in an east-west direction. North-south rows will shade each other as the sun moves across the sky. Taller crops should run along the north side of the garden. Also, be sure to consider including some flowers in your garden plan. They'll make the garden work more enjoyable and will make up for the space they use by attracting valuable pollinating insects.

Throughout the planning stages, try to keep long-range production goals in mind by leaving yard space for the perennial crops, such as rhubarb, asparagus, strawberries, raspberries, and grapes. Place these crops along the north and east borders of your garden where they can grow, undisturbed by yearly garden cultivation. Once established, these plants will become the backbone of your garden.

In the plan above, four 10x10 beds, located close to the back door, produce a steady supply of fresh vegetables and herbs throughout late spring, summer, and fall. Inexpensive concrete paving slabs, laid on strips of black plastic, crisscross the space between plots. The blocks form an all-weather path that makes caring for and harvesting the garden easier and keeps it neatly defined and attractive. Note that much of the space is used twice: the early crops of lettuce, radishes, peas, and spinach are followed by mid-season plantings of bush beans. Herbs are conveniently planted nearest the kitchen door to snip and use at the

last minute to perk up family meals.

When possible, space is saved by gardening vertically. Tomatoes, pole beans, and other crops that like to climb grow on stakes to prevent them from rambling over other lower-growing produce. The resulting harvest is cleaner and demands less stooping for the gardeners.

In the plan below, a strip of land 13 feet wide across the back of the yard was used, so the family's outdoor living and play area would not be broken up. The garden bed was raised above ground level with stacked railroad ties for aesthetic appeal and because a special soil mix was to be added over the poor soil left in the yard by the contractor

who built the home. Besides several truckloads of garden loam, the soil mix included compost, rock phosphate, cottonseed meal, and sand.

But before you plan for a raised-bed garden, there are two facts worth remembering. First, the soil tends to dry out quickly because it's farther from subterranean water supplies. Although the ground-level garden can get by on one thorough watering per week, the raised bed will need water at least every other day. And, second, the soil will compact more easily, which means you should avoid walking on it whenever possible. Use a wide board to stand on when planting seed or weeding between rows.

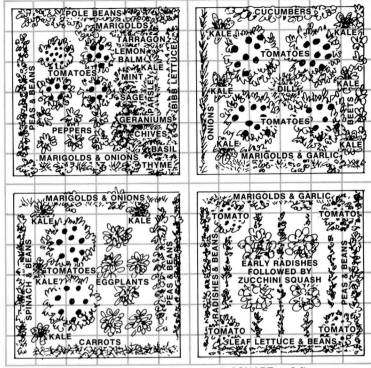

TOTAL GARDEN SIZE 23 ft. x 23 ft.   **ONE SQUARE = 2 ft.**

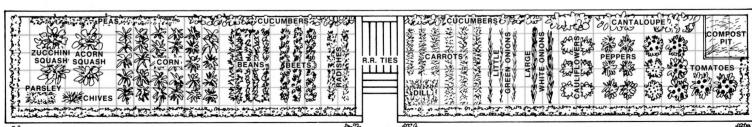

TOTAL GARDEN SIZE 86½ ft. x 13 ft.   **ONE SQUARE = 2 ft.**

Plot Your Lot

Your garden can be more than just a plot of ground with rows of vegetables and a smattering of flowers. Use your imagination to turn it into something memorable—fun, yet good-looking, peaceful and productive.

If you're lucky enough to have an acre plot, you won't have to shuffle space to make room for the vegetables you want. Those gardeners not so happily blessed have to plan carefully to make the most of the space they have.

As you plan your vegetable garden, keep in mind that vegetables are adaptable. They'll grow in almost any location, with little help from you, so long as they get a full day of sunshine. If your yard is small, hilly, or even wooded, don't despair—you can still raise more, bigger, and better vegetables than you probably thought possible and have a good time, too.

Determine the vegetables you'd like to grow, and do some reading on varieties that will adapt to your soil and sun conditions. Seed catalogues are ideal for this purpose. Don't include something just because every vegetable gardener tells you to grow it—if you don't like tomatoes, for example, using precious space to grow them is wasteful and time-consuming. That doesn't mean, however, that you shouldn't experiment—some of the offbeat vegetables can be fun to grow. Keep track of the varieties you plant. If one is a disappointment, switch to another variety next year. Eventually, you'll have a list of personal preferences that will grow well in your backyard with the amount of work you're willing to do.

Remember that every garden—like every gardener—is unique. That's one of the reasons growing your own is so rewarding.

A rooftop garden is one of the best ways to grow vegetables, if there is little or no space in your backyard.

The formal garden (at left) was designed to make the family's vegetable garden fit right in with their home's well-landscaped exterior. It hosts a variety of crops—from cabbage, broccoli, cauliflower, lettuce, tomatoes, and pole beans to dwarf rosemary, thyme, dill, chives, and basil in the bed surrounding the statue of Saint Francis.

Each bed is outlined with railroad ties that not only look good, but also help the soil retain moisture. Tile walkways through the garden provide easy access for weeding, harvesting, and planting the beds. The tomatoes are grown in cages for better harvests and to keep them neatly attractive. Potted dwarf apple trees round out the garden.

Another way to adapt your garden to your own needs is to grow vegetables in boxes and pots. This way, even if you don't have a speck of land to your name, you can get a respectable harvest of homegrown produce.

On the rooftop (above), pots of tomatoes and eggplant enjoy a full day of sun. The planting beds at right include melons, lettuce, and cucumbers. Dwarf and standard-size marigolds add color to every bed. Potted bulb flowers and shrubs can help give your rooftop a penthouse air.

If you decide to container-garden on a balcony, be sure it's strong enough to support the weight of several heavy pots. (They'll weigh even more when watered.) Plastic pots will probably be your best choice because they're lightweight. They'll need drainage, too; simply put a one-inch layer of gravel in the bottom of each container.

Plants in pots, especially on hot, windy rooftops and balconies, require plenty of moisture to replace that which evaporates. Before you start planting, be sure you have a convenient way to water all the pots. During midsummer, most pots need to be watered at least once a day. Morning is the best time.

Another important point to keep in mind before you start a balcony garden is that rooftops, sides of buildings, and fences reflect a fair amount of sun, making it more difficult to grow the cool-season crops, such as lettuce, beets, chard, and spinach. For best results, concentrate on the warm-season crops, such as melons, squash, tomatoes, and eggplant.

Planning Basics

No matter what size vegetable garden you have, your main goal can be high production. Never let space stand empty, and always plant two crops where many other gardeners plant only one.

Before you plant, check the planting dates for your area. These dates vary widely, even within states, so check with the Extension Service for accurate local information. Ask the dates of the last frost in spring and the first killing frost in fall. In frost-free areas, check on times to plant both cool- and warm-weather crops. You can also ask for recommended mid-season planting dates.

Cool-weather crops

The cool-weather crops that can be planted one month before the last frost are:

Beet	Kohlrabi
Broccoli	Leek
Brussels sprouts	Lettuce
Cabbage	Onion
Carrot	Parsnip
Cauliflower	Pea
Celeriac	Potato
Celtuce	Radish
Chicory	Rutabaga
Collard	Spinach
Endive	Swiss chard
Kale	Turnip

Warm-weather crops

The warm-weather crops that should be set out after the last frost are:

Bean	Okra
Celery	Pepper
Corn	Pumpkin
Cucumber	Squash
Eggplant	Sunflower
Ground cherry	Sweet potato
Melon	Tomato

Interplanting

Smart gardeners double up plantings whenever possible. This idea, called interplanting, lets them use the same space simultaneously for two crops. For example, fast-growing radishes are sown between young cabbages. The radishes mature before the cabbage plants need the space. Or sow a package of radishes between rows of corn. You'll get a good harvest of radishes long before the corn is tall enough to block out their sunlight.

Radishes also can be mixed half and half with carrot seeds. The radishes will sprout more quickly than the carrots and will shade the ground where weeds that compete with the carrots might grow. As you pull the radishes, you'll also be thinning the carrots.

Onions you intend to use as young green scallions can be set among cabbage, broccoli, cauliflower, or Brussels sprouts. Fast-growing leaf lettuces and spinach also qualify for interplanting with slower vegetables. Basil grows well around staked or caged tomatoes.

Beets and broccoli are another good combination. The beets grow rapidly in the cool, early spring weather, while the broccoli is just getting established. Later, as the broccoli plants begin to mature, the beets can be harvested.

If you have empty spots in your flower border, tuck in leftover plants of tomatoes, eggplants, or peppers. Many of the more colorful vegetables—such as red cabbage, rhubarb, Swiss chard, or flowering kale—can even be used to edge borders or walkways.

Another way to double your crops is to plant some of the many mini-vegetables. These pint-size vegetables mature quickly and rival their larger cousins for flavor. Team them with flowers, herbs, and normal-size vegetables; or plant them alone in their own special garden. Tom Thumb Midget lettuce forms heads in just 65 days; Tiny Dill and Pot Luck cucumbers grow on two-foot vines and start bearing in 55 days. For even more good eating, try the Golden Midget sweet corn (58 days), Mini Cantaloupe (60 days), or New Hampshire Midget watermelon (65 days).

Second cropping

To get bumper harvests, keep your garden in continuous production. When a cool-season crop, such as lettuce, spinach, radishes, or peas, is done, replant the space with green or wax beans, beets, turnips, Chinese cabbage, or a fast-maturing variety of sweet corn.

Tendergreen mustard, which matures in just 35 days, replaced early cabbage in the garden shown at left. Peas or lettuce can also be used if mustard isn't the family's favorite.

In some cases, it's wise to sow short rows of crops at one-week intervals, instead of a long row that's planted just once. Leaf lettuces, mustard, radishes, and spinach can be used effectively following this plan. Plus, when a short row matures, you aren't swamped with more produce than you need. And by the time you've used the first planting, the second row is ready to be harvested.

In most areas of the country, start seeds of mid-season replacement crops, such as Chinese cabbage, Brussels sprouts, and cauliflower, around the first week of July. Sow the seeds where the plants are to remain in the garden, or start them in an out-of-the-way corner and transplant them to the main garden later, after they've developed their second true set of leaves. Thin or transplant the young seedlings so they stand 12 to 18 inches apart. Then mulch with several inches of straw to keep down weeds and to increase soil moisture.

Give crops such as corn a head start by planting them indoors in peat pots sometime in June. Then, as the earlier crops die down, the corn can take over immediately.

Stretching space

If you're short of growing room, try vertical farming. A sunny section of chain link or woven-wire fence can support a big crop of vegetables. Standard-size cucumbers will completely cover a woven-wire fence by midsummer and be out of the way of other garden crops. Climbing peas, pole beans, melons, and squash also take to vertical growing. Melons and squash need sling supports to keep the weight from pulling the vines off the fence (see page 407). Improvise slings of net and tie to the fence, or use old panty hose.

Another space-saving trick is to grow vine crops on tepees made of lath stakes or bamboo poles. Plant seeds at the base of each stake, and get ready to harvest three times your usual crop. Low-growing, cool-season crops, such as lettuce and beets, can then be planted underneath, where they will remain shaded by the bean foliage during the hottest parts of the day.

If you have a surplus of shrub prunings, you might want to try piling them up in a corner of the garden and letting beans and peas ramble over the stack.

If you're not lucky enough to have a fence already, make a simple, inexpensive substitute out of 2x2s. They don't have to be perfect; the fence isn't decorative, just useful.

Use six-foot 2x2s for the stringers and seven-foot 2x2s for the posts (sink them one foot into the ground). Plan on one stringer six inches from the ground, one three feet up, and one at the top (cucumbers get heavy, so they need firm support). Add a post every six feet.

If your garden boundaries are likely to change in a year or two, don't bother setting the posts in cement. This will also save money spent on the fence. The fence will remain standing at least several growing seasons.

For fencing material, staple on inexpensive, tough plastic grow-netting. Staple the net to the first post, stretch it taut, and staple to the second post. Continue until the fence is complete. If you don't have a staple gun, you can nail on the net with U-shaped nails.

Now, plant the seeds about six to eight inches away from the base of the fence. Most climbers will cling without help. In the fall, the fence can be left in the garden or folded up and stored in a garage or shed.

Think Small

A large garden is nice if you have the time, interest, and space for it, but if you're only a part-time gardener, you'll probably get better results with a smaller, more manageable vegetable garden.

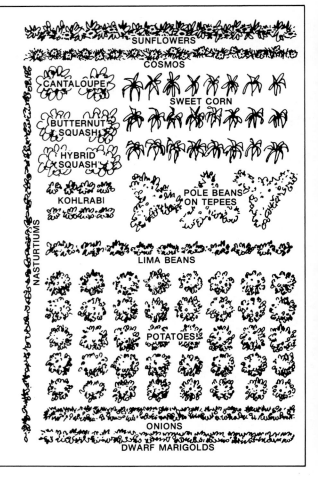

The garden at right measures only about 25x30 feet, yet it produced enough food for a family of four, with plenty left over for freezing and canning. Flowers added color but didn't steal much space.

To save on garden space, the long, rambling vine crops were eliminated. A bush form of butternut squash and the bush Scallopini squash took up little space and produced all summer long. Kentucky Wonder pole beans were also trained up wooden supports to save additional space.

To cut down on weeding and increase soil moisture, a four-inch-thick mulch of straw and grass was laid down between the rows when the seedlings reached two inches in height. By fall, the mulch had almost completely decomposed into the soil, adding valuable organic matter for the next growing season.

For efficient control of the cabbage butterfly, all the cabbage crops were planted together: cabbage, broccoli, Brussels sprouts, cauliflower, and kohlrabi were sprayed at weekly intervals with *Bacillus thuringiensis*. *Bacillus thuringiensis* (or B.t.) is a bacterial deterrent to the cabbage butterfly caterpillar. Savoy Ace cabbage, a recently developed strain of vegetable, seemed especially immune to insect attack and drought.

To keep the garden evenly moist, a 50-foot soaker hose, which could handle about four rows at drip pressure, was used. This system of watering took little time and did a thorough job of soaking the soil. Many vegetables consist of almost 90 percent water, and by soaking the soil around the root zone of the plants, you're ensuring a bigger, better crop.

You'll notice this plan does include some vegetables that ordinarily are not included in smaller gardens because they take up too much space or because they give a low yield in relation to the growing space required. Corn, for instance, yields much less for the space it takes than other vegetables. If you want a really high yield, you're better off giving some growing room to vegetables that produce big crops on compact plants or produce constantly for weeks or both.

Bush beans give you two or three pickings from each planting. With peas, you usually get only one major picking. Therefore, beans are better in a tiny garden because they yield more in relation to the space they take to grow.

Swiss chard continues to produce greens even after hot weather arrives; spinach does not. Broccoli produces several pickings a season, but cabbage can usually be picked only once.

None of this, however, should stop you from planting your favorites. Even in a garden where space is cramped, there should always be room for the vegetables you enjoy. Consider the "space/yield ratio" only when you are undecided about alternative vegetables.

With crops such as beans, peas, lettuce, radishes, beets, onions, carrots, parsnips, and even cabbage, you might want to plant them in wide rows or bands, rather than single file. This system is perfect for small gardens because plants sown close together produce up to four times as much harvest as the same area planted in narrow rows. Individual plants might not produce as much as when they are spaced according to seed pack instructions, but on the whole, the volume produced will be greater. And by planting in a short, wide block, you'll save valuable garden space.

Wide-row planting also helps eliminate that major gardening chore—weeding in the row. Few weeds can break through the solid cover of foliage produced by the closely planted vegetables. The only time you'll have to weed is when the vegetables are small and haven't yet filled in the space.

Another advantage of wide-row planting is the longer season of growth it creates for the cool-season crops. Plants that have a tendency to burn out in midsummer—lettuce and spinach, for example—will shade themselves and keep the soil around their roots cool and moist. This often will extend the harvest.

More food, more fun with more garden

If you have the land and don't mind a little extra work, expand your garden space and bring in a bumper crop of vegetables you'll be proud to feed your family. You'll save on the food budget and have a good time, too.

There are many advantages to thinking big. To begin with, you have enough room to grow the highly rewarding perennial crops, such as asparagus and rhubarb. Even better, you can devote part of the garden to growing small fruit. Eating homegrown strawberries, raspberries, or grapes is a pleasure your family will long remember.

A larger garden also means you can stretch out your harvest by growing plenty of vegetables to store for wintertime use. Potatoes, pumpkins, and the various winter squashes—which demand too much space in smaller gardens—are excellent storage crops.

Although the garden at right measures a whopping 50x60 feet, it still employs a lot of important space-saving techniques. Quick-growing, cool-season crops, such as lettuce, onions, and beets, are all interplanted with the slower-growing broccoli and cabbage plants. As the broccoli and cabbages mature, the cool-weather

crops are harvested from the area. Other vegetables—peas, beans, spinach, lettuce, onions, carrots, and parsnips—are grown in wide rows, rather than in single rows, to increase yields.

Because carrot seeds are so slow to germinate, they are mixed half and half with radish seeds at planting time. The radishes sprout quickly and prevent weeds from getting a foothold. Other space-saving methods include caging the tomato plants and planting mostly bush forms of pumpkins, squash, watermelon, and cucumbers.

To keep the garden producing after the early crops die down, a seedbed was constructed along one edge of the yard. Midsummer backup crops, such as Chinese cabbage, Brussels sprouts, and cauliflower, were then given an early start in this specially treated bed. As the season progressed, they were transferred to the main garden area.

The seedbed was made by laying railroad ties on the surface of the ground to contain a "super-soil" mixture, a combination of garden loam, compost, bone meal, cottonseed meal, and rock phosphate.

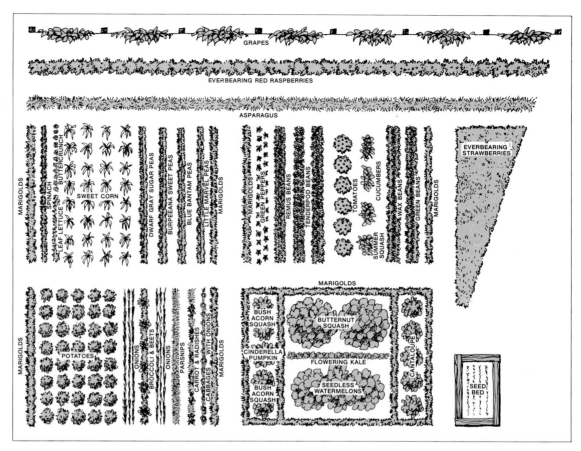

One of the best ways to start carrots from seed is to mix them half and half with radish seeds at planting time. As you pull radishes, you thin carrots.

To save garden space and reduce weeds, plant beets or other quick-growing, cool-season crops with slower-growing broccoli or cabbage plants.

Growing Food in Containers

Growing your own vegetables in containers on the back steps, porch, balcony, or patio is the best way to enjoy homegrown garden produce without taking up a lot of valuable space in the backyard.

Clay pots filled with high-quality potting soil make excellent containers for homegrown harvests.

Anything that will hold soil can be used as a container for growing a healthy, delicious harvest of fresh vegetables. Old kitchen pots, cake pans, plastic hampers, buckets, wood baskets, clay pots, wastebaskets, garbage cans, or even an old sink, washtub, small livestock tank, or wheelbarrow will do. Of course, if you have scrap lumber, you can make containers that will fit the size and shape of your balcony or porch.

Soil is perhaps the key element in a successful, container-grown harvest. It should be lightweight, so plants can be moved around, but it should also be heavy enough to give vegetables needed support, especially in unprotected windy locations, such as a balcony. Stones in the bottom of the receptacle help to keep it from tipping.

Container soil should also be able to retain large amounts of water, with plenty of peat moss, perlite, vermiculite, or well-rotted compost added to prevent drying out and soil compaction. But be prepared to water the vegetables often.

Buy specially prepared commercial soil mixes, or mix your own using equal parts of garden loam, peat moss, and coarse sand. (If your garden soil is already on the sandy side, eliminate the extra sand from the mixture.)

Commercial mixes are sterile, free from soil-borne diseases, and packed with nutrients essential to good plant growth. Although you can sterilize your own soil, it's messy and time-consuming even for a few containers. By using these commercial mixes, you are almost ensured of getting your crops off to a good start, but you do spend a little more money.

Unlike topsoil in your yard, container soil cannot soak up water from the subsoil. All pots and planters will need to be watered frequently (every day during dry, hot spells). Clay pots and hanging baskets are especially prone to drying out. Check them often.

Before you plant, make sure containers have adequate drainage. Poke holes in plastic pots with a screwdriver or ice pick, if necessary. If you are planting in wooden tubs or boxes, be sure there is a drainage hole every three or four inches.

Pots should also be large enough to hold a normal root system. Foliage will quickly turn yellow, due to lack of nutrients, if the pot is too small. Large vegetables, such as tomatoes and zucchini, need plastic tubs at least twelve inches deep. Smaller crops, such as carrots, green onions, and herbs, can get by with nine-inch-deep containers.

Once containers are planted, place them in a location where they will receive at least six hours of sunlight a day. And because your garden will be highly visible in the neighborhood, select plants that are decorative as well as functional, such as rhubarb, chard, or flowering kale plants. Or add some flowers—dwarf zinnias, dwarf marigolds, petunias, alyssum, and ageratum—that will not only provide plenty of color, but will also attract valuable pollinating insects to your container garden. Thyme and borage are two herb species that are colorful and popular with bees. The herbs are useful in cooking too.

CONTAINER VEGETABLES

With proper care, almost any vegetable can be grown in containers or pots, but the vegetable species listed below will stand an even better chance of producing a good harvest.

Beans: bush and pole	Kohlrabi	Potatoes
Beets	Lettuce	Radishes
Carrots	Melons	Turnips
Celtuce	Mustard	Roquette
Swiss chard	Onions, Green	Spinach
Cucumbers	Peas	Squash
Eggplants	Peanuts	Sweet potatoes
Kale	Peppers	Tomatoes

Getting a Jump on the Season

Even though most nurseries and garden supply houses stock a large number of vegetable transplants at planting time, they don't always have the varieties you want. So, to avoid last-minute substitutions in your garden plan, start your own seedlings at home.

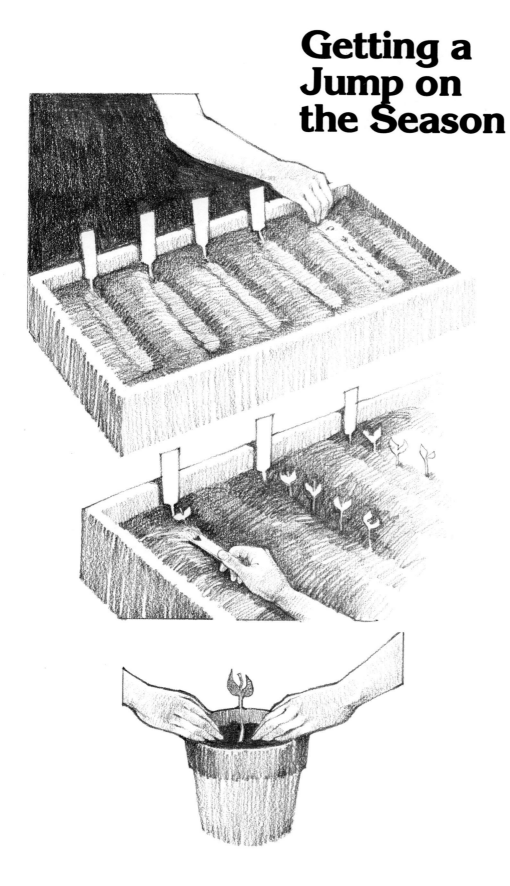

The first thing you'll need to start seedlings indoors is a flat, or shallow container. You can buy inexpensive plastic flats at most garden supply houses, or you can make your own from plywood. Just be sure the flat is only two or three inches deep and that it has plenty of holes in the bottom for drainage.

Fill the flat with an all-purpose potting soil, firming it gently with your hands. Then make a shallow furrow with a stick or pencil, and slowly scatter the seeds into it. Mark the row with a plant label or stake so you'll know what variety you've planted where. Other furrows can then be made at one- or two-inch intervals along the surface of the flat.

After the flat is planted, place it in a sunny window or under artificial lights in a growing unit. If you use a window spot, you'll need to turn the flat occasionally to avoid developing spindly plants. (You'll know when to turn the flat—the plants will lean toward the light.) With overhead artificial lights, you get sturdy plants that take off outdoors without any harmful setback. Keep the flat moist at all times.

Once the plants have developed their second true set of leaves, it's time to move them to a larger container to avoid overcrowding. Or, if you already have more growing than you need, simply thin out every other one, and let the remaining plants go right on growing in the flat. To thin, just snip the plants off with scissors.

Transplanting young seedlings is a lot easier than it sounds. All you need is a forked stick to prick the tiny plants out of the soil; a notched frozen treat stick is ideal. Gently press the stick under the soil around the base of the plant, and lift up.

You can transplant the seedlings to clay or plastic flowerpots, but for the plants to grow best, use commercial peat pots filled with potting soil. These peat pots reduce the shock of transplanting when the plants are introduced into the garden, because the whole peat ball goes into the ground and the roots are not disturbed. A two-inch peat pot is sufficient for most young seedlings. Keep under lights until planting time.

Cold frames

Want a part-time greenhouse to extend your gardening season? It's as easy as building a box. The same basic structure can serve as either a cold frame or a hotbed. The cold frame is a bottomless box. The hotbed is much the same, but with the addition of a soil heating cable. Both frames use the sun's heat to warm the enclosed soil; the hotbed just allows finer control over soil temperature.

The south side of the house or garage is a good spot for the box. Or put it in the shelter of a thick, high hedge or a board fence. But make sure the site you choose has a southern exposure to trap maximum sun and to shelter your plants in the spring from predominantly northern winds. Good drainage is essential, too, so a level site is best. You can use sand or a soil mixture for the top layer within the frame.

If you plan to do most of your planting in flats or pots, sand is fine. Some cuttings also will root

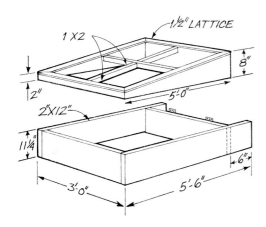

in sand. But if you want to plant directly into the frame instead of into flats or pots, make the top layer a soil mixture. A mixture of one part garden soil, one part sand, and one part peat or leaf mold is perfect.

For the base of either a cold frame or hotbed, build a 3x5½-foot box, letting sides project six inches. Use 2x12 lumber, preferably redwood, cedar, or some other rot-resistant variety. If you choose nonresistant wood, treat it with a preservative other than creosote, which is hard on plants. The top of the frame should measure 3x5 feet, and the sides should taper from two to eight inches.

Inside the top, center and fasten a piece of 1x2 lumber from side to side. It should be flush with the top edge. Center and fasten another piece from front to rear, also flush with the top edge, and notch where the 1x2s cross. This crossed structure will offer support for a piece of clear plastic sheeting in the lid.

Hinge top to base with four-inch butt hinges.

When the top is fully open, it will rest on the six-inch projections of the base sides. Use clear plastic or vinyl sheeting (six to eight mils thick) for the lid. Stretch and staple plastic to the lid edge, and then finish with lattice molding.

For a sun filter, build a frame of 1x2 lumber, and slot it to accept a piece of pierced sheet metal. Attach two eight-inch pieces of 1x3s to the sides of the lid. The filter rests on the edge of the lid and is screwed to the 1x3s. This allows air to pass between filter and lid and also allows the lid

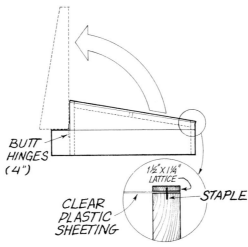

to be propped open to permit ventilation of the frame on especially warm days.

You'll also need covers for times when frosts or freezes are expected. A number of products are

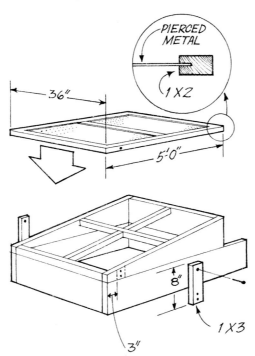

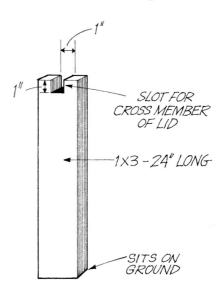

available that will insulate against cold air. They come in rigid sheets, usually 4x8 feet. These insulating materials are similar to composition board that is impregnated with a tar-like substance.

To make a cover, cut the material to fit the lid of the frame. Then lay the cover on the lid, and hold it down with several bricks or stones.

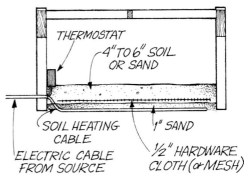

Cut a piece of 1x3 24 inches long to serve as a prop for the lid.

To turn a cold frame into a hotbed, add a soil-heating cable below the layer of sand or soil. Install the cable according to the manufacturer's directions.

To make things easier, select a cable with a built-in thermostat; that way you don't have to tend the hotbed so often. In two or three months, this small space can grow 20 or more trays of seedling varieties that otherwise might not be available at garden supply centers. For best results, try to locate your cold frame or hotbed along a south wall where it is protected from winds. There it can enjoy the warmth of the sun through most of the year. In the fall, use your cold frame to extend the gardening season past the first frost.

Planting How-to

To get a good harvest, you need a healthy, thriving garden. And to get a healthy, thriving garden, you have to give your vegetable seeds and seedlings a little special care at planting time. After that, just stand back and watch your garden burst into life.

Using twine/stake guidelines, mark each row before you sow seeds. Make furrow with a hoe or rake. Check seed packet for furrow depths.

If seeds are big, such as peas or beans, place them in the furrow by hand. If the seeds are tiny, tap gently into the furrow from the opened packet.

Planting seeds

Before you plant a single seed or seedling in the garden, be sure the entire area has been completely prepared. The condition of the soil is about the most vital element in the success of your vegetable garden. The quality and quantity of the crop are directly dependent on what the soil has to offer the plant in the way of good root environment and nutrition. The plant's roots must be able to penetrate the soil easily, and there must be adequate food available if the plants are to thrive.

If you have a vegetable plot, your soil may be in top-notch shape, but if you are breaking new ground for a garden, you may find soil that's less than ideal the first year. However, you can expect a good crop from most of your plants.

You'll find yields during the following years will be better as the condition of the soil improves each season.

Turn the soil a spade deep, or till as deeply as possible. Add all the organic material you can find and turn it under. Leaves, grass clippings, well-rotted manure, compost, straw, and leafy kitchen scraps are all good prospects for organically improving the soil.

If the area is small, add peat moss, vermiculite, or perlite to make the soil more friable, but it's expensive to improve a large garden with these materials.

After the soil is dug and raked level, sprinkle the surface with a vegetable garden fertilizer. Be sure to follow the directions on the bag for the amount needed. Then rake it into the top two inches of the spaded soil.

When planting, try to have all your seeds, stakes, string, and garden tools handy so you don't pack down the soil too much.

Before planting slow-growing crops like carrots, add radish seeds, half and half. The quick-growing radishes will help mark the row so you can cultivate before the weeds get started.

For cabbage or other plants, gently knock sets out of the plant packs. Separate roots and plant singly in holes dug with a trowel.

When young plants are set in the ground, water gently. Use a watering can or a slow-running garden hose to thoroughly soak the area.

Planting transplants

Crops such as cabbage, cauliflower, eggplant, broccoli, Brussels sprouts, tomatoes, and melons can be started directly in the garden, but because they have such a long growing season, many will not mature before the first frost in northern areas. To ensure a harvest, start them early indoors (see page 398), or buy transplants from your local nursery or garden center to be set in the garden when frost danger has passed.

Most nurseries or garden supply stores sell these transplants in shallow plastic flats called six-packs. To remove the plants from the six-pack, turn it upside down, and gently tap the bottom with one hand. With the other hand, be sure to hold onto the plants to prevent them from falling. The plants and soil should slip out. If the plants do not slip out easily, simply break the plastic away from the root ball.

Next, separate the plants and place them in the ground individually. Don't worry if you tear some roots; the plants should recover within a week. After planting, water the plants gently but deeply, and keep them moist for at least a week until they get established. In windy areas, protect the young plants with a board or several shingles stuck vertically into the ground around the plant.

Planting tomatoes

If a vote were taken to determine the most common vegetable in gardens across the country, tomatoes would probably be the hands-down favorite. These delicious vegetables provide rewarding yields in practically any soil and with relatively little care. But because they are a long-season crop and susceptible to cold weather, tomatoes should be started indoors eight to ten weeks before the last expected frost. Or buy started transplants at the appropriate planting time. Avoid spindly plants with yellowing leaves.

Set tomato transplants as deep as their first set of leaves. Run the stem lengthwise just under the surface of the soil so new roots develop.

Stop tomato cutworms by wrapping a two-inch collar of stiff paper around the stem. For complete protection, bury one inch of the paper underground.

Before you buy, be sure you're getting the variety that suits your gardening needs. Check the plant's label for important information. A letter "D" on the plant label means that the tomato variety is a determinate type. This means the plant stops growing after it reaches a certain height. The advantage to this type of tomato is that most of the fruit ripens at the same time—especially important if you plan on canning. Determinate tomatoes require no staking or supporting and should never be pruned.

A letter "I" means that the tomato variety is an indeterminate type. Indeterminate varieties continue growing throughout the season. The plants respond well to staking and pruning and are able to produce fruit over a long period. Most of the indeterminate varieties begin to bear later in the season than determinate types.

Besides these two classifications, most tomato labels will include "F," "V," or "N" after the name. These letters indicate the variety has bred-in resistance to fusarium wilt, verticillium wilt, and nematodes—important characteristics in areas where these problems are widespread. (Call your county extension office if you're not sure about their status.)

Stake at planting time

One of the best ways to get early, blemish-free tomatoes is to stake or support the vines. Tomato vines can be allowed to sprawl over a mulched area in the garden, but this will often result in later-bearing and damaged fruit. Rambling tomato vines also take up a lot of valuable garden space. Insects and diseases may get out of hand before you notice them, too.

Staking is best done immediately when the plants are set into the garden. If you push stakes into the ground after the plants are already growing, you're liable to damage the tender feeder root system.

Single or cross-supported stakes can be used, but single stakes require more work to keep vines

growing. Loosely attach tomato vines to the supports with figure-eight loops of old nylon stockings or strips of cloth. Take care not to damage stem. Because side shoots can become unmanageable and delay fruiting, prune all staked plants so only main stems develop.

Another popular support is to contain the plant within a wire cage. Off the ground, the tomatoes won't rot, and the plant's leaves provide enough shade to cut down on sunscald and fruit cracking. The fruit is also much easier to harvest, and you can see at a glance if it is ripe.

If you only have a few tomato plants, plant several on the outside of a tomato cage. Simply dig a hole two feet deep and the diameter of the cage. Then fill the hole with well-rotted compost, and set the cage around the perimeter, setting it firmly into the ground. Now, plant four tomato plants around the outside of the cage, tying them to the wire as they become taller. The tomato roots will seek out the adjacent compost and feed well. This trick also saves a lot of garden space.

Vegetable Garden Care

Although vegetable gardening is not difficult, some basics of good plant care will help produce better yields—no matter where you live.

Newly transplanted vegetable seedlings will need protection from the elements the first week or so they are in the garden. Strong sunshine or wind will quickly ruin those baby tomato plants you spent weeks nurturing in the kitchen window. Keep your young plants protected with one of the sun- and wind-shields shown below.

Watering

Everyone knows that plants need water, but few people realize that many commonly grown vegetables consist of almost 90 percent water. And to get a respectable harvest, your garden will need at least one thorough soaking a week—by rain or with your help. Watering with a hose is effective if you have the patience to hold one for an hour or so, but soaker hoses (flat and perforated) are better. Soaker hoses can be left in the garden, turned on low pressure, and allowed to run whenever needed. However, soaker hoses may cause flooding in the row.

Many people are turning to trickle or drip irrigation systems, which make a little water go a long way in the garden. The basic principle of drip irrigation is simple. Water is delivered in small quantities under low pressure directly to where it does the most good—the root zones of the plants. The water migrates through the soil by capillary action. Most air passages in the soil remain open, in contrast to the flooding of furrow irrigation or over-sprinkling. Oxygen is always available to the roots, and stresses of overwatering are eliminated.

Trickle irrigation systems vary, but most consist of a half-inch polyethylene header pipe and a roll of thin, tape-like porous tubing.

The header pipe connects to a garden hose and routes the water through the garden. Make small puncture holes in the header pipe at intervals corresponding to each row. The porous tape is connected to the header pipe at each hole. The tape is then rolled out along each vegetable bed and cut to the same length as the row.

To water, simply turn on the garden hose for several hours once or twice a week. Water will continuously ooze from all sides of the porous tape. The porous tape gets best results when it is placed about three to four inches away from the base of the plants. It's often a good idea to plant a double row of vegetables and place the tape down the center. This is especially effective with peas and beans.

Mulching

To save yourself a lot of hard work, time, and money, mulch your garden in late spring. This protective cover insulates the soil against the heat of the summer sun, protects it from drying winds, and all but eliminates weeds. Once the mulch is applied, you don't have to hoe between the rows. During most growing seasons, you have to water only about a third as often. The soil stays evenly moist under the mulch. And as the organic mulches decay, they improve the soil. Another plus for mulches is that they help keep mud from splashing on lower leaves during heavy rainstorms. All told, it makes good sense to mulch, even if you have to buy bales of straw for the job. If you consider the value of your time and energy, the price of mulch is your best buy of the season.

Wait to put the mulch down until after the soil has warmed but before the weeds have started growing. Try to keep most mulches at least three inches thick all season long. You can choose between organic (which will break down eventually) and inorganic mulches. The organic mulches include straw, peat moss, sawdust, dry manure, and bark chips. Inorganic mulches are aluminum foil, newspaper, and polyethylene film. The inorganic mulches are great for vining crops, such as melons and squash.

Gallon plastic milk containers protect individual young plants from low temperatures.

Newspaper tents keep sun and cold air off young row crops. Keep papers in place with stones.

A shingle screen keeps wind from whipping young plants about. Constant stem bending can bruise plants.

Large cans with tops and bottoms removed offer excellent protection for single plants.

If you plan on using a black plastic mulch, spread it over the garden before you plant. Then, cut holes where the seeds or seedlings are to be planted, and sprinkle with a garden hose. After a heavy rain, make punctures in areas of standing water to facilitate quick drainage. With a black plastic mulch, the only place you'll have to weed is near the plants' stems.

Feeding

Pay close attention to the feeding of your vegetable patch, because underfeeding can cause a reduction in crop yield. Some of the biggest problems are caused by gardeners not reading instructions on the bag. Be sure to know the kind of plant food you are applying, the amount of key elements it contains, and the way its nutrients are released. Some are slow-feeding, and one application is all that's needed for the entire season. Others must be reapplied two or three times. Be sure to note how much is needed each time.

If you have applied quantities of dry manure to improve the soil, apply supplemental plant food. If you are late feeding, don't broadcast the food over the growing plants. Apply it in narrow bands down the sides of the rows, and work it into the soil surface. Keep it at least six inches from the plants' stems.

For heavy feeders, such as melons and squash, a good way to feed them automatically is to punch holes in the bottom of a coffee can and sink it into the ground. Plant seeds around the circumference of the can, and fill it with compost or dried bagged manure. This way, the plants will receive a meal whenever you water them.

Vegetable Protection

As a rule, vegetable gardeners are generous people, happy to give away any surplus.

But even the noblest of them take exception when rabbits, raccoons, and birds threaten the entire crop. The best solution to the pesky problem is to cage the vegetables in, the predators out.

The crop cage (above) fits inside a raised-soil vegetable bed; sides of the bed get support from 2x12s. The cage itself measures 72x45 inches; it's made of 2x2s with triangles of half-inch plywood set to straighten each corner. Four hinges attach the lid to the bottom of the cage, and wire-mesh screening is stapled on. Notches on the lid and frame hold a support stick when the lid is up.

Soil inside the bed has received special intensive preparation. It was double-dug to a depth of 24 inches, and organic matter was mixed in. The vegetables can be reached from all sides, so there's no need to walk on the soil and compact it. Also, the plants can be spaced close together for greater yield. A good compost is incorporated with the soil to keep the planting medium productive and healthy. The cage is ideal for the home gardener who wants to produce a big harvest in a small area but has trouble with either poor soil or chewing or nibbling pests.

Companion planting. Too often, in the interest of increased efficiency, the home gardener insists on planting a vegetable checkerboard, where each crop is grown in the same place year after year. Block planting may be simpler in the short run, but in time it can bedevil your garden with a host of problems. Cabbages will shrink and go limp for no apparent reason, corn borers will threaten to overrun the corn patch, or your prize potatoes will be smothered with potato beetles.

In nature, things grow willy-nilly rather than in neat, geometrically placed rows. As a result, insect populations are faced with limited food supplies and can seldom get out of hand. And today, experts agree that diversity is the best defense against bugs and disease.

Through companion planting—combining specific plants so the beneficial qualities of one can be useful to another—you can keep the balance in your own backyard from tipping too far in one direction.

For example, an unusual quality of herbs is their ability to repel insects. Because vegetables are often plagued by bugs, herbs can be a welcome addition. Marigolds, popular because of their colorful flowers, may be especially effective. Planted among beans, they are said to discourage the Mexican bean beetle. Studies have also indicated that large plantings have a way of destroying the root systems of certain starch weeds. Nasturtiums may check aphids, striped cucumber beetles, and squash bugs, while tansy planted with cabbage might help reduce damage from cutworm and cabbageworm.

It will be some time, however, before the benefits of companion planting are scientifically established. So if your crops wilt under an intensive insect attack, chances are a chemical spray may be in order. (See Chapter 16, "Insects and Diseases.") But in your own garden, you might want to try some of the ideas in the chart (at right).

Cagey lettuce

Row-long cages made of welded wire fabric keep wildlife at bay. The 2x4-inch mesh used here is fine enough to keep birds and many animals from snitching seeds or young plants. To make cages, bend the wire at right angles to make a three-sided structure, and close the ends of the rows with a wired-on rectangle of mesh. Push the bottom of the cage into the soil.

Fashion the dimensions to fit your purpose. This cage (above) is 14 inches high and 20 inches wide and covers a 12-foot-long row.

As plants mature, the cages are easily moved to other rows of young vegetables planted later in the season. They can also be folded up easily and stored in stacks for the winter.

COMPANION PLANTING CHART

Plant	Where to Plant	Possible Benefits
Beans or marigolds	With or among potatoes	Discourage Colorado potato beetles
Chives or garlic	Among lettuce or peas	Deter aphids
Geraniums	Near grapes	Discourage Japanese beetles
Marigolds	With beans	Repel Mexican bean beetles
Nasturtiums	Throughout vegetable patch	Deter aphids, Mexican bean beetles, striped cucumber beetles, and squash bugs
Tomatoes	With asparagus	Discourage asparagus beetles
Euphorbias (gopher plant)	Scattered throughout garden	Poisonous to gophers and repugnant to many insects
Potatoes	With beans	Deter Mexican bean beetles
Radishes	With cucumbers	Discourage striped cucumber beetles
Rosemary, sage, thyme, catnip, or mint	Among cabbage plants	Repels white cabbage butterflies
Rue	Between vegetable rows	Bitter leaves are odious to insects
Tansy	Near cabbage	Helps reduce damage from cutworms and cabbageworms

Space-Saving Ideas

No matter how large or small your vegetable garden is, you'll get better production and save valuable garden space if you keep some space-saving methods in mind.

Garden trellis. Attach a sloping trellis to a garage or storage shed and you'll have a ready-made vertical garden spot, perfect for cucumbers, beans, peas, or melons. The fruit from trellis-supported vines is cleaner and straighter than from those on the ground. Improved air circulation helps prevent disease. Cucumbers grown this way are especially good for pickling, because fewer culls form on the vines. Or set grapevines along the base, and

angle the trellis to catch the most sun possible.

To prevent any mid-season mishaps, be sure the trellis is well-anchored before you plant. For a permanently stable foundation that will be rot resistant, sink the support posts into concrete. Use redwood or another kind of durable lumber. You'll want to stain most kinds of wood to cut yearly painting to a minimum. After the trellis is in place, lay a two- to four-inch layer of mulch beneath it to keep weeds choked out, soil moist, and roots cool. Even if you must buy the mulching material, the expense is well worth it; you'd

need the agility of an acrobat to keep the area under the trellis looking tidy.

Bean tepee. Although most varieties of pole beans will quickly grow up even the simplest of supports, you'll have better luck if you give them a support designed just for them. Take three six-foot-long 1x1 laths and assemble them into a triangular tepee, tying the tops together and sinking the other ends into the soil. Be sure all three poles are firmly in the ground before planting. Then, plant six to eight seeds of climbing beans at the base of each lath. When the plants are up and growing, thin them so there are about three healthy seedlings per pole. They won't need to be tied; they'll twine unassisted.

To make the tepee even more functional, use the area underneath the poles to plant cool-weather crops, such as lettuce, spinach, or beets. As the beans grow up the poles, they'll shade the cool-season crops from the direct rays of the sun. Grown in this manner, harvests of lettuce and

the other cool-weather crops can often be extended throughout the summer months.

If you don't want a large bean crop, you can get by with only one pole. Simply sink the pole about one foot into the ground, and wrap a loose cone of chicken wire around it. Secure the chicken wire to the pole so it will not come undone; plant seeds at four-inch intervals around the base of the support. In a few weeks, you'll be enjoying plenty of freshly picked green beans.

Mobile mini garden. The odds are against you if you have a small, hilly, or shaded lot and you want to grow vegetables. But you can build a portable growing unit that can be moved around to catch pockets of sun at different times of the season. The seven-tier design accommodates

six-foot rows of spinach, basil, lettuce, radishes, green onions, and, on the bottom deck, a planting of bush cucumbers. Use only treated, rot-resistant lumber for the unit.

A roll of black plastic, stapled along the top, can be unrolled to shield plants on hot days and to protect them when frost threatens. To provide adequate drainage, be sure to drill holes in the base of each trough every few inches and cover with at least an inch of gravel.

To make the mini garden more portable, use lightweight, commercially prepared soil mixes. Ordinary garden soil will usually pack down and become too heavy for container culture. Also, be sure to add small casters fastened to the corners of the unit to make it easier to move around.

As with any container garden, this mobile unit will need frequent watering. Try to locate it where it can be conveniently watered every day. Or you might try adding an automatic drip watering system to make the job even more efficient. Although the mobile garden unit is built to last for years, you'll have the best luck if the soil mix is changed—in part or completely—each planting season.

Below: Vine crops grown vertically can get heavy close to harvesttime. Avoid "fallout" by making slings for pumpkins, melons, cucumbers, and squash. Use old sheets, nylons, towels, or whatever is available. Cut the material into squares and knot the corners securely. Then, tie twine to each corner, ease the parachute around the fruit, and tie to a sturdy, well-supported fence. Be sure to use thick twine that is resistant to rot. Crops grown in this manner ripen more uniformly and are less prone to rot than fruit produced on unsupported vines.

Above: If your backyard space is really limited, make vegetables do double duty. This attractive privacy screen was made by planting climbing pole beans in an old-fashioned laundry tub. Wooden 4x4s, with mesh garden wire stretched between, provide support for the vegetables. Herbs and flowers add color and fragrance to the planting. If pole beans aren't your favorite, substitute climbing lima beans, melons, or cucumbers. Scarlet runner beans are another good choice because they add brilliant red color, as well as tasty edible beans. The screen will be good-looking from both sides and will let summer breezes through. Container-grown vegetables dry out quickly, so be sure you can water daily before you get started. And don't forget to use a good, nutrient-rich potting soil that won't compact during hot weather.

ABCs of Vegetables

Anyone who claims to hate the taste of vegetables probably hasn't eaten a freshly picked homegrown ear of corn or savored a plateful of early spring peas. Homegrown foods, ripened in the sunshine, really do taste better. That's why gourmet cooks so often pamper their own crops. Besides, as anyone who's grown green beans can tell you, it's more fun to eat food you've raised yourself.

There's no denying you use more vegetables when you have a big crop in your own backyard. A larger percentage of these foods in your diet gives your family a real nutritional boost. Also, they're less likely to eat snacks or less nourishing goodies.

These vegetable entries, arranged in alphabetical order, give you planting how-to and cultural tips for the recommended varieties, plus information on how and when to harvest them.

ARTICHOKE, GLOBE

Seldom thought of as a common garden vegetable, this gourmet's delight is actually relatively easy to grow. But, because of their sensitivity to cooler temperatures, glorious artichoke plantings are not often found in northern gardens.

Varieties: Green Globe is the standard variety.

Planting: Globe artichoke is a perennial vegetable that needs to be planted in a garden spot where it won't be disturbed by yearly cultivation. You can start your own from seed indoors or buy nursery transplants. Set the young seedlings into the garden after all danger of frost is passed, allowing four feet between rows and plants.

Culture: Before planting artichokes, be sure the ground is deeply spaded and enriched with a good supply of well-rotted manure or compost. Plants need full sun to develop properly, so a location that gets at least six to eight hours of sunlight a day is important. After planting, be sure the plants do not dry out. An ample supply of moisture—especially when buds first begin to form—can mean a yield of 12 to 16 buds per plant.

Once plants become established, numerous suckers will appear at the base of the stems. Remove weaker shoots, allowing only five or six to remain for later transplanting.

In the fall, cut stems one foot from the ground, and cover the crowns of the plants with a heavy but porous mulch.

Harvest: As soon as flower buds are visible, check the plants daily, so buds can be picked just before petals begin to open.

ASPARAGUS

An asparagus bed is a lifetime investment. Once this vegetable is established, it will keep on producing yearly for generations. Besides its delicious flavor and nutritious attributes, asparagus is also valued for its quick and early appearance in the spring garden. Its store-bought kin is often expensive.

Varieties: The recommended varieties are the Washington strains, which are resistant to asparagus rust.

Planting: To have a successful asparagus bed, you've got to plan ahead. Dig a trench about 16 inches deep, and fill it with ten inches of manure or compost mixed with soil. Be sure this planting bed is in a spot that will remain relatively undisturbed all season long. It should also be placed in a sunny location.

After the bed is prepared, set out one-year-old crowns in the trenches. (For best re-sults, buy started crowns rather than trying to start the plants from seed.) Cover crowns with several inches of topsoil after planting 18 inches apart. Gradually fill in the trench as the plants develop. By the end of the first season, plants will have reached soil level. Allow five feet between trenches.

Culture: Because asparagus grows so quickly, it is a heavy feeder and should be given yearly applications of fertilizer or nutrient-packed manure or compost. Keep the beds mulched at all times to cut down on weeds and to increase soil moisture. A fall mulch of several inches in cold climate areas is also important to keep the crowns from any winter damage.

If you must hoe, try not to damage the plants' shallow root systems. Only a light scraping of the upper surface of the soil is advisable.

In the fall, after plants have died back, remove the dead foliage to prevent insects and diseases from wintering over.

Harvest: For spears to taste best, pick them when they are no more than eight inches long. Cut the spears at or just below ground level. You can pick a light crop from a newly established bed during its second season, but a full harvest shouldn't be taken until its third year. In midsummer, when spears are the width of a pencil or thinner, stop harvesting and let the plants develop mature foliage. This will help ensure a good crop next season. Remove the dead foliage in the fall to prevent disease.

BEANS

Beans will probably be first on your list of garden favorites. They're a versatile crop and easy to grow. You'll find bush forms and types that grow on vines. There are beans that are eaten fresh and those that are dried and eaten later. Some varieties can even be used both ways.

Varieties: Bean varieties usually fall into two major categories: edible-podded varieties and the shell or tough-podded types. The edible-podded, or snap beans, are eaten pods and all, before they are fully grown.

The shell types are allowed to fully mature, and the beans are then removed from the pod and cooked separately. Beans also vary in growth habit. There are bush forms and those that climb up wooden or wire supports. Popular varieties of bush beans include Tendercrop and Greensleeves. Cherokee and Gold Crop are two varieties of yellow bush wax beans that will do well in home gardens, too.

Commonly grown bush lima bean varieties are Fordhook No. 242 and Henderson. Pole

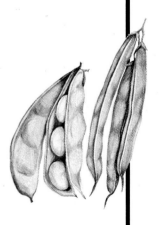

beans include Kentucky Wonder and Romano. A good pole lima bean is King of the Garden. Favorite shell bean varieties are Red Kidney, Fava, White Marrowfat, and Dwarf Horticultural.

Planting: Success with beans begins with warm weather. Beans don't grow in cool, damp conditions, so once your garden soil has warmed up thoroughly, you can make successive sowings of bush beans every two weeks. Pole, lima, and shell beans need only to be planted once.

Space rows 24 to 30 inches apart, with seeds placed two to three inches apart. Pole beans should be planted in hills two to three feet apart, with four or five seeds per pole. After the beans have sprouted, thin to three plants per pole. Lima beans need a little more space, with seeds spaced every eight inches in rows 24 to 30 inches apart. Be sure you plant beans in a sunny, well-drained location.

Culture: Beans are adaptable to a wide variety of soil types but will benefit from side-dressings of fertilizer applied when plants are four to six inches high.

Harvest: To keep the harvests going, don't allow any beans to mature on the plant. Use beans when young and tender. Only shell beans should be allowed to fully mature on the bush. Pick pods before seeds swell enough to cause visible bulges in the shells. To avoid spreading viral diseases to the plants, do not cultivate or harvest when the plants are wet.

BEET

Don't overlook the succulent beet when making your garden plans. If properly cared for, they are one of the easiest vegetables you can grow. Plus, they're a bonus crop—offering tasty roots as well as tops. The red-veined, deep green leaves are also quite decorative, making beets a natural for patio, container, or border planting.

Varieties: Some popular varieties of beets include: Detroit Dark Red, Crosby, Early Wonder, and the new yellow beet, Golden Beet. Most varieties mature in 60 to 70 days.

Planting: Plant your first crop of beets in the early spring as soon as the ground can be worked. Because beets are a root crop, be sure the planting bed has been finely cultivated beforehand. Rough or stony soils will result in misshapen roots.

Sow seeds in furrows about one half to one inch deep, being sure to space rows 12 to 15 inches apart. Space seeds every inch or so in the furrow, and cover lightly with a fine layer of soil. Then water well. Thin the seedlings when they are five inches tall to stand four to

six inches apart. For a continuous beet harvest, sow a new crop of seeds every two weeks until midsummer.

Culture: The key to a successful beet harvest is rapid growth caused by a good supply of water. Rapidly grown beets will taste far superior to those that have been allowed to linger for want of water during their growing period.

Harvest: Harvest beets when the root becomes about two or three inches in diameter. If they are allowed to get any larger, they rapidly lose quality. Harvest the tops throughout the season for tasty boiling greens.

BROCCOLI

An abundant yielder, broccoli is a must for every garden. These easy-to-grow members of the cabbage family will continue to produce side sprouts long after the main head has been picked.

Varieties: The best known varieties include Premium Crop, Green Sprouting, and Waltham 29.

Planting: Because broccoli is a warm weather crop, start it six to eight weeks early indoors. Or buy started transplants from a reliable garden center. Set seedlings outdoors after all frost danger has passed. To prevent cutworm damage, wrap stiff paper around the stems of each plant. At least one inch of the collar should be below the soil line, with two inches above.

Space rows about two feet apart, with at least 20 inches of space between the plants.

Culture: For quick healthy growth, keep plants well supplied with water. A thick mulch will also help ensure an adequate moisture supply for the roots.

Perhaps the worst enemy of broccoli is the cabbageworm, or caterpillar. To combat this pest, spray the broccoli plants at weekly intervals with *Bacillus thuringiensis* (B.t.). *Bacillus thuringiensis* is a bacterial deterrent to the cabbageworm and a naturally safe pest control.

Harvest: Pick flower buds when they are no more than four inches across. The smaller and more compact the head, the better it will taste. Any heads that have the tiny flowerets already opened are past their prime. Pick side shoots later.

BRUSSELS SPROUTS

Brussels sprouts are another relative of the cabbage, but their uniqueness lies in the fact that they produce a tower of miniature cabbages up and down their stems. Brussels sprouts are basically a cool-weather crop that does best planted midsummer for early fall ripening. Some say flavor is actually improved by a few light frosts.

Varieties: For a sure crop, try Jade Cross Hybrid or Long Island Improved.

Planting: For a good-tasting harvest, start your crop of Brussels sprouts in early July. You can sow them where they will remain in the garden, or you can start seeds in a special seedbed and move them into the garden later. If you don't have the time to start them from seed, buy nursery transplants.

Space or thin the seedlings to stand 18 to 24 inches apart in rows about 30 inches apart. Be sure to install a cutworm collar like the one used with broccoli.

Culture: Brussels sprouts are heavy feeders and will be healthier and more productive if you give them a side-dressing of manure or commercial fertilizer every two weeks. When sprouts begin to grow at leaf axils (where leaves join stems), break off lower leaves. The small, cabbage-like sprouts will continue to grow up the stem.

Brussels sprouts are also susceptible to attack by cabbageworms. Spray at weekly intervals with *Bacillus thuringiensis* to keep them at bay.

Harvest: The best-tasting sprouts are compact and only about one inch in diameter. Use a sharp knife to cut off sprouts, leaving enough trunk so new sprouts can grow. If frost threatens, don't worry—the plants will not be harmed.

CABBAGE

No matter what type of soil your garden has, you can still get a respectable crop of cabbage. It's easy to grow and usable in a wide variety of family dishes.

Varieties: With careful planning, you can plant several varieties of cabbage that will give you a long season of harvest. For early cabbage, try Earliana, Early Jersey Wakefield, Early Flat Dutch, Green Acre, Marion Market, or Emerald Cross Hybrid. Big, late cabbages include Premium Flat Dutch, Danish Ballhead, and Penn State Ballhead.

Vary your cabbage crop with a few plants each of red and savoy types. Red Acre is a widely grown early red; Mammoth Red Rock is later but produces a much larger (up to eight pounds) head. A dwarf variety, Dwarf Morden, is a good choice for small gardens. For a gourmet treat, grow the crinkly Savoy Ace Hybrid. It's tender, sweet, and more insect resistant than other varieties.

Planting: To get an evenly spaced crop, sow some seed in early spring as soon as the soil is workable. At the same time, set out some started plants. Space or thin the plants to stand abut 18 inches apart in rows 24 to 30 inches apart. Be sure to place a collar around the stem of each plant to foil cutworms.

Culture: A heavy feeder, cabbage needs rapid growth. Side-dress with nitrate of soda or high-nitrogen fertilizer at planting time and every four weeks thereafter.

Plants should also have a steady supply of moisture to ensure fast growth. A two- to four-inch mulch will help keep the soil cool and moisture content high. Hoeing should be done only when absolutely necessary to avoid disturbing the shallow feeder root system of the plants.

To prevent cabbageworm damage, spray at weekly intervals with *Bacillus thuringiensis*. Be sure the spray coats the deeply folded leaves on both the upper and lower surfaces.

Harvest: To harvest, cut the heads when they are still tight and compact. Use a sharp knife and make the cut near the base of the plant. If left undisturbed, the old stem will produce several smaller but still usable heads. If cracking of the heads occurs before they're harvested, the plants are not getting sufficient moisture. The remedy is to supplement rainfall with thorough drenchings from the garden hose. Some gardeners reduce cracking by severing the roots on one side of the plant with a thrust or two of a sharp spade.

CARROT

One root crop no garden should be without is carrots. Carrots resist cold, grow easily in a small area, and if stored under moist, cool conditions, stay fresh for up to four months. They also give more yield per square inch of garden soil than most other vegetables and are tasty both cooked and raw.

Varieties: If you're lucky enough to have a deep, fine topsoil, you might want to try some of the longer-rooted varieties, such as Trophy, Gold Pak, and Imperator. For shallow soil, try Royal Chantenay or Scarlet Nantes. Medium-size varieties include Pioneer and Nantes Half Long.

Planting: The first thing you should do before planting any carrot varieties is to prepare the soil deeply. All clumps, sticks, stones, and miscellaneous debris should be removed to prevent roots from becoming misshapen. Carrots can be sown two to four weeks before the date of last expected frost. Plant seeds as thin as possible, about a half inch deep, in rows spaced 12 to 15 inches apart. Or, to make later weeding and thinning easier, mix carrot

seeds half and half with radish seeds and plant in a wide row. The radish seeds will be up before the carrots and block out the sun over weed competition. Plus, as you harvest the mature radishes, you will be thinning the young carrots.

Culture: After carrots have sprouted, thin them immediately. With later pulling, it becomes progressively more difficult to separate the plants. Thin the seedlings to stand every three inches. Later, go over the row again so the plants end up about six inches apart. To prolong harvests over a longer period of time, sow seeds continuously every two or three weeks until midsummer.

Harvest: The best-tasting carrots are those that have been grown quickly and harvested while still young. Carrots left in the ground too long are often tough and mealy. For best flavor, pick when the tops of the roots are about a half inch in diameter.

CAULIFLOWER

If you like cauliflower but avoid planting it because you think it's too much work—think again. Cauliflower is no harder to grow than most other vegetables. In fact, if you can grow cabbage, you'll have no trouble with cauliflower.

Varieties: The best known are the Snowball varieties. Burpeeana and Snow Crown are also of high quality. Purple head cauliflower has the advantage of not requiring blanching, but many people say that it tastes more like broccoli than cauliflower.

Planting: Cauliflower grows best during periods of cool temperatures. You can grow it as either a spring or fall crop, but in most areas of the country, you'll have better luck if you plant it during midsummer for early fall ripening. Start plants from seeds sown indoors about six to eight weeks before planting time or in their own special seedbed outdoors. When the seedlings have reached several inches in height, move them to the planting area, spacing plants about 20 inches apart. Rows should be 24 to 30 inches apart. Mid- to late July is a good planting time for most areas of the country.

Be sure to protect stems from cutworm damage by supplying two-inch-wide collars of stiff paper (see page 401). Shade tender plants from direct sun the first few days after transplanting.

Culture: A good harvest of cauliflower depends on cool temperatures, ample moisture, and plenty of rich organic matter. You can't control the temperatures, but you can keep the plants moist and give them a side-dressing of fertilizer every two weeks for continuous

growth. Apply a thick mulch to cut down on watering chores.

Once the flower heads are about the size of a half dollar, the leaves should be gathered together and tied to form a protective canopy. Sunlight striking the bud will cause discoloring. Purple varieties do not require tying.

Spray plants at weekly intervals with *Bacillus thuringiensis* to control cabbageworms.

Harvest: After the heads have been tied, they will be ready for harvesting within three to eight days. Cut stalks with a sharp knife just below the heads.

CELERIAC

Celeriac is one vegetable you don't hear many people talk about. But don't let its relative rareness scare you; it's a tasty, easily grown, celery-flavored plant that is great in soups and salads.

Varieties: The principal varieties are Alabaster and Marble Hall.

Planting: Good-tasting celeriac depends on quick growth, and because these plants are a long-season crop, get seeds started indoors in the early spring. When seedlings are up and growing, move them to the garden. Space plants about six inches apart in rows 18 to 20 inches apart. Be sure to add plenty of well-rotted manure or compost to the planting area before you set out the plants.

Culture: Keep plants moist at all times, using a three- to four-inch mulch when possible. Otherwise, you'll have to make frequent trips with the garden hose. If bulbs begin to push through, cover them with soil to preserve whiteness.

Harvest: Pull plants when the roots are between three and four inches in diameter. For an extended harvest, leave roots in the ground all winter under a thick mulch.

CELERY

Celery has long been considered an overly time-consuming vegetable for the home gardener to grow. It grows slowly; requires a rich, moist, almost mucky soil; and needs to be started indoors at least ten weeks in advance of the planting season. But recently, many garden supply houses have been making the job a lot easier by providing started transplants that can be moved directly into the garden.

Varieties: The two most common varieties include Pascal and Golden Self-Blanching.

Planting: Set out hardened plants for a spring crop as soon as soil is in planting condition. Before planting, be sure to mix in plenty of organic matter—the more the better. Rich soil is a must.

To eliminate any transplant shock, transplant the seedlings on a cloudy day, or shade seedlings with cardboard or newspaper. Be sure moisture supply is constant.

Set plants in rows 24 to 30 inches apart, and space plants at ten-inch intervals.

Culture: Supplemental feedings of manure or fertilizer should be given to the plant every two weeks. Use a mulch to keep soil moisture content high, and give plants at least one thorough soaking a week.

In earlier days, growers used to blanch stalks by hilling earth against the plants with boards. Blanching, however, isn't necessary; in fact, it robs the stalks of their vitamin content. But if white stalks are a must for gourmet recipes, simply place boards on either side of the plants and hold them in place with soil. The trick is to keep out the sunlight. Make sure the top leaves are all that show above the boards.

Harvest: Harvesting your celery crop is not difficult. Simply pull up the plants, shake off the soil, and cut off the roots. You should, however, try to cut the plants when they have become about five inches across at the base. If the plants have gotten too large, their flavor will suffer.

CELTUCE

Celtuce is an unusual and extremely useful vegetable. It's a dual-purpose vegetable, with leafy tops you can use cooked or raw in salads and a central stalk you can use like celery. If you keep it well watered, its rapid, hardy growth will surprise you. It's also a good source of vitamin C.

Varieties: Burpee's Celtuce.

Planting: Celtuce is as easy to grow as lettuce. Sow celtuce seeds in the early spring as soon as the ground can be worked. Drop seeds thinly in a shallow furrow, spacing rows about 12 inches apart. Later, when the plants are up and growing, thin them to stand about ten inches apart. For an even earlier crop, start seeds a few weeks early indoors, and set the developing seedlings outdoors at planting time.

Culture: Rapid growth is essential to this vegetable. Be sure the plants receive plenty of moisture and have a constant supply of nutrients all summer long. A side-dressing of a nitrogen-rich fertilizer every few weeks will help promote rapid development of leaves and stalks.

Harvest: Celtuce leaves can be harvested at any time for use in fresh salads. If tender stalks are desired, wait until plants have reached maturity. Pick stalks and eat either raw or cooked.

CHARD, SWISS

Swiss chard is actually a member of the beet family, but the taste of its cooked tops rivals that of spinach and its substitutes. The leaves are also a flavorful addition to every salad. It's an ideal vegetable, because it is both heat and drought resistant and grows without bolting to seed, right up until frost. It is also packed with vitamins.

Varieties: Swiss chard comes in both red and green forms. Good green varieties are Lucullus and Fordhook Giant. Rhubarb Chard is a popular red variety. Both color forms are attractive enough to mingle easily with flowers in beds and borders.

Planting: Swiss chard is adaptable to a wide variety of soil types and exposures, but, like beets, it will do poorly in an acid soil, preferring a pH of 6.5 to 7.5.

Sow seeds in the garden as soon as the ground can be worked. Space seeds an inch or so apart in the row, because each seed is actually a cluster of three or four seeds and chard can be easily overplanted. Rows should be 18 to 24 inches apart.

Culture: As seedlings emerge, gradually thin the plants to stand about a foot apart. But don't worry if you don't have time to thin; even crowded plants will give you more harvest than you need.

To boost leaf growth, occasionally apply a side-dressing of a high-nitrogen fertilizer.

Harvest: As plants mature, pick the outer leaves and prepare as is, or separate the "chard" midrib from the leaves and serve like asparagus. Do not pick all the leaves from one plant. Managed in this manner, the entire row will last all summer.

In the fall, Swiss chard lends itself to cold frame or greenhouse culture for an extended harvest into the winter. Or simply place protective caps over the plants for pickings well past the first hard frost.

CHICORY

A popular salad delicacy easily enjoyed by everyone, chicory grows best during cooler spring and fall seasons. The tender, creamy-yellow leaf clumps offer a unique flavor that is both tangy and mild.

Varieties: The best-known variety is Witloof, sometimes referred to as French Endive.

Planting: Start chicory from seeds sown outdoors as soon as the ground can be worked, or start indoors for an early crop. As the plants begin to grow, thin them to stand eight inches apart. Rows should be spaced at 15-inch intervals. Keep seedlings moist at all times. A thick mulch will increase needed soil moisture and also eliminate competition from weeds.

Culture: To keep this leaf crop at peak performance, add a side-dressing of nitrogen-rich fertilizer every few weeks. This will promote vigorous growth and healthier plants. The leaves of some varieties can be picked as they mature.

Harvest: Although you can use chicory at almost any time, most gardeners prefer to eat the plants after they have been properly blanched. In the fall, before the threat of frost, dig up the plants and replant in boxes filled with peat moss and sand. Then place it in a warm, dark place where the plants can continue to grow. In about a month, the Witloof variety can be cut. If roots are left in place, new leaves will begin to form for a second cutting.

CHINESE CABBAGE

With the growing popularity of Chinese cooking, Chinese cabbage is becoming increasingly popular in vegetable plots across the country. Mid-season is the best time to start this special cabbage. Plant the seed about three months before the first expected frost in your area.

Varieties: There are two kinds of Chinese cabbage, bok choy, which is loose-leaved, and wong bok, which forms long, narrow heads. Grow Crispy Choy (loose-leaved) or the wong bok types: Michihli, Burpee Hybrid, Springtime, Summertime, or Wintertime. Use Springtime for late spring sowings—it's more tolerant of hot weather.

Planting: Sow seeds in rows spaced 18 to 24 inches apart at least three months before the first expected frost. As plants emerge, thin to stand every six inches.

Culture: Feed young plants with supplemental applications of a high-nitrogen fertilizer every ten days to two weeks until just before harvest. Keep plants as moist as possible for best growth.

Harvest: Pull plants before stalks begin to show.

COLLARDS

Collards are leafy members of the cabbage family that yield heavily over a long harvest season. Collards tolerate starts in hot weather, so they're a widely grown favorite in the South. In northern gardens, they'll grow well as a mid-season crop.

Varieties: The two best varieties are Vates, a compact, dwarf-like variety, and Georgia.

Planting: Seed can be sown any time during the spring, with rows spaced about two feet apart. As plants mature, thin so there is at least six inches of space between each plant. Thinnings make delicious and nutritious additions to the dinner menu.

Keep plants moist and well supplied with nitrogen. Also, if cabbageworms attack, spray with *Bacillus thuringiensis* at weekly intervals.

Culture: Collards are shallow-rooted plants that can be damaged easily by too frequent hoeing. To avoid damaging the root system and to increase soil moisture, apply a two- to four-inch mulch around the plants as soon as they are several inches high. Add side-dressings of nitrogen-rich fertilizer every three or four weeks to stimulate leafier growth.

Harvest: Like chard, you can pick the outer leaves as they develop, leaving the inner leaf buds to grow for later pickings. Don't remove all the leaves from one plant, so the whole row can continue producing leaves. As fall approaches, pick the entire plant; collards will not tolerate frost damage.

CORN

If any vegetable is typically American, corn is. The Pilgrims' staple has since developed into specialized varieties that are extra sweet or extra small and have mixed yellow and white kernels on one ear.

Varieties: For a continuous harvest throughout the summer and into the fall, plant some of the early, mid-season, and late varieties. Popular early varieties (60 to 70 days) are: Spring Gold, Seneca, Illini X-tra Sweet, Explorer, and Early Sunglow.

Among the mid-season choices (70 to 80 days) are: Sundance, Wonderful, Gold Cup, Northern Bell, and Gold Cross Bantam.

For late crops (85 to 95 days), try Seneca Chief and Honeycross (yellow); Silver Queen and Country Gentleman (white); and Honey and Cream and Butter and Sugar (bicolor).

Some of the dwarf varieties are White and Golden Midget, and Midget Hybrid.

For homegrown popcorn, try Peppy, Creme-Puff, Japanese Hulless, Fireside, or Hybrid Gold. Allow 90 to 105 days to maturity for popcorn varieties.

Planting: Heat and water are the two biggest requirements for successful corn growing. For rapid growth, warm days and nights are critical. Most varieties need three months of warm, sunny weather, although early types do mature in as few as 60 days.

Corn grows in average garden soil, but well-rotted manure and compost are a must to provide needed nutrients. Because corn is a tender vegetable, wait until soil is completely warm before sowing seeds. Corn is wind-pollinated, so results will be better if each variety is planted in a block of three or four shorter rows, rather than one long row. Space seeds about eight inches apart in rows 26 to 40 inches apart. If corn is planted in hills, sow five seeds to a hill, and space hills about four feet apart.

To provide an initial food supply for the seed, dig a furrow three inches deep, and sprinkle a band of complete fertilizer along the bottom. Cover with a thin layer of soil, and plant seeds one inch below original soil level.

Culture: After the seedlings have emerged, thin them to stand about 15 inches apart. Keep plants well watered, and occasionally side-dress with manure or compost to boost growth. When the stalk is eight inches high, begin supplemental feedings at regular two-week intervals. To prevent unwanted cross-pollination from ornamental corn or between yellow and white varieties, plant the separate types at least ten feet apart.

Keep an eye out for pests, such as armyworms or corn earworms. If a plant is heavily infected, remove the entire plant, rather than risk the whole crop.

Harvest: Ears are ready to be picked when kernels at the tips are plump and silks have dried out slightly. When the corn is ready for eating, cook it as soon as possible after picking. Corn sugar starts turning into starch when the ear is removed from the plant. To help retard this change, leave the ears unhusked and refrigerate until they can be cooked.

CORN SALAD

Corn salad is a little-known green that can be used as a salad base when the weather is too cool for growing lettuce. Its slightly bland flavor accents tangier greens and is excellent in combination with them.

Varieties: Available varieties are few. Best known is Large Round-Leaved corn salad.
Planting: Because corn salad is a cool weather crop, you'll have better luck if you sow the seeds directly outdoors as soon as the ground can be worked in the spring. Sow seeds again in late summer for a fall crop.

As plants develop, thin them to stand about six inches apart, with rows spaced every 12 inches.

Keep your crop mulched and watered frequently. If plants start to burn out in mid-summer, extend the harvest with a sun-shield made of burlap stretched over the row. The shield should shade the plants during the hottest part of the day and can extend the harvest several weeks.

For rapid leaf development, work plenty of manure or nitrogen-based fertilizer into the soil before planting.
Culture: Other than fighting competition from weeds and keeping the plants moist and well fed, you won't have a lot of work with a crop of corn salad. Where space is limited, plant some in pots or tubs.
Harvest: Leaves may be picked as soon as they reach mature size (about half the size of a lettuce leaf). Pick outer leaves only, so that inner leaves can continue to grow for later pickings.

CUCUMBER

For flavor, abundance, and convenience, the cucumber comes close to heading the list of the most popular crop in the home garden.
Varieties: There are two basic types of cucumbers available to the home gardener: slicing cucumbers and pickling cucumbers. Slicing varieties are developed for table use but also may be used for pickling. Gherkins are cucumbers picked when they are small; however, special varieties that produce only gherkin-size fruit are available. Good slicing varieties include Marketmore Hybrid, Straight Eight, Spartan, Valor, and Burpless Hybrid. Pickling varieties include Mariner, Green Star, Wisconsin SMR 18, and Burpee Pickler.

Bush varieties, Pot Luck and Bush Whopper, are two good petite-size choices for container culture or for gardens where space is at a premium.

Gynodioecious varieties, like Victory Hybrid, bear only female flowers and will often outproduce other varieties. Only one male seed (usually specially marked in the package) needs to be planted for fertilization.
Planting: Under the right conditions, cucumbers will grow and produce a large harvest of fruit. They need plenty of water and organic matter, as well as a sunny location. They are a warm-weather crop, so be sure to plant them only after the soil has warmed up. Cucumbers grow best in well-drained soil. Provide them with a lot of room if you want them to vine along the ground, but you'll get better production and save a lot of space if you train them to a trellis of wire or wooden lath. The fruit from staked cucumber vines is cleaner, straighter, and especially good for pickling, because fewer culls will form on the vines.

Sow seeds in four- or five-seed hills, spaced about six feet apart. Bush varieties can be planted as close as three feet. Place a shovelful of manure or compost under each hill.

Culture: After seedlings have started to develop, thin out all but the three strongest plants per hill. As soon as the plants begin to vine, start training them up a support. Most varieties will quickly take to vertical growth if they get a gentle helping hand at the outset. If necessary, tie the young plants loosely with soft twine.

Keep vines moist at all times and eliminate competition from weeds with a thick mulch. If the vines seem to be getting out of hand at the expense of the fruit, pick off the outermost new growth. As the season nears an end, vines should be pinched back so that existing fruit will mature before frost hits.

Always pick fruits as soon as they are ready, so later cucumbers are not robbed of necessary nutrients. Plus, once a vine succeeds in getting a fruit to mature seeds, that vine will stop producing and die.

Harvest: Cucumbers are best picked when they are small and most tasty. Overripe cucumbers are dry, mealy, and often have developed hard, indigestible seeds. If the skin begins to turn yellow, the cucumber is already too ripe.

DANDELION

Most gardeners would probably scoff at the thought of planting a dandelion on purpose. But this common lawn pest also makes a surprisingly tender, succulent addition to green salads. Wild dandelion can be used, but cultivated varieties will produce more flavorful leaves.

Varieties: Thick-Leaved.

Planting: Sow dandelion in fall or spring in almost any type of soil. You'll get better-tasting leaves, however, if the plants are given plenty of well-rotted manure or compost. Scatter seeds in shallow furrows about 15 inches apart. Cover lightly and water well.

Culture: For best growth, keep plants thinned to stand about six inches apart. Pinch flowers off to prevent the plants from going to seed and spreading. Water during severe drought.

Harvest: Outer leaves can be picked fresh at any time.

EGGPLANT

The oddly attractive eggplant is actually a relative newcomer to home gardens in the U.S., coming originally from India and the Middle East. It's a warm-season crop that needs a long period of warm weather to mature.

Varieties: Over 30 varieties are available; most adapt readily to container growing. One of the recommended large-fruit varieties is Black Beauty. Other hybrids, such as Black Magic, Jersey King, and Burpee Hybrid, are favorites, offering disease resistance, vigor, and quick maturity.

Planting: Start plants indoors from seeds at least eight to ten weeks before the last expected frost. Or purchase started healthy transplants. Harden the plants in a cold frame or on a porch. Then set them out in rows three feet apart in the garden after all danger of frost has passed. Allow two feet between individual plants. Install a cutworm collar (like that used with broccoli) around the stems.

After planting, water generously and protect from high winds or glaring sun for the first few days.

Culture: To get a good crop of eggplant, weeds must be kept at a minimum. Handpick weeds near the plants, and use a hoe to cultivate between the rows and plants. A thick mulch applied after the soil has warmed up will also help control weeds and preserve moisture.

If insects threaten, use an all-purpose spray or pick them off by hand. Check plants daily to prevent any sudden infestations.

Harvest: When harvesting eggplant, look for a glossy coating; brownness indicates overripeness. Remove the fruit with pruning shears, rather than pull the fruit from the plant. As the season draws to a close, pinch off all blossoms and small immature fruit. This will encourage the plants to put all their growing power into the few remaining fruits before frost hits.

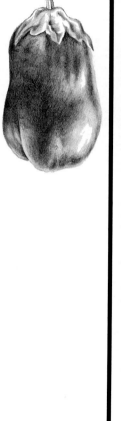

ENDIVE

Endive is another sweet and succulent green crop that can add a special flavor all its own to a salad. It's also used as a garnish, like parsley. Endive is easy to grow and matures in about two months.

Varieties: Two good varieties are Green Curled and Broad Leaved Batavian. For escarole, the wide-leaved version of endive, grow the varieties Full Heart Batavian and Florida Deep Hearted.

Planting: Endive can be grown wherever lettuce thrives. In fact, it's a much hardier green than lettuce and can even tolerate some midsummer heat without bolting to seed.

Sow seed in rows 18 to 24 inches apart. As seedlings emerge, thin them to stand every six inches in the row. You can make succes-

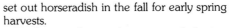

sive sowings every two weeks to ensure a continuous crop. Or treat it as a backup crop for lettuce, sowing it a week or so after the lettuce has germinated. (Endive can be started indoors for an early crop.)

Culture: To encourage extra leafy growth, add a side-dressing of high-nitrogen fertilizer every few weeks. Keep plants mulched to increase soil moisture.

Harvest: Both the broad-leaved and curly-leaved endive must be blanched to produce creamy white centers and to prevent leaves from becoming tough and bitter. As the plants mature, simply gather the outer leaves over the top of the plants, and secure with rubber bands or string. Pull the plants after they have blanched white.

GROUND CHERRY

Also known as the husk or strawberry tomato, ground cherries grow inside paperlike husks. You can eat the deliciously sweet fruit raw or make it into preserves and pie fillings. The fruits can also be dried for use in winter bouquets.

Varieties: Often available only from specialty seed suppliers, ground cherry also may be listed under cape or dwarf gooseberry.

Planting: Grown like tomatoes, ground cherries should be started indoors six to eight weeks before the last expected frost. Set the plants about 15 inches apart in rows 20 inches apart.

Culture: For greatest growth, keep seedlings well watered and free from weeds. Newly planted seedlings should be protected for several days from direct sunlight.

Harvest: Pick husks when they ripen and turn a bright red color. Plants may self-sow readily and can become like a weed in some areas.

HORSERADISH

Horseradish is a prolific perennial you'll enjoy growing. It takes little care, and the grated root makes an excellent condiment.

Varieties: The best-known variety is Maliner Kren.

Planting: Grow horseradish as an annual or as a perennial. As a perennial, all you have to do is plant it in an out-of-the-way garden corner, pulling the roots as you need them. The plants are hardy and will not require any winter protection. They will, however, have a tendency to spread throughout the garden.

If you choose to grow horseradish as an annual, plant the sets in the early spring, and dig up the entire crop in the fall. You can also

set out horseradish in the fall for early spring harvests.

For best results, purchase sets and plant as soon as the soil can be worked in the spring. Space plants 12 inches apart, with the thick ends pointing up. Rows should be at least 24 inches apart. For straight, even roots, be sure the planting area has been deeply tilled before setting out the plants.

Culture: As soon as tiny shoots are visible, remove invading weeds. Pick by hand near plants; cultivate with a hoe between rows. Use a mulch to cut down on weeding chores. Side-dress with a high-potassium fertilizer at ten- to 14-day intervals, to encourage good root growth.

Harvest: Dig up roots as needed.

JERUSALEM ARTICHOKE

Jerusalem artichokes are members of the sunflower family that form edible tubers low in starch and calories. They're a tall perennial that will easily reach ten feet in height.

Varieties: Artichoke tubers may be obtained from a reliable supplier of vegetable seeds.

Planting: Set artichoke tubers 18 to 24 inches apart in rows three to four feet apart. Plant as soon as the soil is workable in the spring. Be sure to cover each tuber with at least four inches of topsoil. A heavy feeder, artichokes will respond favorably to applications of organic or chemical fertilizers.

Culture: As the tubers begin to sprout, handpick competing weeds. Later, as the plants get taller, they'll keep weeds in check by casting a dense shade.

Although the flowers are attractive, it's often advisable to pinch off flower buds to force better tuber development.

Harvest: In the fall, cut stalks to the ground, and dig tubers carefully so the skins aren't damaged. Or leave the tubers in the ground under a heavy mulch for wintertime harvests.

KALE

Another cool-season member of the cabbage family, kale is the perfect early spring or late fall crop. Kale is good tasting and hardy. Its deeply crinkled blue-green leaves make it a natural for striking ornamental plantings.

Varieties: Three of the best varieties for easy growing are Vates, Dwarf Blue Curled, and Dwarf Siberian.

Planting: Because it is hardy and, in fact, improves in flavor after a mild frost, kale can

be grown at either end of the growing season. Or use it to follow an early-season crop, such as green beans or peas.

Sow seed a half inch deep in rows at least 18 inches apart. Or seed can be scatter sown for low maintenance, wide-row cultivation.

Culture: Once planted, kale requires little work other than mulching to keep its roots cool and also to discourage weeds. To increase yield, add side-dressings of fertilizer every few weeks. Constant moisture is also a must.

Harvest: Kale will supply a continuous crop if only the outer leaves are picked as they mature. Or pull entire plants. If you want to harvest the crop all year, cover the plants with a thick mulch during the winter. The plants will stay green all winter, and you'll be able to dig some up at will. Or turn the entire planting bed under in the fall, treating the kale as a green manure crop.

KOHLRABI

Similar in cultural requirements to cabbage, kohlrabi is grown for its unusual, swollen lower stems. Both leaf stalks and the enlarged root stalk are edible.

Varieties: Two popular varieties include Early Burpee Vienna and Early White Vienna.

Planting: Kohlrabi does best when it can mature during cool weather, so your chances of success will increase if you plant it in the garden early in the spring. Sow seeds as soon as the ground can be worked, thinning plants to six inches apart as they emerge. Space rows about 24 inches apart. For an even earlier crop, start seeds indoors six to eight weeks before the average date of last frost.

Culture: Kohlrabi requires plenty of sun and a cool, moist soil. Add a thick mulch as soon as the plants are up and growing to help preserve soil moisture. If you're cultivating with a hoe, be sure to do it gently to avoid damaging kohlrabi's shallow root system, and try not to cover knobs with soil. Spray at weekly intervals with *Bacillus thuringiensis* to prevent cabbageworm attack.

Harvest: Pick before the knobs grow greater than three inches wide. Kohlrabi will become tough and stringy if it ripens beyond maturity. Simply cut the knob from the main root at soil level. Larger, older roots will be tougher but still usable in salads.

LEEK

Coveted for their subtle onion flavor, leeks require about 130 days to mature. They're easy to grow and can be left in the garden for

harvesting all season.

Varieties: The most commonly planted varieties include Conqueror, Tivia, and Broad London.

Planting: Seeds are customarily started indoors eight weeks before outdoor planting. When planting from seed directly into the garden, sow at a depth of a half inch and cover with sifted soil. When plants have reached a height of eight inches, cut off half the tops and plant five inches apart in another row. Rows should be spaced 24 inches apart.

If you are planting transplants, set them into a furrow about six inches below the soil level. As plants mature, gather soil against the stems. This blanching procedure will produce tender, white stalks.

Culture: Nip weeds as soon as they begin to invade the rows. A good mulch will make the job easier. If rain is insufficient, sprinkle with a garden hose to maintain soil moisture. Keep soil on the neutral side (pH 6.5 to 7.5) with periodic applications of agricultural lime. When plants are ready for blanching, pull back mulch and bank soil against the stalks.

Harvest: Pull leeks when the stems are between one and 2½ inches in diameter. For harvest all winter, apply a thick mulch before the ground hardens, and dig stalks as you need them.

LETTUCE

Lettuce is perhaps the most popular and diverse vegetable available to the home gardener. It grows quickly, is easy to care for, and comes in a variety of forms and flavors.

Varieties: There are three major types of lettuce: the loose-leaf variety (leaves can be picked as they mature); head lettuce; and the Cos—or upright—lettuce. Every gardener has a favorite type, but loose-leaf varieties are slightly more popular because they're easier to grow and because they provide a continuous supply of leaves. Good loose-leaf varieties are Black-Seeded Simpson, Salad Bowl, and Oak Leaf. The most popular heading types are Great Lakes, Burpee's Iceberg, and Dark Green Boston. The favorite upright varieties are Romaine and Paris White. And to make matters even more confusing, there is another smaller group of lettuce varieties called butterhead or bibb. The all-time favorite bibb variety is Buttercrunch.

Planting: Lettuce is a short-season crop that is resistant to cold, so for best results, sow seeds as soon as soil conditions permit. Plant seeds a half inch deep in rows spaced 14 inches apart. Or start seeds indoors to get a jump on the outdoor growing season. Be sure to set aside additional rows for successive

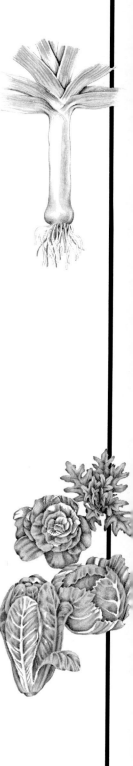

plantings made at two-week intervals. Sow seed in shallow furrows. Because seed is light, pour a small amount into one hand, and grip between forefinger and thumb of the other hand. Cover with no more than a quarter inch of fine soil, and sprinkle with water.

Most lettuce varieties grow well mingled with flowers (the light green is refreshing) or other slower-growing vegetables, such as cabbage, cauliflower, or broccoli. If your garden space is small, let the lettuce crop share its growing space.

Culture: Begin thinning young lettuce plants as soon as they are up and established. When seedlings are about four inches high, thin to three inches between plants; later, six inches; then 12 to 18 inches between mature plants. Use thinnings in early salads, or transplant them to another section of the garden.

A high-nitrogen fertilizer worked into the soil at planting time and applied as a side-dressing during the growing season will encourage abundant leaf growth. Never let fertilizer granules come in contact with the leaves. When cultivating around the lettuce plants with a hoe, avoid getting soil on or against the plants.

Most lettuce varieties will become bitter and unusable during hot midsummer weather, but don't let that stop you from sowing seeds again in early August for a good-tasting fall harvest.

Harvest: Loose-leaf varieties can be used throughout the season, simply by picking the outer leaves as they mature. Pull head, upright, and bibb varieties only after the entire plant has completely matured. To pick leaf lettuce, pinch the leaves off at the base of the plant. Heads are removed by cutting the entire plant at soil level.

MUSKMELON (CANTALOUPE)

A long season of warm days and nights, in addition to ample moisture, are two prerequisites for a good muskmelon (or cantaloupe) crop. But newer, hardier, more compact varieties have recently been developed that make growing muskmelons even easier and less space-consuming.

Varieties: Some of the most reliable varieties are: Ambrosia, Burpee Hybrid, Iroquois, and Delicious 51.

Planting: Because muskmelons are a warm-season crop, they should not be planted until all danger of frost has passed. Sow seeds five to a hill (cluster), about one inch deep. Hills should be spaced at least four to six feet apart. Place a shovelful or two of

compost or manure in each hill before planting to help speed early growth. After seedlings are up and have developed their third set of true leaves, thin them to stand three plants per hill.

Culture: As soon as weeds are visible, remove them from the garden. Keep hoeings shallow to avoid disturbing the shallow root systems of the plants. Add a mulch of black plastic to cut back on weed growth, increase soil moisture, and to keep the soil continuously warm. When fruits begin to appear, place a board, shingle, or roofing paper under fruits to hasten ripening and to prevent rot.

Harvest: Even though a melon may become large, it isn't necessarily ripe. A ripe melon will have an irresistible odor and will slip easily from its stem. Any melons that do not pull away easily from the main vine are not ripe. As the season closes, pinch off small fruits to force the ripening of the larger fruits. Also, pinch off the growing points of all the vines.

MUSTARD

Mustard greens have long been a favorite dish in the South, but their popularity is catching on elsewhere. It takes only about 40 days for the greens to mature, and they make a good spring and fall crop.

Varieties: There are both curly- and broad-leaved varieties. Some favorite curly types are Burpee's Fordhook and Southern Giant Curled. Broad-leaved varieties include Florida Broad Leaf and the flavorful Tendergreen.

Planting: Plan on early spring, fall, or even winter yields because mustard tends to run to seed in warm weather. Sow seeds a half inch deep in rows 18 to 24 inches apart. Some gardeners in the North like to sow seeds in the fall and overwinter young plants with several inches of insulating mulch. In spring, the mulch can be pulled back so the seedlings can resume growth for an early harvest.

Culture: Weed and thin plants as soon as the row becomes visible. Mature plants should stand six to eight inches apart in the row. Because mustard is a leaf crop, it will benefit from occasional side-dressings of a nitrogen-rich fertilizer, either in the form of a commercial preparation or an organic source, such as compost, fish scraps, or blood meal. Be sure to clip off all flower heads as they appear to prevent the mustard plants from setting seed and spreading throughout the garden like a weed.

Harvest: Pick outer leaves as the mustard greens mature, or pull the entire plant as it reaches peak flavor.

OKRA

Traditionally grown in the South, okra requires temperatures well above 60 degrees Fahrenheit and a well-drained, fertile soil. Its elongated seedpods are excellent additions to soups and stews, or they can be cooked and served separately.

Varieties: Tall varieties, such as Clemson Spineless, may grow to four feet. They make an attractive garden hedge, with handsome foliage and showy yellow, hibiscus-like flowers. Shorter varieties, such as Dwarf Green Long Pod, grow two feet tall.

Planting: A slow-growing crop, okra does fine in any fertile, well-drained soil. In regions with short growing seasons, start seed indoors for transplanting after all danger of frost has passed and the ground has warmed. When planting from seed, space rows at least 30 inches apart. Thoroughly prepare the soil, and fertilize it before planting. Indoor sowings should be made at least a month and a half to two months before the last day of expected frost.

Culture: When plants are four to six inches high, thin them to stand six inches apart. Later, as the plants mature, thin them again to stand 18 to 24 inches apart. Occasionally add side-dressings of fertilizer to encourage good growth. Keep the plants mulched and well watered at all times.

Harvest: Pods are ready to be harvested when they are 2½ to seven inches long. The smaller the pod, the more tender it will be. Be sure to keep the pods picked to encourage continuous production. Once a pod is allowed to mature, the entire plant will stop producing.

ONIONS

Onions belong in every garden because they take up little space, are easy to grow, and produce a crop that can be stored for a long period—well into the winter. They also come in a range of shapes, colors and flavors suitable for a multitude of recipes.

Varieties: Good onion varieties to use at the table in mid-season include Red Hamburger, Sweet Spanish, and Yellow Bermuda. Favorite winter storage onions are Ebenezer, Early Yellow Globe, Yellow Globe Danvers, and White Sleeper varieties. Two good bunching onions, or scallions, are Evergreen Long White Bunching and Southport Long White Bunching.

Planting: Start onions by planting sets, seedlings, or seeds. Sets are actually dormant onion bulbs saved from the year before by commercial growers. By planting sets, you'll be sure to get large, well-formed bulbs by the end of the season. They can also be pulled mid-season for table use. Seedlings are young plants that have been started early in the South and shipped to the North for spring planting. These are especially popular because they can be pulled early for use as scallions, or they can be allowed to mature for table use or winter storage. Seeds are slow to germinate, but once started, they produce a late crop perfect for storing.

As soon as the soil can be worked, plant sets or seedlings one inch deep and about four inches apart in rows spaced 12 to 24 inches apart. With sets, be sure the pointed end is facing up. If you're starting your crop from seed, sow as soon as possible in the spring in well-marked shallow furrows. Add a few radish seeds to help identify the location of the slower-growing onions.

Culture: Especially susceptible to weed invasion, onions should be cultivated regularly. As soon as the onions are several inches tall, add a thick mulch around the plants to help cut competition from weeds. Your onion crop will also benefit from plenty of organic matter and moisture. Add side-dressings of rotted manure or commercial fertilizer every two or three weeks during the growing season. Water deeply at least once a week. If plants start to flower, break the buds off to stimulate greater bulb growth.

Harvest: Toward the end of the season most onion stalks will begin to weaken and fall over. When about three quarters of the tops have fallen over, knock the remaining stalks to the ground with a rake or stiff broom. Pull bulbs when stalks are completely brown, and spread them out on the ground for a few days to cure in the sun. This curing process is essential if you want long-lasting onions for storage.

To store, cut off stems about one inch from the top of the bulb, and place the onions in slatted boxes or mesh containers. Set the boxes in a cool, dark place and use onions as needed. Most storage varieties will last up to three months. If you like, weave the dried stems together to make a hanging "onion rope," rather than use the slatted boxes.

PARSNIP

Parsnips are an often-overlooked—but both nutritious and good-tasting—vegetable. They have a sweet, nutty flavor that will improve most any soup or stew. Or use them in many of the same ways you use carrots.

Varieties: The two old standbys are Hollow Crown and Harris' Model.

Planting: Parsnip roots can reach a depth of 15 inches, so be sure to work the soil deeply before planting. Work in compost or manure, break any dense clumps, and remove rocks or other garden debris that might obstruct normal root development. Parsnip seeds take a long time to germinate, so plant them as soon as the ground is workable in the spring. Sow the seed fairly thick a half-inch deep in rows 18 to 24 inches apart. Interplant radishes to help mark the row. To prevent crusting, mix peat moss or dried grass clippings with the soil used to cover the seed.

Culture: When the quick-germinating radish seeds poke through, carefully weed the entire row. Once delicate leaves of parsnips appear and grow to about four inches in height, thin them to stand about six inches apart. Thin again later, allowing eight inches between mature plants. Be sure to keep plants well watered and weed free all season long.

Harvest: Although highly resistant to cold, parsnip roots are generally dug before the ground freezes. Flavor improves after several light frosts, however. If you want plants for wintering over, cover the crowns with a thick layer of straw mulch and mark the bed. You should be able to dig through the mulch layer all winter for a continuous, fresh harvest. Otherwise, the plants can be dug completely in the fall and stored indoors like carrots.

PEAS

A staked row of peas takes little garden space and yields heavily. Peas are a cool-season crop that can be enjoyed in both the spring and the fall. They're also highly ornamental with their graceful vines and delicate, white blossoms.

Varieties: Early varieties (50 to 63 days to maturity) include: Burpeeana Early Dwarf, Little Marvel, Alaska, Freezonian, and Thomas Laxton. Good later varieties (65 to 80 days) are Burpee's Blue Bantam, Alderman, Fordhook Wonder, Green Arrow, and Wando.

Besides the traditional sweet green (or English) pea, snow peas are becoming more popular in home gardens. These edible-podded sugar peas include: Oregon Sugar Pod, Burpee Sweet Pod, Mammoth Melting Sugar, and Dwarf Gray Sugar.

A third type of garden peas is the cowpea or southern table pea. These need warm days and nights. Favorite cowpeas are California Blackeye, Brown Crowder, Mississippi, and Early Ramshorn Black Eye.

Planting: Sow peas as early in the spring as the ground can be worked. Peas will burn out quickly if hot weather strikes while the plants are still small. Plant the seeds every three inches in double rows about 24 to 30 inches apart. Later, as the peas begin to germinate, install a chicken-wire support down the center of each double row.

Other gardeners prefer to plant peas in wide rows. Simply rake an area about 12 inches wide, and broadcast seed. In a few weeks, the peas will be up and almost self-supporting. Planted in this manner, the peas will also choke out a lot of weeds.

Because peas are leguminous (which means their roots develop small nodules that fix nitrogen), stimulate early growth by coating the seeds with a nitrogen inoculate before planting. Most garden supply houses carry pea inoculate as a staple item.

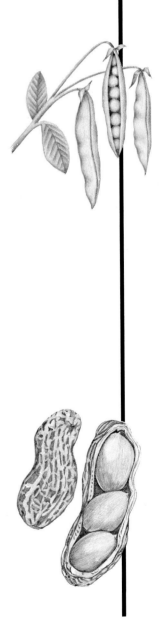

Culture: As soon as seedlings push through the soil, provide support. Nylon netting, chicken wire, or brush pushed into the ground is sufficient. After staking, peas require little maintenance. They are heavy feeders and benefit from an occasional side-dressing of manure or fertilizer, but don't overdo—too much fertilizer will result in plenty of leaves and vine growth but little pod production. Keep the plants moist at all times. Peas planted in rows will benefit from a thick mulch to keep roots cool and conserve moisture.

Harvest: Once pods begin to form, check the plants frequently so the peas don't become overripe. The surface of the pod should feel firm but not hard. Overripe peas will crack and taste mealy. Keep pods picked to stimulate continuous production.

Edible podded peas should be harvested while still thin. If pea bulges are noticeable, the pod will not be at its most flavorful.

Cowpeas may be picked when the peas are fully developed, but not yet hard, and the shells still green. Or allow them to ripen on the plant, and harvest as dried peas to use during the winter.

PEANUT

Often considered a novelty in the North, peanuts are a main crop in many southern areas. They're easy to grow and do surprisingly well in light soil with a light clay content.

Varieties: Jumbo Virginia is the most popular large-podded variety, while the Spanish variety is famous for its small, sweet nuts. The larger varieties will usually require a growing season of at least 120 days.

Planting: Before planting, be sure your ground is well worked and free of stones and debris. Peanuts require a slightly alkaline soil, so work in some limestone if your soil is on the acid side. They are also heavy feeders, so add a layer of well-rotted manure or compost to the soil before you till.

After the danger of frost has passed, plant the seeds four to six inches apart and about two inches deep. Space rows 24 to 30 inches apart. Plant peanuts either with or without the shells.

Culture: After the seeds have germinated and the seedlings are several inches high, thin them to stand about eight to 12 inches apart. Hoe frequently to discourage competition from weeds. Keep plants moist at all times.

Harvest: After peanuts flower, the flowering stalks work their way into the soil where the shells and "peas" develop. In the fall, before frost hits, dig up the row and shake the soil loose from the roots. Hang the plants to dry for several days, and remove the pods from the roots. You can store peanut pods in airtight jars.

PEPPERS

Peppers are warm-weather vegetables that require about 2½ months to fully develop. Somewhat finicky, peppers need even temperatures and warm nights for good fruiting.

Varieties: There are two major classes of peppers: sweet and hot. Sweet peppers can be served raw in salads, cooked, or dried. Hot peppers are dried and used in a variety of spicy recipes. Good varieties of sweet peppers include: Tokyo Bell, Bell Boy, Yolo Wonder, and California Wonder. Favorite varieties of hot peppers are Long Red Cayenne, Hot Portugal, and Hungarian Wax.

Planting: Start pepper seeds indoors four to six weeks before the last expected frost. Or purchase plants for transplanting after the soil has warmed thoroughly. Space plants about 18 to 24 inches apart in rows 20 to 36 inches apart. Be sure to install a cutworm collar, like the ones made to protect broccoli, as soon as possible. After planting, water the seedlings well with warm water and protect from intense sun. Peppers will thrive in any soil that has good drainage.

Culture: Keep pepper plants well watered throughout the summer and free from any weed competition. A straw or black plastic mulch will help choke out weeds and keep soil moisture content high.

Try to avoid adding excessive amounts of fertilizer or organic matter; over-fertilized plants will spend all their time producing foliage rather than fruits. If weather conditions are unsuitable, blossoms drop off, but new blossoms will appear and eventually set fruit.

Harvest: Sweet peppers may be picked at

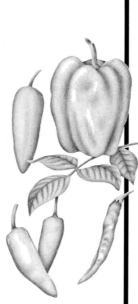

any stage of development, but for sweeter flavor, allow the fruits to ripen to a deep red color. Hot varieties are harvested as needed or used dried.

POTATO

Potatoes should be a staple crop in the home garden because they are easy to grow, take up relatively little space, produce abundantly, and have a superb taste. Grow potatoes for storage all winter long, or harvest them as they grow for mouth-watering "baby spuds."

Varieties: For summertime harvests, try Irish Cobbler, Norland, or Russet. Good long-season varieties that do well in storage are Kennebec and Katahdin.

Planting: To start your crop, obtain certified seed potatoes from your garden supply house. If you use old, grocery store-bought potatoes for planting, you will not get as good a harvest.

Cut the seed potatoes in squares about 1½ inches across, making sure there is at least one "eye," or growing point, per piece. Place them cut-side down in a trench four inches deep. Space the pieces about a foot apart in the row. Potatoes are a cool-season crop, so be sure to get the eyes planted as early in the spring as the ground can be worked. Do not plant if the soil is wet. Potatoes grow best in a slightly acid soil.

Culture: Good soil care around your potato plants is essential for good growth. Pull the soil up around the stems of the potato plants if any tubers begin to show on the soil surface. This will reduce the chances of sunscald and keep the soil in a loose, friable (easily crumbled) condition so harvesting is easier. Potatoes exposed to sunlight turn green and are inedible. Keep the crop well watered and free from weeds.

Harvest: Harvest young potatoes throughout the summer by carefully working them free of the soil. Try not to disturb the mother plant too much. Harvest the rest of the crop after the vines have withered and turned brown completely. Dig tubers with a potato fork or spade, being careful not to puncture the skins. If you're planning on storing the crop for a long time, discard all bruised and damaged fruit, rather than mix it with the rest of the harvest. Dig the tubers on a sunny, dry day, because they are difficult to remove from wet, soggy, soil.

PUMPKIN

Most varieties of pumpkins grow into large, spreading vines that quickly cover a wide area and require more space than the average gardener can afford. They can, however, tolerate more shade than the other squash, so you might find an unused garden corner for them. Or plant them between corn rows or along a fence.

Varieties: Pumpkins come in all sizes. There are the giant-size varieties, such as Big Max, Big Tom, and Howden's Field. And there are the intermediate-size varieties, often used for cooking, Jackpot and Spirit Hybrid. The smaller varieties (Small Sugar and Spookie) are just right for gardens tight on space. Several naked-seed varieties, such as Triple Treat and Lady Godiva, are for devotees of dried pumpkin seeds. A recent introduction is Cinderella, a bush variety that requires much less space than the rambling varieties do.

Planting: After frost danger is past and soil has warmed, gather soil into hills spaced six feet apart. Sow five seeds per hill, and side-dress with plenty of well-rotted manure, compost, and commercial fertilizer. When seedlings are up and growing, thin them to stand three plants per hill. If space is a problem, train the young vines up a trellis or fence, or let the vines ramble down corn rows.

Culture: For a weed-free planting bed, spread a thick mulch before the pumpkins begin to vine. A mulch helps control weeds and keeps the fruit clean. Once the plants have started spreading throughout the garden, it is almost impossible to hoe out weeds. Keep plants well watered, and side-dress with fertilizer or rotted manure every two or three weeks.

Harvest: Allow pumpkins to fully mature on the vine. Then when frost is imminent, remove the pumpkins by snipping stems at least two inches from the fruit. Skins will cure and harden if the pumpkins are allowed to remain in the field several days before storing. Move curing pumpkins to a shed or garage at night to prevent frost damage.

RADISH

The foolproof radish reaches maturity within 20 to 30 days after planting, changing so fast you can almost watch it grow. It's a nearly indestructible crop and can be grown anywhere, from raised beds to flowerpots.

Varieties: Favorite varieties of radishes include Cherry Belle, White Icicle, and Sparkler. Good varieties for fall planting are Black Spanish, White Chinese, and China Rose.

Planting: Sow seeds as early in the spring as the ground can be worked in furrows about three quarters of an inch deep in rows spaced about 12 inches apart. Radishes are a quick-growing crop, so for a continuous harvest, sow small bands of seeds every two weeks, rather than one long row that will mature all at once. If you like, mix the radish seeds half and half with carrot seeds, and plant the mixture in a wide row. The radishes will mark the location of the slower-growing carrots and will also help shade out early weed competition. Plus, as you harvest the radishes, you will be thinning out the young carrots automatically.

The secret to juicy, tender roots is rapid growth. Water the plants generously, and supply them with a continuous nutrient supply by working fertilizer and compost into the garden soil.

When seedlings have sprouted, thin them to stand about two inches apart. Overcrowding produces misshapen, practically unusable roots.

Culture: To help promote vigorous growth, apply a mulch when the seedlings are about three inches high. The mulch will cut weed competition and increase the available soil moisture. Add more fertilizer every other week to keep growth constant.

If root maggots are a problem in your area, treat soil before planting with a pesticide labeled for use in controlling them. Follow manufacturer's instructions carefully.

Harvest: As roots mature, tops will begin to protrude through the soil. Pick while the roots are still young and tender. A split radish is probably an overripe radish.

RHUBARB

An easy-to-grow perennial, rhubarb demands little, if any, attention from the home gardener. Prized for its flavorful stalks, these attractive plants appear unfailingly in the early spring each year.

Varieties: Three commonly grown varieties are MacDonald, Valentine, and Victoria.

Planting: Rhubarb grows best where freezing temperatures penetrate the ground. Because rhubarb is a perennial, plant it in an unused corner of the garden where the plants will not be disturbed by yearly cultivation. They require full sun but will tolerate some shade. Start your rhubarb bed with roots purchased from a reliable nursery, or take root divisions from an established clump. Before planting, turn the soil to a depth of ten inches and fill halfway with well-rotted manure or compost. Then place the roots in the hole, being sure they are at least four to six inches deep. Cover with topsoil and water well. Space plants four feet apart.

You can start rhubarb plants from seed, but it will take at least two years for the plants to grow to a harvestable size.

Culture: Weed control is especially important during the first year. If possible, add a thick mulch of straw or compost as soon as the plants are several inches above the soil level.

If the plants begin to develop a flower stalk, remove it immediately to help channel all growth into the leaves and stems. Later, as the plants get older, the leaf stalks will become more and more spindly. This is the time to split roots for new plantings. Dig the plants in the early spring, separating the plant into several smaller sections. Be sure each section or division has at least three leaf buds and plenty of roots. Replant these divisions as you did the original mother plant.

Harvest: Plants grown from rootstocks can be moderately harvested after the first growing season. Grasp the stalks at the base of the plant, and gently pull from the root crown with a twisting motion. By the second or third year, your plants should be mature enough to stand a full harvest.

Do not use rhubarb leaves. The leaves contain poisonous oxalic acid and should be discarded. Use only the leaf stalks. Never pick more than a third of the plant.

ROQUETTE

Roquette is a tangy salad green well known in Europe. Also called rocket green, it has a distinctly sharp flavor and is at its best when mixed with other greens.

Varieties: There are no named varieties.

Planting: Plant roquette in the spring or early fall because it tolerates heat poorly. Sow seeds in shallow furrows, spacing the furrows about 12 inches apart. Later, as the crop begins to grow, thin the plants to stand about three to four inches apart. Roquette is quick growing, so for a continuous harvest, sow a crop every two or three weeks for a continuous harvest.

Culture: You'll get tender leaves if you encourage the plants to grow quickly. Give them plenty of water, and side-dress with fertilizer or well-rotted manure every other week. If unexpected drought hits, mulch the plants with several inches of hay or leaves.

Harvest: Harvest leaves at any time. Younger leaves usually have a better flavor.

RUTABAGA AND TURNIP

These two flavorful and fast-growing root crops are useful following early-season spinach, peas, or carrots. Harvested in the

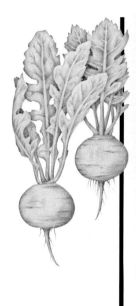

fall, they store well for midwinter meals.

Varieties: The most reliable turnip varieties include: Tokyo Market; Foliage or Shogoin (which is also grown specifically for its succulent greens); Just Right; and Purple Top White Globe. Rutabaga varieties include Macomber and Purple Top.

Planting: Because turnips and rutabagas are both root crops, they demand a well-prepared soil, free of stones and debris, before they can grow well. Work plenty of manure or compost into the soil before you plant. Plant seeds midsummer after the remains of the early crops have died back. Sow seed a half inch deep, and cover lightly with peat moss or sand to prevent the soil from crusting over the small seeds. Both rutabagas and turnips are slow to germinate, so mix in some radish seeds at planting time to help mark the row.

Culture: Using the radish seedlings as a guide, remove early sprouting weeds from the row. Neither rutabagas nor turnips can tolerate weed competition. When the seedlings are about four inches tall, thin the turnips to stand about four inches apart. Rutabagas should stand eight inches apart. Keep the plants well watered at all times and mulched to help combat weeds.

Harvest: Dig turnip roots before a hard frost, while the roots are young and tender. Tops of roots should be about three inches across. Rutabagas can be dug in the fall or wintered over under a protective layer of mulch. Stake the area so the crop can be found under the snow. Harvest turnip tops at any time during the season.

SALSIFY

Salsify, or oyster plant, is the most unusual root crop vegetable you can grow, because, when cooked, the long white roots taste similar to fresh oysters. Salsify is a slow grower that requires about four months to mature fully, but it takes up very little room in the garden. Plant it among other crops, such as lettuce and cabbage, if space is at a premium.

Varieties: The most commonly available variety is Sandwich Island Mammoth.

Planting: Similar in cultural requirements to turnips and parsnips, salsify needs a rich, well-prepared soil, free of clumps, sticks, and stones. As soon as the ground can be worked, sow the seeds in shallow furrows, spaced 16 to 24 inches apart.

Culture: Salsify cannot compete with invading weeds, so keep the row weeded. As soon as seedlings stand three inches tall, thin them to stand six inches apart. At this time, a four-inch layer of mulch should be spread around the plants to increase soil moisture and to combat weeds.

Harvest: Pick roots when crowns are one to 1½ inches in diameter. With adequate protection, the roots may be left in the ground over winter for a spring harvest.

SHALLOT

A member of the onion family, shallots are grown for their mild, delicate flavor.

Varieties: There are no named varieties.

Planting: Shallots are easily grown from bulbs planted as early in the spring as the soil will permit. Place the bulbs in a one-inch-deep furrow, cover with soil, and tamp with the back of a hoe to firm the soil. As with onion sets, bulbs should stand several inches apart, with the pointed end of the bulb facing up. In the South, plant bulbs in the fall for a winter harvest. Before planting, always be sure the soil is well drained and well supplied with nutrients.

Culture: Once planted, shallots require little care other than weed protection. When the plants are several inches high, apply a thick mulch to encourage greatest growth.

Harvest: As the season nears an end, the tops of the plants will brown and die back. Flatten any remaining stalks with the back of a rake or shovel. Pick the bulbs when the stalks have completely turned brown; dry and store as for onions.

SPINACH

Spinach is a dual-purpose vegetable that can be cooked or used raw in salads. With a high vitamin A content, it is also one of the most nutritious vegetables you can grow.

Varieties: Some commonly planted varieties include Viking, Winter Bloomsdale, and Melody Hybrid. New Zealand, which is not a true spinach, is resistant to warmer weather.

Planting: Spinach grows best during the cooler temperatures of spring and fall. As soon as soil preparation is possible, sow seed three quarters of an inch deep in rows 14 to 18 inches apart. If necessary, sweeten an acid soil by applying agricultural lime at the rate of five pounds per 100 square feet of garden. Ideal pH for spinach is between 6.0 and 6.5. For a continuous crop, sow at ten-day intervals until warm weather arrives.

Culture: Quality and quantity of the spinach crop depend entirely on the amount of moisture and nitrogen available to the plants. Keep the plants well supplied with water, and be sure to work into the soil plenty of manure, compost, or fertilizer with a high ni-

trogen content. When the seedlings are about four inches high, thin them to stand three inches apart.

Harvest: Harvest outer leaves as needed, or pull the entire plant. As warmer weather arrives, pull all the crop; spinach bolts to seed in warm weather and becomes unusable.

SQUASH

Squash is a warm-weather crop that takes more room in the home garden than most vegetables but, given the right conditions, will outproduce other choices. Many new bush forms of squash have been developed to replace the old-fashioned, space-taking vining varieties.

Varieties: Of the summer soft-skinned varieties, the most commonly planted are: Early Prolific Straightneck (yellow); Zucchini Elite; Fordhook Zucchini; Cocozelle Bush (green); White Bush Patty Pan; and Scallopini Hybrid. Fall and winter hard-skinned varieties include: Royal Acorn, Bush Buttercup, Bush Acorn, Table King, and Bush Gold Nugget. Spaghetti Squash is a novelty variety that produces tasty, stringlike pulp.

Planting: Plant squash in hills (or clusters) when the soil warms up, spacing seeds about two inches apart. A common misconception is that the soil must be mounded, but this is an unnecessary chore. Be sure to supply the area with plenty of well-rotted manure, compost, or fertilizer. Space the hills about six feet apart. When the seedlings emerge, thin them to stand three plants per hill. If space is at a premium, choose only bush varieties.

Culture: After the young plants have started growing, apply a thick mulch to the entire area. Once vines ramble, weeds will be almost impossible to eradicate. Keep all the plants well watered, and apply periodic side-dressings of manure or fertilizer to boost production. If vines start to get out of hand, try training them up a fence or trellis.

Harvest: Summer squash develops quickly, so check the fruits daily. If they get too big, they lose quality and tenderness. If your fingernail can gently pierce the skin, they are ready to eat. Harvest all you can because any mature fruits left on the bushes will reduce bearing. Winter squash, on the other hand, must be allowed to mature completely on the vine before they are picked.

In the fall, watch the stems for yellowing; this means the fruit should be picked. Cut the fruits from the vines, leaving about three or four inches of stem attached to the squash. Place them in a sunny, dry location in the garden or on a shelf in a warm, well-ventilated room for several days. This curing process allows the shells of the fruit to harden and cure. Then move them to a storage cellar or dark room with temperatures around 55 to 60 degrees Fahrenheit. At no time, should frost be allowed to cover the fruits.

SUNFLOWER

Grown for their bright yellow flowers and tasty nutritious seeds, sunflowers are everyone's favorite. Fun to grow, they're great for the kids' garden. Their seeds also make feed for poultry and wild birds.

Varieties: Several large-flowered varieties are now on the market, including Mammoth, Gray Striped Russian, and Black Striped Russian.

Planting: A warm-weather crop, sunflowers do best when planted after all danger of frost has passed. They need full sun and a rich, well-drained soil. Sow seeds about a half inch deep and about one foot apart.

Culture: Once the plants are up and growing, keep weed competition to a minimum with a good thick mulch. Keep the plants well watered and fertilized. As the plants mature, stake them to prevent the heavy flower heads from breaking the stalk.

Harvest: Before seeds can be harvested, the flower heads must be allowed to mature completely on the plant. When the stem near the base of the flower turns yellow, cut the flower head and hang in a well-ventilated area. Seeds will separate easily when the flowers are sufficiently dry. If birds threaten to raid the flower heads before they can be harvested, cover the entire flower with mosquito netting. Store dried seeds in airtight containers.

SWEET POTATO

Sweet potatoes are a warm-weather crop that has long been grown in southern areas. Now transplants are available in garden supply houses around the country, so you can grow this versatile, long-season vegetable, no matter where you live.

Varieties: Good varieties are: Jersey Orange, Nugget, Nemagold, Centennial, and Goldrush.

Planting: Complete soil preparation is vital for sweet potatoes to grow best. A compact soil should be loosened by thorough digging and addition of compost, peat moss, or well-rotted manure. A moderately fertile, sandy loam is ideal. Sweet potato plants are generally started indoors, then hardened off by moving pots of seedlings outdoors for a few hours a day. Transplant them after danger of

frost has passed. Or buy started, hardened seedlings at your garden supply house at the correct planting time. Transplant the seedlings in rows 3½ to four feet apart and about 12 inches apart in the row.

Culture: Cultivate the plants regularly during the early stages of growth to cut weed growth. Once vines have spread, cultivation can be less frequent because the vines will be thick enough to shade out weeds. Keep plants well watered.

Harvest: Before the first heavy frost in the fall, dig the tubers, taking care not to injure the roots. Allow the roots to dry in the sun for several hours. Then cure by placing them in a warm room (85 degrees Fahrenheit) for about ten days.

TOMATO

Almost a universal vegetable, the tomato will provide rewarding yields in practically any soil and with little care. The tomatoes are a warm-season crop that will grow in nearly any location with at least six hours of direct sunlight a day.

Varieties: Among the smallest varieties are: Tiny Tim, Sweet 100, Small Fry, and Pixie. They're usually less than six feet tall. Yield is red fruit, one to two inches in diameter, 50 to 55 days after setting out. Plants are a good choice for pot culture.

Standard-size plants need 55 to 85 days to produce their larger fruits. By choosing some early varieties, as well as those that take longer to mature, you'll have a long summertime harvest. Among the popular early varieties (55 to 65 days) are Fireball, Early Wonder, Spring Giant, Early Girl, and Valiant. Favorite choices of main-season varieties (70 to 80 days) include: Better Boy, Big Boy, Better Girl, Super Fantastic, Floramericana, Supersonic, Rutgers, and Heinz 1350. Late varieties require at least 80 days of warm weather. Some of these are: Ramapo, Beefsteak, Manalucie, and Tropic.

In addition to the common red fruit varieties, also try the Yellow Pear and Yellow Plum; the pink Oxheart and Ponderosa; or orange Sunray, Jubilee, and Golden Boy. Besides considering the size, color, and growing time of specific plants, check for disease resistance. This is usually indicated on the label. The initial "V" or "F" indicates resistance to the verticillium and fusarium diseases, respectively. An "N" indicates that the plant is resistant to nematodes.

Planting: Because tomatoes are a long-season crop, tomato seed is usually started indoors eight to ten weeks before transplanting. Or well-developed seedlings can be purchased from a garden supply center. Two weeks before transplanting, harden off the plants by putting them in a cold frame or on a porch during the daytime.

Then set the plants about two feet apart in rows three feet apart in the garden. Plant seedlings that are to be caged or staked even closer. Small varieties can be spaced 12 to 15 inches apart in rows 15 inches apart. Be sure to install a cutworm collar of stiff paper, if cutworms are a problem in your area. If the sun seems especially hot, shade new transplants with newspaper or cardboard. Always keep the plants well watered.

Culture: Tomatoes respond well to a properly fertilized soil, but remember that too much nitrogen will result in overdeveloped vines and little fruit. Once plants take hold, control vines by pinching off the suckers that sprout from the joint where leaf stems join the main stem. For support, provide stakes, cages, or trellises before the plants begin to bear fruit.

To eliminate weeds, apply a thick mulch to the tomato bed. Or, to cut weeds and increase soil temperatures, use a black plastic mulch around the plants.

Harvest: Tomatoes are ready to be eaten when they pull easily from the vines. If you have to tug or pull, the tomato is not ready. When the season is nearly over, pinch off vine tips and any flower clusters to hasten ripening of green fruit. When frost threatens, pick green tomatoes, wrap in newspapers, and store in a cool, dark place until they ripen. Destroy spent tomato vines to prevent diseases and pests from overwintering.

WATERMELON

Anyone who has savored the sweet taste of a vine-ripened watermelon will testify there's nothing more succulent and refreshing on earth. Most varieties need a long, warm summer and plenty of soil nutrients to produce a respectable crop, but with proper planning, every gardener can easily savor a harvest of melons.

Varieties: Most watermelons grow well in the South, but northern growers have to take special care to produce a good crop. Always use early-maturing varieties, such as Sugar Baby, Crimson Sweet, Yellow Baby, New Hampshire Midget, and Burpee's Sugar Bush. Other popular varieties include: Burpee's Fordhook, Dixie Queen, Petite Sweet, and Charleston Gray.

Planting: Melons need a loose, rich soil and a warm growing season. Before planting, be sure to work as much well-rotted manure or compost as you can into the soil.

Start seed indoors four weeks before normal planting time, or wait until the ground is warm and sow the seeds outdoors. Plant hills of watermelon six feet apart, starting with six to eight seeds per hill. Later, when the plants are up and growing, thin them to stand only three per hill.

Culture: Keep plants growing vigorously after they've started to vine by watering them weekly and keeping the beds free of weeds. A black plastic mulch will increase your chances of success. If you stunt the plants' growth at an early stage, your beds won't produce as they should. Add side-dressings of manure or fertilizer every two weeks.

Harvest: Picking watermelons is one summertime ritual riddled with theories and old folktales. You'll find advocates of thumping, eyeballing, checking for brown tendril, waiting for the underside to turn yellow, and other techniques.

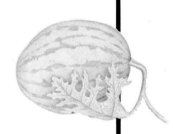

But nearly all home gardeners, even veterans, still will fret over their watermelons. After all, you can't just peek inside.

Here's a hint from the researchers. Make a note the day the female flower blossoms. The female will have a little fruit on it. The male has a similar flower but no fruit. The same day the female blossoms, the plant is pollinated. Small varieties—such as the Petite Sweet—will mature in 28 days. The large ones—such as the Crimson Sweet or Charleston Gray—will be ready in 35 to 40 days. Tag several blossoms and you'll have an accurate test.

If you're not so scientific, be sure to check the round spot on the underside. It should be yellow. If it's still white, wait several more days and check again.

Some old-timers will tell you to pick the melon when the tendril dries. This is a little risky. For some varieties, the inside will be overripe by the time the tendril dries. For others, the tendril can be dead a week to ten days before the melon ripens. When ripe, the top side of the melon will become rough and dull-looking.

And don't sneer at those who believe in the knuckle-tapping or palm-slapping test; these methods have their place. They can't tell you when to pick the melon, but they can tell you when you've waited too long. A hollow sound indicates the fruit is overripe.

There's no point picking a melon too early hoping it will ripen indoors. Watermelons, like any other fruit, have as much sugar in them on the day they're harvested as they'll ever have. They don't get better with age.

As the season draws to a close, pick all the immature fruit, so the vines will put all their efforts into ripening the few remaining large fruits for a delicious treat.

Vegetable Drying

Instead of canning and freezing all those surplus vegetables, why not try the age-old practice of drying? You'll find dried vegetables easy to package and store for use anytime during the winter months.

D ry vegetables three ways: air or sun drying, dehydrator drying, and oven drying.

Sun drying. If you live in the intense, hot, dry sunshine of the Southwest, you can dry vegetables naturally and successfully. However, many sections of the country have humid or rainy days, interspersed with varying degrees of sunshine, which make sun drying of vegetables unpredictable.

Spread thinly sliced vegetables out on trays; cover with cheesecloth or fine screening. Place vegetables in direct sun, then bring indoors at night. This method takes several days.

Dehydrator. Many appliances are available, up to several hundred dollars in price. To cut expenses, consider forming a neighborhood co-op of friends who could share the machine. Follow the manufacturer's directions for drying vegetables in this specialized appliance.

Oven drying. This method provides the easiest, most economical way to experiment with drying. Here's all you do:

1. Spread food evenly in a single layer on trays—between one and two pounds per tray. Make trays of wire screening tacked to a wooden frame (about four inches smaller than oven dimensions), or tack cheesecloth to oven racks.

2. Preheat oven to 150 degrees Fahrenheit (or as low as the oven thermostat will permit). Place lower oven rack about three inches from bottom of oven and other rack above, allowing space between for two trays to be stacked on a rack.

3. Dry vegetables for four to 12 hours. Stir the vegetables several times. See if they are done by referring to the chart below.

After drying. To be sure vegetables are uniformly dried, cure them for a week or two. Place vegetables in a large container in a hot and dry, airy, well-screened room. Stir once or twice a day. Pack in glass jars with lids. Store in a cool, dry, dark place. Before using, soak dried vegetables for several hours, then simmer just until they are tender. Some can be eaten, as is, for snacks or salad toppings. If stored properly, they will still be usable after a year.

For other crops you can store whole, see chart (opposite).

DRYING YOUR CROP

Vegetable	Preparation for Drying	Dryness Test
Beans, Green Lima	Shell. Steam 15 to 20 minutes or till tender but firm.	Shatter when hit with hammer
Beans, Snap	Trim and slice lengthwise or cut in 1-inch pieces. Steam about 20 minutes or till tender but firm. Spread about ½ inch deep on trays.	Brittle, dark green to brownish
Beets	Trim off all but 1 inch of tops and roots. Steam whole 30 to 60 minutes until cooked. Cool and peel. Cut in ¼-inch slices. Spread ¼ inch deep on trays.	Brittle, dark red
Carrots and Parsnips	Scrape or peel. Steam whole about 20 minutes or until tender but firm. Cut in ⅛-inch slices or 2-inch cubes, or shred before steaming. Spread not more than ½-inch deep on trays.	Very brittle, deep orange
Corn	Select tender, mature sweet corn. Husk. Steam on the cob for 10 to 15 minutes. Cut from cob.	Dry, brittle
Mushrooms	Peel large mushrooms. Dry whole or sliced, depending on size. No precooking necessary. If stems are tender, slice for drying; if tough, discard. Spread not more than ½ inch deep on trays.	Leathery to brittle
Onions	Select mature onions. Remove outer, discolored layers. Slice ¼-inch thick. No precooking necessary.	Brittle, light colored
Peas, Green	Shell. Steam 15 minutes or until tender but firm. Stir frequently during the first few hours of drying.	Shatter when hit with hammer
Peppers and Pimiento	Cut in ½-inch strips or in rings. Remove seeds. Steam 10 minutes. Spread rings two layers deep or strips not more than ½ inch deep.	Pliable
Parsley and Other Herbs	No precooking necessary. Hang bunches of whole plant in dry, warm place. When dry, crush leaves and remove stems. Store in tightly closed container.	Brittle
Squash, Winter and Pumpkins	Quarter; remove seeds and pith. Cut in 1-inch strips; peel. Slice strips crosswise, ¼ inch thick. Steam 8 to 13 minutes until slightly soft but not sticky.	Leathery
Squash, Zucchini	Cut in ¼-inch slices. Steam 3 minutes or until tender but firm.	Brittle

STORING YOUR CROPS FRESH

Vegetables	Where to Store	Temperature (Fahrenheit)	Humidity	Comments
Dry Beans, Peas	Any cool, dry place	32-40°	Dry	Leave beans and peas on plants until matured. Spread out in a dry, ventilated place, and allow to dry for 2 or 3 weeks. Shell and store protected in cans or jars.
Fall Cabbage	Outdoor pit or storage cellar	32°	Moderately moist	Place heads, roots up, in trench 2 feet wide by 8 inches deep, lined with straw or hay. Cover with additional straw. Cap trench with 6-inch layer of topsoil.
Cauliflower	Storage cellar	32°	Moderately moist	Raw storage is not reliable. Store like cabbage.
Carrots, Beets	Storage cellar	32-40°	Moist	Place in 10-gallon crocks and cover with burlap to maintain moisture. Carrots may be stored at higher temperature by removing tops completely and storing root in damp sand. Storage beets should have 1 inch of stem.
Fall Celery	Pit or storage cellar	32°	Moderately moist	Dig pit 12 inches wide, 24 inches deep; store plants with root clump. Water plants and allow tops to dry. Construct sloping roof with planks, poles, or old cornstalks. Cover with a layer of straw or hay.
Onions	Any cool, dry place	32°	Dry	Store only fully matured and dried onions. Do not keep in cellar. Arrange in well-ventilated, open-mesh or slatted boxes, and place in attic or unheated room.
Endive	Storage cellar	32°	Moderately moist	Follow storage procedure recommended for celery. Tie leaves together to aid blanching process.
Rutabagas, Turnips, Parsnips, Salsify, Horseradish	Outdoor pit	32-40°	Moist	Parsnips, salsify, and horseradish may be left in ground through winter, if mulched. Rutabagas and parsnips should be either waxed or buried in moist sand.
Potatoes	Storage cellar	35-40°	Moderately moist	Destroy blighted or damaged tubers. Temperatures above 40° F. will induce sprouting. Store in darkness. If too cool, potatoes become sweet. Hold at room temperature for one or two weeks before using.
Peppers	Unheated cellar	45-50°	Moderately moist	Firm, dark green peppers can be kept two to three weeks, if properly handled. Pick just before frost. Wash and sort. Store in plastic-lined containers with 12 to 16 holes for ventilation. Temperatures below 40° F. will cause decay.
Pumpkins, Squashes	Storage cellar	55°	Moderately dry	Select injury-free fruits for storage. Cure at temperatures of 80-90° F. for 10 days. (Acorn squash need not be cured.)
Tomatoes	Cellar	55-70°	Moderately moist	Select tomatoes from vigorous vines for storage. Remove stems, wash, and let dry. Do not wipe; sand scarring may result. Store partially red tomatoes in separate containers. Green tomatoes should be sorted each week and ripened fruits removed.
Sweet Potatoes	Storage cellar	55-60°	Moderately moist	Handle with care because sweet potatoes are easily cut and bruised. Cure for 10 days under moist conditions at 80-85° F., then move bins to cooler area. Do not store at less than 50° F. or in outdoor pits.

chapter 13

FRUITS AND NUTS

In the days of white clapboard houses and quietly moving rocking chairs, almost every backyard had an apple tree. Just a quick listing of the old-world varieties evokes images of picket fences, washboard-like roads, and knickers—names such as Black Gilliflower, Northern Spy, Peck's Pleasant, Maiden's Blush, and Westfield Seek-No-Further. In this day of agribusiness, streamlined production methods have made dabbling in varieties unprofitable. Today our choices are limited. Gone are many of the backyard favorites offering hundreds of shapes, colors, and delicious flavors.

But with home gardening on the increase, amateur growers by the thousands are enjoying the delights of freshly picked fruits and nuts. Peaches, plums, pears, quince, cherries, blueberries, and strawberries are popping up all over suburban United States. The more venturesome are trying their hand at unusual fruits, such as gooseberries and elderberries, or are putting out a nut tree or two.

Mention apple growing to most gardeners and immediately a vision of acres and acres of gently sloping orchards will come to mind. But with modern grafting techniques, dwarf varieties are available. And fruit trees don't have to be tucked away in a weedy corner. Attractive blossoms, graceful growth, and colorful fruit make fruit trees ideal for landscaping.

Before you start a miniature orchard, though, remember that growing fruit will require a little extra time if your efforts are to be successful. Fruit trees need some special care. Bugs, birds, and cold temperatures will threaten. But if you possess a passion for living things and can spare a few hours a week, you can grow delicious, tree- and vine-ripened fruit.

Fruit Tree Basics

Whether you choose peach, apple, pear, or plum, fruit trees are relatively easy to grow, providing certain conditions are present. Once planted, the trees offer years of delicious harvests with a minimum of care. Good planning is important. Fruit trees are somewhat fussy when it comes to location, temperature, and wind. Lingering frosts can wreck tender buds, and sudden thaws can trigger premature growth.

For a bare-root tree, carefully spread the roots out over a cone of soil. Cover with remaining soil.

If possible, keep the family orchard near the house to discourage nibbling rodents. They can seriously injure bark. The trees will be close at hand, too, making spraying and other maintenance simpler. If high winds whistle constantly through the backyard, you might want to plant a windbreak of evergreens to protect fruit trees from winterkill.

Choosing a variety

After years of genetic tinkering by scientists, almost any shape, size, or type of fruit tree is available. There are even novelty trees that have been grafted to produce four different kinds of fruits on one tree. Others combine the qualities of two fruits to offer the best of two worlds. The plumcot, for example, is a mix of plum and apricot.

To select a fruit tree, first match the fruit you want to grow with the climate in your area. Growing a tender tree in an area buffeted by cruel winters will only lead to disappointment. Most varieties of peaches, for example, suffer bud damage when temperatures in the early spring dip low. On the other hand, most apples need a period of cold for their growth cycle to continue.

Another important consideration is the amount of space available. If a vast expanse of fertile ground is not at hand, don't despair. The wide selection of dwarf varieties is just as rewarding in a fraction of the space. And harvests are plentiful, too. A single dwarf no higher than eight to ten feet can yield up to six bushels of fruit. If you prefer a happy medium between the dwarfs and the space-consuming standard trees, which grow to heights of 15 feet or more, you can always plant a semi-dwarf type. At an average height of about 13 feet, semi-dwarfs offer a perfect middle-size tree. In short, somewhere in the pages of a fruit tree catalogue is the ideal tree for your backyard.

Because the product of growing fruit trees is the fruit, care should be taken to ensure proper pollination. Some fruits, such as nearly all varieties of grapes, are self-fruitful, which means blossoms can be fertilized by pollen from blossoms on the same plant. But other types, such as apples, pears, most plums, and some peaches, need a little help from neighboring varieties. Blueberries, although self-fruitful, generally do better when other varieties are nearby. Chances are good there are enough plantings in your area to pollinate the trees. But the best bet is to have more than a single variety within 100 feet, so bees can easily travel between. Or set a bucket of blossom-filled branches of one variety beneath a tree of another variety. Most catalogues and garden center personnel can tell you which varieties of each kind of fruit are self-fruitful and which two (or three) varieties make the best partners. If bees are scarce, the harvest isn't doomed. With miniature trees, take matters into your own hands and pollinate the blossoms yourself by shaking blossoms of one variety over those of another.

The key to growing fruit successfully depends on the right blend of conditions, together with the abiding care of the home gardener. If bugs and disease are nipped before they become a plague and fruits are insulated from the ravages of wind, cold temperature, and marauding birds, your orchard will be a thing of beauty. Before investing in your favorite fruits, keep these additional requirements in mind:

Sun. Fruit, whether it ripens on a branch or bramble, needs plenty of sun. When plotting your orchard, be sure to place trees where there is unobstructed sun all day.

Soil. Almost all the fruits do best in a slightly acid soil, somewhere between 5.5 and 6.5 in pH reaction. The exception is blueberries, which prefer a soil of even greater acidity (pH between 4.0 and 5.0). Location has a lot to do with just how acid your soil is, because rainfall naturally percolating through the soil tends to make it acid. If in doubt about your soil, send a sample to the nearest county extension office or soil testing laboratory for help with analysis, or try your hand at home analysis by purchasing a small soil testing kit, available at most garden supply centers. If soil is alkaline, it can be brought to the proper level by adding powdered sulfur. Be sure to follow manufacturer's directions carefully; applying too much can be deadly to plants.

Drainage. Whatever fruit you plan to grow, adequate drainage is a top prerequisite. When scouting the backyard for a suitable site, avoid low-lying areas that collect water or are slow to drain in the spring. If choices are limited, however, correct poor drainage by installing drainage tile or digging a small ditch for runoff.

Planting

If ever a fruit tree needs intensive care, it is during those critical hours when the tree is about to be lowered into its new home. The trouble is, roots exposed to a searing sun and drying wind will succumb in no time if left unprotected. Try to prepare the planting hole before the tree is brought home from the nursery. If a delay of several days is impossible to avoid, simply "heel in" the roots by digging a shallow trench and leaning trunk and rootball against the side. Cover the roots with soil.

At its permanent site, dig a hole twice the width and depth of the rootball. As you excavate, put dark topsoil in one pile and lighter color subsoil in another. Mix equal amounts of the topsoil and sphagnum peat moss, then fill the hole halfway. Thoroughly drench with water. After the water has drained, place the tree in the hole, setting it at the same level it grew in the nursery unless otherwise noted in the planting information of "ABCs of Fruit," pages 440 to 453.

For balled-and-burlapped trees, loosen the wrap from around the trunk, but do not remove. The wrap can be used to help lower the tree into the hole (later the burlap will decompose gradually). When the tree is in place, fill around rootball with remaining peat moss and soil mixture. Tamp the soil firmly with your foot to make certain no air pockets remain. Water thoroughly. Now check to see if the tree is standing straight. If it is leaning, straighten it. A slight depression around the base of the tree will help catch rainfall and direct it toward the roots. Keep the young tree supplied with moisture.

Most fruit trees are best planted in the spring so the roots become well established before winter. Apple, plum, cherry, and pear can often be planted in late fall, however.

The distance separating trees depends on whether they're dwarf or standard. Generally, dwarfs should be planted at least ten feet apart; standards need as much as 25 feet between.

Care after planting

The care fruit trees get during the first season can make or destroy the orchard. Most fruit trees need some support to prevent tender trunks from bending and possibly snapping in high winds. Excessive swaying can also prevent roots from getting a solid grip on the soil. Drive an iron pipe or 2x2-inch stake well into the ground beside the tree at planting time. Then loop rope or wire around trunk and pipe. Avoid injuring the bark by passing wire or rope through a piece of rubber hose or plastic tubing.

Newly planted trees will need moderate pruning. Thin out all but a few branches, and cut back the top. As for fertilizers, most trees of any age do better if underfed. Too much fertilizer can lead to jungle-like growth and a scarcity of fruit. Keep trees tidy by mulching with an ample layer of straw or other organic material. Pull the mulch several inches away from the trunk to discourage rodents from gnawing on tree bark.

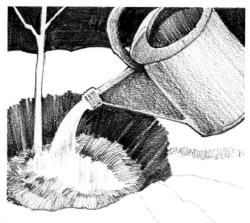

Drench soil thoroughly with a watering can or garden hose, so soil settles in and around roots.

Most trees need pruning at planting time. Remove weak or dead growth.

Wrap tender trunk bark with special tree tape to deter chewing animals and prevent sunscald.

How to Prune Fruit Trees

TRAINING METHODS

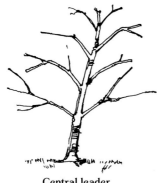

Central leader

Open center

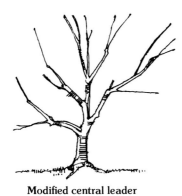

Modified central leader

Fruit growers have experimented with shaping to determine which method leads to the most fruit. The above are most common.

Careful training in early years may be wise advice for parents of young children; it's a good hint for gardeners planting fruit trees, too. Proper pruning and training yield quality fruit and a longer-lasting tree. Follow these basic procedures when shaping trees:

• Whenever you use pruning shears, make sure edges are sharp and tools are in good working order. Nothing is more conducive to disease than a tree with mangled stumps caused by dull pruning shears. In removing a branch, make the cut close to and parallel with the supporting limb.

• Reserve pruning for late winter or early spring when fruit trees are still dormant and sap has not begun to move. At that time, wounds heal best and flower buds can be easily located.

Remember that a wide-angled branch is stronger and healthier than a branch with a narrow crotch. Instead of cutting off branches to produce this wide angle, spread the branches to help produce fruit earlier and, at the same time, improve the tree's form. Bend branches growing upright down to a 45-degree angle, and hold them there with a brace for at least a year. The more horizontal branch has healthier fruit along its entire length than an upright one because of vigor and even distribution of light.

• Make cuts just above a strong outwardly growing lateral branch. Take care not to leave a stub; it can become diseased.

• Fruit with poor color is a clue pruning is needed. Remove branches that are severely shaded and will bear few spurs (the short, woody, fruit-bearing stems).

• As a general rule, promote healing by treating wounds larger than two inches in diameter with a coat of paint especially made for this purpose; it's available from nurseries and garden supply centers. Smaller cuts will heal nicely by themselves.

Three training methods get best results:

Central leader system. Sometimes referred to as the pyramid form, the central leader system means a single central trunk is allowed to predominate while lateral or scaffold branches develop at regular intervals. Trees tend to withstand heavy weather and heavy fruit. Thin annually, so the center of the tree gets good light.

Open center system. A central leader does not dominate. Three or four main limbs of similar size are encouraged to grow at wide angles. In turn, these branch outward with six or so secondary limbs. Peach, nectarine, apricot, plum, and sour cherry are adaptable to this system.

Modified central leader system. The central leader and scaffold or lateral branches are equally important in the modified central leader method. If branched one- or two-year-old trees are planted, then pruning involves selecting three or four widely spaced, wide-angled branches and removing the rest. The leader or any scaffold branch should not be allowed to dominate for the first two years.

How to Prune Cane Fruits

As anyone who has ever been scratched in a berry patch knows, nothing can become so tangled as a thicket of bramble bushes. Unless kept under strict control, cane fruits dwindle in yield, ripe fruit ready for plucking becomes inaccessible, and only wildlife can appreciate your planting. Proper pruning is the only way to bring easy picking to the berry patch.

Many growers combine pruning with a system of support that helps keep canes off the ground and, at the same time, makes the ripe berries easier to approach. For blackberries, tie canes to a trellis constructed of posts nailed in a "T" arrangement and connected with wire (see opposite page). Then anchor the canes to the wire with twine or cloth ties. Plants are neater, less susceptible to disease, and produce more fruit. The same system of posts, with crosspieces supporting wire, can also be used for raspberries. Instead of tying, allow canes to grow inside the twin wires. Canes supported this way remain upright and are easier to harvest.

Whatever support system you use, a session or two with the pruning shears is necessary. Judicious snipping prevents the rapidly growing canes from becoming a tangle, helps improve air circulation (which reduces the chance of disease), boosts yields, and makes maintenance and berry picking easier.

The bramble fruits—red raspberry, black or purple raspberry, and blackberry—are biennial in their habit of growth and pattern of setting fruit. That means young canes or suckers sprout and flower from perennial crowns or roots and set fruit the following year. Once fruiting has occurred, canes wither and die while new canes take their place. The purpose of pruning is to make room for the upcoming shoots by removing all old and spent canes. Generally, prune brambles twice every season. Do it once in early spring to remove old and weak canes and snip back tips of canes to a height of about 24 to 30 inches to remove winter-killed tips and encourage more vigorous growth. Schedule the second pruning for after the harvest. Again, remove old or broken canes.

Treat blackberries the same way as raspberries, but add an extra pruning of lateral growth. In spring, before new growth starts, snip back lateral branches to a length of ten to 12 inches. When removing old and dead canes, be sure to destroy wood (rather than leaving it as mulch) to prevent diseases and insect larvae from wintering over and invading young, emerging canes. Burn the cuttings or bag them for garbage pickup soon after you prune.

TAME THOSE CANES

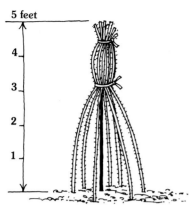

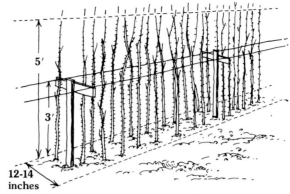

An excellent way to keep raspberries from taking over house and home is the hill or tepee system. Drive a six-foot stake at least ten inches into the ground, and gently tie canes together with soft twine.

Another popular way to introduce order to the bramble patch is the hedgerow system of posts, using crossties and wire. Canes grow up between wires and are pruned to a height of no more than five feet.

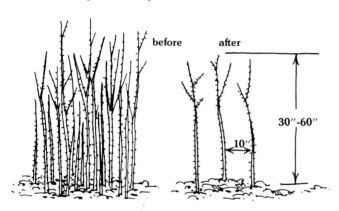

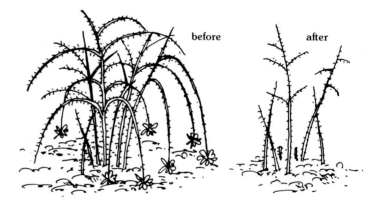

Pruning raspberries is as simple as working a pair of shears, so long as you remember how canes grow. Biennial fruiting canes sprout from perennial crowns. Once you pick the berries, remove old canes.

Blackberries have central canes that produce much longer side shoots, called laterals. Because fruiting occurs on the laterals, cut back the growth and trim back the tips of the plants.

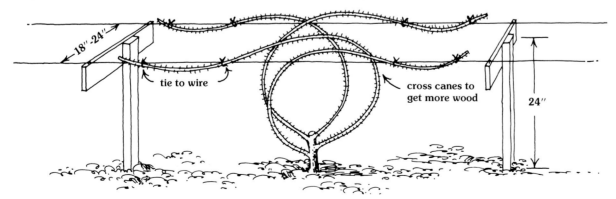

One of the more effective ways to keep blackberries within bounds is to train young canes on a wire trellis. Tie laterals to wire with soft twine or cloth. Erect varieties can be trained to a single wire.

Espalier Basics

Once roots have settled into the soil, a young fruit tree will send fresh green sprouts in almost every conceivable direction. How it grows and where it grows is largely a matter of chance. The main need is sun and plenty of it.

Because branches and leaves consistently reach toward the warm magic of the sun, you can snip, bend, and twist trees to grow in nearly any pattern you want. Espalier is the art of shaping trees into special patterns. And the possibilities are practically infinite if you keep some basic tips in mind. There are candelabra, tiered, grid, arched, "U," and "Y" patterns.

Shaping trees is not something dreamed up by idle gardeners; it is a practice developed by European fruit growers to get more fruit from less space. For the home gardener cramped for space, espalier growing can mean bushels of delicious fruit where fruit culture was previously thought out of the question because of a mini-size yard.

What to grow. Though almost any plant can be nudged and snipped into a new shape, the most popular for espalier growing are dwarf fruit trees, especially apples, pears, peaches, and nectarines. The dwarf varieties have the advantage of developing to a moderate height of eight to ten feet. At the same time, they set fruit early and in abundance. When buying a tree for espalier, seek the advice of a reputable nursery in your area so you get the right variety for your climate and best size for your space.

Where to grow. No matter how you shape your tree, fruit trees still need plenty of sun. Be sure to place the tree where it receives at least six hours of unobstructed sun per day. A wall or fence can make an ideal location for an espaliered tree, but, remember, a wall facing directly south can become sizzling hot when summer reaches its peak. Temperatures above 90 degrees Fahrenheit may damage the tree. A southeast or southwest wall is better. As for soil, fruit trees thrive in slightly acid conditions.

Planting the tree. In early spring as soon as the ground can be worked, dig a hole at least twice the diameter of the tree's rootball. Make sure the hole is centered on the trellis and slightly in front of cross wires that will support the branches. Mix ample amounts of sphagnum peat moss with the removed soil. Then plant the tree, making sure it is planted no deeper than it grew at the nursery. If the previous soil level is difficult to determine, set a dwarf tree in so that the graft union (visible as a distinct bulge in lower part of trunk) is about two inches above the soil surface. Cover roots with soil, tamp firmly to remove air bubbles, and moisten thoroughly.

Making a support. Most trees are adept at supporting themselves, but, because you want twigs and branches to grow in a certain pattern, you'll need to tie the branches to something. The most efficient support can be easily constructed by sinking two stout posts into the ground at least eight feet apart. (Width will vary depending on the shape you want the tree to take.) Stretch 14-gauge wire at one-foot intervals between the posts. Be sure the trellis is at least one foot away from the house or wall to allow you plenty of working room in back of the tree. Steady the posts by connecting them to the house with metal brackets.

Pruning and shaping. Trees produce hundreds of buds, some of which develop into blossoms and finally fruit, while others form new branches. Usually fat, bulging buds are the fruiting buds; narrow ones are leaf buds. The key to shaping a tree is identifying the leaf buds and choosing the ones that will contribute to the espalier design you have chosen. For example, if you are aiming for the simple tier system, a cut is made just above two buds on opposite sides of the trunk, about 12 inches above the ground (in line with the first wire on the trellis).

Then, as horizontal branches elongate, tie them to the wire with soft twine or strong cloth. The tree will continue to grow vertically, eventually reaching the second wire of the trellis. This is the time to select another pair of buds for the lateral development. Remember, however, that buds have no idea what's going on and will sprout willy-nilly if not pinched back. Keep an eye on new growth throughout the growing season. If buds begin to send out new unwanted growth, pinch them off with your fingers. To achieve the tier shape, plan growth so the bottom tier is healthy and strong. Each succeeding tier should be somewhat shorter in length to balance the overall shape.

To achieve the palm or grid shapes (see illustration, this page), the training procedure is a trifle more complicated because the branches will have to be gently bent to conform to the pattern. To accomplish this, use short sections of bamboo or other wood to form a temporary horizontal support to which developing branches can be tied. Then bend new growth to the desired direction, and tie to wood sections.

Espalier care. Once the tree is shaped the way you want it, you still will have some work to do. Half the joy of sculpturing a tree is the added bonus of fresh, tree-ripened fruit. To improve fruiting, keep after rampant growth by cutting back new growth to half its length in the beginning of the season.

In midsummer, stubs will put out additional growth. Pinch this back to the last two leaves so the branch will produce even more fruiting spurs. Chances are these insistent branches will send out even more new growth, which again should be pinched back. A new tree, however, should be encouraged to use all its energy for developing roots and branches, rather than setting fruit. The first year remove all the fruit buds. By the third year, the tree should begin producing a limited amount of fruit.

It's true espalier gardening requires more effort per tree than other methods; the results, however, are bountiful, as well as attractive, enough to stop a passerby.

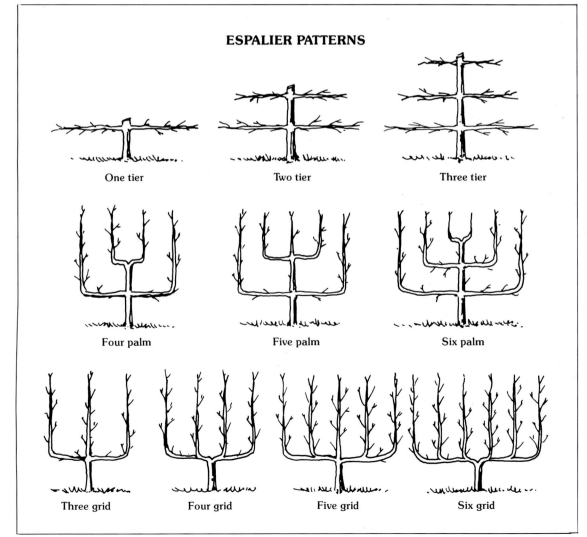

ESPALIER PATTERNS

One tier

Two tier

Three tier

Four palm

Five palm

Six palm

Three grid

Four grid

Five grid

Six grid

Fruit Tips

Many of your favorite ornamental plants can be shifted from place to place until you hit on the ideal conditions. But a fruit tree, once it is planted, staked, and trimmed, can only be moved with difficulty; choosing the right spot is critical. Perhaps the most important requirement is good drainage.

Plant fruit trees only where excess water can drain out of the soil freely so tree roots don't suffocate. If you are planning an orchard, you can get a good idea of drainage conditions by observing your selected spots for several months. If water sits in puddles after a rainfall or if the side yard resembles a lake during the spring, then drainage is poor and must be corrected.

Take a close look at a sample of soil. Squeeze a handful and then check to see whether it crumbles easily. A clay soil will remain a compact mass, and an overly sandy soil will disintegrate into granules. Clay feels somewhat slimy when moist, and sandy soil feels gritty. Both are unsatisfactory: clay resists water and sand cannot retain moisture. In short, a suitable soil will have an open, friable (crumbly) structure that allows moisture to pass through but, at the same time, retains enough to provide a constant supply to roots.

Don't give up hope just because soil conditions aren't ideal. There's a lot you can do to improve drainage and soil structure so your fruit garden can thrive. Nothing beats organic matter for bringing soil up to snuff. By working compost, sphagnum peat moss, and manure into the top eight inches of topsoil, structure will improve dramatically and, at the same time, nutrients essential for healthy plant growth eventually will be plentiful. If drainage problems are severe, special drainage tile or pipe might be the only answer. Good soil structure by itself isn't enough. Trees and plants also need essential nutrients in order to grow, blossom, and later explode into bushels of succulent fruit. The big three when it comes to growing things are nitrogen (essential for leaf growth and chlorophyll formation); phosphorus (necessary for fruit and root development); and potassium (helps strengthen stems and contributes to disease resistance). Although these are the chief elements, calcium, magnesium, and sulfur are needed in lesser amounts. There is also a need for the trace elements, including molybdenum, iron, boron, manganese, zinc, copper, and chlorine. It's evident these elements are nec-

essary because they are found in the tissues of plants. But to juggle each one would mean becoming entangled in the complex rigors of chemistry. The best approach combines conscientious observation with a carefully thought out program of soil management. Fertilizer is worth little or actually is harmful if not used properly. Read labels carefully, and spend enough time in the garden to become aware of what plants need for good growth.

There are two ways to get needed nutrients into the soil. You can mix organic materials, such as dried blood, bone meal, cottonseed meal, or manure into the topsoil, or you can purchase chemically prepared fertilizer. Chemical fertilizers are quicker acting and offer greater convenience. Organic materials are slower to release their nutrients and may be difficult to obtain. But manure and other organic materials are unsurpassed for their ability to improve soil structure. Whether fertilizer is organic or inorganic makes no difference to the fruit tree. The decision is yours. However, organic fertilizers alone are not balanced sources of nutrients without additional juggling, and their contents of the three major elements is low.

Rodent guard

No matter where you live, there will also be a rabbit, mouse, or squirrel waiting to sink its teeth into the succulent bark of a young fruit tree. Especially in winter when other sources of food are scarce, the damage from rodents can be severe enough to kill your tree. (Keep branches trimmed; piled snow can bring branch tips within easy reach of hungry animals.)

Construct a rodent guard to protect bark by wrapping a cylinder of wire mesh around the tree trunk. Or use special tree tape. Make sure the guard extends into the ground and at least 24 inches up the tree. Make the cylinder several inches wider than the trunk so animals can't nibble from outside.

Fruit limb support

Fruit trees occasionally bear more fruit than they can hold. As a result, limbs droop under the increasing weight until they snap. The entire tree may threaten to split down the middle if major branches on opposite sides of the trunk are heavy. One of the best ways to lighten the load is to remove some of the fruit.

Grow fruit for shade

An excellent way to enjoy disease-free grapes is by training vines on an arbor. Raised plants create an attractive canopy of cool green leaves and, at the same time, fruits will get plenty of ventilation. As young vines develop, tie canes to posts with soft twine or strips of cloth.

Dwarf varieties especially will benefit from regular thinning.

Inspect the tree about four to six weeks after blossoming, and remove all those fruits that appear diseased, shriveled, or wormy. Later, thin again so fruits will be six to eight inches apart for apples, pears, and peaches and four inches apart for plums and nectarines. If branches still sag, use a pole or stake, driven an inch or two into the ground, as a support (see above drawing).

Battles with bugs

Somewhere, crouched in the dark recesses of weeds and woods, is an ever-present horde of beetles, bugs, and flies eager to inspect the newest addition to your garden. Fruits, of course, are a special treat for insects. Maggots like to burrow through the pulp, the coddling moth is quick to zero in on apples, and uncountable crowds of soft-bodied aphids swarm over buds and leaves. For small infestations and a few trees, pests can be hand-picked; on cloudy days, tent worms will cluster together. Heavily infested branches can be sawed off and burned.

When large numbers overrun your fruit trees, you'll have to decide how important a harvest is to you. You have several choices: do nothing (and likely lose the crop); remove insects and wormy fruit often (and get a few usable fruits); or spray (and get a fair-size harvest). The backyard has an effective arsenal of chemical sprays available, which, if used intelligently, can handle most bugs.

It's possible to match a spray to each particular insect and disease problem. But such a program would be complicated. A good—and safe—bet is to rely on an all-purpose spray mixture. With the right combination of chemicals, a combination of problems—from scale to scab—can be kept under control. Many chemical companies sell prepared mixtures that contain one or two fungicides and two or more insecticides. Or you can buy materials separately and combine your own. For a general-purpose spray, add the following to one gallon of water:

Captan (50 percent wettable powder)—two tablespoons

Malathion (25 percent wettable powder)—three tablespoons

Methoxychlor (50 percent wettable powder)—three tablespoons

Both methoxychlor and malathion keep insects at bay, and captan is effective against most fungus diseases. If you prefer to buy a pre-mixed, all-purpose spray, be sure to check the label so you know what you are getting and the pests it will control. Some of these sprays will be in dust form that can be applied as is. Unfortunately, although dusts are convenient, they do not adhere or cover as well as sprays and are especially risky on windy days when dust is carried beyond the afflicted plant.

As a rule, application times are governed by the various budding, blossoming, and fruiting stages of fruit trees. Avoid spraying when trees are in full bloom because chemicals will harm bees. Refer to individual fruit entries (on pages 440 to 453) for specific instructions.

Without chemicals, growing large quantities of unblemished fruit in the backyard would be practically impossible. But chemical sprays also can be harmful to things besides insects, if handled carelessly. Keep these safety tips in mind when handling spray materials.

● Store chemicals in original containers and keep them out of the reach of children.

● Discontinue spraying at least ten days before you plan to harvest.

● Clean sprayer thoroughly after each use. Do not dump leftover spray where it can collect in puddles.

● Read manufacturer's directions line by line and follow recommendations carefully.

Planting ideas for dwarf trees

Luckily for the homeowner cramped for space, fruit trees aren't all business. Attractive, perfume-scented blossoms and pleasing shape make dwarf varieties perfect for your landscaping plans. Keep in mind, though, that some fruits will need companion trees for proper pollination.

Fruit trees don't always have to be planted in the regimented rows of an orchard to bear fruit. Use pears, peaches, or dwarf apple varieties as accent plantings near the house, garage, or barn. Because most fruit trees cast inviting shade, they are perfect companions for a host of foundation and ornamental plants.

Protect from birds

If you think your yard is strangely devoid of birds, wait until your prize fruit is ripe and ready for picking from the vine. Birds of all descriptions will descend on your berry patch. Before you are overcome with rage, though, remember that birds are one of your best allies when it comes to staving off bugs and other insects.

Drape bird netting or cheesecloth over the entire tree. Bush and vine fruits may be protected with chicken wire or netting material over the top and down the sides.

ABCs of Fruit

No matter how you freeze, gas, crate, or ship fruit, something happens when it is picked before it has ripened properly. Witness the all too often dry, pulpy taste of store-bought produce. Small wonder that thousands of homeowners across the country are devoting more and more backyard space to growing their own apples, pears, apricots, peaches, strawberries, blueberries, and raspberries. Once you have enjoyed a plump, sun-ripened berry just off the vine, you'll want to double your planting. And fruits are easy. In this section you'll find the information you need to get a fruit garden underway: selecting the best varieties, planting, pruning, feeding, and harvesting.

APPLES

Ever since Johnny Appleseed set out to dot America with apple trees, the apple has been as much a part of our history as the bald eagle. Of course, commercial production and urban growth have limited the number of trees grown and the number of varieties available. But with interest in home gardening burgeoning, nurseries are offering more and more types each year.

Homeowners usually have to be careful about what goes where to get the most from their gardens. Trees take up a good deal of room, especially standard-size apple trees; a single tree can gobble up as much as 1,600 square feet. For this reason, it's often best to opt for the dwarf varieties. Bushel for bushel, dwarfs will offer excellent produce and, at the same time, are easier to plant, prune, and maintain. Because of the smaller size—about nine feet high for a dwarf and between 13 and 14 for a semi-dwarf—picking fruit is much easier, spraying against bugs and disease is simplified, and pruning is a cinch because nearly all the branches are within easy reach.

Varieties. You'll find one or another of the apple varieties for just about all 50 states. Among the most popular of the early-fruiting or summer-harvesting apples are Anoka, Lodi, and Stark's Earliest. Fall varieties include the ever-popular Cortland, Delicious, Gravenstein, McIntosh, Northern Spy, Winesaps, and Wealthy. Apples require cross-pollination to set good fruit, so plant two or more varieties to ensure proper pollination.

Most apple trees need an extended period of cold during dormancy to leaf out and eventually set blooms; Tropical Beauty is one exception and is suited to southern states. But some varieties are better at withstanding the temperature variations than others. Check with nursery staff or the county extension office to find out the best varieties for your area. Catalogues, too, should list recommended zones along with variety descriptions.

A dwarf is a union of two or three trees. One type, often a crab apple, is for the rootstock, with a standard tree grafted or budded on top. The place where they join is called a graft union and looks like a bulge or kink in the lower part of the trunk. Some apple trees are created from three trees: a full-size tree for the rootstock, the dwarfing tree as the mid-piece, and a standard tree for fruit.

All three sizes of mature trees—dwarf, semi-dwarf, and standard—may be grafted onto hardy rootstocks. Red and Yellow Delicious, Winesap, Wealthy, and Jonathan come in all three sizes. Fruit trees have been budded or grafted for desirable features, so

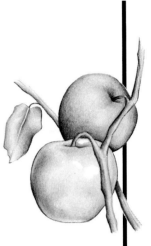

trees you start from seeds may not be as sturdy or productive as purchased ones.

Planting. Plant apple trees in early spring in the North and late autumn in the South. The roots are the most vulnerable part of the fruit tree, so get the spadework started before trees arrive in the mail or before you select them from the nursery.

Dig a large enough hole, making sure it's at least twice the estimated size of the tree's rootball. Plant the tree as deeply as you can, while leaving the graft union or mid-piece above soil level. This may put it somewhat deeper than the tree was planted at the nursery. But be sure the graft union or mid-piece is above ground. If it is covered with soil, it could sprout and you could end up with a large tree because the dwarfing segment was bypassed. Allow 25 feet between semi-dwarfs and ten feet between dwarfs.

Provide support for the young tree. Drive a pipe, iron stake, or 2x4 into the ground, and anchor the trunk to the stake with soft twine.

Depending on variety, dwarfs will bear in three to four years, and semi-dwarfs bear in four to five years. Standards take somewhat longer. Remove blossoms for the first couple of years after planting so the tree can direct vigor into establishing root and trunk.

Care and feeding. You'll find reasonably priced nursery stock as year-old whips (without branches). Trim top. As branches develop, train to the central leader for dwarf trees and modified leader for semi-dwarfs. Prune while dormant. Remove dead, broken branches, crossed limbs, and water sprouts. (For pruning advice, see "How to Prune Fruit Trees," page 434.)

The process for feeding the apple tree is often more a matter of resisting temptation. The young tree, especially, should not be given huge doses of fertilizer, because over-application may lead to excessive leaf and branch growth, leaving the tree susceptible to disease and breaking.

As soon as the apple tree is planted and staked, cover the surrounding soil with a four- to six-inch layer of mulching material, such as hay, dried grass clippings, wood chips, sphagnum peat moss, or partially decomposed compost. Add more throughout the season to maintain a two- to three-inch layer. As vegetative matter breaks down, nutrients will be gradually released into the soil. At the same time, decayed matter will improve the structure of the soil, which means its ability to retain water and nutrients will be greatly enhanced. Mulch keeps weeds down, too.

Mulches do, however, provide a handy cover for mice, so leave a four- to six-inch space around the base of the tree. A wire screen placed around the trunk will also dis-

442

APPLES (continued)

courage chewing animals from damaging the bark. (See "Rodent Guard," page 438.)

Insects and diseases. Next to bone-chilling cold, the more serious obstacles to growing tasty fruit are bugs and diseases. Spraying is practically unavoidable. Use the general-purpose spray formula given on page 439. As a rule, seven to 12 applications are necessary, and all should be timed according to the growth stages of the tree: dormant (before buds begin to swell), prepink (blossom buds show pink), pink (just before full bloom), petal fall (blossom petals drop off), and then every ten to 14 days thereafter for up to six more applications. To protect the bee population, avoid spraying when trees are in full flower.

Keeping apple trees clean and avoiding overfertilization will help keep fire blight disease under control. (Symptoms include a burnt appearance of young leaves, twigs, and blossoms.) Cut out and burn (or bag for garbage pickup) diseased limbs, fruit, and leaves. Avoid heavy pruning or overapplication of nitrogen fertilizer, which stimulates rapid growth.

Harvesting. Summer apples will ripen in late July or early August, fall apples in September, and winter ones in late fall. Try to be patient so fruit can reach peak flavor while on the tree. Check the seeds: fruit is immature while seeds are white, ripe when they're brown. Fruit should also part easily from stem. If you plan to squirrel away a bushel or two for midwinter use, be sure you select only those apples free of dents, cuts, or bruises.

APRICOTS

A ripe apricot bulging with sweet juices is undoubtedly one of the most pleasurable rewards from the fruit garden. But the apricot is extremely tender and, therefore, often unable to cope with frigid winters. Apricot lovers, however, find ways to beat the cold by selecting trees developed for far northern zones (see "Varieties"). Also, plant the tree behind a protective hedge of evergreen or on a northern slope. If a dwarf variety is grown, the tree can be planted in a tub or oversize container, then moved indoors when winter winds arrive. Its attractive blossoms also make the apricot a popular landscaping tree.

Varieties. Among the more popular varieties are Blenheim, Hungarian, Moorpack, Royal, Tilton, and Wilson Delicious. Most will pollinate themselves, but others (Moongold and Sungold) need a second variety nearby. All tend to have a larger crop if you plant two

varieties. Check with nursery staff for pollination needs of the tree you buy. In cold winter zones, try Hardy Iowa, Manchu, Moongold, Scout, and Sungold.

Planting. Plant in early spring, preferably on a northern slope. On southern exposures, warm spring sun will encourage early buds that inevitably succumb to late frosts. Dwarf varieties will grow to eight to ten feet tall and may be grouped as close as ten to 15 feet apart; they begin to bear in about two years after planting. Standards begin bearing in about three years and will stand about 15 feet high; they need at least 30 feet between trees.

Care and feeding. Once the tree is planted, prune out misshapen and weak wood, leaving at least three healthy branches. Remaining limbs should be eight to twelve inches apart and facing in opposite directions. Keep in mind that wide-angled growth means stronger, weight-resistant branches. After the tree is established, pruning will consist mainly of removing oldest spurs, deadwood, and those branches that cause crowding.

As a rule, the rambunctious apricot will set much more fruit than its branches can support. To prevent limbs from breaking and to reap better fruit, pick off stunted and diseased young fruit about six weeks after blossoming. Thin again later, allowing one fruit for every six to eight inches of stem.

Insects and diseases. Apricots tend to be remarkably disease and insect resistant. For best results, spray tree with an all-purpose spray at dormancy, at prepink, at petal fall, and for three additional applications after petal fall (at ten- to 14-day intervals).

Harvesting. Pick fruits when golden yellow in color and fairly soft to the touch.

BLACKBERRIES

The true blackberry (including boysenberries, dewberries, and loganberries) devotee will brave snakes, thorns, bees, and whatever else may inhabit the bramble patch for a single bowl full of ripe berries swimming in cream. Usually found wild and sprawling over hill and dale, blackberries can also be brought under control and cultivated in neat, well-disciplined rows.

Varieties. There are two types of blackberries—the trailing type (sometimes called dewberry) and the erect type. The upright growing varieties form stiff canes, requiring little support. Trailing types, on the other hand, will become a tangled nuisance and berries will be difficult to reach if canes are not trained on a trellis or other form of support.

When and how fruits form also differ somewhat. Trailing forms produce smaller fruit clusters that generally ripen up to two weeks earlier than erect types. The best known erect varieties are Bailey and Darrow. Trailing varieties include Boysen (boysenberry), Logan (loganberry), and Cascade.

Planting. When choosing a site for the blackberry patch, look for a well-drained soil that retains plenty of moisture. Sometimes weeds can be better controlled if the soil is prepared the year before and used for an annual vegetable crop. Remember, young plants brought home from the garden center and left lying around can dry out. Roots will shrivel and die. If a delay is unavoidable, heel in plants by setting in a temporary earth trench and covering roots with loose soil.

At planting time, it helps to soak the roots in water an hour or two if roots appear dry. Then set out the plants in rows spaced eight feet apart. Plants should be three to five feet apart in the row. Trailing varieties need at least ten feet between rows. Next, make holes deep enough to accommodate roots, and set in plants to a depth equal to the depth they were planted at the nursery. Cut back canes to about six inches after firming soil around the roots.

Care and feeding. After several years of solid growth, blackberries can hold their own. But the new planting must be carefully tended to prevent weeds from choking young plants. Some gardeners, eager to use every square inch of soil, plant vegetables such as cabbage, beans, cauliflower, and potatoes between blackberry rows the first year. This intercropping means bonus vegetables for the dinner table and a cleaner berry patch because of the extra cultivation.

It will be just a matter of months before some method of cane support will have to be constructed for young plants. Trailing varieties, if left to sprawl, become a thicket. The erect types are self-supporting, so long as the proper pruning techniques are followed. Most growers like to support all bramble fruits to keep them healthier and to make picking easier. All that is needed is a simple trellis consisting of wire and poles. For trailing types, nail a crosspiece about 18 to 24 inches wide on posts placed at either end of the row and about 24 inches off the ground. Then simply train canes to grow up in between wires. Erect types can be tied with soft twine to a single wire stretched between the posts. (For more tips on training cane fruits, see pages 434 and 435.)

Whatever method you use, fruiting and good growth depend on a regular pruning schedule. Keep in mind how blackberries grow. The crowns are perennial, but the canes that emerge each year are biennial. The first year they mature and send out lateral

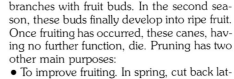

branches with fruit buds. In the second season, these buds finally develop into ripe fruit. Once fruiting has occurred, these canes, having no further function, die. Pruning has two other main purposes:
• To improve fruiting. In spring, cut back lateral branches to a length of about 12 inches.
• To encourage fuller growth, improve ventilation, and contain growth. As root suckers appear during the growing season, pull them out of the ground to prevent ordered rows from dwindling into a thicket. When erect types exceed a height of 30 to 36 inches, cut back tips so the plant will form stronger canes. Then, at the conclusion of the season, cut out all spent canes at soil level and destroy them. If new emerging canes are especially numerous, thin to four or five healthy canes per plant. For trailing varieties, leave 12 to 16 canes per plant.

To keep the blackberry planting vigorous, supplemental applications of a complete 5-10-10 fertilizer will keep yields high and plants strong. Apply side-dressings along the row at blossoming time and a lighter application shortly after fruiting.

Insects and diseases. As a rule, insects and diseases seldom present a serious problem to the blackberry grower. Occasionally, aphids will be found sucking on leaf juices. Most berry ills can be kept under control by planting only disease-resistant varieties, removing and destroying weak and diseased canes immediately, and keeping the surrounding area free of weeds where diseases and insects can gain a foothold.

Harvesting. As soon as berries begin to turn color, keep an eye on the patch so you can harvest fruit at peak ripeness. Berries should be sweet but still firm. Once ripening occurs, berries should be picked each day and preferably during the morning hours. Take care not to crush or otherwise damage fruit, and it's ready to wash and eat.

BLUEBERRIES

Bright blue blueberries tumbling over a heap of rich vanilla ice cream or bobbing in a bowl of cream is a treat few fruit growers want to pass up. But blueberries are loners in the fruit world because they do best in acid soil that would probably spell doom for almost any other crop. In fact, a pH as low as 4.0 is not too acid for them.

Varieties. A wide range of blueberry varieties means you can choose early, midseason, and late season types. But keep in mind that your blueberries are not self-pollinating, which means you'll have to plant at least two different varieties. A popular early

BLUEBERRIES (continued)

variety is Earliblue; Stanley and Blue-crop are high-producing mid-season types. For late harvest, try Jersey or Coville.

Planting. When planning on a row or two of blueberry bushes, naturally the first consideration is soil acidity. If, after testing, your soil is too close to the neutral mark (pH 7.0), then increase acidity. Mix generous amounts of sphagnum peat moss with the soil, and mulch heavily with an acid material, such as oak leaves or pine needles. If drastic measures are needed, apply powdered sulfur. Four pints of powdered sulfur per every 100 square feet of garden soil will lower pH approximately one point. Be sure to have soil tested, though, before attempting to juggle the pH level one way or the other.

Blueberries, like many other fruits, need ample amounts of soil moisture for an abundance of well-formed fruit. But soggy conditions should be avoided.

Purchase three- or four-year-old plants from a reliable nursery, and set them out as soon as possible to avoid injury to roots. Dig a hole at least twice the diameter of the rootball. Then loosen the burlap root covering. If the bush is in a plastic container, slit plastic with a sharp knife, and carefully remove the rootball. Place exposed roots over a cone of soil heaped in the bottom of the hole. Cover with a mixture of equal parts sphagnum peat moss and topsoil.

Be sure to firm soil thoroughly so air pockets are eliminated. Then water generously so soil settles in and around roots. A mulch of sawdust, peat moss, wood chips, or shredded leaves will help soil retain moisture and protect the plant from invading weeds.

Care and feeding. A well-established blueberry bush is usually a relatively maintenance-free bush. But pruning is important if the best fruiting and yield are expected. An unattended shrub tends to pack every inch of stem with berries. In time, this overproduction will result in small, inferior fruit.

Good pruning provides three benefits: the chief bearing branches are given plenty of room in which to develop, air circulation is increased (this is one of the best defenses against disease), and leaves and ripening fruit are exposed to the beneficial rays of the sun. But save your pruning chores until the third year of growth. Then, in early spring or late winter, remove weak or deformed branches. Thin out some of the many side shoots that sprout. As the bush increases in age, it may be necessary to remove tough, old wood to give room for newer growth just coming along.

Recently planted shrubs require little in the way of supplementary feeding. Once plants

are established, a dose of ammonium sulfate fertilizer at the rate of about one-half cup per bush may be applied. Later, the amount can be increased to one-quarter pound, applied as soon as buds begin to swell in spring.

Insects and diseases. Oddly enough, birds can be a greater threat to the blueberry grower than bugs. Ripe berries are choice morsels and will soon dwindle to nothing if countermeasures aren't taken. The most effective protection is a canopy of nylon or cheesecloth netting placed over each bush when berries show signs of ripening.

Shriveled, dried up blueberries, called "mummy berries," indicate the presence of a fungus disease. Spray bush with a fungicide recommended for use with this problem, according to label instructions. Good ventilation and adequately spaced plantings will go a long way toward preventing the spread of the fungus.

Harvesting. Resist plucking just-turned blueberries, because change of color by itself doesn't mean harvesttime has arrived. Allow berries to remain on the bush two or three days longer. Then berries will drop off easily.

CHERRIES

Cherries have the delightful habit of ripening earlier in the season than many other fruits, but the blossoms alone make this tree a prize.

Varieties. You can pick from two kinds of cherry trees: sweet or sour. (Sour is also sometimes called tart or pie cherries.) The needs and characteristics of the two are somewhat different.

Sweet cherries need a second variety for pollination. (Stella is an exception.) Bing, Lambert, and Napoleon will not pollinate each other; they need another variety, such as Black Tartarian, planted with them. Or set out Yellow Glass—a yellow-fruited variety.

Sweet cherries are generally available only in standard size. The trees tend to be larger than sour cherries and branching is more upright. Train branches of new trees to grow horizontally—instead of upright—by bracing them apart with a board; you'll get fruit on younger trees. Sweet varieties grow more slowly than other fruit trees and require less pruning to keep them productive.

Sour cherries are best known for their use in pies and preserves. They're hardier in cold climate areas, more resistant to drought, and more compact and spreading than their sweet relatives. Pie or sour cherry trees will bear well without a pollinator. They come in dwarf and semi-dwarf sizes, as well as standard. Among the standard-size sour cherries, Montmorency is one of the best. Early Richmond and

Suda are also good. Dwarfs North Star and Meteor are best for small lots. (You'll also find a somewhat taller semi-dwarf North Star.)

Planting. All cherry varieties need well-drained soil. Sweet cherries are especially sensitive to soggy soil.

Plant sour types in late fall in mild climates and in early spring elsewhere, 20 to 25 feet between trees. Sweet varieties should be set in the ground in the spring, 25 to 30 feet between trees.

Standard sour cherry trees need three to five years until they will bear; standard sweet take four to seven; genetic dwarf (those bred for small size) take only two or three.

Care and feeding. After planting young trees, cut back branches to three or four strong, wide-angled limbs on opposite sides of the trunk. Keep both sweet and sour kinds trimmed to a modified central leader. Prune annually in late winter or early spring. Sour cherries may become so dense you'll have to remove limbs in the center to allow sunlight to reach the middle of the tree.

No fertilizer is needed while the young tree is taking hold. Once established, yearly applications of a 5-10-10 or 10-10-10 commercial fertilizer will keep growth vigorous and the yields mouth-watering.

Insects and disease. Flocks of birds are by far the greatest pests attacking the cherry tree. The most effective deterrent is nylon or a cheesecloth netting draped and tied over the tree just as the fruit begins to ripen.

Harvesting. As cherries ripen, their color gets deeper. Both sweet and sour varieties should be left on the tree until mature.

CHERRIES, BUSH

Many a fruit grower's dreams have been dashed by the skimpy dimensions of a backyard. But there is a way to beat the problem. Bush cherries produce clump after clump of luscious red fruit on attractive shrubs that seldom grow more than ten feet in height. Some ground-hugging types, in fact, are under six feet. The bush cherry's blossoms are no less spectacular than those of its skyscraping counterpart, making it an excellent choice for border or hedge plantings.

Varieties. The best known varieties of bush cherry are the Nanking and Hansen types. Both are dense shrubs ideal for screen or border. Or a single bush may be placed as an accent planting. The plants are self-fertile so cross-pollination is not essential.

Planting: For border or hedge, space young shrubs eight to ten feet apart. In areas where winters are severe, early spring planting is best. When choosing a site, check for

good drainage. If soil is compact, mix in a shovelful of sphagnum peat moss for every shovelful of soil.

Care and feeding. As with most fruits—whether bush or tree—soil should be kept free of weeds for the first few years of growth. A well-maintained mulch will help keep soil friable and, at the same time, hold in moisture. If fertilizer is used, keep applications small.

Insects and diseases. Bush cherries seldom need sprays. Birds tend to leave them alone, too.

Harvest. When berries begin to ripen in midsummer, check shrubs daily to catch fruit at peak flavor. Remove cherry and stem from bush, taking care not to injure tiny fruit spurs.

CITRUS

Think of citrus, and soon warm, sunny thoughts crowd your mind—with good reason. This collection of tree species and their hybrids thrive only in warm weather areas—southern parts of Zone 8, but most successfully in Zones 9 and 10. All varieties of oranges, lemons, limes, grapefruits, and tangerines are frost tender.

In borderline areas, develop a microclimate by planting citrus near a south or west wall, painting walls nearby a light color to reflect heat, and making a raised bed of railroad ties or concrete blocks (filling the space inside with improved soil).

Varieties. Pick from several important species of oranges. The common or sweet orange *(Citrus sinensis)* is most widely grown and includes the thick-skinned navels.

Orange varieties vary widely in their bearing season, so plant several to extend the length of time you can enjoy fresh squeezed juice. For example, you could try tending Washington, Hamlin, Pineapple, and Valencia—listed here in order of their bearing times. Most citrus varieties are self-fertile, so you can get fruit even if you have space for only one tree.

With an exotic red pulp, but no more difficult to grow, are the blood oranges; outstanding are Ruby, Torocco, Temple, Moro Blood, and French Perfume.

Grapefruit, most successful in desert-like regions, is available in pink and white. Marsh is an excellent seedless white; Foster and Ruby are pink and bear early in the season.

Tangerines, decidedly subtropic fruits, are small and easy to peel. Both Dancy and Fremont are hardy, but Fremont appears earlier (November), with Dancy in December.

Libson and Eureka (bearing most heavily October to May) are top lemons in California,

CITRUS (continued)

but Meyer has the best cold tolerance.

Best known lime varieties include Persian (also called Tahiti) and Bears. Mexican is hardiest and can take temperatures down to 30 degrees Fahrenheit.

Planting. Good drainage and high temperatures are citrus trees' chief needs. Continuously soggy soil inhibits growth. The trees do need heat, but can get by in shade for part of the day.

Californians can plant citrus trees March to May, but Floridians set trees out somewhat later—spring and early summer. Plant trees no deeper than they grew at the nursery; the bud union should be about four inches above ground. If the young tree was not headed back at the nursery, prune it after planting. No more pruning is needed for a couple years. Rub off any young sprouts that appear beneath the bud union.

Wrap trunk in tree tape to prevent sunscald, and make a ridge around base to direct water toward roots. Young trees need deep waterings about every two weeks, but let the soil dry out between waterings.

Care and feeding. Citrus fruits do best in soils with a pH between 6.0 and 6.5. Take a soil test every few years, and apply dolomitic limestone when pH drops below 5.8. Fertilizer is applied three times a year, just before the appearance of new leaves. Only nitrogen will be needed in most parts of California, but nitrogen, phosphorus, and potassium may be needed in Florida.

Take care to deeply water even mature trees about every two weeks. Watering sufficiently to keep the lawn healthy isn't enough.

Insects and diseases. Usually an all-purpose spray will protect citrus against most hungry invaders. Spray in early spring, just after petal fall, and again four to six weeks later. At the first flush of growth—late February or early March—spray for aphids with a mixture of 1½ tablespoons of malathion per gallon of water. If thrips infest during hot weather, control them with the same mix used for the aphids.

Harvesting. Citrus specimens are ready for harvest for a long time. Often they can stay on the tree more than three months before becoming overripe. But, for peak flavor, pick fruits as soon after they mature as possible. Cut them from branches; don't pull them.

CURRANTS

The hardy and easy-to-grow currant has a tart flavor that makes it a favorite for homemade jellies and jams.

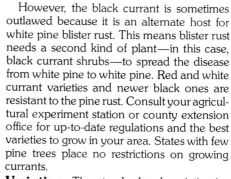

However, the black currant is sometimes outlawed because it is an alternate host for white pine blister rust. This means blister rust needs a second kind of plant—in this case, black currant shrubs—to spread the disease from white pine to white pine. Red and white currant varieties and newer black ones are resistant to the pine rust. Consult your agricultural experiment station or county extension office for up-to-date regulations and the best varieties to grow in your area. States with few pine trees place no restrictions on growing currants.

Varieties. The standard red varieties include Wilder and Red Lake, both vigorous and with tart berries. Cascade and Perfection are also popular reds. White Grape is a productive white (or yellow) variety. Currant varieties are self-fertile, so you can get good fruit with only one bush.

Planting. A hardy plant, currants do best in cooler regions and in soil that is moist but well drained and well supplied with nutrients. Set out young plants in the fall or early winter, because they leaf out early in the spring. If winters are brutal in your area, wait until spring to plant currants. Pick a lightly shaded area or spot shaded from the hot afternoon sun. Allow five feet between plants, trim tops back to six to 12 inches after planting, and mulch. Shrubs will bear in about two years.

Care and feeding. Many gardeners claim that currants respond better to organic fertilizers, such as manure and compost, than to commercial fertilizers. Keep four to six inches of mulch around plants. Prune out oldest branches, along with weak, crowded, or bushy twigs each year while the currant shrubs are dormant.

Harvesting. Pick berries for jellies or jams before they are fully ripe to preserve pectin content. Break or twist off the cluster stem and remove currants.

ELDERBERRIES

Elderberries are often found growing wild in damp areas. Small, dark, almost purple-black berries ripen in clusters. Their cane-like shrubs seldom grow more than six to ten feet in height. Elderberries' tart flavor makes them especially suitable for wines, jellies, and jams.

Varieties. Several varieties are adaptable to backyard growing. Nova, Johns, York, and Adams No. 2 are all vigorous. Although some varieties are self-fertile, research indicates you'll get a better yield if at least two varieties with overlapping bloom time (such as Adams and Johns) are included in the planting.

Planting. When choosing a site for the elderberry patch, look for a spot in full sun or

partial shade that can be kept moist but not soggy. Set out plants in early spring as soon as the ground can be worked. Allow at least five feet between shrubs. They'll bear two years after planting.

Care and feeding. Little pruning is required for elderberries, although deadwood, weak stems, and broken or diseased branches ought to be removed. Prune during late winter when plants are dormant. After planting, cultivate frequently to keep weeds at bay. A mulch four to six inches deep will help preserve moisture. Add more mulch to maintain proper depth. Prune to hedgerow or hill (see page 435). Remove dead, broken, bushy, or weak branches in early spring before leaves appear.

Insects and diseases. Insects and diseases seldom bother elderberries, but the fruit will need protection from birds. Cover shrubs with nylon or cheesecloth netting.

Harvesting. Gather berries when plump and in full color. Berries should not be allowed to soften.

GOOSEBERRIES

Similar to currants in their growth and cultivation, gooseberries thrive where winter temperatures drop below zero Fahrenheit. Hardy and easy to grow, the small tart berries make excellent jams.

Like some currants, the gooseberry plant can be an alternate host to the white pine blister rust fungus. The fungus doesn't harm them as much as it does white pine trees; other pines don't seem to be bothered by the disease, so gooseberries can be grown near them.

Varieties. Among the best known red types are Poorman, Fredonia, and Pixwell. Oregon Green and Downing are popular varieties with green berries. All are self-fertile so may be planted singly.

Planting. Plant one- to two-year-old shrubs early in the spring. Place them in a cool, moist, well-ventilated spot. Plan on at least five feet between plants, six to ten feet between rows, and two years from planting to bearing.

Care and feeding. Keep shrubs supplied with four to six inches of mulch. Prune in late winter or early spring to remove dead or broken branches, old wood, and weak stems. Gooseberries respond well to applications of organic materials, such as rotted manures or compost. Yellowing leaves may mean an application of nitrogen is needed.

To start new plants, bend a low branch over and cover it with soil, with the tip sticking out. Trim the new plant away from its parent after roots have formed.

Harvesting. Pick berries when somewhat on the green side for peak tart flavor and pectin content. Wear gloves for protection against thorny varieties.

GRAPES

For centuries a symbol of "the good life," grapes fit even postage-stamp size (but sunny) gardens because they grow up—not out. After careful planting, grapes reward you luxuriously with plump fruit in two to three years.

When calculating how and where to raise grapes, keep in mind that at least 150 days of frost-free weather are needed.

Varieties. Although most grapes are self-fertile (Scuppernong is an exception), you'll get best results by planting two different varieties in your yard or garden. Choosing the right variety for your part of the country is important. For the Northeast, try Beta, Blue Jay, Red Amber, or Concord; for the middle states, Concord, Catawba, Blue Lake, Delaware, and Niagara are recommended; for the West and coastal states, plant Campbell Early, Concord, Niagara, and Niabell; for the South, Blue Lake, Catawba, Concord, Delaware, and Niagara are best. Some seedless varieties include: Himrod, Interlaken, Concord Seedless, and Romulus.

Planting. Choose a site that offers protection from strong winds and unexpected late frosts. A northern slope is perfect because temperatures are generally more even there. If possible, run vines in an east-west line to cut down on shade cast on vines by the trellis. This also will help dry up rain or dew quickly, cutting down on diseases.

Grapes need a nutrient-rich and well-drained soil. Before planting, work in moderate amounts of rotted manure or compost. But don't overfertilize. Rampant vines are soft and tender and will succumb easily to severe weather.

In spring, as soon as the soil will accept a spade, plant one- or two-year-old vines obtained from a reliable nursery or garden supply center. Set vines in the soil so that the soil line matches original planting depth at the nursery. Then cut back all vines and branches to a single stem with at least three remaining buds. If plants are planted in rows, allow seven to eight feet between vines.

Care and feeding. Grapevines will twist and twine around everything within reach unless snipped and trained to grow where you want them. If you want shade for a patio or screening for privacy, limit pruning to the removal of scraggly growth and old canes. For quantities of luscious clusters, serious

GRAPES (continued)

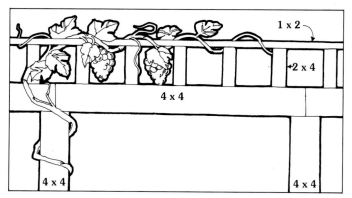

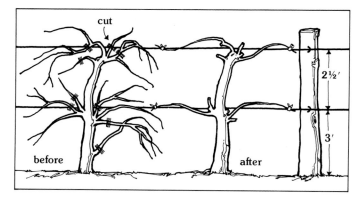

Above. *A good grape arbor provides ventilation around canes to discourage mildew diseases. Make the arbor sturdy enough to support vines all year.*
Below. *If fruit production comes first with you, use the four-arm kniffen system described below. Trim off all but four canes and four stubs.*

pruning is in order each year. The most popular training method is called the *four-arm kniffin system.* The idea is to prune vines in such a way that four canes are allowed to develop and bear fruit, while four spurs are carefully preserved for the following year.

First, construct a trellis consisting of two stout posts sunk into the ground. Then stretch two wires so the bottom wire is about 30 to 36 inches from the ground. The second wire should be 24 to 30 inches above the first. After the first season and during midwinter or very early spring when the plant is dormant, tie the central cane to the top wire. If there is a confusion of canes, select the most vigorous for the central stem. Cut the cane off slightly above the wire, and snip off all other growth. If the cane doesn't quite reach the top wire, fasten a piece of bamboo or lath as a bridge between the wires and tie cane to wood.

After the second or third season, new growth will be vigorous enough to select four

of the best canes for the "arms." Cut back to about ten buds per cane, and tie to upper and lower wires. Also, leave stubs with two buds each to become next year's renewal canes. Then remove all other canes and stubs. Every winter the previously bearing canes are removed to make room for the renewal growth.

Well-rotted manure is the best fertilizer for grapes. If none is available, use a good garden fertilizer—a pound and a half for each mature vine.

Insects and diseases. Thwart the host of diseases and bugs with prevention. Plant vines in a sunny, fairly open spot where good air circulation is assured. To protect against fungus diseases, use a reliable fungicide at rates recommended on the label. If insects threaten to defoliate the vine, spray thoroughly with an insecticide labeled for use against them. Some growers shroud the ripening clusters in paper bags as a defense against wasps and bees.

Harvesting. Don't be fooled by a purple grape. Most varieties change color well before they have arrived at peak ripeness and flavor. Let taste be your guide. A fully ripe grape, ready for picking, will be sweet and bursting with juice. To harvest, cut the entire cluster from vine.

PEACHES

Although they have a reputation for being touchy, peaches can be grown in at least 30 states. Take care before planting peaches north of Zone 5, but don't rule them out. Check with your county extension office or nursery to find out if your part of the state and your favorite variety are compatible.

Varieties. Peaches come in two general categories: clingstone types have pits that stick to the flesh, even when the peach is fully ripe, and freestones—the more popular varieties—separate easily. You'll find a range of sizes, too. Some dwarf varieties grow no taller than four feet and resemble a bush. Semi-dwarf trees grow to about nine feet; standard, to around 18 feet.

Select a variety for your climate. Popular peach varieties include: Belle of Georgia, Elberta, Harbinger, Garnet Beauty, Sunhaven, Cresthaven, and Madison. Compact Red Haven is a reliable dwarf variety. For colder regions, try Oriole and Veteran. Reliance and Sunapee can take temperatures far below zero Fahrenheit, particularly in a protected spot, and are candidates for colder zones.

Nectarines, or fuzzless peaches, grow where other peaches do and take the same care. For early fruit, plant Pocahontas. Cherokee, Lexington, Redbud, and Sure-

crop are fairly frost resistant.

Most peaches are self-fertile, so you can plant only one tree and still get a harvest. J.H. Hale, Mikado, Honeydew Hale, and Hal-Berta Giant are exceptions and will need a second variety planted nearby. Check a catalogue carefully because some of the newer varieties will need a partner to bear a crop of fruit.

Planting. Keep peach trees out of the direct path of winter. A slope facing north is ideal; trees won't be lured into premature growth by a warm spring day only to be crippled by an unexpected frost. Nestling trees near a building or behind a windbreak of evergreens helps protect them from the freezing effects of high winds.

The trees require well-drained soil. If soil is clayey, add sphagnum peat moss to soil in the planting hole. Choose well-branched and well-rooted year-old nursery stock about four feet tall. Plant them in early spring as soon as the frost danger has passed. Allow 25 feet between standard-size trees and ten to 15 between dwarf varieties. Next, cut back the main stem of the new trees to about three feet from the ground. Prune off all other twigs, and stake trees until they're well established. Resist fertilizing new trees. Expect fruit the third season after planting.

Care and feeding. Keep mulch of straw, hay, sawdust, or similar material about six inches deep around peach trees. But pull the mulch away from the base in the fall to discourage rabbits and mice from nesting there. For additional protection, keep a rodent guard (see page 438) on the tree the year around.

Train peach trees to an open center (see page 434), and keep the center of the tree free of dense growth. Prune annually while the tree is dormant. The part of the branch where the peaches grew last year won't fruit again, so prune to encourage new growth and top-notch peaches.

As the young fruit begins to form, thin them to about seven inches apart.

Insects and diseases. Tree borers and bacterial cankers can become serious problems. The preventive approach calls for regular applications of an all-purpose spray at pink and petal fall stages, and at least three times thereafter at three-week intervals. To control leaf curl, apply ferbam (available from most garden centers and nurseries) when trees are dormant.

Harvesting. Allow peaches to ripen fully on the tree. Yellow-fleshed varieties are generally ready for picking when the skin changes from light green to yellow. To be certain, sample a peach or two before hauling out the bushel basket.

PEARS

The pear—like the ubiquitous apple—was much a part of early America. Few colonial gardens were without the long-bearing and easy-to-grow Bartlett or the innocent-looking, but spicy, Seckel. As for flavor, the pear is a culinary specialty. It can be marinated, sliced, canned, candied, or enjoyed straight off the tree. If space is scarce, put a pear tree on the list of ornamental plantings scheduled for the backyard or lawn.

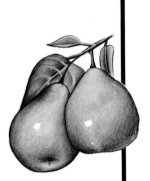

Varieties. When mulling over the various varieties, keep in mind that a second tree should be planted nearby to ensure proper pollination. Two favorite early bearing varieties are Clapp Favorite and Early Seckel. Bartletts, Buerre Bosc, and Magness are outstanding mid-season types. Dwarf varieties are also available.

Planting. Where winters are severe and the growing season short, plan on setting out pear trees in early spring. In warmer regions, you can choose either spring or fall for planting. A suitable soil will be heavy and definitely on the moist side. But drainage should be good, so roots don't suffocate in standing water. After the tree is planted and mulched, provide a stake for support against strong winds until tree is established.

Care and feeding. Most growers like to snip branches just above an outward pointing bud to encourage open center growth. Otherwise, pear trees are pruned in the same way as apples, that is, according to the central leader or modified central leader method.

Pears have a reputation for making do with the conditions facing them, so large amounts of fertilizer are not usually necessary. Let a soil test be your final guide. The tree's appearance can be a clue, though. If leaves begin to show a yellow cast, the tree may need a light application of a complete 5-10-10 fertilizer.

Once trees reach the fruiting stage, keep an eye on branches so they don't become overloaded. Pick off excess fruit allowing one pear for every eight inches of wood.

Insects and diseases. Fire blight is the principal disease that haunts the pear. It's often brought on by overabundant growth, such as that resulting from application of too much fertilizer. For blemish-free fruit, spray with an all-purpose spray at blossom pink and petal fall stages, as well as four times thereafter at ten- to 14-day intervals.

Harvesting. Pears are one of the few fruits that are not allowed to fully ripen on the tree. Harvest when the small spots on the skin turn brown and when the fruit separates easily from the branch. Then wait a few days before tasting a sample.

PLUMS

Plums can be grown in any state in the country, but they vary so widely in hardiness that no one variety can be grown everywhere. The search for a suitable variety is worth the effort: the small size, even of standard trees, simplifies pruning, spraying, and harvesting.

Varieties. Double-check two details as you select plum trees: are they suitable for your climate? will they need a second variety planted nearby for cross-pollination? Although many varieties of plums are available, Abundance, Burbank, Ember, Pipestone, Purple Heart, Stanley Prune, Mt. Royal, and Underwood were all developed in northern areas and can withstand tough winters. Most varieties can be found only in the standard size (up to 20 feet tall), but Abundance, Burbank, and Stanley Prune are also in dwarf form. If your winters aren't brutal, consider the tasty Damson, Superior, or Green Gage (also called Reine Claude).

Many catalogues will differentiate between European or Japanese plums. European varieties tend to be best for cold weather areas. Japanese varieties, such as Shiro, are a reward for gardeners in areas seldom surprised by late frosts; they bloom earlier than European.

Only a few plum varieties are self-fertile. Stanley is one, but it also makes a good pollinator of other varieties. Others, such as Underwood, Redheart, Shiro, or Santa Rosa, benefit if two or more trees of the same variety are planted in the same area. Or they will act as pollinators for other varieties.

Planting. Most plum trees are best planted in early spring, as soon as the soil will allow. European varieties can also be set in the ground in late fall. Space standard-size trees 20 feet apart, with graft union above the soil line. A northern slope is ideal, especially for the early blooming Japanese varieties. Good drainage is essential.

Most standard and dwarf plums take at least three years from planting to reach the bearing stage. But standards will last up to 20 years, dwarfs up to 15.

Care and feeding. Mulch is an aid to plum trees all year. In early spring, it can keep roots cool so the tree doesn't impatiently send out blossoms on the first sunny days (only to be nipped by a late frost). During hot weather, mulch helps keep soil moisture from evaporating and keeps weeds down.

Prune Japanese varieties to an open center; others, to the modified central leader (see page 434). The idea is to allow plenty of sunshine to fall on ripening fruit. Thin some of the developing fruit because most varieties set more fruit than they can support. In general,

leave one fruit for every three to four inches. Don't thin Damson and prune plums.

Once trees are established, a regular feeding program can be started. Plan on about one pound of ammonium sulfate for young trees and about two to three pounds for the mature tree. Cut rate about in half for dwarf varieties. All applications should be reserved for early spring.

Insects and diseases. Black knot and brown rot can plague the plum. Spray with an all-purpose spray at petal fall and thereafter at least three times at ten-day intervals. Wood with large, dark swellings is likely suffering from black knot and should be removed.

Harvesting. Because color varies with the type of plum, you'll have to be your own judge when it comes to determining ripeness. Fruit should detach easily with a slight twist of the stem.

QUINCE

Unless you are an incurable jelly connoisseur, any thought of growing quince will probably dart in and out of your mind. But jelly lovers wouldn't dream of being without a quince tree. The large, golden color fruit makes excellent preserves.

Varieties. Because the demand is low, the varieties available are limited to Orange, Van Deman, and Burbank Jumbo. Although not actually dwarfs, they are diminutive in size, hardly getting much above 12 feet. Because of their compact growth and showy blossoms, quince trees are good choices for accent plantings.

Planting. Quince is adaptable to a wide range of soils, requiring good drainage and regular cultivation to keep down weeds. Because quince is self-pollinating, a single tree will have no difficulty setting fruit.

Insects and diseases. As a rule, quince will manage the diseases and bugs on its own. But, occasionally, blight or insect pests will invade the tree. If the crop is threatened, spray with an all-purpose mixture, according to the schedule used for apples.

Harvesting. In late fall when fruit is mature, they may be picked over an extended period as needed.

RASPBERRIES

Nothing caps a summer evening better than a raspberry cobbler heaped with vanilla ice cream. Or sprinkle the ripe berries on cereal for a morning treat. Homemade jam is always a welcome gift, too. Because of their delicious uses and ease of growing, the perennial raspberry ought to be in every garden.

Varieties. The most commonly grown raspberry is the red. But the purple and black types make interesting variations on the raspberry theme. All can be grown in most parts of the country, and all are self-fertile. The most popular red varieties are Fallred, Hilton, Indian Summer, Latham, Newburgh, New Heritage, and Thornless Canby. For black raspberries, try Bristol, Allen, Black Hawk, or Morrison. Purple varieties include Clyde, Amethyst, Sodus, and Purple Autumn. Some, such as Latham, are termed everbearing because when pruned properly they will provide two yields per season.

To make the most of your raspberry patch, check with your nursery or county extension office to make sure the variety you want to buy will thrive in your area. Resist the free offerings of well-intentioned neighbors who appear on your doorstep with a handful of seedlings culled from their own patches. The small amount of money you may save is not worth the risk of diseased plants.

Planting. Moisture and plenty of rich organic matter in the soil are essentials. It pays to grow a high cultivation crop, such as any of the root vegetables, the year before in order to get the ground in proper condition. When deciding on a location, look for a spot that gets some protection from the blustery cold winds of winter. To improve the soil's ability to retain moisture, work in plenty of well-rotted manure or sphagnum peat moss.

Set bushes in the ground as soon as you bring them home from the nursery. If roots appear dried out, soak them in water for an hour or two before planting. Red raspberries can be planted two or three inches deeper than at the nursery; black and purple varieties should be planted at the same depth. Space plants three feet apart and rows five to eight feet apart.

Care and feeding. After canes have been set out, cut back central canes to a height of six inches. Then mulch to conserve moisture. Also, keep the hoe handy so weeds can be nipped before they invade the row. Remember, though, that deep hacking with the hoe can do considerable injury to shallow raspberry roots.

Like blackberries, raspberries need a thorough going-over with the pruning shears to maintain some semblance of order. When plants are dormant in early spring, remove weak and spindly canes. Then remove any suckers that have grown up between rows. Ideally, rows should be no more than about 12 inches wide so that berries are always accessible and plants benefit from good air circulation. If properly pruned, raspberry canes are self-supporting. Head back your black

raspberry varieties to 18 to 24 inches; purple and red varieties, to 30 to 36 inches. The amount and the quality of the fruit will be greatly improved if lateral branches are trimmed back to at least four to six buds. Finally, after the harvest is in, remove all old, spent canes, and destroy them.

If your winters are especially deadly for fruit-bearing plants, you can overwinter raspberry canes by bending them gently to the ground and covering them with a deep layer of mulch. Then when the warm winds of spring return, remove protective mulch, and allow canes to return to their normal upright position again.

Most growers like to keep raspberry rows open and fruit accessible by training the canes to grow within a trellis arrangement constructed of posts and wire. Plants may be grown between double wires or merely tied to a trellis or single wire. (See "Blackberries" for hints on how to make the various supports.)

Insects and diseases. Raspberries are hardly immune from disease and insect attack, but problems will be few if you practice good garden hygiene. Purchase only healthy, disease-resistant plants from a trustworthy nursery or garden supply center. And make sure the variety grown is the right one for your weather zone. Because weeds can lead to an assortment of miseries, keep area clean and mowed. Make sure, too, that old canes are removed and destroyed so insect larvae and fungus spores don't overwinter. If a plant appears doomed because of disease, remove it immediately so other plants aren't infected.

Harvesting. As berries approach ripeness, they change color rapidly. Check the raspberry patch each day. A deep red color on red varieties and a dull coating on others means harvesttime has arrived.

STRAWBERRIES

If you want to break into the fruit growing business in gentle stages, strawberries are the perfect introduction. Many a backyard grower, thrilled by the vegetables nurtured just outside the kitchen door, plants strawberries as a first step toward growing fruits. Easy to grow and rich in rewards, strawberries can be either tucked into the vegetable patch or used as an ornamental plant. The white blossoms and deep green, attractively-shaped leaves, plus low growing habit, make them a natural for borders or rock gardens. Or convert the children's sandbox into a raised strawberry garden, or punch holes in a rain barrel for a makeshift strawberry jar.

Varieties. Befitting its popularity, strawberry varieties exist in abundance and all are

STRAWBERRIES

(continued)

self-fertile, so you can get by with a single variety. There are early season kinds, mid-season types, and varieties that barely manage to ripen their fruit before fall frosts arrive. You'll also find everbearing plants that give you a fairly heavy harvest early in the season, then offer a second picking just before the season comes to an end.

For early season strawberries, try Earlidawn, Red Rich, or Fairfax. Catskill, Empire, Guardian, Midway, Robinson, Surecrop, and Redchief are reliable mid-season types. Late season varieties include Jerseybelle and Sparkle. The double bonus varieties, termed "everbearing," include Ogallala, Dunlap, Geneva, Ozark Beauty, and Superfection. Some varieties are better at surviving winter's ravages than others. Consult your local nursery or county extension office for the best varieties for your area, and for the amount of work you're willing to do.

Planting. Because of their shallow root systems, strawberry plants are easy victims to heaving caused by the alternate thawing and freezing of the ground in many parts of the country. The plants can be practically pushed out of the ground where roots die. Look for a patch of ground that slants gently toward the north but which receives plenty of sun. Proper location means the strawberry bed will not be tempted into premature blossoming by a warm spring sun. At the same time, cool, frosty air masses will drain away from the plants into lower regions.

Soil slated for the strawberry bed must be well drained for the plants to thrive; a slope is often a good choice. Spade soil to a depth of eight to ten inches, and mix in compost or dry, bagged manure. Some gardeners plan on two stages. The first year they break ground and sow a vegetable crop. By the time the second season rolls around, their ground will be in excellent shape and generally free of stubborn weeds. Then they work in generous amounts of manure and organic soil conditioners, such as sphagnum peat moss or compost.

When purchasing plants, find a dependable nursery where you can buy disease-free, reliable plants that will reward you with abundant yields. Strawberry roots are numerous and tender. If not planted right away or if exposed to bright sun, they can dry out. If too many roots are destroyed, the plant cannot recover.

Set out plants in early spring at the proper depth. If too deep, the crown will smother and the plant will die. If too shallow, roots will stick out and dry. The trick is to match the new soil line with the depth the plant grew at the nursery. Or simply make sure the soil covers all the roots but does not cover the crown. As you work, protect unplanted ones by covering them with wet burlap or several layers of newspaper.

The strawberry grower has three planting methods from which to choose, depending on the variety grown and the yield desired. Close, dense planting, as a rule, results in heavy yields of smaller berries, and the open, well-spaced method offers a lower yield but larger berries. The chief difference between each system has to do with what you do with the runners, those tethered baby plants that develop from the main plant.

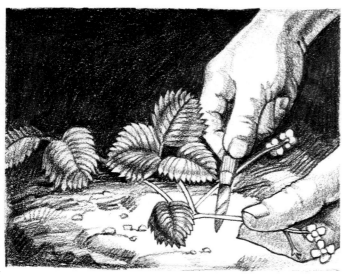

On June-bearers, remove all flowers that form the first season after planting. Strawberry starts need energy to establish and grow runners. Remove runners that develop in late summer. Use a sharp knife; don't pull blossoms off.

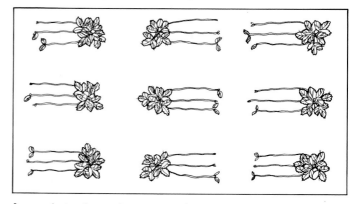

Leave plenty of space between strawberry rows. Encourage the runners from each parent plant to grow in the center aisle. After the parent plant dies, reverse the process and set the second generation runners back into the original bed.

Hill planting. For jumbo berries and the manicured strawberry bed, set plants 12 inches apart in rows spaced about 18 inches apart. Pinch off all runners when they appear to encourage a strong central plant.

Matted row. Many commercial growers opt for the matted row system because it requires the least care and maintenance. Set plants 18 to 24 inches apart in rows at least three feet apart. Allow runners to sprout willy-nilly and take root wherever they happen to land. In no time, the rows will expand into a tangled sea of leaves and overlapping runners. But when harvesttime comes, there will be berries galore for your enjoyment.

Hedgerow planting. The hedgerow system combines the best of the matted and the hill methods of planting strawberries. Nursery plants are set out 24 inches apart in rows about 24 to 36 inches apart. For a single row, allow two runners per plant to take root. The double row allows four runners per plant to become established. Sometimes the young runner plants must be coaxed into taking root within the row. Use a clothespin or forked stick to anchor the tiny plant to the soil.

Care and feeding. The chief aim during the first season is to concentrate on getting the plants well established. Since a strong root system is essential, make sure all blossoms are removed so the plant's energy is channeled into root formation. Nip weeds as they appear so all available nutrients are used by plants, and keep soil moisture high by frequent watering. In the fall, after growth has ceased, spread a three-inch mulch over the entire bed to insulate plants against alternate freezing and thawing.

As soon as the soil begins to warm the following spring and the likelihood of a surprise frost has diminished, use a rake to pull mulch off the plants. Proper timing is important because plant leaves will turn yellow if left under the mulch too long. A good indication of renewed growth is a fresh green color to the leaves. Gather mulch into space between rows so weeds are thwarted and soil moisture retained. Once the air warms, the bed will become a sea of white blossoms.

Insects and diseases. A bright red, ripe strawberry is a neon sign to birds. If plants aren't shrouded under netting or wire, your crop might vanish. Use nylon netting, chicken wire, or treated cheesecloth as a deterrent. If the soil is properly prepared beforehand and the bed is kept reasonably clean, insects and diseases will seldom threaten. However, grub control and good soil drainage are critical.

Harvest. The veteran strawberry grower can tell by the sweet fragrance in the air that picking time is just around the corner. Once ripening is under way, the process is rapid. Check the bed each day and pick berries as they ripen. They won't store well for long, so be prepared to cook or freeze them soon—or nibble them as is.

Encourage runners to form new plants every nine inches. Pin down runners with U-shaped pins, or simply bury them with soil, making sure the tips peek out. Remove unwanted runners. Root no more than six runners around a plant.

In cold climates, mulch the entire bed heavily in winter; add mulch after the first frost. In spring, loosen the mulch as plants turn green, but don't remove completely until weather is at least ten degrees Fahrenheit day and night.

ABCs of Nuts

No Thanksgiving celebration would be complete without a bowl heaped with crunchy walnuts, pecans, filberts, and almonds. Nuts are as much a part of fall festivities as pumpkin pie and cranberry sauce. When putting together your garden blueprint, be sure to reserve a choice location for a miniature grove of nut trees. Attractive and easy to care for, a well-placed nut tree can provide years of shady splendor as well as tasty nuts.

ALMONDS

Because almonds bloom almost a full month before peaches, they will succumb to spring frosts where winters are slow to make way for warmer temperatures. As a result, most are grown in California. Almonds are, by and large, not self-pollinating, which means companion trees should be planted nearby.

Planting. A well-drained soil on the sandy side is practically a must for successful almond culture. Wet, soggy roots will lead to declining yields and, ultimately, a failing tree. Because lingering frosts are a constant hazard, place the tree on higher ground or in a protected area. Nut trees generally have a sizable taproot, which makes them slightly more difficult to transplant than shallow-rooted trees. Dig a large hole, making sure it is deep enough to accommodate the taproot. Then fill the planting hole with soil, taking care to firm soil around roots.

Care and feeding. Immediately after planting, head back tree, but leave three or four healthy branches growing at wide angles. Once the tree is established, pruning will consist mainly of removing old wood or inwardly growing branches. As for fertilizer, the almond can get along nicely on the nutrients naturally present in the soil. An occasional dose of a well-rotted manure, though, will contribute to good growth.

Harvesting. In late fall, the hardened husks will drop easily to the ground when the branches are gently shaken. Remove kernels from inner shells and allow to dry before using in your favorite recipes.

BUTTERNUTS

Often referred to as the white walnut, the butternut is adaptable to a wider range of climates than are most nut trees. The rich, buttery kernels are used primarily in cooking and for eating as a snack.

Planting. Although most nut trees lean toward slightly acid soils, the butternut likes soil on the alkaline side. Its roots also range far and wide, which means soil needs to be deeply worked and fairly well cultivated. Drainage must not be neglected because soggy conditions will affect the yield. Like other nut trees, butternut produces a long taproot that must be carefully set in the ground so that it is not bent or damaged. Dig a deep hole and, after planting tree, refill with soil that has been mixed with an equal amount of sphagnum peat moss. Tamp soil as you backfill so all air pockets are eliminated. Then saturate soil with water. Finally, remove at least one third of the treetop so a strong central leader will develop.

Care and feeding. Most nut trees are shaped to follow the pyramid, or central leader, form. After the severe pruning when tree is planted, subsequent pruning consists mainly of removing dead or injured wood and cutting out branches that threaten to crowd main limbs. Soil moisture can be kept high by applying a generous mulch around tree. But bark is susceptible to rodent damage, so a protective guard (see page 438) should be provided.

Harvesting. Nuts will fall naturally to the ground when mature, or they may be shaken from the tree. Husk and allow to dry before storing in airtight containers.

CHESTNUTS

Veteran gardeners have fond memories of gingerly gathering prickly chestnuts and then roasting the shiny kernels over the glowing coals of a fire. The American chestnut, of course, has been reduced by blight to a scattering of sprouts growing desperately from old and decaying stumps. But other varieties are not so susceptible to disease. The Chinese chestnut, with its low growth, attractive blossoms, and unusually shaped leaves, is especially useful for landscaping purposes.

Planting. For more abundant harvests, experts recommend planting two different varieties in order to ensure proper pollination. Plant trees in early spring as soon as the soil will permit. Then train to the central leader system by cutting back the top of the tree so that three or four of the strongest branches are left. For soil, the chestnut will thrive in a

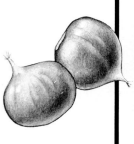

wide variety of loams, but low, soggy ground should be avoided. Be sure to dig the hole deep enough to accommodate the taproot.

Care and feeding. To keep soil moisture high, a thick, regularly maintained mulch is helpful. If a chestnut tree is featured in your lawn and a mulch strikes you as unsightly, simply cultivate the area thoroughly so weeds won't compete for valuable nutrients. To help the young tree survive blustery winter winds, drive a stake into the ground; then tie the tree to the stake with soft twine.

Harvesting. As nuts mature in the fall, they will drop to the ground. To prevent mold and insect injury, gather husks immediately. Kernels should be allowed to dry before being stored.

FILBERTS

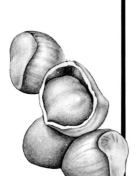

For the home gardener whose activities are limited to a sliver of yard tucked between the garage and the back door, the filbert, or hazelnut, can be the answer to a nut lover's dreams. The smallest of the nut trees, filberts are satisfied with almost any soil as long as sufficient moisture is present.

Planting. Because roots are shallow and fibrous, soil should be well prepared before planting. Mix in ample amounts of rotted manure or compost together with sphagnum peat moss.

Care and feeding. Because weeds and rampant grasses can rob the soil of nutrients needed by the tree, it's important to cultivate the soil regularly. A mulch will help nip weeds and, at the same time, hold in soil moisture. Moldy hay, wood chips, or partially decomposed compost are all suitable mulching materials.

Harvesting. Gather nuts as they drop to the ground. Dry husked nuts by spreading them out on a tray or rack.

PECANS

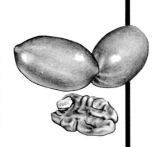

Count on a growing season of at least 200 days if the flavor-packed pecan is part of your nut-growing plans. Sensitive to temperature extremes, trees exposed to wild and woolly weather will have tiny—or no—yields. But the decorative branch and leaf structure of the pecan make it especially popular as a landscaping specimen.

Planting. Planting a pecan can present something of a challenge because the tree produces a lengthy taproot, which may be as long as 2½ feet when dug in the nursery. Be sure the planting hole is deep enough to allow the root to continue its downward growth.

The tree can be set out two to three inches deeper than it grew at the nursery. But great care should be taken when replacing the soil so that air pockets don't remain. Replace soil a little at a time, then moisten thoroughly with watering can or garden hose, so soil settles snugly in and around roots.

Care and feeding. After initial planting, cut the tree back to a height of about two feet. Because insistent weeds and grass can cripple—if not kill—a young tree, cultivation should be frequent and thorough until the tree is established.

Harvesting. Gather nuts as they fall to the ground, or shake them gently from the tree. They may be husked and stored in the freezer or dried, then stored in their shells in airtight containers.

WALNUTS

If there is such a thing as the king of nuts, then the English walnut certainly takes all honors. Coveted for its delicious fruit and ornamental value, the English walnut tree grows best wherever winters are moderate and springs free of late frosts. The black walnut is native to much of the eastern half of the United States and grows best in that area. For successful pollination of either type of walnut, plant at least two varieties. Grafted trees generally will bear several years earlier than native trees grown from seed.

Planting. In most areas, trees are planted in early spring as soon as the soil can be worked. In warmer regions, however, trees may be set out in the fall. Dig a hole deep enough to accommodate the lengthy taproot. Be sure the planting site is well drained. When replacing soil that has been mixed with compost or sphagnum peat moss, be sure you press soil firmly around roots so air pockets are eliminated. Sometimes an occasional watering as you fill helps settle loose soil. Tree should be planted at the same depth as at nursery.

Black walnut trees tend to bear heavily every second year with a light crop in between.

Care and feeding. Weeds and invading grass should be periodically removed so the tree has access to all the soil nutrients. Keep an eye on the soil surface to determine moisture content. If dry, water thoroughly. A bark or hay mulch can do wonders when rainfall is scarce.

Harvesting. Walnuts are ready to harvest when the hulls crack open. Shake the nuts from the tree. A ripe nut will be easy to crack, allowing easy removal of the kernel. Husk immediately and wash kernels to remove stains. Dry and store in airtight containers.

chapter 14

HOUSEPLANTS

Nothing makes you feel closer to nature than plants. And when you reside in a high-rise apartment or have a tiny yard, tending lots of plants may be about as close to nature as you'll get. Think of plants as vital, growing individuals; they'll strengthen your ties with the out-of-doors and give you pleasure—no matter where you live. As you get to know different plant species, you'll find diversity—and be endlessly fascinated. Quiet and unobtrusive, plants still manage to establish a relationship with their owners—care for a plant, watch it respond, and you'll understand.

Houseplants need help if they're to remain healthy and thriving. They depend on you for water, food, soil, and placement in proper light. But plants are remarkably adaptable. They're amazingly tough and resilient; almost any plant will break so-called rules when given just a few of their favored conditions. Kitchens and bathrooms, for example, with their high degree of humidity, form natural havens for many plants. Give your leafy beauties their other "must have"—lots of light—and they'll reward you with thriving foliage and bountiful bloom.

Trim a window with plants hung at different levels and treat yourself to a living, green drapery; you'll also please your sun-loving plants. But don't despair if you don't have good natural light available, or if you've run out of places close to window areas. With grow-lights widely available and simple to install, there's no reason why you can't garden in any room of the house.

Don't hesitate to try new kinds of plants: cactus, bromeliads, ferns, or palms, for example. You'll be delighted to learn that some are as easy to grow as your old favorites. Check the charts in this chapter for tips to make them flourish.

Containers and Potting

Proper potting techniques are easy to learn, so there's no excuse for strangling plants in too-small pots. To make things easy, set aside a corner of the basement or garage where you can store containers, fertilizers, and soil mixtures. Make a point to check all plants every spring; move those needing more space into larger pots.

The first thing to consider when getting ready to repot a plant is the type of container to use. This is especially important for plants, such as ferns, orchids, and cactus, whose roots need more air than some other plants.

The pots used most often are made from clay (or terra-cotta), ceramic, and plastic. All three work well, if you understand how they retain moisture. Clay and unglazed ceramic pots let a plant's roots breathe but also let moisture escape more quickly than plastic. This is an advantage for plants that need to dry out between waterings, such as cactus and other succulents.

Conditioning new clay pots is a step beginning gardeners often overlook—then wonder why their newly potted plants wilt, in spite of proper watering. The reason is that clay absorbs water. A pot that isn't conditioned tends to draw water out of the soil, robbing the plant. To avoid this, completely immerse the pot in a pail of water. Let it remain there until all bubbling and hissing stop. The hissing is barely audible, but you will hear it if you lean close to the water.

Plastic and glazed ceramic pots hold moisture longer; they are often preferred for plants that need a lot of water and like evenly moist soil, such as fittonia, pickaback plant, and miniature roses. This is a plus if you're a little forgetful about watering. Plastic pots are also ideal for small plants that tend to dry out rapidly, too. When using plastic pots for other plants, be careful not to water excessively. This can present problems when plants are potted directly in decorative glazed ceramic containers and jardinieres. To avoid waterlogging, pot the plant in a clay or plastic container with drainage hole, and set it inside the decorative receptacle. Or place a layer of gravel or pebbles in the bottom of the fancy pot before adding the soil and plant.

All standard-size pots and most plastic or ceramic pots have bottom drainage holes that let surplus water drain away and provide an entry for air into the lower root area. Before planting, this hole should be covered by a shard, a broken piece of pottery (right). This prevents soil from washing out along with the water. A small square of screening or a bottle cap may also be used.

Put a pot saucer under the container to catch any water running out of the hole. Use glazed ceramic or plastic saucers to protect wood surfaces or carpeting. To simplify moving large plants around the floor, choose saucers with built-in casters, too.

Most pots for hanging houseplants are plastic or ceramic; check for drainage holes and attached saucers before buying them.

Soil

Remember, your plant will live or die depending on the soil you give it. Always use good soil that's moist—neither soggy, nor completely dry. It's difficult to pot a plant when the soil is powder dry and equally hard to get the soil remoistened once it's in the pot.

You can buy packaged potting soil or mix your own using two parts garden loam; one part leaf mold or peat; and one part sand, perlite, or vermiculite. Sterilize parts of the mix that weren't sterile when purchased by spreading them in a baking dish or cookie sheet and cooking them in a 200-degree Fahrenheit oven for 45 minutes. Store the soil mix in a plastic bag or closed container to retain the moisture. Special soil blends can be purchased for certain plants with special characteristics, such as cactus, African violets, and orchids.

Sometimes the need for repotting is obvious: the plant wilts between normal waterings. Another sign is when new leaves are quite a bit smaller than older ones. Any plant growing spindly or not growing at all in a two- or three-inch pot is also a likely candidate. (However, remember that many plants are naturally dormant during the short days of winter.)

Repotting is in order, too, if you buy a small plant and discover you have to water it daily because the soil is too porous and won't hold the moisture.

It's normal for a few small roots to grow through the drainage hole, but when several large roots crowd their way through, you know they need more growing space.

Check plants that have been in the same container for two or more years to see if they're root-bound. Turn the pot and plant upside down, and grasp the base of the stem between your fingers. Tap the rim of the pot to remove the plant. If the soil ball is filled with roots, repot the root-bound plant in a slightly larger container.

Some plants, ferns and palms in particular, prefer being slightly root-bound and shouldn't be repotted too frequently.

Repot, also, if you receive a gift planter crowded with four or five young plants. They'll

Cover the hole in the bottom of the pot with a shard. This keeps the soil in the pot from washing out as the surplus water drains away.

have a better chance for survival in individual pots. When the massed roots are free of the original receptacle, separate the plants gently. Put each plant in a four-inch pot, and water thoroughly. Keep all of them away from direct sun until they've recovered from the shock of transplanting.

How to repot

Follow this potting procedure step by step:

1. Lay out all your supplies (remember to condition new clay pots). Choose the size pot to be used. Generally, plants should be shifted to a container no more than an inch larger in diameter. For cuttings and offshoots, a four- or five-inch pot will do.

Place a pot shard, piece of screen, or bottle cap over the drainage hole of the pot, and put a layer of pea gravel or small stones in the bottom of the pot. For small pots, a half-inch depth is fine. One to three inches is best for pots over ten inches in diameter. Fill approximately one-third of the pot with soil, pressing it lightly with your fingers.

2. Remove the plant from its old pot by tipping it upside down and tapping it against a counter or tabletop (top right, second illustration). Run a knife around the rim of the pot, and pull gently at the roots if the plant is difficult to get out. This is easiest if you haven't watered the plant for several days. Retain as much soil around the roots as possible.

Removing a big plant from a heavy pot often requires a helper. Start by running the long thin blade of a knife all the way around the soil ball to separate it from the pot. Then, with one person holding the pot down, the other should be able

Use a packaged soil mix or make your own, following the guidelines below. Be sure to sterilize garden loam you dig yourself.

To remove the plant, simply turn the pot upside down, holding your hand against the soil. Firmly rap the pot rim against a solid surface to loosen the plant.

Once the plant is loosened (you may need to run a knife around the rim of the pot), grasp the plant by the stem near the soil and pull gently.

to lift the soil ball out by firmly pulling up on the trunk. For large plants, it's also important to measure the soil ball to be certain that it will sit at the proper depth in the partially filled new pot. Allow for the depth of the soil ball plus a half inch of space between the soil surface and the rim of the pot. Add or remove soil from the pot before setting in the plant.

3. Center the plant in its new pot, and hold it in place with one hand while you add the remaining soil. Make sure you fill in thoroughly around the roots. Firm the soil by lightly pressing downward with your fingers. Continue adding and pressing until you have the proper level. Remember to leave about an inch (or less if the pot is small) at the top of the pot for water that will soak into the soil.

4. Give the plant a thorough soaking. Water the soil slowly from the top, or set the pot into a saucer of water for about an hour. Then let the plant drain.

5. Set newly potted plants in indirect light for several days so they can adjust to their new home.

Many plants, such as philodendrons, devil's ivy, and some of the begonias, need additional support to keep them from sprawling unattractively. Bamboo stakes and fern-root totems are strong enough for small plants, but you'll need a sturdy stake for big philodendrons and monsteras. A cedar bark slab makes a good totem for large plants.

You can use totem pins to secure stems to fern-root totems, but there's a little trick to tying plants to a bamboo stake or other thin stick. Use a plastic-covered wire tie or strip of nylon hose, and tie a loose loop around the stem; tie tightly around the stake so the loop won't slip down.

Center the plant in the pot with one hand and add soil by handfuls, pressing lightly with your fingertips to avoid damaging roots.

It's easy to make your own compost to use as the leaf mold or peat moss in the potting soil formula. See complete directions below.

Trim the ends of the ties so they are inconspicuous. You don't need to wrap your tying strip around and around a cedar slab to secure the plant. Just insert screws deep into the bark and tie the stems to them. Or drill holes through the slab, and, after tying the loop around the stem, thread the other end through a hole and tie it to a screw sunk into the back of the slab.

Make your own compost

You can make your own compost to serve as the leaf mold in the basic potting mixture. Mix a small amount in your basement or garage, and keep it on hand for use as needed. To make compost, you'll need a container (such as an old dishpan), plastic bags, plant food, and organic scraps (sawdust, leaves, or vegetable trimmings). Place the scraps in the pan, add a couple of cups of soil (to provide bacteria for decomposing the organic material), and one-fourth cup of plant food containing at least 15 to 20 percent nitrogen, and mix well. Moisten with water, and stir until all is moist. Fill the plastic bags, tie shut, and set in a spot where the temperature is about 70 degrees Fahrenheit. The compost will be ready in three to four months. Or use compost from your outdoor compost pile.

Care for Houseplants

Keeping your plants healthy and happy is a simple matter of knowing how much light, water, and fertilizer they need. Ask questions when you purchase or receive a new plant. Try to provide your plants with as nearly perfect growing conditions as you can—then just sit back and enjoy them.

Help your plants survive by finding out their light needs: direct or bright sunlight; bright, indirect light; or medium light.

Watering is another plant need to know—especially if the plant is one that should never be allowed to dry out or that should be bone-dry before watering.

Light

Proper light is critical for success with houseplants. You can compensate for incorrect watering or feeding, but there's little you can do about poor lighting. Check charts in this chapter to find out what kind of light a plant needs before you purchase it. If it needs more than you have available, pass it up until you can provide it with the necessary light through grow-lights or additional windows.

You often see terms like "bright sunlight," or "bright, indirect light," or "medium light." Direct sunlight means just that: sun shining directly through a window, often from the south. This light is too strong for most plants, except cactus and other succulents. You can filter the light with a sheer curtain or drapery for more sensitive plants.

Bright light is less intense than direct sunlight. Plants should be placed in a southeast, southwest, or west exposure or a few feet away from a south window. Croton, schefflera, and coleus are a few of the plants that need this kind of light.

Bright, indirect light is reflected light—usually from white walls. The intensity of this light is roughly equivalent to east or west sun, or south sun filtered with a sheer curtain. This is the kind of light most foliage plants need.

Medium light is light strong enough to read by. A northern exposure gives medium light. It's roughly equivalent to light a few feet away from an east or west window. Most ferns and a few foliage plants require this kind of light. Few houseplants can survive in light that's not strong enough to read by. Regardless of its light requirements, turn the plant occasionally so it doesn't lean toward the light.

Watering

How much water does the plant need? This is probably one of the first questions you ask a salesclerk. And the stock answer seems to be, "Water when it's dry." Generally, that's good advice, but some plants should never be allowed to dry out completely, but others shouldn't be watered until the soil is bone-dry. A bit of experience and a drooping plant or two will teach you quickly when it's time to water again.

Varying conditions determine how often you should water your houseplants. For instance, if the air in your home is dry, you'll have to water more frequently than if the air is humid. Plants in small pots need water more often than those in large pots. A plant in bloom needs extra water.

There is one golden rule to follow: when you water, be thorough. Supply enough moisture to soak the soil all the way to the bottom of the pot and into the saucer. But don't let the plant stand in this excess water.

Thorough watering once a week is better than shallow watering every other day. More plants perish from overwatering than from underwatering. Excessively wet soil crowds out the oxygen needed by the roots, and the roots can't support the leaves if they don't have oxygen. Even plants needing a lot of water can be killed if they are kept soggy. *If in doubt, don't* is a good rule to follow until you've established a successful watering schedule.

Checking plants twice a week is a good habit to adopt. Check early in the week, and water the plants that are dry—coleus, pickaback, hemigraphis, and small specimens will probably need it. Water the rest once a week or so (or more if your home is very dry). Cactus and other succu-

Most plants need more humidity than the average home offers. Group plants on a tray of moistened pebbles. Keep the water below the pot bottom.

Daily misting is another way to help give plants more humidity. For best results, mist the plants several times during the daylight hours.

Don't overfertilize! A little plant food goes a long way—too much can burn the roots and kill the plant. Always follow directions on the plant food label.

lents may go ten to 14 days between waterings. Every month or two, water your plants by immersion to be sure that all of the soil gets watered. To immerse a plant, fill a pail or dishpan with water deep enough to come just under the rim of the pot. Set the pot under water and leave it until bubbling stops. The time this takes depends on the size of the soil mass and how dry it is. Remove the pot from water, and set it in the sink to drain completely. Meanwhile, clean the foliage. Don't go away and leave a plant immersed for longer than necessary. Too much water over a long period of time prevents oxygen from getting to the roots.

Containers should also be considered when watering plants. A clay pot presents the fewest dangers because it absorbs moisture from the soil, lessening the danger of waterlogging at the bottom of the pot. When the surface of the soil in a clay pot feels dry, you can safely assume that the soil in the bottom of the pot is dry and that the plant needs water.

Most plastic pots have drainage holes in the bottom so excess water can escape. But, because the plastic isn't porous, the water held by the soil doesn't evaporate as fast as it does from a clay pot. The soil surface can feel dry while the soil at the bottom of the pot is still wet. Water plants in plastic pots less often.

Ceramic containers are the riskiest to use. They usually have solid bottoms, so there's no way excess water can escape. Water carefully— just enough to moisten the roots—never let water run over the rim of the pot. Water more often but not as thoroughly.

An easy way to water plants, especially when you want to use ceramic containers, is a technique called double-potting. Simply take a plant in a clay pot and set it inside a ceramic pot two sizes larger. Line the space between pots with sphagnum moss. Keep the moss moist by soaking it once a week. The moisture will seep through the inner clay pot wall to provide even moisture.

If you have plants potted in clay or plastic containers and set inside ceramic containers, be sure to lift out the inner pot after watering and empty the water from the jardiniere.

Adding humidity

Most plants need more humidity than is normally found in the home—especially during the dry, heating season. The colder the air outside, the drier the air inside, and dry air can be disastrous for plants accustomed to tropical conditions. Most plants require 30 to 40 percent humidity; your home may have less than ten percent humidity when it's extremely cold outdoors.

More frequent watering will help plants somewhat, although the dry air will still cause the leaves to transpire (lose water they've absorbed) at a faster rate. The trick is to supply more water to the leaves. Humidifying your entire house is ideal, but you can increase air moisture around your plants in other ways.

Frequent misting will provide some relief; you might run a cool vaporizer in rooms where plants are kept. Or hand mist in the morning, so plants will dry off and not stand damp overnight.

Plants that require constant humidity, such as ferns, can be placed on a moistened tray of pebbles, which will increase humidity as the water evaporates. Keep your plants in a close group, rather than scattered about, to help ease their need for humidity. Set pans of water near heat registers, and if you don't mind company when you shower, take your plants into the bathroom with you so they can share the steam.

Feeding

Knowing when and how often to feed your plants can be terribly confusing. Generally, most plants should be fertilized in spring and summer when they are putting out new growth or blooms. At the same time, most need to rest over the winter months and shouldn't be fed.

Certain plants grow throughout the year and should be fed lightly year round. They usually prefer to be fed smaller doses each time than other plants.

There are many kinds of plant food available, from time-release capsules to liquids and powders. Any balanced fertilizer specifically designed for houseplants is fine. On the label you'll see a set of numbers, such as 10-20-10 or 12-6-6, describing the blend of nitrogen, phosphorus, and potassium (or potash) in the fertilizer. Nitrogen gives the plant lush foliage, and phosphorus keeps roots and stems strong and healthy. Potash encourages more colorful blooms.

Follow the directions on the container for proper dosage and frequency, or establish your own feeding schedule based on what your individual plants need. Make sure the soil is sufficiently moist before applying fertilizer. Applied to a dry soil, fertilizer can burn roots and stems. Remember, too much fertilizer can produce weak stems and leaves. Hold up feeding of new or repotted plants for eight weeks until they've had time to adjust to their move.

If you prefer organic fertilizers, fish emulsion or bone meal will give good results.

Problem Solving

It's easy to tell when there's something troubling your plant, but it's not so easy trying to decide exactly what it is. Sometimes a simple cleaning and pruning will revive the plant. But if the plant is diseased or infected, more drastic measures will be necessary.

Cleaning and pruning

Periodically remove the dust from plant leaves, so the plants can breathe. Clean many plants quickly by putting them under the bathroom shower if you have unsoftened water. Use a gentle lukewarm sprinkle. To avoid washing soil out of the pot, wrap a plastic sheet around the base of the plant and over the pot. After their shower, let the plants drip a while before taking them back to where they belong. If chemical residue in the water makes white spots, remove them with a clean, soft cloth.

Large-leaved plants can be easily cleaned by wiping the leaves with a damp cloth. Support the underside of the leaf with one hand while gently wiping the upper side with the cloth.

To remove dust from hairy-leaved plants, such as African violets and gloxinias, rub gently with a dry cotton swab or pipe cleaner. A watercolor brush works well for this job, too.

A little judicious trimming will keep your plants the size you want. Without pruning and pinching, a plant can become tall and leggy.

Pinching off the tip growth of a branch encourages side branches to develop and results in a thicker, bushier plant. No tools are necessary for this simple operation; just use your thumb and index finger. New branches generally arise from buds at the bases of the remaining leaves.

Treat your plants to a periodic cleaning. Support the underside of large leaves with one hand, while gently wiping the upper side with a warm, damp cloth.

To clean hairy-leaved plants, such as African violets, use a dry cotton swab or pipe cleaner to gently dust the top side while supporting the underside.

Encourage naturally branching plants to develop into thicker, bushier plants by pinching off the tip growth. Energy is then channeled to the side branches.

Avoid overwatering. These two coleus were the same size when potted. The right one was soaked daily, while the left was watered only when the soil started to dry.

Insufficient light over a long period of time results in spindly stems, new leaves that are smaller, yellow foliage, and leaf drop.

Pinching improves the shape of branching plants, such as wax begonias and coleus. Single-leader plants, such as dieffenbachia, rubber tree, and dracena, shouldn't be pinched.

Often a major branch must be removed, either to keep the plant the size you want or to improve its shape. Study the plant carefully before cutting off all or part of a major branch. Use clippers to get a smooth cut, and make the cut just above a bud. The best times to prune a plant are when it is actively growing (usually in the spring) or soon after it has bloomed.

Trouble signs

Many symptoms have more than one cause, so it's often difficult to tell exactly what the problem is. Here are some major trouble signs and what you can do about them.

• **The symptom:** Leaf tips turn brown; lower leaves turn yellow and drop off. Stems get soft and mushy, then turn brown. Soil is soggy, and slimy scum forms on edges of pots.

The cause: Plant is getting too much water.

The cure: Allow soil to dry completely before watering again. Repot, if soil is hopelessly soggy. Make sure plant has adequate drainage. Don't let it sit in water in saucer. Water less often.

• **The symptom:** Leaf tips turn yellow, then turn brown and dry up. Bottom leaves of plant turn yellow. Cactus fades and sometimes turns yellow.

The cause: The plant is getting too little water and is showing the effects.

The cure: Water plant thoroughly by immersing the whole pot in water. Let excess drain away. Then start watering more often on a strict schedule.

• **The symptom:** Leaves look faded or have yellow or brown "burned" spots. Foliage plants turn brown, cactus pales.

The cause: Plant is getting too much light.

The cure: Move plant out of bright light. Ease up on artificial light.

• **The symptom:** Plant develops long, spindly stems. New growth is weak and pale; leaves are undersized.

The cause: Plant is getting too little light.

The cure: Move plant to a location that gets more light. Supplement natural light with artificial light, if necessary.

• **The symptom:** Plant grows quickly, but new growth is weak and spindly or streaked with yellow. A crusty scum may have formed on pots.

The cause: Plant is getting too much fertilizer.

The cure: Flush fertilizer buildup out of the soil and off pot rims by watering the plant several times an hour with tepid water. Let excess moisture run out the bottom. Stop fertilizing for a while, and reduce dosage or frequency.

• **The symptom:** Leaves look yellow but veins are green. New growth is weak and droopy.

The cause: Plant is getting too little fertilizer.

The cure: Set up a fertilizing schedule based on the plant's needs, the season, and its size. Then stick to the schedule.

• **The symptom:** Edges of leaves curl under and turn crispy and brown.

The cause: Plant is getting too little humidity or temperature is too high—or both.

The cure: Add humidity to the air by misting plants or installing a home humidifier. If you think temperature is too high, move plant to a location with cooler temperatures.

Houseplant pests

Mealybugs. These white cottony blobs are apt to be your worst headache. They're sometimes hard to eradicate because they're protected by a water-resistant wax. Dab each bug with a cotton swab dipped in rubbing alcohol, and rinse leaves with clear, cool water. Or use a houseplant miticide, and rinse plants when mealybugs are eradicated.

Red spider mites. These tiny bugs feed on the undersides of leaves, spinning fine webs along veins and leaves. They give a plant a gray webby look with anemic foliage. If possible, take plant outside and flush bottoms of leaves with a light spray from a garden hose.

Or mix a mild soap (not detergent) into a pan of lukewarm water, producing a lather. Cover the top of the pot with foil to hold the dirt, upend the plant, and swish the foliage through the suds. Rinse well with clear water. Follow this procedure once a week until pests are gone. If you use a miticide, wash the leaves to remove the webs.

Scale. Scale looks like little green or brown ovals. Scales line up along the main veins of the plant and cause it to lose color, yellow, and die. Gently scrape the scale off with a soft toothbrush or your fingernail. Wash the plant with lukewarm, soapy water.

Aphids. These greenish-white or black insects cluster in the open where they're easily detected. Use the tepid, soapy water wash and clear rinse recommended for red spider mites. Or spray with a miticide and rinse when pests have been eradicated.

At least once a year give your houseplants and their pots a thorough housecleaning. Throw out sickly plants before their ailments spread to healthy ones.

Red spider mites spin fine webs along veins and the undersides of leaves. Swish in a pan of soap (not detergent) and lukewarm water; then rinse with clear water.

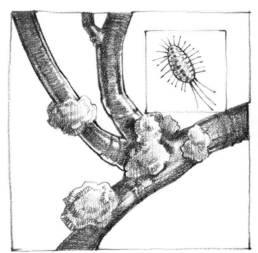

Mealybugs appear as white cottony blobs clustered on leaves and stems. Use a cotton swab to dab area with rubbing alcohol; rinse with lukewarm water.

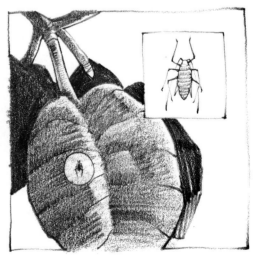

Aphids appear as greenish-white or black insects clustered on plants. Treat as you would red spider mites, but treat again when successive generations hatch.

Propagation Techniques

The easiest, most inexpensive way to add plants to your collection is to propagate those you already have. Multiplying them yourself will give you the added pleasure of watching baby plants grow to maturity. Just follow these guidelines.

Stem cuttings

Propagating houseplants from cuttings is probably the most common method of multiplying houseplants. Do this clipping in the spring. Almost any plant with trailing stems can be propagated from stem cuttings. Try coleus, wandering Jew, Swedish ivy, and the philodendrons for quick results.

Select a mature, healthy stem; use a sharp knife or blade to cut just below a leaf node (the place where a leaf grows from the stem). The cutting should be several inches long and have four to six healthy leaves. Remove leaves from the bottom of the piece so they won't be buried in the rooting medium; dip the cuttings in a rooting hormone, if you wish.

Many cuttings will root in plain water, but roots grown in water tend to be brittle and fragile; they often break off as you pot the plant. You'll have better luck using a soilless medium, such as perlite, vermiculite, sand, peat moss, or any mixture of these. Equal portions of perlite and peat moss make a good combination.

If you're rooting only two or three cuttings, a small clay pot works well. If you're rooting more, use a clear plastic shoe box or other larger flat, covered container.

Moisten the soil mixture and poke holes in it with a knife or pencil. Slip the cuttings in and gently firm soil around the stems. Mist lightly and cover with the lid or encase in a plastic bag and close tightly. This will help retain vital humidity and keep the leaves from wilting as the stems root. Place under fluorescent lights or in indirect light.

In several weeks, check to see whether the cuttings have rooted by giving each a gentle tug; if the cutting resists, it should be sufficiently rooted to pot. (There should be an inch or two of roots.) If the cutting isn't sufficiently rooted, just slip it back into the medium.

Woody-stemmed plants, such as the dieffenbachias and dracenas, can be propagated from pieces of stem. This is an especially good technique to use after you've air layered the plant. Simply take a

AIR LAYERING

Plant	Comments
Chinese evergreen	Also can be propagated from stem cuttings.
Croton	Propagate in spring and summer.
Dieffenbachia	Wash your hands after working with the plant; its acrid sap can cause temporary loss of voice.
Dracena	Also can be propagated from stem cuttings or sections.
Ficus	Rubber plant, weeping fig, and fiddle-leaf fig all can be air layered.
Monstera	Also can be propagated from stem cuttings.
Philodendron	Also can be propagated from stem cuttings.
Ti plant or Cordyline	Also can be propagated from stem sections.

SPORES

Plant	Comments
Bird's-nest fern *Asplenium*	The species A. *bulbiferum* also can be propagated from plantlets growing on the fronds.
Hare's-foot fern *Polypodium*	Spore mounds are larger than most; also can be propagated by root division.
Holly fern *Cyrtomium*	Also can be propagated by division.
Leatherleaf fern *Rumohra*	Wait to propagate until spores turn deep brown.
Maidenhair fern *Adiantum*	Spores are obvious on small, delicate leaves; also can be propagated by root division.
Rabbit's-foot fern *Davallia*	Also can be propagated from its creeping, hairy rhizomes; simply cover lightly with soil.
Staghorn fern *Platycerium*	Suckers or offshoots sometimes develop at the base of fronds.

sharp knife and cut the remaining stem into pieces several inches long. Lay pieces on their sides and barely cover with a moist, sandy soil mixture. In several weeks, new growth will sprout from the side of the stem. Remove and repot in a larger container when roots are sufficiently strong.

Leaf cuttings

Follow the same procedure for rooting leaf cuttings as described for stem cuttings. Take leaf cuttings of such plants as peperomia, hoya, begonia, African violet, and many of the succulents. Simply cut off a mature, healthy leaf at the stem base with a sharp knife, and insert it in a moist rooting medium. The leaves of some of the succulents (such as sedum and *Crassula argentea*) will have to be partially buried in the medium. In several weeks, tiny leaves will push their way up through the soil. When leaves and stems are strong and healthy, sever plantlets from the parent leaf and pot up individually.

If you're rooting only one leaf, especially the woody-stemmed ones, you can put it in a small plastic bag filled with rooting medium. When the leaf has developed strong roots, pot it and watch for baby leaves to emerge. When they do, remove and discard the old leaf.

Many leaf cuttings also will root in water. Simply cover a jar or cup of water with aluminum foil, poke holes in it, and insert one or more leaf cuttings.

With pickaback plants, use a combination of the stem cutting and runner processes. Choose a mature leaf that has a plantlet piggybacking atop. Pin the plantlet down into a small pot filled with loose soil (a mixture of equal parts packaged soil and sharp sand works well). Do not remove the leaf from the parent plant yet. In several weeks, the plantlet will have developed its own roots; then you can sever the runner and remove the parent leaf.

To root cuttings of sansevieria, cut a mature, healthy leaf into three-inch segments; place upright in growing medium so that half the section is buried. (Sections will not root if upside down.) In a couple of months, new shoots will form at the side. Remove when roots are sufficiently strong.

Rex begonias can be rooted by placing the whole leaf flat on the surface of a pot of soil (use the same mix as for pickaback described earlier). Pin it down and make cuts across the main veins with a sharp knife. New plants will develop at the slits. Pot when rooted, taking a good portion of leaf with each plantlet.

Air layering

Air layering isn't so much a way to propagate plants as it is a way to revitalize them. Through air layering, top-heavy, woody-stemmed plants are induced to grow new roots higher up on the stem.

You can air layer schefflera, dieffenbachia, ficus, and dracena species that have lost their bottom leaves. Use a sharp knife to make a cut approximately one-third of the way down the stem; make an upward slit, cut a notch out of the stem, or just scrape away enough of the bark to expose the plant tissue. Don't cut more than halfway through the stem. If you simply slit the stem, hold the cut open with a toothpick or matchstick.

Next, wrap a baseball-size clump of sphagnum moss around the stem where you've made the cut; wrap with plastic and secure with wire twists or string.

Periodically check the moss for moisture; if it has dried out, mist lightly and rewrap the plastic. In several weeks (or months, depending on the species of the plant), you'll see roots forming. When they fill the plastic wrap, cut the stem off below the new roots; then plant, moss and all.

The leafless stem can be left to sprout new shoots, or in the case of the dieffenbachia and some of the dracena and cordyline species, the stem can be cut up and planted. New plants will eventually grow from each of the cuttings.

Spores

Almost all ferns can be propagated from spores, but it's no simple task. It's a challenge to grow a full-sized

CUTTING

Plant	Stem	Leaf
African violet		x
Chinese evergreen	x	
Coleus	x	
Crassula	x	x
Devil's ivy or Pothos	x	
Dracena	x	
Echeveria		x
Euphorbia	x	
Fittonia	x	
Gloxinia		x
Grape ivy	x	
Hoya	x	x
Monstera	x	
Nephthytis	x	
Peperomia		x
Philodendron	x	
Pickaback		x
Pilea	x	
Purple velvet plant	x	
Sansevieria		x
Sedum	x	x
Swedish ivy	x	
Wandering Jew	x	

Propagation Techniques

(continued)

plant from a dust-sized spore; you need exacting temperatures and sterile conditions to be successful. There is no greater feeling of accomplishment, however, when all your tiny ferns finally do emerge.

Ferns, unlike most members of the plant kingdom, don't flower or reproduce themselves by seeds. Ferns are ancient plants, still clinging to their primitive method of reproduction. Their pale green spores appear periodically on the undersides of the fronds. As the spores mature, they turn brown or black. If you see a plant that has symmetrical or evenly spaced rows of brown dots (or brown fuzz along the edges of the fronds), the dots are merely ripe spores.

You can use several methods to grow ferns from spores. One option is to "plant" the spores in a covered jar or pan; or you can use a clay pot, as described for growing seeds. Make up a soil mix of equal parts garden soil, peat moss or leaf mold, and sharp sand. Sterilize parts that weren't sterile when purchased by baking in a 200-degree Fahrenheit oven for at least 45 minutes.

If you opt to use a jar or pan, boil the container to sterilize it, also. Let it dry, then add a layer of soil several inches deep. If you use a clay pot, condition by immersing the pot in boiling water. Then fill it three-fourths full of soil. Save the boiled water to use later to moisten the soil.

When spores are mature, remove a frond from the plant and let it dry for several days between papers or in a bag. Then shake the spores off onto a sheet of paper, and make a funnel so you can evenly tap them onto the growing medium. Or sprinkle them on the surface with your fingers. Mist spores in pans or jars using the cooled, boiled water. If you're using the clay pot method, set pots in a pan of water (boiled, then cooled; or distilled) until they take up enough moisture to dampen the surface. Cover with plastic wrap or place in a closed plastic bag. Put in indirect light or under fluorescent lights for 14 to 16 hours per day. The temperature must remain a constant 65 to 75 degrees Fahrenheit.

Mist with sterile water whenever the soil starts to dry out. In several days (or weeks, depending on species), a green slime will appear. Several months later tiny fronds will push up from the soil. Transplant them from the pot or jar into a plastic shoe box or other flat, covered container. Or simply rearrange them so they aren't crowded. Maintain high humidity to keep the fragile leaves from drying out. When plants are one or two inches tall, transplant into separate pots, and in a year or two you'll have full-grown ferns. Then follow fern care advice for your specific kind, as described on pages 482 and 483.

SEEDS

Plant	Comments
Asparagus fern	Will germinate in 1 to 2 months.
Banana	Can grow up to 3 feet tall the first year.
Coleus	Grow outdoors in spring from seed; take cuttings in fall.
Cyclamen	Will flower a year after germinating.
Herbs	Try lemon balm, chervil, and mint in a sunny window.
Hoya	Prefers to germinate in a peat soil mix.
Lithops	Prefers a sandy germinating medium.
Palms: *Livistona, Chamaedorea, Howea, Phoenix, Chrysalidocarpus*	Temperatures should be around 80 degrees Fahrenheit for best results; seed may take several months to germinate.
Polka-dot plant	Seeds germinate quickly.
Rubber plant or *Fiscus elastica*	Prefers temperatures around 70 degrees Fahrenheit.
Mimosa or Sensitive plant	Needs a warm growing medium; will grow quickly from seed.

Seeds

Houseplants are easy for anyone—even beginners—to grow from seeds. Use new clay pots that have been conditioned by immersing in water. Soak until the clay has absorbed all the moisture it can hold—until the bubbling and hissing stop.

You'll need a well-balanced soil mixture for good germination—a rich commercial potting soil will work fine. Fill the pot with soil and gently sprinkle seeds across the surface. Cover the seeds with a layer of soil no deeper than twice their diameter. Don't pack them down.

Set the pot in a pan of shallow water until it soaks up enough moisture to make the soil surface damp. Then remove the pot from the water, let excess water drain out, cover with a plastic bag, and place it in a bright east or west window where the temperature is relatively stable. Don't water at all during this time.

When seedlings appear, remove the bag and begin watering the surface whenever the soil starts to dry out. Nighttime dampness encourages mold and fungus, so water early in the morning. Turn the pot periodically—or set under grow-lights—to keep plants growing straight, instead of leaning toward the window.

Thin out the seedlings if you plan to keep the plants in the same pot. If not, remove the seedlings when the first true pair of leaves appears, and plant them in their own small pots.

Root division

Root division is actually the splitting or cutting up of one plant into two or more parts.

For a while you'll have small plants, but these divisions grow just as any normal plant and eventually become larger. Almost any plant that grows from several stems in one pot can be divided; this includes pileas, peperomias, most of the ferns, aspidistras, and marantas.

To divide a plant, gently knock it out of its container; you may have to run a sharp knife around the edge of the pot to loosen the soil. Remove the rootball and shake off as much soil as you can. Then gently break the rootball apart to see how the roots are growing and to determine the way to divide it.

For example, airplane plants actually put out new stems and plants next to the original plant, similar to a sucker or offset. These plants can be separated and potted up individually. The roots of the sprengeri asparagus fern, on the other hand, simply build on each other to make one large rootball. In cases like this, you'll have to cut the plant apart. Don't be afraid to use your knife; it's actually better to cleanly sever the roots than to tear them into pieces. Sometimes asparagus ferns have so many roots you simply have to cut some off and discard them.

Put the divisions into smaller pots. Water thoroughly, and set in indirect light for a week or two while the plant adjusts to life on its own. Early spring is the best time to divide plants.

Bulbs also are propagated by root division. The amaryllis and oxalis form offsets that can be cut from the parent plant and potted up individually. Propagate before new growth starts in the spring.

The tuberous begonia and caladium can be propagated by dividing their tubers into two or more parts and potting them separately. Spring is the best time for dividing.

The gloxinia and cyclamen will grow from the "eyes" of their tubers, just as a potato plant grows from eyes. Cut the tuber while dormant so that each piece has an eye, and pot the pieces individually.

Runners and offsets

Many plants reproduce by runners and offsets. Runners (or stolons) are long stems sent out by the parent plant, with a new plant at the tip.

You can root the plantlets several ways. The safest method is to fill several small pots with loose, moist soil and pin the plants to the surface with a hairpin or bent paper clip. In three weeks or so the plantlet should be rooted; check to see by giving it a gentle tug. If it resists, roots have developed and the runner can be severed. Or you can cut off several plantlets, root them in water, and pot them. Easier yet is to cut off the plantlets and pot them immediately into individual pots.

Offsets (or suckers) are somewhat more difficult to propagate successfully. Many succulents, as well as most of the bromeliads, reproduce by this method. Offsets develop at the base of the plant and look just like miniatures of the plants themselves.

Cut the offset from the parent plant with a sharp knife, getting as many roots with it as possible. Be careful, however, not to take so many that the parent plant hasn't enough to live. Be especially careful with cactus—they're usually reluctant to give up their offsets. Put the offset into a small pot filled with loose, moist soil. Even if you can't get many roots, the offset may still survive. In the case of bromeliads, you can take as many roots as you want because the parent plant will die anyway soon after it blooms and produces suckers.

ROOT DIVISION

Plant	Comments
Airplane plant	Separate offsets that grow from base of parent plant.
Asparagus fern	Divide when fleshy roots appear on soil surface.
Aspidistra	Make sure each division has several leaves.
Ferns: *Nephrolepis, Polypodium, Pteris, Adiantum, Cyrtomium*	Nephrolepis species also can be propagated from runners.
Moses-in-a-boat	It may be several years before plant can be propagated.
Maranta	If the plant looks top-heavy, divide in spring.
Peperomia	Divide when plant appears too big for its pot; it also can be propagated by cuttings.
Pilea	Divide when plant appears scraggly; it also can be propagated by cuttings.

RUNNERS AND OFFSETS

Plant	Method	Comments
African violet	offset	Root as you would a leaf cutting when the offset has several leaves.
Airplane plant	runner	Plantlets also can be removed and rooted in water.
Bromeliad	offset	Cut sucker from parent plant when it's large; parent plant will then die.
Cactus and other succulents: *Mammillaria, Agave, Echeveria Echinopsis, Aloe*	offset	This can be difficult because the plant's roots are hard to reach; propagate at any season.
Episcia	runner	Don't sever the plantlet from the parent plant until it's well rooted.
Palms: *Caryota, Cycas, Rhapis, Chamaerops*	offset	Palms don't produce suckers until they're several years old.
Pandanus or Screw pine	offset	Don't confuse the offset with the screw pine's natural surface roots.
Strawberry saxifrage	runner	Don't sever the plantlet until it's well rooted.

Houseplants Under Lights

Too few windows needn't deter you from growing houseplants indoors. With artificial plant lights (often called grow-lights), you can garden in the darkest corners on the cloudiest days. Grow-lights have the added advantage of giving foliage plants a richer, darker color and flowering plants brighter blooms.

What is light? Pure "white" sunlight is made up of all the colors you can see, plus some you can't see. Passing white light through a prism breaks it down into the specific wavelengths called visible colors. A rainbow does this naturally.

Plants don't use all the wavelengths in the visible spectrum. They do use those we see as blue for good foliage development and those we see as red, at the other end of the spectrum, to produce blossoms. They don't use the colors in between—those from orange through green.

It doesn't take long to learn that plants don't do as well in normal household artificial light as they do in sunlight. And it's easy to understand why. Incandescent bulbs are strong in the red end of the spectrum but lack the blue needed for foliage. The reverse is true with fluorescents; they produce ample blue light, but they lack the red needed to make flowering plants bloom.

Commercial growers, who have been aware of this fact for years, solve the problem by growing plants beneath a combination of incandescent bulbs and fluorescent lamps. But this presents a problem for home hobbyists who usually can't easily combine fluorescent and incandescent light in their homes.

Fortunately, there's an easier solution: simply use grow-lights, special incandescent bulbs and fluorescent lamps designed to produce wavelengths in the spectrum the plants actually need—reds and blues. They emit very little of the midrange wavelengths, so they appear less bright than regular bulbs or tubes, and they glow with a pinkish or bluish hue.

Using grow-lights

If you plan to build a grow-light setup similar to the one shown at left, first determine how many lamps you'll need. It's easiest to figure in watts per square foot. For example, using two standard 20-watt bulbs 24 inches long, you'll need a tray that's 1x2 feet in size to get 20 watts of light per square foot. In the same way, you will need four bulbs for an area that's 2x2 feet for 20 watts per square foot.

Depending on what you're planning to grow under your lights, you can get by with less than 20 watts of light per square foot. Foliage plants do well in ten to 15 watts, but blooming plants need all 20. Cactus, other succulents, and orchids need much more than 20 watts per square foot—even up to 30. Naturally, plants placed directly under lamps receive more light than those along the edge of the trays.

There's one more condition to take into consideration when building a grow-light. That's distance from the light, measured in footcandles. Don't be scared by the technical term. You probably won't use it unless you become a real grow-light specialist. Footcandles are measured by a footcandle meter. Light follows an inverse-square law of diminishing brightness, which means that when you double the distance from a light source, you reduce intensity to one-fourth. For example, if you moved a plant that should be six inches from the light to 12 inches, you'd be reducing the light to one-fourth (not one-half) the light it used to get.

Foliage plants should be placed no farther than 15 inches from the light; flowering plants, no more than ten inches. You can help increase light intensity by using reflectors. Using perlite in the bottom of the plant tray helps, too, as perlite is highly reflective. The chart below will advise you on best distances from the light for your plants.

If you decide to design a unit using incandescent bulbs, you may have problems caused by heat. Incandescents heat up (unlike fluorescents), so most should be kept about two feet above plants to lessen the chances of burning the foliage. Experiment with different light levels to see where you get the most intense light without burning the plants. Incandescents are most efficient when used to spotlight a few favorites; you'll have best luck with the hardier foliage plants. By moving plants around under the lights, you'll have success with flowering specimens, too.

Darkness is important

Although plants can't grow without light, they can't grow properly without periods of darkness, either. Most plants respond best to normal cycles of day and night—14 to 16 hours of light and eight to ten hours of "sleep." Sometimes varying the periods of light and dark by specific plant needs can increase growth.

It may be hard to remember to turn your grow-lights on and off at the same time every day, so invest in an inexpensive timer. You have a choice of tabletop models or those that plug directly into the outlet. Make certain the timer you buy has a 1,875-watt capacity. It will then be able to carry the same load as safely as any other outlet on a 15-amp household circuit.

LIGHT CHART

Category	These Do Well	Light Needed	Comments
Foliage plants	Pilea, peperomia, coleus, devil's ivy (pothos), philodendron, grape ivy, and Swedish ivy	Fourteen to 16 hours of light per day; place 6 to 12 inches below lights.	If using incandescent light, keep plants 18 to 24 inches below lights.
Ferns	Asparagus, *Pteris* sp., and *Nephrolepis* sp.	Fourteen to 16 hours of light per day; place 8 to 12 inches below lights.	Be careful so foliage doesn't burn under lights.
Flowering plants	Blooming florists' plants, such as cyclamen, mum, calceolaria, gloxinia, geranium, and begonia	Fourteen to 16 hours of light per day; florists' plants should be 6 to 10 inches below lights, geraniums 6 to 8, and begonias 6 to 12.	Geraniums and begonias are special; you'll need to experiment before you find what's right.
Cactus and other succulents	Echeveria, haworthia, agave, aloe, kalanchoe, sedum, euphorbia, and sansevieria	Approximately 16 hours of light per day; keep succulents no more than 6 inches from light; in the fall, gradually reduce to 12-hour days.	Desert cactus, such as the golden barrel, opuntia, and mammillaria, should be no more than 4 inches from the light.
Gesneriads (such as African violet and achimene)	Almost all respond beautifully under lights	Fourteen to 16 hours of light per day; place 4 to 10 inches from light, depending on species being grown.	Gesneriads are probably the most popular plants for grow-light cultivation.

FOLIAGE HOUSEPLANTS

Plant Name	Light			Moisture		Propagation Method						Comments
	Bright (sunny)	Bright, indirect	Medium (filtered)	Water when soil dries	Keep evenly moist	Air layering	Runners or offsets	Leaf cuttings	Stem cuttings	Root division	Seeds	
AGAPANTHUS **Lily-of-the-Nile** *Agapanthus africanus*	x	x			x					x	x	Fertilize in spring only. Blooms best when root-bound. Divide roots in spring.
AIRPLANE PLANT **Spider plant** *Chlorophytum comosum*		x		x			x			x		Leaf tips often turn brown because humidity is too low; trim them to keep plant looking tidy. Root baby plantlets in water to start new plants. Variegated varieties available.
ALUMINUM PLANT **(See pilea)**												
ARALIA *Dizygotheca* or *Polyscias* sp.												
Balfour *P. balfouriana*	x	x		x					x			Available in variegated species. Needs fairly high humidity.
False *D. elegantissima*		x		x					x			Has dark brown lacy leaves.
Ming *P. fruticosa*	x	x		x					x			Can grow to several feet tall. Needs fairly high humidity.
ARROWHEAD VINE **(See nephthytis)**												
ARTILLERY PLANT **(See pilea)**												
ASPARAGUS FERN *Asparagus* sp.												
Myers fern, **Foxtail fern** *A. densiflorus* 'Myers'		x		x						x	x	Foliage resembles a fox's tail. Least common asparagus fern.
Plumosa fern, **Lace fern** *A. setaceus*		x		x						x	x	Has the most delicate foliage of all asparagus ferns. Needs high humidity.
Sprengeri fern *A. densiflorus* 'Sprengeri'		x		x						x	x	Very hardy indoors. Has small white blooms and red berries. Divide when fleshy roots appear on soil surface.
ASPIDISTRA *Aspidistra* sp.												All species very hardy. Easily survives forgetful watering, poor light, and low humidity.

Coleus

Rieger begonia

Aralia

Aspidistra
(Cast-iron plant)

Yucca

Caladium

Gardenia

Spathiphyllum

Episcia

FOLIAGE HOUSEPLANTS (continued)

Plant Name	Light			Moisture		Propagation Method						Comments
	Bright (sunny)	Bright, indirect	Medium (filtered)	Water when soil dries	Keep evenly moist	Air layering	Runners or offsets	Leaf cuttings	Stem cuttings	Root division	Seeds	
ASPIDISTRA **Barroom plant** A. elatior		x	x	x						x		Ideal in dim apartments or offices.
Cast-iron plant A. elatior 'variegata'		x	x	x						x		Do not overfertilize.
AUCUBA Aucuba sp.												Plants tolerate lower temperatures than most. Produce insignificant blossoms and red berries.
Gold-dust tree A. japonica 'variegata'		x			x				x			Foliage is speckled with yellow.
Japanese aucuba, Japanese laurel A. japonica		x			x				x			Foliage is solid green.
AVOCADO Persea americana		x		x							x	Can easily be grown from the pit of a ripened fruit. Insert several toothpicks into the pit, and suspend it large end down in a jar of water. Pot in soil when sufficiently rooted.
BABY'S-TEARS Soleirolia soleiroli		x			x				x	x		Ideal creeping ground cover in a terrarium. Prefers soil high in humus.
BANANA PLANT Musa acuminata		x			x		x				x	Propagated by suckers that appear at the base of the plant. Remove and pot separately.
CALADIUM Caladium sp.			x		x					x		Known for its colorful foliage. Flowers are insignificant.
CHINESE EVERGREEN Aglaonema sp.		x	x		x	x			x			Solid green and variegated varieties available. Tolerates low light and humidity. Makes a good office plant—much friendlier than plastic greenery. Also can be grown in water.
COLEUS Coleus sp.	x	x			x				x		x	Available in many different varieties and a wide range of color combinations. Droops quickly when it needs water. Pinch tops and blooms back to induce bushy growth. Take stem cuttings often from houseplants or from coleus growing in your garden.

Plant Name	Light			Moisture		Propagation Method						Comments
	Bright (sunny)	Bright, indirect	Medium (filtered)	Water when soil dries	Keep evenly moist	Air layering	Runners or offsets	Leaf cuttings	Stem cuttings	Root division	Seeds	
CORN PLANT (See dracena)												
CROTON *Codiaeum* sp.	x	x			x	x			x			Needs good light to maintain leaf markings. Available in many different varieties.
DIEFFENBACHIA Dumb cane *Dieffenbachia* sp.		x	x	x		x			x			Nicknamed dumb cane because the sap can cause loss of voice and swelling of vocal cords. Air layer when the plant grows tall and loses its bottom leaves. If your house is dry, move the dieffenbachia into a steamy bathroom occasionally.
DRACENA *Dracaena* sp.												
Corn plant *D. fragrans 'massangeana'*		x	x		x	x			x			Nicknamed corn plant because it resembles one. Very hardy. Variegated variety available.
Dragon tree *D. draco*		x	x		x	x			x			Has thick, gray-green leaves. Can reach 4 feet tall indoors; 70 feet outdoors.
Gold-dust *D. surculosa*		x	x		x	x			x			Has wiry stems and leaves speckled with yellow or white.
Red-margined *D. marginata*		x	x		x	x			x			One of the most common species. Long, thin leaves are edged in red.
Sanderana, Belgian evergreen *D. sanderana*		x	x		x	x			x			Has long, wide leaves edged in white.
Warnecki, Striped *D. deremensis 'Warnecki'*		x	x		x	x			x			Has long, green leaves striped in white.
DRACENA, TRICOLOR *Cordyline terminalis 'tricolor'*		x	x		x	x			x			Has long, thin, pale leaves edged in pink and yellow.
DUMB CANE (See dieffenbachia)												
EMERALD RIPPLE (See peperomia)												

FOLIAGE HOUSEPLANTS (continued)

Plant Name	Light			Moisture		Propagation Method						Comments
	Bright (sunny)	Bright, indirect	Medium (filtered)	Water when soil dries	Keep evenly moist	Air layering	Runners or offsets	Leaf cuttings	Stem cuttings	Root division	Seeds	
ENGLISH BABYTEARS **Bead plant** *Nertera granadensis*		X			X				X	X		Distinguished from baby's-tears (*Soleirolia soleiroli*) by larger, more waxy leaves.
EUONYMUS *Euonymus sp.*												
E. fortunei		X			X				X			Has green leaves edged in white.
E. japonica		X			X				X			Has pale green leaves narrowly edged in white.
FATSIA *Fatsia japonica*	X	X			X				X			Has large, lobed, shiny leaves. Grows to 5 feet tall indoors.
FICUS *Ficus sp.*												
Creeping fig, Climbing fig *F. pumila*		X			X	X			X			Clings to poles or totems by rootlets. Variegated variety also available.
Fiddle-leaf fig *F. lyrata*		X			X	X						Leaves are shiny green and are shaped like a violin. Can become 6 feet tall indoors.
Mistletoe fig *F. deltoidea*		X			X	X						Has dull green leaves with yellow spots; bears orange berries. Sometimes found under species *F. diversifolia* or *F. lutescens*.
Rubber plant, India rubber tree *F. elastica*		X			X	X					X	Variegated varieties available. Tolerates low humidity.
Weeping fig, Benjamin tree *F. benjamina*		X			X	X						Leaves tend to drop if conditions are unsatisfactory. Can grow to 6 feet indoors.
FITTONIA **Nerve plant** *Fittonia verschaffelti*			X		X				X			Droops quickly when it needs water. Pink-veined and white-veined varieties available. When flowers appear, they grow erect as white spikes.
HEMIGRAPHIS **Waffle plant, Red ivy, Red flame** *Hemigraphis sp.*	X	X			X				X			Droops quickly when it needs water.

Variegated Swedish ivy

Pickaback plant

Variegated rubber plant

Ponytail

Dracena

Variegated pittosporum

Dieffenbachia

Fatsia

FOLIAGE HOUSEPLANTS (continued)

Plant Name	Light			Moisture		Propagation Method						Comments
	Bright (sunny)	Bright, indirect	Medium (filtered)	Water when soil dries	Keep evenly moist	Air layering	Runners or offsets	Leaf cuttings	Stem cuttings	Root division	Seeds	
IVY **Devil's,** **Pothos** *Epipremnum aureum*		x		x					x			Has variegated heart-shaped leaves. Tolerates low humidity. Culture is same as for philodendron. Grows easily and vigorously.
English *Hedera helix*		x			x				x			Dozens of varieties available. Needs fairly high humidity.
German, **Parlor** *Senecio mikanioides*		x			x				x			Has thin shiny green leaves. Benefits from summering outdoors.
Grape *Cissus rhombifolia*		x			x				x			Nicknamed grape ivy because of its vining tendrils. Grows quickly. Tolerates lower humidity than most ivies.
Kangaroo *Cissus antarctica*		x			x				x			Closely related to grape ivy. Tolerates low humidity.
Swedish *Plectranthus sp.*		x			x				x			Several varieties available. Grows quickly. Has shiny green leaves.
LILY-OF-THE-NILE **(See agapanthus)**												
MARANTA **Prayer plant** *Maranta leuconeura*	x	x			x					x		Nicknamed prayer plant because its leaves fold up at night as if in prayer. Leaf edges brown if humidity is low.
MIMOSA **Sensitive plant** *Mimosa pudica*	x	x			x						x	Nicknamed sensitive plant because its leaves fold up if touched. Needs more water than most plants.
MONKEY-PUZZLE *Araucaria araucana*	x			x					x			Grows slowly. Has spiny, shiny green leaves.
MONSTERA **Split-leaf** **philodendron** *Monstera deliciosa*	x	x			x	x			x			One variety nicknamed Swiss cheese plant. Can be propagated by aerial roots. Culture as for philodendron. Tolerates low light and humidity.
MOSES-IN-A-BOAT **Moses-in-the-cradle,** **Purple-leaved** **spiderwort** *Rhoeo spathacea*	x	x			x					x		Nicknamed moses-in-a-boat because boat-shaped leaves appear at the base of the plant cradling tiny flowers.

Plant Name	Light			Moisture		Propagation Method						Comments
	Bright (sunny)	Bright, indirect	Medium (filtered)	Water when soil dries	Keep evenly moist	Air layering	Runners or offsets	Leaf cuttings	Stem cuttings	Root division	Seeds	
NEPHTHYTIS **Trileaf wonder,** **Arrowhead vine,** **African evergreen** *Syngonium podophyllum*		x			x				x			Grows very quickly and can soon become unmanageable. Take cuttings often.
NORFOLK **ISLAND PINE** *Araucaria heterophylla*		x		x					x			Resembles a miniature pine tree. Water less often in winter.
PANDANUS **Screw pine** *Pandanus veitchi*		x		x			x					Can be propagated by offsets that appear at the base of the plant.
PEACOCK PLANT *Calathea makoyana*		x			x					x		Several varieties available, all with multi-colored, almost luminous leaves. Culture as for maranta.
PEDILANTHUS **Devil's-backbone,** **Redbird flower,** **Japanese poinsettia** *Pedilanthus tithymaloides*		x			x				x			Stems have an acrid sap that can cause skin inflammation. Plant may bear birdlike red flowers.
PELLIONIA **Trailing watermelon** **begonia** *Pellionia daveauana*			x		x				x			Plant grows slowly.
PEPEROMIA *Peperomia* sp. **Baby rubber plant,** **Blunt-leaved** *P. obtusifolia*		x			x			x		x		Several varieties available, including *P. obtusifolia 'albo-marginata'* with silver margins and *P. obtusifolia 'variegata'* with white margins.
Emerald-ripple *P. caperata*		x			x			x		x		Has distinctive rippled leaves. One of the most common species. Variegated variety available.
Silver-leaf, **Ivy-leaf** *P. griseoargentea*		x			x			x		x		Leaves are silvery green.
Watermelon *P. argyreia*		x			x			x		x		Species *P. arifolia* similar, but leaves aren't silver striped.

FOLIAGE HOUSEPLANTS (continued)

Plant Name	Light			Moisture		Propagation Method						Comments
	Bright (sunny)	Bright, indirect	Medium (filtered)	Water when soil dries	Keep evenly moist	Air layering	Runners or offsets	Leaf cuttings	Stem cuttings	Root division	Seeds	
PHILODENDRON Philodendron sp.												
Fiddle-leaf, Horsehead P. bipennifolium		x	x	x		x			x			Has large, violin-shaped leaves. Slow-growing.
Florida P. squamiferum		x	x	x					x			Has large, deeply lobed leaves.
Heart-leaf, Common P. scandens 'oxycardium'		x	x	x					x			Most common philodendron. Grows quickly and vines easily. Can tolerate neglect better than many other plants. Train to climb a totem or place in a hanging basket. Sometimes called P. cordatum.
Imbe P. imbe		x	x	x					x			Has large, arrowhead-shaped leaves.
Saddle-leaf P. selloum		x	x	x					x			Has large, sprawling, deeply lobed leaves. Can reach 6 feet across.
Spade-leaf P. domesticum		x	x	x					x			Has large, spade-shaped leaves.
Velvet-leaf P. scandens 'micans'		x	x	x					x			Has small, dark green, velvety leaves.
Wendland P. wendlandi		x	x	x					x			Has thick, glossy leaves forming a cluster. Stays low.
PICKABACK PLANT **Piggyback plant** Tolmiea menziesi		x		x			x	x				Droops quickly when it needs water. Low humidity can cause leaf edges to brown. Propagate baby plantlets that appear at the base of mature leaves.
PILEA Pilea sp.												
Artillery plant P. microphylla		x		x					x	x		Has tiny, dense leaves on thick stems.
Creeping charlie P. nummulariifolia		x		x					x	x		Trails more easily than other pileas. Plant in a hanging basket.
Friendship plant, Panamiga P. involucrata		x		x					x	x		Has bronze green foliage.
Aluminum plant P. cadierei		x		x					x	x		Has leaves variegated with creamy white.

Airplane plant

Red-margined dracena

Creeping fig ficus

Croton

Watermelon peperomia

Tricolor dracena

Hairy-leaved begonia

Wax begonia

Aechmea bromeliad

FOLIAGE HOUSEPLANTS (continued)

Plant Name	Light			Moisture		Propagation Method						Comments
	Bright (sunny)	Bright, indirect	Medium (filtered)	Water when soil dries	Keep evenly moist	Air layering	Runners or offsets	Leaf cuttings	Stem cuttings	Root division	Seeds	
PITTOSPORUM **Japanese pittosporum** *Pittosporum tobira*	x	x		x		x			x			Often incorrectly called schefflera. Prune back in spring before new growth appears.
PLEOMELE *Dracaena sp.*		x			x				x			Has thick, swordlike leaves edged in creamy white.
POLKA-DOT PLANT **Freckle-face** *Hypoestes phyllostachya*		x			x				x			Becomes more colorful in bright light, but avoid full sun. Prefers high humidity. Pinch back often to induce bushy growth.
POTHOS **(See ivy)**												
PODOCARPUS, CHINESE **Buddhist pine** *Podocarpus macrophyllus*	x	x			x				x			Has shrubby, needlelike leaves. Can grow to 6 feet tall.
PONYTAIL **Elephant-foot tree** *Beaucarnea recurvata*	x	x		x							x	Can tolerate low humidity and infrequent watering. Slow-growing.
PRAYER PLANT **(See maranta)**												
PURPLE VELVET PLANT *Gynura aurantiaca*	x				x				x			Has velvety, purple leaves. Purple Passion variety also available.
ROSARY VINE **String-of-hearts** *Ceropegia woodi*		x		x					x			Has long, trailing stems that bear heart-shaped, speckled leaves.
RUBBER PLANT **(See ficus)**												
SANSEVIERIA **Snake plant, Mother-in-law's tongue** *Sansevieria trifasciata*		x	x	x				x		x		Thick, swordlike leaves. Favorite plant for low-light areas. Very hardy. Tolerates low humidity. Cuttings of variegated varieties may revert to all green. Root leaf sections in sand. Rosette form, Hahni, also popular.

Plant Name	Bright (sunny)	Bright, indirect	Medium (filtered)	Water when soil dries	Keep evenly moist	Air layering	Runners or offsets	Leaf cuttings	Stem cuttings	Root division	Seeds	Comments
	Light			Moisture		Propagation Method						Comments
SCHEFFLERA *Brassaia actinophylla*	x	x		x		x						Grows slowly, but will eventually attain ceiling height. Has glossy leaves.
SILK OAK *Grevillea robusta*	x	x		x							x	Has fernlike foliage. Grows rapidly. Prune in early spring.
SPATHIPHYLLUM **White anthurium,** **Spathe flower** *Spathiphyllum clevelandi*		x			x					x		Has arching leaves resembling aspidistra.
SPIDER PLANT **(See airplane plant)**												
STRAWBERRY **SAXIFRAGE** **Strawberry geranium** *Saxifraga* sp.		x		x			x					Bears dainty white flowers in summer. Foliage is edged in reddish pink; leaf centers are cream colored.
TI PLANT **Good-luck plant** *Cordyline terminalis*	x			x		x			x			Variegated varieties available. Needs high humidity. Closely related to dracena. Propagate from stem sections.
TRILEAF WONDER **(See nephthytis)**												
UMBRELLA PLANT *Cyperus alternifolius*	x	x			x					x		Prefers porous soil kept moist. Has thin stems and leaves.
WANDERING JEW *Tradescantia* or *Zebrina* sp.												
Giant white inch plant *T. albiflora 'albovittata'*		x			x				x			Has dark green leaves with white stripes.
Purple *Z. pendula*		x			x				x			Has purple, green, and light green leaves with purple undersides.
Variegated *T. fluminensis*		x			x				x			Has pale green leaves with white stripes. Similar to *T. albiflora* but with purple underside. Also similar to *Z. pendula,* except has white flowers.
White-velvet *T. sillamontana*		x			x				x			Has dark green leaves with velvety white hairs. Undersides are purple.
YUCCA TIP **Adam's-needle** *Yucca* sp.	x	x		x			x					Has sharp, pointed foliage. This succulent needs porous soil.

Ferns

Don't let the delicate appearance of ferns discourage you from growing them. They are deceptively sturdy and have only a few needs.

Give your ferns bright, indirect light but no exposure to direct sunlight. A sheer curtain pulled across a sunny window usually offers adequate protection.

Use potting soil that is high in organic material (two parts peat moss or leaf mold to one part each sterilized garden loam and perlite or vermiculite).

Ferns like a moist soil but should never be waterlogged. Put an inch of pebbles or other drainage material in the bottom of the pot. Never allow your fern to stand in water. Misting fronds daily will be appreciated.

FERN CHART

Plant name	Light		Moisture			Propagation method		Comments
	Bright, indirect	Medium (filtered)	Keep barely moist	Keep fairly wet	Keep evenly moist	Root division	Spores	
BEAR'S-PAW *Aglaomorpha meyeniana*					x	x	x	One of the larger ferns.
BIRD'S-NEST *Asplenium nidus*	x	x			x		x	Fronds can reach 4 feet long. Tolerates less humidity than most ferns.
BOSTON *Nephrolepis exaltata*	x	x	x			x		Also propagated by runners. Cultivars include: Dreyeri, Compacta, Fluffy Ruffles, Norwoodi, Smithi, Whitmani, and Wicheri.
BRAKE **Table** *Pteris sp.*		x	x			x	x	Several available, including: *P. cretica* (Cretan brake), *P. ensiformis* (sword brake), *P. multifida* (spider brake), and *P. tremula* (Australian brake). Delicate foliage; require high humidity.
BUTTON *Pellaea rotundifolia*		x	x				x	Several less common species also available. Native to rocky areas.
CLIMBING *Stenochlaena palustris*		x			x		x	Only species commonly available.
CLIMBING, JAPANESE *Lygodium japonicum*		x			x		x	Most commonly cultivated species.
HARE'S-FOOT **Golden polypody** *Polypodium aureum*	x		x			x	x	Sometimes incorrectly called rabbit's-foot fern. Has hairy creeping rhizomes along soil surface. Fronds are large and wavy edged.

FERN CHART (continued)

Plant name	Bright, indirect	Medium (filtered)	Keep barely moist	Keep fairly wet	Keep evenly moist	Root division	Spores	Comments
HEDGE *Polystichum setiferum*		x	x			x	x	Develops plantlets on its mature fronds. Several varieties available. Avoid extremes in temperature.
HOLLY *Cyrtomium falcatum*		x	x			x	x	Hardier than most ferns. Tolerates low humidity and poor light.
HOLLY *Polystichum tsus-simense*		x	x			x	x	Closely related to hedge fern. Fairly compact.
LEATHERLEAF *Rumohra adiantiformis*	x	x			x		x	Commonly used as green accent in floral arrangements. Tolerates low humidity.
MAIDENHAIR *Adiantum* sp.		x		x		x	x	Some of the most delicate species of ferns. All need high humidity. Keep away from hot air register.
MOTHER *Asplenium bulbiferum*		x			x		x	Develops plantlets on mature fronds. Remove and pot plantlets to form new plants.
PEACOCK *Selaginella willdenovi*	x	x			x		x	Not a true fern. Can also be propagated by cuttings.
RABBIT'S-FOOT *Davallia fejeensis*		x	x			x	x	Has hairy rhizomes along soil surface that form roots if pinned to soil. Foliage is deep green and feathery.
SQUIRREL'S-FOOT *Davallia trichomanoides*		x	x				x	Culture as for rabbit's-foot fern.
STAGHORN *Platycerium* sp.	x				x		x	Also can be propagated from small plantlets appearing at the base of the plant. Usually grown vertically on a bark support. Water by immersing support and base of plant in water. Mist early on sunny days.
SWORD *Nephrolepis biserrata*	x	x			x	x	x	Closely related to Boston fern. Hardier than most ferns.
TREE, AUSTRALIAN *Sphaeropteris cooperi*	x	x			x		x	Grows rapidly and can reach large size.
TREE, MEXICAN *Cibotium schiedei*	x	x	x				x	Can also be grown in plain water. Can grow to large, sprawling size.
TREE, WEST INDIAN *Cyathea arborea*	x	x		x			x	Only species commonly cultivated. Can reach large size.

Palms

Palms create a lush tropical atmosphere indoors. Unlike some houseplants, palms put out new growth during the winter. Every three or four months give them slow-release houseplant food, following manufacturer's directions. When they near the maximum size you want, feed just once a year in spring. The potential giants (fishtail and fan palms), plus the wide spreaders (such as *Howea* sp.), will need less per feeding than the shorter palms (parlor and bamboo).

Palms like plenty of moisture, but be sure to use a porous soil, and don't let pots stand in water.

PALM CHART

Plant name	Light			Moisture			Propagation method	Comments
	Bright (sunny)	Bright, indirect	Medium (filtered)	Water when soil dries	Keep evenly moist	Runners or offsets	Seeds	
ARECA (See butterfly)								
BAMBOO *Chamaedorea erumpens*	x	x			x		x	One of the most widely available palms. Cannot tolerate bright light.
BUTTERFLY **Areca, Yellow, Madagascar** *Chrysalidocarpus lutescens*	x				x		x	Has long, thin, drooping leaves. Native to Madagascar. Should be kept fairly wet but not soggy.
CHINESE FAN *Livistona chinensis*	x				x		x	Should be kept fairly wet but not soggy. Leaves resemble open fans.

PALM CHART (continued)

Plant name	Light			Moisture		Propagation method		Comments
	Bright (sunny)	Bright, indirect	Medium (filtered)	Water when soil dries	Keep evenly moist	Runners or offsets	Seeds	
EUROPEAN FAN *Chamaerops humilis*	x	x			x	x		Needs approximately half a day of full sun but will survive with less. Should be kept fairly wet. Main stem covered with dark hair.
FISHTAIL *Caryota mitis*		x			x	x		Leaves have ragged edges and resemble the tail of a fish. Should be kept fairly wet.
FORSTER **(See sentry)**								
KENTIA **(See sentry)**								
LADY **Bamboo** *Rhapis excelsa*		x			x	x		Main stem covered with dark hair. Should be kept fairly wet.
MADAGASCAR **(See butterfly)**								
MINIATURE DATE **Pygmy date** *Phoenix roebeleni*		x			x		x	Should be kept fairly wet, so check soil often. Can reach 6 feet tall but seldom grows over 2 feet indoors.
NEANTHE BELLA **(See parlor)**								
PARLOR **Neanthe bella** *Chamaedorea elegans*		x	x		x		x	One of the most widely available palms. Cannot tolerate bright light; this makes it an elegant office plant or one perfect for a living room corner.
PYGMY DATE **(See miniature date)**								
SAGO *Cycas revoluta*		x		x		x		Not a true palm, but appearance is similar. Grows from a short trunk resembling a pinecone.
SENTRY **Kentia, Forster** *Howea forsterana*		x			x		x	One of the most widely available palms. Very attractive. Cannot tolerate overwatering. Curly palm *(H. belmoreana)* also available.
YELLOW **(See butterfly)**								

Flowering Houseplants

Nothing brightens a cold dreary day better than a primrose, *Primula x polyantha* (right). African violets, begonias, and a host of other flowering houseplants also provide spots of color. Keep your flowering houseplants at their happiest with the right amount of light and humidity.

When choosing flowering plants, remember there are several types: those that bloom almost continually (such as African violets); those that bloom only at certain periods of the year but have attractive foliage throughout the year (Christmas cactus is one); those that produce large blossoms once a year and then go dormant (gloxinia and others); and the brightly colored greenhouse-produced plants, which die after blooming (calceolaria, for example).

FLOWERING AND ORNAMENTAL CHART

Plant name	Light			Moisture			Propagation method					Comments
	Bright (sunny)	Bright, indirect	Medium (filtered)	Keep on dry side	Water when soil dries	Keep evenly moist	Runners or offsets	Leaf cuttings	Stem cuttings	Root division	Seeds	
ACHIMENES Magic flower *Achimenes* sp.		x				x			x		x	Blooms spring through fall. Blue, pink, yellow, red, purple, and rose flowers. Dormant after flowering.
AFRICAN VIOLET *Saintpaulia* sp.		x			x			x		x		Single and double blooms of pink, lavender, or white. Fuzzy leaves may have ruffled edges. Leaves or stems that touch edge of pot may rot; crimp strip of foil over pot edge. Demands good drainage. Take care not to get water on leaves. Water with lukewarm water. Touch mealybugs with alcohol-soaked cotton swab.
AGAPANTHUS Lily-of-the-Nile *Agapanthus* sp.	x	x				x				x	x	Blooms best when root-bound. Blooms are blue, purple, or white. Propagate in the spring.
AMARYLLIS (Also see page 498) *Hippeastrum* sp.	x	x			x	x	x				x	Lilylike flowers. Keep plants out of direct sun while blooming. After blooming, cut off stalk. Continue to water until late summer when foliage yellows; then put pot in dark place for 6 to 8 weeks. Repot bulb, water well, and set on sunny windowsill to wait for new blooms.
ANTHURIUM Flamingo flower, Tailflower *Anthurium* sp.		x			x	x	x					Glossy bracts are orange-red, pink, white, with yellow taillike structures called spadices; spadices contain two flowers. Blooms during all seasons. Attractive foliage.

FLOWERING AND ORNAMENTAL CHART (continued)

Plant name	Light			Moisture			Propagation method					Comments
	Bright (sunny)	Bright, indirect	Medium (filtered)	Keep on dry side	Water when soil dries	Keep evenly moist	Runners or offsets	Leaf cuttings	Stem cuttings	Root division	Seeds	
APHELANDRA Zebra plant *Aphelandra squarrosa*		x				x			x			Yellow-orange flower clusters 4 to 8 inches high. Blooms in fall for about 6 weeks.
AZALEA *Rhododendron* sp.	x	x				x			x			Blooms winter through spring. Red, pink, white, and multicolored. Blooms last 2 to 4 weeks.
BEGONIA *Begonia* sp.												
Rex *B. x rex-cultorum*		x				x		x	x		x	Pink or white flowers in spring. Prized for foliage in shades of green, red, bronze, silver, or rose.
Tuberous *B. x tuberhybrida*		x				x			x	x	x	White, pink, red, yellow, or orange blooms in summer.
Wax *B. x semperflorens-cultorum*		x				x			x		x	White, pink, or red flowers bloom all seasons. Colorful foliage.
BIRD-OF-PARADISE *Strelitzia reginae*	x				x					x	x	Multicolored flowers shaped like the heads of tropical birds. Usually blooms in summer and fall.
BOUGAINVILLEA Paper flower *Bougainvillea glabra*	x				x				x			Noted for its papery petallike bracts in many colors. Most varieties bloom in early spring until late summer.
BROWALLIA *Browallia* sp.	x	x				x			x		x	Trailing or upright plant that bears masses of trumpet-shaped blossoms all year.
CALCEOLARIA Pocketbook flower *Calceolaria* sp.		x	x								x	Blooming in spring, the plant has saclike blossoms. Red, pink, maroon, bronze, or yellow flowers. Dies after blooming.
CAMELLIA *Camellia* sp.		x				x			x			Blooms all through spring, for 4 to 6 weeks at a time. Pink to red flowers.
CHRISTMAS CACTUS *Schlumbergera bridgesi*		x		x					x		x	For blooms, stop watering in the fall for a month. Resume watering in November. Starting in October, keep plant at night where it's 60 to 65 degrees Fahrenheit.
CLIVIA Kaffir lily *Clivia miniata*		x			x					x		Bears clusters of lilylike flowers on stalks. Repot only when extremely overcrowded.
COLUMNEA *Columnea* sp.		x				x			x	x	x	Blooms all seasons. Trailing plant; great for hanging baskets. Many colors of blossoms.

FLOWERING AND ORNAMENTAL CHART (continued)

Plant name	Light			Moisture			Propagation method					Comments
	Bright (sunny)	Bright, indirect	Medium (filtered)	Keep on dry side	Water when soil dries	Keep evenly moist	Runners or offsets	Leaf cuttings	Stem cuttings	Root division	Seeds	
CROSSANDRA **Firecracker flower** *Crossandra infundibuliformis*	x	x				x			x		x	Salmon-orange flowers, blooming all seasons. Keep in direct light except for hottest part of the year.
CROWN-OF-THORNS *Euphorbia mili*	x	x			x				x			Woody-stemmed with prickly spines. Has pink, rose, red, coral, or yellow bracts around the petals. Water sparingly in winter.
CYCLAMEN *Cyclamen persicum*		x				x					x	Blooms in late fall through spring. White, pink, or red flowers with colorful foliage.
EPISCIA **Flame violet** *Episcia sp.*		x				x	x		x			White, pink, red, or yellow flowers, blooming spring through fall. Trailing plant.
FUCHSIA *Fuchsia sp.*	x	x				x			x			Blooming all seasons. Has hoopskirt-shaped, pink to red blossoms.
GARDENIA **Cape jasmine** *Gardenia jasminoides*	x					x			x			Waxy, white flowers, blooming winter to spring. Fragrant blossoms.
GERANIUM *Pelargonium sp.*	x				x				x			Pinch back tall stems to promote branching. Pink to red flowers; often with horseshoe-shaped, soft, plush leaves.
GLOXINIA *Sinningia sp.*		x				x		x				When stops blooming, withhold water gradually until foliage dries. Store tuber and its pot in a cool, dark place until new growth starts. Repot in rich, well-drained soil and set pot in a warm, lighted spot. Take care not to get water on leaves.
HIBISCUS *Hibiscus sp.*	x					x			x			Papery flowers, blooming all year long. White, cream, yellow, salmon, orange, and scarlet.
HOYA **Wax plant** *Hoya carnosa*	x	x			x				x			Sweetly fragrant, star-shaped blossoms. Two- to 4-inch shiny leaves. Vines.
HYDRANGEA *Hydrangea macrophylla*		x				x			x			Large clusters of soft-textured flowers in a variety of colors.
IMPATIENS **Patience plant** *Impatiens wallerana*		x	x			x			x		x	Has soft, flat flowers in many colors. Shiny leaves in green, maroon, or a variegated green and white.
JERUSALEM CHERRY *Solanum pseudocapsicum*	x				x						x	Starlike blooms from July through September. Cherry-size orange, scarlet, or yellow fruit following. Fruit is poisonous.

Plant name	Light			Moisture			Propagation method					Comments
	Bright (sunny)	Bright, indirect	Medium (filtered)	Keep on dry side	Water when soil dries	Keep evenly moist	Runners or offsets	Leaf cuttings	Stem cuttings	Root division	Seeds	
LILY **Calla** *Zantedeschia sp.*	x					x				x		Divide tubers in late summer. Blooms all seasons. Yellow to orange, waxy, single petals are rolled and flaring. Foliage is shaped like arrowheads.
Easter *Lilium longiflorum*		x				x				x		Snowy white flowers. Sweet fragrance. Flowers last about a week. Blooms in spring.
Eucharist, Amazon *Eucharis grandiflora*		x				x				x		White, fragrant flowers. Blooms in clusters of three to six flowers. Plant will blossom two or three times a year.
ORCHID CACTUS *Nopalxochia ackermanni*		x		x					x			Multicolored, fragrant blossoms. Stem has no leaves or spines.
ORCHID **Brassavola, Lady-of the-night** *Brassavola nodosa*		x			x					x		Blooms all seasons. Bears long-lasting, fragrant, white, yellow, or pale green blossoms.
Cattleya *Cattleya sp.*	x				x					x		Pot in fir bark or tree fern chunks. Mist foliage daily. Mauve, white, pink, or lavender blooms.
Cymbidium *Cymbidium sp.*	x					x				x		Blooms in fall through spring. Mahogany, bronze, maroon, green, yellow, pink, and white blossoms.
Epidendrum *Epidendrum cochleatum*		x				x				x		Multicolored, fragrant flowers shaped like clamshells. Blooms all seasons.
Oncidium, Dancing-lady *Oncidium sp.*	x	x			x					x		Clusters of yellow to orange long-lasting flowers. Blooms in fall and winter. Keep shaded from midday sun.
ORNAMENTAL PEPPER *Capsicum annuum*	x				x						x	Valued for its masses of colorful fruits. Two- to 3-inch-long peppers appear in summer and fall.
PASSIONFLOWER *Passiflora sp.*	x					x			x		x	Keep soil moist during growing season; dry, during resting periods. Blooms in spring through summer. Fragrant, multicolored blossoms. Vines.
POINSETTIA *Euphorbia pulcherrima*	x				x				x			Has bright red, petallike bracts. Blooms fall through winter. Traditional Christmas plant.
PRIMROSE *Primula sp.*		x				x					x	Multicolored flowers appearing in tiers or clusters. Winter flowering. Requires cool temperatures.
VENUS'S-FLYTRAP *Dionaea muscipula*	x					x				x	x	Traps insects inside of leaves. Digests the insects to obtain nutrients necessary for growth. Spring blooming.

Bromeliads

No wonder the bromeliad is a favorite of hobbyists: it's exotic but almost foolproof. Dozens of varieties are available. (The *Vriesea splendens* is below, left; the variegated *Guzmania zahni* is below, right.)

The secret is in the watering. Keep water in the center cup of the plant, and water lightly around the base once a week.

Bromeliad roots need little space, so the plants can be put in small clay pots that may seem out of proportion with the plant. Although they prefer osmunda or shredded tree fern, bromeliads also thrive in a mixture of fir bark, sphagnum moss, and commercial soil. Another mix that works well is half perlite and coarse sand with soil. The goal is good drainage.

Bromeliads prefer bright— not full—sun and can tolerate poor light. Direct sun will burn the foliage. But the stiffer the leaves, the more light they need.

Bromeliads produce new plants by suckers. The parent plant turns brown as it dies, and leaves can be peeled away. Divide the plant, potting offsets individually in three- or four-inch pots.

BROMELIAD CHART

Plant name	Light			Moisture			Comments
	Bright (sunny)	Bright, indirect	Medium (filtered)	Keep water in center cup	Water when soil dries	Keep evenly moist	
AECHMEA Urn plant *Aechmea* sp.		x		x	x		Common species include: *A. chantini* (Amazon zebra plant), *A. fasciata* (silver vase), *A. fulgens* (coralberry), *A. orlandiana* (finger-of-god), and *A. caudata.* Flowering spike rises from center cup. Hardy.
ANANAS Pineapple *Ananas comosus*	x	x				x	Prefers good sun but grows well in indirect light. Group includes the common edible pineapple.
BILLBERGIA *Billbergia pyramidalis*	x	x		x		x	Easiest of all bromeliads to grow. Flowering spike rises from center cup.
CRYPTANTHUS Earth-star *Cryptanthus* sp.		x	x		x		Common species include *C. bivittatus* 'minor' (dwarf rose-stripe star) and *C. zonatus* (zebra plant). Blooms small and insignificant. Foliage flat and spreading.
DYCKIA Pineapple dyckia *Dyckia brevifolia*	x				x		Usually grows in clumps. Blooms appear in summer on long, slender stalks.
GUZMANIA *Guzmania* sp.		x	x	x		x	Common species include *G. lingulata* 'cardinalis' (scarlet star) and *G. lingulata* 'minor.' Blooms last for several months.
NEOREGELIA *Neoregelia* sp.	x	x	x	x		x	Common species include *N. carolinae* (blushing bromeliad) and *N. carolinae* 'Tricolor.' Center foliage turns color before blooms appear.
NIDULARIUM *Nidularium regelioides*		x	x	x		x	Tolerates lower light than most bromeliads. Very hardy.
QUESNELIA Grecian-vase *Quesnelia marmorata*		x		x		x	Plant becomes slightly fragrant before blooms appear. Flowering spike is made up of many tiny blooms.
TILLANDSIA *Tillandsia* sp.	x	x					Largest genus of bromeliads. Common species include: *T. caput-medusae* (medusa's-head), *T. argentea* (silver pincushion), *T. punctulata* (Mexican blacktorch), *T. circinnata* (pot-bellied tillandsia), *T. usneoides* (Spanish moss), and *T. cyanea.* Usually grown on bark or driftwood. Water by misting.
VRIESEA *Vriesea* sp.		x	x	x		x	Common species include *V. splendens* (flaming-sword) and *V. x rex.* Bloom usually bright colored.

Succulents

Sunlight suits cactus and other succulents best; they can usually adapt to any window except north. Plant in a clay pot with equal parts coarse sand, potting soil, and leaf mold. Succulents should dry out between waterings. Graft cactus by cutting off the top of one plant to form a base or rootstock; cut off the bottom of another and center it on the base. Tie a string around the top of the grafted part and the pot until the two parts join.

CACTUS AND OTHER SUCCULENTS

Plant name	Light			Moisture		Propagation method				Comments
	Bright (sunny)	Bright, indirect	Keep on dry side	Water when soil dries	Water sparingly in winter	Runners or offsets	Leaf cuttings	Stem cuttings	Seeds	
AEONIUM **Black tree** A. arboreum	x			x	x		x		x	Quick-growing rosette form. A. arboreum 'atropurpureum' and 'foliis purpureis' have reddish-purple leaves.
Pinwheel A. haworthi	x			x	x		x		x	Leaves covered with waxy powder. Often grown outdoors in warm climates. Edged in pink.
Nobile A. nobile	x			x	x				x	Flowers only once; dies after flowering. Leaves are olive green.
AGAVE **Century plant** A. americana	x			x	x				x	Nicknamed because of the long time plant takes to flower. Marginata cultivar has variegated leaves.
Parviflora A. parviflora	x			x	x				x	Popular dwarf species.
Queen victoria century plant A. victoriae-reginae	x			x	x				x	Leaves form small, tight rosettes.
ALOE Candelabra A. arborescens	x	x		x	x	x			x	Stems form a clump. Can grow quite tall (up to 10 feet). Toothed leaves.

CACTUS AND OTHER SUCCULENTS (continued)

Plant name	Light		Moisture			Propagation method				Comments
	Bright (sunny)	Bright, indirect	Keep on dry side	Water when soil dries	Water sparingly in winter	Runners or offsets	Leaf cuttings	Stem cuttings	Seeds	
ALOE **Common** *A. barbadensis*	X	X		X	X	X			X	Has long, fleshy leaves with soft-toothed edges. Leaf sap commonly used to treat minor burns.
Partridge-breast, Tiger *A. variegata*	X	X		X	X	X			X	Has triangular, toothed leaves with dark splotches.
Spider, Crocodile-jaws *A. humilis*	X	X		X	X	X			X	Stemless. White, toothed leaves. Grows in dense rosette. Several varieties available.
Torch plant, Lace *A. aristata*	X	X		X	X	X			X	Stemless. Toothed leaves. Grows in compact rosette.
ASTROPHYTUM **Bishop's cap** *A. myriostigma*	X			X	X				X	Small, globular plant. Nicknamed bishop's cap because of its resemblance to a bishop's miter.
Sand-dollar *A. asterias*	X			X	X				X	Small, globular plant. Several varieties available.
BORZICACTUS **Old-man-of-the-mountains** *Borzicactus celsianus*	X			X					X	Some species can be propagated by cuttings. Withhold all water in winter.
CEPHALOCEREUS **Old-man cactus** *Cephalocereus senilis*	X	X		X	X			X	X	Popular because of its long white hairs. Take cuttings in spring.
CEREUS **Peruvian apple** *Cereus peruvianus*	X			X	X			X	X	Has thick, upright stems edged with spines. Blooms at night.
CHRISTMAS CACTUS **(See page 487)**										
CRASSULA **Airplane plant, Propeller plant** *C. falcata*	X	X		X			X			Has gray-green leaves that resemble airplane propellers.
Bead vine, Necklace vine *C. rupestris*	X	X		X				X		Popular because of its unusual bead-like leaves. Grows slowly.
Jade plant *C. argentea*	X	X		X			X			Most popular crassula. Easy to grow. Several varieties available, including variegated types. Plants usually live for years, even when root-bound. Repot at any season.
Rattail *C. lycopodioides*	X	X		X				X		Popular with collectors.

CACTUS AND OTHER SUCCULENTS (continued)

Plant name	Light		Moisture			Propagation method				Comments
	Bright (sunny)	Bright, indirect	Keep on dry side	Water when soil dries	Water sparingly in winter	Runners or offsets	Leaf cuttings	Stem cuttings	Seeds	
ECHEVERIA **Mexican-gem** *E. elegans*	x	x		x	x	x	x	x		Leaves covered with white, waxy powder.
Rosy hen-and-chickens, Plush plant *E. pulvinata*	x	x		x	x	x	x	x		Densely growing. Several varieties available.
ECHINOCACTUS **Golden barrel cactus** *E. grusoni*	x			x	x				x	Large, round plant with golden yellow spines.
Large barrel cactus *E. ingens*	x			x	x				x	Large, round blue-gray plant with brown spines.
ECHINOPSIS **Easter-lily cactus** *Echinopsis multiplex*	x	x		x	x				x	Hardy outdoors to Zone 5. Bears fragrant pink flowers in spring.
EPIPHYLLUM **Orchid cactus** *Epiphyllum* sp.		x						x		Keep soil slightly moist. Various species bear colorful, often fragrant, blooms. Ideal for an attractive hanging basket.
EUPHORBIA **Candelabra cactus, Hat-rack cactus** *E. lactea*	x	x		x				x		Has long stems with many branches. Looks like a candelabra or hat rack.
Crown-of-thorns *E. mili* **(See page 488)**										
Medusa's-head *E. caput-medusae*	x	x		x				x		Nickname comes from plant's resemblance to a head with branches radiating from it.
FEROCACTUS **Fishhook cactus** *Ferocactus acanthodes*	x			x	x				x	Globular plant with pinkish, curved spines. Grows slowly.
GASTERIA **Cow-tongue cactus** *Gasteria* sp.		x		x		x	x		x	Plants grow in clumps with thick leaves facing each other. Various species have colorful markings. Don't use vermiculite in the potting mix; it retains too much moisture.
GYMNOCALYCIUM *Gymnocalycium* sp.	x	x		x	x				x	Commonly used as a grafting rootstock.
HAWORTHIA **Zebra** *Haworthia fasciata*		x		x			x		x	Most popular haworthia. Has white markings on undersides of leaves.

Plant name	Light		Moisture			Propagation method				Comments
	Bright (sunny)	Bright, indirect	Keep on dry side	Water when soil dries	Water sparingly in winter	Runners or offsets	Leaf cuttings	Stem cuttings	Seeds	
KALANCHOE **Christmas** *K. blossfeldiana*	x	x		x			x		x	Has small, waxy leaves with clusters of colorful flowers. Cut back after blooming. Commonly sold in florists' shops during Christmas and Easter seasons.
Velvetleaf, Velvet elephant-ear *K. beharensis*	x	x		x			x	x		Has hairy stems covered with brown felt. Leaves are large and triangular.
LITHOPS **Living-stones** *Lithops sp.*	x		x	x					x	Cannot tolerate high humidity. New leaves grow from the cleft formed by present leaves; old leaves then shrivel and die.
MAMMILLARIA **Bird's-nest cactus** *M. camptotricha*	x			x	x	x			x	Grows in a compact cluster. Has long, twisted yellow spines.
Feather cactus *M. plumosa*	x			x	x	x			x	Covered with thick, feathery spines.
Lace cactus, Golden-star cactus *M. elongata*	x			x	x	x			x	Has long, fingerlike stems covered with yellow spines.
Old-woman cactus *M. hahniana*	x			x	x	x			x	Covered with long, white hairs. Spines are also white.
Snowball cactus, Powder-puff cactus *M. bocasana*	x			x	x	x			x	Grows in a compact cluster. Covered with white hairs.
MELOCACTUS **Turk's-cap cactus** *Melocactus sp.*	x	x		x	x				x	Nicknamed Turk's-cap because of the woolly crown at the top of each plant.
OPUNTIA **Bunny-ears** *O. microdasys*	x			x	x			x	x	Spineless, but has tiny, sharp bristles. Most popular opuntia. Large, fan-shaped leaves resemble bunny ears.
Prickly pear *O. vulgaris*	x			x	x			x	x	Variegata cultivar (Joseph's-Coat Cactus) is mottled.
SANSEVIERIA **(See page 480)**										
SEDUM **Burro's-tail** *S. morganianum*	x	x		x			x	x		Leaves are fragile and often drop if bumped. Ideal plant for a hanging basket.
Jelly bean, Christmas-cheer *S. x rubrotinctum*	x	x		x			x	x		Shiny, succulent leaves have reddish tips.

Terrariums and Dish Gardens

Terrariums had their start with Dr. Nathaniel Ward in London in the 1800s. In his experiments with growing plants indoors, Ward found they grew well in closed containers. His discovery let to the craze for "Wardian cases," as terrariums were then called. Bell jars were the commonly used containers, but now almost any glass container is fair game for creating miniature landscapes and mossy woodlands; a dish garden is even simpler.

Glass containers are the best choices for terrariums. Clear plastic ones can also be used, but they tend to discolor in time. To start, clean the container and dry it thoroughly—inside and out.

Packaged soils especially for terrariums are available; or use any standard packaged soil mixed with additional sand for better drainage. Use only sterilized materials.

Put a layer of small stones, gravel, or coarse sand in the bottom of the container. Sprinkle a one-fourth-inch layer of charcoal pieces over it to help keep the soil sweet. Add from one to four inches of soil to hold the plants. Moisten the soil before planting.

Landscaping

While the plants are still in their pots, determine how they should be placed in the container. Arrange and rearrange them on a counter top as you visualize them in the container. Give the miniature garden perspective by adding at least one plant that is taller than the others. Variegated-leaved plants also add interest.

Start planting from the center and work your way out; or start in one corner and work to the opposite corner. Make a hole in the soil for the first plant. Knock it out of its pot, shake off the excess soil, and set it into the hole. Mound soil around the roots and tamp it down firmly. Keep the leaves of the plant above the soil as much as possible. Continue with the rest of the plants.

Before watering use a small sable brush to remove soil clinging to the sides of the container. Brush soil off leaves and stems of plants. Add decorative stones, driftwood, gravel, bark, or ceramic animals for interest, if desired. (Or position them as you set in the plants.)

Water and light

Water the plants lightly. Use a poultry baster for hard-to-get-at plants in a bottle. Give plants in a closed terrarium or small-necked bottle about a tablespoon of water. Plants in open terrariums or dish gardens will need more.

Set your newly planted terrarium in medium light for a week. Then move the terrarium into bright, indirect light—not full sun. Move it into full sun if it's a succulent dish garden (such as the one at right), with its miniature jades, sedums, and echeveria.

Water terrariums when the soil is dry. This will probably be every month or two for covered terrariums. Open ones should be checked every week or so. Succulent dish gardens should be watered as often as any normal potted succulent.

Tops for terrariums

Aucuba	Gesneriad
Baby's-tears	Grape ivy
Begonia	Maranta
Chinese	Peperomia
evergreen	Philodendron
Creeping fig	Pickaback plant
Dracena	Pilea
English ivy	Polka-dot plant
Fern	Purple velvet plant
Fittonia	Strawberry saxifrage

Bulbs Indoors

You don't have to wait for spring to enjoy colorful tulips and daffodils or sweet-scented hyacinths and paper-white narcissus. By using a technique called forcing, you can enjoy these spring bloomers in the dead of winter—indoors. Forcing speeds up the normal blooming time of bulb plants—from six or seven months to three or four months. Follow the general directions for most bulbs.

Buy bulbs that are recommended for forcing in the fall from a nursery or greenhouse. Choose bulbs that are large, firm, and free of bruises and blemishes. Generally, the larger the bulb you use, the better the results.

Use a pot that is at least twice as tall as the bulbs you're using—that way you're sure there'll be room for the roots to develop properly. It doesn't matter what the pot is made of—plastic, terra-cotta, ceramic—as long as it has a drainage hole. Wash the pot, and place a shard over the hole to prevent the soil from washing out.

Use a porous potting soil—equal parts of vermiculite, peat moss, and packaged potting soil work well. Don't reuse soil that has already been used to force bulbs. Fertilizing is unnecessary because the bulb has all the nutrients the plant needs for its first season.

Fill the pot halfway with soil mix-ture, but don't pack it down. Then, place the bulbs on top, and filter more soil to cover the bulbs. Let the bulb tips peek out. Fill the pot with as many bulbs as possible for the best effect, but leave at least a pencil's width between each bulb.

Plant tulip bulbs with the flat side of the bulb to the outside. Label each pot with the date and variety of bulb you've planted. You may want to list color, too.

The next step is to create an artificial winter by placing the bulbs in cold storage for several months (see the chart below for exact times). A refrigerator, window well, and an unheated basement or garage are all good places. Temperatures should be from 35 to 50 degrees Fahrenheit but should never drop below freezing. Cover the pots with newspapers or a box so no light reaches them. Water every two or three weeks or whenever soil dries out.

Check the pots for root development in eight weeks. If roots are visible through the drainage hole and stems are about two inches high, the bulbs are ready for a simulated spring. Some should be moved into a cool room with no bright light for a few weeks; others are ready for good light immediately. In a few weeks, buds will appear, followed shortly by blooms. To prolong the life of your plants, keep them out of direct sun and away from hot or cold drafts. Put them in a cool room at night. Water regularly.

To get your bulbs to bloom in January, you should pot them in early October. For February, pot in October or November; for March bloom, pot in mid-November.

As the blooms fade, move the crocus, daffodil, or hyacinth pots to a cool window and continue to water. When the garden thaws, plant the bulbs in the ground.

FORCING

Plant	Potting	Comments
Amaryllis	Buy treated bulb that's ready to flower. Plant in a 6-inch pot, leaving half the bulb above soil.	Set potted bulb in a sunny window or in a warm room with good light. Keep the soil evenly moist. Stems may need to be tied to stake. Flowers can be red, pink, white, or coral; some are striped.
Crocus	Plant ten corms in a 6-inch pot. Crowd the corms to get better display.	Water the pot after you've planted crocus, then place pot in a refrigerator or cool closet for 8 weeks, keeping the soil moist. Next, place pot in cool room where the light is strong.
Daffodils	Set six daffodil bulbs in an 8-inch pot. Plant bulbs so their necks peek out of soil.	After you've set daffodils in pot, water soil well, then put pot in refrigerator for 8 to 12 weeks until roots fill bottom of pot. When cold treatment is over, put pot in a sunny window.
Hyacinths	Use one bulb for a hyacinth vase or three bulbs in a 6-inch pot with soil.	If you use a vase, fill with water, then put in refrigerator for 7 weeks. If you pot in soil, water pot, then put in refrigerator for 7 weeks. With both, put in partial sun a week, then move to a spot with full sun.
Paper-white narcissus	Start with a 6-inch-diameter, pebble-filled bowl and wedge in four bulbs. Add water to cover bases.	Store planted bowl in a cool, dark closet or basement for two weeks, replenishing the water in bowl as necessary. Then bring bowl to sunny location. The flower spikes will shoot up in a hurry.
Tulips	Plant bulbs in a pot, setting each bulb with its nose showing above the soil level.	After bulbs are planted, water thoroughly, then set pot in the refrigerator for 12 weeks; water weekly. Next, move the pot to a cool, dark closet or basement for 2 weeks. Put them in a warm, sunny spot.

chapter 15

GREENHOUSES

There is a certain magic to the sweep of white that winter puts on things. But it isn't long before the spirit craves a touch of life, even if it's only a tiny green leaf sprouting from a twig. And nothing satisfies that craving faster than a greenhouse. Brimming with blossoms nestled among leaves, the greenhouse resembles a part of paradise attached to the side of your house.

In the old days, greenhouses were restricted to the wealthy upper classes; keeping the warmth in and the cold out required nothing less than a small miracle of engineering. But today, with lightweight materials, improved glazing, and readily available sources of heat, launching a greenhouse demands little more than getting the right angle of the sun. And because of the mushrooming interest in gardening, greenhouses are well within the limits of the average family's budget. Many are available in prefabricated units that can be put in place in less than a day. Others can be attached to the second story or fitted over a sunny window. You can select size and complexity to fit your interest.

As for plants, you can grow almost anything—from the most exotic of passionflowers to a modest row of carrots. The palm, cactus, geranium, primrose, fern, begonia, and African violet all thrive in a greenhouse. If you have a weakness for cut flowers, old favorites—such as the carnation, aster, snapdragon, chrysanthemum, pansy, and sweet pea—will provide a continuous supply of blossoms for every room of the house.

And because the greenhouse can offer close to ideal conditions for plants, growing things is almost as easy as picking up a watering can. All you need is at least three hours of sun per day and an undying passion for living things.

Greenhouse Basics

For some, the whir and squeaks of motors, ventilators, and blowers—mingled with the clicks or snaps of thermostats—are a little terrifying. But a greenhouse is nothing more than a mechanical way to provide a place where plants can grow under optimum conditions.

Modern greenhouses, equipped with automatic devices, are about as simple to operate as your refrigerator. But an understanding of a few basics will make initial construction less confusing and, at the same time, keep your greenhouse from dwindling into a wasteland of shriveled plants.

Temperature. Some plants have their roots in the tropics, which means they require semitropical conditions. Others resemble relatives from the desert or cool, moist woodlands. The temperature needs of plants are divided into three categories:

Cool
40 to 45 degrees Fahrenheit (minimum temperature at night); 55 to 60 degrees Fahrenheit (maximum temperature during the day)

Temperate
50 to 55 degrees Fahrenheit (minimum temperature at night); 65 to 70 degrees Fahrenheit (maximum temperature during the day)

Warm
62 to 65 degrees Fahrenheit (minimum temperature at night); 80 to 85 degrees Fahrenheit (maximum temperature during the day)

Seldom is the greenhouse temperature so uniform that only one group of plants can be grown. Through trial and error—combined with careful observation—you can identify cool and warm spots, or microclimates, which are suitable to a wide variety of plants. The northwest corner, for example, is bound to be considerably cooler than an elevated shelf centered on the south wall. Cooler areas under the growing benches can be a perfect starting place for forcing spring bulbs. Or plan on a cascading vine that will provide attractive leaf patterns and, at the same time, protect your favorite foliage plant from searing rays of the sun.

Location. Half the glory of a greenhouse is its profusion of color and foliage, regardless of the weather outdoors. Sun—and lots of it—is the key to greenhouse success. Unfortunately, the tilt of the earth in winter means the sun barely slides along the treetops before disappearing below the horizon. Days are shorter, and the increased distance and widened angle weaken the sun's warming rays. Therefore, the greenhouse has to be cleverly placed to capture the most sun possible.

Because the sun spends most of its winter days in the southern sky, the ideal direction for a greenhouse to face is south. Next, in order of preference, are southeast, southwest, and west. A northern exposure is satisfactory if you're growing only foliage plants. As a general rule, plants will need at least three hours of sunlight per day.

Keep in mind that trees, buildings, and other obstructions can rob plants of valuable sun. Deciduous trees (which lose their leaves in the fall) often are valuable allies because they offer filtered shade in the summer. Wind can be a factor, too. A greenhouse constantly buffeted by frigid winds is difficult to heat and often drafty. Plan on planting an evergreen screen or constructing a fence if winds are a problem.

Construction. Almost all greenhouses are variations of two basic designs: the even-span and the lean-to. The lean-to looks like a full greenhouse that has been sliced down the middle and attached to an existing structure. The even-span is a complete enclosure capable of functioning independently of other buildings. Beginners often find the lean-to ideal, because it can be incorporated into the living space. As a rule, it is easier to heat and supply with electricity; systems already in the home can be tapped. Because your home is the other half of your greenhouse, the lean-to is generally less expensive to construct than an even-span.

The even-span, although designed to be a self-contained unit, also can be treated as a modular unit and attached to a house or slipped between kitchen and garage. The even-span is more expensive than a lean-to, but it offers more growing room.

A greenhouse is basically a translucent bubble engineered to admit the sun but keep out the cold. This means it can be made of a wide variety of materials—from aluminum and glass to a wood frame covered with a thin plastic film. Aluminum and glass structures are most popular because of their strength and durability. Plastic structures are not so attractive and must be recovered every year or two. But their lower price and simple construction make them a tempting alternative.

Both the even-span and the lean-to are available in glass-to-wall or glass-to-ground models. Whether the glass extends to ground level or joins a short wall depends on the severity of winters in your area. All glass structures, however, require a solid footing extending below the soil's frost line. But a wall of stone, brick, or wood about two or three feet high increases the ability of the greenhouse to retain heat. Growers in more temperate regions often opt for the glass-to-ground type because of the additional growing area beneath the plant benches.

Size. Although construction costs increase with the size of the greenhouse, it may pay to think big. For example, the climate of a larger greenhouse may be easier to maintain than a small one simply because large spaces are less prone to rapid temperature changes. Starting large is also less expensive than adding sections later.

Greenhouse types

The lean-to greenhouse is a favorite. Growing space is accessible from indoors, so you can work whenever you wish. Often, the indoor heating system can be used, and plumbing and electrical hookups are easy to do.

A freestanding greenhouse can be located facing any direction you wish. All you need to do is find a spot with at least three hours of winter sunlight per day. You have room for potting benches on both sides. In warm-winter zones, glass goes all the way to the ground.

A window greenhouse takes little space, is low in cost, and is easy to install. If you have a pair of windows side-by-side, order two of these units and double your growing room. Window greenhouses come in a variety of sizes—all the standard dimensions are available.

An indoor, freestanding greenhouse is perfect if you plan to move it. Placed to receive east light, this plant center gets help from an overhead light, too.

A porch with a southern exposure becomes a greenhouse during winter months, thanks to plastic panels attached to a redwood frame.

Good for Growing

Adorning your home with vines and blossoms doesn't necessarily take thousands of dollars or an army of expensive architects. A sunny window, patio, entrance way, or even a neglected corner can become a small forest of lush plants.

Because your improvised greenhouse is often part of the home, it will present some of the hazards common to growing plants indoors. Most homes are kept warm, which means the moisture content of the air is low. As a result, many plants, especially those requiring cooler temperatures, may eventually languish and die. Also, most homes are a patchwork of cool nooks and warm crannies. To us, they may be troublesome fluctuations. But to plants, they represent miniature climates—perfect for some but slow death to others.

A little pre-construction observation can spell the difference between success and failure. Place thermometers and humidity indicators wherever you think plants will grow, and take note of the prevailing conditions. The trick is to construct a sun trap, so plants can enjoy life-giving light and warmth. How you accomplish this is limited only by your ingenuity. Here are some possibilities:

The window greenhouse. One of the quickest routes to greenhouse gardening allows you to convert a sun-drenched window into a miniature greenhouse by installing a specially designed, glassed-in unit. Available from several manufacturers, the units usually are reasonably priced, as well as quick and easy to assemble. Two such units placed over a double or picture window will provide a surprising amount of growing room. Some window greenhouses can be constructed from readily available materials as do-it-yourself projects. (For example, see project below.)

The plant wall. No matter how your house is situated, chances are that one wall or entrance gets an abundance of full sun each day. Or the door of an unused garage may face south. An attractive plant wall can be built, using discarded storm windows (see photo on page 506) or heavy-duty plastic stretched over a wood frame (see opposite page). Some homeowners incorporate a solarium into their building plans or convert a living room wall to glass when they remodel. Heating is a simple matter because the plant wall is an integral part of the house.

Sun dome or skylight. For a hanging garden effect, let light in through the roof. Clear or translucent domes are fairly simple to install. Or a glass sash may be fitted to the opening. Of course, proper insulation and weatherproofing are critical. Skylight gardens get plenty of sun but may become overheated on bright, sunny days. Ventilation should be provided.

Top candidates for growing under skylights are the trailing vine plants, available in both blossoming and foliage varieties. Ferns have delicate fronds and offer a host of trailing types perfect for the ceiling garden.

The cold frame. Primarily a temporary structure designed to provide a transition for plants before they are plunged into the outdoor garden, the cold frame can be altered to protect plants all winter long. Attach the cold frame to a basement window with a southern exposure, and insulate the glass as much as possible. Some heat from the basement will escape into the frame, but additional heat can be supplied by installing a portable heater or heating cable. Try to make the excavation as deep as possible, so you can take advantage of deeper, frost-free soil. The cold frame (considered a "hotbed" once heat is provided) will hardly match the splendor of a greenhouse but will keep plants thriving and help reduce the gloom of winter.

Fourteen inches in front of any sunny window are all you need for this plant haven.

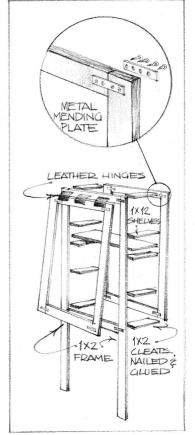

To make this plant house, cut the components to fit the width of your window, then assemble the three frames with metal mending plates. Secure cleats with glue and nails or screws. Shelves rest atop. Fasten door with hinges or with strips of rubber or leather. Staple plastic to frame.

Discarded storm windows get a second life as a budget-price greenhouse.

More growing ideas

If mere glass strikes you as a pitiful barrier against winter's fury, go underground and build a pit greenhouse. Resembling a root cellar with a glass top, the pit greenhouse combines the warmth of the sun with the insulating protection of the subsoil to create a friendly climate for plants.

A pit greenhouse is a structure half above ground and half below ground. In some ways, it could be considered a walk-in cold frame because it doesn't depend on artificial sources of heat to keep plants from freezing, except, on occasion, in cold climates. Dig to a depth of at least four feet, so the floor is well below the frost line. Then construct walls of concrete block or fieldstone. Finally, attach the glass roof and gable ends. If possible, the glassed-in section should face south; in winter, the sun never

leaves the southern hemisphere. Cover the north roof with shingles. To aid drainage, spread a layer of stones or rough gravel a foot deep over the floor.

Thorough insulation is the key to a successful pit greenhouse. The sun is the primary source of heat, so you must be sure to keep trapped heat in and cold out. A good way to insulate the glass section is to place a layer of plastic film over the sash, so a dead-air space is created. Or attach bubble plastic (used for shipping fragile items) directly to glass. Doors should fit tightly and be insulated. The roof and gable ends are generally double constructed with ample insulating material between.

If—in spite of all your precautions to conserve heat—supplemental heat is needed, put incandescent bulbs under the benches. Or use small electric heaters with blowers and automatic thermostats.

Remember, though, that the pit greenhouse is decidedly cool and not suitable for heat-loving plants. Reserve the space for primroses, camellias, rhododendrons, azaleas, and hardy bulbs, such as tulips, daffodils, and hyacinths. Or specialize in the unending varieties of geraniums. The pit is an excellent place to grow cool-season vegetables, such as lettuce, chard, beets, or carrots. Certain annuals, such as petunias, chrysanthemums, and sweet peas, are also excellent candidates for pit growing.

Good air circulation is essential for robust plant growth. Install small fans at both ends to maintain the flow of air. The glass sash should be hinged to the ridge so panels can be propped open, allowing fresh air to enter and overheated air to escape.

Light, too, is crucial, especially during the winter months when sunny days are often the exception rather than the rule. Fluorescent fixtures can be installed directly over benches for supplemental lighting. If seedlings or cuttings are planned, fluorescent lighting will encourage the development of healthy roots.

Because the pit is usually unheated, maintaining temperatures above the freezing mark on cold nights may require extra effort. Keep quilts, canvas, and extra plastic on reserve, so glass can be quickly covered. A backup electric heater can be a plant-saver when temperatures and high winds are especially brutal.

Space-savers

Be sure your plans include a work space where potting and other duties can be completed easily. Traditionally known as the "potting bench," the area should consist of a storage rack for tools, shelves for pots, containers for soil mixes, soil amendments (such as bone meal, lime, and fertilizer), and a sink with running water.

Here are some ways to get the most from your indoor garden space—whether it be skylight, pit greenhouse, or another variety:

● Because sun is all important, increase the amount of sunlight available by placing reflective material where it will toss light back onto plants. Some growers construct movable mirrors that adjust to the sun's movement across the sky. Movable screens painted flat white can go a long way toward increasing light intensity.

● Before winter sets in, check your landscape plantings, and prune back those shrubs or trees blocking the sun.

● Construct planter boxes for starting seeds of vegetables and annual flowers.

● Put sun-loving plants on portable stands or trays that can be shifted for maximum exposure to the sun.

● Use shelves made from clear acrylic plastic, glass, or wire mesh. This way plants can grow in the middle of the window as well as around the sides.

A section of glass on hinges can be opened for ventilation on warm days.

Warmth captured during the day keeps this energy-saving greenhouse warm at night. Good insulation is the secret.

Hydroponics: A Soilless Growing Technique

There was a time when the sprouting of leaves and flowers was considered magic. However, scientists have been able to isolate many of the chemicals that contribute to plants' growth and development. Since these discoveries, gardeners have tinkered with methods of doing away with soil. The result has been hydroponics, growing plants in a solution of necessary nutrients. Many commercially prepared units are available, or you can make your own.

Once you get a taste of homegrown winter vegetables, you'll want to expand your hydroponic system.

Hydroponics is defined as growing plants in a nutrient solution without using soil. Most methods of hydroponics use inert materials as a growing medium and as support for the plant. This is sometimes referred to as nutriculture, too.

The idea is to short-cut the complicated chemical exchanges that take place in ordinary soil and make the crucial nutrients directly available to plants. The basic nutrients required by plants include potassium, phosphorus, and nitrogen, plus several trace minerals. In gardening with soil, potassium, phosphorus, and the trace minerals are provided by the soil, and nitrogen is provided by decaying organic matter. Water dissolves the nutrients and supplies them to the roots of the plants. In hydroponics, all the nutrients are supplied to the plants by the solution, thus eliminating many chemical exchanges.

One way to make the nutrients directly available to plants is to set plants into an artificial aggregate soil, such as perlite, vermiculite, coarse sand, or gravel, and then add a specially prepared nutrient solution. Or the artificial soil can be eliminated and the plants grown by suspending the roots in the nutrient solution.

For the indoor or outdoor gardener, hydroponics can offer bonanza yields with maximum use of available space. With proper support, plenty of light, and conscientious care, a small pot can support a six-foot tomato vine. Most garden centers stock prepared nutrient mixes containing the critical elements. Or you can purchase the basic ingredients and mix your own nutrient solution; if the water contains chlorine, let the water stand overnight. Most of the chlorine will evaporate.

Use of a soilless medium is an ideal introduction to hydroponics, because washed sand, gravel, vermiculite, or perlite provides support for plants and allows air to penetrate properly. At the same time, the nutrient solution can wash around roots without eliminating valuable air.

Any container will do as long as it drains thoroughly. The container should be at least four inches deep. You might use flowerpots, plastic dishpans, or cat litter trays. Punch or drill holes in the bottom, if necessary, and cover the holes with cheesecloth, netting, or a piece of window screen, so growing materials will not be flushed from the container. Fill the container to within a half inch of the rim with perlite or other artificial soil, and tamp gently. Seeds should be started in a separate flat, then shifted to a hydroponic unit when seedlings are large enough to transplant easily without injury to the roots.

Big-time hydroponics. The greenhouse on the opposite page produces vegetables year round. Besides holding strawberries, peas, cabbage, lettuce, cucumbers, and cherry tomatoes, the greenhouse has room for marigolds, carnations, and sweet peas for cutting, as well as a host of houseplants. The nutrient solution is automatically pumped into the growing medium in the plant trays two or three times a day. When the trays are full, the pump automatically shuts off and the solution drains back into the nutrient tank. The solution can be reused for about two weeks, and then it's time to throw it out and add fresh solution.

Small-scale hydroponics. The junior-size hydroponic system (right) can accommodate bougainvillea, tomato plant, chives, and lettuce. In the summer, it is perfect for the deck, porch, or any place where you have 1½x3 feet of space to spare. The greenhouse top is optional—depending on unpredictable weather conditions in your area, insects, and your preferences. In fall and winter, the compact unit moves to a sunny window location indoors.

Made of kiln-dried redwood, the planters consist of two stacked boxes that fit snugly together. The sides are 2x12s attached to a half-inch plywood base. The lower compartments work as water/nutrient reservoirs; the uppers are filled with growing medium. Both compartments are lined with 20-mil vinyl.

The right side of the growing bed is boxed in to house the pump and to make adding nutrients easier. A cover with a half-inch grooved perimeter fits over the opening to prevent excessive evaporation. The nutrient solution is automatically pumped through twice a day.

Because roots don't have to stretch for food, less space is required than in conventional gardening.

Plants are watered daily with a nutrient solution.

For a compact unit, try perlite as growing medium.

Miniature varieties work best in small spaces.

Try a New Kind of Gardening

Start with a simple hydroponic setup, and your interest will grow as plants flourish. The systems shown on these pages are inexpensive but vary in the time they will require to put your mini-farm together.

The least expensive hydroponic system is also the easiest to operate. In fact, your children may become experts in hydroponics with this beginner's special. Fill an ordinary flowerpot with perlite. Add the young, sturdy plant, gently covering bare roots with the perlite. Pour a cup of nutrient solution through the perlite once or twice a day, depending on the strength of the solution, and catch the drainage in a bowl. The solution can be reused for a week. (Old solution may be used on the lawn or garden.) Although hydroponic gardening is not completely free of problems, you won't have to fertilize regularly to get healthy plants.

If you're more adventurous, try one of these other ways of applying the nutrient solution.

Siphon-feed method

A variation of the basic watering method described above makes plant care almost automatic, allowing you to leave plants unattended for several days at a time. Place a container (such as a glass jug, available from wine-maker supply stores, or an old thermos jug with spigot at the bottom) of nutrient solution above the plant container's soil level, and connect tubing so liquid can be either gravity-fed or siphoned (see illustration at right). A clamp (such as those available from sickroom supply stores and some hardware or automotive equipment stores) attached to the tubing will regulate the flow; this way just the right amount of solution goes through. Be sure to set the planter on a tray or something similar to catch drips.

Bucket and tray method

Siphon-feed method

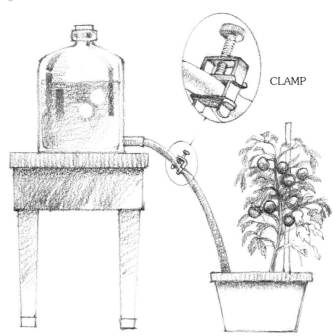

CLAMP

Wick system

Here's another way to escape daily watering. This system provides feeding through the bottom of the planter, using wicks dipped in a container of the nutrient solution. The wicks or cords should be made of synthetic fiber, either nylon, rayon, or polyester. First, test the wick to see whether it draws moisture up its entire length by placing the end of a six-inch cord into water.

The end of the wick inserted into the artificial soil should be spread out on the bottom of the plant container so nutrients will be distributed evenly throughout. The wick then is passed through the drainage hole into the second receptacle filled with the solution. For best results, place the container of nutrient solution directly underneath the planter. Several wicks can be used to supply the solution to the plants; simply drill holes in the bottom of the planter. The wicks will carry the solution up to keep the medium moist.

Soluble salts from the water in the nutrient solution will build up gradually in the growing medium because of evaporation. This will eventually inhibit plant growth. To avoid the problem, clean the grow-ing medium thoroughly every few months by running tap water through the medium several times.

Bucket and tray method

A quick and easy way to provide daily saturations of nutrient solution is to connect the bottom of a pail to the bottom of a plant box or tray with half-inch plastic tubing (see illustration at left). Seal the connections with silicone rubber cement. Cover the drainage holes of the plant box with a piece of netting before adding the plants and the growing medium. Fill the pail with the liquid food. Once a day, lift the pail above soil level until the surface of the growing medium becomes well dampened. Then lower the bucket so excess solution can drain back into the pail.

Remember that the nutrient solution should be shielded from light, so algae and other organisms don't spoil the mixture.

Pump and timer method

An entirely automatic system can be built using an aquarium pump and a household timer. The timer triggers the release of the nutrient solution from a sealed reservoir into the growing tray or planter.

Connect a plastic dishpan to a five-gallon plastic gas can (used for the reservoir) with flexible half-inch tubing (see illustration below). Apply silicone rubber cement to make the openings around the tubing airtight. Run the tubing to the bottom of the sealed reservoir. Next, attach the aquarium pump to the top of the reservoir with aquarium tubing. Seal the connections with silicone rubber cement. By plugging the air pump into the timer and setting it for a two-hour "on" cycle every 24 hours, you'll have an easy-care setup for a crop of vegetables or flowers.

Remember to cover the planter's drainage hole with netting. Then add the rooting medium. Pour the solution through the dishpan

planter to fill the reservoir.

When the timer turns on, air will blow into the reservoir, forcing the solution into the planter. The solution will drain back into the reservoir when the timer is turned off. Add new solution every two weeks. The used solution can be poured around outdoor plants.

Recycling drip system

In this system (see illustration at right), nutrient solution is pumped up through the growing medium from a reservoir in the bottom of the planter. However, unlike the pump and timer method, this procedure does not require the timer or sealed reservoir. The solution is pumped up by an aquarium pump with a bubbler valve submerged in the solution. This valve sends solution, plus air bubbles, up to the top of the

Recycling drip system

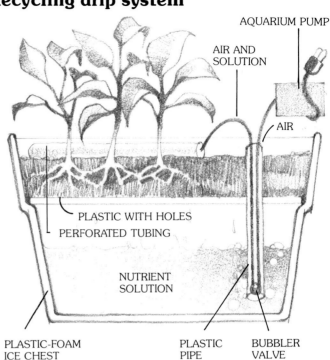

AQUARIUM PUMP

AIR AND SOLUTION

AIR

PLASTIC WITH HOLES

PERFORATED TUBING

NUTRIENT SOLUTION

PLASTIC-FOAM ICE CHEST

PLASTIC PIPE

BUBBLER VALVE

growing medium, where it continuously drips through, returning to the reservoir through drainage holes.

Build this low-cost system with two stacked pans, or use a plastic-foam ice chest. To use an ice chest, cut a piece of one-eighth-inch-thick plastic sheeting to work as a second bottom; fit it where the ice chest narrows. Then run a piece of plastic pipe (about two inches around) through a hole drilled in the plastic insert. Make drainage holes in the insert at the same time. Cover the insert with window screen, and fill the top growing space with perlite. Next, add solution until the reservoir below is full.

Insert the bubbler valve into the tube, and connect one end to the aquarium pump. Connect the other to a piece of perforated half-inch tubing. Lay the tubing along the top of the growing medium. Holes in the tubing permit the nutrient solution to spread evenly.

Plug in the aquarium pump, and you're ready to grow. The solution will rise and drip out across the growing medium.

Add new solution each week to replace that which evaporates.

Every two or three months, pump the old solution into a bucket and use outdoors in the garden. Replace the fluid in the reservoir.

Hydroponic hints

• The secret of getting the biggest crops from your hydroponic garden is to keep planting. Seedlings should be started and ready for transplanting into the unit.

• Sow seeds of leaf lettuce, spinach, or some of the miniature vegetables in small hydroponic setups. Cherry tomatoes work well, as do chives, thyme, oregano, and parsley.

• Start houseplant cuttings in a pot or flat filled with growing medium, such as moist vermiculite. When roots form, transplant to the hydroponic system.

• In the late winter, use your hydroponic garden to start seeds of flowers to be transplanted outdoors when the weather turns warm.

• You can use nursery-started transplants in your hydroponic system. Remember to remove all soil from the roots by gently rinsing them before you replant.

Pump and timer method

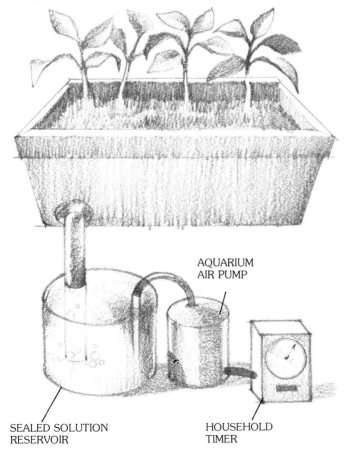

AQUARIUM AIR PUMP

SEALED SOLUTION RESERVOIR

HOUSEHOLD TIMER

Indoor Gardening

In the expanse of backyard soil, all the elements crucial to healthy plants achieve a balance on their own. But the greenhouse gardener who scoops up backyard soil for a flowerpot faces a host of challenges. Ventilation, soil, water, humidity all must be managed.

Because a pot in a greenhouse is practically suspended in midair, there isn't a water table to offer additional moisture when the weather is dry. At the same time, because clay pots are porous, moisture rapidly leaves the soil and plant. Air circulation is reduced to near zero, and temperature fluctuations are dramatically flattened out. So you have to step in and, through proper greenhouse management, supply these conditions artificially.

Heat. What separates the greenhouse from other kinds of growing is the need for artificial heat. In more temperate regions, heat built up from a full day of sun will be enough to carry plants through dips in temperature during the night. The sun, of course, is a critical heat source in northern locations, but cloud covers and drastic drops in temperature at night make supplementary heating necessary. Some greenhouse buffs further protect their collections with a battery-operated alarm system that sounds when the temperature becomes too low or too high. In addition, many keep a backup oil heater on hand should the power fail or regular heater malfunction.

Traditional methods of getting heat to the greenhouse include tapping the home heating system or using a gas-fired space heater or an electric heater. Because keeping plants warm is by far the most expensive aspect of greenhouse gardening, the lean-to design is especially attractive. Once attached to the house, it's simple to add a separately controlled heating extension—provided the present home system is not already operating at peak capacity.

Gas heaters are efficient, compact, and fairly inexpensive to operate, but the exhaust must be vented outside. Uncombusted fumes can be deadly to plants and humans. Electric heating is more than adequate but may be expensive in those areas where rates are high.

Solar heating relies exclusively on the tremendous energy flow from the sun. With proper collection and storage, it's possible to heat part of your home, as well as the greenhouse.

Heating a greenhouse, whether lean-to or freestanding, is a tricky business. Mistakes in planning may lead to unplanned expenses later, not only in the form of high fuel bills, but also in lost plants. For best results, get expert advice from a greenhouse manufacturer.

Whatever system you choose, keep greenhouse management chores from causing headaches by installing the proper thermostatic controls. Specially designed thermostats will keep conditions at almost the exact levels you want. Remember to place the thermostat in a central location and keep it shaded from the direct rays of the sun. For economical operation, settings should be maintained at the minimum night temperatures required for the plants you plan to grow. If the frigid winds of winter make heating difficult, take steps to insulate wherever possible.

Ventilation. Ironically, too much heat can be as much of a problem as too little. A bright, unobstructed sun burning from sunrise to sunset can turn the greenhouse into a steam room. As a result, some way to ventilate excess heat must be provided. Most greenhouses are equipped with hinged ridge panels, powered by a motor or operated by hand. Because temperatures will fluctuate, thermostatically controlled motors can prevent overheating automatically—whether you are there or not.

But too much heat is not the only reason for proper ventilation. Good air circulation, even during the winter months, increases the supply of carbon dioxide to plant leaves and stems, prevents the spread of disease, and contributes to the even distribution of heat. Small vents can be installed under the benches to allow fresh outside air to enter. Remember, though, that strong drafts can affect plants adversely. It's also a good idea to put screening material over all vents so insects won't invade the greenhouse.

Some form of shading, especially during spring and summer, can be an effective way to keep excessive heat under control. Reflective paint, colored plastic film, or slatted curtains are easy to install and provide relief from intense sunlight. If the greenhouse will be used in summer, some form of air conditioning may be necessary when temperatures are not sufficiently reduced by shading and ventilation.

Water. The greenhouse is an isolated environment encased in glass. This means the normal sources of water are not present. As a result, the greenhouse gardener must know how and when to provide moisture. However, the needs of plants vary. Some, originating in dry, arid regions, have developed a built-in resistance to drought. Others, such as African violets, are accustomed to the luxury of damp, tropical soil.

There are several ways to tell just how thirsty a plant is. The most obvious sign is wilting. If the leaves begin to droop, it's time to water. Or inspect the soil surface. If it is dry to the touch when you scratch a half inch or so beneath the surface, a thorough watering is needed. Old hands at plant care often can tell when to water by the color of the soil or by the sound of the pot when it's tapped with the knuckles.

Here are some important tips for watering:
- Schedule watering for the morning, so plants can dry off before nightfall. Wet plants exposed to cooler temperatures at night are more susceptible to disease. Watering in the morning also means plants get moisture during daylight hours when they grow most.
- On bright, sunny days, the loss of water through evaporation and transpiration is greater than on cloudy days. Give plants an extra dose on bright days, and hold back a little on dark days.
- Coarse, sandy soil cannot retain moisture as well as humus-rich, well-structured soil. Watering may have to be more frequent for sandy soil, so check pots often.
- Keep water from collecting on leaves, where disease could get a foothold.
- Keep in mind that plants prefer too little water to too much. Roots stuck in swampy soil will suffocate.
- During the winter, cold water directly from the tap may be so cold it will shock roots into temporary inactivity. Although plants look doomed, they often will recover.

Keeping a careful watch on temperature is one key to good management.

pots. Capillary action pulls water up into the soil. The amount of water supplied can be regulated by increasing or decreasing the distance between water source and plant containers. Flats are usually kept no more than four inches above the reservoir pans, while pots may be as far as eight inches away.

For catering to the needs of individual plants, nothing beats watering by hand.

Humidity. There is more to watering than simply pouring water on soil. Plants lose moisture through small openings in their leaves at a surprising rate. Trouble is, if the air is too dry, more water will be lost than can be taken in by the roots. An imbalance results, and the plant begins to droop. To prevent the loss of too much water, the ideal relative humidity is between 50 and 70 percent. To keep track of air quality, place a hygrometer (humidity indicator) in a protected place. When moisture drops, replace it by sprinkling walks and floor, syringing or misting plants, installing a portable humidifier, or placing pans of water under benches.

Keeping bugs in check. Nothing is more inviting to a horde of insects than a greenhouse that has been allowed to become a jungle of sickly, mold-infested plants. Prevention is the best way to keep pests at bay; a healthy, thriving plant is less inviting.

Start by managing the greenhouse correctly. Try these hints.
● Keep benches and all work areas clean. After potting or fertilizing, remove spilled soil and liquids.
● Remove and destroy dead leaves and spent blossoms.
● Give plants plenty of room to prevent overcrowding and poor ventilation.
● If an infested plant has no hope of survival, suppress sentimental attachments and throw it out. A terminally ill plant will only threaten the well-being of other plants.
● At least once a year (preferably during the summer when plants can be moved outside), give the greenhouse a thorough cleaning.

Getting rid of insects doesn't always require a battery of devastating sprays or chemicals. Most can

be easily controlled, if detected early enough, by simply spraying with water or by dunking the affected plant into a bath of mild soap (not detergent) and water and then rinsing. If these initial methods fail, use an organically derived pesticide, such as rotenone or pyrethrum. Both are nonresidual and relatively safe. For a small greenhouse, a hanging insecticide strip or two placed near plants usually can provide all the control you need. When insects threaten, follow these remedies:
● **Aphids.** Small, soft-bodied insects that cluster on the undersides of leaves and near tender leaf and flower buds, aphids can be discouraged by spraying plants with a forceful stream of water. Or dunk plants gently into a tub of mild soapy water, and rinse. For severe infestations, spray plants, especially undersides of leaves, with rotenone or pyrethrum.
● **Whitefly.** A telltale sign of whitefly attack is a cloud of white specks that appears when you jostle the plant. Fuchsia, geranium, basil, coleus, and tomato are some of the susceptible plants. Rotenone or malathion, if used regularly, will effectively control the whitefly.
● **Spider mites.** Difficult to see because of their small size, mites can be detected by the wispy webs located at leaf axils. Thorough control is not easy, and sometimes it's best to dispose of the plant. If you decide to spray, use a miticide labeled for the purpose. If infestation isn't severe, a weekly bath in lukewarm, soapy water is often effective. Rinse with clear water.
● **Mealybugs.** Cotton-like clumps on flower stems or in leaf axils signal the presence of mealybugs. Use malathion as directed by the manufacturer. Dabbing each mealybug with a cotton swab and rubbing alcohol is also effective, though tedious with large plants or heavy infestations. Rinse with clear water.

Keep in mind that a languid plant doesn't mean insects are necessarily the culprit. In many cases, poor cultural practices—water, fertilizer, light, pollution—are to blame. Inspect the plant carefully, and identify the trouble before trying to correct it.

Avoid shocking roots by mixing warm water with cold. Ideal temperature is around 60 degrees Fahrenheit.
● Because they are non-porous, plastic pots retain water better than porous clay pots. Consequently, fewer waterings are necessary.
● If a garden hose is fastened to the faucet, prevent the soil from spattering by using a water bubbler attachment or misting device.

With the wide variety of greenhouse accessories available, watering can be fully automated and temperature controlled. Water can be misted, applied directly to the surface, or irrigated from un-

derneath. For overhead or surface watering, mist nozzles are installed on vertical pipes attached to a feeder pipe located along the perimeter of the bed. A solenoid valve activated by a timer allows you to make watering fully automatic. Overhead misting is useful for the cutting or propagating bed. For seedlings or mature plants, surface watering is best because foliage generally needs to remain dry to avoid disease.

An uncomplicated, inexpensive way to maintain soil moisture is through the wick system. Wick material suspended in water reservoirs is inserted into flats or individual

Soil for Greenhouse Plants

One of the most important parts of a plant is the part you seldom see: the roots. Without that fuzzy network of white shoots and tiny, almost invisible root hairs, nothing would happen above ground. Below ground, hundreds of processes are taking place. Air and water alternately occupy pore spaces, bacteria reduce organic matter to manageable dimensions, and roots are constantly trading useless ions for nutrient ions.

A good greenhouse soil will be open and friable (easily crumbled) enough to allow air to penetrate and, at the same time, permit water to drain freely. It is spongy so a constant supply of moisture will be on hand for plants. The soil also functions as a nutrient storehouse where plant food is kept available and provides a means of physical support for the plant.

Some gardeners make a lifetime avocation of juggling soil ingredients to come up with the ideal mixture for each plant. But experts have found that most plants grow well in a single basic mix. The time-honored formula calls for two parts soil, one part peat moss and one part perlite, coarse sand, or vermiculite. Many succulents need a different mix; see the photograph below. Because "damping off" (see Chapter 16, "Insects and Diseases") can make a shambles of your seedlings, sterilize any soil brought in from the garden. Place a pan of soil in an oven set at 200 degrees Fahrenheit, and bake for 45 minutes. Because sterilization can be a nuisance and thorough mixing somewhat tricky, it may be worth the extra expense to buy premixed (and sterile) soil at a garden supply center. Several have been developed to provide all your plants will need for initial growth.

Potting ins and outs. There are all kinds of pots, from plain to fancy, but a good pot must have three essential features: a sturdy receptacle for soil, a place for water to go in, and a place for excess water to drain.

Often, a gardener's first impulse is to throw a bunch of soil into the nearest container and then plunge a plant into the soil. But proper size is crucial. A medium-size plant faced with an excess of nutrient-rich soil in a too-large pot may produce only roots at the expense of stem, leaves, flowers, and fruit. Some plants prefer

For cactus and other succulent plants, try a soil mixture of equal parts coarse sand, sterilized potting soil, and leaf mold. Sand helps keep them drained.

having slightly crowded roots, but if the plant seems to be languishing, carefully remove it from its pot by knocking the rim against a counter. Turn the pot upside down with your hand over the soil and around the stem. If the rootball is a solid mass and soil is hardly visible, repot.

Garden variety pots range in size from two to 18 inches (diameter of the inside rim). From two to seven inches, the sizes increase in half-inch increments; from seven to 12 inches, in one-inch increments. Beyond 12 inches, pots are generally available in 14-, 16-, and 18-inch sizes.

Materials vary almost as much as size. Clay, or terra-cotta, is the traditional material. But plastic is making great strides because it retains moisture and is lightweight, unbreakable, and less expensive. Die-hard gardeners, however, swear allegiance to clay, citing porosity and more pleasing appearance as the chief advantages.

Once seedlings have lost their baby or cotyledon leaves, young plants should be planted in two- or 2½-inch pots and placed in a sunny location. Be sure small stones or broken crockery are placed in the bottom of the pot, so good drainage is assured. As plants develop, they can be shifted to larger pots. As a rule of thumb, a plant's new quarters should be no more than two inches larger than its previous one.

Feeding know-how. For the greenhouse, both dry and wet forms of fertilizer are used. The dry is usually mixed with the growing medium, while the wet is diluted with water and applied with a watering can or by a special attachment to a garden hose. "Slow-release" fertilizers are valuable because their nutrients are released gradually, providing a little at a time.

Keep in mind, though, that fertilizer comes in concentrated form. Too much is worse than too little. If over-applied, it can burn roots and stems or result in plants that produce all leaves and no blossoms or fruits.

As you become more and more familiar with your plants and how they look when hungry or dried out, you can adjust your feeding schedule to individual needs.

Here are some hints to keep in mind:

● Make sure the soil is moist before applying fertilizer. If soil is dry, plant food can burn roots.

● Mix fertilizer at half strength for plants that demand less feeding, such as geraniums and most herbs.

● Do not fertilize dormant plants. Most growing things lapse into a period of inactivity when days shorten and nights lengthen. (Christmas cactus is a notable exception.) When days begin to lengthen, plants renew activity and will welcome a fertilizer.

● Avoid the buildup of salts (whitish deposits on soil and pot rims) by periodically "leaching." To leach, drench soil with tepid water until excess runs out at bottom. If deposits are heavy, repeat two or three times at half-hour intervals.

HOME GREENHOUSE PLANT GUIDE

PLANT	GREENHOUSE TEMPERATURE AND WHEN TO START PLANTS*		
Annuals/Perennials	**Cool** Night minimum: 40-45°F. Day maximum: 55-60°F.	**Moderate** Night minimum: 50-55°F. Day maximum: 65-70°F.	**Warm** Night minimum: 62-65°F. Day maximum: 80-85°F.
Agapanthus	Seeds: March-April	Seeds: March-April	—
Ageratum	—	—	Seeds: July-August
Allamanda	—	—	Cuttings: March-April
Anemone	Seeds: May-June Bulbs: September-October	Seeds: May-June Bulbs: September-October	—
Aphelandra	Cuttings: March-April	Cuttings: March-June	Cuttings: March-June
Ardisia	—	Cuttings: March-June Seeds: May-June	Seeds and cuttings: March-June
Aster, China Callistephus chinensis	—	Seeds: July-October	—
Azalea Rhododendron sp.	Cuttings: July-December	Cuttings: July-December	Cuttings: November-December
Begonia Begonia sp.	Seeds: March-April	Seeds: January-April	Seeds: January-June
Bellflower, Italian Campanula isophylla	Cuttings: January-February	—	—
Bellis Bellis perennis	Seeds: July-August	Seeds: July-August	—
Beloperone Justicia sp.	Cuttings: March-April	Cuttings: March-December	Cuttings: March-June, September-December
Bloodleaf Iresine sp.	—	Cuttings: July-August	—
Blue lace flower Trachymene	—	Seeds: July-October	Seeds: January-February, September-October
Bougainvillea	—	Cuttings: May-June	Cuttings: May-June
Bouvardia	—	Cuttings: May-June	Cuttings: March-June
Browallia	Seeds: March-April	Seeds: March-June	Seeds and cuttings: January-February
Bulbs, Hardy (for forcing) Also see specific bulbs.	Bulbs: September-December	Bulbs: November-December	—
Caladium	Bulbs: March-April	Bulbs: November-December	Bulbs: March-April
Calceolaria	Seeds: January-February, July-December	Seeds: September-October	—

*NOTE: Most seeds like warm temperatures for germination. Once seedlings are established, they should be moved to a location with the proper temperature.

HOME GREENHOUSE PLANT GUIDE (continued)

PLANT	GREENHOUSE TEMPERATURE AND WHEN TO START PLANTS		
Annuals/Perennials	**Cool** Night minimum: 40-45°F. Day maximum: 55-60°F.	**Moderate** Night minimum: 50-55°F. Day maximum: 65-70°F.	**Warm** Night minimum: 62-65°F. Day maximum: 80-85°F.
Calendula Calendula officinalis	Seeds: January-February, July-December	Seeds: January-February, July-August	—
Calla lily Zantedeschia sp.	—	Bulbs: January-February, September-October	Bulbs: March-April, September-October
Camellia	Seeds: May-June	Cuttings: July-August	Seeds: March-April
Campanula	—	Cuttings: January-February	—
Candytuft Iberis sempervirens	Seeds: January-February	Seeds: January-February, November-December	Seeds: November-December
Carnation Dianthus sp.	Seeds: January-February	Cuttings: January-February	—
Cathedral bells Cobaea scandens	Seeds: March-April	Seeds: March-April	—
Celosia Celosia sp.	—	Seeds: March-April	Seeds: January-February, July-August
Centaurea Centaurea montana	Seeds: July-December	Seeds: January-February, September-October	—
Cerastium Cerastium tomentosum	—	—	Cuttings: March-June
Chrysanthemum	Cuttings: January-February	Cuttings: May-June	—
Clerodendrum	—	Cutings: March-April	Cuttings: January-April
Coleus	Seeds and cuttings: March-April	Seeds: March-June Cuttings: March-April, July-August	Seeds: July-October Cuttings: March-April, September-October
Columnea	—	—	Cuttings: March-June
Crocus	—	Bulbs: September-October	—
Crossandra	—	Bulbs: September-October	—
Cuphea Cuphea	Seeds: March-April	Seeds: March-April	—
Cyclamen	—	Seeds: September-December Bulbs: July-August	Seeds: July-August, November-December
Daffodil Narcissus sp.	—	Bulbs: September-October	—
Delphinium	Seeds: September-October	—	—
Dimorphotheca	—	Seeds: July-August	—

PLANT	GREENHOUSE TEMPERATURE AND WHEN TO START PLANTS		
Annuals/Perennials	**Cool** Night minimum: 40-45°F. Day maximum: 55-60°F.	**Moderate** Night minimum: 50-55°F. Day maximum: 65-70°F.	**Warm** Night minimum: 62-65°F. Day maximum: 80-85°F.
Dipladenia *Mandevilla* sp.	—	Cuttings: March-April	Cuttings: March-April
Eranthemum	—	—	Cuttings: May-June
Exacum	—	Seeds: May-June	Seeds: May-June
Felicia *Felicia amelloides*	Seeds: January-February	Seeds: January-February, May-August Cuttings: May-June	—
Fuchsia		Cuttings: July-August	Cuttings: September-October
Gardenia	—	—	Cuttings: January-April
Gazania	—	Seeds: May-June	Seeds: May-June
Geranium *Pelargonium* sp.	—	Cuttings: May-October	—
Gerbera *Gerbera jamesoni*	—	Seeds: January-February	—
Godetia *Clarkia* sp.	—	Seeds: January-February, November-December	—
Gypsophila	Seeds: May-October	Seeds: January-February, May-October	Seeds: January-February
Haemanthus	—	Bulbs: March-April	—
Hibiscus	—	Seeds: January-April Cuttings: March-June	Cuttings: March-August
Hyacinth *Hyacinthus* sp.	—	Bulbs: September-October	—
Hydrangea	—	Cuttings: July-August	—
Impatiens	Seeds: March-April	Seeds: January-August Cuttings: July-October	Seeds: January-February
Iris, Spanish *Iris xiphium*	Bulbs: September-October	Bulbs: September-October	—
Ixia	—	Bulbs: September-December	—
Jasmine *Jasminum* sp.	Cuttings: March-April, September-October	Cuttings: September-October	—
Leadwort *Ceratostigma* *plumbaginoides*	—	—	Cuttings: May-August
Lobelia *Lobelia cardinalis, L. erinus*	Seeds: January-February	Seeds: January-February	Seeds: November-December

HOME GREENHOUSE PLANT GUIDE (continued)

PLANT	GREENHOUSE TEMPERATURE AND WHEN TO START PLANTS		
Annuals/Perennials	**Cool** Night minimum: 40-45°F. Day maximum: 55-60°F.	**Moderate** Night minimum: 50-55°F. Day maximum: 65-70°F.	**Warm** Night minimum: 62-65°F. Day maximum: 80-85°F.
Marigold *Tagetes* sp.	—	Seeds: January-February, September-October	Seeds: January-February
Mignonette *Reseda* sp.	Seeds: July-August	—	—
Morning-glory *Ipomoea* sp.	Seeds: March-April	Seeds: March-April	—
Myosotis or Forget-me-not *Myosotis* sp.	Seeds: May-August	Seeds: May-August	—
Nasturtium *Tropaeolum* sp.	—	Seeds: September-October	—
Nicotiana	—	Seeds: July-August	—
Nierembergia	Seeds: January-February	Seeds: January-February, November-December	Seeds: January-February
Oleander *Nerium oleander*	Seeds: May-June Cuttings: May-August	Seeds: July-August Cuttings: March-April, July-August	—
Ornithogalum	—	Bulbs: September-October	—
Oxalis	—	Bulbs: July-August November-December	—
Pansy *Viola* sp.	Seeds: January-February, May-August	—	—
Paper-white narcissus *Narcissus tazetta*	—	Bulbs: September-December	Bulbs: November-December
Passionflower *Passiflora* sp.	—	Cuttings: March-August	Cuttings: March-June
Petunia	—	Seeds: January-February, July- August, November-December Cuttings: September-October	—
Primrose *Primula* sp.	Seeds: March-April, July-August	Seeds: March-August	Seeds: May-August
Ranunculus	Bulbs: September-October	—	—
Reinwardtia	Seeds: March-April	Seeds: March-April	—
Rudbeckia	—	—	Seeds: March-April
Salpiglossis	—	Seeds: January-February, September-October	—

PLANT	GREENHOUSE TEMPERATURE AND WHEN TO START PLANTS		
Annuals/Perennials	**Cool** Night minimum: 40-45°F. Day maximum: 55-60°F.	**Moderate** Night minimum: 50-55°F. Day maximum: 65-70°F.	**Warm** Night minimum: 62-65°F. Day maximum: 80-85°F.
Salvia Salvia sp.	—	Cuttings: March-June Seeds: May-October	—
Schizanthus	Seeds: January-February, July-October	Seeds: January-February, July-October	—
Smithiantha	—	Seeds: May-June	Seeds: March-June
Snapdragon Antirrhinum sp.	Seeds: July-December	Seeds: January-February, July-December	—
Stephanotis Stephanotis floribunda	—	Cuttings: March-June	Cuttings: March-June
Stock Matthiola sp.	Seeds: September-October	Seeds: July-August	—
Streptocarpus	—	Seeds: March-April	Cuttings: March-April
Sweet pea Lathyrus odoratus	Seeds: January-February, July-December	Seeds: January-February	—
Throatwort Campanula trachelium	—	Cuttings: May-June	Cuttings: July-August
Tibouchina	Cuttings: March-April	Cuttings: March-June	—
Tuberose Polianthes tuberosa	—	—	Bulbs: January-February
Tuberous begonia Begonia x tuberhybrida	—	—	Bulbs: March-April
Ursinia Ursinia sp.	—	Seeds: July-October	—
Violet Viola sp.	Seeds: January-February	—	—
Wax begonia Begonia semperflorens— cultorum	—	—	Cuttings: September-October
Zinnia Zinnia sp.	—	—	Seeds: November-December
Houseplants	**Cool**	**Moderate**	**Warm**
Abutilon Abutilon sp.	Seeds: March-June Cuttings: September-October	Seeds: March-June Cuttings: September-October	—
Acalypha	—	—	Cuttings: March-June

HOME GREENHOUSE PLANT GUIDE (continued)

PLANT	GREENHOUSE TEMPERATURE AND WHEN TO START PLANTS		
Houseplants	**Cool** Night, minimum: 40-45°F. Day maximum: 55-60°F.	**Moderate** Night minimum: 50-55°F. Day maximum: 65-70°F.	**Warm** Night minimum: 62-65°F. Day maximum: 80-85°F.
Achimenes	Bulbs: March-April	Bulbs: March-April	Bulbs: March-April Seeds: November-December
African violet *Saintpaulia* sp.	—	—	Seeds: January-August, November-December Cuttings: July-October
Amaryllis	Seeds: March-April	Seeds: March-April	Bulbs: January-February, September-December
Anthurium	—	—	Seeds: March-April
Asparagus fern *Asparagus* sp.	Seeds: March-April	Seeds: March-April	—
Begonia	—	—	Seeds: November-December
Bird-of-paradise *Strelitzia reginae*	Seeds: March-April	Seeds: March-April	—
Cactus; other succulents	—	—	Seeds: March-June
Cineraria *Senecio* x *hybridus*	Seeds: May-October	Seeds: March-October	—
Clivia *Clivia miniata*	—	—	Seeds: March-June
Crassula	—	Cuttings: January-December	Cuttings: January-December
Croton *Codiaeum* sp.	Seeds or cuttings: March-April	Seeds: March-April	Cuttings: March-June
Crown-of-thorns *Euphorbia mili*	—	Cuttings: March-June	Cuttings: March-June
Cyclamen	—	Seeds: May-June, September-October	Seeds: July-August
Dracena	Cuttings: March-April	—	—
Echeveria *Echeveria* sp.	—	Cuttings: March-June	Cuttings: March-June
Episcia	—	—	Cuttings: March-April
Ferns (See Chapter 14, "Houseplants")			
Freesia	—	Bulbs: July-August, November-December	—
Gloxinia *Sinningia speciosa*	—	—	Seeds or bulbs: January- February

PLANT	GREENHOUSE TEMPERATURE AND WHEN TO START PLANTS		
Houseplants	**Cool** Night minimum: 40-45°F. Day maximum: 55-60°F.	**Moderate** Night minimum: 50-55°F. Day maximum: 65-70°F.	**Warm** Night minimum: 62-65°F. Day maximum: 80-85°F.
Hoya *Hoya carnosa*	—	Cuttings: March-June	Cuttings: March-June
Ixora	Cuttings: March-April	Cuttings: March-April	Cuttings: March-June
Kalanchoe *Kalanchoe blossfeldiana*	—	Seeds: January-February, May-August	Seeds: January-February May-August
Lantana *Lantana camara*	—	Cuttings: March-April, September-October	Cuttings: July-August
Maranta	—	Seeds: May-June	—
Palm (many species)	Seeds: March-April	Seeds: March-April	—
Peacock plant *Calathea sp.*	—	Seeds: May-June	—
Poinsettia *Euphorbia pulcherrima*	—	—	Cuttings: May-June
Spathiphyllum *Spathiphyllum clevelandi*	—	—	Seeds: March-April
Stevia *Piqueria trinervia*	Cuttings: May-June	Cuttings: March-April	—
Wandering Jew *Tradescantia sp.* or *Zebrina sp.*	Cuttings: March-June	Cuttings: March-June, September-October	Cuttings: May-August
Vegetables and Fruits	**Cool**	**Moderate**	**Warm**
Broccoli	Seeds: March-April	Seeds: March-April	—
Brussels sprouts	—	Seeds: May-June	—
Cabbage	—	Seeds: January-February	—
Celery	—	Seeds: January-February	—
Citrus	Seeds: March-April	Seeds: March-April Cuttings: May-June	Cuttings: May-June
Eggplant	Seeds: March-April	Seeds: March-April	Seeds: March-April
Head lettuce	Seeds: January-February	—	—
Pepper, Garden	Seeds: March-April	Seeds: March-April	Seeds: March-April
Pepper, Ornamental *Piper ornatum*	Seeds: March-April	Seeds: March-April	—
Tomato	Seeds: March-April	Seeds: March-April	Seeds: March-April

chapter 16

INSECTS AND DISEASES

One frustration of raising a home garden is damage, loss, and annoyance caused by insects and plant diseases. It is a normal part of the intricate world of living communities that plants are attacked by insects and plant diseases. There are thousands of insects and diseases that may attack growing things. But it is unlikely the home gardener will encounter more than a few of them during a season.

The yard and garden have the same cycles and changes experienced in all of nature. The plants, insects, and diseases all are influenced by each other and by other factors, such as rainfall, humidity, temperatures, parasites, and pathogens. One of the major determinants in garden production and pest problems is our own activity. Often, we can be our garden's worst enemy by inadvertently limiting the health and vigor of our plants or by promoting pests through the wrong practices. However, we can also work with nature and manage the garden ecosystem for a successful harvest.

One of the first lessons is not to panic at the sight of pests. Many of us have a low tolerance for pests (especially insects) and will take hasty—and often inappropriate—actions. The loss of a portion of the leaf or the root system does not usually kill the plant and will probably not significantly reduce the harvest. Gardeners with a wise attitude about insect pests and diseases adopt the philosophy of "planting a little extra for the bugs!"

Garden Pests

Pest management encompasses all activities for reducing damage and losses caused by insects, plant diseases, weeds, and nematodes. It is an attitude about pests and pest control in the garden that reflects an understanding of the interrelationships of factors in the environment. As experienced gardeners know, it's impractical to eradicate every pest.

Many factors determine the number of pests and the damage they will cause. The aim of pest management is to use gardening techniques that will reduce their numbers. This way, loss and inconvenience are limited, while yield and enjoyment are increased.

Pest management helps to prevent and cure insect and disease problems. Often, the preventive portion of the program is the most important. But sometimes early detection of problems is just as critical. A regular inspection of the garden and yard is the surest way to discover a problem in time to try effective controls. Know what to look for, when specific problems may appear, and how to recognize signs of damage. Consider alternatives and evaluate consequences.

Many of the problems attributed to insects or diseases are not caused by them at all. Yellowing, discoloration, wilting, stunting, and curling or deformation of the plant foliage *may* be symptoms of another common problem, such as nutrient deficiency; toxic chemicals (air pollution, some pesticides, salts, or too much fertilizer); lack of water or too much water; too much sunlight or not enough; or frost damage. Of course, there is no response to usual pest treatment. Some can be corrected (with more water, for example), but others can't. Yield may be reduced or the garden ruined.

Pest management activities can be divided into chemical and nonchemical categories. Some people interpret pest management to mean "pesticide elimination." Although one goal of a home garden pest management program is to reduce the use of pesticides as much as possible, insecticides and fungicides will likely remain a part of any pest management system.

Nonchemical control

Nonchemical control (both prevention and cure) includes cultural, biological, and mechanical activities. Cultural control involves our manipulation of the plants' environment to reduce the chance of pests surviving and reproducing. It also means limiting the amount of damage caused by their attack. First, though, cultural control requires maintaining good plant health and vigor. Plant health is dependent on many factors. Moisture (proper watering conservation techniques, such as mulching) and available soil nutrients (proper fertilization) are under our control.

Selection of proper plant varieties can reduce pest problems. Plant only species and varieties adapted to your area, climate, and soil type. Where possible, choose varieties labeled as resistant to insect and disease attack. When buying plants for transplanting, carefully inspect for insects and diseases. Look for certified disease-free seeds and plants.

Other gardening activities can influence pest populations, too. For example, plant rotation is an important way to prevent buildup of insects and disease organisms. In most cases, allow three years between plantings of a certain vegetable in any one spot.

Sanitation and weed control can influence pest numbers. Many insects survive on weeds and tall grasses in and around the garden, then attack the growing crops. Garden residues, such as stems, leaves, or unusable fruit, may harbor insects or disease and should be plowed under, composted, or burned as soon as the harvest is complete. If they've been treated with insecticide, burn the refuse or bag it for garbage pickup.

Interplanting, or growing certain plants next to each other, can sometimes reduce pest problems. Certain planting combinations or companion plantings tend to have fewer problems. For example, chives and garlic planted near lettuce and peas may discourage aphids, while radishes in cucumber hills are unpleasant for striped or spotted cucumber beetles.

Biological control involves the use of natural enemies to eliminate part of the pest population. Natural enemies of insects include predators, parasites, and pathogens. Some birds, toads, mantids, and lady beetles are well-known predators. Lesser-known predators include the lacewings, ground beetles, syrphid flies, and spiders. Learning to recognize them and promote their existence is an important step in pest management.

A parasite is an insect that lives part of its life inside another insect, eventually killing the host. Often, there is no external evidence of the parasite until the host-pest dies. Some parasites leave clues; the braconid wasps, for example, leave white, egg-shaped wasp cocoons attached to the back of the parasitized caterpillar.

Other parasitic wasps include the trichogramma wasps (tiny, but effective, parasites of insect eggs) and the ichneumonid wasps. The stinger of these small wasps is used only to insert the eggs into the host. They do not sting people, as do the more familiar paper and mud dauber wasps. But even these stinging wasps are beneficial in the yard and garden; the females capture and paralyze caterpillars to provide food for their offspring. Many flies, such as the tachinids, are valuable as parasites of insects, too.

Use of pathogens to combat pests is a part of pest management. There are many disease-causing organisms occurring in nature that work to our benefit. Among the bacteria, fungi, viruses, and nematodes are many that attack garden pests, especially insects, causing them to sicken or die. This type of biological or natural control is often referred to as microbial control.

There are a few commercially available pathogens that can supplement the naturally existing controls of some pests. For example, the bacterium, *Bacillus thuringiensis,* causes disease in moth and butterfly caterpillars. The material is effective after caterpillars eat foliage coated with the bacteria spores. Another bacteria product causes milky spore disease in white grubs.

Mechanical control is simply attacking the pest directly. In our fascination with technology, we often overlook the simplicity of picking off insect pests with our fingers, or using traps and barriers to stop them. When only a few plants are involved and when infestations are not too heavy, remove insects or diseased leaves with your fingers, and discard the pest. To prevent transmitting plant disease pathogens, wash your hands and avoid touching healthy plants. For many insect problems, a stream of water from the hose will dislodge enough insects to reduce the population.

By knowing the habits of insect pests, you may be able to keep them away from your crop or capture them before they do much damage. Barriers, such as screens or coverings, are other ways to keep insects from reaching the plants.

Chemical control

Sooner or later, you may have to apply pesticides to get the yield you want. However, you can reduce their use if you follow the techniques described above.

When you do use pesticides, be careful to use the proper material for the problem. The pesticides currently available are safe and effective when used as directed. Carefully follow the directions on the label to mix and apply them.

The directions will specify the plants that can be treated, the rate of mixing and application, safety precautions to follow, and the time you need to wait between application and harvest. Read and follow the directions each time the pesticide is used.

Specific recommendations on particular insecticides and fungicides are not included in the following descriptions of insects and diseases or their control. Garden pest management is a rapidly changing scene, due to changes in legislation, regulations, and registrations relating to pesticides; development of new products and techniques; breeding of new pest-resistant plant varieties; and discovery of nonchemical control activities practical for use in the home garden. The gardener has to stay abreast of these rapid changes.

Sources of current garden pest control recommendations and information about pests and pest management include: Federal and State Departments of Agriculture, the Cooperative Extension Service (headquartered at your state land-grant university, with local offices in nearly every county), newspaper and magazine gardening columns, and garden supply stores.

Dragonflies

Dragonflies are both lovely and beneficial. As they fly, their legs form basket-like nets to capture small insects. Young dragonflies also consume vast quantities of mosquitoes and other water insects.

Lady Beetles

Probably the best-known of the garden benefactors is the lady beetle, ladybug, or ladybird. One of the more common varieties has 12 or 13 spots on its reddish back. Both the adult and larva eat large amounts of soft-bodied insects, such as aphids, mealybugs, leafhoppers, and scale insects.

Controlling Foliage Diseases

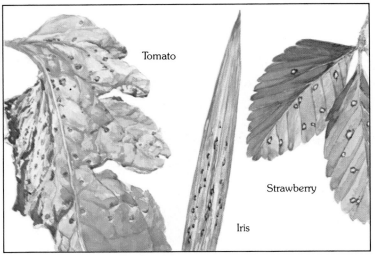

Tomato

Iris

Strawberry

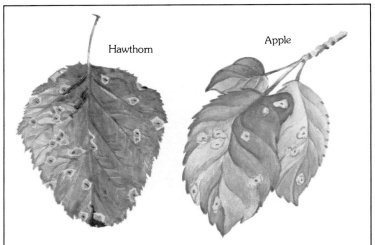

Hawthorn

Apple

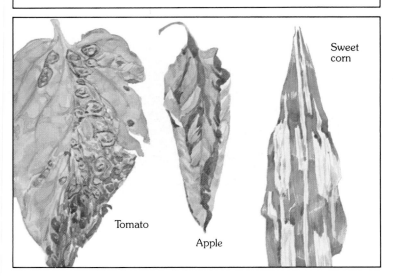

Tomato

Apple

Sweet corn

Leaf spots

Leaf spot diseases attack practically all plants, especially those in more humid regions. Spots appear on lower leaves and progress upward. Spots may later enlarge and run together, forming leaf blights. Spots usually have light centers and dark margins. Infected leaves may be killed or drop early.

Control with general sanitation, such as collecting and burning fallen leaves. Plant rotation is also useful. Use of recommended fungicides must begin soon after the disease strikes.

Rusts

Rust diseases are caused by highly specialized fungi. Some complete their life cycle on one plant (for example, hollyhock rust, raspberry rust, and asparagus rust). Other rusts require two different and alternating hosts (such as white pines and currants or junipers and apples).

Rusts are not reddish discolorations of the leaf but are, instead, the rust-colored spores present in powdery pustules or gelatinous-like horns. The rusts appear on the leaves, twigs, or fruits, causing the leaves to deform or drop off prematurely.

Control by repeated application of recommended fungicides, beginning at the first sign of rust. Destroy alternate hosts that you don't need, and you may be able to stop the cycle. Plant resistant varieties when available.

Leaf blight

Leaf blights are caused by a wide variety of pathogens. They are characterized by a sudden and conspicuous wilting and death of leaves and shoots. Blights progress more rapidly in humid, wet weather.

Control is the same as for leaf spots. Thorough application of fungicide spray is essential, especially to undersides of leaves.

Shot hole

Shot hole occurs when leaf spots drop out, giving the leaf a ragged appearance. It's common on stone fruits and may be caused by fungi, bacteria, or viruses. Control as for leaf spots.

Leaf and bud nematodes

Leaf and bud nematodes are microscopic roundworms that attack many plant species—especially strawberries, ferns, chrysanthemums, and lilies. Nematode injury may occur on flowers, leaves, stems, and roots. It appears as malformation, stunting, or galls.

Control by purchasing disease-free plants and resistant varieties. Destroy infected plant parts and rotate plantings.

Potato

Cherry

Smuts

Smuts generally produce dusty, irregular, sooty black spore masses on leaves, stems, flowers, and seeds. They are common on corn, onions, and certain grasses. Plants may be stunted, with withering of affected parts.

To control, cut and destroy infected plants. Do not use diseased material in compost. On onions, start with disease-free transplants, and rotate from areas where disease has occurred. Use resistant sweet corn hybrids and maintain plant vigor.

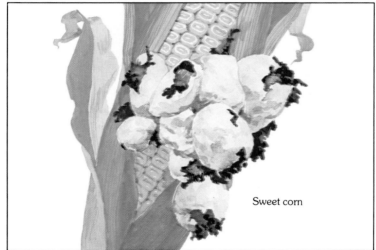

Sweet corn

Leaf galls and curls

Leaf galls are swellings caused by bacteria, fungi, viruses, and insects. They're common on azaleas, rhododendrons, and camellias. Handpick and burn the affected plant parts.

Leaf curl, also called leaf blister, is a yellow to red arched, curled, puckered, or distorted leaf that will drop early. The curls are common on peach and plum trees where fruits become swollen and bladder-like. Dormant oil spray and other recommended sprays are often effective. Remove and destroy affected leaves.

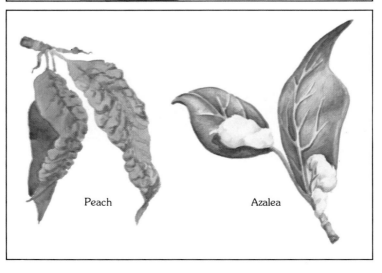

Peach

Azalea

Controlling Foliage Diseases

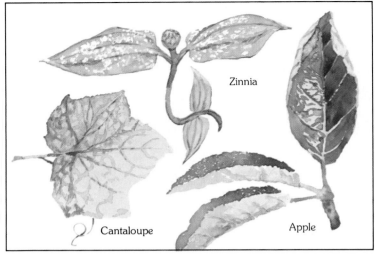

Zinnia

Cantaloupe

Apple

Powdery or downy mildews

Powdery or downy mildews are flour-like patches on the surface of leaves, buds, young stems, and fruits. They cause dwarfing, stunting, and deformation. The mildews are common on roses, zinnias, phlox, lilacs, cucurbits, apples, and grapes in shaded, crowded areas.

To control, avoid crowding to improve air circulation and reduce shade. Control weeds that harbor the disease. Apply recommended fungicides.

Pine

Linden

Apple

Sooty mold

Sooty mold shows as black blotches on surface of leaves, stems, and fruits, following attack by sap-feeding insects (see pages 530 to 533). Mold grows on the honeydew secreted by these insects, and control is directed at the insects, rather than the resulting mold.

Mosaics

Mottled leaves of yellow and light or dark green are the symptoms of mosaics. Plants are often stunted. Flowering and fruiting are reduced. Leaves often are cupped or distorted. Hundreds of different plants are attacked.

Control the virus-transmitting insects (such as aphids and leafhoppers), and destroy infected plants. Plant certified, virus-free seed or resistant varieties.

Squash

Apple

Ring spot

Ring spot is a virus disease characterized by rings, spots, or irregular patterns on young foliage. Plant growth and fruit set are often reduced. Ring spot is common on dahlia, delphinium, tomato, peony, and cabbage plants. Spotted wilt—a virus common in western states—is found on many vegetables and ornamentals. Control as for mosaics.

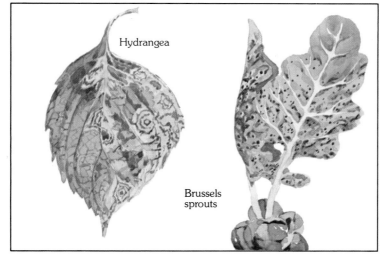

Hydrangea

Brussels sprouts

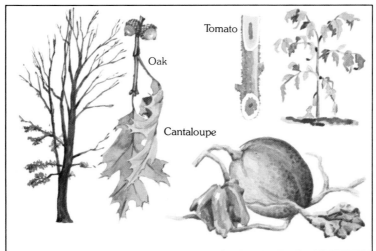

Oak

Tomato

Cantaloupe

Wilts

Wilts cause part or all of the plant to droop, often yellow, wither, and die. The plant may die gradually or rapidly. Water-conducting tissues often become discolored and nonfunctional, causing permanent wilting and death. Wilts may be the result of insect damage (borers or root feeders) or may be caused by certain viruses, bacteria, or fungi.

To control, use disease-free planting stock, and destroy infected plants. Control wilts by controlling insect vectors (those playing a part in the spread of wilt, such as flea beetles or cucumber beetles). Use wilt-resistant varieties and a three- or four-year plant rotation. Avoid wounding the plant. Destroy plant residue.

Yellows

Yellows are due to various causes, including lack of soil nutrients, crown or root rot, insects, fungi, and viruses. Virus-yellows cause plants to be stunted and to have yellow, bunchy growth. Flowers may be greenish, aborted, or lacking altogether.

Yellows occur frequently on asters, chrysanthemums, lettuce, and carrots. Control by using healthy plants and by limiting insects and weeds. Use crop rotation and destroy infected plants.

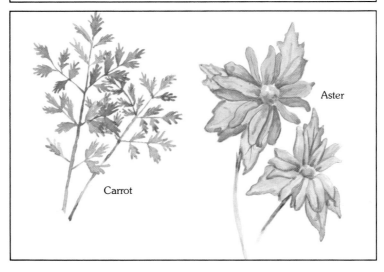

Carrot

Aster

Leaf and Sap-Feeding Insects

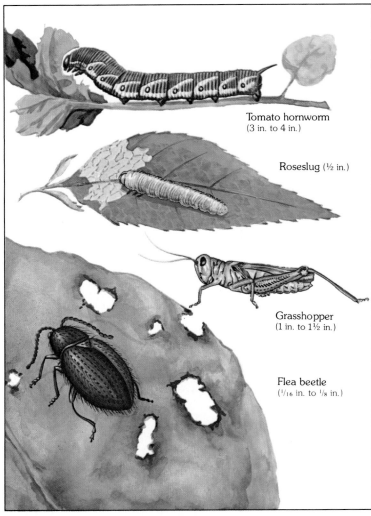

Tomato hornworm
(3 in. to 4 in.)

Roseslug (½ in.)

Grasshopper
(1 in. to 1½ in.)

Flea beetle
(¹/₁₆ in. to ⅛ in.)

Gall makers

Psyllids, other insects, and mites attack leaves or stems, causing the formation of galls that house the insects. Such galls are unsightly but relatively harmless. Control is usually unnecessary.

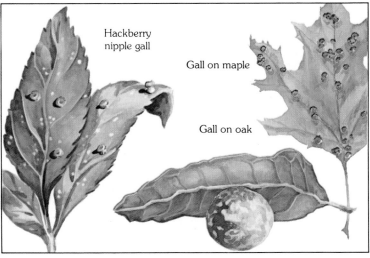

Hackberry
nipple gall

Gall on maple

Gall on oak

Leaf feeders

Leaf feeders have chewing mouthparts they use to remove portions of the leaf tissue. All or part of the leaf may be consumed, and the remainder may be ragged or filled with holes. The symptoms always consist of missing leaf material.

Many different groups of insects are leaf feeders. These include caterpillars of moths and butterflies, beetle adults and larvae, the immature stage of certain wasps, and grasshoppers. All have chewing mouthparts and cause defoliation. Many of the common garden pests are leaf feeders: tomato hornworms; cabbageworms (the imported cabbageworm, the cabbage looper, and the diamondback moth); flea beetle adults; roseslugs; and Colorado potato beetles (both as larvae and adults).

Many different ways can be used to control leaf feeders. Cabbageworms can be handpicked; treated with the pathogenic bacterial spray, *Bacillus thuringiensis*; or sprayed with one of several garden insecticides. Flea beetle populations are reduced by eliminating weeds in and around the garden, where adult beetles spend the winter.

Another set of leaf feeders, hornworms, are seldom a problem because of parasitic wasps that attack these caterpillars. As with all efforts at controlling pests, effectiveness comes with early detection and timely application of controls.

Leafrollers and leaftiers

Leafrollers are caterpillars that roll a leaf into a tube held by silk strands, or they may tie several leaves together. The well-protected larvae then feed within the tied leaves. In addition to defoliation, twig tips may be destroyed or fruits deeply scarred. To be effective, insecticide must be applied before the leaves are tied.

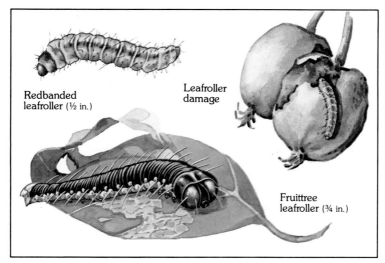

Redbanded leafroller (½ in.)

Leafroller damage

Fruittree leafroller (¾ in.)

Bagworms

Bagworms overwinter as eggs inside tough silken bags constructed of bits of stem and leaf. Larvae hatching in early summer form new bags as they feed. Control bagworms by handpicking bags during the winter or by spraying when new bags appear.

Bagworms (2 in.)

Snails and slugs

Snails and slugs abound in moist environments, often feeding at night or on cloudy days. A shiny, iridescent trail and irregular feeding holes mark their presence. Control with snail and slug baits, or trap under boards or in shallow pans of stale beer.

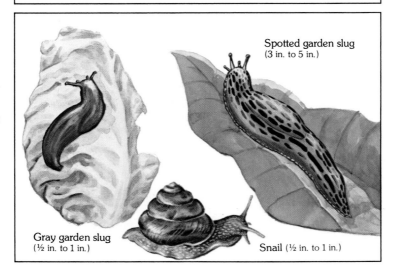

Spotted garden slug (3 in. to 5 in.)

Gray garden slug (½ in. to 1 in.)

Snail (½ in. to 1 in.)

Leaf and Sap-Feeding Insects

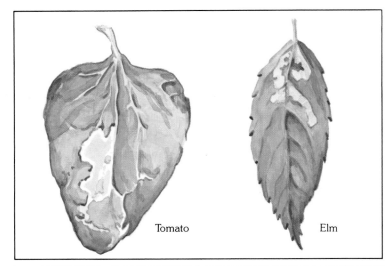

Tomato   Elm

Sap feeders

To get their food, sap feeders pierce the plant with needlelike mouthparts and suck out the juices. Loss of sap and the damage caused by piercing the plant cells do not create holes in the leaves. Instead, injury can result in stunting, deformation (such as curling), twisted foliage, and discoloration, often in the form of speckles. Another major consequence of sap-feeding insects is the spread of organisms causing diseases in plants.

Leafhoppers

Leafhoppers are small, active insects, typically wedge-shaped and green. Blight-like browning and curling of foliage, called "hopperburn," is a symptom on potatoes. Other attacked plants will show loss of color, often in a dotted or spotted pattern. Reduced plant vigor and lower yields result from severe loss of sap.

Effective control requires early detection of the leafhoppers before severe damage occurs. Frequent, thorough applications of common garden insecticides may be needed.

Leafminers

Leafminers are immature stages of flies, wasps, beetles, or moths. The larvae make winding or large blotch mines on the foliage of broad-leaved plants. Or they may tunnel into evergreen needles.

Plants commonly infested with leafminers include hawthorn, holly, locust, birch, elm, and vegetables, such as spinach, beets, and tomatoes. Control by picking and destroying infested leaves. Or thoroughly spray the foliage at times recommended for your area.

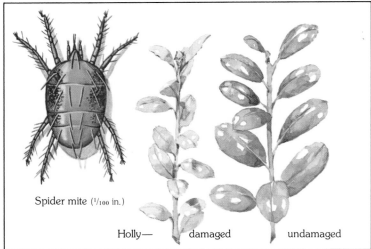

Spider mite (¹⁄₁₀₀ in.)

Holly—   damaged   undamaged

Spider mites

Mites are close relatives of spiders and ticks and are not true insects. Most are too small to see with the naked eye.

Their feeding causes reduced plant vigor and discoloration or bronzing of the foliage. Use a recommended miticide (mite-controlling pesticide) at times recommended for your area.

Leafhopper
(⅛ in. to ½ in.)

Damage on potato leaves

Aphids

Aphids, or plant lice, are small round, soft-bodied sap feeders commonly found on foliage and stems. Different species are variously colored: green, white, pink, black. Besides reduced vigor, damage often appears as wilting or curling of foliage or stunting and deformation of buds and flowers. Aphids reproduce rapidly, making early detection and frequent monitoring important.

Aphids can be controlled naturally in several ways: parasitic wasps, predators, pathogenic fungi, rain, and wind. Aluminum foil stretched under the plants may repel aphids from the plants. If insecticides are needed to control aphids, spray thoroughly, starting when aphids appear to be increasing; repeat as needed.

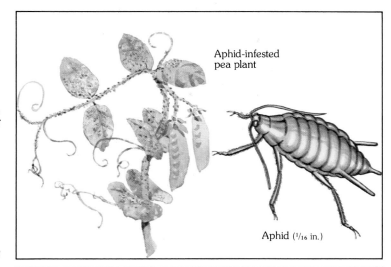

Aphid-infested pea plant

Aphid ($^1/_{16}$ in.)

Plant bugs

The rapid plant bug, tarnished plant bug, and related pests suck plant juices and inject substances toxic to plants. The substance interferes with development, causing one-sided strawberries, cat-faced peaches or apples, and lopsided flowers. Regularly apply insecticides labeled for use in controlling plant bugs.

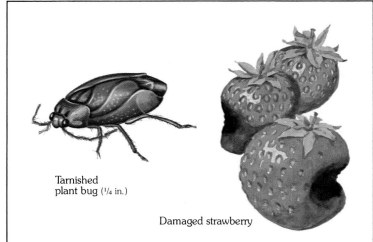

Tarnished plant bug ($^1/_4$ in.)

Damaged strawberry

Whiteflies

Whiteflies are common pests of greenhouse vegetables and flowers. In warmer climates, they attack citrus and many ornamentals. Nymphs—found on lower leaf surfaces—are oval, flat insects with short, sucking beaks. Sweet, sticky honeydew dropped by nymphs attracts ants and may lead to the growth of sooty mold.

Carefully inspect purchased plants grown in greenhouses. Combat with thorough coverage of insecticides labeled for use in controlling whiteflies.

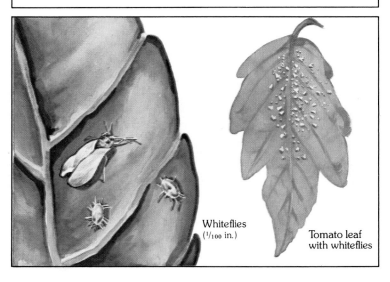

Whiteflies ($^1/_{100}$ in.)

Tomato leaf with whiteflies

How to Prevent Stem Diseases

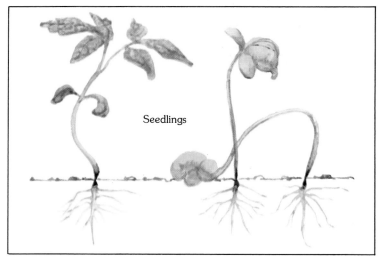

Seedlings

Damping off and seed rot

Just before or after seedlings emerge, the seeds may rot or seedlings weaken and wilt or collapse because of decay at the soil line or below. This is most common in cold, wet, poorly drained soil.

To control, plant disease-free, fungicide-treated seeds. Start seeds in a sterile medium indoors, or outdoors in well-drained soil. Avoid overwatering, crowding, and poor air circulation.

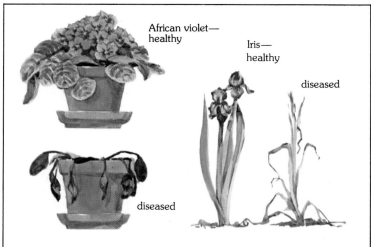

African violet— healthy

Iris— healthy

diseased

diseased

Crown rots

If the base of a stem, petiole, rhizome, or tuber rots (becomes slimy and soft or hard and dry), the problem may be crown rot. Many kinds of plants are attacked and often collapse and die.

To control, plant disease-free stock at the correct depth in clean, well-drained soil. Avoid wounding, overfertilization, and heavy, wet mulch. Control stem borers, stem and root-feeding insects, and nematodes. Practice crop rotation. Remove and destroy diseased plants.

Stem canker and dieback

Stem canker and dieback cause discolored, often slightly sunken, lesions on stems, twigs, and branches. Cankers kill water-conducting tissues, so dieback (wilting and death of foliage) spreads beyond the canker. The entire plant may be killed.

Canker and dieback are common on many shrubs, flowers, and trees. Prune dead and weakened branches several inches below the affected area. Disinfect shears between cuts. Burn the prunings. Destroy badly affected plants.

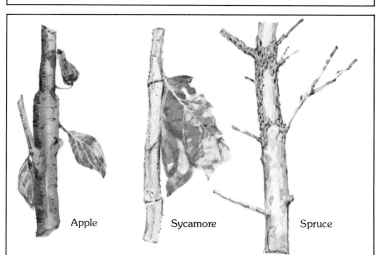

Apple

Sycamore

Spruce

Galls

Round, rough-surfaced over-growths near soil line or graft of plants are crown galls. They are often caused by a bacterium.

Control by using disease-free stock. Avoid plant injuries. Cut galls and infected branches, then burn them.

Cedar-apple galls appear on junipers as orange tentacles attached to a brown ball. The disease does little harm to junipers but causes a rust on apple trees. The results: deformed fruit and leaf loss. To prevent, don't grow junipers near apple trees.

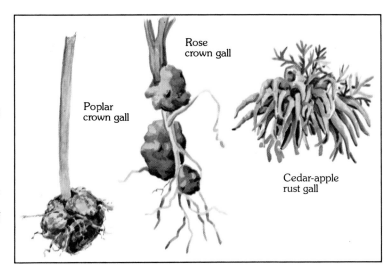

Poplar crown gall

Rose crown gall

Cedar-apple rust gall

How to Control Stem Insects

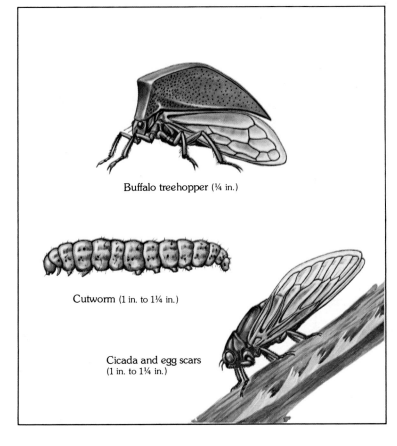

Buffalo treehopper (¼ in.)

Cutworm (1 in. to 1¼ in.)

Cicada and egg scars (1 in. to 1¼ in.)

Treehoppers and pruners

Treehoppers, cicadas, and tree crickets insert eggs inside woody stems, twigs, or canes, causing unsightly scars and split or broken twigs. Cicada nymphs drop to the ground and burrow to tree roots, where they feed on sap—some for as long as 17 years. Treehopper nymphs drop from twigs to feed on legumes and grasses.

Control with recommended insecticide or dormant oil sprays. Tree crickets may damage berry fruits but are easily killed with insecticide sprays early in the season.

Cutworms

These moth caterpillars feed at night, chewing on plant stems at soil surface. Control by hand-picking or by using a recom-mended insecticide. Prevent damage to tomato transplants by placing paper collar around stem.

How to Control Stem Insects

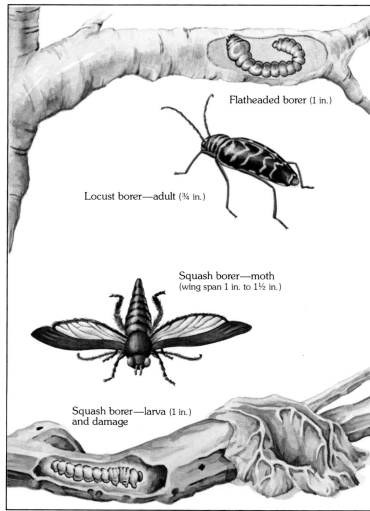

Flatheaded borer (1 in.)

Locust borer—adult (¾ in.)

Squash borer—moth
(wing span 1 in. to 1½ in.)

Squash borer—larva (1 in.)
and damage

Stalk, vine, and wood borers

Borers cause damage by weakening the structure supporting the plant. They also prevent fluids from moving between roots and leaves. European corn borer is a common insect pest that tunnels in corn stalks and ears. This reduces yields as stalks break off or ears fall off. Lilac, dogwood, and rhododendron borers (caterpillars of clearwing moths) frequently weaken or kill host plants.

A similar insect tunnels into squash stems, killing portions of the vine. Sometimes a vine can be rescued if the borer is removed and the damaged part of the vine covered with soil.

Flatheaded and roundheaded wood borers (beetle larvae) attack apple, poplar, locust, and other trees, especially unhealthy ones or trees under stress. Bronze birch borers persistently kill white bark birch trees planted as ornamentals.

To reduce problems caused by wood-boring insects, maintain the health and vigor of trees. Wrap young transplants with a high-quality tree wrap. Spray tree bark, squash plants, and sweet corn when adults are laying eggs. Use a yard and garden insecticide labeled for controlling plant boring insects.

Scale insects

Scale insects are sap feeders that live under a shell-like covering on the stems, twigs, and branches of many different plants. The scale may be hard and shellac-like, soft and waxy, or cottony.

Scale crawlers can move for a short time after hatching before they settle down to feed and secrete a new cover. During this time, crawlers are vulnerable to insecticide sprays and are more easily killed. A spray of superior oil during the dormant season will also control scale insects. Prune heavily infested stems and branches. Destroy prunings.

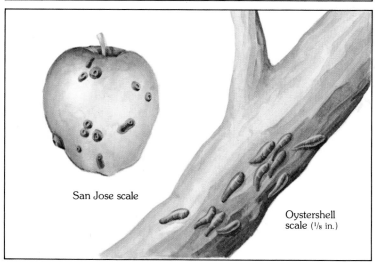

San Jose scale

Oystershell scale (⅛ in.)

Flower and Fruit Diseases

Tomatoes

Apple

Peach

Sweet potato

Spots and rots

A wide variety of flower and fruit spots and rots attacks almost all plants during wet, humid weather. Azalea, camellia, gladiolus, and many vegetables and fruits suffer most. Spots are small, black, scabby patches. Rots are decay, decomposition, or disintegration of plant tissue. Flowers may be blighted or not set fruit.

Spray or dust plants regularly during flowering. Collect and destroy affected parts. Avoid overcrowding and over-fertilization. Plant crops on a four-year rotation in well-drained soil.

Scab

This appears as an overgrowth, sunken area, or spot on fruit (apple, pear, peach, citrus, pecan); vegetables (potato, beet, peas, cucurbits); and leaves of many plants.

Follow recommended program of spraying for fruits. For other plants, treat same as for leaf spots and blights. Control weeds and insects in and around the garden. Destroy plant refuse, and rotate non-wood plants at three-year intervals.

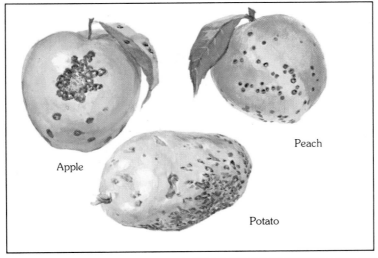

Apple

Peach

Potato

Strawberries

Tulip

Peony

Mold and botrytis blight

These diseases are widespread in humid areas, especially on strawberry, peony, lily, tulip, rose, dogwood, and geranium plants. They attack flowers, buds, fruit, and tender shoot growth. Molds grow profusely on plant surfaces, similar to rots. Botrytis is common on soft, ripe fruits, especially after they're picked. But they may appear before harvest in humid weather.

Flower and Fruit Diseases

Gladiolus

Tulip

Flower breaking

Abnormally streaked or striped flower petals are a symptom of flower breaking. The problem is common on tulips, gladiolus, and lilies. It is caused by viruses that may also produce mosaic, stunting, and other symptoms. The virus is spread by insects (especially aphids); by diseased stock; and by the handling of a healthy plant after working with a diseased one. The health of the plant is not frequently damaged, though appearance is affected. Plant disease-free stock, and control insects and weeds. Destroy infected plants.

Insects Infesting Flowers and Fruits

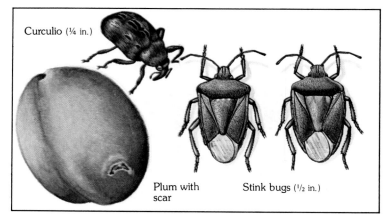

Curculio (¼ in.)

Plum with scar

Stink bugs (½ in.)

Thrips

Thrips are tiny insects that lacerate or rasp plant cells and suck the juices. Fruit, flowers, and foliage may be attacked, producing colorless streaks. To control, remove infested flower buds and all blossoms that have begun to fade. Recommended sprays for thrips will give some protection but must be repeated frequently. Rotate planting, if possible, and maintain sufficient moisture by proper watering and mulching.

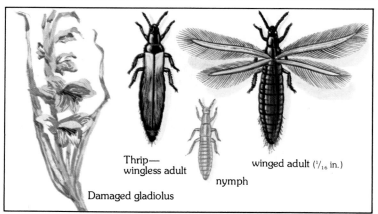

Thrip— wingless adult

nymph

winged adult (¹⁄₁₆ in.)

Damaged gladiolus

Stink bugs and curculios

Stink bugs are sap feeders that feed on developing flowers, berries, or fruits, thus causing them to grow unevenly or become deformed.

Curculios (snout beetles) chew into developing fruits of apple, pear, quince, and stone fruits. The hole made is used for feeding or as a site for eggs. Curculio larvae develop inside the attacked fruits, often causing premature fruit drop.

The number of curculios in succeeding years can be reduced by gathering and destroying dropped fruit daily. Otherwise, spray to control curculio and stink bug by following a schedule developed for your state.

Aphids

Aphids, commonly found on leaves and stems, may also feed on flowers and blossoms. This sap feeding in buds or flowers sometimes causes distorted shapes or discoloration and may affect blossoms so no fruit sets. Aphids also frequently transmit diseases to healthy plants. Sooty mold may grow on the sweet, sticky honeydew secreted by the aphids.

Despite many natural controls, such as parasites and predators, chemical control is sometimes necessary. Treat aphids when you notice they're increasing rapidly. Use an insecticide labeled for use in controlling them.

Infested pea plant

Apples— distorted

healthy

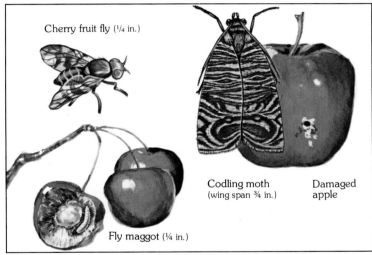

Cherry fruit fly (¼ in.)

Codling moth (wing span ¾ in.)

Damaged apple

Fly maggot (¼ in.)

Codling moths, fruit flies, and fruit maggots

Wormy fruit is inevitable after an invasion by larvae of codling moth, oriental fruit moth, and the like. Apple maggots and cherry fruit fly maggots are larvae of flies. Eggs of these pests are laid on, in, or near the fruit. The immature insects feed and develop inside the fruit, often ruining it and causing the fruit to drop off prematurely.

Thorough covering sprays, begun when the insects first become active and repeated frequently, are usually needed for control. Collecting dropped fruits may reduce apple maggot populations for the following year. Banding tree trunks with several thicknesses of corrugated paper is a way to trap many codling moth larvae as they move down the tree trunks to their pupation sites. Remove and destroy the bands in late fall.

Japanese and cucumber beetles

These beetles are flower and fruit feeders. The larvae feed underground on roots. Control is difficult. Applying insecticide frequently to infested foliage may be required. Protect small trees, roses, and vegetables by covering with plastic or cloth netting as soon as beetles begin to appear.

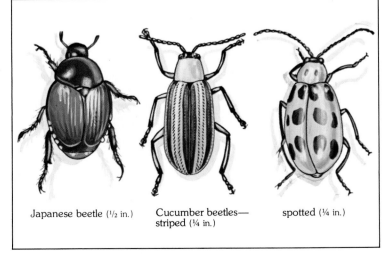

Japanese beetle (½ in.)

Cucumber beetles— striped (¼ in.)

spotted (¼ in.)

Root Diseases

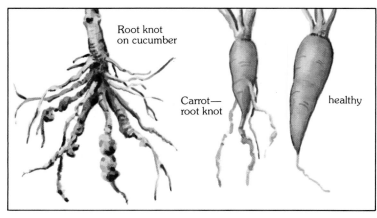

Root knot on cucumber

Carrot— root knot

healthy

Root rots

Affected plants show decline in vigor; are stunted or discolored; and later wilt, die back, or die completely. Roots rot away or change color and small plants are easily pulled up. Nearly all plants can be attacked by this disease. The disease is caused by fungi common in most soils.

Plant disease-free stock of resistant varieties in well-drained soil. Avoid injuries to roots from deep cultivations. Rotate plantings.

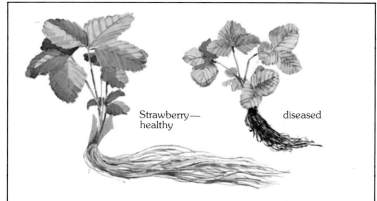

Strawberry— healthy

diseased

Root knot, clubroot

Nearly all kinds of plants in northern greenhouses and outdoors in southern states are attacked by root knot. Plants are stunted, often wilt, yellow, and die. Round nodules or long, irregular, highly branched swellings on roots are caused by nematodes and block the flow of water and nutrients. To control root knot, plant nematode-free plants using a four-year rotation. Use sterilized soil in greenhouses. Plant resistant varieties.

Clubroot has symptoms similar to root knot, but roots become a mass of club-shaped galls caused by a fungus. Affected plants have yellowed leaves and may wilt during the day. All plants in the cabbage family are attacked. To control clubroot, use healthy transplants and seedlings of a resistant variety in soil corrected to a nonacidic pH.

Root and Root Crown Insects

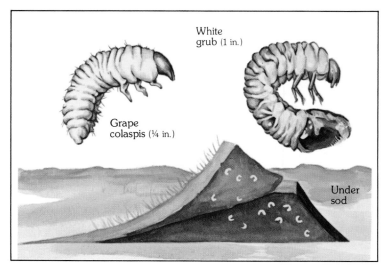

White grub (1 in.)

Grape colaspis (¼ in.)

Under sod

White grubs

The C-shaped larvae or grubs of many beetles develop from eggs laid in the soil. These grubs feed on fibrous roots of grasses, strawberries, or other plants.

Greatest garden infestations occur when planting follows sod. If sod cannot be avoided, treat soil before planting with an insecticide labeled for use in controlling grubs. In turf areas, an application of milky spore disease provides a biological control.

Root weevils and crown borers

Root weevils and crown borers feed on the main roots and plant crown. Infested plants are weakened or killed. Certain mites find the dense crowns of plants ideal habitats. There they feed on the plant sap, causing stunting and distorted growth.

An insecticide labeled for use to control your plant's problem may be required. Rotate planting locations, and use pest-free planting stock. Maintain plant health and vigor.

Root maggots

Root maggots, the immature stage of flies, tunnel in the roots or underground parts of cabbage, radishes, and similar vegetables. Damage may cause the plant to wilt or die or make the produce unusable. Use a soil insecticide prior to planting.

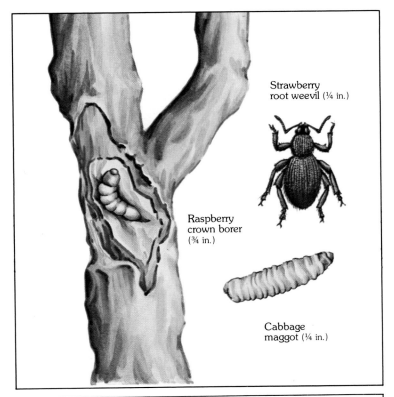

Strawberry
root weevil (¼ in.)

Raspberry
crown borer
(¾ in.)

Cabbage
maggot (¼ in.)

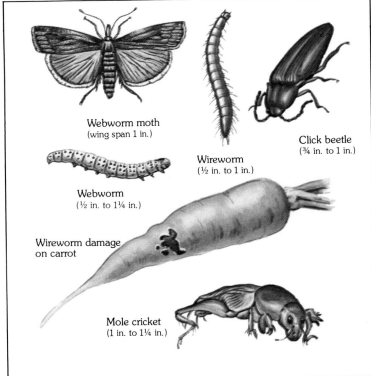

Webworm moth
(wing span 1 in.)

Webworm
(½ in. to 1¼ in.)

Wireworm
(½ in. to 1 in.)

Click beetle
(¾ in. to 1 in.)

Wireworm damage
on carrot

Mole cricket
(1 in. to 1¼ in.)

Webworms

Webworms, larvae of small moths, construct silken channels leading to shelter in the soil. They feed close to crowns of grasses and certain vegetables and flowers. Control by spraying a recommended turf grass insecticide timed to the hatch of moth eggs.

Wireworms

The larvae of click beetles, or wireworms, are able to locate germinating seeds in the soil. They chew into softened seeds or destroy seedlings. Use a soil insecticide before planting.

Mole crickets

Mole crickets are brownish, hairy insects with flat, shovel-like forelegs. They tunnel into roots and seedlings. To prevent damage, apply insecticide labeled for use in controlling soil insects.

Index

A-B

Abelia, 46, 142, 154, 353
Abutilon, 519
Acalypha, 519
Achimenes, 469, 486, 520
Acidanthera, 300
Acroclinium, 258
Actinidia, 159, 165, 166
Adder's tongue, 341
Adonis, 186
Aechmea, 491
Aeonium, 492
African violet, 465, 467, 469, 486, 520
Agapanthus, 301, 470, 486, 515
Agave, 469, 492
Ageratum, 173, 175, 180, 181, 228, 229, 235, 236, 241, 247, 249, 258, 365, 367, 396, 515
  hardy, 186
Air drying flowers, 383
Air layering, 465
Airplane plant, 247, 466, 467, 470
Ajuga, or carpet bugle, 32, 78, 185, 365, 367
Akebia, five-leaf, 80, 156, 167
Alba rose, 321
Alder, 94
Alkanet, 186
Allamanda, 515
Allium, 54, 184, 270, 286-287
Almonds, 454
Aloe, 369, 469, 492-493
Althaea, 118, 123, 155
Aluminum plant, 478
Alumroot, 191, 340
Alyssum, 179, 180, 182, 185, 186, 365, 366, 396
  sweet, 75, 180, 228, 229, 237, 243, 247, 249, 258, 365
Amaranth, 228, 258, 369
  globe, 233, 262
Amaryllis, 467, 486, 498, 520
Amethyst, 259
Ammobium, 233, 258, 369, 380
Ananas, 491
Anchusa, 184, 185, 186, 241, 367
Andromeda, 142
Anemone, 175, 184, 185, 270, 285, 515
  rue, 340
Angel's-tears, 78
Anise, 358
Annuals, 15, 29, 170, 172-173, 178-179, 182, 226-227

Annuals (continued)
  border, 230-232
  climbing, 233
  color, 229, 230, 241
  combining, 235, 241
  container plants, 246-249, 377
  cutting, 245, 379, 380
  in desert gardens, 368, 369
  drying, 233
  edging, 229
  fragrance, 229
  in greenhouse, 506, 515
  layered, 231
  light, 228, 230, 238, 366, 367
  pinching back, 245
  in rock garden, 229, 363, 365
  and roses, 315
  starting, 242-245
  thinning, 244-245
  uses, 228-231
  vines, 161, 162-164, 233
Anthemis, 175, 186-187
Anthurium, 486, 520
Ants, 73
Aphelandra, 487, 515
Aphids, 313, 405, 439, 463, 513, 524, 528, 533, 538, 539
Apple maggots, 539
Apples, 389, 430, 432, 433, 436, 441-442, 528, 535, 536, 537, 538
Apricots, 442
Aquilegia, 191
Aralia, 123, 470
Arbor, rose, 319, 332
Arborvitae, 32, 94, 140
Arbutus, trailing, 340
Arctotis, 228, 258, 369
Ardisia, 515
Areca palm, 484
Armeria, 85, 221
Armyworms, 73
Arrow arum, 372
Arrowhead, 372
Arrowhead vine, 477
Artemisia, 84, 179, 180, 182, 184, 185, 187, 358, 363, 365
  (see also Dusty-miller)
Artichoke, globe, 409 (see also Jerusalem artichoke)
Artillery plant, 478
Arundo donax, 351
Ash, 42, 88, 94
Asparagus, 386, 394, 405, 409
Asparagus beetle, 405
Asparagus fern, 466, 467, 469, 470, 520

Aspen, 51, 88
Aspidistra, 466, 467, 470, 472
Aster, 173, 179, 180, 235, 369, 529
  China, 258, 515
  hardy, 175, 181, 184, 185, 187
  heath, 369
  stokes', 220
  wood, 343
Astilbe, 175, 178, 184, 185, 187, 367
Astrophytum, 493
Aucuba, 142, 472, 496
Avens, 199
Avocado, 472
Azalea, 24, 34, 54, 55, 119, 120, 180, 487, 506, 515, 527, 537

Baby's-breath, or gypsophila, 175, 184, 185, 187, 241, 262, 369, 517
Baby's-tears, 78, 472, 474, 496
Bachelor's-buttons, 229 (see also Centaurea; Cornflower)
Backyard, landscaping, 54-57
Bacteria, 12, 13, 331 (see also Disease)
Bagworms, 531
Bahia grass, 63
Balloon flower, 175, 184, 185, 187-188
Balm, lemon, 357, 360
Balsam apple, 163
Balsam pear, 163
Bamboo palm, 484
Banana, 466, 472
Baneberry, 175, 340
Baptisia, 175, 184, 188, 369
Barbados-pride, 123
Barberry, 29, 34, 46, 118, 123, 142, 143, 155, 353
Basil, 180, 356, 357, 358, 389, 390, 406, 513
Basket-of-gold alyssum, 179, 180, 185, 186
Bauhinia, 94
Bay, 358
Bayberry, 55
Beans, 390, 391, 395, 396, 405, 409-410
  bush, 386, 392, 428
  dry, 429
  lima, 407, 409
  pole, 386, 389, 392, 407, 409-410
  scarlet runner, 407
Bean tepee, 406

Bearberry, 76, 77, 78
Bear's-paw fern, 482
Beautybush, 47, 115, 123
Bees, 432, 439
Bee balm, or monarda, 175, 178, 184, 185, 188, 340, 367
Beech, 32, 42, 94, 180, 354
Beech fern, 344
Beet, 380, 389, 390, 391, 392, 394, 396, 410, 428, 429, 506, 532, 537
Beetle,
  asparagus, 405
  Colorado potato, 530
  cucumber, 529, 539
  flea, 529
  fuller rose, 313
  Japanese, 313, 539
  Mexican bean, 405
  spotted cucumber, 313, 539
  striped cucumber, 405, 539
Beetleweed, 81
Begonia, 228, 229, 230, 237, 238, 242, 247, 249, 258, 367, 459, 465, 469, 487, 496, 515, 520
  tuberous, 268, 295, 365, 377, 467, 487, 519
  wax, or fibrous, 178, 245, 366, 463, 487, 519
Bellflower, 184, 185, 365, 515
  (see also Campanula)
Bellis, 515
Bells-of-Ireland, 233, 258
Bellwort, 175, 340
Beloperone, 515
Bent grasses, 62, 65
Bergamot, 188
Bergenia, 175
Bermuda grass, 61, 63
Berries, growing for birds, 353
Betony, 82 (see also Stachys)
Biennials, 170, 184, 223-225, 379
Billbergia, 491
Billbugs, 73
Birch, 42, 47, 94, 532, 536
Bird-of-paradise, 487, 520
Birds
  and fruit, 353, 439
  in garden, 352
Bird's-foot trefoil, 78
Bird's-nest fern, 482
Bishop's-cap, 340
Bishop's weed, 78, 175, 182, 367
Bittersweet, 156, 166, 353, 354
  dried, 383
Blackberry, 354, 434, 442-443

Black-eyed susan, 163, 340
Black medic, 68
Black spot disease, 311, 313
Bladder senna, 123
Blanket flower, 198, 262 (see also *Gaillardia*)
Bleeding-heart, 175, 178, 181, 184, 185, 188, 365, 366, 367
Bloodleaf, 515
Bloodroot, 175, 340, 345, 365
Blood-trumpet, 166
Bluebeard, 123
Bluebells, 340, 346
Blueberry, 123, 432, 443-444
Blue gentian, 341
Blue grama grass, 64
Bluegrass, 61, 62, 65
Blue lace flower, 259, 515
Blue oats, 350
Bluet, mountain, 190
Bogbean, 372
Borage, 358, 396
Borax, for drying flowers, 383
Border, flower
  annuals, 230-232, 241
  bulbs, 270, 282
  perennial, 178-185
  roses, 315
  shrubs, 118-119, 122
Borers, 536
  cane, 313
  corn, 405, 536
  crown, 541
Borzicactus, 493
Boston fern, 482
Botrytis blight, 537
Bottlebrush, 143
Bougainvillea, 166, 487, 509, 515
Bourbon rose, 321
Bouvardia, 515
Box elder, 94
Boxwood, 112, 143, 144, 180, 353
Bracken fern, 344
Brake fern, 482
Broccoli, 389, 390, 392, 394, 400, 410, 521
Bromeliads, 467, 490-491
Broom, 47, 123, 124
Browallia, 247, 259, 369, 487, 515
Brown patch, 72
Brunnera, 184, 189
Brussels sprouts, 390, 391, 392, 395, 400, 410-411, 521
Buckeye, 95, 124
Buckthorn, 124, 353
Buddleia, 154

Buffalo grass, 64
Bugleweed, 77, 78, 367
Bugloss, Siberian, 189
Bulbs, 15, 29, 34, 268-303, 467, 506, 515
  as annuals, 289
  blooming times, 270-271, 272, 284-286
  care after blooming, 289
  color, 270-271, 291, 303
  container plants, 302-303, 377
  cutting, 379
  forcing, 498-499
  hardy, 270-289
  hardy lilies, 290-291
  height, 271
  light, 288-289, 366
  with perennials, 179, 182, 270
  planting, 288-289
  for rock garden, 363, 365
  and roses, 315
  soil, 289
  tender, summer, 292-301
Bulrush, 372
Burnet, 175
Burning bush, 52, 229, 259
Bush clover, 124
Buttercup, 68, 185, 189, 340, 346
  shrub, 117
Butterfly bush, 115, 124, 154
Butterfly palm, 484
Butterfly weed, 175, 184, 185, 189, 340, 348, 369
Butternut, 95, 454
Button fern, 482

C

Cabbage, 389, 390, 392, 394, 400, 405, 411, 429, 509, 521, 529, 540
  Chinese, 391, 395, 414
Cabbage butterfly, 392, 405
Cabbage rose, 321 (see also *Centifolia*)
Cabbageworm, 405, 530
Cactus, 249, 368-369, 458, 460, 467, 469, 492-495, 520 (see also *Succulents*)
Caladium 182, 294, 365, 366 472, 515
Calceolaria, 469, 487, 515,
Calendula, 170, 173, 228, 229, 235, 238, 516
Calliopsis, 229, 241, 259, 367
Camellia, 46, 144, 366, 487, 506, 516, 527, 537

Campanula, 173, 175, 180, 189, 516 (see also *Bellflower; Canterbury-bells*)
Canary-bird flower, 163
Canby pachistima, or Paxistima canbyi, 47, 83, 365
Candytuft, 80, 175, 184, 185, 190, 229, 247, 249, 259, 365, 516
Cane fruits, pruning, 434-435
Cantaloupe, 419 (see also *Melon*)
Canterbury-bells, 170, 223, 259 (see also *Campanula*)
Cape plumbago, 166
Caraway, 357, 358
Carbaryl, 73, 74
Cardinal climber, 159, 163, 233
Cardinal flower, 340, 372 (see also *Lobelia*)
Carex morrowi 'variegata,' 351
Carmel creeper, 78
Carnation, 259, 509, 516
Carolina jessamine, 166
Carpet bugle, or ajuga, 32, 78, 185, 365, 367
Carpet grass, 61, 64
Carpetweed, 68
Carrot, 380, 390, 392, 395, 396, 400, 411-412, 428, 429, 506, 529
Castor aralia, 95
Castor bean, 259
Catalpa, 95
Catananche, 191
Catchfly, or lychnis, 208, 365, 369
Caterpillar, 530
Cathedral bells, 163, 516
Catnip, 175, 358, 365, 405
Cat's-claw vine, 166
Cattail, 372, 383
Cauliflower, 389, 390, 391, 392, 395, 400, 412, 429
Cedar tree, 51, 88, 94, 95
Celeriac, 390, 412
Celery, 390, 412-413, 429, 521
Celosia, 228, 233, 241, 260, 369, 377, 516
Celtuce, 390, 396, 413
Centaurea, 190, 516 (see also *Cornflower*)
Centifolia rose, 321, 324
Centipede grass, 61, 64
Centranthus, 206
Cephalocereus cactus, 493
Cephalotaxus, 140
Cerastium, 175, 190, 365, 516 (see also *Snow-in-summer*)

Ceratostigma, or leadwort, 82, 175, 184, 206, 367, 517
Cereus, 493
Chamomile, 79, 356, 357
Chaparral broom, 79
Chard, Swiss, 389, 390, 392, 396, 413, 506
Chaste tree, 124
Cherries, 119, 433, 444-445, 539
Chervil, 359
Chestnut, 42, 95, 454-455
Chickweed, 68
Chicory, 390, 413-414
Chinaberry, 95
China rose, 321
Chinch bugs, 73
Chinese evergreen, 464, 465, 472, 496
Chinese fan palm, 484
Chinese forget-me-not, 163
Chinese-lantern, 190-191
Chinese trumpet creeper, 169
Chionanthus, 117
Chionodoxa, 270, 285, 365
Chives, 356, 357, 359, 389, 405, 509, 511, 524
Chokeberry, 124, 353
Christmas cactus, 487
Christmas fern, 344
Christmas rose, 367 (see also *Helleborus*)
Chrysanthemum, 56, 179, 180, 181, 182, 184, 185, 192-193, 229, 230, 234, 245, 260, 280, 363, 380, 381, 469, 506, 516, 527, 529
Cicada, 535
Cigar flower, or cuphea, 229, 260, 516
Cineraria, 520
Cinnamon fern, 344, 372
Cinquefoil, 117, 125, 340, 377 (see also *Potentilla*)
Citruses, 445-446, 521, 537
Clematis, 55, 156, 159, 166, 167 316
Cleome, 180, 241, 260, 369
Clerodendrum, 516
Climate, 8-9 (see also *Temperature; Weather*)
  and grasses, 61
  and landscaping, 36
  and shrubs, 46
Climbing fern, 482
Climbing rose, 161, 307, 308, 309, 311, 315, 316, 319, 324

Climbing rose (continued)
332-333, 335
rambler, 158, 169, 307, 315, 333
Clivia, 487, 520
Cloud grass, 351
Clover, 68
Clubroot, 540
Cockscomb, 260 (see also Celosia)
Codling moth, 539
Colchicum, 270, 287
Cold frame, 174, 399
Coleus, 182, 228, 230, 237, 241, 242, 245, 247, 260, 367, 377, 460, 463, 464, 465, 466, 469, 472, 513, 516
Collards, 390, 414
Color
annuals, 229, 230, 241, 244
annual-perennial garden, 170-173, 178-179
bulbs, 270-271, 291, 303
flowering shrubs, 119
landscaping, 36, 51
planning for, 172-173, 182
Columbine, 51, 175, 184, 185, 191, 365, 367
wild, 341
Columnea, 487, 516
Comfrey, 357, 359
Compost, 12-13, 14
houseplant, 459
Coneflower
prairie, 341
purple, 341, 348
rudbeckia, 175, 179, 180, 184, 185, 215, 235, 241, 265, 269, 518
Conifers (see Evergreens)
Container garden, 54, 56
annuals, 236-238
bulbs, 302-303
herbs, 357
and landscaping, 25
mobile mini, 406
roses, 307, 309, 319, 334
in shade, 366, 377
vegetables, 389, 396-397, 407
Containers for houseplants, 458-459
Convolvulus, 260
Copper spot, 72
Coralbells, 170, 175, 184, 185, 191, 367
Coral-gem, 83
Coral vine, 167

Cordyline, 464, 465
Coreopsis, 175, 181, 184, 185, 191, 369
Coriander, 357, 359
Corms, 268
Corn, 390, 391, 392, 414-415, 428, 527, 536
Corn borer, 405, 536
Cornflower, 229, 241, 243, 260, 369 (see also Centaurea; Dusty-miller; Sweet-sultan)
Corn plant (see Dracena)
Corn salad, 415
Corsican pearlwort, 79
Corticium, 72
Cosmos, 229, 235, 241, 260, 315, 369
Cotoneaster, 47, 55, 76, 78, 115, 125, 144, 155, 354, 363
Couch grass, 71
Coyote brush, 79
Crab apple, 32, 42, 47, 52, 53, 56, 88, 90, 95, 115, 180, 354, 441
Crabgrass, 68
Cranberry highbush, 115, 121
Crape myrtle, 46, 90-91, 118, 125
Crassula, 465, 493, 520
Creeper, 159, 167
Chinese trumpet, 169
Creeping charlie, 83
Creeping fig, 167, 496
Creeping jennie, 83
Creeping mazus, 79
Creeping speedwell, 79
Cress, garden, 359
Crimson star-glory, 163
Crocus, 178, 179, 184, 185, 241, 268, 270, 284, 287, 288, 365, 498, 516
Crossandra, 488, 516
Cross vine, 167
Croton, 460, 464, 473, 520
Crowfoot, 340 (see also Buttercup)
Crown borer, 541
Crown-of-thorns, 488, 520
Crown rot, 534
Crown vetch, 80
Cryptanthus bromeliad, 491
Cryptomeria, 140
Cucumber, 389, 390, 391, 395, 396, 405, 406, 407, 415-416, 509, 524
wild, 164
Cucumber beetle, 529, 539
Cucurbits, 528, 538

Cultivating soil, 60
Cuphea, 229, 260, 516
Cupid's-dart, 191
Cupressocyparis, 140
Curculios, 538
Currants, 446
Cutting garden, 229, 378-381
Cuttings for propagation, 174, 245, 464-465, 506
Cutworms, 74, 405, 535
Cyclamen, 366, 466, 467, 469, 488, 516, 520
Cynoglossum, 260, 367
Cypress, 80, 88
Cypress, false, 96, 140
Cypress vine, 163

D-E

Daffodil, 24, 178, 179, 241, 268, 270, 271, 280-281, 289, 303, 379, 498, 506, 516
Dahlia, 180, 185, 228, 229, 235, 245, 261, 268, 292-293, 315, 380, 381, 529
Daisy, 85, 182, 271
African, 228, 258
blue, 197
cape, 261
dahlberg, 261, 365
English, 173, 179, 180, 223
gloriosa, 265 (see also Rudbeckia)
michaelmas (see Aster)
oxeye, 69, 200, 338
painted, 184, 209
shasta, 180, 182, 184, 185, 219
Swan River, 229, 266
tahoka, 269
transvaal (see Gerbera)
Dallis grass, 69
Damask rose, 321
Damping off, 242, 534
Dandelion, 69, 416
Daphne, 115, 118, 125, 126, 144
Daylily, 175, 179, 181, 182, 184, 185, 194-195, 230
Decks, 40-41
Dehydrator, 428
Delphinium, 176, 179, 181, 184, 185, 196, 315, 382, 516, 529
Desert garden, 368-369
Deutzia, 115, 118, 126, 155, 377
Devil's-paintbrush, 69
Dianthus, 184, 185, 196, 229, 235, 242 (see also Pink)
Diazinon, 73, 74

Dicentra
bleeding-heart, 175, 178, 181, 184, 185, 188, 365, 366, 367
Dutchman's-breeches, 341, 345
Dichondra, 80
Dictamnus (see Gas plant)
Dieffenbachia, 463, 464, 465, 473
Dill, 180, 357, 359, 389, 390
Dimorphotheca, 261, 516
Dipladenia, 517
Disbudding roses, 311
Dish garden, 496
Disease (see also Bacteria)
flower and fruit, 537
foliage, 526-533
lawn, 72-73
root, 540
roses, 311, 313
stem, 534-535
Dividing perennials, 177
Dock, curly, 69
Dog-tooth violet, 341
Dogwood, 24, 32, 47, 52, 55, 88, 91, 93, 96, 354, 536, 537
shrub, 115, 126, 153
Dollar spot, 72
Doronicum, 185, 196-197
Dove tree, 96
Dracena, 463, 464, 465, 473, 496, 520
Dragonfly, 525
Dragonhead, or physostegia, 175, 214
Drainage, 28, 29, 39, 43, 60, 438
Dried flowers, 233, 382-383
Dried vegetables, 428
Dripstone, 370
Driveway, landscaping, 47, 53
Dropwort (see Meadowsweet)
Dumb cane (see Dieffenbachia)
Dusty-miller, 182, 241, 249, 261, 369 (see also Artemisia; Cornflower; Sweet-sultan)
Dutchman's-breeches, 341, 345

Echinocactus, 494
Echinops (see Globe thistle)
Echinopsis cactus, 494
Echeveria, 465, 469, 494, 520
Eel grass, 372
Eggplant, 389, 390, 396, 400, 416
Elaeagnus, 127, 145, 354
Elderberry, 127, 353, 354, 446

Elephant's-ear, 372
Elm, 88, 96, 532
Emerald ripple (see *Peperomia*)
Endive, 390, 416-417, 429
Entry, landscaping, 22, 34, 36, 50, 52, 53, 316
Epiphyllum, 494
Episcia, 467, 488, 520
Eranthemum, 517
Eranthis, 270, 271, 284, 365
Espalier, 436-437
Eucalyptus, 97
Euonymus, 22, 46, 47, 52, 76, 83, 93, 115, 122, 127, 145, 151, 180, 353, 474
Eupatorium (see *Spurge*)
Euphorbia, 261, 465, 469, 494
European fan palm, 485
Evening primrose, or oenothera, 175, 209, 241, 341
Evergreens, 15, 42, 51, 88, 363, 366
    landscaping, 32, 34
    pruning, 154
    shrubs, 32, 46
Everlasting (see *Strawflower*)
Exacum, 517

F

Fairy rings, 72
False dragonhead, or physostegia, 175, 214
False miterwort, 341
False spirea, or astilbe, 175, 178, 184, 185, 187, 367
False sunflower, or helenium, 175, 184, 185, 200
Fatsia, 145, 366, 474
Felicia, 197, 369, 517
Fence (see also *Privacy; Vines*)
    roses, 315
    vegetables, 391
Fennel, 359
Ferns, 175, 178, 247, 339, 344, 345, 365, 366, 377, 458, 460, 465-467, 482-483, 496, 505, 520, 527
Ferocactus, 494
Fertility, soil, 14-15, 60
Fertilizer, 11, 14-15
    annuals, 243, 245
    applying, 14-15
    bulbs, 289
    compost, 12, 13
    container gardens, 377
    desert gardens, 368-369

Fertilizer *(continued)*
    fruit trees, 433, 438
    greenhouse, 514
    houseplants, 461
    lawn, 67
    roses, 308
    trees, 111
    vegetables, 400, 403
Fescue, 61, 63, 65, 77, 78, 350, 365
Feverfew, 180, 184, 197, 241, 261, 369
Ficus, 464, 465, 474 (see also *Rubber tree*)
Fiery skippers, 74
Fig, 81, 97, 167, 496
Filbert, 128, 455
Filipendula, or meadowsweet, 208, 367
Fire thorn, or pyracantha, 114, 115, 145, 155, 156
Fir tree, 24
    douglas, 97
    white, 97
Fishtail palm, 485
Fittonia, 465, 474, 496
Flag, blue, 341
Flame flower, 163
Flame vine, 168
Flax, 184, 197-198, 261, 369
Fleabane, 198
Floating-heart, 372
Floribunda roses, 307, 308, 309, 310, 314, 315, 328-329, 330, 335
Flossflower (see *Ageratum*)
Flower breaking, 538
Flowering rush, 372
Flowering trees, 42, 43, 90-91
    pruning, 108
Flowers and landscaping, 32
Fluorescent light
    and houseplants, 469
Foamflower, 341
Foliage
    and annuals, 237, 238
    drying, 383
    and perennials, 182
Forget-me-not, 80, 173, 175, 180, 223-224, 241, 260, 341, 348, 365, 372, 518 (see also *Myosotis*)
    Siberian (see *Brunnera*)
Forster palm, 485
Forsythia, 46, 47, 115, 118, 119, 127, 128, 155
Fothergilla, 128

Fountain grass, 350
Four-o'clock, 228, 229, 261, 369
Foxglove, 170, 176, 184, 224, 261
Foxtail millet, 351
Fragrance, flower, 51, 229
Franklin tree, 128
Freesia, 315, 520
Fringe tree, 97, 116-117
Fritillaria, 270, 286
Fruit flies, 539
Fruits, 15, 42, 430-453, 521, 537
Fuchsia, 375, 377, 488, 513, 517
Fungicide, 73, 313, 439, 525, 528
Fungus, 72, 73 (see also *Disease*)
Funkia (see *Hosta*)
Fusarium blight, 72

G

Gaillardia, 175, 180, 181, 182, 184, 185, 198, 228, 229, 235, 241, 262, 369
Galanthus, 270, 271, 284, 288, 365
Galax, 81, 175
Galaxy, 81
Gallica rose, 323
Galls, 535, 540
Gardenia, 46, 145, 488, 517
Gardens, special, 336-383
    container, 336, 374-377
    cutting, 378-380
    desert, 336, 368-369
    grasses, ornamental, 350-351
    herb, 356-361
    landscaping, 55, 56, 57
    miniature, 24-25, 316
    rock, 362-365
    shady, 366-367
    water, 336, 370-373
    wildflower, 339-349
    wildlife, 352-355
Garland flower, 365
Garlic, 69, 359, 524
Gas plant, 175, 181, 184, 185, 198
Gasteria cactus, 494
Gay-feather (see *Liatris*)
Gazania, 81, 241, 262, 517
Gentian, 199, 367
    closed, 341
Geranium, 56, 180, 184, 199, 228, 236, 237, 242, 245, 247, 256-257, 262, 380, 405, 469, 488, 506, 513, 517, 537
    cranesbill, 175
    rose, 357, 359-360
    wild, 69, 341

Gerbera, 199, 517
Germander, 81
Gesneriad, 496
Geum, 185, 199
Ginger, wild, 81, 178, 341, 366
Ginkgo, 88, 92, 97
Gladiolus, 268, 296-297, 315, 537, 538
Globeflower, 175, 200, 367
Globe thistle, 175, 184, 185, 200
Glory-of-the-snow, or chionodoxa, 270, 285, 365
Gloxinia, 465, 467, 469, 488, 520
Glycerin, for drying flowers, 383
Goatsbeard, 372
Godetia, 262, 517
Golden-chain tree, 97
Golden-club, 372
Golden-rain tree, 97
Goldenrod, or solidago, 179, 184, 219
Gomphrena (see *Amaranth, globe*)
Gooseberries, 447
Goose grass, 68
Gourds, 158
Goutweed, or bishop's weed, 78, 175, 182, 367
Grade, land, 28-29, 60
    changing, 28, 43
    drainage, 28-29
    and landscaping, 53
    (see also *Slope*)
Grafting cactus, 492
Grandiflora roses, 307, 309, 310, 330, 335
Grape hyacinth, 184, 185, 270, 271, 283, 288, 365
Grapes, 447-448
Grasses, 16, 61, 62-64, 336, 350-351, 527
Grasshoppers, 530
Gray leaf spot, 72
Grease spot, 72
Greenbrier, common, 168
Greenhouse, 500-521
    construction, 502, 506
    humidity, 513
    insects, 513
    soil, 514
    temperature, 502, 505, 512, 515-521
    vegetables, 506, 509, 521
    ventilation, 512
    watering in, 512-513
Ground cedar fern, 344
Ground cherry, 390, 417

Ground cover, 75-85
  annual, 75
  desert garden, 369
  landscaping, 32
  maintaining, 76
  planting, 76
  propagating, 76
  roses, 315
  shade, 366
  slopes, 29
  wildflower, 339
Ground pine fern, 344
Grow-lights, 468-469
Grubs, 72, 540
Guzmania bromeliad, 491
Gymnocalycium, 494
Gypsophila, or baby's-breath, 175, 184, 185, 187, 241, 262, 369, 517

H

Hackberry, 98, 353
Haemanthus, 517
Hanging basket, 237, 246-247, 334
Hare's-foot fern, 482
Harlequin bugs, 313
Hawkweed, 69
Haworthia, 469, 494
Hawthorn, 42, 48, 88, 92, 98, 353, 354, 532
Hay-scented fern, 80, 344
Hazelnut, 128, 455
Heading back, shrubs, 152-153
Heal-all, 70
Heath, 84, 146
Heather, 84, 146, 365
Hedge, 15, 46-47, 120-121
  privet, 46, 132, 148, 151, 155
    353, 366
Hedge fern, 483
Helenium, 175, 184, 185, 200
Helianthus, 175, 184, 200
Heliopsis, 175, 181, 184, 185, 200-201
Heliotrope, 175, 229, 262
Helleborus, 175, 185, 201
Hemerocallis (see Daylily)
Hemigraphis, 460, 474
Hemlock, 98, 154, 353
Hen-and-chickens, 365 (see also Sempervivums)
Hepatica, 185, 341, 345, 365
Herbicides, 66
Herbs, 229, 249, 336, 356-361, 386, 396, 405, 407, 466

Herbs (continued)
  in containers, 357
  drying, 428
  and vegetables, 357
Hibiscus, 46, 115, 118, 128, 146, 155, 175, 184, 488, 517
Hickory, 88, 98
Holly, 32, 46, 88, 98, 147, 353, 483, 532
  shrub, 146
Hollygrape, 79
Hollyhock, 179, 184, 224, 235, 245, 262, 315
Honesty, 224-225
Honey locust, 98
Honeysuckle, 46, 77, 81, 115, 118, 128, 129, 155, 159, 168, 353, 354, 377
Horehound, 360
Hornbeam, European, 99
Hornworms, 530
Horse chestnut, 99, 353
Horseradish, 417, 429
Horsetail, 372
Hosta, 170, 175, 178, 182, 184, 185, 202-203, 365, 366, 367
Hotbed, 399
Houseplants, 15, 456-499
  bulbs, 498-499
  flowering, 486-489
  foliage, 470-481
  outside, 247
  propagation, 464-467
  repotting, 458-459
  rooting, 464-465
  succulents, 492-495
  terrarium, 496
Hoya, 465, 466, 488, 520
Huckleberry, 353
Humidity
  greenhouse, 513
  and houseplants, 461
Humus, 11
Hyacinth, 51, 184, 185, 241, 270, 271, 282-283, 289, 498, 506, 517
  bean, 163
Hybrid foetida rose, 323
Hybrid perpetual rose, 323
Hybrid rugosa rose, 323
Hybrid spinosissima rose, 323
Hybrid tea rose, 307, 309, 310, 326-327, 330, 335
Hydrangea, 46, 115, 129, 153, 155, 168, 377, 488, 517
  hills-of-snow, 153
Hydroponics, 508-511

Hypericum, 175, 201, 365

I-K

Iberis, or candytuft, 80, 175, 184, 185, 190, 229, 247, 249, 259, 365, 516
Ice plant, or mesembryanthemum, 85, 229, 262, 369
Impatiens, 178, 228, 230, 236, 237, 238, 241, 242, 245, 249, 263, 366, 367, 377, 488, 517
Incandescent light
  for houseplants, 469
Indigo (see Baptisia)
Insecticide, 66, 73, 74, 313, 439, 525, 530, 531, 533, 535, 539
Insects, 396, 405, 522-525, 528, 529, 530
  biological control, 524
  chemical control, 525
  flowers and fruits, 434, 439, 538-539
  in greenhouse, 513
  and houseplants, 463
  and lawn, 74
  mechanical control, 524-525
  nonchemical control, 524
  root, 540-541
  and roses, 313
  stem, 533-536
  and wildlife, 353
Interplanting, 390, 394, 524
Interrupted fern, 344
Iris, 175, 181, 182, 184, 185, 204-205, 230, 241, 270, 280, 365, 373, 517
  reticulata, 271, 285
Irrigation (see Watering)
Ivy, 24, 76, 165, 247, 366, 377
  476
  Algerian, 78, 168
  American, 85
  Baltic, 55, 78
  Boston, 156, 168
  devil's, or pothos, 459, 465, 469, 476
  English, 32, 156, 168, 496
  geranium, 82
  grape, 465, 469, 476, 496
  ground, 70
  Japanese creeper, 156, 168
  kenilworth, 365
  Swedish, 247, 464, 465, 469, 476
Ixia, 517
Ixora, 521

Jack-in-the-pulpit, 339, 342, 345
Jacob's-ladder, 175, 201, 206, 342, 367
Japanese hop vine, 164
Japanese pagoda tree, 88, 99
Japanese spurge, 83
Jasmine, 84, 156, 169, 517
Jerusalem artichoke, 417
Jerusalem cherry, 488
Job's-tears, 263, 351
Jonquil, 280 (see also Daffodil)
Joseph's-coat, 182
Juneberry, or serviceberry, 42, 104, 353
Juniper, 29, 32, 43, 46, 51, 53, 54, 76, 99, 112, 114, 140, 141, 154, 353, 363, 535
Jupiter's-beard, 206

Kalanchoe, 469, 495, 521
Kale, 390, 396, 417-418
Katsura tree, 99
Kentia palm, 485
Kerria, 115, 130
Kniphofia, or poker plant, 181, 214
Knotweed, 70
Kohlrabi, 390, 392, 396, 418

L

Lady, northern, fern, 344
Lady palm, 485
Lady-slipper, 342
Lamb's-ears, 82
  (see also Stachys)
Lamb's-quarters, 70
Landscaping, 20-57, 114
  annuals, 232-234
  backyard, 35, 38, 54-57
  drainage, 28-29
  driveway, 47
  entry, 22, 34, 36, 50, 52, 54
  garden, 24-25, 55, 56, 57
  grade, 26-29
  lot analysis, 30-31
  patio, 54
  planning, 26-27, 32, 34-35
  for privacy, 54
  and shrubs, 112-122
  surveying, 26-27
  and trees, 88
Lantana, 82, 228, 237, 263, 521
Larch, 88, 99
Larkspur, 235, 241, 242, 245, 263, 382, 383
Laurel, 147

Lavender, 184, 206, 360, 365
  cotton (see *Santolina*)
  pillows, 383
Lawn, 58-74
  care, 67
  diseases, 72-73
  fertilizing, 15, 67
  grasses, 62-65
  ground cover, 75-85
  insects, 74
  landscaping, 32, 35
  leveling, 67
  mowing, 67
  rejuvenation, 66-67
  soil, 60
  starting, 61, 65, 66
  water, 66, 67
  weeds, 66, 68-71
Lawn leaf, 80
Leadwort, 82, 175, 184, 206, 367, 517
Leaf blight, 72, 526
Leaf curl, 527
Leaf-cutting bee, 313
Leaf feeders, 530
Leaf galls, 527
Leafhopper, 74, 528, 532
Leafminers, 532
Leafrollers, 313, 531
Leaf spots, 526
Leaftiers, 531
Leatherleaf fern, 483
Leek, 390, 418
Lenten rose, 367 (see also *Helleborus*)
Leopard's-bane (see *Doronicum*)
Leopard plant, 372
Lettuce, 386, 389, 390, 391, 392, 394, 395, 396, 405, 406, 418-419, 506, 509, 511, 521, 524, 529
Leucothoe, 147
Liatris, 175, 181, 184, 185, 207, 369
Light
  bromeliads, 490-491
  container plants, 375
  fruit, 432, 436-437
  gardens, shady, 366-367
  greenhouse, 502, 505, 506
  houseplants, 460, 468-469
  perennials, 175, 178-179, 203
  rock garden, 365
  terrarium, 496
  vines, 159
  wildflowers, 345-346, 348-349
Lilac, 46, 51, 55, 115, 118, 121

Lilac *(continued)*
  130, 131, 155, 377, 382, 528, 536
Lily, 177, 179, 180, 184, 185, 381, 489, 527, 537, 538
  calla, 268, 298, 303, 489, 516
  canna, 299, 315
  gloriosa, 298
  hardy, 290-291
  pineapple, 300
  plantain (see *Hosta*)
  and roses, 315
  spider, 299
  torch, or poker plant, 181, 214
  trout, 341
  water, 370, 373
Lily-of-the-Nile, or agapanthus, 301, 470, 486, 515
Lily-of-the-valley, 55, 77, 82, 175, 365
Lilyturf, 79, 83
Linaria, 229, 263, 365
Linden, 42, 43, 51, 99
Linum, or flax, 184, 197-198, 261, 369
Liriope, 79, 351
Lithops, 466, 495
Lobelia, 175, 180, 184, 185, 207, 229, 230, 235, 237, 241, 242, 247, 249, 263, 342, 366, 367, 377, 517
Locust, 532, 536
Locust, honey, 47, 98
Loosestrife, 175, 178, 181, 182, 184, 185, 207
Lotus, 370, 372
Love-lies-bleeding (see *Amaranth*)
Lungwort, 175, 207, 367
Lupine, 176, 184, 207-208, 263
  Carolina (see *Thermopsis*)
Lychnis, 175, 208, 365, 369
Lythrum (see *Loosestrife*)

M-N

Madagascar palm, 484
Maggots, 439, 539, 541
Magnolia, 25, 32, 52, 100
Mahonia, 79, 112
Maidenhair fern, 344, 345, 483
Male fern, 344
Mallow, rose, 342
Maltese-cross, or lychnis, 175, 208, 365, 369
Mammillaria cactus, 495
Mandrake, or mayapple, 339, 342
Maple, 32, 42, 43, 52, 54, 55, 88

Maple *(continued)*
  92-93, 100, 354, 366
Maranta, 466, 467, 476, 496, 521
Marble vine, 164
Marguerite
  blue (see *Felicia*)
  golden (see *Anthemis*)
Marigold, 173, 175, 179, 180, 182, 228, 229, 235, 237, 238, 241, 243, 247, 249, 250-251, 263, 280, 348, 353, 365, 377, 380, 389, 396, 405, 509, 518
  marsh, 342, 346, 372
Marjoram, 360
Matrimony vine, 169
Maurandia, 164
Mayapple, 339, 342
Mayday tree, 57
Meadow beauty, 372
Meadow rue, or thalictrum, 175, 220, 342
Meadowsweet, 208, 367
Mealybugs, 463, 513
Melocactus, 495
Melon, 389, 390, 391, 396, 400, 403, 407
Mertensia, or Virginia bluebell, 175, 184, 185, 222
Microclimate, 8
Micronutrients, 15
Mignonette, 229, 263, 367, 518
Mildew, 72, 313, 528
Milfoil, 71
Milkweed pods, 383
Mimosa, 466, 476
Mimosa tree, 104
Miniature date palm, 485
Miniature rose, 307, 308, 309, 311, 315, 334-335
Mint, 79, 356, 357, 360
Miscanthus sinensis, 350
Mist flower (see *Ageratum, hardy*)
Misting houseplants, 461
Mites, clover, 74
Mobile mini garden, 406
Mock orange, 46, 51, 115, 118, 131, 151, 155, 353
Mold, 73, 528, 537, 539
Mole cricket, 74, 541
Monarda, or bee balm, 175, 178, 184, 185, 188, 340, 367
Mondo grass, 83
Moneywort, 83
Monkey flowers, 241
Monkey-puzzle, 101, 476
Monkshood, 175, 209
Monstera, 464, 465, 476

Montbretia, 301
Moonflower, 162, 164
Morning-glory, 81, 164, 233, 237, 245, 260, 316, 518
Mosaics, 528, 538
Moses-in-a-boat, 476
Moss, Irish, 79, 83
Moss rose, or centifolia, 324
Moss rose, or portulaca, 75, 180, 229, 241, 249, 265, 280, 365, 369
Moss sandwort, 83
Mother fern, 483
Mountain ash, 101, 353
Mowing, lawn, 67
Mulch, 13, 17-19, 51, 57, 65, 245, 316
  bulbs, 289
  cutting garden, 379
  ground cover, 76
  fruit trees, 433, 441
  rock garden, 363
  roses, 308, 334
  trees, 107
  vegetable garden, 391, 393, 406
Mullein, or verbascum, 174, 185, 221
Mum (see *Chrysanthemum*)
Muscari (see *Grape hyacinth*)
Mushrooms, 72, 428
Muskmelon, 419
Mustard, 391, 396, 419
Myosotis, 229, 235, 264, 518 (see also *Forget-me-not*)
Myrtle, 46, 76, 83, 147, 365

Nandina, 147
Nannyberry, 354
Narcissus, 184, 280, 498
Nasturtium, 156, 164, 180, 229, 233, 237, 241, 243, 247, 264, 280, 380, 405, 518
Neanthe bella palm (see *Parlor palm*)
Nectarines, 448-449
Nematodes, 74, 527, 534, 540
Nemesia, 241, 249, 264
Nemophila, 243, 249, 264
Neoregelia bromeliad, 491
Nephthytis, 247, 465, 477
Nettle, 70
New York fern, 80, 344
Nicotiana, 180, 228, 229, 230, 241, 264, 518
Nidularium bromeliad, 491
Nierembergia, 229, 247, 249

Nierembergia *(continued)*
264, 365, 518
Nigella, 243, 264
Nimblewill, 70
Ninebark, 115, 131
Nitrogen, 14, 15, 60, 61, 67
Noisette rose, 324
Norfolk Island pine, 477
Nut grass, 70
Nutrients, plant, 14-15 (see also *Fertilizer; Hydroponics*)
Nuts, 430, 454-455
Nut sedge, 70

O

Oak, 24, 32, 42, 43, 51, 88, 101, 354
Obedience, or physostegia, 175, 214
Oenothera, or evening primrose, 175, 209, 241, 341
Offsets, 467
Okra, 390, 420
Oleander, 46, 147, 518
Olive, Russian, 22, 88, 104, 121
Onion, 69, 390, 392, 394, 395, 396, 406, 420, 428, 429, 527
Ophiobolus patch, 72
Opuntia, 369, 495
Orange clock vine, 164
Orchid, 372, 458, 489
cactus, 489
Oregano, 360, 511
Oregon holly grape, 47
Organic plant foods, 14
Ornamental grasses, 350-351
Ornamental pepper, 489
Ornamental shrubs, 32, 34
Ornamental trees, 32, 34
Ornithogalum, 518
Ostrich fern, 344, 345, 373
Oxalis, 271, 286, 467, 518
Oxeye, or heliopsis, 175, 181, 184, 185, 200-201
Oyster plant, or salsify, 424-425, 429

P-Q

Pachysandra, 32, 51, 75, 77, 83
Palm, 466, 467, 484-485, 521
Pampas grass, 351
Pandanus, 467, 477
Pansy, 225, 229, 230, 235, 236, 237, 241, 242, 247, 249, 264, 271, 518

Papaver (see *Poppy*)
Paper plant, 373
Parasites, 524
Parlor palm, 485
Parrot's-beak, 83
Parsley, 356, 357, 361, 428, 511
Parsnip, 390, 392, 395, 420-421, 428, 429
Partridgeberry, 342
Pasqueflower, 342
Passionflower, 169, 489, 518
Pathogens, and insect control, 524
Patio, 38-39, 54, 236
Paxistima canbyi, or canby pachistima, 47, 83, 365
Pea, 386, 390, 391, 392, 395, 396, 421, 428, 429, 509, 524, 537
Peaches, 432, 436, 448-449, 527, 537
Peacock fern, 483
Peacock plant, 477, 521
Peanuts, 396, 421-422
Pears, 432, 433, 436, 449, 537, 538
Pearlbush, 131
Pecan, 101, 455, 537
Pedilanthus, 477
Pellionia, 477
Pennywort, 71
Penstemon, 175, 209
Peony, 131, 170, 175, 179, 182, 184, 185, 210-211, 230, 241, 529, 537
Peperomia, 465, 466, 467, 469, 477, 496
Pepper, 380, 390, 396, 422, 428, 429, 521
Pepper vine, 169
Pepperidge, 102
Perennial pea, 175
Perennials, 15, 170-222
bloom dates, 185
border, 178-180, 182, 185-186
and bulbs, 270
color, 172-173
for cutting garden, 379
in desert garden, 368, 369
dividing, 177
greenhouse, 515-519
ground cover, 76
heights, 178-180, 184
planting, 176-177
preparing soil, 176
propagating, 174
in rock garden, 363

Perennials *(continued)*
and shade, 175, 178-179, 203, 366-367
and soil, 175
and vegetables, 386, 394
vines, 161, 165-169
winter protection, 177
Periwinkle, 76, 77, 83, 164 (see also *Vinca*)
Pesticides, 313, 525
Pests (see also *Insects*)
and bulbs, 289
and lawn, 66, 68-74
and young trees, 106, 107
Petunia, 22, 56, 75, 173, 179, 180, 228, 229, 231, 235, 236, 237, 241, 242, 247, 249, 252-253, 264, 280, 377, 380, 396, 506, 518
pH, soil, 11, 15, 60
Philodendron, 247, 459, 464, 465, 469, 478, 496
Phlox, 79, 175, 179, 182, 184, 185, 212-213, 229, 230, 235, 243, 265, 280, 342, 365, 369, 528
moss, 79, 175, 182, 363, 365
Phosphorus, 14, 15, 60, 61, 67
Photinia, 131, 148
Physalis, 190-191
Physostegia, 175, 214
Pickaback, 460, 465, 478, 496
Pickerel weed, 373
Pilea, 465, 466, 467, 469, 478, 496
Pimiento, 428
Pincushion flower, or scabiosa, 218, 228, 266, 380
Pine, 32, 88, 102, 354, 363
shrubs, 112, 114, 141, 154
Pink, 79, 82, 85, 170, 265, 365
moss, 79, 175
swamp, 373
(see also *Dianthus*)
Pink patch, 72
Pittosporum, 148, 480
Plantain, 71
Plant bugs, 533
Plant food, 14-15
Planting (see also *Interplanting*)
annuals, 243-245
borders, 178-185, 230, 314-315
bulbs, 288-289
combinations, 405, 524
fruits, 432-433, 437 (see specific fruit)
ground covers, 76

Planting *(continued)*
lawns, 61
perennials, 176
roses, 306
shrubs, 121, 151
tomatoes, 401
trees, 106-107
vegetables, 400
vines, 161
Plant lice, 533
Platycodon, or balloon flower, 175, 184, 185, 187-188
Pleomele, 480
Plugging grass, 61
Plums, 90, 432, 433, 450, 527
Plumbago, or leadwort, 82, 175, 184, 206, 367, 517
Plumcot, 432
Plume grass, 351
Podocarpus, Chinese, 480
Poinsettia, 489, 521
Poker plant, 181, 214
Polemonium, or jacob's-ladder, 175, 201, 206, 342, 367
Polka-dot plant, 466, 480, 496
Pollination, fruit, 432
Polyantha rose, 328, 329, 335
Polypody fern, 344
Pomegranate, 132
Ponytail, 480
Poplar, 42, 102, 536
Poppy, 177, 184, 185, 228, 230, 235, 241, 265, 369, 381
California, 75, 180, 243, 259, 342, 348
Iceland, 170, 173, 201, 365
Oriental, 175, 181, 216-217
Spanish, 365
Portland rose, 324
Portulaca, or moss rose, 75, 180, 229, 241, 249, 265, 280, 365, 369
Potash, 14, 15
Potassium, 60, 61, 67
Potato, 390, 394, 396, 405, 422, 429, 537
Potato beetle, 405
Potentilla, 117, 184, 214-215 (see also *Cinquefoil*)
Pothos, or devil's ivy, 459, 465, 469, 476
Potpourri, 357
Pots, for houseplants, 458
Prairie rose, 343
Prayer plant, or maranta, 466, 467, 476, 496, 521
Predators, and insect control, 524

Pressing flowers, 383
Primrose, 175, 184, 215, 365, 367, 489, 518
  evening, or oenothera, 175, 209, 241, 341
Privacy
  fence, 48-49
  hedge, 46
  landscaping for, 54
  screen, 50, 54-55, 319, 407
Privet hedge, 46, 132, 148, 151, 155, 353, 366
Propagation (see also *Cuttings*)
  ground covers, 76
  houseplants, 464-467
  perennials, 174
Pruning
  cane fruits, 434-435
  fruit trees, 433, 434, 437
  ground covers, 76
  houseplants, 462-463
  roses, 308, 310-311
  shrubs, 152-155
  trees, 107, 108-109
Prunus, 103, 132-133
Pumpkin, 390, 394, 395, 407, 422-423, 428, 429
Purple velvet plant, 465, 480, 496
Puschkinia, 270, 285
Pussy willow, 133, 383
Pygmy palm, 485
Pyracantha, or fire thorn, 114, 115, 145, 155, 156
Pyrethrum, or daisy, painted, 184, 209

Quack grass, 71
Quaking grass, 265, 351
Quesnelia bromeliad, 491
Quince, 34, 46, 115, 117, 133, 353, 450, 538

R

Rabbit's-foot fern, 483
Radish, 386, 390, 391, 392, 395, 396, 400, 405, 406, 423, 524
Rambler rose (see *Climbing rose*)
Ranunculus, 300, 518
Raphiolepis, 117, 148
Raspberry, 386, 394, 434, 450-451
Rattlesnake fern, 344
Redbud, 32, 42, 50, 54, 88, 103, 119, 133, 353
Red mulberry, 353
Red spider mites, 313, 463

Red thread, 72
Redwood tree, 103
Reinwardtia, 518
Repairs, lawn, 66
Repotting houseplants, 458-459
Resurrection fern, 80
Retaining walls, and landscaping, 28
Rhizomes, 268
Rhododendron, 24, 50, 53, 112, 122, 134, 148, 149, 150, 155, 180 365, 506, 527, 536
Rhubarb, 386, 390, 394, 396, 423-424
Ring spot, 529
Rock cress, 175, 369
Rock garden, 362-365
  annuals, 229
  bulbs, 271
  light, 365
  rocks for, 363, 364, 365
  and shrubs, 122
Rocky Mountain garland, or godetia, 262, 517
Rodents, 432, 438
Root division, 466-467
Rooting houseplants, 464-467
Root knot, 540
Root maggots, 541
Root rot, 540
Root weevil, 541
Roquette, 396, 424
Rosary vine, 480
Rose, 51, 82, 304-335, 528, 537, 539
  care of, 308-309
  for containers, 307, 309, 319, 334, 375, 377
  cutting, 331, 381
  disease, 311, 313
  drying, 382, 383
  fertilizing, 15
  hybrid perpetual, 311
  light, 306
  miniature, 307, 308, 309, 311, 315
  old garden, 308, 309, 311, 321-325
  pillar, 307
  planting, 306
  polyantha, 309, 311, 328, 329
  pruning, 308, 310-311
  shrub, 307, 308, 309, 311, 314
  soil, 306, 309
  types, 307
  uses, 314-319
  winter protection, 309

Rose *(continued)*
  (see also *Climbing; Floribunda; Grandiflora; Hybrid tea; Tree*)
Rose acacia, 134
Rose canker, 313
Rose chafer, 313
Rosemary, 150, 356, 357, 361, 389, 405
Rose midge, 313
Rose-of-sharon (see *Hibiscus*)
Rose scale, 313
Roseslug, 313, 530
Rot, 72, 534, 537, 540
Royal fern, 344
Rubber tree, 463, 466 (see also *Ficus*)
Rudbeckia, 175, 179, 180, 184, 185, 215, 235, 241, 265, 369, 518
Rue, 405
Rugosa rose, 46, 353
Runners, 467
Rust, 73, 313, 526
Rutabaga, 390, 424, 429
Ryegrass, 61, 63, 65

S

Sage, 356, 357, 360, 405 (see also *Salvia*)
Sago palm, 485
St. augustine grass, 61, 64
St.-john's-wort, or hypericum, 175, 201, 365
Salpiglossis, 265, 518
Salsify, 424-425, 429
Salvia, 181, 184, 185, 215, 229, 241, 242, 266, 369, 519 (see also *Sage*)
Sand verbena, 343
Sansevieria, 465, 469, 480
Santolina, 218
Sanvitalia, 365
Saponaria, 365
Sap feeders, 532
Sawtooth sunflower, 343
Scab, 537
Scabiosa, 218, 228, 266, 380
Scale insects, 463, 536
Scarlet kadsura, 169
Scarlet runner bean, 164
Scarlet star-glory, 164
Schefflera, 460, 481
Schizanthus, 266, 519
Scilla, siberica, 185
Screen (see *Privacy*)
Screw pine, 467, 477

Sea pink, or thrift, 85, 221, 365
Sea thrift, or thrift, 85, 221, 365
Second cropping, 391
Sedum, 55, 84, 173, 175, 180, 185, 218-219, 363, 365, 369, 465, 469, 495
Seedbed, vegetable, 395
Seeding, lawn, 61, 65, 66
Seedlings, 397, 400, 506, 511
  annuals, 242-243, 244, 245
  vegetables, 398
Seed rot, 534
Seeds
  annuals, 242-243
  for birds, 353
  ground cover, 76
  houseplants, 466
Self-heal, 70
Sempervivums, 369 (see also *Hen-and-chickens*)
Sensitive fern, 344
Sensitive plant, or mimosa, 466, 476
Sentry palm, 485
Serviceberry, 42, 104, 353
Shade (see *Light*)
Shade tree (see *Tree, shade*)
Shallot, 425
Sheep fescue, 350
Sheep sorrel, 71
Shellflower (see *Bells-of-Ireland*)
Shepherdspurse, 71
Shooting-star, 343
Shot hole, 527
Shrubs, 112-155
  colors, 119
  container gardens, 375, 377
  desert garden, 369
  evergreen, 32, 46, 140-150
  fertilizing, 15
  flowering, 116-117, 118
  garden planning, 180
  ground cover, 76
  hedge, 46
  height, 46
  landscaping, 32, 47
  planting, 121, 151
  pruning, 152-155
  rock garden, 363, 365
  shade, 366
  transplanting, 151
  and trees, 43
  watering, 151
  for wildlife, 353, 354
Siberian pea tree, 134
Silica, for drying flowers, 382
Silk oak, 481

Silk tree, 90, 104
Silver lace vine, 169
Skimmia, 150
Sky vine, 169
Slope (see also *Grade, land*)
  ground cover, 75, 76
  planting on, 65, 232
  rock garden, 362, 365
Slugs, 531
Smithiantha, 519
Smoke tree, 104
Smuts, 73, 527
Snails, 531
Snake palm, 301
Snakeroot, 343, 345
Snapdragon, 173, 180, 229, 235,
  242, 245, 266, 382, 519
  baby (see *Linaria*)
Sneezeweed, or helenium, 175,
  184, 185, 200
Snowberry, 118, 354
Snowdrop, or galanthus, 270,
  271, 284, 288, 365
Snow-in-summer, 77, 84 (see also
  Cerastium)
Snow mold, 73
Snow-on-the-mountain, or
  euphorbia, 261, 465, 469, 494
Sodding grass, 61
Sod webworms, 74
Soil, 10-11
  amendments, 11, 16
  annuals, 242, 243
  artificial, for hydroponics, 508
  bromeliads, 490
  bulbs, 289, 498
  cold frame, 399
  composition, 10-11
  container garden, 238, 377,
    396, 406
  cultivating, 60
  cutting garden, 379
  daffodils, 281
  desert garden, 368
  fertilizers, 11
  fruit, 432, 438
  greenhouse, 514
  ground cover, 76
  hanging baskets, 246
  houseplants, 458
  hyacinth, 282
  lawn, 60
  perennials, 175, 176
  pH, 11
  roses, 306, 309, 334, 335
  succulents, 492
  terrarium, 496

Soil (continued)
  testing, 11, 14, 60
  tilling, 11
  trees, 88, 106
  tulips, 273, 288-289
  vegetables, 386, 400, 404
  water garden, 370
  wildflowers, 339
Solidago, 179, 184, 219
Solomon's-seal, 175, 343
Sorrel, 71
Spartina pectinata, 350
Spathiphyllum, 481, 521
Spearmint, 356
Species rose, 324
Speedwell, or veronica, 170, 175,
  184, 185, 221, 365
Spicebush, 134
Spider mites, 463, 513, 532
Spider plant,
  houseplant, or airplane plant,
    247, 466, 470
  annual, or cleome, 180, 241,
    260, 369
Spiderwort, 175, 184, 185, 343
Spinach, 386, 389, 390, 391,
  392, 395, 396, 406, 425, 511,
  532
Spirea, 46, 54, 57, 115, 118, 119,
  134, 135, 155
  false, 135, 136
Spleenwort fern, 344
Spores, 465-466
Spotted cucumber beetle, 524,
  539
Sprigging, grass, 61
Spring adonis, 186
Spring-beauty, 343
Spruce, 104, 141, 154, 354, 365
Spurge, 175, 219, 369
Squash, 389, 390, 391, 395, 396,
  403, 407,
  summer, 392, 425-426
  winter, 392, 394, 425-426,
    428, 429
Squash bugs, 405
Squill, 270, 271, 285, 365
Squirrel's-foot fern, 483
Squirreltail grass, 351
Stachys, 175, 220 (see also
  Betony; Lamb's-ears)
Staghorn fern, 483
Star-of-Texas, 369
Statice, 175, 233, 235, 266, 380
Stem canker and dieback, 534
Stephanandra, 136
Stephanotis, 519

Sternbergia, 270, 287
Stevia, 521
Stewartia, 136
Stink bug, 538
Stock, 229, 266, 519
Stokesia, 184, 220
Stolonizing grass, 61
Stolons, 467
Stonecrop (see *Sedum*)
Storing vegetables, 429
Strawberry, 81, 85, 249, 386,
  394, 451-453
Strawberry jar flower garden, 248-
  249
Strawberry saxifrage, 467, 481,
  496
Strawflowers, 233, 266
Streptocarpus, 519
Stripe, 73
Succulents, 249, 363, 368-369,
  460, 465, 467, 469, 492-495,
  520
Suckers, 467
  bromeliad, 490
Sumac, 47, 53, 93, 115, 136, 353,
  354
Summer savory, 357, 361
Summersweet, 136
Sun (see *Light*)
Sundrop (see *Oenothera*)
Sunflower, 235, 241, 266, 343,
  353, 369, 390, 426
  false (see *Helenium*)
  Mexican (see *Tithonia*)
  perennial (see *Helianthus*)
Sun rose, 365
Surveying, and landscaping,
  26-27
Swamp milkweed, 175
Swamp pink, 373
Swamp rose mallow, 175
Swamp saxifrage, 175
Sweet alyssum, 75, 180, 228,
  229, 237, 243, 247, 249, 258,
  365
Sweetbrier rose, 323
Sweet cicely, 361
Sweet flag, 373
Sweet gum, 43, 88, 93, 98, 353
Sweet pea, 164, 180, 229, 233,
  243, 266, 506, 509, 519
Sweet potato, 390, 396, 426, 429
Sweet rocket, 182
Sweet shrub, 136
Sweet-sultan, 267 (see also
  Cornflower; Dusty-miller)
Sweet william, 170, 175, 225

Sweet william (continued)
  229, 235, 267
Sweet woodruff, 175, 361
Sword fern, 483
Sycamore, 42, 104
Symphoricarpos, 137

T-U

Tamarisk, 51, 137, 154
Tansy, 361, 405
Tarnished plant bug, 313
Tarragon, 357, 361
Tartarian dogwood, 373
Tassel flower (see *Amaranth*)
Tea, herbal, 357
Tea roses, true, 324 (see also
  Hybrid tea rose)
Temperature (see also *Climate;
  Weather*)
  cut flowers, 331
  fruit, 432
  greenhouse, 502, 515
  trees, 88
  vegetables, 390
Tent worms, 439
Terrace flats, 234
Terrarium, 496
Teucrium, 365
Texture, and landscaping, 36, 51
Thalictrum, 175, 220 (see also
  Meadow rue)
Thatch, lawn, 66
Thermopsis, 185, 220-221
Thinning
  fruits, 439 (see also specific
    fruit)
  shrubs, 153
Thistle, Canada, 71
Thrift, 85, 221, 365
Thrips, 313, 538
Throatwort, 519
Thunbergia, 316
Thyme, 32, 80, 175, 356-357,
  361, 365, 396, 405, 511
Tibouchina, 519
Tickseed, perennial, or coreopsis,
  175, 181, 184, 185, 191, 369
Tillandsia bromeliad, 491
Ti plant, 464, 481
Tithonia, 229, 267
Tomato, 386, 389, 390, 395, 396,
  400, 401, 405, 508, 513, 521,
  526-527, 529, 532
  cherry, 509, 511
Tomato hornworm, 530
Tools, pruning, 107-111, 155, 310

Toothwort, 343
Torch lily (see *Poker plant*)
Torenia, 229, 230, 267, 365, 367
Transplanting
  and hydroponics, 511
  seedlings, 242-243, 245, 397, 400
  shrubs, 151
Trees, 86-111
  drainage, 43
  evergreen, 32, 42 (see also specific tree)
  fertilizing, 15, 32, 111
  flowering, 42, 43, 90-91
  landscaping, 20, 32, 35, 47
  maintaining, 106-107
  planting, 42-43, 106-107
  pruning, 107, 108-109
  selecting, 88
  shade, 32, 42-43, 88
  wildlife, 353, 354
  winter protection, 110
  wounds, 110-111
Tree cricket, 535
Tree fern, 483
Treehopper, 535
Tree-of-heaven, 105
Tree rose, 307, 309, 311, 335
Trellis, 406
Trileaf wonder (see *Nephthytis*)
Trillium, 343, 345
Trollius, or globeflower, 175, 200, 367
Trumpet vine, 165, 169
Tuber, 15, 268
Tuberose, 519
Tulip, 24, 55, 178, 179, 182, 184, 185, 241, 268, 270, 271, 272-279, 289, 365, 379, 381, 498, 506, 537, 538
  blooming time, 272-273, 277
  chrysantha, 279
  cottage, 275
  darwin hybrid, 274
  double, early, 277
  double, late, 277
  eichleri, 279
  fosterana, 273
  greigi, 273
  horned, 278
  kaufmanniana, 272
  lily-flowered, 274
  mendel, 276
  parrot, 275
  single, early, 277
  species, 270, 272, 278-279
  tarda, 278

Tulip (*continued*)
  triumph, 276
  whittalli, 279
Tulip tree, 105
Turnip, 390, 391, 396, 424, 429
Turtlehead, 343

Umbrella plant, 481
Urban areas, trees in, 88
Ursinia, 519

V-W

Valerian
  Greek, or jacob's-ladder, 339, 342, 345
  Red, 206
Vegetable garden, 386-429
  care, 402-407 (see also specific vegetable)
  planting, 400-401
  starting seedlings, 398
  and temperature, 390
Vegetables, 15, 384-429
  container gardens, 25, 375, 389, 396-397
  in cutting garden, 379, 380
  drying, 428
  greenhouse, 506, 509, 512, 521
  herbs, 357
  irrigation, 17
  storing, 429
Venus's-flytrap, 489
Verbascum, 174, 185, 221
Verbena, 75, 180, 229, 247, 267, 357, 360, 365
Veronica, 170, 175, 184, 185, 221, 365
Viburnum, 46, 57, 115, 137, 138, 139, 150, 151, 180, 354
Vinca, 32, 175, 230, 237, 267, (see also *Periwinkle*)
Vines, 15, 156-169
  annual, 161, 162-164, 233
  grape, 168, 377
  greenhouse, 505
  ground cover, 76
  landscaping, 158-159
  perennial, 161, 165-169
  and roses, 316
  in shade, 366
  starting, 161
  tomato, 401
  training, 160
  vegetable, 391, 407
Violas, 170, 173, 175, 182, 184, 185, 221-222, 235, 249, 267

Violet, 85, 175, 343, 346, 519
Virginia bluebell, 175, 184, 185, 222
Virginia creeper, 85, 353, 354
Vriesia bromeliad, 491

Wahoo, eastern, 353
Walking fern, 344
Wallflower, 225, 365
Walnut, 105, 455
Wandering Jew, 247, 464, 465, 481, 521
Wasps, 530
Water arum, 373
Water canna, 373
Water chestnut, 373
Watercress, 373
Water garden, 370-373
Water hyacinth, 373
Watering, 16-17
  bromeliads, 490
  bulbs, 289, 498
  container garden, 238, 375, 389, 396, 406
  cut flowers, 381
  desert garden, 368
  in greenhouse, 512-513
  ground cover, 76
  houseplants, 460-461
  lawn, 66, 67
  rose, 308
  seedlings, annual, 245
  shrubs, 151
  terrarium, 496
  trees, 107
  vegetable garden, 386, 392, 402
Water lettuce, 373
Water lily, 373
Watermelon, 395, 427
Water milfoil, 373
Water plantain, 373
Waterweed, 373
Weather (see also *Climate; Temperature*)
Weather and rose pruning, 311
Webworms, 74, 541
Weeds, 245
  ground cover, 76
  lawn, 66, 68-71
  pests, 524, 530
  rock garden, 363
  among seedlings, 243
  vegetable garden, 392, 395
  water robbers, 16
Weigela, 115, 139, 155
White Dutch runner bean, 164

Whitefly, 513, 533
Wild cucumber, 164
Wildflowers, 336, 339-349
  light requirements, 345-346, 348-349, 367
Wildlife
  garden, 352-355
  and vegetables, 404-405
Willow, 20, 42, 51, 88, 105, 365
Wilts, 529
Window boxes, 236 (see also *Container garden*)
Winged everlasting (see *Ammobium*)
Winter care
  desert garden, 368
  perennials, 177
  roses, 309
  shrubs, 154
  trees, 110
  wildflowers, 339
Winter aconite, or eranthis, 270, 271, 284, 365
Winterberry, 139, 354
Winter creeper, 47, 50, 52, 63, 64, 65, 76, 83, 156, 169
Wireworm, 541
Wisteria, 24, 156, 159, 169, 377
Witch hazel, 53, 93, 115, 118, 139
Woodbine, 85
Woodruff, sweet, 84
Wormwood, satiny, 84

X-Z

Xeranthemum, 267, 380
Xylosma, 150

Yarrow, 71, 85, 175, 179, 184, 185, 222, 241, 365, 369
Yellow-root, 85
Yellows, 529
Yellowwood, 105
Yew, 32, 46, 51, 84, 112, 114, 120, 141, 142, 154, 180, 353, 365
Yucca, 175, 181, 184, 222, 369, 481

Zebra grass, 350
Zelkova tree, 105
Zinnia, 173, 179, 180, 182, 235, 237, 241, 243, 247, 254-255, 267, 280, 338, 339, 353, 369, 380, 396, 519, 528
Zone map, 8-9
Zoysia grass, 61, 64
Zucchini, 380, 396, 425, 428